Find It Online

The Complete Guide to Online Research

3rd Edition

DATE DUE

BRODART, CO.   Cat. No. 23-221-003

2003 By Facts on Demand Press
206 W. Julie Drive, Suite 2
Tempe, Arizona 85283
(800) 929-3811
www.brbpub.com

Find It Online
The Complete Guide to Online Research
3rd Edition
2nd Printing

©2003 by Facts on Demand Press and Alan M Schlein
206 W. Julie Drive, Suite 2
Tempe, AZ 85283
(800) 929-3811

ISBN 1-889150-29-0
Cover Design by Robin Fox & Associates
Edited by J.J. Newby and Peter J. Weber

Schlein, Alan M.
    Find it online : the complete guide to online
research / [by Alan M. Schlein]. – 3rd ed.

        p. cm.
        Includes index.

        1. Electronic information resource searching.
    2. Computer network resource.   I. Title

    ZA4375.S35 2002   025.04
                        QBI02-200262

Acknowledgments

I could never have gotten this book done without the incredible help and inspiration of a lot of people.

Researching this book was both challenging and incredibly rewarding, giving me the opportunity to tap into the knowledge of some of the best minds in the online world.

I should discharge my debt to them by absolving them of blame for any error or biases. Any mistakes are mine. Having established that all problems are mine, I am deeply grateful to all those who have helped along the way.

First, to my contributors, listed on the back cover whose insights, guidance, and willingness to share your knowledge have taught me much of what I know. Many of you are simply the best in your fields and I thank you for your willingness to share your knowledge with me and contribute to this book. Special thanks to Greg Notess, Nora Paul, Barbara Quint, Mary Dee Ojala, Mary Ellen Bates, Amelia Kassel, Mark Goldstein, Gary Price, Danny Sullivan, Reva Basch, and Chris Sherman who have repeatedly contributed to my growth as well as to specific points of this book. A special note to Carole Lane and Don Ray, I can never thank you enough for your expertise, guidance and support.

Next, I want to acknowledge that, at least for me, a reporter is nothing without a good editor. In the first two editions, I had the guiding hand of Shirley Kwan Kisaichi. In this edition, I could never have done this without the skilled work of J.J. Newby. You outdid yourself this time, making me continue to do better.

Thanks also to my team at BRB Publications – Mike and Mark Sankey, editors Peter Weber, Ivy and Christine Bailey for having the continued faith in me to get this book into a third edition and for all their help along the way. I would also like to thank my friend and web site designer Dan Levy; Vince Ricardel for the back cover photo; my many friends at the National Press Club; and of course, a few journalists who have always helped on my career path, Charlie Thomson, Brian Buchanan, Ian Brodie, and Hugh Davies.

On a personal front, I dedicate this book to my Dad, Richard, who I think about all the time and who inspired me to thoroughly enjoy the career I've chosen and whose memory and spirit continues to thrive among all those he touched.

To keep this to a reasonable length, I'd like to give a blanket thanks to all my friends, family, clients and colleagues. Thanks for your patience and understanding.

To my mom, Betty, my brother Michael and his wife Jordan, my sister Carol and her husband Craig and their children Margaret and Jamie, you all give me great joy.

To my wonderful stress-relief team -- you know who you are -- for helping distressed me when needed, and to my A-team (listed alphabetically) for keeping me motivated, relaxed, focused and smiling:

Angela Betters, Randy Blumenfield, Lisa Day, Kelli Emerick, Katherine Feldmann, Corinna Ferrer, Christopher Fotos, Mitch Gerber, Holly Haines, Cynthia Hunter, Heidi Klamath-Moore, Holly Klotz ,Cheri Lacey, Ken Marks, Ginny McNair, Sarah Memari, Jackie Merrick, Julie Montgomery, Kevin "Kebmo" Moore, Belinda Norton, Donna Parolini, Cheryl Peppers Heather Pedersen , Helena Rey, Rory Robertson, Marsha Shaikh, Donna Sager, Gina Simpson, Paul Skalnick, Stephanie Spong, Karen Spranklin, Theresa Howell, Stephanie Viers, Terri Williams, Britt Wilsen. Lorrie Worley, and the many other friends in LA and Washington DC whose ears I bent in the course of this book. You should only know how important you are to me.

To Lora Ware, thanks for continuing to always be the calm in the storm. And of course to my growing family of cats – Moose, Murph, Kali and Sammi – who always know the perfect moment to crawl onto my lap and give me unrivaled joy and affection.

Alan Schlein, January 2003

Contents

Chapter 3 - Framing Your Search Strategy 69

Chapter 4 - General Search Tools 79

Contents

Contents

Foreword

By Alan M. Schlein

The Internet has opened up a new world to millions of people. Think of the advantages. The Internet enables you to be your own researcher and find information critical to making decisions that affect your life. The Internet allows us to instantly tap into amazing information sources. It allows people to answer questions they never could before, and communicate like never before.

Still, as "super searcher" Mary Ellen Bates often says, many researchers look at the Internet as a gardener looks at a field of wildflowers. There's a ton of great material there and you know it's there, but you still need to pick your way through the huge amounts of weeds and nasty pests to find what you want.

Find It Online is your field guide, a constant companion to help you zoom past the weeds and head straight to the best of the Internet. It will show you what is really out there, how it can be useful to so many areas of your life, and how to get the results you want quickly and efficiently. It is a practical, how-to guide, updated every year, with pages and pages of the best web sites and commercial databases, plus tips from some of the world's leading researchers.

This edition has new features. Over the past few years I've traveled all over the world, training folks on how to find information and use the Internet. As a result of seeing how the Internet is used around the world, I've made this edition considerably more global in focus than previous editions, highlighting not only the online resources from several countries, but also providing tips for finding resources in other countries, how to translate those results, and all the other important considerations for performing truly global research.

We *are* seeing a new sophistication in the many search tools available to us, a world of tools no longer limited to just search engines and subject directories. This edition of Find It Online provides the latest in search strategies in addition to teaching you the basic tenets of sound research such as developing a search strategy, and also how to verify the information you find. You will learn about the many tools in your research arsenal, why they are effective, and how you can use them. For example, you will learn how to properly select from search engines, subject directories, meta-search tools, and more to find just what you need when you need it.

Find It Online – something you keep next to your computer and flip through the chapters as you need them. Whether you are a newbie to the 'Net or a professional researcher, you are bound to find tips and tricks, and useful resources that are relevant to your searching needs.

- **Chapter 1** gives you a look at how people all over the globe are creatively using the Internet to change the world around them.

- **Chapter 2** gives you the basics you need to understand how your computer finds information, and why your search works or doesn't work.

- **Chapter 3** helps you frame a strategy to find what you are looking for.

- **Chapters 4 and 5** give you a look at search engines and the many other specific tools you can use to find information. These chapters also focus on ways to tap into the "invisible web" and get to hard-to-find information that search engines may not locate. Learn the importance of "the human element" – finding experts or people knowledgeable about the subject you care about, who can guide you quickly to the best information.

- **Chapter 6** examines the amazing collections of information found on governmental sites.

- **Chapter 7** looks at the expanding selection of public records available on the Internet.

- **Chapter 8** looks at the myriad of news resources available online and where to find breaking news online.

- **Chapter 9** focuses on business information and how you can research companies, competitors, and potential new markets around the world.

- **Chapter 10** looks at the international landscape and shows you how to find information in foreign places. This chapter includes locating translation tools enabling you to read pages in foreign languages and find out what they mean in your native language.

- **Chapter 11** examines managing and filtering information. Here you will find tips and tricks for triaging the overwhelming amount of information you get when you research. This chapter also highlights some effective strategies for narrowing the barrage of information by using alerting tools to track information that is important to you.

- **Chapter 12** offers techniques and insights into determining if the information you find is accurate, credible, and the most up-to-date available.

- **Chapter 13** gives you some specific searching examples and problem-solving techniques you can apply to your own search requests.

- **Chapter 14** offers a reality check on how your privacy is being violated when you search for information. Learn ways you can protect yourself from prying eyes!

- **A bonus chapter** – The Cutting Edge – looks at how all this technology is changing and where we are going in the near future, with the latest on wireless search tools, and hotlinks directly to the best sites. But, you can only view this chapter online at www.deadlineonline.com.

In addition, <u>Find It Online</u> offers a series of valuable indices, and at the ends of chapters are additional web sites to take you a few steps further. Not all information can be found for free online, so we've included profiles of vendors who have public records for purchase.

--

Looking for more innovative ways to help you and your company research more effectively, contact me and maybe I can show you and your staff how to do it with a hands-on demo. Conversely, I'm always looking for the latest techniques and tricks and the best sites, so if you have suggestions, or comments, go to my web site www.deadlineonline.com or email me at alan@deadlineonline.com

- Alan Schlein

Chapter 1

Creative Uses of the Internet

Browser Beware — A World of Knowledge at Your Fingertips — Have You Heard About...? — I Can't Get Away From The Web — More Creative Uses of the Internet — Not All That Glitters Is Gold — When Private Information Becomes Public — Data Mining — Online Technology: Picking Up Where Direct Marketing Leaves Off — How Much Is Too Much, and When? — The Letter You'll Never Get — Personal Information from the Marketer's Point of View — You Can Level the Playing Field!

In Karoo National Park in South Africa, Namibia, and the Congo, modern technology has partnered with an ancient art to help protect the wildlife.

Preserving the legacy of the Kalahari bushmen, today's bushmen trackers continue to successfully track game. They can follow nearly invisible animal tracks and identify the animals that made them, when they made them, and even what they ate along the way. These bushmen, like their ancestors before them, are an invaluable resource of information about the local environment. For generations, conservationists have sought to tap that knowledge.

Now, despite their inability to read and write, the bushmen can record what they see and share their unique wisdom with the rest of the world by using handheld computer devices linked with satellites in space. Information that has never been written down is now being logged, cataloged, and used to map the environment. Under this program – developed by Louis Liebenberg, Director of Cybertracker Projects in South Africa, Namibia, and the Congo – these wired trackers are enabling conservationists to accurately follow the wildlife across the African bush.

It works like this: when a tracker sees a black rhinoceros or other endangered species, he matches it with a picture icon on his handheld computer. The attached global positioning system or GPS – a technology used around the world by planes, cars, and boats for positioning and mapping purposes – pinpoints the tracker's signal to a ground location within seventy-five yards of his position. When he returns to camp, he uploads the information to a central computer. The information is mapped so that park and conservation officials know precisely where endangered animals are located. This helps the everyone drastically reduce threats from both predators and poachers.

Add an internet connection into the mix, or wireless capability, and that information can be sent anywhere in the world in a matter of seconds.

This is not so unusual. The work of cybertrackers and the African bushmen is just one example of the technological revolution reshaping our world.

But, do *we* really know how to use the Web? Consider this: a January 2002 Outsell (www.outsellinc.com) study of over 20,000 knowledge workers found that:

- 86 percent said they don't know what information is available on the Internet,

- 79 percent said they don't know which sources are reliable,

- 70 percent said they think information is "too hard to find," and

- 66 percent said they don/t know how to evaluate sources.

And 88 percent of these people say they are "skilled" or "very adept" 'net users!

Perhaps this feeling of being overwhelmed is due to rapid advancements in information technologies – the Internet, electronic notepads, a never-ending fount of publicly-accessible information.

Browser Beware

While the Internet offers remarkable opportunities to learn, the future also comes with the need for caution. For better or worse, online technology is making it easier than ever for personal information to be collected, disseminated and accessed by a mind-boggling array or people and entities. Even if you don't use a computer, your privacy is being violated on a regular basis. You are a part of the online world, whether or not you actively participate in it.

In order to retain some control of the information that can be found about you, it is incumbent on you to learn exactly what someone else can uncover about you and how you can protect yourself from being exploited.

So while a new world of information is easily available, the very information you want to know about someone else may also be found about you. If you feel vulnerable, the best way to protect yourself is to learn what others can find out about you.

But first you need to understand how to use these resources. Think of the Internet as the world's largest library, available whenever you need it.

A World of Knowledge at Your Fingertips

Veteran journalist Don Ray tells a story about a lonely man who went to his community library to find a book that would teach him how be more affectionate.

Being standoffish and unapproachable, he didn't want to consult with the knowledgeable reference librarian who could have instantly pointed him to many affection-related resources. So instead, he wandered for hours and hours trying to find a book on how to hug. Finally, after almost an entire day walking around the library and looking at nearly every title in the entire library, he found a book labeled *How-to-Hug*.

"You can't take that book out," snapped the librarian as the man handed her the book at the counter. "That's volume seven of the encyclopedia, How-to-Hug."

The lesson is if you keep looking hard enough, eventually you can find what you need. But to be smart and time-efficient, it is always better to learn how the system you are using works.

Despite the myth to the contrary, you can't find "everything" on the Internet. But if you learn how to use the search tools and understand how the Internet works, you can avoid spending hours aimlessly looking for that one site in a million and quickly pinpoint exactly what you want to find. In the process, you can protect your privacy by learning what information can be found about you and how to keep that information out of the hands of prying marketers.

Over the past couple of months, I've looked to the Internet to discover:

- how to calculate the difference between South African rand and American dollars
- the blue book value of a car
- the most popular words people search for on the Internet
- how to check the weather report in Hawaii (sunny and warm, surprise)
- a synonym for the words "amplitudinous"
- if a specific lawyer has been sued for malpractice
- absolutely everything I can about an alleged terrorist
- the patient safety records of some nursing homes
- the proper way to fix a plumbing problem
- how to buy dinner for someone while they are honeymooning on a remote island
- a vegetarian restaurant in the Netherlands
- the gravesite of someone's ancestor
- how to write a grant request and a business plan
- the location of the nearest ATM machine
- how to track my packages being shipped across the world
- who was born and what happened in history on a friend's birthday
- how to compare the cost of living in different cities for friends who were looking for jobs
- the rules of a long-forgotten childhood game

Another creative use of the Internet, at least for me, is to let its strengths compensate for my weaknesses. A confession. I am hopelessly geographically-impaired. When people tell me to go west, I'm in trouble. But now, because I routinely look at map sites like www.mapquest.com or www.mapsonus.com, I can find my way. These sites provide turn-by-turn directions, telling you to make a left at this corner and a right at that one.

You can use the Internet as your personal learning tool. The Internet opens the world to your fingertips, allowing you to be an armchair globetrotter or a space explorer, letting you look closely at Mars and outer space.

Some people suggest the Internet's time has already come and gone. I think otherwise. An estimated 605.6 million people are online as of September, 2002 and those numbers keep skyrocketing according to Nua.com – see `www.nua.com/surveys/how_many_online/index.html`.

Can you find everything you want on the Internet? Using computers in research is a big step in the direction of finding information. And vast stores of information are on the Internet, but locating exactly what you want requires some forethought about how to search for it. Unquestionably, computers can manipulate huge volumes of information, but getting exactly what you want when you want it requires more than putting in a keyword and praying you come up with the right answer.

Have You Heard About... ?

Nonetheless, the Internet is transforming the way we work, learn and play, from cradle to grave, with some innovative and creative uses of the technology.

-- Parents use computers with videoconferencing equipment to watch their premature infants in neo-natal intensive care and talk with the doctors and nurses at the same time. Couples looking to adopt can search the Internet for children available worldwide, while couples looking for the latest fertilization techniques can find a virtual catalog of sperm and egg donors online. Across the United States, parents are using small video cameras strategically placed in their community daycare centers to watch their children and even talk with their children while the parent is at work and the child is at daycare. The Internet has also revolutionized placement services for finding daycare and live-in nannies.

-- Computer access is only now really coming to Japan. In January, 1998, a Nikkei Market Access survey counted almost nine million people online, or less than seven percent of the country. By March of 2000, twenty-one million people were online, or seventeen percent of the population. But that number has shot up dramatically over the past three years, to 56 million people or thirty-seven percent of the country and the vast majority of them do not use a PC computer to gain access to the Internet, according to NUA. The largest growth has been by teenagers using wireless I-mode cellular phones. Roughly seventeen million of the twenty-seven million new Internet users in Japan are using I-mode phones acquired in the past two years. Teenagers send email messages, talk, of course, and send photos of themselves to their friends, using the digital camera included within the phone.

-- As you get older the Internet has more and more useful resources. Education, from distance education to home schooling, is available worldwide, including entire classrooms with wireless laptops.

-- For the working person, the Internet's usefulness is obvious – getting everything from the latest news to the latest stock information to checking to see if someone you want to do business with has a criminal record.

-- For those nearing retirement (or just dreaming of it), there are many excellent financial planning, retirement planning and other investment sites.

-- Death is big business on the Internet. There are tributes to people who are dead, those who just refuse to admit they're dead – The Dead Psychics Line at `www.geocities.com/Athens/Forum/6909/dead.html` – and even pages to the "living dead." There are even betting pools on when certain celebrities will die. Seriously, on Stiffs.com (`www.stiffs.com`). And if you like quirky sites, there's the American Funeral Museum (`www.roadsideamerica.com/attract/TXHOUfuneral.html`).

-- There are serious pleas from those who need life-saving organs and perhaps the most unusual, kiosks on the Internet tied to cemeteries where biographers and families write and film video tributes to honor those who have recently passed away.

From the serious to the ridiculous to the sublime, you can find it online.

I Can't Get Away from The Web…
…Or Do I Want To?

By J.J. Newby

I use the Internet all day long to research writing projects for my professional life, but in recent years, I've found that it has insidiously worked its way into being an increasingly important tool in my personal life, so much so that an ISP or access line outage escalates to a priority one emergency in my household!

In 1995 there wasn't as much out there as there is today, but that didn't stop me from finding the Serial Killers Home Page, now at `www.mayhem.net/Crime/serial.html`. It was a personal favorite because it fulfilled a disturbing fascination the journalist in me developed.

These days most of my favorite pages are decidedly more domestic as I plan a wedding and a home purchase in the same year, but I still find that the Web is a terrific way for me to satisfy many of my information and entertainment needs ranging from the macabre to the mundane.

Here are just a few of the many ways you can use the Web for more than just research.

Love Links

I first found out how my life-long best friend and new husband felt about me when I received an email which led to a web site he constructed that told me he loved me. If you don't have a steady mate in your life, I know many couples who found true love on the Web via dating sites such as Match.com (`www.match.com`) or Matchmaker.com (`www.matchmaker.com`). On these sites, you can post a photo and a profile then sift through those of other members until you find your match. Think of it as a relationship search engine. The site hides your real email address so you can safely communicate via protected email before you give out any identifying information. Once it's time to go out on that first date, Yahoo! Yellow Pages (`http://yp.yahoo.com`) will help you two find restaurants or other businesses/services nearby (mini golf, bowling, whatever your pleasure is) allowing you to search by name or category and by proximity to an area or address. Most importantly, it allows you to get directions, which you can double-check at MAPBLAST (`www.mapblast.com`). Nothing kills a first impression like being late or getting lost.

For a night at the movies, you can search movie listings online at your local paper or use a regional entertainment guide. There you can read the reviews and find the closest theater with the best show times. Resources vary by area, but a Washington DC area example is `http://eg.washingtonpost.com/section/movies`. Many movie theaters now sell tickets online, so you can skip the long lines at the box office.

Once you get to the "comfortable" stage with your date, you can plan a quiet dinner with what you already have in the pantry with recipe searches at Busy Cooks (`http://busycooks.about.com` and go to Recipe Box), or `www.recipes.com`. Enjoy a steady stream of DVDs by subscribing to NetFlix (`www.netflix.com/Default`). Provide them with a list of your movie requests and you'll receive new DVDs each time you mail back the old ones.

Keep the romance alive by sending flowers and gifts (`www.800flowers.com`, `www.ftd.com`, `www.thepopcornfactory.com`) and the occasional silly card (`http://greetings.yahoo.com` or `www.flowgo.com`).

And once you know this is forever, learn about the four C's of diamond ring shopping and even try your virtual hand at ring design at `www.adiamondisforever.com`. Once she says "I do" however, expect her to disappear for hours at a time when she logs onto The Knot (`www.theknot.com`) which is *the* destination site for cyber-savvy brides because it provide a personalized online checklist, seating chart software, articles, chat rooms, a place to host a wedding web site, a virtual gallery of wedding dresses, bridesmaids dresses and other wedding attire, and tons more. She will rapidly overtake the bookmarks section of your browser marking wedding favor places (`www.bridalink.com`), registry sites (`www.weddingchannel.com`), places to order invitations (`www.wedding.orders.com`) and much, much more. If you are the groom, you should encourage this, however, because otherwise *you* will have to go from store to store and vendor to vendor with her, so letting her work it all out online means you can stay sane and use your weekends for your own activities.

Problem Solving

Many times, when I haven't known where to turn, I've turned to my trusty tool — the Web. When our cats dug up a neighbor's garden, I found many resources on the Web including tips at `www.gardenfoundation.com/pets/pets2.htm`, do-it-yourself methods for keeping them from climbing fences at `www.corporatevideo.com/klips/details.htm`, instructions for building a kitty kennel at `www.just4cats.com`, and the solution I finally went with, Cat Fence-In at `www.catfencein.com/index.html`. There are tons of resources for just about every kind of pet and every kind of pet crisis. Need a company that specializes in ground transportation of pets? Try `www.feathersandfurvanlines.com`.

Unexpected babysitting duty for a friend? Thank goodness for coloring pages printed from the Web, which you can find through this coloring book search engine `http://ivyjoy.com/coloring/search.html`.

When I suddenly broke out in a mysterious rash at the office, I quickly ruled out the possibility of it being anthrax by going to the Centers for Disease Control: `www.cdc.gov`. I also discovered it was a case of stress-induced hives by visiting the Skin Rash Flowchart at `http://familydoctor.org/flowcharts/545.html`.

When an out-of-state meeting ran long, the fact that I had downloaded the airline's flight schedule from the Internet to my Palm Pilot proved to be a time saver. I was able to call and switch my tickets to the exact flight I wanted in a matter of minutes.

I'm convinced there are few everyday problems that can't be solved via the Web.

Ultimate Entertainer

Since I am often asked by friends and families to plan and organize parties for milestone events, I've found so many helpful resources on the Web. I've found baby shower games (`www.dfcreations.com/BabyShower.html`), guidelines for age-appropriate parties for kids (`www.parenting.com`, `www.parents.com`, `www.amazingmoms.com`), and for a real party twist, found a How To Host a Murder party kit (`www.mystery-games.com/murmyspar.html`). It is easier to shop online for party decorations and goodies than running from store to store, and the selection is much better. A frequent stop is Birthday Express (`www.birthdayexpress.com`) and for the murder party, I found several things at Marshal Moody (`www.marshalmoody.com/50s.asp`).

Home Is Not Just a Browser Button

Get a taste for what kind of home your money will buy in a particular area by looking online at `www.realtor.com`. You can search by zip code, by area, or, if you want to know more about a specific house, by MLS listing. You put in some parameters and get back prices and listings of homes in that area, usually with pictures and detailed square footage information, perhaps even a 360 degree "virtual home tour." Before you shop for a mortgage, be sure to check your FICO score — the credit score most lenders use to calculate your creditworthiness — at `www.myfico.com`. Comparison shop for mortgages with online services such as eLoan (`www.eloan.com`), or your bank or credit union may have an online application. You can practically find a new home without, well, leaving home!

Once you've found the home, there are a ton of packing and moving resources, including a Relocation Wizard (`www.homefair.com/homefair/wizard`) that allows you to plug in a moving date and other factors (kids, pets, etc.) and spits out a prioritized and dated task list for planning and executing a move. Once you've settled in, find organization and decorating tips at Organized Home (`www.organizedhome.com`) and maintenance tips such as how to fix your toilet at sites like Toiletology (`www.toiletology.com/index.shtml`).

Thoughtfulness at the Click of a Mouse

Online registries and wish lists (one of the best is at `www.amazon.com`) make gift buying easier for both the buyer and the recipient — no more chartreuse turtlenecks from Aunt Hilda. With family and friends spread out around the nation, I love online shopping sites for the simple fact that I can shop at any time of day or night, and they will gift wrap and ship it overnight. I can buy a gift at the last second. With its partnerships with companies such as Toys 'R Us, Amazon.com is popular as a one-stop shopping center for gifts for people of all ages. For collectibles and other quirky gifts, Ebay's auction site (`www.ebay.com`) is a great place to find just about anything. Often the items are new and in the original box. For the person who has everything, a Super Certificate allows you to buy one gift certificate that is good at hundreds of stores and web sites (`www.giftcertificates.com`). For a gift of luxury, don't miss SpaFinders (`www.spafinders.com`) where you can either find a spa service or buy a gift certificate good at spas around the world. Catalog shopping has never been easier thanks to a variety of catalogs online including Solutions (`www.solutionscatalog.com`) and gourmet shop Harry and David (`www.harryanddavid.com`).

Keeping In Touch

This is not site-specific, but it shows you how the Web can bring far-flung family members closer. My father used to joke that I was the hub of a communications network — the Newby Network — and that I could hear and disseminate family news in a matter of hours. Thanks to the Internet, now it takes seconds. Literally every member of my family has an email address, including the infants and the elders. Most even have their own web sites. And all of them have Instant Messaging accounts through AOL. So when my sister went into labor, my mother in Florida called my father in California who, unable to find me by phone, IM'ed me, so I could IM my then-fiancé Jeff, who IM'ed his family in Florida, while at the same time my father IM'ed my aunts, uncle, and grandparents. When we decided to call the hospital, I looked it up online, found out the room extension, talked to my sister to get the details (a boy, seven pounds, nine ounces, healthy, 20 inches long), and was able to broadcast this news in real time to all my anxiously awaiting relatives. The IMs were chiming loudly on my screen while I talked to her, and I was able to answer their questions: Does he have hair? Eye color? How is the father holding up? It didn't take long for the proud daddy to upload digital photos to the new baby's web site.

When we see photos on the web site we like, we can easily move them over to Shutterfly (www.shutterfly.com) which allows you to order dye-sublimation ("real" photo prints) copies of digital photos. You can also try Ofoto.com at www.ofoto.com. I made the proud parents a brag book of their baby, and copies for all the grandparents.

If you want your family to be able to peek into your life, but don't have the skills or desire to maintain your own web site or web log, you may want to look into a no-programming-skills-required online diary site at http://diaryland.com.

Plan Your Life

Yes, you can find tools for just about every stage of life. Many are positively silly, like the love calculators at www.lovetest.com, some claim to be based on proven methods, like the Chinese baby gender calendars at www.thelaboroflove.com/chart, and others are tools for serious topics like the online funeral planner at www.funeralplan.com/funeral plan/preneed/personalplan.html. There truly is a checklist for everything, and you can find just about all of them at www.checklists.com.

-- J.J. Newby is a former television journalist and has spent the past seven years as a ghostwriter and consultant to Silicon Valley executives as well as a self-professed web addict. Email: jjnewby@aol.com

More Creative Uses of the Internet

As the Internet matures, more and more creative uses of the 'Net develop.

Using online phone books and people-finding tools, refugees all over the world use the Internet to reconnect their families. In Kosovo, relief volunteers set up web sites and distributed pamphlets to help reunite families who were separated during the fighting. In the Middle East, displaced Palestinians in refugee camps are able to use the Internet to communicate with family members. Free speech and Internet usage is a difficult problem in some parts of the world. In China, despite government opposition, anti-government dissidents have used the Internet to spread their message. This has prompted the Chinese government to order Internet service providers to screen private emails for political content. The Chinese government suggests it will hold the companies responsible for subversive postings on their own web sites.

The Internet has also served to bring a sense of community to ex-patriots living far away from their homelands.

Great innovations have been made because of the wireless capability of the Internet – especially for the military and law enforcement. In the war on terrorism in Afghanistan, the U.S. military used handheld wireless computers to let soldiers know instantly where they were, where they needed to go, and where the enemy might be. Using orbiting satellites, soldiers view digital maps of the landscape including three-dimensional contours that give a precise overview of the battlefield.

Firefighters now use computerized maps combined with satellite communication and global positioning (GPS) devices to chart the landscape. They can also devise a fire-fighting strategy using mathematical calculations like wind speed and the direction of the fire to limit potential damages and casualties.

Crime fighting has taken on new dimensions because of technology. Many U.S. and British towns have video cameras around busy downtowns and intersections to monitor crime. Most American police officers' vehicles are wired with sophisticated computers allowing the officer to quickly check a suspect's background.

The Internet's increased usage and the huge surge in the popularity of chat groups, particularly among teenagers, has led to great concern about the access sexual predators have to children. So, law enforcement and even vigilante groups have worked to catch these people, and state governments in the U.S. now post web sites with lists of convicted sexual offenders and their addresses to warn communities. In the United States, possessing photographs of a child engaging in a sex act is illegal, as is sending such photos over the Internet or downloading them onto a computer. So officers pretend to be teenage girls, chatting online with suspects and then luring them to a public place where an arrest can be made. Some law enforcement agencies have aggressively pursued this kind of internet policing, while others have gone so far as to arrest anti-porn vigilantes.

Real estate is another industry that has dramatically changed as a result of the Internet.

At least in the U.S., the Internet has become a great time saver in buying a house or shopping for a place to live. In 2000, almost forty percent of U.S. home buyers used the Internet to shop for a house and most of them used it to find information about specific areas and neighborhoods. A few years ago, the head of a realtors group pronounced the Internet as a major "threat" to realtors. When the Internet generated more business, they changed their opinion. Most realtors use the Internet to "show" houses. This helps cut down the number of actual house visits a realtor makes, giving them more time for other aspects of their business.

Paper blueprints are on their way out in the construction industry as are fax machines, replaced by handheld devices complete with wireless modems and mapping software. Several of the biggest construction companies are using linked web sites, making it easier for contractors, builders, and subcontractors to collaborate on everything from design and engineering, to management, to buying materials, posting schedules and bidding for jobs.

While the Internet's use is now widely accepted in real estate, the medical field has been slow to endorse the inevitable changes. Now, physicians are starting to use handheld computers to assist them in various procedures — writing prescriptions, keeping track of billable hours, checking drug interactions, measuring appropriate doses and identifying side effects for patients. The wireless computers have also prevented some pharmacies from accidentally giving patients the wrong medicine.

Patients are taking advantage of the Internet by downloading software that will provide analytical data to help them decide on a hospital, doctor, or nursing home. Now patients can use web sites to compare prices and quality of online drugstores, and put search engines to work to find quality medical information.

Dozens of companies have transformed travel arrangements by setting up web sites for electronic ticketing, discounted airfares, and registration for hotels. Pre-select your meals, too. Even more changes are envisioned for the travel industry in the near future.

More and more airports have kiosks that provide travelers with easy Internet access, but soon internet-enabled technologies will appear throughout the airports. Airlines such as Alaska Airlines have test-marketed internet-enabled conveniences such as letting their frequent flyers print boarding passes from their own computers or scanning in driver's licenses and linking them to boarding passes via a bar code – thus allowing the gate agent to identify the passenger without the traveler having to reach into their pocket for ID. In the future, digital fingerprinting and eye scan technology may be added for identification purposes.

With people turning to the Internet to find the perfect sofa or even a car, then why not online therapists? To the excitement and alarm of some experts in the field, new mental health web sites are offering the type of counseling once available only in the intimacy of a therapist's office. Several allow you to email your therapist for guidance and advice, for a fee.

Farmers across the world have also seen major changes in the way they do business, shopping for the best deals on machinery and supplies, especially chemicals to kill bugs and weeds. Also farmers are exploring the Internet to find the best prices for their crops. In China, over 30,000 farmers in the coastal city of Ningbo peddle their plums, peaches, and peacocks on the Internet. According to the *People's Daily* newspaper, the Ningbo farmers praise the Internet, a medium they call "a bridge" that leads the farmers "to fortune." Chinese officials say the farmers are selling their produce to more than twenty countries.

Perhaps the most profound changes caused by the Internet have been in how people find jobs.

Not only are dozens of web sites collecting resumes, posting job openings, and providing job-seekers with guidance and advice, but many companies have taken to saving travel money by using the Internet's video conferencing capability to conduct job interviews online. Target, Macy's, Home Depot, and other big-name retailers – even the Mirage Resorts Casino – have replaced paper applications and in-person interviews with computer kiosks for the initial screening of applicants.

Not All That Glitters Is Gold

Forward-looking Internet experts like John Patrick of IBM predict that one day the Internet may become a utility – every bit as life changing as electricity. That it will deliver instant information anytime, anyplace, and will be fast, natural, easy, intelligent and trusted. But, as Patrick notes, the technical reality keeps pulling that transformation back. The Internet remains in a messy global build-out stage and people are finding themselves the human guinea pigs for this technology.

But not-quite-there-yet technology is not the only downfall of the Internet. There is the human impact as well – which is still being studied and measured. Initial academic studies of the Internet's effects on society in the mid-1990s found that it dramatically increased stress, was addictive in its usage, and caused loneliness, isolation and depression. A 2001 study from Carnegie Mellon University finds that the more people use the Internet, the more stress and hassles they have in their daily lives. While the researchers can't pinpoint why stress levels increase, the study countered the previous conclusions and found that the Internet no longer appears to induce feelings of loneliness and depression. In fact, other studies, like a 2001 UCLA report, found that the Internet helps people feel more connected to their family and friends and were slightly less likely than non-users to experience feelings of alienation, loneliness and powerlessness.

So the long-term impact of the Internet on global society is still undetermined, and most likely will change along with how our use of the Internet changes.

One clear area where the Internet has proven to have negative consequences is in the area of privacy. What follows here will begin to explain the unseen information caching aspect of the business that is the Internet. Also, Chapter 14 illuminates privacy and protection issues, and what you can do to protect your best interests.

When Private Information Becomes Public

There is no doubt, the Internet is changing our lives in significant ways. But at what price? The ease with which information can move around in the digital age means more information is shared and disseminated than ever before – and that includes information you do not want everyone in the world (literally!) having access to.

From the skeptic's viewpoint, the Internet's future is closing in on us. It is a future in which every detail of our lives is noted, stored and, more often than not, sold to marketers and advertisers, conscientious service-providers and con-artists alike.

If you feel vulnerable, you should. Your privacy is being violated on a daily basis by the companies you buy from and the organizations you interact with. They may be recording information about you on *their* computers.

If you think you can avoid the online world, you are sadly mistaken. Like it or not, the online world has already found you. Chapter 14 will open your eyes to how the Internet affects your life.

Data Mining

The process of harvesting information, referred to as "data mining," is a huge, booming business. When you register your pet, your house, or your car, pay your taxes, use a credit card, send in a warranty, subscribe to a magazine or conduct any of the hundreds of activities that comprise normal life, you leave behind information about yourself. In recent years, the quality and detail of information about our lives has skyrocketed.

In the old days – what we can call "B.C." for "before computers" – credit card bureaus and junk mailers collected information about people from the purchases they made and the warranty cards they mailed in. But the companies had to record the information by hand, and cross-referencing of the material was an inaccurate and unwieldy process. They were able to target market groups by gender, age, ethnicity, neighborhood and so on, but with nowhere near the precision they do now. Today, every time you use a supermarket discount card, the store tracks your purchases, builds a profile on you and, most likely, sells that profile to marketing companies – for a surprisingly hefty price. This is a component of "direct marketing." Many companies offer incentives to stores in order to be able to buy this data from them.

Magazines sell their subscription lists to direct marketers, too. Increasingly, so do other institutions such as schools, churches, banks, insurance companies, and mail order companies. They do it mostly without your knowledge and, in some cases, contrary to your consent. To these companies, information about their customers belongs to them, not you. They consider the money they make from selling the information to be part of their profit stream.

Businesses are not immune to the same kind of targeting. There is such interest in business profiles that many companies build extensive databases, company profiles, and reports on industries and competitors. In addition, companies target specific businesses and follow their every movement to get new sales leads, and scour publications and all kinds of information to get a jump on a trend or to stay a step ahead of the competition.

Three of the leading U.S. data mining companies – Metromail, First Data Corporation, and Acxiom – control huge databases with demographic, geodemographic, psychographic and behavioral information. First Data claims to maintain a database of more than 160 million individuals, and ten million U.S.-based businesses. Metromail Corporation claims to sell data on ninety-five percent of U.S. households.

This data includes our birth dates, how often we travel, what we buy, prescriptions we use and whom we telephone. In the U.S., some companies also gather, store and sell Social Security Numbers – numbers that uniquely identify every U.S. citizen and are essentially the golden key to a cache of private information. The major U.S. credit bureaus – Experian, Equifax, and Trans Union – maintain databases with information about people's jobs, income, bank accounts, credit limits and *most significantly*, credit card transactions.

Direct marketers who buy wholesale or custom-made databases from credit card companies and other sources use the information to develop more product marketing and targeting strategies. You know those telemarketing calls that keep your home phone ringing off the hook? Guess how they got your name, number, and buying habits? Right. Read on.

Online Technology:
Picking Up Where Direct Marketing Leaves Off

There is one big difference between traditional direct mail and the Internet. Internet target marketing starts where direct mail ends. Online technology enables *almost anyone* to access information contained in one or more databases and combine them in a nanosecond. This allows the marketers and their clients to zero in on your specific interests.

In fact, some of the largest commercial sites on the Internet have agreed to feed information about their customers' reading, shopping and entertainment habits into a system developed by Engage Technologies of Massachusetts. Engage is already tracking the moves of more than thirty million Internet users, recording where they go and what they read – often without the user's knowledge. This enables webmasters to track users so that advertisements can target the likeliest consumers of goods and services.

Not surprisingly, this technology disturbs privacy-rights advocates who worry about the increasing ability of online companies to collect and store personal data.

> **Example:** A cat food company wants to introduce a new line of gourmet food products. Using traditional direct marketing techniques, they could contact a data miner and purchase lists of people who precisely fit their target profiles. The data would include home addresses, phone numbers, the names of their pets and contact information for the nearest pet store to their homes.
>
> They could also purchase lists of cat owners and people who buy cat products from supermarkets and pets store companies. Using the Internet, they could purchase lists of email addresses of people who visit cat-related web sites or those who use cat-related newsgroups and mailing lists. Such discussion groups are in abundance on the Internet. The cat-related groups include `alt.animals.felines`, `alt.cats`, and `rec.pet.cats.misc`. (Discussion groups are discussed in Chapter 5, Specialty Tools.)

In addition, there are other discussion groups, called mailing lists, where people subscribe to receive correspondence about specific subjects. One cat-related group is called the PURRS mailing list, which dubs itself "a purrfect place for all cats and kittens to chat."

Marketers are only beginning to tap into these groups as sources of information.

How Much Is Too Much, and When?

Some companies advertise their ability to obtain the past and current addresses, phone numbers, birth dates, driving records, bankruptcy history and other information on just about anyone in the United States. But it is access to these kinds of records that let people make important "public safety" connections between databases – things like exposing drunk-driving schoolbus drivers and pinpointing where the unsafe bridges and roads in your community are.

You could be a customer. You could also be a target. You could be both at the same time without knowing it. That's because the Internet relays information from one computer to the next until it reaches its destination computer. Anyone who can view your data can grab it, copy it and keep it. They can do anything they want with it: alter it, sell it, pass it off as someone else's personal history – you name it.

→ *hot tip:* **Most people don't realize that what you thought was a private email between you and a friend could actually be seen by others along the route. At every step along the way your information footprint passes across the screens of numerous online handlers whose staff (permanent, temporary, subcontracted, ex-convicts, whomever) can read your data — information that you never intended for unauthorized viewing.**

Unauthorized collection and abuse of personal data happens all the time. What follows is a humorous letter that illustrates the depth of data collections.

The Letter You'll Never Get

By Don Ray

Dear Average Customer:

Just a long-overdue note to say thanks for all the information you gave us yesterday — information we computerized and are making available to hundreds of other marketers like us. You're our prime source of information, and income.

In case you weren't paying attention, here's where you dropped loose "information change" into our little "information piggy bank:"

When you turned on your cellular phone this morning, we noted that you got a late start to work. We didn't sell the information, but we're working on it.

You stopped to get gas and used your electronic credit card to pay for the gas and a quart of oil. I see you bought that new synthetic oil. We sold that information to the manufacturer. They said they may send you a coupon for the next one before they sell your address to someone else. You might want to drop them a thank you note.

Did you miss breakfast again? You stopped at the chain fast-food place and used your ATM card. You actually had them put mayonnaise on your potato nuggets? We'll alert the condiment manufacturer. They may want to track the rest of your eating habits.

We were wondering if you were running low on cash. Sure enough, you stopped at the ATM for a $60 withdrawal. Oh, I hope you don't mind, but we notice from the security camera there that you're a bit overweight. Too much mayonnaise and potatoes? Just kidding. We sent the information from your bank account to a couple of weight-reduction clinics. We do our best to keep you in good health.

Hey, thanks for dropping your business card into that fishbowl at the restaurant. Listen, don't count on getting a free lunch, but we were able to see from your card that you work in retail sales. At your age, you should be doing better. We took it upon ourselves to give your name and address to a couple of trade schools. For a minute we thought you might want to go to a truck driving school, but with your driving record you might be better off as a dental hygienist.

While you were at work, we received that warranty card you mailed last week when you bought the new DVD player. Thanks for letting us know that you like to play tennis, you enjoy gardening, and you and your spouse have a combined income of $72,000. We'll let the appropriate people know. There are some telemarketers who'll call you tonight to tell you about some promising stock options.

Oh, wait. Tonight's your bowling night. We just got the list from the bowling center. Is your spouse going to their creative writing class tonight? After using their credit card to buy $115 worth of textbooks, they had better go.

You went to the supermarket on your way home last night. You saved $3.80 by using your handy Preferred Customer Card, and we were able to learn a lot about your family. You've been buying disposable diapers for over a year. You were buying the pink brand, with the protection at the bottom. Now you're buying the blue brand with the protection in front. A baby boy, eh? I confess, we checked the birth certificates to learn the little tyke's name. Brandon, eh? Named after your mother's father. How nice.

You know, we really value all the wonderful marketing information you're giving us. We have visions of tracking you for the next twenty years.

Again, thanks so much to you, your spouse, your kids and Rascal for all you've done for us.

Sincerely,

Your Neighborhood Marketing Folks

p.s.: Forgot to mention that Rascal needs his rabies vaccination before the end of the month.

-- Don Ray is a multimedia investigative journalist and a sought-after speaker in information gathering, privacy and public records. He's written books on sources of information, interviewing, checking out lawyers and on document interpretation. His email address is `donray@donray.com`

Believe it or not, some people don't mind marketing. In fact, the following piece illuminates the bright side to advertising on the Internet.

Personal Information from a Marketer's Point of View

By Robbin Zeff

Before you get all worked up and conclude that the use of personal information by marketers is a bad thing and has no direct benefit to you, consider this:

❖ When is a quarter-page print ad in a magazine not just filler on a page?

❖ When is a billboard not just scenic junk?

❖ When is an ad on the radio not just noise on the airwaves?

The answer: when it's information you want!

Having someone know what you like and how you like it can simplify the buying process. I like it when I go to my favorite coffee shop and Bill behind the counter knows just how I like my latté and has it ready for me when I get to the front of the line. Bill can do this because I've been there before. He remembers how I like my latté. Bill also knows that I like scones, and his recommendation of the day's choice of scones will often result in a sale. This personalized service makes me feel at home and results in my returning again and again. In short, it's good business.

Targeting and personalization in advertising on the Internet has the same effect. Through the sophisticated technological capabilities of the Internet, an advertiser can deliver the right ad to the right person at the right time. In the example above, when Bill recommends a scone as he hands me my coffee, he knows that it is the right time to hit me up for an additional purchase. This strategy works just as well in selling books or CDs. If you are purchasing the latest murder mystery novel by John Grisham, you might be interested in an ad for a similar page-turner by a different author. In which case, the ad becomes a source of information.

This is precisely the strategy behind targeting and personalization in Internet advertising: put the right ad in front of the right person at the right time to increase the relevancy of the ad to the individual. For the marketer, personal information allows the advertiser to maximize the efficiency of the advertising and make each ad a piece of relevant information to the consumer. Targeting like this has been the age-old dream of advertisers. What the Internet brings to the forefront is the ability to deliver on this promise.

Targeting Based on Content and Context

The first level of targeting in marketing is based on content and context. For example, when you first read a fashion magazine like *Vogue* or *Glamour*, you expect to see fashion ads for clothing and cosmetics. The content of the magazine is about fashion as are the ads. When you read the *Los Angeles Times*, you expect to find ads for businesses in the Los Angeles area. Moreover, the ads in the *Los Angeles Times* not only represent business in that geographic area, but also narrow in on specific interests so that in the automotive section you find ads directly relating to cars: car dealers, automotive repair, car washes, etc. Likewise, when you watch a baseball game on television, the commercials reflect the audience demographics so that you see beer and car ads instead of ads for diapers or back-to-school sales.

Targeting based on content and context is easily achieved on the Web by placing ads on specific web sites and on particular pages within those sites. Search engines do this through keyword ad placement. For example, an advertiser can buy a specific keyword like "allergy" and every time that keyword is requested, an ad for its allergy relief medicine appears on the page. But, this is only the beginning of the targeting capabilities for internet advertising. (See the Paid Placement sidebar in Chapter 4, Search Engines.)

Targeting Based on Analyzing Web Site Log Files

The next level of targeting information comes from analyzing the log files of web sites. Log files hold all the on-site activity records: who entered the site, what browser was employed, the user's entrance and exit pages, etc. This information is useful for understanding the traffic and usage patterns on a site, but it doesn't provide *demographic* information. Why? The log file identifies *only* the Internet address of the computer that visited the site, *not* the individual behind the computer. The only real way to get demographic data on the Web is to ask the user for this information. Sites gather data through registration forms, subscription forms, contest registration forms, and the like. The strategy works.

Example: A major newspaper chose to make its online access free to all registered users. Why? The value of the demographic information provided by the viewers was deemed to be more valuable than the potential income from subscription fees. Information about the demographic profile of its readership enabled the newspaper to charge a premium for its ad space.

But, online targeting can do even more. The backbone of direct mail is using databases to target consumers with specific interests and then exposing them to products that their profile might find of interest. These databases are built on previous buying patterns, magazine subscriptions, and even Zip Code analysis. Marketers rent these lists and then send their material to the targeted lists. Internet marketers compile their own lists in addition to overlaying existing database information. The result is that soon Internet marketers will be able to do everything online that traditional direct marketers do by mail. But, online targeting can go even further.

The next level of targeting is unique to the technological capabilities of the Internet. Through a technique called "collaborative filtering," companies are learning the buying preferences of consenting searchers and then using this information to recommend books, music, and even movies. The result is that an enabled site can function as an old and trusted sales clerk who knows your taste in music and movies and, consequently, knows just what to recommend.

Then there is a method of Internet targeting based on actual behavior in which special software analyzes the user's behavior on the site and then presents ads based on analysis of the user's behavior during that particular online session. Each user session is unique and the software does have to store the data. For example, a web searcher who behaves like a thirteen-year-old girl will receive ads that appeal to thirteen-year-old girls. Later, if that person comes to the site and acts more like an adult, different ads will be shown.

So, is it a bad thing to have an advertiser know what you like and how you like it?

When the issue of access to personal information is put in this light, the answer for most consumers is "no." Targeting in advertising is actually a service to the customer. One way or another, ads will be shown on web sites. Personally, I appreciate the fact that when I visit my favorite web sites, I'm only shown ads for products and services of interest to me. Likewise, I like the fact that when I walk into my favorite coffee shop, Bill behind the counter knows just how I like my latté. My only hope is that someday my computer will be able to brew up a great latté while I'm on the Web.

-- Robbin Zeff is president of the Zeff Group, a research and training firm specializing in Internet advertising and marketing. She wrote the best-seller *Advertising on the Internet* and *The Nonprofit Guide to the Internet*. Her email address is `robbin@zeff.com` web site is www.zeff.com

You Can Level the Playing Field!

Before you can regain control of how people may be perusing your information, you must understand the online landscape. You can protect yourself by using the same technology that people are using to find information about you. Chapter 14, Privacy & Protection, will show you how to protect yourself and how you can use the information collected about you or someone else to your advantage.

It's a matter of understanding the kind of access that you have in a given situation. Examples:

Example 1: **You work for a company that solicited and received bids for a large contract. The lowest bid looks good … too good. So, you go online and discover some interesting facts: the low-bidding company incorporated just two years ago, and its CEO's previous companies were tangled in numerous lawsuits, liens and bankruptcies. Clearly, the CEO had a habit of changing companies every time he ran into trouble – and he ran into trouble regularly.**

Example 2: **You're a divorcée and your alimony checks have been shrinking. You're due a specified percentage of your ex's income, and something seems amiss. So, you start digging online and discover through public records that he has remarried and is in the process of transferring his assets to his new wife. Clearly, his strategy is to reduce his assets and reduce his alimony payments. You have a right to file a court appeal, and do, and the court is made aware of his hiding of assets. You fought back by using public records, which cost you almost nothing to access.**

The list of everyday applications is endless. As you read this book you will become familiar with tools and concepts that enable you to move freely and effectively online. Web sites are constantly changing, but the techniques to master searching on the Internet will continue to work as the Internet evolves. These techniques enable you to find more recent sites on subjects that interest you. Chapter 14, Privacy & Protection, lays out a number of ways for protecting your privacy.

Additional Web Sites for Creative Uses of the Internet

Bone Marrow Donors Worldwide
www.bmdw.org
Worldwide links for blood marrow donors.

Care Scout
www.carescout.com
This site permits you to access some comparative data on nursing homes by Zip Code or area in the U.S. Fee for detailed reports.

Citadon
www.citadon.com
Construction company that uses online tools for business.

Citadon CW
www.bidcom.com
Centralized bidding system for online construction industry.

Cybertracker
www.natureoutlet.com/cybertracker
American version of South African cyber tracking tool.

Cybertracker
www.cybertracker.co.za/
Joint bid network of several construction companies.

Destination RX
www.destinationrx.com
A search engine that scours most leading retail drug sites for the products – prescriptions, OTC, and non-drug items.

Expat Access
www.expataccess.com
Resource for ex-patriots In Europe and around the world.

Expat Singapore
www.expatsingapore.com
Resource for ex-patriots in Asia.

ExpatExpert
www.expatexpert.com
Resource for ex-patriots.

Health Notes
www.healthnotes.com
provides balanced information on supplements, vitamins and alternative therapies Provides time-limited access.

Here2Listen.com
www.here2listen.com
helps you locate mental health professionals.

Japan In Your Palm.com
www.japaninyourpalm.com
Resource for ex-patriots who use Palm Pilots.

Kdnuggets
www.kdnuggets.com
Newsletter for the data mining industry and research site.

Life Saving Organs & Marrow Requests
www.marrow.org
Life saving organs and bone marrow requests.

Mental Healthline
www.mentalhealthline.com
Offers counseling through email.

National Marrow Donor Program
www.marrow.org
National blood marrow donor program.

Natural Pharmacist
www.naturalpharmacist.com
Info on supplements, vitamins, and alternative therapies.

One Medicine
www.onemedicine.com
Provides balanced information on supplements, vitamins and alternative therapies. Provides time-limited access.

People Going Global
www.peoplegoingglobal.com
Resource for ex-patriots.

Rent a Priest
www.rentapriest.com
Allows you to find a priest or religious person to marry you. More than 2,500 available for referrals.

Studies with Government Funding
www.clinicaltrials.gov
Starting place to find where clinical trials are available.

Traffiic School Online
www.trafficschoolonline.com
Central clearinghouse for traffic school's online.

Chapter 2

The Basics

Basic Internet Terminology and Concepts

~~~~~~

The Mechanics of The Internet — Browser Software — Making It All Work — Ad Blocking Software — Everything About Email (Almost) — Saving Your Results — How Does Uploading/Downloading Work? — Identifying File Types — Field Guide to File Formats — How to Save Files — Virus Protection — Good Resources About Viruses — Virus Hoaxes — Additional Internet Basics Resources — Your Rights & Copyrights — Downloading Databases & Spreadsheets — Additional Sites: Basics

~~~~~~

First, in this book there will be no talking about "surfing" unless it relates to the beach. There will be no talk of "cyberspace" or the "information superhighway." These terms have been used to the point of being meaningless when discussing online research. Okay, maybe we'll let the information superhighway reference go because it can be a useful metaphor...

Second, while this book contains thousands of useful sites, the wonder as well as the frustration of the Internet is that it changes every single day. New sites are added on the Internet at a frantic pace, and existing sites can disappear without warning. So the focus of this book is not to be the definitive index of web sites, but to get you pointed in the right direction and teach you how to reason your way through the Internet and find what you are looking for quickly and efficiently.

Finally, a caution: think carefully before you write, send, or post anything on the Internet. Don't post anything you wouldn't post on, say, a grocery store bulletin board, or as journalists say, don't say anything you wouldn't want to see attributed to you on page one of the newspaper. While most of your email discussions will be private, mistakes happen and if you live online by the public standard – meaning that everything that happens will be broadcast to the masses – your caution will give you some peace of mind.

This chapter is designed to give anyone – novice or expert – a quick understanding of the basics of how the Internet works and tips for using it more effectively. The chapter is divided into subsections and uses the question and answer format to allow more experienced web users to skip around to only the answers that interest them. Hopefully, this book will become a steady companion with you as you work your way around the Internet. Feel free to skip around to the chapters most relevant to your searching needs.

The Mechanics of The Internet

What's the Difference Between The World Wide Web and The Internet?

If you've ever visited New York City, or looked at it on a map, you know that when people talk about the city, they mean Manhattan Island. But as New Yorkers quickly point out, New York City is actually five boroughs — Manhattan, Queens, Brooklyn, The Bronx, and Staten Island. Nonetheless, anytime anyone except a New Yorker talks about New York, they mean Manhattan. Most people tend to use the words "the Internet ('Net)" and "the World Wide Web (Web)" interchangeably. But they are not the same. Much like Manhattan is just a part of New York City, the Web is just the dominant part of the Internet.

The Internet is a set of rules that allows computers to connect and communicate with other computers easily, a development by the U.S. Defense Advanced Research Agency (DARPA) in 1969 as a way for researchers and defense contractors to exchange information.

The World Wide Web (www) was developed in 1990 by Tim Berners-Lee, who was a computer programmer working for CERN, the European Organization for Nuclear Research. Berners-Lee constructed a graphic interface that allowed you to see photos and graphics, hear sounds, and view videos by simply clicking on a hypertext link.

So the Web is only a part – yes, the dominant part – of the Internet. In most cases, when you look at your email, technically you are doing it separately from the Web. When you talk in chat rooms, you can do that without accessing the Web. When you share files, like swapping music or text files, that too can be done without the Web. All of these things can also be done using the Web, which is why things get confusing. Again, think of Manhattan Island and realize that the Web is just a part of a much larger Internet.

What Equipment Do I Need to Start Using the Internet?

First, it helps to understand that "the Internet" is not a singular thing. It is a collection of computers around the world connected via phone and data lines. There is no single point of entry to the Internet – it's a crazy quilt of computers and connections.

So to get "on" you need to have a way to reach the other computers. You need a phone number that can connect you to the Internet, an interface device and software that does the mechanics of dialing that phone number so that the computer network can understand it, and you need a password that lets the system know that it's really you who wants to get started on an internet journey. The phone number and password information are provided in advance to you by your Internet Service Provider (ISP).

The third thing you need is that interface device that can talk to other computers, and also a device or software that displays this information so you can see it. Just a couple of years ago, the answer to "what do you need to get online?" was straightforward: a personal computer, a modem that hooks into your telephone line, an account with an ISP, and some software. That's still the starting point for most of us, but now there are many ways to connect your computer to the Internet.

Now, people can access the Internet from dial-up phone lines, dedicated digital high-speed phone lines, cell phones, and other mobile devices such as personal digital assistants (PDAs). So the answer is a little more complex, but the formula is the same. You still need a device that has a computer's capabilities, a way to connect to the computer network, plus software such as a web browser, email client and possibly other software components. Much of this software is preloaded on your computer (we'll use the term "computer" to universally mean whatever device you are using to connect to the Web) and only requires you to enter a few pieces of information from your ISP in order to get you up and running.

How Exactly Do Computers "Understand" Each Other?

Computers can't see, hear, or comprehend – they basically just compute numbers. So everything on a computer – words, sounds, images – is translated into a series of ones and zeroes so that the computer can "see" or "hear" what it receives. Telephone lines, however, rely on sounds. So when you use a modem to connect to the Internet via the telephone line, your computer or device sends out digital information (ones and zeros) and the modem converts them into special sounds the phone line can understand. The act of your modem "talking" to another modem is called a handshake. Once your modem connects to another computer, it can then talk with any other computer that is also connected.

What's an ISP?

Because there is no single gatekeeper to the Internet, an internet service provider creates a secure entry point into one of the many computers that comprise the Internet. They provide accounts for individuals and companies to access the Internet. These accounts include a unique ID and password, and a phone number or connection your computer can use to connect to the ISP's main computer. There are a variety of pricing plans and ways you can connect to the Internet.

Usually your ISP will provide software programs including a web browser, electronic mail or email program, and sometimes additional software. They also tend to provide customer support and technical information. Many also offer a wide array of other services including hosting web pages. Most ISPs will work with the browser and email programs already installed in your computer. But some internet companies like America Online (AOL) and Microsoft Network (MSN) provide their own proprietary software to get you online. This includes a way onto the Internet as well as a range of other online services from news to travel information, to chat rooms – available only to their members. AOL, the largest of these online services, has thirty-three million subscribers.

Internet Service Providers, telephone and cable companies have different methods of charging for internet access. In the United States, the standard has become unlimited access for between US$20-$25. High-speed unlimited access costs nearly double that much. In parts of Europe, Asia and Latin America, access is charged on a per-minute basis, so the costs of spending time on the Internet can vary dramatically. As a result, the way someone researches a subject will change based on their budget. Also, when faced with per-minute charges, people tend to go where they are familiar instead of exploring new sites.

Because some plans offer unlimited usage, and others charge you by the minute, take some time to shop around for the ISP that best suits your needs. Ask yourself what's important – do you just need access to the Internet or do you also need email? Do you expect to spend more than a few hours online each week? Are you also looking for a place to host your web site? Look over the pricing plans to see what service best matches your needs. A good place to start your research is The List of ISPs (`http://thelist.internet.com`).

What Are Internet Protocols? What Is TCP/IP?

Internet jargon is an alphabet soup of acronyms. TCP/IP refers to the method computers use to communicate via data lines — phone lines, cables, satellites. You probably won't need to know much about this in order to start your research, but it is helpful to understand when someone starts talking to you about things like "lost packets."

When computers connect to send information back and forth, they do so using a system in which the data is sent in chunks of information, known as packets. The packets are numbered and given an address to the target computer. They are then sent through the Internet to be delivered. On the receiving end, the target computer grabs up the packets and reassembles them in their original order. The nice part is when you send something, you don't have to worry about the packets and how they work. The Internet routes the packets through different routes, allowing the system to operate efficiently. The receiving computer tests to ensure that all the packets arrive correctly, and if errors are found, it asks the original computer to send the packet again.

The specification standards by which all these computers send each other information – or "talk" – are called protocols. There are hundreds of different types of protocols including ones to send email and ones to copy files from one place to another.

Lots of researchers are able to conduct their business without ever understanding the following few paragraphs. However, there may come a time when you need to understand the system of protocols and how they work in order to pass your information around the Internet.

The two most important protocols are the ones that allow data to be transported as packets. They are called IP or Internet Protocol, which moves the packet data from one place to another, and TCP or Transmission Control Protocol, which manages the flow of packets and ensures they arrive without errors. Together they are called TCP/IP.

A few other protocols are important depending on what you are sending. When you are setting up your domain name, you will use a DNS or Domain Name System, which translates domain names like `cbs.com` to IP numbers. FTP is File Transfer Protocol, which allows you to copy entire files between computers. HTTP is the Hypertext Transfer Protocol, which allows the distribution of web data through hypertext, the language that gives you the ability to link one site to the next. POP is the Post Office Protocol, which is needed to get email messages from a mail server. When you use a POP, you check your email and download the email to your computer before you can access them. SMTP is Simple Mail Transfer Protocol, which allows you to send messages to a mail server and finally MIME or Multipurpose Internet Mail Extensions, encodes different types of data so you can send them via email. Other programs that may work instead of using POP are web mail, IMAP4, and mail forwarding.

IMAP servers, or Internet Message Access Protocol servers, are sometimes used as alternatives to POP. POP is great when you are using your own computer, because you must download the email before you can read it. But if you travel or don't take a computer with you, then downloading your messages onto other people's computers can be a big problem. That's where IMAP comes in handy. With IMAP, you leave the email on the server, so you can read the messages at your convenience. They stay on the server until you delete them. That way you can check them from the office and again from home, or when traveling, before you delete them. Most ISPs prefer you use a POP server, so they don't have to store your messages.

You can also use web-based email services that allow you to send and receive mail using only your web browser.

Web mail works through the World Wide Web instead of using a separate email program. The information rests on a server on the Web, and you never download it to your hard drive. Under web-based mail, the browser acts as your simple email program. The big advantage of using web mail services is they tend to be free since you already have the browser, and you can access them from almost any computer in the world. It also allows those without their own computer to receive email. It also provides a modest level of privacy or anonymity, allowing you to write email from your office when you don't want to use your work email address. I strongly recommended that you get a web-based email address as a backup to any POP-based email service in case your regular email is not working.

There are a few downsides however to web-based email services. These services can be extremely slow at times, and are often loaded with advertisements. Even worse, some of these services put advertisement tags on the bottom of every piece of email so even your recipients will see the ads. And the worst part of this is that they are notorious for being the recipients of spam and there's almost no way around it. (See the spam section below for more information.)

Mail forwarding is another option. With this type of email, your mail is redirected to wherever you choose. This allows you to switch Internet Service Providers without losing your regular email address. This can also be accomplished by setting up what is called an alias.

A *few* of the better web-based mail services include:

Hotmail	**Lycos Mail**	**Yahoo! Mail**
www.hotmail.com	www.mailcity.lycos.com	www.mail.yahoo.com

What Is an IP Address?

When you are connected, your computer will be assigned a unique internet address, called an IP address. This is the official location of your computer while it is on the Internet and allows other computers to route information to you. No two computers can use the same IP address simultaneously. Some ISPs give you a static IP address – your computer will always have the same address, while others assign a dynamic address to you each time – a different number each time you log in. The reason for dynamic IP addresses is that there are so many computers accessing the Web at various times, that eventually it would run out of numbers. Dynamic addresses allow web users to recycle addresses that aren't in use at that particular time. Your computer at work most likely has a static IP address assigned to it so your information technology staff always knows where your computer is on the network and what it is doing.

The IP address or IP number is a code made up of a series numbers separated by dots that identifies a particular computer on the Internet. Every computer requires one to connect to the Internet. A web IP address looks like 216.147.47.134 and if you put http:// in front of that particular IP address in the location bar on your browser, you can go to that specific page, which belongs to a terrific glossary on computer terms by Sharpened.net. Domain names are the word-based addresses for web sites and are usually much easier to remember than the IP address. A domain name doesn't become active until it is matched to an IP address. Before you can send something to someone, your email program must ask your Domain Name Server to convert their email address to its IP address. This process is called a DNS lookup. Coincidentally, DNS lookup is a valuable tool for finding web sites that are no longer active.

In addition to allowing computers to route information back and forth, IP addresses can be used as investigative tools. Law enforcement agencies around the world have been able to track criminals directly to specific computer IP addresses, even dynamic ones. (See the Chapter 14, Privacy & Protection for more details.)

Who Runs The Internet?

What makes the Internet so disorganized is also one of its great strengths. Nobody runs the Internet. That's because it's really a collection of many smaller networks, not one giant network. There are groups that manage *parts* of the Internet but no one manages it as a whole. It probably won't make a big difference to you, the user, one way or the other. But without a centralized system, legislative efforts to regulate the Internet by local or even national governments are extremely difficult to accomplish. What's permissible in one country can be prohibited in another. While you may have the ability to express your opinion about another country's rules and laws, someone from that country may not have that luxury. Information may flow from one country to another across the Internet, but local governments can enforce their own laws. With millions of people online from nearly every country in the world, and its incredible diversity, it's almost impossible to design laws or guidelines that work worldwide. But as it grows, etiquette, and standards of acceptable behavior have developed.

It's not all chaos. There are some groups that help establish policies for the Internet. ICANN, (the Internet Corporation for Assigned Names and Numbers at www.icann.org) coordinates domain names, while the Internet Society (www.ISOC.org) acts as a clearinghouse for technical standards. The Internet Engineering Task Force (www.IETF.org) works to establish Internet protocols and iron out problems. The Web Consortium (W3C) (www.w3c.org) acts as a forum to discuss specifications, guidelines, tools and software to develop what it calls a "collective understanding." For more details on the way the Internet is loosely organized, go to the ICANN web site.

On a more practical level, a handful of companies – like Microsoft, America Online, Yahoo!, Intel, and Cisco have undue influence over how the Internet works simply because these companies and their products greatly shape the infrastructure of the Internet and therefore, how we use it.

While we may enjoy the Web's incredible ability to disseminate information and, as a result, its freedom of speech, it also requires great effort and some skill to avoid pornography and other materials frequently considered offensive. But while you may stumble across something disturbing, it is that same free exchange of information and ideas that allows Chinese dissidents to get information over the objections of the Chinese government. With this freedom comes an increased need for each of us to develop our own sense of information discrimination – judging what we want to look at and what we choose to believe or dismiss.

How Many People Are Online and Who Are They?

That number is constantly changing. The best "educated guess" from NUA, an Irish-based internet statistics company, puts it at about 605.6 million. Country-by-country breakdowns and ethnic makeup are also available from these sources.

One other statistical note worth mentioning. Often I am asked, is it still a male bastion on the Internet? If the U.S. is an indication, the answer is no. In the U.S., women now outnumber men online, and the rest of the world is not far behind.

To find out the latest numbers on how many people are online and where they are from, here are some links to sites that follow that information:

Cyberatlas
www.cyberatlas.internet.com/big_picture/geographics

Internet Stats
www.internetstats.com

Nielsen Net/Ratings
www.nielsen-netratings.com/hot_off_the_net_i.jsp

Nua Internet Surveys
www.nua.org/surveys

What Is a URL?

A web address is also called a URL or Uniform Resource Locator. Every web page has a unique URL that can be broken into three parts: the protocol, the domain name, and the file path. While in the early days many pronounced this "earl," the common pronunciation is to spell it out "u-r-l."

How Do You Read A Web Address (URL)?
How Do Domain Names Work?

Domain names can tell you who the entity is, what kind of entity (company, individual, government) and sometimes what country they are from.

Let's say we're looking at the following address: `http://www.whitehouse.gov`.

The letters before the ": //" describe the way a browser can get to the resource. The "`http://`" stands for Hypertext Transfer Protocol, which is the way the Web moves data around. Following the colon are two slashes (always forward slashes, never backward slashes). The "`www`" indicates a computer that acts as a web server, which just means it is a computer that stores and provides or "serves" web content up to any computer that connects to it. Next comes the name of the host computer on which the resource exists – in this case, the "White House."

Some addresses may start out with `https://` or `ftp://` – these are just different types of connections or protocols to computers on the Web.

At the end of the domain name (after the . or "dot") is a two- or three-letter abbreviation that indicates the top-level domain. This part of the domain tells you the kind of organization the web site you are looking at is or the country where the host server is located.

.com — refers to a commercial site (most companies use this extension)

.edu — refers to an educational institution

.gov — refers to a government agency in the United States

.mil — refers to a United States military organization

.net — refers to a network (most dot-nets have been reserved for organizations like ISPs)

.org — refers to a non-profit or non-commercial organization

Beginning in 2001, ICANN, one of the governing organizations of the Internet, approved seven additional domain names scheduled to be rolled out over time. Three are already being used:

.biz — refers to any business

.info — refers to any individual or company

.name — refers to any individual

And four more are being considered:

.aero — refers to airlines

.coop — refers to business cooperatives

.museum — refers to museums

.pro — refers to business professionals like doctors, lawyers, accountants, etc.

To find out more, you can visit the ICANN web site (`www.icann.org`).

What Are HTML Tags and How Do They Work?
Will They Be Around for a Long Time?

Hypertext Markup Language (HTML) is a set of special codes referred to as "tags," which instruct a web browser how to display a hypertext document. It's like a collection of styles that define the different parts of a web page. All HTML documents are written in plain text (ASCII) format, making them universally readable by different web browsers running on different computer platforms.

HTML tags consist of a left angle bracket (< or "less than" symbol) followed by the name of the tag and closed by a right angle bracket (> or "greater than" symbol). Most tags are paired, with a beginning (or open) and an ending (or close) tag. You can see the HTML coding on your browser by clicking on "View," then "Source."

HTML coding is what makes the Internet easily readable to crawlers. But it has many weaknesses. So the creative minds behind the Internet have been looking to a newer language to help move the Internet into its next phase. It's called XML.

As Internet expert John December explains, XML (eXtensible Markup Language) is a method for defining structure in documents. The philosophy behind XML is that the information (text, images, etc.) of a document can be identified through a set of rules. With these rules, a variety of software applications (like browsers) can interpret, display, or process data in documents.

XML, similar to HTML, was created to specifically address the issue of writing documents for the Web. And as in HTML, XML authors use elements bracketed by open and close tags. But unlike HTML, XML does not limit you to a fixed set of elements and entities, giving you much more flexibility and allowing the documents to include context and have structural relationships in your documents. XML is the next big language.

Using XML, you will be able to define your own elements, which allows you to create a logical structure in documents. So instead of being locked in by HTML coding, you can add elements (like an image or a person) to help define structures that are in complex relationship. This flexibility will ultimately help organize web pages and how they relate to one another. For more on how this works, see John December's excellent site www.december.com

What Are Those Two-Letter Codes at the End of an Address?

As the Internet is truly a global experience, email addresses and web sites outside the United States often carry a two-letter country code from IANA, the internet assigned numbers authority.

Here is the comprehensive list of country and territory codes. For updates, visit www.iana.org/cctld/cctld-whois.htm

.ac – Ascension Island	.al – Albania	.as – American Samoa
.ad – Andorra	.am – Armenia	.at – Austria
.ae – United Arab Emirates	.an – Netherlands Antilles	.au – Australia
.af – Afghanistan	.ao – Angola	.aw – Aruba
.ag – Antigua and Barbuda	.aq – Antarctica	.az – Azerbaijan
.ai – Anguilla	.ar – Argentina	.ba – Bosnia and Herzegovina

.bb – Barbados	.ec – Ecuador	.io – British Indian Ocean Terr.
.bd – Bangladesh	.ee – Estonia	.iq – Iraq
.be – Belgium	.eg – Egypt	.ir – Iran (Islamic Republic of)
.bf – Burkina Faso	.eh – Western Sahara	.is – Iceland
.bg – Bulgaria	.er – Eritrea	.it – Italy
.bh – Bahrain	.es – Spain	.je – Jersey
.bi – Burundi	.et – Ethiopia	.jm – Jamaica
.bj – Benin	.fi – Finland	.jo – Jordan
.bm – Bermuda	.fj – Fiji	.jp – Japan
.bn – Brunei Darussalam	.fk – Falkland Islands/Malvina	.ke – Kenya
.bo – Bolivia	.fm – Micronesia, Federal State	.kg – Kyrgyzstan
.br – Brazil	.fo – Faroe Islands	.kh – Cambodia
.bs – Bahamas	.fr – France	.ki – Kiribati
.bt – Bhutan	.ga – Gabon	.km – Comoros
.bv – Bouvet Island	.gd – Grenada	.kn – Saint Kitts and Nevis
.bw – Botswana	.ge – Georgia	.kp – Korea, Demo. People's Rep.
.by – Belarus	.gf – French Guiana	.kr – Korea, Republic of
.bz – Belize	.gg – Guernsey	.kw – Kuwait
.ca – Canada	.gh – Ghana	.ky – Cayman Islands
.cc – Cocos (Keeling) Islands	.gi – Gibraltar	.kz – Kazakhstan
.cd – Congo, Democratic Republic	.gl – Greenland	.la – Lao People's Demo. Republic
.cf – Central African Republic	.gm – Gambia	.lb – Lebanon
.cg – Congo, Republic of	.gn – Guinea	.lc – Saint Lucia
.ch – Switzerland	.gp – Guadeloupe	.li – Liechtenstein
.ci – Cote d'Ivoire	.gq – Equatorial Guinea	.lk – Sri Lanka
.ck – Cook Islands	.gr – Greece	.lr – Liberia
.cl – Chile	.gs – South Georgia/S Sandwich Is	.ls – Lesotho
.cm – Cameroon	.gt – Guatemala	.lt – Lithuania
.cn – China	.gu – Guam	.lu – Luxembourg
.co – Colombia	.gw – Guinea-Bissau	.lv – Latvia
.cr – Costa Rica	.gy – Guyana	.ly – Libyan Arab Jamahiriya
.cu – Cuba	.hk – Hong Kong	.ma – Morocco
.cv – Cap Verde	.hm – Heard and McDonald Islands	.mc – Monaco
.cx – Christmas Island	.hn – Honduras	.md – Moldova, Republic of
.cy – Cyprus	.hr – Croatia/Hrvatska	.mg – Madagascar
.cz – Czech Republic	.ht – Haiti	.mh – Marshall Islands
.de – Germany	.hu – Hungary	.mk – Macedonia, Yugoslav Republic
.dj – Djibouti	.id – Indonesia	.ml – Mali
.dk – Denmark	.ie – Ireland	.mm – Myanmar
.dm – Dominica	.il – Israel	.mn – Mongolia
.do – Dominican Republic	.im – Isle of Man	.mo – Macau
.dz – Algeria	.in – India	.mp – Northern Mariana Islands

.mq – Martinique	.ps – Palestinian Territories	.tj – Tajikistan
.mr – Mauritania	.pt – Portugal	.tk – Tokelau
.ms – Montserrat	.pw – Palau	.tm – Turkmenistan
.mt – Malta	.py – Paraguay	.tn – Tunisia
.mu – Mauritius	.qa – Qatar	.to – Tonga
.mv – Maldives	.re – Reunion Island	.tp – East Timor
.mw – Malawi	.ro – Romania	.tr – Turkey
.mx – Mexico	.ru – Russian Federation	.tt – Trinidad and Tobago
.my – Malaysia	.rw – Rwanda	.tv – Tuvalu
.mz – Mozambique	.sa – Saudi Arabia	.tw – Taiwan
.na – Namibia	.sb – Solomon Islands	.tz – Tanzania
.nc – New Caledonia	.sc – Seychelles	.ua – Ukraine
.ne – Niger	.sd – Sudan	.ug – Uganda
.nf – Norfolk Island	.se – Sweden	.uk – United Kingdom
.ng – Nigeria	.sg – Singapore	.um – U.S. Minor Outlying Islands
.ni – Nicaragua	.sh – St. Helena	.us – United States
.nl – Netherlands	.si – Slovenia	.uy – Uruguay
.no – Norway	.sj – Svalbard/Jan Mayen Islands	.uz – Uzbekistan
.np – Nepal	.sk – Slovak Republic	.va – Holy See (City Vatican St)
.nr – Nauru	.sl – Sierra Leone	.vc – Saint Vincent/the Grenadines
.nu – Niue	.sm – San Marino	.ve – Venezuela
.nz – New Zealand	.sn – Senegal	.vg – Virgin Islands (British)
.om – Oman	.so – Somalia	.vi – Virgin Islands (USA)
.pa – Panama	.sr – Suriname	.vn – Vietnam
.pe – Peru	.st – Sao Tome and Principe	.vu – Vanuatu
.pf – French Polynesia	.sv – El Salvador	.wf – Wallis and Futuna Islands
.pg – Papua New Guinea	.sy – Syrian Arab Republic	.ws – Western Samoa
.ph – Philippines	.sz – Swaziland	.ye – Yemen
.pk – Pakistan	.tc – Turks and Caicos Islands	.yt – Mayotte
.pl – Poland	.td – Chad	.yu – Yugoslavia
.pm – St. Pierre and Miquelon	.tf – French Southern Territories	.za – South Africa
.pn – Pitcairn Island	.tg – Togo	.zm – Zambia
.pr – Puerto Rico	.th – Thailand	.zw – Zimbabwe

➜ *hot tip:* **When you look at a domain name address, look to the right side of the name after the dot. If the name has three or more letters, it is an organizational domain, like `.org` or `.gov`. But if it has two letters, it is a geographical domain, probably representing a country, like `.gov.au`.**

What Are Second-Level Domain Names?

Earlier you learned about top-level domain names, the .coms, .nets, etc. They are called top level because if you drew a diagram of host names with the most general names at the top, they would be the top level. But some host names have several parts to the name, all to the right of the www. These tend to be second-level domains like `mail.verizon.net` and `news.verizon.net`. Both of those would belong to the main domain: `verizon.net`.

The URL `www.ges.gov.uk` is for the government economic service in the UK. The URL `www.gpa-ni.gov.uk/home.htm` is for the government purchasing office of Northern Ireland in the U.K. Both of these are second-level domain names of the `gov.uk` domain.

Why Do Some Domain Names Have .US in Them?

In the early years, the Internet was primarily U.S.-centric. Top-level domain names like `.com` and `.edu` were set up and then country names were added. Originally it was designed that the U.S. would have a .us at the end. But by the time the geographical ones were introduced, people had been using the organizational domains for so long that few U.S. companies or people were willing to change. So, in the U.S., organizational domains are used, and everywhere else, geographical domains are used, except where non-U.S. companies have purchased organizational domains. So, ".us" is used primarily by local schools and local governments in the United States and by the different states. Using abbreviations like "cc" for community college and "ci" for city, Broward Community College in Florida can be found at `www.broward.cc.fl.us` while the City of Los Angeles' web site is `www.ci.la.ca.us` and San Francisco is `www.ci.sf.ca.us`.

But as always with the Internet, there are exceptions to the rules. For example, most U.S. federal government sites use `.gov` as their top-level domain. Or if a company got onto the Internet late and their domain name was taken, in many cases they tried to get .net or .org if .com was taken. That leads to some confusion. If you can't find the company you are looking for with `.com`, check out `.net` or `.org`. But be aware that early Internet advocates grabbed up thousands of domain names with the idea of later selling them to the companies that actually use the name. The U.S. Congress had to step in and pass legislation requiring companies that regularly use the company name in business to get first access to the proper domain name. Nonetheless, many companies were already established as `.net` and `.org` domains. In addition, some scammers bought up hundreds of domain names. They guessed that some people would make typing mistakes and others wouldn't know the difference between a `.gov` and a `.com` and so would accidentally go to the `.com` site. Most of those were X-rated sites and they set up revenue streams based on the number of hits to the site. WhiteHouse.com is the most notorious example.

How Is It That So Many Companies Have .TV?

Some two-letter country codes have different meanings based on language. In the United States, television stations wanted to have the easy to remember `.tv` at the end of their domain name. The extension `.tv` is the geographic designation for the little country of Tuvalu. To generate revenue for its government, Tuvalu began selling the domain name to companies around the world. The country code belongs to that country and they can do with it what they want. For the most part, they've used them for companies within their nation. Several more valuable codes are: `.to` for the small South Pacific nation of Tonga, `.it` for the country of Italy, and `.md` for the country of Moldova. Moldova has established an arrangement to license .md domain names to medical doctors.

Tricks to Reading an Address or URL

One good trick is: when you get an error message or a "can't reach that web site" notice, take the address and work backwards toward the domain name, removing the text between the slashes one section at a time. This is known as truncating.

For example, this news story on CNN will likely not be there by the time you read this: `www.cnn.com/2002/LAW/01/11/enron/index.html`, but if you keep working backwards toward the domain name slash (for example, start by deleting "`index.html`"), you will eventually find the main site — `www.cnn.com` — and may be able to find the page you were looking for.

If you see a tilde (~), it means the web site resides on a UNIX system – most often used at universities – and is most likely contained in the home directory of someone on that system.

Browser Software - Making It All Work

What Is the Browser?

Think of your browser as your window to the world. Almost everything you do on the Internet will revolve around the browser. It is the software program you need to graphically access the World Wide Web. The easy-to-use point-and-click browser, developed in the early 1990s, helped popularize the Web, although few imagined the incredible growth it would spur.

Although many different browsers are available, the two most popular ones are Microsoft's Internet Explorer (IE) and Netscape's Navigator. Both companies' browsers are based on the first browser, Mosaic, developed by the National Center for Supercomputing Applications. For a few years, Netscape dominated the browser world. But now Microsoft's browser thoroughly dominates the market. Both Microsoft and Netscape (now owned by AOL) have put so much money into the browser battle, few other companies want to compete. The intense, costly battle has prompted steady improvements to the browsers. Both companies provide free versions and if you have one, you should definitely check out the other as each has different features. There are differences between the Mac and Windows versions. In general though, they are similar and easy to learn. Microsoft and Netscape both offer help menus on their respective web sites.

Browsers consume a lot of disk space, especially if you choose to load all the added accessories. They also use a lot of RAM and require a reasonably fast processor. PC users need at least a 486-speed processor with 16MB of RAM to get Internet Explorer to function under Windows 95, 98 and 3.x and even more under Windows NT, 2000, ME and XP. The Netscape browser is comparable. A third browser, called Opera, from a Norwegian company, was designed to be slim but extremely usable and has a version designed for cell phones and other mobile devices.

You can find the latest versions of each of these browsers throughout the Web, but good places to start include:

CNET Download

`http://download.com`

Microsoft

`www.microsoft.com`

Netscape

`http://netscape.home.com`

Opera

`www.opera.com`

How Do I Use My Browser?

When you first launch your web browser, a pre-defined web page appears on your screen. Once this is loaded, you can look for the "location" or "address" bar at the top of the screen and replace the existing URL with the URL of the web site you would like to visit. Then press the "Enter" key and your browser will take it from there. Then, using the navigation keys at the top of the screen, you can skip around to different pages, print pages, and even save pages to your hard drive. (See questions and answers below for more detailed information about these functions).

How Do I Customize My Home or Start Page?

The first page that automatically loads onto your screen when you start your browser is the home page or start page and it is set to a default page by the manufacturer. This will be the page that will automatically open each time you start the application, so you may want to change it to a page you want to see every day (for example, your favorite web site) or even set it to open to a blank page to begin with so you don't have to wait for a page to load before you can point your browser to your destination. To customize this, click on the "Tools" Internet options button on Explorer, or click on "Edit and Preferences" on Netscape and indicate which, if any, URL you would like it to open first.

How Do I Use Those Buttons to Navigate The Web?

At the top of both browsers, in the section known as the toolbar, there are several buttons designed to help you navigate your way around the Web. "Back" and "Forward" allow you to toggle between pages you have already looked at in the current session. "Home" takes you to the page you have designated as the start page (see the above question and answer). "Stop" will stop a page from continuing to download, and "Print" is a shortcut to send a page to your printer.

Two very important buttons are "Reload" and "Refresh" because when you download a web page, sometimes all of the elements of a page don't load the first time. When a page loads onto your screen, the data is cached (pronounced "cashed") – meaning it is temporarily stored in your computer's memory. The next time you go to that same exact page, your browser pulls it from its cache memory so that the page will load more quickly since you already have the text and image files sitting on your hard drive. The problem is that if it is a page that changes frequently, a news page for example, you won't get the most current information until you hit the reload button, which tells your computer to go and get the most recent page. Caching is also how other people (like your information technology department at the office) can see information you looked at on your computer.

If you find you do not like the caching feature, you can turn caching off, or change the rules of how your computer caches. In IE (Internet Explorer) go to "Tools," then "Internet Options" and click on the "General" tab. Go to the section called "Temporary Internet Files" and click the "Settings" button. Here you can tell it when you would like the computer to check for a new version (refresh) of a page. In Navigator go to "Edit," then "Preferences," and click on "Advanced," then "Cache." Here you will see an area for editing your caching preferences.

Both IE and Netscape have buttons that allow you to connect to directories and search tools on their web sites. Don't do it. You will get limited versions of those search tools. Instead go to the dedicated search engines and directories as they will provide you with more options for searching. (See Chapter 4, Search Tools.)

How Do I Keep Track of My Favorite Web Sites?

Netscape calls them "Bookmarks" and Microsoft Internet Explorer calls them "Favorites," but these tools are similar and very valuable for keeping track of sites you would like to visit again by maintaining a list of them right in your browser. Since Netscape was around first, everyone calls saving these sites "bookmarking."

To bookmark a web site, go to your toolbar and click "Bookmark" or "Favorites," and then "Add." It's that simple. Once you have added a URL to your list, you can simply go back to "Bookmarks" or "Favorites," click on the link in your list, and you will go directly to that page, without having to remember and retype the address. Starting with versions 4.0 and up, both tools allow you to store these bookmarks/favorites in folders that you can organize and even write descriptions to tell you more of what they are. Note that some webmasters either give very long names or very generic names to their web pages, so for example, you may want to change a page that shows up as "`index.html`" to "cool pet site" in your bookmark list so you can easily remember what it is.

Beware of the temptation to put hundreds and thousands of sites into your bookmark list. Often when people do this, they can't locate the one site they really need when they are looking for it. Instead you may want to pick the handful of sites you will regularly use and bookmark those.

You can create an even faster link to your favorite sites by simply dragging a URL from the location bar (look for the small icon to the left of the URL) to the space beneath it – this creates a custom button right there under your location bar – saving you a couple of clicks of the mouse.

You can easily rename, delete, or change these buttons by editing your "Bookmarks" or "Favorites" list.

What Does the Location Bar on the Browser Do?

Just under the toolbar is a box called the "Location" bar, or "Go To" or "Address." This is where you enter an address, press "Return" and go to the web page you have entered.

If you click on the small triangle or downward arrow to the right of the address or location box, you will get a drop-down list of the most recent web sites you have visited. To revisit a site, but get the latest version, all you have to do is click on the address in the list.

Sometimes you may find that you have inadvertently hidden this bar from your view. To get it back, just go to the "View" menu and click "Toolbars," then "Address Bar" in IE, or "Show," then "Location Toolbar" in Navigator.

What Is the Menu Bar?

On the browser, the menu bar is located along the top of the browser window. The menu bar gives you a variety of options to do things like save files to your hard drive, change the size of the browser pages and even translate languages. All of the tools use drop-down menus.

How Do You Know If the Page Is Still Loading?

On each browser there are two indicators of a page loading on to your browser. Both Navigator and IE have a small picture in the upper right hand corner of the browser. When the image is moving, the browser software is pulling your data from a remote computer called a server. The browser downloads these files (sometimes temporarily into memory, sometimes permanently to your hard drive) to your computer and displays them on your screen. How fast that process is depends on several factors – the size of the file you are downloading, the speed of your modem connection, how busy the server is and how busy the Internet is at the moment you are downloading.

The second indicator is the status bar at the bottom of your browser. It tells you what percentage of the site has loaded as well as the address that you are loading. It has a tendency to jump around, so you may see it say "10%" for a while, then suddenly surge to "30%." That is normal!

What Is the Scroll Bar and Why Do I Need It?

Not all of the content of a single page may be visible on the computer screen, so you may have to use the scroll bar tool on the right hand side of your screen, and if the page is very wide, use the scroll bar at the bottom of your screen. A scroll bar is simply a slider that allows you to move up and down or side to side. You can also use your arrow keys or Page Up and Page Down keys to move around a page. If a page does fit on one screen, the scroll bar will disappear.

How Does the History Work?

As you move from web site to web site, your browser remembers where you've been by keeping a history of your actions. With Navigator, select "History" from the drop-down list under the Communicator menu. With IE, click the "History" button on the toolbar. Up will pop your recent history on the left side of your browser. To revisit a page, just click on the address. But there is a definite downside to history. If, for example, you are playing around on sites you shouldn't be looking at while at work, they will be listed in your history. So to protect yourself and cover your tracks, make sure to clear your history. More on this in Chapter 14, Privacy & Protection.

How Do I Block Out Advertising?

Much of the content that is on the Web is available for free because advertisements on the sites generate revenue for the companies providing them. These free sites are critical to the continued growth of this technology. And the ads that pay for them are also critical to that growth. However, sometimes these ads get in the way of your research. These are ads that pop up another window (hence the name *pop-up ad*) to sell you something you probably don't care about. To make you look at them, usually these ads cover the site you were looking at. If you hate advertising, and many people do, there are a couple of ways to research on the Web without being overwhelmed by advertising. Some web site ads, as *Detroit Free Press* columnist Heather Newman suggests, are like department store perfume salespeople. "They come on too strong, won't leave you alone, and just when you think you've gotten rid of them, another one appears," she says.

People have grown to hate pop-ups so much that there are lots of web sites devoted exclusively to their extinction. See Popups Must Die (`www.4degreez.com/popupsmustdie`).

While these ads are routine on web sites, now they are starting to overwhelm people as web-page style HTML email as well. They automatically fire up your browser program to display more of their ads. If this happens to you, there are a few things you can do to stop it.

In Internet Explorer browsers, pull down the Tools menu and select "Internet Options." Click on the "Advanced" tab. Then go down to the "Multimedia" section and uncheck the box next to "Show Pictures." Reload or open a new browser and you will see no ads on your browser's page.

In Netscape, go to "Edit," then select "Preferences." In the "Category" box, click on "Advanced." Then uncheck the box next to "Automatically Load Images."

But be aware – sometimes you will want to see photos. Rather than regularly overriding that setting each time you want to see a photo, all you have to do is go to the photo or ad you have blocked, click on your right mouse button on your PC and select "Show Picture" using Internet Explorer or "Show Image" using Netscape.

Ad Blocking Software

Another way to avoid ads is to purchase software that will block ads. This can be especially valuable if you have children and want them to avoid overexposure to ads.

Sites that can prove useful on this include:

NoAds

`www.firase.com`

Click on "Software," then on "NoAds."

PopUp Killer

`http://pop-up-killer.net`

PopUp Killer is especially fun because you can pick a sound for it to make as it nukes the pop-up windows.

interMute

`www.intermute.com`

Free for personal use.

Internet Junkbusters

`www.junkbusters.com/ht/en/ijb.html` `(free)`

Beware that some pop-up ad killers also inadvertently kill relevant windows that will pop up when browsing a site. For example, some sites open a new window for you when you pursue a hyperlink to another topic or web site, so that you won't lose your place on their web site and some of these programs would automatically suppress that window.

How Do I Speed Up Page Loading?

While text downloads quickly, images can really slow things down. There are two ways to speed things up. Like the ad blocking scenario above, you can view web sites in text-only mode by turning off the auto-loading of images function under the Options menu. It's in the same place as the blocking advertising is on the two browsers.

The next way to speed things up is to let the text appear and then simply click the "Stop" button. That will stop the page from loading anything beyond where you stopped it. You can always add the image by right-clicking your mouse and then selecting the "View Image" button.

___

browser tip #1: On Internet Explorer, one time-saving trick is the partial address trick. Usually an address requires you to type out `www.phonebashing.com`. Because IE will fill in the rest of the site, all you need to type is "phonebashing" and hit "Ctrl+Enter" and IE will bring you to whatever the domain you chose by automatically adding the .com part.

Be careful *not* to try this if you don't intend to go to a `.com` address.

___

browser tip #2: Multi-tasking means to do several things at once. Some internet users like to look at several things at the same time. One thing you can do on any browser is use multiple browsers at the same time. There will be times when you want to look at more than one page at a time. It's also a great way to compare how Microsoft's Internet Explorer and Netscape's Navigator work. You can also use multiple windows on the same browser at the same time. Using IE, you pull down the File menu, select "New" and then "Window." Using Netscape, pull down the File menu, select "New" then "Navigator Window." You can also press "Ctrl+N" in both programs and it will do the same thing.

Remember to close the browsers when you are finished – "Alt+F4" will do that.

browser tip #3: This is really a Windows tip. Every web browser has a "Find" feature. Once you've accessed a web page, click on the "Edit" button and use the "Find On This Page" feature to quickly locate the particular term you are looking for. It will save you time from scrolling through and reading the entire document. For example, if you have done a search on a particular word, say "frog," and you get back a page that doesn't seem to be about frogs, using the find feature will show you where that word appears on the page. This is also a great way to find threads or names of posters on cluttered message boards.

Everything About Email (Almost Everything)

How Popular Is Email and How Does It Work?

At every major computer gadget show around the world, people are always looking for what they call the "killer app" or "killer application" – that device, gadget, gizmo or program that will revolutionize the world. An International Data Corporation study in 2000 estimated that worldwide, ten billion pieces of email are sent daily. That figure should grow to thirty-five billion a day by 2005. Now that's a killer app.

The power of electronic mail, or email, becomes abundantly clear when you see a grandmother get an email from her grandchild, or a man getting an email from the woman he loves. Email is the tool that reunites families. Of course, it can also be used in a negative way. More on this later.

Email is time efficient, easy to use, and for many people, it's a money saver, eliminating long distance phone calls and costly express delivery charges. It negates the time delays of what computer geeks lovingly call "snail mail" – the postal service. Hands-down, email has become the most popular tool used on the Internet.

Email has the immediacy of a phone call, the permanency of a letter, and a style all its own. You can send an email to one person or 100 just as easily – and you can send it at your convenience and the recipient can enjoy it at their pleasure. It is an informal, immediate way to communicate. People tend to be less formal about what they write and how they write it, but there are established do's and don'ts in communicating online. In fact there are even entire books on the subject. Here are a few basic rules:

- Remember who you are talking to and that it is a public experience – you never know whose eyes will see it along the way once it has been sent.

- Don't forget that what you say can come back to haunt you – emails are often saved on hard drives and servers around the world, and can easily be forwarded.

- Similarly, remember that when you send information to people, you are taking their time and bandwidth. Don't overwhelm people with too many emails, respect people's privacy, and don't abuse the power of having a forum to talk to people.

- And one very simple rule, while typos and punctuation errors are more easily forgiven, NEVER TYPE IN ALL CAPS – this is considered "yelling." Not only is it rude and insulting to the reader, it is difficult to read.

For more information on proper "netiquette" see:

Albion Netiquette Page
`www.albion.com/netiquette/index.html`

The Net: User Guidelines and Netiquette
`www.fau.edu/netiquette/net/`

How Does Email Work?

Email, in its simplest form, is an electronic message sent from one computer to another. With the latest technology not only can you email people photos, music and other attachments, you can even send video emails.

Just as web site information is passed in packets from one computer to another, email works the same way, going from a mail server to another as it travels over the Internet. When it arrives at the destination mail server, it is stored in an electronic mailbox until the recipient retrieves it. The process can take seconds, usually longer, depending on the connections between all the servers involved. What makes it so useful is that you can open it and answer it on your schedule. So, unlike a phone call, you can fit it in whenever it is convenient for you.

To have email, you must have an account on a mail server. It's like having a street address for receiving letters. To send email you need a connection to the Internet and access to a mail server that either has your mail or can forward your mail. The standard protocol used for Internet email is an SMTP, or Simple Mail Transfer Protocol. It works along with another protocol, POP or Post Office Protocol.

When you email something, your computer routes it to an SMTP server, which looks at the email address and then forwards it to the recipient's mail server. Then you either retrieve your mail from the server, or read it on that server.

Just like you can dissect a URL to learn more about its origins, you can gain a few clues from an email address. The user name usually comes before the @ sign. After that sign comes the domain name of the mail server. For example: `alan@deadlineonline.com`. We can reasonably deduce that Alan is the recipient and `deadlineonline.com` is the domain name. Keep in mind there are a lot of strange user names out there, but studying the pattern of an email name will help you figure out how to send email to other people at the same place. For example, if you know that Bob Smith's email address at Company XYZ is `bsmith@companyxyz.com`, it's likely that Sue Barker's email address at the same company is `sbarker@companyxyz`. It's not foolproof, but it's helpful in a pinch.

What Is an Attachment and What Do I Do With It?

An attachment is an additional file separate from the body of the text. Common attachments include digital photos, word processing documents, sounds or music files, even jokes and cartoons.

It used to be difficult to attach documents on the Internet. However, today's common encoding standards now developed ensure your email will not appear as gibberish. The two standards are MIME (Multipurpose Internet Mail Extension) and UUencode. As long as your computer uses one of them, you can easily attach messages, photos, sound, and videos with your email. Both encoding standards are now routinely used, so almost all recent computer systems can understand these attachments. Keep in mind the following:

- That the person on the receiving end needs to have the technology to open or decode what you've sent. If your computer program doesn't automatically decode attachments, upgrade and get an email program that does.

- It's a good idea to ask the person you're sending to if they have the software to open your attachment.

- Name the file something that will be meaningful to the person you are sending it to.

- When you send an attachment, in the accompanying email, make sure you explain what you are sending. Because of viruses, many people will not open attachments without understanding exactly who it came from and what it is. That's just being cautious.

The protocols used to attach messages involve complex math in which files are converted to text, encoded into a form that other computers can read, and then converted back. Understand that encoding a file is different from encrypting a file. Encrypting adds a layer of sophisticated security to a file, but anyone with the right decoding software can read an encoded file. Because computer programs get more and more sophisticated every year, many computers can now recognize and automatically detect an attachment, decode it and open it or tell you to save it to your computer's hard drive. With MIME compliant or UUencode email programs, this is fairly automatic.

Another type of file, binary, is also something most computers will recognize, but with all files, you need to make sure the person on the receiving end can accept binary files and understands what to do with them if you send them. This is especially true if you encrypt a file.

To attach a file, first compose your email, then look for the "attach" or "send file" function in your particular email software – it is generally a fairly obvious button or menu option. It will then prompt you to point the email program to the file you want to attach, so just as when you are looking for a file on your computer, you click through your individual layers of folders and files until you find the one you want to send. Generally you click an "OK" button and then send your email as you normally would. Some email programs even allow you to send multiple attachments at one time.

When you receive an email message with an attachment, your mail program usually indicates that something is attached. Usually, your program saves the attached file as a separate file in the folder or directory you specify. After it has been saved, you can read and use it like any other file. The key is in saving the attachment with the proper extension. If it is a picture or image, chances are it is a .jpg file or a .gif file. Usually your email program will automatically put in the correct extension, but sometimes your email program may not recognize a file format. See the Field Guide to File Formats later in this chapter.

If you receive an unknown attachment, it will appear as a large message in your mailbox. If it contains text, it may be garbled but still readable. In this case, you can try saving the message as a file and then extracting the contents of it through a separate program. However, if the garbled text represents a botched attempt at sending a sound or picture, you will not be able to recover the information. Be especially careful before you open an attachment from someone you don't know.

Email is the most common way that viruses spread, so let me say this again because it is extremely important: *avoid opening files with attachments from people you don't know*. Even if you know someone, always run the attachment through a virus checker. If you get an attachment and want to avoid the risk of a computer virus, check it out before you open it.

Make sure you have the most recent anti-virus software, as you need to stay current to preventing your computer from becoming infected. See the section on viruses, pages 55-58.

Other Ways to Send Files and Information – Telnet, FTP, Digital Fax, and Voice Mail

Sometimes you want to send a really large file that is too big for email, or from a computer where your email is not set up. There are three possible ways of doing this.

Via Telnet

Telnet is a software program that lets you use the resources of a distant computer somewhere else in the world – meaning that you can tap into your computer from anywhere. You can log onto a "host" computer, issue commands as if you were on your own computer, and gain access to all of that computer's resources. Telnet works by running a piece of software on your computer that tells the distant computer that you can use its resources. This other computer is called the host.

The host computer allows many different computers to simultaneously access its resources. To use Telnet, though, you will need to know the address of the internet host whose resources you want to access.

When you use Telnet, you must log in and "take over" the host computer. Usually, host systems will let you sign in as "guest," but some require a user name and password.

You can Telnet into many different computers and computer systems. Each one works differently. When you contact the host computer, the distant computer and your computer negotiate how they will talk with each other. To make things easier, many hosts use a menu system allowing you to mimic the host's computer. This is called terminal emulation.

Via FTP — File Transfer Protocol

FTP is particularly good for transferring very large files. Many software companies incorporate FTP into their web sites to enable you to download program files and software patches quickly and easily. If you have your own web site, you will want to have an FTP program for transferring files you create on your computer to your ISP's server.

When you connect to the other computer using an FTP program, you get a split screen, with the files on your computer's hard drive on the left side and the files of the computer you dialed into on the right. In the middle of the screen are arrows. Highlight the file you want to transfer and then click on the arrow — the left one if you want to download or receive something, the right arrow if you want to upload or send a file from your computer.

FTP can transfer enormous quantities of data. It is used to transfer computer software and upgrades, anti-virus utilities, games, graphics and so forth.

If, for example, you wanted to download a copy of *Alice in Wonderland* from the Internet, it is available for a fee at `www.literatureproject.com/best-sellers/children-young-adults.htm`. You would likely use FTP to download it. Simply saving it from a web page directly without FTP would take much longer.

Via Digital Fax and Voice Mail

All faxes can sent or received digitally. This used to require configuring fax software on your computer, but now you can send and receive faxes via email. Several companies now offer this service. Two of the better ones are Jfax (`www.j2.com`) and Efax (`www.efax.com`). These are especially helpful to people who travel a great deal. Callers can also leave voice messages, which are then sent to your computer as an audio file. And both companies now also provide interaction with cell phones, pagers, and mobile devices like PDAs.

➔ ***hot tip:*** **There are many places to get shareware FTP programs. WS_FTP and Breeze FTP are two easy to use Windows FTP programs. For locating all kinds of valuable shareware and freeware computer files, here are a few sites. They all are terrific sites for information about all-things related to computers, and offer extensive software libraries – both free and for a fee – that you can download.**

CNET Software Library
`www.cnet.com`

Tucows
`www.tucows.com`

Jumbo! Download Network
`www.jumbo.com`

ZDNet Software Library
`www.zdnet.com/downloads`

Shareware.com
`www.shareware.cnet.com`

What Is a Bounced Email and What Should I Do?

A "bounced email" is an undeliverable email. There are several reasons why an email can be bounced by either your mail server or the receiving server. The file size is too large, the mailbox is full, the server is down, the address was typed incorrectly – these are just a few of the possible reasons. If you send an email and it bounces, you will receive an email from the mail server telling you so, and often (usually in technical jargon) the reason it bounced. Some mail servers will automatically retry sending the email in a few hours for you – some won't. Depending on the reason given for the bounce, you may need to check the way you typed the address, carve up the attachment into smaller files, or find another way to send your information.

How Private Is My Email?

Unlike regular mail sent by the postal service, email is not totally private. In most countries, if you send an email from your work, your employer has the right to read it. There are ways to protect and keep email totally confidential. For that you need special software to encrypt the message. (See Chapter 14, Privacy, for details).

How to Deal with All that Spam Mail

First, email spam has absolutely nothing to do with the spiced meat Spam. Nor is it a laughing matter like Monty Python would have you think. Being "spammed" on the Internet means you are getting large amounts of unsolicited email from lists gathered without your consent. It can also mean receiving or sending emails to multiple discussion groups that are inappropriate to the subject of that discussion.

If you are overwhelmed with unsolicited email, there are steps you can take to control it. First, see Managing and Filtering Information, Chapter 11. After screening, filtering and deleting unwanted email, one thing you should do is look at who sent you the information. If you don't recognize the name and the subject heading doesn't mean anything to you, chances are you can simply delete the email. If it is really important and you inadvertently delete it, someone will likely contact you again.

Spammers get your address from a variety of methods. They harvest it from places you've posted it or left it on the Web, they guess randomly, they trick you into revealing it, or they buy it from a mailing list broker. What can you do to prevent getting spammed? Be careful how you display your email address in public. Most spammers have programs called scavenger bots that gather email addresses. So if your email address appears on a list of addresses on someone's web site – even your own – the spammers find those and put you on their target lists. The best thing you can do to stop it is to prevent it from happening in the first place. Set up a free secondary email address. Use your secondary address to post on discussion groups, and even to register for conferences, they are notorious for selling their mailing lists. Even registering software should be done with your secondary address.

Complaining won't do you a lot of good. Writing to these companies usually makes the situation worse. They don't send their information out from addresses that you can write back to. However, since few ISPs will tolerate spamming from their company, your first task is to find out who their ISP is and write to them. Several computer programs can assist you in going after spam. These include:

Internet Junkbusters
www.junkbusters.com

SpamCop
www.spamcop.net

Coalition Against Unsolicited Commercial Email
www.cauce.org

Fight Spam on the Net
http://spam.abuse.net

⌨ *email tip:* Learn how to display the full header of a mail message for important clues as to the origin of an email. If you are using Microsoft's Internet Explorer, all you need to do is pull down the "View" menu and select "Headers," then "All." This can be very valuable when people email you things you don't like or find distasteful or dangerous. The keys to tracking where that email came from are in the header of the message. Specifically, one of the lines in a header is the message ID line. While people can forge email addresses, you must control the mail server to change the ID line, so it can be a good way to track down email that bothers you. To investigate further, send an email to the postmaster at that address and ask for help and be sure to include the entire original message and the full header. This is a good starting point for the postmaster's investigation.

⌨ *more email tips:* Learn how to use your mail program well enough so that you don't accidentally send a private email intended for someone special to everyone you know. Make sure that the subject line is filled out when you send an email – and has a meaningful description. With viruses being spread occasionally through email, and lots of companies sending out emails to massive numbers of people as a marketing strategy, smart researchers look at the subject line of an email to decide whether or not to open or delete it. So a simple "Hi" from an email address you don't recognize will likely get deleted, not opened. Remember that the subject line may be the only part of the email that your recipient looks at to identify if it's worth opening. It makes a big difference to you when you get an email with the subject line: "Changes in office policy on potted plants" and one that says, "Your check will bounce."

Saving Your Results

How Does Uploading and Downloading Work?

Typically, downloading is the process of accessing and saving files to your computer from another computer. If you wanted to send something from your computer to another computer, the process would be referred to as "uploading." Most of the time, though, you'll be on the receiving end, downloading.

For instance, when you access a web page, you're actually downloading the page of text and all the associated graphics from a server. In fact, when you receive electronic mail – email – that contains an attachment, you have actually downloaded both the email message and the attachment. The files you download can be documents or programs that let you:

- Update your computer's software
- See graphics
- Hear sounds, music
- See video pictures
- Read text

Downloading is the process that creates your own copy of a file by copying it from another computer to yours. Once a file is downloaded, it's a simple matter to use it or change it. But first, you must identify the file type (also called its format).

Identifying File Types

In the Windows environment, the file extension lets your computer know which program opens that file. This is the piece of text at the end of a file name, preceded by a period, which identifies the file type.

For example, the .txt extension means the file is a plain text file. It is also sometimes referred to as an ASCII file. Any program that can read ASCII text can open this file and read it.

Most file extensions are three or four characters long. On some operating systems, such as UNIX, they are four characters. Normally, each file has only one file extension, but some operating systems like UNIX and most Windows programs allow multiple extensions as well as extensions with more than three characters.

For the most part, on the Internet, every file has a three or four character extension. Macintosh files don't require a file extension and instead have an identifier built into the file that is visible only to the computer. Mac files on the Internet, however, do have extensions, like .sea.

Most image files end with .jpg and .gif. The former stands for JPEG, which is a popular compression standard for photos and other still images. The latter extension stands for Graphics Interchange Format, a standard that was developed by CompuServe in the late 1980s. Both of these graphics formats can be used on PCs, Macs, or UNIX machines as long as viewing software has been installed. Also, your word processor can work with these files using the "Insert Picture From A File" option in Microsoft Word or "Insert Graphics From File" in WordPerfect.

Popular extensions for video files are `.avi` for the PC, `.mpg` (short for MPEG), `.mov` and `.qt` for QuickTime movies.

Sound files come in `.aiff` for Macintosh; `.au` for Mac and UNIX; `.wav` for the PC; and `.ra` for Real Audio, which is a Web proprietary system for delivering and playing real-time audio.

Field Guide to File Formats

The software needed to read these files comes with most standard browsers. The "file formats" are also called file extensions.

File Format	Type of File It Identifies
.aiff	Sound files for the Mac
.arj	A common format for MS-DOS machines used especially in Europe
.asp	Stands for active server pages, usually customized from a server
.au	Sound files for Mac and UNIX
.avi	Video for Windows
.bin	A Mac binary II encoded file
.bmp, .pcx	Common bitmap graphics formats
.cgi	A CGI script or common gateway interface
.doc, .dot	Microsoft Word files from Word for Macintosh, Word for Windows and Windows WordPad
.exe	A program file or a self-extracting archive file in DOS/Windows
.gif	Graphic Interchange Format files are often found in web pages, most commonly used for photos.
.hlp	Windows help files
.html, .htm	Hypertext Markup Language is the language in which web documents are authored and saved.
.jpg .jpeg, .jpe	JPEG graphics files often used for photos on web pages.
.mid	Music files used for creating your own music
.mpeg, .mpg, .mpe, .m1v	MPEG (Motion Pictures Expert Group) video formats, used for movies

.mpe, .m1v .Mp3	The most popular file format on the Web for distributing CD quality music. (But you will need an MP3 player, which is available for Mac and Windows.)
.mov., .qt	Movie files for Quicktime, originally developed for the MacIntosh, but now plays on Windows and UNIX
.pdf	Portable Document Format, an Adobe Acrobat hypertext file. This format is a popular means of distributing electronic documents.
.png	A new image file format
.ppt	Microsoft PowerPoint presentation
.ram, .ra	Real Audio. This sound format plays while it's being transmitted.
.rtf	Rich Text Format. These word processing files are readable by a variety of word processors.
.sea	A Macintosh self-extracting archive
.sit	Stuffit is the Mac's primary compression file. (To unstuff it, you need a program called Stuffit Deluxe or Stuffit Expander for the Mac or for Windows.)
.tar, .tar.gz .tar.Z, .tgz	Tar files, short for tape archive, can archive files but not compress them. `.tar` files are often gzipped, which is why you may see file extension `.tar.gz`
.tif, .tiff	A common graphics format used for very large high quality images.
.txt, .text	A text or ASCII file, readable by most word processing programs.
.uu	UUencoding allows the user to convert binary data into text so it can be sent via email. You usually don't see the `.uu` extension, because most programs can decode it automatically.
.wav	The standard Windows "wave" sound format
.wpd	A WordPerfect document file
.xls	A Microsoft Excel spreadsheet file
.zip, .sit, .tar	A compression file used by many Windows (and some MacIntosh) compression utilities to bundle files together into a single archive.

For more details on file formats and how to use them, see:

About.com - Internet for Beginners
www.learnthenet.com/english/html/34filext.htm

Stack.com
www.stack.com

TechTutuorials
www.techtutorials.com/fileformats.shtml

Whatis?com
http://whatis.techtarget.com/fileFormatA/0,289933,sid9,00.html

How To Save Files

A web page may look like a seamless unit, but actually it's a compilation of several files and several types of files. The words are either .text or .html. The photos are image files such as .gif or .jpg. That animated banner like rolling waves in water may be a Java file or something similar. A video file is often an .mpeg. An audio file can be a .wav or another type of sound file.

How you download a file depends on its size, format, and your reason for downloading it. Generally, you can choose where to store the file (i.e., on a floppy disc, zip drive or hard drive), what to name it, and what type to save it as. Today's browsers are intuitive and will often walk you through the process.

The first type of file most people download is a program file. Perhaps it's a software "patch" to fix a bug or glitch found after the original product was shipped, or maybe it is a program that allows you to view other types of files. Web pages that download software usually ask you to click to start the process. At this point, your browser will ask you if you want to "save to disk." Tell it where you want to store the file, and note the location so you can retrieve the file later. The computer will then automatically begin the download process.

What you will have downloaded is usually an "executable" file, such as .exe, which you can double-click on to install. For some files you may have to use the "Run" feature instead of double-clicking. When the program file is comprised of several files or is compressed (such as a .zip file), you will need another software program to open it before it can be downloaded (see the Compressing and Decompressing Files section later in this chapter).

Saving Text and Documents

Maybe you have found an information-loaded web site and you want to download some of its material. While bookmarking is always a good idea, a web site may disappear without notice, so it's best to grab and save material when you can. Remember, though, that this is someone else's work and there may be copyright issues to be resolved before you can use the information. (See Stephanie Ardito's copyright sidebar later in this chapter.) For this example, let's assume the information you want to download is some form of text. The text could be embedded in the web page itself, or it could be a separate file that can be downloaded in its entirety.

If the text is part of the overall web page, you can simply save the page. Actually, when you go to your browser and choose "Save," you will only be getting a portion of the page. Remember: all those banners, dancing dogs and other eye-catching graphics are separate image files. If you "Save As" .html, you can re-open the file while offline using your browser, and usually the page will look like it did online, except sections with graphics will become little boxes. If you "Save As" .txt, you will have a plain text file which can be opened in your computer's most basic text editor, such as Windows Notepad. Depending on your computer's configuration, you can later convert this.

Now, you can revert to the old "cut and paste" method to manipulate text information as you can with any text file. If you have inadvertently copied some of the document's HTML code, then you may see some strange symbols. After you've pasted the text into your document, simply delete any extraneous characters.

Sometimes the text is stored as a separate file that can be downloaded in its entirety. One of the most popular formats for this is .pdf (Portable Document Format or PDF), which uses Adobe Acrobat software. Acrobat is a popular format for several reasons:

- It is a quick way to put information on the web rather than converting existing files to HTML.

- It is a convenient way to preserve formatting that is important either for integrity or aesthetics.

- It is a good way to store very large files.

You must have an Adobe Acrobat Reader to view these files. The U.S. government has endorsed using PDF files, and its usage is widespread, especially since the Reader program is free – download it from Adobe Systems at www.adobe.com/products/acrobat/readstep.html.

Downloading documents such as PDF files is very similar to downloading a program. Again, you may actually be downloading from an FTP site. Usually there will be a link that you can click on that will make your browser do most of the work.

Let's say you want to send something to someone via an email. First you must highlight – select – what you want to send. There are several ways to do that.

If you want the entire text of the document on the screen, you can hit "Select All" under "Edit" on your browser, you will be able to highlight all the text you want to send. Or, you could press "Ctrl+A" to select *all* of the text.

If you want *only a portion* of the entire text, you can click the mouse at the beginning of a section and drag the mouse to the end of the selection or, you can also click at the beginning of a section – anywhere, actually – and hold down the "Shift" key on the keyboard, and use the arrow keys to select the text you want to copy.

Once you have the text highlighted, you can choose the Copy command from the "Edit" menu. Alternatively, you can use "Ctrl+C" to copy the selected text into the Windows clipboard.

Once the text is in the clipboard, you can switch to another program (i.e., an email program or a word processing program) and use the Paste function to incorporate the text (or graphic) into that program. If the program doesn't have an icon or menu option for Paste, you can use "Ctrl+P" to paste from the Windows clipboard or "Command+P" from a Mac This technique of copying from a web page and pasting into a word processing document is a very effective way to enhance your documents and avoid retyping information that is already available on your computer.

Saving Images and Sounds

To save an image, move your mouse directly over the image itself then right click button on your mouse. You will be presented with a menu of options. Choose "Save Image As" or "Save Picture As" from the menu that appears. If it is a JPEG file, you will probably want to save it as a `.jpg`. You can change the file name — the part before the extension — to a name you can better recognize. The suggested names for image files are usually pretty cryptic, like "`x32yT.jpg`." You could rename this "`charlie.jpg`" and you'll know from the extension `.jpg` that it's an image of Charlie.

If changing the names is too much work, just keep a list somewhere of what the file is called and where you put it. Some people keep a running log of the files they download and where they saved them.

Most sound files feature a link that initiates the download process. Again, you will probably want to preserve the format and file extension as you would an image file, as explained above.

To open image and sound files, your computer must be configured with the right programs to do so. Usually, when you double-click on a file, the appropriate program will probably launch, opening the file onto the screen.

What If I Want to Save an Entire Web Page?

There are several reasons you may want to save an entire web page. Perhaps you want to read it while you are offline. Maybe you're giving a presentation and would like to show the page as an example of something. Again, the intended use determines the format in which you should save the file. Always be aware of the copyrights associated with web pages – and use web material accordingly. (See Stephanie Ardito's sidebar on copyrights later in this chapter.)

If you copy the entire page to your computer, you must save each file on that page separately, using the techniques outlined above. Usually, you begin by using the "Save" function of your browser — saving to `.html`. Then you have to individually save each of the image and sound files. All of them must be stored in the same folder and must maintain their original names. If you do this properly, you will be able to double-click on the "main" file (the one you saved as .html) and the other files will load automatically. In the newer versions of the Internet Explorer browser only, Microsoft has added a most convenient feature – "File, Save As Complete," which allows you to capture the entire web site including the photos and graphics in one click. Netscape does not offer this feature.

If you merely want to save the "look" of a web site, it may be easier to do a screen capture. To capture a screen, press "Alt+Prt Scr" (Print Screen), which copies the active window, then paste it into the application of your choice (perhaps a paint or graphics program). To paste, press "Ctrl+V" or go to the "Edit" button and hit "Paste." Then save the file as a bitmap or `.bmp` file.

If you want to get fancier and be able to copy parts of a page including their graphics, so you can play with the images size and shapes, you will need special software to do what's known as "screen capturing" of a page. There are dozens of companies that provide free, low-cost or high-cost capturing software. If you need a more sophisticated program, try a program like Jasc's Paintshop Pro (`www.jasc.com`), which costs about US$100 orr Snagit (`www.techsmith.com/products/snagit`), which is free to try for 45 days, US$39.95 if you decide to register.

These programs allow you to control what part of the screen you want to capture and also let you edit the image or convert it to a large number of formats. Some of these programs cost money, others are shareware – where you pay a modest fee to keep the company in business. A good resource for shareware programs to screen capture is `www.webattack.com/shareware/gmm/swscreen.shtml`. A good collection of the free ones is found at `www.webattack.com/freeware` or (`www.zdnet.com/downloads/`) ZDNet Downloads, or Tucows (`www.tucows.com`) by searching for "screen capture."

Saving Web Links

Once you get comfortable with downloading, you may want to make a connection to the actual page. A hypertext link connects your computer to a site on the Internet through HTML coding.

You can save a linked page without going to the link itself. Put your pointer over the link and click your right mouse button (or hold down the mouse button if you are a Mac user). From the pop-up menu that appears, select "Save Link As." That will give you the "Save As" dialog box where you can select a folder and drive for the page.

Using Compression and Sending Compressed Files

Program files on the Internet can be very big. If you couldn't shrink files, you'd waste time sending and receiving huge files. Compressed files do just that, reducing files to as little as two percent of their normal size, depending on the type of file and the program you are using. Normally, compression reduces files between forty to seventy-five percent of their size. If you want to transfer a file or group of files across the Internet, it's a lot faster to transfer a compressed file than an uncompressed one.

How does it work? It gets kind of techno-geekish, but all compression programs rely on the fact that there are many instances of lengthy, repeated information in program code. They can all be abbreviated as they are being sent, and then restored when the item is decompressed.

Most compressed DOS and Windows files are in .zip format, which were created by a program called PKZIP or WinZip. There are other compressed formats as well. If it is a UNIX program, `.Z`, `.gz`, and `.tar` are common archive formats. On the MacIntosh, they are called `.sit` (Stuffit) and `.pit` (Packit).

One thing that makes compressed files valuable is that you can package many files inside one file. If a program, for example, needs ten files in order to run, it's convenient to compress them as a single file rather than transfer each of the ten files individually.

Compression programs can also create files that can run themselves automatically. These are called self-extracting files and usually end with `.exe`. They are very useful for sending a compressed file to someone who you are not sure has the capability to decompress the file. So, if you receive a compressed file with an `.exe` extension, you can run that file directly from the DOS prompt or from the Run prompt in the Start menu, just by typing its folder and filename then pressing Enter or by double-clicking in the Windows Explorer File Management program. When you do these tasks, all the compressed files pop out. If you know there are going to be several files inside the main compressed file, it's a good idea to create a temporary folder and copy the compressed file into it before unzipping or expanding it into its separate component pieces. On a Mac, the `.sea` (self-extracting archive) does the same thing.

If you use a `.zip` file, you must have a program that can read zip files and extract the archived files from within. You may already have such a program. Some Windows file management programs, for instance, can work with zip files. Otherwise you'll need a decompression program.

There are many places where you can download freeware and shareware that will unzip files. Among the most popular programs are PKZIP/UNZIP and WinZip.

➜ *hot tip:* **Make sure you download a copy of the appropriate program so you have it in case you need it. If you are sending a compressed file to someone, first ask them if they have the capability to decompress the file — and if they know how to.**

Virus Protection

What Are Viruses and How Do They Work?

As the number of people using computers grows, so does the number of viruses and the ease with which they are spread. If the names Anna Kournikova, the Magistr, Code Red, Nimda, and Sircam don't mean anything, they should – they were all viruses that affected and wreaked havoc on personal and company computers in 2001.

First, computer viruses are not real viruses, but a metaphor for a serious problem. A computer virus is a program that makes copies of itself and infects diskettes or files. Viruses can spread to other computers and files whenever infected diskettes or files are exchanged. Often infected files come as email attachments – even from people you know. And often, the email sender has no idea that he or she has passed on a file with a virus in it.

Some computer viruses can erase or change the information stored on your computer, while others may do little or no harm to your computer system. According to CERT (www.cert.org/stats/cert_stats.html), the Carnegie Mellon University virus-monitoring center, more than 73,000 incidents of separate viruses were reported in 2002, more than double the amount from the previous year. A recent study from Rip-Tech (www.riptech.com/indsexfl.html) said it verified at least 128,678 cyber attacks from July to December of 2001, but the Alexandria, Virginia-based company noted that few posed a severe threat.

A computer virus is a program that can "infect" other programs by modifying them to change how your computer operates. Viruses can spread themselves without your knowledge or permission on your computer or to potentially large numbers of programs on many machines. Unlike most other programs, viruses are specifically designed to spread themselves and they can without your knowledge. A virus program can contain instructions on when or how to activate. Several of the worst viruses have triggered on a specific calendar date.

One way to protect your computer is to run an anti-virus program, which scans your hard drive looking for signs of these viruses.

The way you get a virus on your computer is to accidentally run a program that already contains the virus. Viruses can be passed along by email, also on floppy disks that have been in a public computer at a library or internet café. In email, viruses are usually in an attachment that, when opened, unleashes the virus program. Since you must run the program in order for the virus to take effect, you should make it a policy never to open an attachment someone sends you until after you are certain it does not contain a virus.

Do I Really Need an Anti-Virus Program?

Yes. If you limit your activities to commercial software and to programs you download from places that have credibility on the 'Net (see Chapter 12, Evaluating Accuracy…), you may never encounter a virus. But that is the exception. If you work on a network of computers where people regularly use their own floppy disks, like at a school, or you have questions over who might have access to that computer, then an anti-virus program is a smart investment. Viruses have been known to display messages, erase files, scramble data on your hard drive, cause your computer screen to behave differently, and some have prevented computers from starting up. Many viruses do nothing obvious at all except spread! You cannot rely on strange behavior as an indication that you have a virus. The most reliable way to find viruses is to use competent anti-virus software. The rule you should live by is if anyone else ever touches your computer, connects to your computer or sends you email, you should have a virus checker and make sure it is the most up-to-date version available.

How Can I Protect My Data?

Viruses are a threat, but data loss can also occur from other factors, usually mechanical failures. If you have files you can't afford to lose, make sure you have more than one copy of them. The best way to do that is to copy hard disk files to disk/tape with a reliable backup utility program. You should also create an emergency boot disk, and keep it with your backup disks/tapes in a safe place, with write-protect tabs secured.

Tips On Catching Viruses Before They Infect Your Computer

- Any executable has the potential to harbor a virus infection. So be careful with `.exe` files.

- Beware of attachments received unexpectedly, even if from a known source. Always run them through the latest anti-virus software or don't open them.

- Don't open files that have double extensions, unless you know what they are.

Make sure you have file extension viewing enabled. For most Windows programs, go to the Windows Explorer program, then click "View," then "Options" and, depending which program you have, either uncheck the box for "Hide file extensions for known file types" or check the box. In Windows 2000, users will find the settings under the "Tools" menu, then click "Folder Option," click on the "File Types" tab and then select whichever programs you want to see the extension on and click the "Advanced button." Then check the box "Always Show Extension." In Windows XP, users will find the settings under the Tools menu, then select "Folder Options" and "View," and uncheck "Hide Extensions for known file types."

Good Resources About Viruses

→ *hot tip:* **Before you open that attachment, cross-reference it in the Infected Attachments list** `http://antivirus.about.com/library/attachments/blenext.htm` **to see if it's related to a virus. This site has details on all the viruses, and most important, the file extensions associated with these viruses.**

Another excellent source for details on viruses and the most likely place to find a quick fix for a virus can be found at CERT, the Carnegie-Mellon University Software Engineering School's CERT coordination center at `www.cert.org`

These three sites AVG, McAfee, and Symantec (owners of Norton Anti-virus) all offer anti-virus information and products on their web sites. Remember: they are trying to sell you their products.

AVG Anti-virus
`www.grisoft.com/html/us_index.htm`

McAfee
`www.mcafee.com/anti-virus/default.asp`

Norton Anti-virus
`www.symantec.com/avcenter/`

Virus Hoaxes

Virus hoaxes spread like wildfire all over the Web. People tend to spread these like gossip, without question, causing unnecessary anguish. From time to time, a real virus does spread. One thing you can do is check computer-related news sites like CNET (`www.cnet.com`), ZDNet (`www.zdnet.com`), or by checking web sites like Virus Myth (`www.vmyths.com`) or About.com's excellent anti-virus section (`www.antivirus.about.com`).

Additional Resources for Internet Basics

There are some incredibly good resources on the Internet to teach yourself more detail on the basics of using the Internet, everything from how to use email to designing web pages. Here are a few of the best:

About.com - Internet for Beginners
`www.netforbeginners.about.com`

A terrific starting spot for anyone who is new on the Internet. It is loaded with good and easy-to-find information.

BBC - WebWise
`www.bbc.co.uk/webwise/`

The BBC site is a wonderfully easy, well-written and nicely designed site, which the British Broadcasting Company says is the Internet made simple. And it is.

Ithaca College - ICYouSee
`www.ithaca.edu/library/Training/ICYouSee.html`

Ever wonder how many millions of things you can do online? This may be the most thorough list anywhere.

Learnthenet.com
`www.learnthenet.com/english/index.html`

This is a really easy-to-understand and creative site that explains the complexity of computers in a fun and innovative way.

NetLearn
`www2.rgu.ac.uk/~sim/research/netlearn/callist.htm`

Net Learn, from the Robert Gordon University in Aberdeen, Scotland, is another good beginner's guide to the 'Net.

Northville District Library - New User Tutorial
`http://northville.lib.mi.us/tech/tutor/welcome.htm`

This site is particularly good for first-time internet users.

The HelpWeb
`www.imaginarylandscape.com/helpweb/`

Another good beginner's guide to the Internet.

University at Albany Libraries - Internet Tutorials
http://library.albany.edu/internet/

Useful, well-written and simple guide to getting started on computers and on the 'Net.

University of California - Berkeley Library - Internet Tutorial
www.lib.berkeley.edu/TeachingLib/Guides/Internet/FindInfo.html

This is one of a series of tutorials on all aspects of using the Internet. These are excellent training sessions.

Your Rights & Copyrights Online

by Stephanie C. Ardito

In the U.S., the Copyright Act of 1976 and its major revisions enacted in 1978 and 1998 (www.loc.gov/copyright/title17/), govern the use of copyrighted works. Works are protected from the moment of their creation and remain in effect during the author's life plus seventy additional years after the author's death. Works made for hire, anonymous, and pseudonymous works are protected for 95 years from publication or for 120 years from creation, whichever is shorter.

In 1989, the U.S. joined the Berne Convention (www.wipo.org/treaties/ip/berne/index.html), which guarantees copyright protection for authors in all member nations (nearly 180 countries). The Berne Convention does not require registration, a copyright symbol, or notification of any kind on authors' publications. In other words, one should assume that *all worldwide* Internet works are copyrighted and protected by the Berne Convention.

To determine what can be legally downloaded, copied, and printed from the Web, users should look for terms and conditions and/or links detailing the site owner's permission for reproducing content. Generally, commercial sites (those ending in .com and including content from companies, databases, newspapers, newswires, and magazines) permit reproduction for personal use or for non-profit educational purposes. Commercial sites do not permit the making of multiple copies to be distributed to individuals other than one user. Copyright violations potentially exist if web content is passed on within a user's organization for commercial reasons. It is best to seek the site owner's permission for such reproduction. A second option is to forward the web site's address, also known as a URL, to other users so each viewer's use will be legal.

U.S. federal government web sites are not protected by copyright and can be copied freely. The contents of these sites are considered to be in the public domain. Content of state government web sites may be protected by copyright laws; as with commercial sites, users should be careful about making more than one copy. Content from U.S. patent documents and federal legal documents can also be copied without fear of copyright violation; however, any proprietary information from private parties attached to federal documents is protected by copyright law.

Other countries' copyright laws are more restrictive. Canada and the U.K., for example, *do* protect their government publications, so users should observe copyright terms and conditions before making multiple copies of non-U.S. government documents.

The U.S. Supreme Court has ruled that telephone directory information is not protected by copyright law, but users should be cautious about what they download and reuse. One can copy directory listings, but not "value-added" information such as indexing terms, descriptors, abstracts, and formats.

Non-profit groups, such as associations, also copyright their materials. Seek permission before distributing multiple copies, especially if the material may be used for commercial purposes.

There is no clear-cut legal decision on whether linking is protected by international copyright laws. Many industry experts believe that the Internet was established to link individuals and organizations with common interests, and that to copyright links would severely restrict the Internet's great strength. On the other hand, many organizations do not want indiscriminate linking of their web sites, and are threatening lawsuits and/or requiring periodic royalty or licensing payments in order to control their content.

The practice of placing the content of other people's web sites into your own web page is called "framing" or "inlaying," and can also be a copyright infringement. When in doubt, seek permission from the content owner.

In searching the Web and sites furnished by online service providers, I recommend the following:

- **Look for and read copyright notices** (keeping in mind that content does not have to have a copyright notice to be protected), **terms and conditions, and vendor licensing agreements** (generally, a commercial online provider's fees include copyright permission to type, print, and view each document as a one-time use).

- There are three things you can do when in doubt about what can and cannot be done: **contact the web site owner**, **contact the U.S. Copyright Clearance Center** (www.copyright.com), or **contact the relevant licensing agency in your country**. In the U.S., it is still safe to download or print content if for personal use – i.e., one copy for your own non-commercial purpose.

- **Refer other users within your organization to Internet URLs** to retrieve information. If each individual logs on and downloads his or her own version of web pages, then reproduction may be viewed as personal use copying.

- Know that **you are consenting to a contract** that is legally enforceable **when you click on a terms and conditions agreement** in order to access an Internet document. Violations could result in lawsuits.

- **Don't frame web sites** that you do not personally own.

- Information brokers, librarians, or other intermediaries conducting research on behalf of another individual or company should **search commercial databases** for full-text articles or **use a document supplier who pays royalties** to the U.S. Copyright Clearance Center or other international licensing agency. Content is not free; however, signed terms and conditions are quite clear about reproduction rights. Unlike terms and conditions agreements on web sites, many commercial online vendors furnish special clauses that clearly explain the rights of librarians and independent information professionals.

- When downloading online search results, **keep all copyright notices with each record**. In other words, do not delete copyright notices when post-processing search results. The notices will serve as reminders to users that the content is copyrighted and any further reproduction is forbidden unless permission has been received from the copyright holder.

Additional Resources:

- Copyright Law of the United States of America and Related Laws Contained in Title 17 of the United States Code at `www.loc.gov/copyright/title17/`

- Berne Convention for the Protection of Literary and Artistic Works `www.wipo.org/treaties/ip/berne/index.html`

-- Stephanie C. Ardito is President of Ardito Information & Research, Inc., an information firm specializing in pharmaceutical, medical, and business information research, as well as intellectual property and copyright matters. She is co-author of the Legal Issues column published in *Information Today*, and a past president of the Association of Independent Information Professionals. Email: `sardito@ardito.com`

For the more adventurous data mavens, Drew Sullivan shows you how to handle the nuances of downloading databases and spreadsheets.

Downloading Databases & Spreadsheets: A Practical Introduction

By Drew Sullivan

As the Internet has matured, it has become a treasure trove of electronic databases from organizations and government agencies around the world. It's inexpensive now for organizations to put gigabytes of data on a server that can be downloaded into a sophisticated analysis tools like a spreadsheet or a database.

Simply defined, a database is information structured in a particular way. A good example of a database is your phone book. The first line of a phonebook is always the name sorted alphabetically by the last name. The second piece of information is the address and the final piece is the phone number. Data is stored in tables with rows (called records) and columns (called fields).

Database programs allow you to manipulate the information in different ways. You can sort, filter, or aggregate the data. Using our example, you can search by a particular first name, last name, address, phone number or by any combination of the above.

A spreadsheet program is similar to a database program. It's an electronic ledger sheet that makes it easy to add, subtract, or multiply rows or columns. Like a database program, a spreadsheet program lets you sort, filter or graph data.

Many of these databases can be searched via the Web or downloaded for more complex analyses. For instance, an interested person can go to the U.S. Occupational Safety and Health Administration's site and look at how many violations of workplace standards a company has had. Or they can look at how much money a particular celebrity has given to a gubernatorial candidate in Florida or the number of accidents a railroad company has had. Internationally, you can look up life expectancy in Andorra, look up a phone number in Croatia or even study the budget for the city of Sarajevo in Bosnia and Herzegovina.

These seemingly disparate bits of information are all stored on the Web in a database. Sometimes the information is easy to get to; sometimes it requires a bit of work. It all depends on how the information is stored and the means provided to retrieve it. In general, we can define three ways in which information is stored and retrieved:

- As a searchable database with a front-end or tool designed to help you search the data.

- As a set of structured data designed to be downloaded and imported into a database or spreadsheet program

- As a set of data that can be downloaded and converted into a database or spreadsheet program.

Searchable Databases

If you've been on the Web at all, you know there are thousands of searchable databases available. Many may have already been mentioned in this book. These tools may allow you to search by some fields. Some are sophisticated. Others are not.

Here are just a few examples of these types of sites:

OSHA workplace violations: www.osha.gov/oshstats

Do an establishment search and search by the company you work for in the U.S.. The U.S. Occupational Safety and Health Administration will tell you whether your company has violated any rules.

Aircraft safety: `http://nasdac.faa.gov/asy_internet/safety_data/`

Want to know what accidents or incidents your local airline was involved in? Select "FAA Incident Data System" and select an airline or other criteria on the search form.

A problem with these sites is that you can only search the data in ways the site creator has made provisions for. Thus you might be able to search by name but not city. Or you may not be able to use wildcards, special characters that can be used to represent any letter.

Also, a database search is a sophisticated process and there are many potential problems that can give you wrong results. Look for documentation about the database and the search engine. Unfortunately, documentation of databases is not very good on many web sites. Here are a few data problems you might encounter:

- Is all the data really in the database? What date range is included? Is the most recent data in the database? Is the old data in the database?

- How clean is the data? Are there misspellings of key names? Is the data consistent? For instance, is IBM listed as IBM, I.B.M Inc., International Business Machines, or even Computer Division/IBM?

- Does the search engine account for different names, look for plural as well as singular or use common variation (i.e., looking for "Mike" when you search by "Michael")?

- What information is not included? A list of fines levied against companies might include only companies that have agreed to pay and not companies that are disputing the fines.

- Is the data just plain wrong? Data in some states is input by prisoners, lowly paid clerks, or interns. It's common to find errors.

Don't base a lawsuit on information you find on the Internet. Always trace the information back to the original signed paper copy.

Structured Data Sets

To get a better handle on some of the above problems, you can sometimes download a database rather than search it on the Internet. This often allows you to use the full power of a database program or spreadsheet to mine the data and to do searches or tests on the data that a web front-end might not allow you to do. This is for the power user who wants to get the most out of the data.

These datasets reside on servers that have an FTP (file transfer protocol). This is the way the Internet lets you transfer files between computers. The data is stored in computer files and you simply download them. This may be as easy as clicking on a link, though sometimes you may have to right click on a file name and choose to save it to your disk. If your web browser is configured correctly, it may open Excel or Access automatically and display the file when you click on one of these files. Files that are saved to your hard drive may be downloaded into a spreadsheet or database program. Look for either the documentation on the web page to tell you the file format or look for these file extensions:

`.xl*` or `.xls`	Excel spreadsheet file
`.wk*`	Lotus 1-2-3 spreadsheet file
`.wq*`	Quattro Pro spreadsheet file
`.dbf`	FoxPro or dBase database file
`.mdb`	Access database file
`.db`	Paradox database file
`.txt` or `.asc`	ASCII text file (can be imported into database or spreadsheet)
`.csv`	ASCII comma-separated file (can be imported)

Below are some examples of government sites where you can download complete files. In each case, the procedure is a little different depending on how your browser is configured. Your browser should do one of two things:

1. It may try to display the file if your browser recognizes the file extension (file extensions can be set in Microsoft Internet Explorer by opening "My Documents" and selecting "Tools" and then "Folder Options" from the menus. There is a tab for file types.) If it recognizes the correct file type, you will be able to see the data.

2. If your browser does not recognize the file type, it will ask you to either save the file to your hard drive or to display it using your default text editor. Choose to save it because an Access or Excel file will not display correctly in all text editors.

Try downloading the data from the following sites:

International demographic data
`www.census.gov/ftp/pub/ipc/www/idbacc.html`

The U.S. Bureau of the Census also tracks international data that you can download in a spreadsheet. Very nice.

Older Populations Chart
`www.aoa.dhhs.gov/aoa/stats/AgePop2050.html`

The Administration on Aging has nice demographic information on the growing adult population. This site has a link to an Excel file near the bottom where you can download all the data easily.

Finding Data

Databases and spreadsheets are not stored on the Web as web pages or HTML files. The data is stored in a database server or as a separate file on a file server. You are either querying the database file on a database server or downloading a file. You can't search in those files using a search engine like Lycos, AllTheWeb, or AltaVista. Search engines usually only find web pages.

The key is to find the web page that refers to the database or file using standard search techniques such as Boolean search logic or HTML tag searches (this is explained in the Search Engines Chapter).

Another trick is to use a feature often found in search engines: searching by file type. For instance, if you type the phrase "aircraft filetype:mdb" in the Google (`www.google.com`) search engine, you will search for Access database files on the Internet associated with the word aircraft. You can build sophisticated searches with many other qualifiers but the key is you limit your results just to spreadsheets or database files.

Converting Data

The final method for downloading data from the Web is to import data into a spreadsheet from tables or charts displayed on a web page.

On the Web there are two table formats: HTML (hypertext markup language) or ASCII text. An ASCII text format is simply a table entered using common text. An HTML table uses hypertext tags to create the table. You can find out which format a page uses by looking at the page's source. In Internet Explorer, this is done by selecting "View" and then "Source" from the menus.

If a table on a web page has a series of tags (such as <TR> or <TD>), it is an HTML table. Excel and other spreadsheets will often recognize these tags. A table can be imported into Excel simply by saving the page on your hard drive and then opening it with Excel. You must specify the file type as HTML. An example of an HTML table can be found at:

`www.census.gov/hhes/poverty/poverty96/pv96state.html`

If the table shows up as you see it on the page, it is a ASCII text table. An example of an ASCII text table can be found at:

`www.census.gov/population/estimates/nation/intfile1-1.txt`

These files can be imported into spreadsheets or databases using the text import features found on most of these programs, or by cutting and pasting the text.

PDF Files

PDF files are files generated by the Adobe Acrobat program. It is a program that allows the user to generate documents in a word processing program and then quickly convert them to a web page or a non-editable electronic report for wide scale distribution. To a user, the PDF file appears almost like a picture of a report.

Since pictures can't be edited, you will have to convert the document into an editable text. This can be done by purchasing the Adobe Acrobat software. Acrobat allows you to select the text from the tables and copy it to another program such as Excel. You can use the "Text To Columns" feature in Excel to separate the data. Be aware that this may not work in all cases depending on how the tables were formatted.

Adobe also lets you submit an email with a PDF file or the URL where you found it online and it will send you back the text version. See http://access.adobe.com/onlinetools.html for more information.

Third-party vendors also make plug-ins or software that will convert a PDF file to either text or a spreadsheet. See Infodata's Aerial (www.ambia.com/aerial.asp) or ScanSoft's OmniPage (www.scansoft.com) for more information.

For more ideas on data you can find, see my Journalists Database of Databases at www.drewsullivan.com/database.html.

-- Drew Sullivan is the media advisor for IREX ProMedia in Sarajevo, Bosnia and Herzegovina. Email: drew@drewsullivan.com

Additional Sites for The Basics

Census State Poverty Rates
www.census.gov/hhes/poverty/poverty96/pv96state.html
HTML tables of U.S. Census information.

Fight Spam on the Net
http://spam.abuse.net/
Anti-spam site.

Finding Data on the Internet: A Journalist's Guide
www.nilesonline.com/data/index.shtml
Reporters' guide to finding stats and sources of data.

Government Economic Service (UK)
www.ges.gov.uk/
Is for the government economic service in the U.K.

Hotfiles.com
www.hotfiles.com
Thousands of shareware, freeware and demo programs for windows, PC, Mac and PDA devices.

Infodata's Aerial
www.ambia.com/aerial.asp
Fees for some content. Third party vendors also make plugins or software that will convert a PDF file to either text or a spreadsheet.

interMute
www.intermute.com
Filtering software company.

International demographic data
www.census.gov/ftp/pub/ipc/www/idbacc.html
Excellent collection of international population data.

Ithaca College - ICYouSee
www.ithaca.edu/library/Training/ICYouSee.html
Ever wonder how many millions of things you can do online? This is the most thorough list I've seen anywhere.

Life on the Internet
www.screen.com/loi/guide/default.html
This is another excellent beginners guide. It walks you through the basics.

Lycos Mail
www.mailcity.lycos.com
Example of web-based email program.

McAfee
www.mcafee.com/anti-virus/default.asp
Fees for some content. Pre-eminent anti-virus and firewall prootection software maker.

National Aviation Safety Data Analysis
http://nasdac.faa.gov/internet
FAA site for plane safety databases.

NetLearn
http://www2.rgu.ac.uk/~sim/research/netlearn/callist.htm
Net Learn, from the Robert Gordon University in Aberdeen, Scotland is another good beginner's guide to the 'Net.

NoAds
www.firase.com
Software the blocks pop-up ads.

Northville District Library - New User Tutorial
http://northville.lib.mi.us/tech/tutor/welcome.htm
This site is particularly good for first-time internet users.

Online Conversion Tools for Adobe PDF documents
http://access.adobe.com/onlinetools.html
Adobe lets you submit an email with a PDF file or the URL where you found it online and it will send you back the text version.

RealNetworks
www.real.com
RealNetworks provides a variety of multimedia editing and playing solutions for the Internet.

ScanSoft's OmniPage
www.scansoft.com
Fees for some content. Third party vendors also make plugins or software that will convert a PDF file to either text or a spreadsheet.

SpamCop
www.spamcop.net
Fee-based site. Anti-spam software.

Stack.com
www.stack.com
File format types and how to use them.

TechTutorials
www.techtutorials.com/fileformats.shtml
File formats list.

The HelpWeb
www.imaginarylandscape.com/helpweb/
Another good beginners guide to the Internet.

The Net: User Guidelines and Netiquette
www.fau.edu/netiquette/net/

The Web Consortium (W3C)
www.w3c.org
Acts as a forum to discuss specifications, guidelines, tools and software to develop what it calls a "collective understanding."

U.S. Census Information
www.census.gov/population/estimates/nation/intfile1-1.txt
Monthly estimates of the United States population.

University at Albany Libraries - Internet Tutorials
http://library.albany.edu/internet/
This is a really useful, well-written and simple guide to getting started on computers and on the 'Net.

University of California - Berkeley Library - Internet Tutorial
www.lib.berkeley.edu/TeachingLib/Guides/Internet/FindInfo.html
Excellent web training classes and tutorials from librarians at Cal-Berkeley.

Virus Myth
www.vmyths.com
Find the truths about hoaxes, urban legends, computer viruses.

webTeacher
www.webteacher.org/winexp/indextc.html
An online tutorial for a variety of internet topics ranging from the very basic functions to coding. Also serves as a resource for educators and professional development trainers who need training materials for classes.

WhatIs.com
http://whatis.techtarget.com/fileFormatA/0,289933,sid9,00.html
Comprehensive list of file formats.

ZDNet
www.zdnet.com
ZDNet is an excellent computer news site.

Zen and The Art of the Internet
www.cs.indiana.edu/docproject/zen/zen%2d1%2e0%5ftoc%2ehtml
An online guide to the Internet and internet technology, dated 1992.

Chapter 3

Framing Your Search Strategy

The Crucial First Step to Staying Afloat in a Sea of Data

Blending Skill, Common Sense, and Clever Intuition — Why The Internet Is So Tough to Index — What Is a Search Strategy? — Framing Your Question — Determining Your Information Resources — Other Search Strategy Considerations — A Little Perspective — Sources, Friends and Enemies — Boolean Operators and Keywords: Bloodhounds of Online Searching

Searcher Magazine editor Barbara Quint likens computers to dogs "faithful, friendly but not very bright." She also thinks they're like children at the "one joke" age in which the punch line is always the same. No matter how many times you complain about something they didn't do, the response is, "Because you didn't ask me" meaning: "Because you didn't ask me right!"

If you've ever looked for information about a specific subject on the Internet, you probably went to a search engine, input your subject and received a zillion results, called hits. "Wow!" you might have thought, "The Internet is great. Look how much information I found!" A closer look at the results made you think, "Oh, no, I need useful information within the next ten minutes!"

How do you reduce the number of hits to a manageable and relevant number of twenty sites? That's the goal of this chapter. Anyone can come up with a zillion hits. The real goal of research is *quality* information. For that, there are tools – lots of them – each with its own strengths, shortcomings and peculiarities.

Blending Skill, Common Sense, and Clever Intuition

Why The Internet Is So Tough to Index

You're reading this book because you want to figure out how to quickly and efficiently get from 200,000 results to the six things you need. People often approach searching the way they play slot machines at a casino. You just throw in a few keywords, pull the lever, and wait for your prize. Your odds are about as good. Effective searching requires a blend of learned skills, common sense and a bit of clever intuition.

In order to understand how the search tools work and why sometimes they don't, you need to understand a little history about the Internet.

As mentioned in Chapter 2, most people interchangeably use the words "Internet" and "Web." But they are really different things.

The Internet – or The 'Net – is a series of rules that allows computers of all types to connect and then communicate with other computers. The World Wide Web – The Web – is a software protocol that runs on top of the Internet, allowing users to easily access files stored on Internet computers. In the pre-Web days of the early 1990s, you had to use incredibly long complicated addresses to find specific information on the Internet. The Web changed that, making it easy to retrieve all kinds of different files from pictures, sound, and video, and text by simply clicking on a hypertext link.

One tool that transformed the Web into an easy-to-use system was the development of hyperlinks – a system all but taken for granted now. A hypertext link allows computerized objects like images and sounds to be linked together at a specific place tied to the text. When you click the hypertext link, it opens the file associated with the object.

In the 1980s, with the help of the U.S. Department of Defense, a network of computers emerged. When the network adopted a universal standard of communication called TCP/IP, the Transmission Control Protocol/Internet Protocol, the Internet became widely available. This new network was used mostly by governments and universities.

It wasn't until 1990 when Tim Berners-Lee developed several key components of the Web, including hypertext markup language (HTML), that the Web really took off.

The early internet search tools were very raw. There were two methods for retrieving information. First, you needed to establish a connection to the remote computer where the file you wanted was located. This was called Telnet, a terminal emulation program. Then you needed to transfer the file you wanted back to your computer. To do that you needed an FTP client, or a File Transfer Protocol, which standardized the way files were sent and received.

For a long time, to get what you wanted, you had to know both the address of the location you were looking for and the specific file name you wanted to find once you got there. But while the 'Net took evolutionary turns, commercial online services like Dialog and Lexis-Nexis offered advanced search and information retrieval networks on closed or proprietary systems, where sophisticated research could be done.

It was Berners-Lee, then working at CERN, a world-famous, high-energy physics laboratory in Geneva, Switzerland who – through a series of important innovations – created what would become the World Wide Web that we now use. Among other things, he created a way for all computers to use a common language that display identically on any computer. He also created a set of rules for computers to use to communicate with one another and to allow documents to be retrieved without worrying about where the computer was located. Berners-Lee also created what is now called URL, the Uniform Resource Locator system, which gave unique addresses and then pulled it all together into an early version of what is now the Web.

Interestingly, the first web directory is still online and can be viewed at www.w3.org/History/19921103-hypertext/hypertext/DataSources/bySubject/Overview.html. Be aware that most of the links listed there no longer work!

In the early 1990s, search "robots," now better known as "crawlers" or "spiders," were developed. These were computer-generated and didn't need people to help them locate and index content. 1994 was the watershed year for the Web's takeoff. In addition to the first sophisticated crawlers, two Stanford University graduate students used crawlers to find links and then hand-selected them and built the directory that now Yahoo! (www.yahoo.com). The next year, the first search engines appeared – Infoseek (http://infoseek.go.com), AltaVista (www.altavista.com), and Excite (www.excite.com) – with each offering different things they could do.

Search engines, compiled by computers, and subject directories, compiled by human beings, were developed to find and index documents and to point you to the most relevant documents in response to your keyword query. That worked initially because the Internet pages were mostly text and were simple hypertext markup language documents.

Gary Price and Chris Sherman, authors of the outstanding book *The Invisible Web*, say, as useful and necessary as search tools were for finding documents, they shared a common weakness – keyword query design. Quickly, web pages developed with information available in many formats, including sound and video. The search tools began to fall behind in keeping up with both the Web's impressive growth and the ability to recognize and index non-text information, like graphics.

These pages that fall through the cracks are part of what Price and Sherman describe as the "invisible web," an area that is growing considerably larger than the huge growth of the Internet. A Cyveillance.com study of July, 2001 estimated the size of the Internet at 2.5 billion documents and growing by a rate of 7.5 million documents per day. Another study, by Bright Planet.com[1] estimated the number of pages not indexed by search tools to be a whopping 400 to 550 times larger than what is already indexed. Price and Sherman and others believe the Bright Planet study is overstated, speculating that the "invisible web" is two to fifty times larger than the visible web. They have developed methods and innovative ways to search for "invisible web" resources (see Chapter 4, General Search Tools).

---

[1] Bright Planet study: Data collected between March 13 and 30, 2000. The study was originally published on Bright Planet's web site on July 26, 2000. Some of the references and web status statistics were updated on October 23, 2000, with further minor additions on February 22, 2001.

To become a top searcher, you need to understand the many tools in your researcher's arsenal and how to use them. To properly frame your search – something you do before you touch the keyboard – you also need to understand the difference between browsing and searching.

Browsing is the process of following a series of hypertext links, pointing and clicking your way through a collection of documents. It is good way to look through a limited amount of information on a particular subject. But it is an inadequate method if you are looking at a huge number of documents. Searching relies on software that matches keywords you specify in order to locate the most relevant documents in its index.

So when you are looking at an organized category of information, browsing can be a useful technique. But if you are looking at a large number of documents in an unorganized way, searching is a more efficient method of finding information.

This is important because search tools use two different methods to help you find what you are looking for. Subject directories, organized by human beings into hierarchical categories, are a great way to study a small number of subjects in its proper context. You look at one category and within it are several sub-categories of that subject. Search engines, by contrast, are organized by computers using keywords or phrases, and offer no context but allow you to research large numbers of subjects. They have no hierarchical structure. Instead they are organized by a search engine using mathematical formulas and algorithms to find relationships and compute correlations between subjects.

In searching, documents judged by the computer to have the most relevance are presented first in an indexed list.

Both techniques – browsing and searching – are very important in your efforts to find what you are looking for quickly and efficiently.

Despite the increasing sophistication of internet search tools, none of the thousands of search tools in existence can keep up with the mushrooming number of pages on the Internet. At best, the latest studies show that the top search tools index only about fifteen percent of the sites out there.[2]

As it stands now, no single search tool comes close to indexing even a quarter of the Internet, and taken together, many of the best tools combined get only a limited amount of what's out there. The level of sophistication of the search tools continues to increase, but is dwarfed by the numbers of pages being added daily to the Internet.

And the search engines have little overlap. Greg Notess, a highly respected search engine guru, found that only rarely did any of the major search engines come up with the same findings and there was surprisingly little overlap between the major search engines and directories. But Notess' tests, which can be found on his excellent web site `www.searchengineshowdown.com` were done with obscure words.

---

[2] *Nature Magazine* July 8, 1999; Study by computer scientists Steve Lawrence and C. Lee Giles at the NEC Research Institute in Princeton, NJ.

➔ *hot tip:* If you are searching for something unusual, you will need multiple search tools to find what you are looking for. On more popular searches, you may get some overlap.

This overwhelming, exponential growth is the source of a lot of frustration for would-be researchers. By the time you've devised your own methods for getting around the Internet, things will have changed. Keeping up is, in itself, a full-time job. But there are rules of thumb that will stand you in good stead.

While online research can be frustrating, it can also be fascinating. As we all know, there's usually more than one way to reach an intended destination. If you're stymied in one direction, the trick is to devise another way to get there.

What Is a Search Strategy?

Most good researchers have developed their own ways to focus their searches. The habit dates back to the early days when access was far more restricted and searches cost more because only fee-based tools were available. At the time, you paid for the usage in by-the-minute charges. Consequently, researchers developed the habit of thinking things through before placing an order that would set the meter ticking.

Today, so much data is available that, without a plan, you can easily find yourself swimming in an ocean of information. The trick is to stay clearly focused on your goal while also being flexible and creative enough to revise your approach, based on the results you encounter.

One of the best approaches is the one devised by Nora Paul, a nationally recognized lecturer and now the director of the Institute for New Media Studies at the University of Minnesota. She has taken the "five Ws and H" (who – what – when – where – why – how) of reporting and devised a simple checklist that will help you formulate a search strategy by providing many avenues that can take you to the answer you're seeking. Framing your research strategy is critical to finding what you are looking for. A good, clear question will save you hours of work.

The first major step for almost any research project is to visualize your destination. Before you touch the computer, think through what you are looking for, where it might be available, and prepare a temporary roadmap. If you imagine your perfect search result – exactly what you want to find on the exact page you are looking for (if it exists) – then you can focus your search strategy to find it. If you have no idea what you are really looking for, you won't find it. One of the most important questions to ask yourself is: what is the purpose of the search?

Nora Paul's excellent questionnaire is a great way to figure out what you are looking for before you waste time trying to find it.

Framing Your Question

By Nora Paul

First and foremost, frame your question. Putting your question into words forces you to think about what you want. By taking the time to identify the key phrases and visualize the ideal answer, you'll be more likely to recognize that answer when you find it online.

The following checklist will help you think through the details of your information quest.

Who:

- Who is the research about: a politician, a businessperson, a scientist, a criminal?

- Who is key to the topic you are researching? Are there any recognized experts or spokespersons you should know about?

- Who do you need to talk to: someone who has experienced something, someone who knows someone, someone who is an expert?

- Who have you already talked to? Who do they know who might help you?

What:

- What kind of information do you need: statistics, sources, background?

- What kind of research are you doing: an analysis, a backgrounding report, a follow-up?

- What type of information will be useful: full-text articles or reports, specific facts, referrals to a person, public records?

- What are you trying to do: confirm a fact you've been given, find someone to interview, get up to speed on a topic, background somebody, narrow a broad topic, fill in a hole in your knowledge?

- What would be the best source of the information: an association, a government agency, a research center, a company?

- What information do you already have: what do you already know about the topic or person?

- What would the ideal answer look like? Envisioning the perfect answer will help you recognize it when you find it!

When:

- When did the event being researched take place? This will help determine the source to use, particularly, which information source has resources dating far enough back.

- When did the event being researched end?

- When will you know you should stop searching? (When you have the answer!)

Where:

- Where did the event you're researching take place?

- Where are you in your research: just starting (looking for background), in the middle (looking for verification of information found), towards the end (looking to tie up loose ends)?

- Where have you already looked for information?

- Where is the biggest collection of the type of information you're looking for likely to be: university research center, association files, a specialty database?

- Where did the person you're backgrounding come from?

- Where might there have been previous coverage: newspapers, broadcasts, trade publications, court proceedings, discussions?

Why:

- Why do you need the research: seeking a source to interview, surveying a broad topic, pinpointing a fact?

- Why must you have the research: to make a decision, to corroborate a premise?

How:

- How much information do you need: a few good articles for background, everything in existence on the topic, just the specific fact?

- How are you going to use the information: for an anecdote, for publication?

- How far back do you need to research: the current year, last two years, ten years ago?

-- Nora Paul is now the Director of the Institute for New Media Studies at the University of Minnesota, former Library Director of the Poynter Institute, a former *Miami Herald* librarian, a nationally recognized lecturer and co-author with Margot Williams of the *Great Scouts! Cyberguides For Subject Searching On The Web*, published by Cyberage Books (www.infotoday.com)

Once you know what you're looking for, it then becomes a matter of determining where to find it.

Determining Your Information Resources

By Nora Paul

Once a question has been formulated clearly, then you can select the information resources you need to answer the question. Those resources may include online resources (commercial data services, Internet, etc.) as well as conventional tools (phone calls, books, interviews, etc.).

Every project requires a different combination of resources. Sometimes you'll have more than a library at your disposal. Sometimes you'll have a hefty research budget but a tight deadline, and so forth. All of these factors come into play when you examine your information resources. This checklist will help you determine which information resource can best be of service.

Who:

- Who might have the kind of information I'm seeking?

- Who has the data I need? Does the database I'm considering include information from the time period I want?

What:

- What kind of database should I use: am I looking for full-text articles, public records, statistics?

- What services are available to me?

- What does each offer? At what cost?

When:

- When are the services available: will they be accessible when I need them?

- When should I use another service: at which point does it make sense to try a different one?

Why:

- Why might I choose one service option over another? Determining factors include cost, range of material, ease-of-use.

Where:

- Where am I most comfortable searching: which service is most familiar to me?

- Where do I have the best deal? Database services offer varying options at varying prices.

- Where can I get the search support I need?

How:

- How can I select the most logical resource? Sometimes the best way is to consult a specialist familiar with the range of choices and their features.

Other Search Strategy Considerations

Here are a few more tips and things to consider as you work through your strategy for searching.

When you begin searching on the computer, make sure you select words that would actually be on the page you are looking for. For example, if you are looking for the children of U.S. presidents or children who lived in the White House, don't search for words like "presidential progeny." The words are accurate, but not the kind of words you would find on a web page about the children of presidents. Instead, words like "children" and "white house" are obvious. But ask yourself, what words *must be* on a page about children of the White House. If you pick "Chelsea Clinton," "Amy Carter," and "John F. Kennedy, Jr.," you increase your chances of finding a page that focuses on the children of presidents who lived in the White House.

You will find the pages you are looking for using keywords like "president," "children," and "white house." But you will also get a whole lot of unrelated information. When I did this search on AltaVista, I got more than 296,000 results, the top one being the White House site itself and another being a bio of President George W. Bush, but none about his kids, who don't actually live at the White House. When I put the names of presidents' kids in AltaVista, I got seven results, one of which was an ABC TV news report about the children of presidents. Try a search like this on another search engine and see how you do.

A Little Perspective

Remember when you are searching, a search engine doesn't know what you are looking for, doesn't know your business, how you want the information results packaged, what to highlight, and what to leave out. It doesn't know what's important to you. Only you can provide that.

Sources, Friends and Enemies

Information comes from people. If you're looking for information that really matters to you, the ultimate source is often other people. Generally, people can be classified as friends, observers, or enemies. If you can't get information directly from one person, talk with someone who knows that person well, such as a friend. Or try someone who spends a significant amount of time observing that person – perhaps a work colleague. Another potential information source is someone who dislikes the person. If someone doesn't want to talk to you, ask yourself who else might have the information you seek. Former employees often know a company's secrets and have no inhibitions about sharing them, if asked. But, while online research can help you locate sources, it's no substitute for actually talking to real people. Do not forget that people are an incredible resource in helping you find information. (See the Human Element Tools Section of Chapter 5, Specialized Tools.)

Boolean Operators & Keywords: Bloodhounds of Online Searching

At the beginning of this chapter, editor Barbara Quint said that computers were like dogs, "friendly, but not very bright." Like dogs, computers obey specific commands.

Here are the commands. They are simple. It's unfortunate that such simple commands were given a name straight from outer space – Boolean. But if you can get through the next two paragraphs, you'll be well on your way to online proficiency.

There are three major Boolean operators:

AND   NOT   OR

Some search engines substitute symbols for words such as (+) for "AND" and (-) for "NOT."

Say you are interested in the rose industry, and you want to focus on thornless roses. Your primary search word would be "roses." If you submit "roses" as your primary search term on the search engine HotBot, you would get 147,940 hits, and on Infoseek, another search engine, you would receive about 1.4 million hits. The number of hits is too large to be manageable. That's where the Boolean operators AND and OR come into play.

If you submit "roses" OR "thornless," you'll get even more hits. In fact, you will get a list of every available reference that mentions *either* of those two words. However, if you submit "roses AND thorns," you'll get *only* the hits that contain both of those words.

If you do this example and find that the numbers for "thornless" OR "roses" and "thornless" AND "roses" are the same, it is because the search engine includes all search terms by default, so the "and" and the "or" are unnecessary.

Many search trainers advise people not to use Boolean operators at all. They suggest that because people don't understand how to do it properly. My suggestion is this – just use it wisely. Search guru Greg Notess agrees, saying you don't want to use a Boolean phrase like this:

> Which (way OR path) does the (water OR liquid) go down the (drain OR sink) in the (southern OR south) hemisphere

Instead, Notess suggests to use it for simple ANDs, ORs, and to keep the sentence simple, not too complex. For example:

> Yellowstone AND (Buffalo OR Bison)

Chapter 4 introduces the basic search tools. These tools accept Boolean operators and keywords.

Chapter 4

General Search Tools

Search Engines, Subject Directories, Portals & Meta-Tools

Search Engines — How a Search Engine Works — Relevancy Ranking — A Million Hits, Profitability and Other Half-Truths — Natural Language Search Engines — When to Use a Search Engine — Subject Directories — How Directories Work — When to Use a Subject Directory: General Topics, Popular Topics, Targeted Directories, Current Events, Product Information — Search Engines vs. Subject Directories — Portals and Hybrid Search Tools: Vortals and Focused Crawlers — Meta-Tools — Advantages and Disadvantages of Meta-Tools — Paid Placement Inclusion — Best Search Engines — Best Subject Directories — Best Hybrid Search Tools: Academic, Bibliographies, Business, Environment, Genealogy, General to Specific, Government, Health and Science, Legal, News, Politics, Statistics, Technology — Best Meta-Tools — Search Tools to Watch — Value-Added Search Tools — Accessing Hidden Content — The Best of the Invisible Web — Telephone Numbers — Mapping Tools — Tips from a Search Engine Guru — Resources on Search Tools — Must Reads — Search Engine Books and Charts

Each day, vast numbers of new web sites are created. The numbers are so large that they are incomprehensible, and the growth rate is so explosive that some companies spend all their time simply tracking Internet development. When searching in this furiously expanding universe of information, first prepare by following these four steps—

First step:	WHAT:	Define the data you want.
Second step:	WHERE:	Figure out where it's likely to be found.
Third step:	WHICH:	Select the search tool most likely to provide it.
Fourth step:	HOW:	Learn how to interpret your results.

In this chapter, we'll introduce the general search tools, subject directories and some of the other search tools you can use to find information. We'll also discuss easy strategies and techniques for using these tools and why search engines don't find everything. Understanding that will enable you to select the best tool to retrieve the information you want.

The two most basic and commonly used search tools are search engines and subject directories. A thorough understanding of how they work and how to use them will make you a far more effective researcher. Unless you're a veteran or specialty researcher, you should try these tools first, once you've developed your question, framed your research strategy and determined your search terms.

Many people think of search engines and subject directories as the "big guns" of internet research, often ignoring the many other types of search tools available. In the book *The Invisible Web*, Gary Price and Chris Sherman notes that other search tools to include in your arsenal are: targeted directories, focused crawlers, portals, vortals, meta-tools, and value-added search services. This chapter will introduce you to each of these types of tools, explain what they can do for you and why you need to know them.

Searching & Search Tools: An Introduction

In pre-computer days, a library's card catalog was a chest of drawers that contained a card for each book. On each card was the book's name, author, publisher and other information. In other words, a card catalog was a database; each card was a record and each piece of information (name, author and so on) was a field.

Every search tool is made up of one or more databases that contain records and fields. With electronic databases, you can isolate the information you want by specifying the fields you want to search. For example, you can search through all the books by Tom Clancy and then specify or limit the result to books published in 2002, or only those from a certain publisher. You can do this because you're searching through information (fields) common to each card (record) – in this case, the fields containing the author's name, the books' publication dates, and the publishers.

As Cheryl Gould suggests in her excellent book *Searching Smart on the World Wide Web*, "the database of a search tool can be visualized as a gigantic, never-ending three-dimensional tic-tac-toe board with unlimited boxes. Each box contains a piece of information that relates to information in other boxes. The relationships built between the pieces of information are created by the database provider and serve as one of the ways the search tools differentiate themselves."

➔**hot tip:** **Take the time to learn how a search engine works and take full advantage of the capabilities it offers. The best way to do this is to use help screens. Before you begin using a search tool, consult the Help, How To, or Tips page linked to its front page. Each search tool has one.**

➔**hot tip:** **1. Become familiar with several major search engines. That way when a research topic doesn't show up in one engine, you should be able to find it using another. 2. Study the simple and advanced instructions. 3. Review the instructions on how the search tools work frequently – they change constantly, usually for the better.**

Search Engines

A search engine is an enormous database of web sites compiled by a software robot that seeks out and indexes web sites (and sometimes other Internet resources as well). There are thousands of search engines, and they vary in speed, skill, depth of indexing, size of database, advanced search features and presentation of results. Every search engine's method of searching is proprietary; the depth and breadth and realm of its database is unique, and each search engine possesses its particular strengths and idiosyncrasies.

Data is collected according to a unique mix of criteria. These criteria – also called variables – are weighted and trigger tradeoffs that make each database dramatically different from its counterparts. For example, when you use HotBot (`www.hotbot.com`), you're using one database that was organized in a specific way, and when you use Google (`www.google.com`), you're using another database, which was organized differently. Consequently, you may get wildly different results. This is true for the many different search engines.

An eye-popping number of search engines claim to be the best, the largest, or the most thorough. Several claim to be comprehensive. You can ignore the claims because every search engine database is woefully incomplete. While the most comprehensive study on this was back in 2000, professors Steven Lawrence and C. Lee Giles at the NEC Institute found that the top search tools indexed less than twenty percent of the available web material. With the Web's continued growth and the increased sophistication of the web search tools, those percentages are probably about the same or lower today.

➔ *hot tip:* **Because each search engine is constructed differently, they may return different results, even if you use the exact same phrase or words. So never do just one search, always do the same search using several different search tools for the best results.**

➔ *hot tip:* **Many searchers make the mistake of using one search engine for all their searches. If you don't get the results you want on a search engine, don't keep trying different variations on the same words until you get it. A better approach is to get to know several search tools and if you don't get results after a couple of tries, move on to another search tool or step back and re-evaluate what words you are using to find the information.**

How a Search Engine Works

When you use a search engine, you are not searching the entire Web for the latest information. You are searching the full-text index of that search engine. In other words, you are not searching the Web itself, just what pages and web sites the search engine has already categorized and stored.

Search engines consist of three major elements – the crawler, the indexer, and the query process.

Crawler

A crawler – also known as a spider, robot or worm – is an automated tool that visits a web page, finds the information on the page, and then follows links to other pages within that site. The job of the crawler is to find the information and hand it off to the search engine's indexers. Web crawlers don't actually search the Web at all. They work much the way your browser does, sending a request to a web server for a web page, downloading everything on that page and giving it to the indexer. But they do it a lot faster than a browser.

Crawlers find information in two ways. Early on, you could send the search engine your information and it would be added to the database. The crawler would take the information it was sent, and go retrieve the web pages. But people overwhelmed the "add URL" pages on the search engines with bogus posts and the search engine companies started to phase out that way of notifying them.

Now, what the crawlers do is look at the URL links on the web pages it finds and goes back over all of those links. This cuts down on the bogus URLs and helps the crawler be thorough.

The search engine crawls and indexes information, but search engines do further refinement before the information is available to the public. The companies perform spam detection and removal, duplication detection and removal, and also do some database quality testing. So, the information found on a web site and indexed is not available in your search for several weeks. Greg Notess calls this the "black box process."

But this all comes at a cost. Crawling is extremely expensive for the search engine companies, so most search companies limit the number of pages that will be crawled on one web site. That means that search crawlers may look at an entire web site, but may only crawl a part of it, leaving a lot of valuable information not indexed. These are sites that can be located, but are intentionally not included in the search engine indices. They are what Gary Price and Chris Sherman like to call the "opaque web." These are not part of the "invisible web," just ones that simply can't be indexed.

Besides cost, the other major issue with crawlers is the time it takes to log all this information. While some crawlers can index millions of pages in a day, there's sometimes a significant amount of time between when the information is put on the Web, when it is found by the crawler and when it recrawls looking for new material. These time lag issues lead to inaccuracy in your results. There's an ongoing debate about the "freshness" of the search engines. Most search engine companies claim they constantly crawl and have only the freshest of information. But analysis by Gary Price and Greg Notess found that the search engine companies tend to be weeks behind on a regular basis, and many search tools are months behind in their efforts to recrawl and index material.

Indexer

Everything the crawler finds goes into the second part of the search engine: the index.

The indexer takes every word on a web page, logs it, categorizes it and then stores the results in a huge database. Indexing every word allows most search engines to go beyond keyword searches and allows proximity searching for words close to each other. Most of these can be utilized in the advanced search areas of nearly all the major search engines. Some indexers also index the HTML coding which allows the search engine to look by web page categories like URLs or titles. The help section of every search tool will show you how to get maximum results from that specific search engine. Sometimes there's a time lag, so that a web page may have been crawled but not yet indexed.

Until it is indexed, it's unavailable to search engine users. If a crawler finds changes on a web page, then it updates the index to include the new information. The word "index" implies categorization and classification – activities that require human assessment and interpretation. In reality, the indexing for a search engine is done by computer (software, actually), and the rankings of the responses, or hits, are calculated by mathematical formulas as well. To improve performance, many search engines eliminate certain common words like "is," "and," "or," and "of." These are called "stop words" that add no real benefit to the search. Search engines also have taken other steps to focus their searches by eliminating punctuation and converting all letters to lowercase. It's important to remember that each search engine has different rules and ways of working.

➜ *hot tip:* **Receiving too many hits? If your initial search returns an overwhelming number of hits, visually scan the results for keywords that can narrow the returns from your second search. Get maximum returns. Most search engines will let you determine the number of hits returned on your screen. Set the Display Option (which you'll find almost always under the Advanced Search feature) to the maximum number, which usually varies from 10-100 at a time, depending on the search tool.**

Query Process

The third part of a search engine is its query processing capability, the complicated part of the process. What happens is the query is taken by the search engine, the index is searched, and all kinds of different factors are weighed in deciding what is relevant, what is not, and the results are returned. The exact process differs with every search engine and the search engine companies closely guard the specific mathematical algorithms used to make the calculations.

The big difference is the way relevance is calculated.

Relevancy Rankings

When you give a search engine a keyword, how does it know which of the millions of pages in its index to sort through? It follows a set of rules known as search algorithms. As mentioned before, each particular search engine closely guards the exact mathematical formula it uses as a trade secret. But most search engines follow some general rules.

As search expert Danny Sullivan chronicles in his *Search Engine Watch* newsletter at www.searchenginewatch.com, one of the key ranking rules is using the location and frequency of keywords on a web page. So, pages with the search words in the HTML title tag are assumed to be more relevant to the topic than other pages. In effect, title tags are like a headlines of a news story. Another major factor in how search engines determine relevancy is how keywords appear in relation to other words on the page. The higher the frequency, the more relevant the page is viewed. All the major search engines follow that rule, Sullivan notes, "in the same way cooks may follow a standard chili recipe. But cooks like to add their own secret ingredients."

Nobody does it the same, which is why you get different results when you do a search, even the exact same search on two different search engines.

Some search engines like Google put extra emphasis on what sites are linked to the primary site, ("link analysis"), while Infoseek (http://infoseek.go.com) ranks sites that appear in its human-developed directory higher.

Search engines have found some creative ways to deal with bad queries from you and me. Certain phrases become very popular and are repeatedly sent to the search engine. So most search engine companies have developed pre-programmed results. For example, the 2002 movie *Black Hawk Down* is based on the true story of American soldiers in the battle of Mogadishu trying to capture two Somalian warlords. So several search engine companies have developed standard responses to queries about the movie, directing you to that movie's web site, details about the true events, bios of the stars, details on the lives of the real people involved in the real incident and Mark Bowden's original book and reporting from *The Philadelphia Inquirer*, which inspired the movie.

Search engines differ in the way they work. Say you want more information about chocolate-flavored peanut butter. One search engine or subject directory might search its database first for "chocolate." Then it takes those results and searches them for the additional word "peanut." Then it takes those results and scans for the word "butter," and presents you with the results.

➜**hot tip:** **When you click the Search button on your browser — especially Netscape Navigator and Internet Explorer — you'll go to special miniature versions of selected search tools. These mini-versions aren't as powerful or as comprehensive as the real search engines. Search results from the browser versions aren't the same as results from the original, full-size search engines. The same thing happens when a subject directory, America Online a portal or any other site kicks you through a button to a search engine. For example, the Lycos access via a browser is a limited version of the full-size Lycos engine.**

Another search tool might require you to submit a term using a plus sign (+), so your search term would be "chocolate+peanut+butter." Another might require you to submit "chocolate AND peanut AND butter." And a fourth search engine might conduct three simultaneous searches – one for each word – and extract only the documents that the three sets have in common. Other search tools might utilize a combination of these approaches.

All of this isn't very important until you're clear about what you want. For now, it's enough to understand that every one of these search engines works differently. Consider them different tools for different purposes. For example, AltaVista (www.altavista.com) is especially good for finding foreign sites and information in foreign languages because it has a built-in translation component. HotBot allows you to opt for image-only and graphics-only hits. Teoma (www.teoma.com) and Wisenut (www.wisenut.com) customize your results into folders – essentially an automatic grouping feature that makes for easier searching.

→ *hot tip:* **Use phrase searching to narrow or expand a search on a search engine. If you're interested in the puffer fish and search the word "puffer," you'll get thousands of hits, most of them irrelevant. But if you search for the phrase "puffer fish," you'll get more relevant hits. You can phrase search in AltaVista, Google, AllTheWeb, Lycos, Wisenut, MSN Search, and Teoma by putting your phrase within double-quotations, "like this," and do the same in HotBot through a drop-down menu. And, when you search for the puffer fish's scientific name, tetradon, your hits will be far more specific. Also, on many engines, a + sign can denote a phrase, "puffer+fish."**

Search engines also vary in their presentation of results. Some search engines list their results alphabetically, others by relevance ranking, and some use a combination of both criteria or different criteria altogether. Search engines are programmed to rank results according to many factors, including the location and frequency of keywords on a page.

For example, depending on the search engine, pages with keywords appearing in the title are assumed to be more relevant, and pages with keywords located higher up on a web page – in a headline or the first few paragraphs of text – are ranked higher than pages where the keywords appear lower on the page. Also, the more frequently a keyword is mentioned, the more relevant a web page is considered to be.

→ *hot tip:* **Search engines treat numbers and other non-alphabet characters such as a forward slash "/", a numeral or a hyphen in differing ways. If a search term includes special or non-alphabet characters, try incorporating it into a search phrase. If that doesn't work, try using a "wildcard" character in place of the special character. Consult the search tool's help screen to identify that search tool's wildcard character. For example, on AltaVista, submit wish* to find**

wish, wishes, wishful, wishbone and wishy-washy. The ^ in this example is considered a wildcard character.

→**hot tip:** The link search feature of some search engines (namely Lycos, MSN Search, AltaVista, and HotBot) can also serve as a quick credibility check because the links identify other sites that consider this site to be credible. For example, a site linked to universities and government agencies is more credible than a site linked to the Jerry Springer TV show home page. Credibility checking is discussed in Chapter 12 - Evaluating Accuracy, Credibility & Authority.

The Search Engine World

A Million Hits, Profitability and Other Half-Truths

What you see is not always what you get when it comes to search engines. For example, when you run a search and get 1.2 million hits, you think "Wow, that's a lot of links!" But you will never see 1.2 million hits at one time, even if you were willing to try to scroll through that many. Most major search engines restrict your actual list or results to 1,000. According to Sullivan's *Search Engine Watch*, AllTheWeb, also known as FAST (www.alltheweb.com), is the only search tool that will let you get more than 1,000 results, and even it only allows 4,010 results to be displayed. Directories limit displayed results to 199.

Why do they limit the displays? And why do they claim to show much more? It comes down to the economics of running a web site. The more frequently a search engine database is updated, the more reliable its results will be. But frequent updates cost a lot of money, so more and more, how good a search tool is can depend on how much money its owners are putting into it and how good its partners are. Most of the major search engines claim to index 500 million documents. Wisenut says it indexes 1.5 billion pages and Google claims it has searched more than three billion pages, including 2 billion web pages, 800 million Usenet posts, and 330 million images. So the big numbers are meant to lure you into believing they have the most comprehensive databases, but knowing that no one will actually go through a million hits, search engines save time, money, and bandwidth by only serving a up a portion of those results.

However, even those claims to the number of indexed pages can be questioned. Notess, a search engine expert who runs tests to determine accuracy, puts the numbers at well-below a billion, and notes that the search engines list how many documents they've found, not how many they've indexed. But whatever the numbers, the search engines have gotten much better at finding information, much more accurate and much more sophisticated in how they do their jobs. That means you have a better chance of finding what you are looking for.

→ **hot tip:** You need to do an "on-the-fly" analysis when you view search engine results. Always question your results for accuracy. Evaluate and compare the different search tools. You can do this, Greg Notess suggests, by doing your own search engine comparison by using a unique, low-posted term and then do the same test a few weeks or months later and watch for changes over time.

Initially search engine sites were not concerned about profitably, believing that after they established a loyal following, the money would follow from advertisers and other commercial ventures. However, the great lesson of the dot-com crash of 2000 was that companies need to have a profitable business base to survive on the Internet. Many search engines have come and gone, others are simply a shell of their former selves. But there is still room for growth in the search tool market and a few new search tools, Teoma and Wisenut, show great promise.

The search tools market is an ever-changing landscape as companies thrive and fail, expand through acquisition or disappear altogether without so much as a blip. Excite, Go.com and Infoseek (both owned by Disney), iWon, NBCi, are no longer powerhouse search engine leaders, if they are around at all. Many of the meta-search tools have also died or been bought out or merged with other ones. Include in casualty list Inference Find, Savvysearcher, Webcrawler, and Magellan.

The biggest loss to researchers was the announcement in January, 2002 that Northern Light had been sold to Divine Inc., which provides content management and delivery solutions to business customers. Worse news was that Northern Light was closing as a free public search tool. While its database was the fourth largest searchable database, what made it outstanding were two features: its "special collection" documents that allowed you to buy news and research documents on a pay basis from an extensive collection, and its auto-classification of results, which allowed you to look at the search several ways using custom search folders created on the fly. Luckily that auto-classification technique is now being used by the two major newcomers, Teoma and Wisenut, and another meta-search tool to watch, Vivisimo (`www.vivisimo.com`). What is left of Northern Light is the special collections section, which you can still search on, but will have to pay for your results. Divine also announced that Yahoo! will offer that special collection through a new "premium documents search." The loss of Northern Light is a blow to the research world.

What is left after the fallout from the dot-com crash are six major players:

- AltaVista, `www.altavista.com`
- FAST, `www.fastsearch.com` which powers AllTheWeb and a Lycos
- Google, `www.google.com`
- Inktomi, `www.inktomi.com` which powers HotBot and MSN
- Teoma, `www.teoma.com`
- Wisenut, `www.wisenut.com`

Natural Language Search Engines

One of the hottest techniques is so-called "natural language search engines," which allow users to submit search terms in English rather than using Boolean operators, quotes, + signs and other search terminology. Many search engines claim natural language processing when what they actually mean is that Boolean operators aren't required – there is a difference.

According to Dr. Elizabeth Liddy, an expert on natural language searching and the director of the Center for Natural Language Processing at Syracuse University, a true natural language search engine extracts the meaning of the document by reprocessing it and pulling out relevant terms. Then it compares potentially relevant documents and finds similarities. The pages are isolated. Then, the engine summarizes and analyzes potentially relevant documents. Finally, it finds commonality among the relevant documents.

> **Example:** If you submitted the word "Robert," a natural language search engine might look for "Bob" as well. Natural language searches evaluate proximity of terms, phrase recognition, capitalization and keyword occurrence in titles, subheads and text. If you wanted to know where Winston Churchill delivered the "Iron Curtain" speech, a natural language search engine would search for items containing the following words: winston, churchill, iron, curtain and speech.

Inktomi and many other search tools like Oingo (www.oingo.com), Simpli (now part of www.NetZero.com), Lexiquest (www.lexiquest.com) and Manning and Napier Information System's Map-It (www.mnis.net) offer phrase detection and more advanced natural language products including concept mapping to find what you mean, not what you say.

A special word about Oingo, which refers to itself as a meaning-based search tool. It tries to pull together words, meanings, and their relationship to other words, then give you back concept-based answers. It is worth looking at.

When to Use a Search Engine

Search engines have several strengths. They can:

- Search large numbers of documents and provide large numbers of results.

- Provide huge numbers of links in their results and as noted earlier in this chapter, you can use those links to find other valuable resources.

- Allow you to search the full text of most of the pages on a web site.

So with a carefully thought-out request, a search engine will help you find information you may not find elsewhere.

Search engines are the preferred tool when you:

- Are looking for something very specific.

- Need to pin down a quick fact or two.

- Need to know if any information exists at all on a subject.

- Want mass quantities of links, but are not concerned about quality control.

- Are doing an exhaustive search (remember, though, you want more than just one search engine).

➔ *hot tip:* **When do you walk away from the search engine (or a subject directory)? Amelia Kassel, an excellent business searcher who runs her own company Marketingbase.com (`www.marketingbase.com`) offers this tip: "Don't spend hours using search engines just because they're free." Or, as Amelia puts it, pick your favorite cliché, because in this case they are all true: You can't make a silk purse from a sow's ear. —You can't improve the quality of junk. —You can't make gold from iron. —You can't squeeze blood from a turnip. So her final point is "move on and get over it" or find it another way.**

Subject Directories

A subject directory is a database of titles, citations, and web sites organized by category – similar to a filing cabinet containing folders with files. Categorization and indexing are performed by humans, not by machines or software. Users travel down a series of menus arranged by subject.

Unlike search engines, where a computer attempts to rank the most relevant results first, subject directories present results in categories, usually alphabetically, and the category titles vary from one subject directory to the next. The information is organized, evaluated and cataloged by a person – not software – who ranks the material using pre-determined criteria. The entire process of collecting, arranging, HTML coding and annotating requires a great deal of human effort. As a result, subject directory databases tend to be much smaller than those of search engines. Subject directories are designed for ease of browsing.

The largest and most well known subject directory is Yahoo!, which categorizes subjects into fourteen topics and hundreds of subtopics.

Example: If you want to know more about Caribbean vacations, searching for the phrase "Caribbean vacation" may not be the best way to go. Instead of keyword searching, which will get you some links to hotel web sites and other commercial sites, you are better off browsing through Yahoo!'s categories to find specific references and results, such as first person accounts of traveling in this area, reviews of hotels and restaurants, or suggestions of things to do in the area. In this case, you would click through the following categories:

```
Home > Recreation > Travel > By Region > Regions >
     Caribbean
```

… to get to a series of on-target Caribbean vacation resources and information.

Most subject directories are organized in similar ways. Subject directories effectively use hypertext links, enabling you to work your way from broad categories to specific topics. Most subject directories allow you to keyword search them, but then you are *not* searching the full-text of the documents contained on the specific pages the link is pointing to. So you could miss important documents altogether by using the search function in a directory.

Most directories' databases tend to be much smaller than search engines' databases. To make up for that, most directories supplement their results with additional results provided by search engine partners. So, for example, a search on Yahoo! will list additional results from its partner, Google. MSN uses Inktomi as its partner., so does About.com, while LookSmart (`www.looksmart.com`) uses AltaVista. When the directory search fails to provide any results, the search engine partner's results are listed as primary results.

Another benefit of using a subject directory is in how results are listed. When you use a search engine, you get ten or twenty results per page and must keep flipping through to get all the results. A subject directory will list all its results on one page with descriptions of all the links and direct links to the sites you want to see.

But, there are some downsides to subject directories besides the size limit. Timeliness can be an issue. With the constant changes of the Web some directories get out-of-date quickly because the editor does not regularly monitor all the changes on pages. Bias can also be an issue, depending on the subject. This problem is much more prevalent on directories in politically charged areas like the Middle East, the Balkans, India, and Pakistan.

How Directories Work

By hypertext-linking the pages, these directories can be very topic-focused. Most subject directories provide summary descriptions for every link, allowing you to get an idea of what's on the page without having to actually look at it.

For the most part, directories are either closed models or open ones. Closed model directories, exemplified by Yahoo! and LookSmart, are pulled together by professional editors who select the links and set up the categories. While the quality does vary some, generally you can expect high quality results from closed directories.

Open model directories such as the Open Directory Project (`www.dmoz.org`) depend on volunteer editors to compile the category and subject information. The Open Directory project is the directory for AOL. Search engines Google, HotBot and hundreds of other also have extensive directories, and depend on volunteer editors as well. With open directory models, you will find that the level of quality can vary widely from editor to editor. You will still find some very good volunteer editors, but the range of quality can be quite a bit wider.

In either case, a good way to test the overall quality of a subject directory is to start with a topic you are familiar with and look at the quality of the resulting links.

When to Use a Subject Directory

Subject directories are useful when you want to know more about broad-based subjects, such as:

- General topics
- Popular topics
- Targeted directories
- Current events
- Product information

Subject directories have two great strengths: they are organized and they are selective. When you are not sure of the exact term to search for, browsing subject categories will help you find those keywords. At the same time, if you are looking for a subject and you think a search engine will return an overwhelming number of hits, a subject directory can suggest the best keywords to use and good resources on the subject.

Remember, these directories are usually smaller than search engines, have much more focused and higher quality links, but are poor for exhaustive searching.

Let's consider each of these in turn.

General Topics

Say, for example, you're thinking about a beach vacation and want to evaluate some choices. On Yahoo!, for instance, you would choose the travel category and browse away, finding beaches all over the world. But, if you start out in search of a specific black-sand beach on Grenada, you'll have to go down many multiple-choice paths before concluding that a particular subject directory does or doesn't have information about it. If you're set on going to Grenada, you'd be better off submitting "Grenada" to a search engine.

Popular Topics

Let's say you're looking for information about American basketball superstar Michael Jordan. Logically, you would start looking under basketball. Due to a subject directory's file-within-a-file system, you'd have to start at recreation, then go to sports, then basketball then National Basketball Association, then players, then Michael Jordan. Using a keyword search of either a subject directory or a search engine in this case would quickly get you to pages about the Washington Wizards superstar. When comparing search directories and search engines, here's the difference: in a subject directory tool like Yahoo!, you'll find more than a dozen categories in which Jordan pops up, all presorted and indexed by a human being. A search on the Google search engine for "Michael Jordan" would retrieve more than 477,000 hits – more than you have time to sort through.

Targeted Directories

Sometimes you need to find a directory that is focused on a specific subject. These are time-saving devices that help you find very specific information quickly. The advantage of using these targeted directories is they tend to be more comprehensive than general directories, are much smaller in size and often more current. Perhaps the best advantage is that because these directories are so focused, they are compiled by experts on the subject and often updated with the most current sites on the subject.

But finding these targeted directories can be difficult.

Say you are looking for information on the Bronze Age archeological period of Mainland Greece and Crete. What you need to find is an ancient historical site that is devoted to that time period. The perfect page for your search is http://clvl.cla.umn.edu/chloris/

But how do you find it? Obviously, this will require help from the academic world. So the first place to start is an academic-focused subject directory, like InfoMine at http://infomine.ucr.edu/ which links to about thirty targeted directories focusing on ancient history, two good directories about the "bronze age" or you can find the "Classics Resources on the Web" at www.classics.cam.ac.uk/faculty/links.html, a directory from the humanities faculty at Cambridge University. Both will get you to your destination. (More targeted directories are listed below.)

Current Events

Most subject directories have preset categories for news topics of general interest that link related information and recent news stories. News resources are also available in other places (see Chapter 8, News Resources).

Subject directories are especially valuable when you're trying to determine the key players in a specific industry or locate specific kinds of information. Chances are that a subject directory – because it's organized by people – will bring you to the best one-stop site for that industry.

Product Information

If you know exactly what you want, a search engine is the place to go. But, if you're looking for information about types of products or specific product information and had no luck at manufacturer web sites, try a subject directory. Using a subject directory works especially well if:

- You're hunting for information about a group of products.

- You don't know the name of the manufacturer.

- You suspect the product information is on the web site of the manufacturer's corporate owner or parent company.

Search Engines vs. Subject Directories

Should you use a subject directory or a search engine? Often the answer is both.

- If you're just beginning to research a subject, use a subject directory to find search words, phrases, and keywords that you can submit to other search tools.

- If you're trying to find the most current information on a subject that's already familiar to you, try a search engine. Since computers update them, search engines tend to be more current than subject directories, which are updated by hand. Targeted directories are the exception.

- When you don't know exactly what you are looking for, but you would recognize it if you saw it, a subject directory is the preferable tool.

- The broader the subject, the better off a subject directory is to start with. It will help you narrow what you are looking for because you can look around a subject area and find a variety of topics that might be useful to your research, or eliminate non-essential information.

A good rule to follow is the more specific you are, the less likely you'll be to find what you're looking for in a subject directory. However, while many novices will reach for a search engine first, veteran searchers will start with a subject directory to obtain the right phrases and keywords. Some subject directories don't have search capabilities; in those cases, your only choice is to browse through the categories and subcategories. With search engines, the approach is reversed: use keywords that are as unusual as possible. Narrow your search even further by using combinations of unusual words and by using advanced features. Make lists of words that you think may help you narrow your query. Submit unique keywords first, since some tools rank the order of words submitted.

Search engines tend to be more effective than subject directories for searches with unusual keywords, for combining keywords, for using advanced features like field searching, and for finding pages buried inside a web site.

➔ *hot tip:* **When narrowing a subject, try putting the rarest or most unusual keyword first. For example, if you're looking up the Dow Corning Company, you'll get fewer misses if you submit it as: corning dow. When juggling word order, however, be sure not to use quotation marks or + signs around the entire group, which would require the search tool to return hits that contain words only in the exact order they're submitted.**

Portals and Hybrid Search Tools

To differentiate themselves – and make more money – many search engine and search directory companies have enhanced their offerings by adding other services. Their intention is to ultimately direct you somewhere else, but hope that they offer enough information – news, sports, weather, reminders, latest stocks, TV listings, search tools, key links, bulletin boards, chat groups, discussion groups, and links to other sites, etc. that you come back often to their home page. Like a Swiss army knife, you select the tools you want to use. AOL, MSN, Yahoo, Excite, and Netscape, are good examples of this portal phenomenon. Portals make money from advertisers who pay according to user "ratings" which are tallied each time you click on a linked web page.

Most of the ten most-looked-at sites on the Internet are portals. Many of these portals also try to be both search engines and subject directories. They offer the ability to search for subjects of interest to you and also offer recommended sites on commonly-researched subjects. While Yahoo! is still predominately a directory, three of the other most used sites America Online, MSN and Netscape are portals, and combination search engines and directories at the same time.

Vortals

An even newer trend in search engines is the development of specialty portals, commonly called vertical portals or Vortals. They are very specific on particular topics, so they tend to accurately filter out irrelevant documents.

A vortal is a mini-version of a search engine or subject directory, focused on a particular subject or topic. What differentiates most vortals from other tools is that it usually offers an online marketplace for providing goods and services to that industry. That means vortals can be excellent resources for finding business information and testing the climate of a business field. These can also be extremely pro-business and will likely have a bias when compared to other topic-specific directories.

A good vortal example is Yahoo!'s Business-to-Business Marketplace (http://b2b.yahoo.com) where you will find excellent business resources for small businesses. A great collection of vortals is SearchKing (www.searchking.com). Vortals are usually made up of a targeted directory, and also offer listings compiled by a focused crawler.

Focused Crawlers

Focused crawlers are the search engine equivalent of targeted directories. Like a targeted directory, a focused crawler only looks for and indexes web pages about a specific subject. However, they do so not with human editors, but with automated crawlers. So they have the focus of a targeted directory and the searching and indexing capabilities (and increased volume of information) of a search engine. They crawl a limited number of web sites on that particular subject and tend to crawl them more thoroughly and more often.

Focused crawlers allow you to find information quickly on a very specific topic. Just as your best source for the latest and most accurate news online is the web site for a newspaper or a television or radio station, rather than, say, a discussion group, your best source of information for a topic is a focused crawler. Sure, you could still find information about a news story from a general search engine or a discussion group, but it is not the most reliable or efficient way to search. Search engines are not the ultimate tool for your information needs. Why go for a generalist, when you can get topic-specific help?

Some of these focused crawlers are superb research tools. SearchMil.com is a focused search engine that is a great resource for military information around the world, one of several such tools pulled together by MaxBot.com.

Sometimes targeted directories are matched with focused crawlers, and lead to a very powerful hybrid tool. An excellent example of this focused crawler/targeted directory is one pulled together by the U.S. government – FirstGov.gov – which is an excellent starting point for information about or from the U.S. government.

Meta-Tools

You can access multiple search engines and subject directories simultaneously through meta-search tools – meta-tools, for short.

Meta-tool examples include CNET's Search.com, Dogpile (www.dogpile.com), Ixquick (www.ixquick.com), and Vivisimo.

Meta-tools don't create their own databases, rather they rely on databases gathered by other Internet search engines. They allow you to submit searches to multiple search tools, obtaining results quickly from more than one general purpose search tool. While it would seem logical that you would cover more of the Internet quicker with a meta-tool, that's not necessarily the case. You don't get significantly broader results because all the search engines limit the number or results you get and most have arbitrary cut-off points for timing out when they don't get results. You ultimately get results that are less precise.

They do, however, serve a valuable purpose. When you want to get a lay-of-the-land search, a quick overview of what may be available and also as a way to test your keywords, a meta-tool is a big help. The other real value in using a meta-search tool is to compare how the different search engines do against one another. If you run a search using a meta-search tool and find that Teoma gives you much better results than say Lycos, you may want to go to Teoma directly for much more results. Most importantly, remember that meta-search tools use different combinations of search engines. So make sure the engines you want to use are included in that meta-tool.

Not all the meta-tools operate in the same way. The all-in-one approach used by Beaucoup! (www.beaucoup.com) lets you use various search engines, but keeps you on the meta-tool's search page. You can conduct only initial, simple searches, meaning you can't further refine, or limit your search. This is one of the big problems with most meta-search tools. To get wide access to many search tools, you give up several things, including the ability to do any kind of sophisticated or advanced searching. It also sharply limits the number of hits retrieved to no more than, say, thirty. That means if the search tool ranks its results and your desired item doesn't show up among them, you won't see it at all.

However, if you consult the actual search tool directly, you will get many more hits and more comprehensive results. In other words, if you search Lycos, AltaVista, or any other major search tool through a meta-search tool, you will sacrifice exhaustive results for a quick glance at several search tools. The multi-dimensional approach allows you to search many search engines and subject directories simultaneously, resulting in quicker, shallower and more broad-based searches. Along the way, you can stumble on new search engines and subject directories that you may not have tried before.

Yet another type, exemplified by Intelliseek Profusion (www.profusion.com) and Dogpile, lets you select the search tools through pop-down menus. Some will even select the search features for you.

Advantages & Disadvantages of Meta-Tools

The biggest advantage of meta-searching is the ability to simultaneously access multiple search engines. Another advantage is you can cover more ground and obtain a more complete picture of what is available on the Internet. Some meta-tools, like Dogpile, also remove duplicate hits and sort the remaining results by host, keyword, date or search engine.

Meta-tools have weaknesses, too. In addition to the restrictions of simple searching, meta-tools are unable to use field searching and other advanced features. You are often limited to making a single request, and some can't accommodate Boolean terms.

And, here is one very serious warning: Many times when you do a search, some of the results from search engines come from those that accept paid placement of results or paid inclusion of results. This issue is particularly prevalent in meta-tools.

In fact, a *Search Engine Watch* survey shows that some meta-search services are providing results where more than half of their listings are paid links. Although many major search engines also include paid listings, they do so on a smaller scale and typically separate paid listing content from non-paid listing content. (See the paid inclusion/paid listings section later in this chapter for some detail.)

For example, Google, clearly displays a "sponsored links" banner to denote where paid listings are. Yahoo! lists paid listings visibly under the headline "sponsored matches," but on HotBot and Lycos, they are listed as the first results you see under the headings "products and services" and "search partners." In contrast, the meta-search services generally do not have such delineation, making it impossible to tell which links are paid for and which are not. (These details are explained in the charts on the following pages.)

When I conducted my own search recently on "breast cancer" using Dogpile, I received results from the following search engines:

Overture (www.overture.com), LookSmart, Sprinks (www.sprinks.com), Find What (www.findwhat.com), About, Ah-Ha (www.ah-ha.com), Kanoodle (www.kanoodle.com), Direct Hit, Open Directory Project (http://dmoz.org), E-pilot (www.epilot.com), Search Hippo (www.searchhippo.com) and Yahoo!. In addition, Dogpile often draws results from AltaVista and FAST (via Lycos) among the major search engines, and Bay9 (www.bay9.com),

BrainFox (www.brainfox.com), and ValleyAlley (www.valleyalley.com) among the paid search engines.

As a result, of the seventeen search tools available, nearly seventy percent of the results came from paid placements or paid inclusion.

A recent study by *Search Engine Watch* found that Dogpile, Mamma (www.mamma.com), Metacrawler (www.metacrawler.com), qbSearch (www.qbsearch.com), and Search.com each drew more than fifty percent of their results from paid placements. And few if any of the meta-search tools identified the results as paid for. So it's searcher beware.

Paid Placement or Paid Inclusion? Researcher Beware!

Before the year 2000, you couldn't buy your way to the top of a search engine. But that year a company called GoTo.com, looking for a different revenue model, started to sell placement in its search engine.

Initially, it was chastised by search engine purists arguing it was corrupting the way researchers evaluated web sites. At the time, GoTo's CEO said that they were like a glorified yellow pages, allowing those with money to pay for bigger positioning.

But this was all before the dot-com crash. GoTo, now Overture, is no longer seen as a pariah, but as a trailblazer. Now paid placement in search tools is a common practice, although one you may not know about. It is so widespread, that at a mid-2001 conference run by *Search Engine Watch* editor Danny Sullivan, the vast majority of the companies presenting their technologies were firms specializing in getting listings put into search engines, a field they dub "search engine optimization." Those people who viewed placement as a violation of the spirit of search engines were a tiny minority amid a wave of placement proponents.

So, since then, how much have meta-search tools endorsed paid positioning? A *Search Engine Watch* study in late 2001 found that more than fifty percent of the results returned from using meta-search tools were paid results. Though not all meta-search tools will sell placement directly in their listings, most of them will let you purchase banner ads for advertising and content deals where the search engine promotes the advertiser's content in specific areas of the engine's web site. Many search engine companies are careful to separate the ads from the results, but others make no such distinctions.

Now there are three different ways that search engines sell positioning in their results. Here they are, according to Danny Sullivan:

1. Paid Placement

Several major search engines carry paid listings. Where they position these listings varies. Sometimes they are contained within the actual results, other times they're listed in separate categories, in boxes above the editorial results and or in separately marked boxes along the side of the editorial content. If you want to be number one for a particular search term at

GoTo.com/Overture – which is a paid placement search engine – you simply agree to pay more money than any other advertiser for the term. To its credit, Overture notes how much money the advertiser makes every time someone clicks on the site, with a little note under the search result "cost to advertiser $.031" for example.

2. Paid Inclusion

Paid inclusion is where an advertiser is contained directly in the search results. But, unlike paid placement, paid inclusion doesn't guarantee a specific position in the main search results, only that it will be included. Sullivan explains it like a lottery. In a lottery, the more tickets you have, the more likely it is you'll win something. Similarly, with search engines, the more listings you have, the more likely you'll rank well for various searches, and thus the higher and more visible your "inclusion" will be.

3. Paid Submission

Many search engines and directories are paid a fee to process requests for inclusion in their listings. Usually, these programs do not guarantee to list your site, only to review it and possibly include it.

Below is an example of how a paid inclusion works at Ask Jeeves. You will also find a list of what the major search engines allow, as well as a list of some of the paid positioning search tools. Remember these tools when you are trying to assess the credibility of the search results. The following information is all courtesy of Sullivan's *Search Engine Watch* ; details can be found on the web site, www.searchenginewatch.com.

Ask Jeeves sells paid inclusions, through its question and answer search tool, by writing useful questions to point people to the ad as an answer. When you ask the search engine a question, it points you to several potential answers, including these inclusions. To see a paid inclusion in action at Ask Jeeves, Sullivan suggests a search for "what should my blood pressure be?" The top link leads to a page from OnHealth, an Ask Jeeves advertiser, and one of about twenty "basic knowledge" providers that include companies such as Ticketmaster-CitySearch, Verizon, GE Financial, ImproveNet, and AllBusiness. Ask Jeeves also has several hundred advertisers for e-commerce topics, such as Sears, Best Buy, Land's End and Garden.com. There is absolutely no disclosure that an advertiser is benefiting from the activity.

One more thing to watch about paid placement: a lawsuit filed in February, 2002, has the potential to shake up the search engine world – especially the meta-search tools. Mark Nutritionals, owners of the weight-loss program Body Solutions, filed lawsuits seeking $440 million in damages for alleged trademark infringement and unfair competition against AltaVista, FindWhat, Kanoodle and Overture. The four search engines named have paid placement listings that appear when searches are conducted for the term "body solutions." The company believes the ads are misleading consumers and infringing upon its trademark on the Body Solutions name. Since this is the first lawsuit of its kind, the relationship between how search engines display keyword phrases – paid for or not – seems to be an issue. Because of the pay-for-placement practice, the Body Solutions site (of Mark Nutritionals' product) gets buried in the search engines, the company's lawyer charges. The message as Sullivan sees it, seems to be, "Don't bury our site, and you won't get sued over ads." Google escaped being sued because its paid placement lists the Body Solutions site above the results and therefore is highly visible. The underlying issue at stake has profound consequences. While this case is about keyword-linked text ads, the question could be determined in a broader way: can any word be trademarked? "Orange" is the name of a mobile phone company in the U.K., while "Apple" of course is the name of a computer company. Sullivan raises some tough legal questions that could result from this case:

- Can searches for these words not carry ads without the permission of Orange or Apple?

- Do search engines need to conduct a trademark search any time they sell an ad, then ask the trademark holder to determine if the proposed ad is acceptable?

- And how do you do this for all the trademarks that are unregistered in the country of the search engine origin, but still entitled to trademark protection?

The Body Solutions case will likely focus on what appears on a search engine's results page. Watch this legal dispute. It could be precedent setting.

Who are the Paid Placement and Paid Inclusion Search Tools?

...and how do the major search engines deal with paid placement?

Here's a list of paid placement engines followed by a chart of how the majors handle the wording of placement and inclusion:

Ah-ha.com
www.ah-ha.com

Billed as a kid-safe service powered by FAST Search, paid listings appear at the top of its results – a distinction most kids won't make.

Espotting.com
www.espotting.com

Major paid placement service that targets users in the United Kingdom and Europe – wide distribution on U.K. search engines such as Lycos, Netscape and Ask Jeeves.

FindWhat.com
www.findwhat.com

FindWhat is an important paid placement service because the company distributes its results on the Excite search engine as well as on many major metacrawlers.

Go (Infoseek)
www.go.com

Go is the former portal site that grew out of the old Infoseek search engine. Owned by Disney, the company abandoned further development of Go in March, 2001. Search is still available at Go; however, the results are simply paid listings provided by Overture.

Godado

www.godado.tv

A European based paid placement search tool.

NBCi

http://nbci.msnbc.com

NBCi provides listings from Dogpile, a meta-search engine that is dominated by paid listing services. NBCi has provided paid listings since mid-2001. It was previously called SNAP.

Overture (GoTo)

www.overture.com

Overture is the oldest and most important paid placement search engine because it distributes its listings to a wide range of major search engines, including AltaVista, AOL Search, Lycos, HotBot and Netscape Search.

Sprinks

http://sprinks.about.com

Paid placement service that posts links to appropriate areas within the About.com network of subject sites. Listings are also available by searching at the Sprinks site itself. They are also distributed to some meta-search engines.

Other paid listings that are most often found on meta-search sites include:

Bay9.com

www.bay9.com

eFind.com

www.efind.com

ePilot (see the paid inclusion/paid listings later in this chapter for some detail

www.epilot.com

Kanoodle

www.kanoodle.com

theinfodepot.com

http://theinfodepot.com

Valley Alley

www.valleyalley.com

Win4Win

www.win4win.com

Beside Sullivan's excellent resources, another place to find information about paid positioning:

PayPerClickSearchEngines.com
`www.payperclicksearchengines.com`

Major Search Engines' Paid Listing Programs

On the next page is a chart from *Search Engine Watch*[1] that details how the different major search tools allow paid listings and how they note them in your results.

Search Engine	Program	Notes
AllTheWeb (FAST)	<Paid Placement>	"Start Here" links are paid links sold by Lycos or Kanoodle
	Paid Inclusion	May occur in main results
AOL Search	<Paid Placement>	"Sponsored Links" section at top of page are paid links from Overture
	Paid Inclusion	May occur in some crawler-based results provided by Inktomi
AltaVista	<Paid Placement>	Exact label often changes, but "Products and Services," "Featured Sites" and "Partner Listings" have all been used for paid links sold by AltaVista or from Overture
	Paid Inclusion	Occurs in main results and directory listings
Ask Jeeves	<Paid Placement>	"You may find these sponsored links helpful" links from Overture
	<Paid Placement>	"Click below to see results from other search engines" option usually leads to listings from paid placement search engines
	<Paid Placement>	"Featured Sponsor" links on right side of page sold by Ask Jeeves
	Paid Inclusion	May occur in "Click below for your answers" area at top of page
Direct Hit	<Paid Placement>	"Partner Search Results" at top of page are paid links from Overture
Excite	<Paid Placement>	First fifteen results of all searches typically from Overture
Go (Infoseek)	<Paid Placement>	All results listings are from Overture
Google	<Paid Placement>	"Sponsored Link" ads sold by Google appear at top of page and to right of main listings
HotBot	<Paid Placement>	Exact label often changes, but "Products and Services" and "Featured Listings" have both been used for paid links from Overture

---

[1] "Reprinted with permission from *Search Engine Watch*, Copyright 2001 INT Media. All Rights Reserved." Note: the chart changes often, but the online version's always being updated.

HotBot (con't)	**Paid Inclusion**	May occur in any results from Inktomi (look for Inktomi logo at bottom of page)
Inktomi	**Paid Inclusion**	Paid inclusion program allows sites to be crawled more deeply in Inktomi's listings
iWon	\<Paid Placement\>	"Featured Listings" from Overture
	Paid Inclusion	May occur in results from Inktomi
LookSmart	\<Paid Placement\>	"Featured Listings" are sold by LookSmart; also, paid inclusion listings given ranking boost
	Paid Inclusion	LookListings program allows web sites to be deeply listed in LookSmart's listings
	\>Paid Submission\<	All commercial sites required to pay to be considered for listing
Lycos	\<Paid Placement\>	Exact label often changes, but "Products and Services," "Featured Listings" and "Sponsored Search Listings" have all been used for paid links from Overture
	Paid Inclusion	May occur in main results provided by FAST
MSN Search	\<Paid Placement\>	"Sponsored Sites" from Overture
	Paid Inclusion	May occur in "Web Directory" information from LookSmart or "Web Pages" information from Inktomi
NBCi	\<Paid Placement\>	Listings are from Dogpile, where first page of results usually all paid links
Overture (GoTo)	\<Paid Placement\>	Listings with "Cost to advertiser" note after description are paid
Netscape	\<Paid Placement\>	"Partner Search Results" from Overture

Best Search Engines (listed alphabetically)

AllTheWeb (FAST) www.alltheweb.com

Looking for the next Google? FAST is one of the ones to watch. AllTheWeb, also known as FAST search, is pushing hard to rival Google as the must-use search engine. It now has the second largest database among search engines, according to search expert Greg Notess, with 580 million pages.

Since its debut in 1999, the Norwegian-based company's goal has been to index the entire public, "indexable" Web. It has done a good job pushing the envelope and has forced other search tools to refocus efforts on increasing their index sizes. FAST offers large multimedia and mobile-wireless web indexes available from its web page. It has added several new features – speed and customization capabilities. These new features include dynamic clustering of results, real-time news search, a "pre-analysis" tool that helps refine search queries, an enhanced user interface, and customization options. Perhaps the best feature of this search engine is its educational effort to teach you how to search better via its pre-analysis tool. It trains you on how to better write your search queries by taking your search query and rewriting it. Also, you can turn off the rewrite feature. One of the best new advanced features is its news capability. You can search all the news categories, or pinpoint which news resources you want it to search.

One possible weakness is that you can only get ten results on a page in the simple search. However, in the advanced search, you can get as many as 100.

FAST is now powering Lycos' search and has added paid site inclusion on the Lycos site.

What AllTheWeb Does Best	Ties together its clustered results with the latest news stories on your query. Huge, frequently updated indexed database to pull from.
Search Tips	AllTheWeb has added a new "search tips box" that may appear to the right of search results. It's a very helpful set of suggestions.
Media Specific Searches	FAST claims an impressive 70 million listings in its multimedia picture and video catalogs, huge MP3 music listings, and a good FTP search. FAST has the unique ability to tie all of these tools together in its "universal search."
AllTheWeb Special Features	Some new features are excellent additions, including dynamic clustering of results and real-time news search. The clustered results appear at the top of a result page in a box labeled "Beta FAST Topics." Each result is displayed as a hyperlinked category topic next to a yellow folder. The clustering helps you pinpoint and target your results, like providing headlines on news stories. They also link you to news stories on your subject of choice.
	This site also offers more than 45 language limits, more than any other search tool. You can't search in specific languages, but you can limit your results to only those from specific languages.
	They pledge to refresh their entire database every nine to twelve days, but so far no database has successfully executed that kind of a pledge.
	AllTheWeb recently added a specialized news search, covering full text stories from more than 3,000 sources – crawling and indexing them continuously. It offers a more impressive advanced "News Search."

AltaVista www.altavista.com

Around since 1995, this easy-to use search engine is one of the largest and best. According to Greg Notess, the search engine has more than 397 million pages indexed. It is powerful, fast, has great flexibility in its advanced search, and allows users to conduct precision searches for specific information by looking for phrases, specifying keywords, using case-sensitive matches, or restricting searches to titles or other parts of a document.

Now owned by CMGI, AltaVista was the largest and best search engine for years. Although it's fallen back into the pack, it is still an excellent choice. It offers the ability to search news, images, MP3 audios, and videos.

It uses its own search engine, but has partnerships with human-powered directory information from LookSmart, paid listings from Overture (formerly GoTo.com) and news headlines from Moreover (www.moreover.com). One of the best features on AltaVista is Babelfish, a translation tool powered by Systran.

Unlike many of the other search tools, AltaVista has never really found its niche. It is a search tool looking to understand its mission. It has experimented with being a portal, offering a directory as well as a search engine, and gone through several owners. This constant revision of direction has caused problems and created confusion for users.

What AltaVista Does Best	AltaVista is very good at retrieving specific phrases. It digs down into the page and finds actual words and phrases from within the full-text of the web site. As a result, if you can pin your search down to one word or a unique phrase, you can find it – quickly. It offers a broad range of search functionality and when it returns results, it highlights the matching search term – a time saver.
Search Options	Two search options are offered: Simple and Advanced. To do a Simple Search, you must submit +, - or " " signs to narrow and focus the search. The Advanced Search option requires you to type the actual Boolean operators (AND/OR/NOT). Don't forget to use the ranking capability in the Advanced Search mode.
Search Tips	AltaVista has terrific field searching ability. You can search for title and/or URL in both the Simple Search and Advanced Search modes. Restricting by URL will allow you to limit your hits to government or education sites and focus your hits overall credibility. To use this tool, simply write Title:<subject> (example: Title:tree) and you will get sites that have "tree" in their titles.
Media Specific Searches	The image and news search tools are excellent. AltaVista is also capable of searching newsgroup postings.
AltaVista Special Features	One strong feature of its advanced search function is a "sort by" box, allowing you to rank your search terms. You can also add a term to an already-run search that way, which is often useful.
	AltaVista's advanced search engine is one of the few search tools that lets you search by range of dates, helping you find the latest information.

AltaVista was the first search engine to offer a Link Search feature that allows you to find any web pages linked to a particular site. It's a valuable way of conducting competitive intelligence on rival companies, and evaluating credibility.

AltaVista offers several unique features, including a photo-finding tool using Corbis' extensive photo library, and a family-friendly version so that you can bar access to pornographic sites.

AltaVista's language translation capability is excellent. It allows you to translate part or all of a web page. It also offers country-specific search engines – in 22 countries around the world, including Australia, Brazil, France, Germany, India, Korea and the U.K. But all the information is stored in one master international database, so you get the same results, with that country's material given higher ranking.

Another superb translation option is the world translation keyboard. It allows you to write in another language, making your final, non-native language message to be grammatically accurate.

AltaVista has added a directory from Look Smart, allowing searches by category in pre-selected subjects. AltaVista also offers access to a comparison-shopping site.

Google www.google.com

Google is the best of the search engines, and the largest, with Greg Notess crediting Google with 968 million pages indexed. Google is one of the more innovative web search engines. Launched in 1999 and developed by two Stanford University graduate students (same school as the founders of Yahoo! and Excite), Google has made its mark for its relevance-ranking based on link analysis.

It uses its own database for searching; the directory listings are from the Open Directory.

What Google Does Best

Google uses what it calls a popularity engine, ranking its database based on the degree to which other pages refer or link to a page. As a result, Google tends to find "things" that other users have already searched. The results are directly relevant to what you're looking for. What separates it from others is that it is simple to use and its top few results tend to be remarkably accurate. Its deceptively simple basic interface give you little control, but great results. For more control, use its advanced features.

Search Tips

Google's search features are limited, but they've added phrase searching. Google always searches for pages containing all the words in your query, so you do not need to use + in front of words. To eliminate things in your search, you must use "for NOT." Its advanced search function overcomes that problem and offers extensive language searching.

Google Special Features

Google allows field searching by URL, date, location and media type. It has also added map searching, stock searching, and adult-content filtering. Its "caching" option allows you to find earlier versions of pages, or pages no longer online, a feature unique to Google. It offers translation features and highlights terms when it returns results.

Google purchased the well-known former Deja News database of Usenet postings, and continues to maintain it. You can see it in the "Google Groups" section of the web site. Google also recently added the ability to search over 13 million PDF files, which allows you to get better results from U.S. government sites and other organizations that depend on PDFs.

Google has other terrific features, including links to the latest news stories, a top-of-the-line image finder, and its latest addition a catalog search tool. The family filtering feature is automatically on. Google has also added asterisk searching for missing words, so you can search for "Lord ** Rings" to bring up references to the book and movie *Lord of the Rings*. Google also has a neat phonebook finding feature where you can put "phonebook:starbucks,los angeles" in the search box and it will bring up the phone numbers.

What helps make Google so good is that it keeps pushing the envelope.

HotBot   www.hotbot.com

One of the larger search tools around, HotBot offers basic searching with limited options, and an advanced search with all kinds of sophisticated capabilities. HotBot, owned by the Terra Lycos Network, provides its users with information from three main sources: the Open Directory, Direct Hit (a popularity-based search tool) and Inktomi – the behind-the-scenes provider of search data for several major search engines. What separates HotBot from the others is its easy to-use search options. Greg Notess lists it as the sixth largest index with 332 million pages

What HotBot Does Best

HotBot's power lies in its Advanced Search Options, which allows innovative searching – everything from looking for images and audio on specific pages, to limiting your search by date, to searching for when pages were updated. In the simple search mode, HotBot's Exact Phrase and Must Contain combination is especially effective to narrow and focus a search.

Search Tips

One unique and very helpful feature is HotBot's automatic search for first name followed by last name. You can also limit results by date, which can be helpful when you are looking for time-specific material.

Media Specific Searches	For media specific searching, HotBot is great for pulling up images and graphics. It was the first image-focused search.
HotBot Special Features	HotBot also offers a family-content filter, site clustering (to find sites similar to those you like) and a Direct Hit top ten list of the most popular web sites on a given subject. The last is a great way to find out the popularity of search terms and follow the searches of others who have already looked for what you want to find.

Lycos www.lycos.com

Lycos is another "hybrid" combination search tool. It has had a series of ups and downs over the past few years, but is again a useful search tool. It offers a web search engine, several subject directories, and many other services. Its database is much smaller than other search engines, but now that it is powered by AllTheWeb/FAST, it once again provides useful results.

What Lycos Does Best	Lycos' best feature is its advanced search capability. It has an extensive directory and content resources, including local content from more than a dozen countries.
Search Options	Lycos' Advanced Search mode offers more search options and many advanced features geared to research. These include using drop-down menu "filters" that allow you to limit your searches by words, URLs or sites, and languages.
Search Tips	Lycos allows you to click on its "fast forward" link, and it brings you a search comparison chart of other sites in the list. Its advanced search filters are included in your search results, allowing you to rerun the search and refocus it using original terms.
Media Specific Searches	Like several other search tools, Lycos can do image-only, sound-only, video-file and multimedia searches.
Lycos Special Features	Lycos' Advanced Search features – especially the filters – are a great new resource for focusing and refocusing a search.

Teoma www.teoma.com

Teoma, which debuted in the Spring of 2001, is definitely a search tool to watch. Recently, it was purchased by Ask Jeeves; thus giving Jeeves' question-and-answer search tool an outlet and a database to draw from. It started publicly using the Teoma database in January 2002. Ask Jeeves also purchased Direct Hit, which is used on HotBot and other search tools to rank the top ten most popular hits. The Ask Jeeves collaboration means it will have financial resources behind it. At this writing, it only has a database of about 150 million pages, but that is expected to grow. It offers intelligent grouping of search results into topic groups that focus on exactly what you are looking for. Teoma has a unique method of analyzing links to determine relevance ranking, and it also discovers content hubs that show in the results as "Experts' Links." This helps you quickly locate useful links on your subject and is the primary reason to regularly use Teoma in your research arsenal.

What Teoma Does Best	One of Teoma's best features is its ability to point you to expert links or super sites on your subject.
Search Options	It has a small database and no real advanced search functions. No Boolean searching is available. But phrase searching is available by using quotes and you can use pluses and minuses.
Search Tips	This tool provides wonderful groupings of topics – by topic, by sites that have several links in your results and by "experts' links" – which help point you to authority sites on that subject.
Media Specific Searches	No special multimedia or targeted searches.
Special Features	The "experts' links," as discussed above, provide easy sorting of results.

Wisenut   www.wisenut.com

Wisenut, which debuted in July, 2001, was founded by Yeogirl Yun, co-founder and former CTO of mySimon, one of the first online comparative shopping sites. Wisenut was recently purchased by LookSmart, which should give it the financial footing to grow rapidly. It is big, fast and flexible. It claims a database of 1.5 billion documents, although Notess puts it more accurately at 579 million, large enough to place it second behind Google. It lets you customize settings, like number of results you want on a page, what languages to search and whether to group pages from the same site together. Its WiseGuides are guides linked by keywords into categories from your search, similar to the customized folders of the late Northern Light. They give you a quick way to zero in on the most relevant material within a search that turns up hundreds or thousands of results.

What Wisenut Does Best	Its customized folders, called WiseGuides help you group results in your search to see easy patterns and overlapping subjects. For a newcomer, it has a huge database.
Search Tips	Like Teoma and Google, Wisenut offers the same pared-down query syntax of phrase matching, "+" and "-", no Booleans. But, it does offer phrase searching using quotation marks. No advanced searching options. It does offer a series of display, language and results options, under the "set search preferences" category.

Media Specific Searches	WiseNut does not offer video or audio-searching, but can limit searches in twenty-five languages and offers a family filter.
WiseNut Special Features	Much like Google's cached pages, WiseNut offers a feature called "Sneak-a-Peek" that lets you get a preview of a page without leaving WiseNut's results page.

Search Engine Comparison

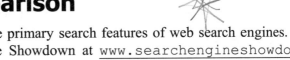

The chart that follows summarizes the primary search features of web search engines. For more detailed reviews, visit Search Engine Showdown at `www.searchengineshowdown.com`. The search engines here are grouped according to size, as measured by statistical comparisons published on Search Engine Showdown.

Name	Boolean	Default	Proximity	Truncation	Case	Fields	Limits	Stop	Sorting
Google	-, OR	and	Phrase	No	No	intitle, inurl, more	Language, filetype, date	Yes, + searches	Relevance, site
WiseNut	- only	and	Phrase	No	No	No	Language	Yes, + searches	Relevance, site
AllTheWeb	+, -, or with ( )	and	Phrase	No	No	title, URL, link, more	Language, domain,	No	Relevance, site
Lycos	+, -	and	Phrase	No	No	title, URL, link, more	Language, domain	No	Relevance
Northern Light	and, or, not, ( ), +, -	and	Phrase	Yes * %, auto plurals	No	title, URL, more	Doc type date, more	No	Relevance, site, date, folders
AltaVista Simple	+, -, AND, OR, AND NOT, ( )	and usually	Phrase, NEAR	Yes * < 6 ** unlimited	No	title, URL, link, more	Language	No	Relevance, site
AltaVista Advanced	and, or, and not, ( )	phrase	Phrase, near, within, <, <~	Yes * < 6 ** unlimited	Yes	title, URL, link, more	Language, date	No	Relevance, if used
HotBot	and, or, not, ( ), +, -	and	Phrase	Yes *	Yes	title, more	Language, date, more	Yes	Relevance, site
MSN	AND, OR, NOT, ( ), +, -	and	Phrase	No	Yes	title, link	Language, date, more	Yes	Relevance
Teoma	- only	and	Phrase	No	No	No	No	Yes, + searches	Folders, Relevance, metasites

Best Subject Directories (listed alphabetically)

There are some truly wonderful subject directories. We discussed what they are and how they work earlier in this chapter. Depending what you are looking for, these subject directories are your best starting point.

4Anything.com www.4anything.com

This is an excellent, but little-noticed new directory. What they do – and do well – is link you to other excellent sites. The quality of the recommendations is terrific and the links seem fresh.

About.com www.about.com

If you need collections of exhaustive links on specific topics, About.com is a great site. Formerly known as the Mining Company, it has excellent evaluative guides in 23 categories with over 50,000 subjects. Owned by Primedia, this site's unique tool is that each category has a guide – a person – whom you may contact for guidance. Some guides are excellent but not all the guides are at that level. A note of caution; they make money every time you click on a hyperlink, called clickthroughs, so the more you click around on the site, the more money their guides make. That's not a problem as much as a bother. When you want to go to a site, you must learn to read the address from their combined URL. Here's an example:

http://websearch.about.com/gi/dynamic/offsite.htm?site=http%3A%2F%2Fwww.audiofind.com%2F

To pull the correct web address out of this dynamically generated page, you need to click through the URL. You will see that it is www.audiofind.com. The other downside is every time you click around, their advertising arm, Sprinks, opens up another window. I often find myself with twenty or more windows open by the time I'm done, but I figure I'm earning Kevin a some income, and learning a great deal. So its worthwhile.

Britannica www.britannica.com

Britannica.Com's first web effort was an extensive subject directory based on its encyclopedias, which date back to 1768. Formerly known as Eblast and eBig, the site is now an online version of the entire encyclopedia and also offers resources including the *Merriam-Webster's Dictionary* and a thesaurus. The page links to more than 150,000 sites in hundreds of subject areas and is more academically focused than some of the other popular directories. The advanced options combine features of several search engines. You can view results from the Encyclopedia for free, but considerably more detail is available for those who subscribe. A one-year subscription is US$95 or a month-to-month option of US$7.95 per month. Many times they offer a free fourteen-day trial subscription and a discount on the annual subscription price. An excellent resource.

Internet Public Library www.ipl.org

This excellent directory has recently added the archived collection of the Argus Clearinghouse, which will no longer exist as an ongoing, separate project. That makes the IPL an increasingly good tool to work with. It's a small directory, but it is maintained by volunteer librarians and the selections are good ones.

Joe Ant `www.joeant.com`

An up-and-coming new web directory, it is easily searchable and well organized and pulled together by some of the folks who worked for Disney's Go.com before its demise.

The Librarians Index to the Internet `www.lii.org`

This directory is simply outstanding. Pulled together by librarians Carole Leita, Karen Schneider, and their team at the University of California-Berkeley, it is a must-see tool when you are looking for anything academic or research-oriented. It's not a huge directory, but the links are so good that you need to look at it or you are doing yourself and your clients a disservice. It could be labeled a specialized directory (see below), but it is such a gem that it needs to be listed with the major directories. It stands apart for two major reasons: it's constantly being updated, and its collection of resources and reviewed sites is simply levels above other collections. All materials are evaluated, annotated, and selected for content and reliability. Its weakness is that it is not as good when you are looking for pop-culture. But, when LII gives something a "best" mark, you can count on it being outstanding. Lots of resources from the LII are included in this edition.

LookSmart `www.looksmart.com`

This excellent subject directory began as a specialized venture funded by *Reader's Digest*. It has grown to be comparable in size to Yahoo!, but considerably better organized, featuring over 250,000 categories and subcategories. In fact, LookSmart is the directory that AltaVista, MSN, Excite and others turn to when it can't find a subject in its own index. LookSmart also offers LookSmart Live, a service that offers personalized email responses to questions. Be aware that LookSmart accepts both paid inclusion in its listings (in other words, you can buy a random spot in the listings) and paid placement (where you can buy a specific place in its listings – see the paid placement/paid inclusion Section near the end of this chapter).

Open Directory `http://dmoz.org`

Like LookSmart and Yahoo!, Open Directory is one of the largest directories in existence. It also tends to have fewer dead links than Yahoo!. Like About.com, Open Directory uses over 35,000 volunteer editors to catalog the Web, so Open's quality varies with the editor in charge of that specific section. Formerly known as NewHoo, the Open Directory is owned by Netscape, now a division of America Online. Open is also the directory for Netscape, AOL, Google, Lycos and Lycos-owned HotBot.

Yahoo! `www.yahoo.com`

Yahoo!, the largest and most comprehensive of all the subject directories, is very good at providing information for the masses. If the subject is trendy, Yahoo! is a great place to start; and Yahoo! offers more than just trendy information. More than any other directory or engine, Yahoo! has become a true portal and content site. Its personalization features are top-of-the-line. Yahoo! offers current news, sports scores, stock quotes, and has subject directories in thousands of categories. But, if you are looking for content evaluation, then Yahoo! is not the best place to go. Yahoo! contains over a million web site listings – some evaluated, some not. (Yahoo! uses a sunglasses icon for non-commercial listings that are evaluated, but the majority are taken as they're found.) If your search finds nothing, then Yahoo! takes you to the Google search engine database. To make money, Yahoo! is now charging an annual fee (used to be a one-time fee) of

US$299 for new sites to get listed, more for adult-related sites. It is also offering Northern Light's Special Collection of news articles on a per-pay basis.

Subject Directory Comparison

This chart summarizes the primary search features of web subject directories. For more detailed reviews, visit Search Engine Showdown (`www.searchengineshowdown.com`). The directories are arranged in hierarchical topics and sizes as measured by statistical comparisons published on Search Engine Showdown.

	Selection	Size	Boolean	Truncation	Fields	Sorting
Yahoo	User Submitted, 100+ editors	1,700,000+	+, -	Automatic, except in phrase	t:title u:url	Categories, sites, then Google
Open Directory	30,800 editors	2,152,000	and, or, andnot, +, -	Yes, *	None	Categories then sites
LookSmart	Selected	2,300,000	Automatic AND	Automatic stemming	None	Random sites, then AltaVista
Britannica	Selected	125,000	AND, **OR**, NOT, ( )	Automatic stemming	Title	Relevance
NBCi	User submitted	1,000,000+	+, -	Automatic stemming	None	Categories, sites, then Inktomi

Reprinted with permission from Search Engine Showdown, copyright at notess.com web site ©1999,2000,2001 by Greg R. Notess, all rights reserved. Note: chart update is noted at the site.

Best of Portals and Hybrid Search Tools

(Listed alphabetically by category)

Academic:

Academic Info

`www.academicinfo.net`

This is an easily searchable, education-focused subject directory geared for colleges and universities. It also provides specialized and advanced research options.

Best Information on the Net (BIOTN)

`http://library.sau.edu/bestinfo/`

While this directory is aimed at college students at St. Ambrose University, it is a great place to find academic-oriented research sites.

BUBL LINK

`http://bubl.ac.uk/link/`

This British-based searchable subject directory (focused on British Internet resources) is education-oriented and internationally focused. It is very well organized and easy to use.

InfoMine: Scholarly Internet Resource Collections
http://infomine.ucr.edu

This site contains scholarly Internet resources pulled together by librarians for the University of California and Stanford University campuses. InfoMine is terrific for academic and scholarly resources, but isn't designed for other purposes. It is searchable by keyword and category.

PSIgate - Physical Sciences
www.humbul.ac.uk

A super clearinghouse site for humanities information from the British Humbul Humanities Hub.

Bibliographies:

C&RL NewsNet Internet Resources
www.ala.org/acrl/resrces.html

The American Library Association's Association of College and Research Libraries has pulled together this solid collection of Internet bibliographies, called webliographies. It covers a wide range of topics and gives you specific subject-oriented directories to look at.

Business:

Internet Intelligence Index
www.fuld.com/i3/index.html

An excellent tool for finding competitive intelligence information, the stuff you want to know about your business competitor or a company you are interested in buying. It contains links to over 600 intelligence-related Internet sites. It is maintained by the Fuld Company, a leader in competitive intelligence work.

Environment:

University of Brussels Library - Environmental Resources Directory
www.ulb.ac.be/ceese/meta/cds.html

This excellent site was established by the Belgian government's Office of Scientific, Technical and Cultural Affairs.

Genealogy:

Cyndi's List of Genealogical Sites on the Internet

www.cyndislist.com

Cyndi's List is very good starting point for genealogy research with over 130,000 links to genealogy-related sites.

General to Specific:

Digital Librarian

www.digital-librarian.com

Like the superb Librarians Index to the Internet, this directory is maintained by Margaret Vail Anderson, a librarian in Cortland, New York. This is an excellent collection of links on many specific topics. Like Fossick (listed below), it will help you find topic-specific subject directories.

Fossick.com

www.fossick.com

As discussed in the international chapter, Fossick is a link to more than 3,000 subject-specific search engines. It is particularly good for finding internationally targeted directories. A superb directory of subject-focused search engines.

Searchability - Guides to Specialized Search Engines

www.searchability.com

This is a site geared to helping you find the specialized search tool you are looking for – call it a collection of specialized search sites. It is a targeted directory to get you to other directories and search tools, but it's a good one.

WWW Virtual Library

www.vlib.org

Another good place to find subject-specific directories. This is the oldest directory on the World Wide Web, begun by web founder Tim Berners-Lee. Quality varies, but it's a good way to find specific resources.

Government:

University of Michigan Documents Center

www.lib.umich.edu/govdocs/

This University of Michigan site, from which the Statistics Resources is a small sub-directory, offers a series of excellent U.S. and non-U.S. government resources in directory form.

Health and Science:

BIOME Health and Life Science

http://biome.ac.uk/biome.html

BIOME offers free access to a searchable catalog of internet sites and resources covering the health and life sciences. It is also browsable as a targeted directory, one of several superb British-based science directories and focused crawlers.

HealthAtoZ - Your Family Health Site

www.healthatoz.com

This is a focused crawler offering quick access to medical information online. It has subject-oriented directories and can be searched easily.

Legal:

FindLaw

www.lawcrawler.lp.findlaw.com

FindLaw is an excellent targeted directory and its law crawler lets you search and maneuver around this top legal site's database. It offers law-oriented web pages, a terrific free database of full-text U.S. Supreme Court cases, a directory of online law reviews, a collection of state codes, and continuing discussions about education as well as law. The law crawler is powered by AltaVista, so it offers advanced search functions. The longer this site is around, the better it gets, and it's definitely the place to start for U.S. legal information. I just wish it would add international components.

University Law Review Project

www.lawreview.org

Offers information on law journals, some in full text, and lots of legal-related documents. It's a nice companion site for FindLaw.

News:

Net2one

www.net2one.com

This is a focused crawler primarily looking at news information (see Chapter 8, News Resources for details).

Politics:

Political Information.Com

www.politicalinformation.com

This focused crawler is a great site for high-quality political information. It offers both a web directory and a searchable database of information. It was started, according to its founders, because the information they were looking for was often 600 links into a search. They decided that a focused crawler would be a better way to help locate political information.

Statistics:

Statistical Resources on the Web
`www.lib.umich.edu/govdocs/stats.html`

This extensive resource contains valuable statistics, mostly from federal government sources. It also lists other resources and other subject directories of value.

Technology:

SearchIQ - Directory of Specialty Engines - Technology
`www.zdnet.com/searchiq/subjects/`

This is another directory of specialized search engines. It's owned by ZDNet, a company that produces magazines and newsletters about technology. It is another excellent collection of collections.

Best Meta-Tools (listed alphabetically)

Beaucoup! `www.beaucoup.com`

This site contains links to one of the most thorough collections of search engines, directories, finding aids and indexes on the Internet so far – 2500+ at last count. You can browse from broad categories or via specialized search tools. Beaucoup! also provides great summaries of difficult-to-locate resources on topics like arts, politics, education and music.

Actually, Beaucoup! isn't really a meta-tool because it doesn't run searches through multiple search engines. Technically, it's a one-stop shopping site to a plethora of other search tools.

Dogpile `www.dogpile.com`

The most complex, but by far the most thorough of all the meta-tools, Dogpile is extremely flexible. It permits searches of many search tools simultaneously – you can even designate which ones. Regardless, keep your Dogpile queries as simple as possible in order to accommodate the query standards of the various search tools being accessed. Be aware of the paid inclusion warning mentioned earlier.

Intelliseek ProFusion - Advanced Search `www.profusion.com`

Intelliseek's Profusion is an excellent meta-tool, offering a combination of nine search engines and directories. It allows you to select all nine, or any combination of them and it draws from many of the major search tools. In addition, it will run a check to make sure or verify that the results you see are still live sites on the Web.

Ixquick www.ixquick.com

A new meta-search tool, Ixquick offers some innovative features, including natural language or complex Boolean searches. It also translates your search into each engine's preferred syntax and allows you to customize which of the fourteen search tools you want results from, then gives you a ratings list showing how many sites list a particular result, allowing you to evaluate your results.

MetaCrawler www.metacrawler.com

It gives you a choice of eleven search tools, including Google and AltaVista, then combines the results into one master list with duplicates deleted. It also allows you to set the timeout duration, which will result in changes to your searches.

Metor.Com www.metor.com

What makes this tool so useful is that it combines most of the major search engines, adds in an excellent European one – Euroseek – and using the "Specific Search" function allows you to search for topic-specific engines focused on subjects like business, finance, health, job searching and even recipes.

Proteus www.thrall.org/proteus.html

Proteus is very easy to use and offers all kinds of help to show you how to maximize your results.

QB Search www.qbsearch.com

An offshoot of the terrific QuickBrowse personalized news-gathering tool, qb Search presents your results in a single, long page of results; so don't ask for too many engines or it will take a long time to load your page.

Query Server Web Search www.queryserver.com/web.htm

This site clusters your results under subject headings or site headings and also offers focused meta-searches on subjects like news and money.

Researchville www.researchville.com

Researchville uses an excellent collection of search tools, gives you good results and allows you to target reference sites, dictionaries, encyclopedias and discussion forums. The more you use this tool, the more you like it for its focused meta-searching.

Search.com www.search.com

Owned by CNET, this meta-search tool has been combined with the former SavvySearch. What's good about this tool is you can customize it – choosing exactly which search tools to use. This allows you to get a pure non-paid-for search, if you know which tools allow paid placement and which don't. In addition, you can add in the latest headlines. (Refer to the Paid Placement chart, page 101.)

Surfwax `www.surfwax.com`

Completely revamped and refocused, Surfwax separates itself by giving you control over which search tools you want to look at. You develop personalized search sets and as a result you can maneuver the results and refine them.

Vivisimo `www.vivisimo.com`

Vivisimo has an easy-to-use front page. What makes it so valuable is it sorts your results into folders allowing you to choose which search engines to use (in the "Advanced Search" only). Your results come back in folders that list shows where a web site appears on multiple sites.

Search Tools to Watch

A few other search tools worth pointing out:

Anzwers `www.anzwers.com.au/`

Anzwers, or the Australia and New Zealand Web Enquiry Research System, is an Inktomi-powered search engine geographically focused on those two countries. It can be searched on a world basis. It is worth mentioning again that in addition to many options, like HotBot, it offers the largest and most thorough version of the Inktomi databases.

Ask Jeeves `www.askjeeves.com`

A unique subject directory, Ask Jeeves allows the user to enter a question in plain English, or select from the list of the most popular questions. Jeeves searches its knowledge base of already-researched questions, returns possible question matches, and runs your question through several search engines and subject directories. Results are presented in drop-down selection boxes. It has recently purchased Direct Hit and Teoma, and its database of information from which the questions are answered will grow dramatically and get considerably better.

Daypop.com `www.daypop.com`

Daypop is a current events search engine that crawls the Internet at least once a day, thus bringing you the latest information relevant to your searches. It also searches results from web blogs that may direct you to unique and valuable web resources.

Direct Search `www.freepint.com/gary/direct.htm`

One of the best search tools available is Gary Price's amazing Direct Search. It is one of several sites Price maintains and if you check out one, you will find yourself spending hours checking out several of his other sites. It offers links to several thousand specific search tools to help you find the "invisible web" resources not indexed or found by traditional search tools. Price has a knack for finding the best of the best. Included are excellent collections of speeches, transcripts and audio and visual resources online. Direct Search is a Web "must-see." More on Price's "invisible web" resources later in this chapter.

Google's Groups www.groups.google.com

This is the ultimate collection of Usenet postings. The collection has over 800 million postings in more than 35,000 categories going back to 1994 and is searchable using the advanced search. It used to be owned by Deja.com. See more on Usenet in Chapter 5, Specialized Tools.

iLOR www.ilor.com

As good as Google is, iLOR manages to step it up a notch. iLOR licenses Google's database and technology, and provides nearly identical results. But it adds some really useful interface innovations that make results easier to work with.

Infopeople - Best Search Tools Page
www.infopeople.org/search/tools.html

Want easy access to many of the best tools all in one easy to use page? This is the page to start with, from the Infopeople project of the California State Library system.

Kid's Tools for Searching the Internet www.rcls.org/ksearch.htm

Another collection page, this one is geared for kids or parents trying to educate kids. It pulls together many of the best children's search engines and directories onto a single page, including KidsClick!, Yahooligans!, Awesome Library, Ask Jeeves for Kids, and Searchopolis.

Moreover.com www.moreover.com

Moreover is one of the best news search tools on the Web. It brings together a massive index to news stories posted elsewhere and pulled together into an easy-to-use format. It uses 3,000 news sources around the world. See more information in Chapter 8, News.

Orientation www.orientation.com

This international search uses the motto "think globally, search locally." What makes this noteworthy is that it has locally-focused search engines in hundreds of countries around the world. See Chapter 10, International, for more details.

Value-Added Search Tools

Another category of essential tools are those that offer resources available on the Web combined with ones requiring a fee. Many of these are discussed in different areas of the book, for example, see the specialized search discussion of fee-based databases like Dialog (www.dialog.com), Factiva (www.factiva.com), and Lexis-Nexis (www.lexis.com and www.nexis.com) in the following chapters.

Some resources allow you to purchase resources on a per-piece basis or a limited time basis instead of requiring a subscription. These are value-added resources and offer some material you can't get elsewhere. A few examples:

Northern Light's Special Collections
www.northernlight.com (Highlight "Special Collection" in the drop-down box.)

This former web search engine, now only offers its special collection of full-text news stories, journals, magazines, transcripts and business reports on a per-item basis at a very reasonable price.

KnowX

www.knowx.com

KnowX provides access to public records on a pay-per-page basis. Several business resources fit this category and offer value-added content in the area of business, including Hoovers.com, some of the Thomson Financial resources, and sites like EDGAR (www.edgar-online.com).

Tips From a Guru

Greg Notess follows the nuances of search engines, how they work and their strengths and weaknesses. And as a reference librarian, writer, and internet trainer, he's learned a few tricks to help you maneuver the search tools. Here's a guru's perspective

Tips from a Search Engine Guru

By Greg R. Notess

1. Learn What You Can Expect to Find on the Internet — and What Isn't Likely to be Posted

What kind of information do organizations typically make available on the Web? Product information, public relations material, collaborative scientific project reports, staff directories, mission statements, library catalogs, current news, government information, selected article reprints and press releases are just some of what is commonly accessible on the Web. Trade secrets, strategic plans, commercial databases and most copyrighted published material (except some news and magazine articles) are not readily accessible.

2. Go Straight to the Source

Consider what organization is most likely to provide the kind of information being sought. Then go directly to that organization's web site.

For example, rather than searching all over the Web for the population of a U.S. town, go straight to the web site for the U.S. Census Bureau. Or, for detailed information on one side of the gun control debate, check out the National Rifle Association web site.

3. Locate a URL the Easiest Way

Doing some simple URL guesswork before trying subject directories and the larger search engines can save you time. Guessing the unofficial standard address (`www.nameofcompany.com`) can, as often as not, take you directly to a company's main web page where you can see what information is available at the site and how it is organized.

Both Netscape Navigator and Microsoft's Internet Explorer automatically take a host address and add the common `http://` at the beginning. Sometimes an address will not work without the `http://`, usually it is because there is no www in the address. So to save typing a few strokes, just leave that part of the URL off. Since www is the most common way to begin a host address, start with that when guessing. After the www, try the organization's name, acronym, or abbreviated name, and then add the appropriate top-level domain. While most commercial sites now have the .com domain, don't forget the other common U.S. endings: .edu for educational institutions, .gov for U.S. government, .mil for U.S. military and .org for other organizations. Using these, it becomes relatively easy to guess that the U.S. Census Bureau is at `www.census.gov` and that the National Rifle Association is at `www.nra.org`.

4. Slice — or Truncate — a URL to Find a Page's New Location within a Web Site

Since web sites are being reorganized continuously, the dead-end message "file not found" pops up frequently. One strategy is to use the site's own organization to find a page's new location. Slice off parts of the URL, starting on the right hand side and stopping at every slash. A page formerly located at `www.yourco.com/products/sales/needthis.html` may have been renamed, moved to another directory, or completely removed. If it is still available, try `www.yourco.com/products/sales` to see if any files are still available in that directory. If you still get an error message, next try `www.yourco.com/products`. If the page pointed to a product on sale, it may still be available under the regular section now. If all else fails, try the root URL at `www.yourco.com` as your tracking base. Web sites are altered continuously, but relatively few pages are deleted altogether.

5. Use a Subject Directory for Difficult-to-Find URLs

Some associations and companies have names that overlap with the names or acronyms of other companies, making it harder to track their URL. For example, the American Marketing Association was the first to claim `www.ama.org` so the American Medical Association decided to go with `www.ama_assn.org`. For URLs that are more difficult to guess, try a quick search in a subject directory such as Yahoo! or LookSmart. Most subject directories link to the top-level pages of web sites, rather than to all the pages at the site.

6. Use a Subject Directory for Product Information Searches

Subject directories should also be the first step in a product information search. While the strategy of going to the company's web site may work, searching a directory for product information is especially helpful when searching for a group of products, or for products where the company's name isn't known.

7. Run a Phrase Search on a Search Engine

The best search engines have enormous databases that index not only main pages but also lower-level or subsidiary pages. For example, AltaVista has well over 397 million individual web pages fully indexed in its database. With a database this size, a single word search will often result in far too many hits to be useful, unless the word is infrequently used. Chemical names, taxonomic categories, unique small business names or personal names may be unusual, but not unusual enough to limit the returns to a manageable number.

All the major search engines support phrase searching to some degree. Surround the search phrase in double quote marks (" "). By running a phrase search, the search engine is looking for the exact term in exactly the word order specified. If you can express information needs with a phrase (at least two words are required), try the search with the phrase first, before broadening out to other strategies. For example, submitting the phrase "digital frequency hopping" can get far more precise results than searching it without the double quotes, which will elicit thousands of additional pages that don't contain that exact phrase but rather contain only one or more of those words.

-- Greg R. Notess is a reference librarian at Montana State University, a columnist for *Online* and *Database* magazines and the author of the *Search Engine Showdown*. He is also the author of the first three editions of *Government Information on the Internet* (www.bernan.com), Email: notess@notess.com, Web: www.searchengineshowdown.com and www.notess.com.

The Invisible Internet:
What Search Tools Can't or Don't Access

Search engines miss a lot of material. The reality is there is a vast area of material that either isn't found by the search tool or is intentionally neglected by the search engine for size or other limits. For example, when you use a search engine do a search on *The New York Times*, their content never shows up because it is not indexed by a search engine crawler. *The New York Times* requires you to fill out a registration form, and the search engine can't crawl past the registration barrier. So while the content of *The New York Times* is available on the Internet, it falls into an area of content that has become known as the "invisible web."

That barrier to entry – and there are several other barriers – blocks the material from ever being crawled by the search engine crawler, and causes an extraordinary amount of great material to be "invisible."

Part of the reason is simply an economic one – search engines crawling costs money to search, index, and store the results. So many search engines limit the number of pages on a web site they search, or limit the number of pages indexed, dumping older ones and replacing them with new ones, or restrict the kinds of pages they crawl by cataloging only certain types of domain names. So as many as 500 pages on one site may be crawled and still thousands more are never even looked at.

Sometimes pages are crawled and simply omitted or forgotten about. What makes this so important is that studies show that this "invisible web" dramatically dwarfs the size of all the material you see on the World Wide Web. A Bright Planet study in 2000 found the "invisible web" to be as much as 500 times larger than the visible web.

So what is the "invisible web?" It is all the material that is behind these gates as well as certain kinds of file formats that simply are not cataloged by the search crawlers. With the notable exception of Google, most PDF files – a format used intensively by the U.S. government – are not indexed by search tools. That's because PDF is not a HTML text, which is what these crawlers index. Flash animations and streaming media files also fall into the "invisible web." Same goes for most real-time data, like stock quotes, weather information and airline flight information. Those are not indexed because they tend to change so quickly that no crawler will get back and re-index them regularly.

Gary Price and Chris Sherman, authors of *The Invisible Web*, the definitive book on the subject, estimate this informational chasm to be between two to fifty times larger than the visible web. They claim that resources in this portion of the Web tend to be much higher quality than the ones search engines find on the visible web. Sherman and Price have categorized four types of invisibility, which they have graciously allowed us to reprint below:

Opaque Web

The "opaque web" consists of pages that can be found by search tools, but for one reason or another are not included in search engine indices. This includes pages that are "hidden" behind dynamic navigation codes. For the most part, the data you find on an opaque database tends to be subject-focused, can't be easily found on a general purpose search engine and are more precise, more current and more authoritative than what you would find using more general tools.

Private Web

This second group of files consists of technically indexable pages that have deliberately been excluded from research engines by web page designers. These "private web" pages are ones where a password has been set up to protect the page from crawlers.

Proprietary Web

A third group, the "proprietary web" are pages that have been roped off or blocked access to and are only accessible to people who have agreed to special terms in exchange for seeing the content. These include agreeing to fill out a registration form to get access to *The New York Times* pages.

Perhaps the biggest difference between the private web and the proprietary web is money. In most cases the "invisible web" material is free, or inexpensive, where proprietary web sites can be very expensive. Proprietary pages include companies like Hoovers.com or *The Wall Street Journal* http://online.wsj.com/public/us, which charge fees to get access.

Truly Invisible Web

The "truly invisible web" includes pages that use file formats that current-generation web crawlers aren't programmed to handle. Most search engines were originally designed to focus on text. So pages that just have photos, graphics files, sound or video and no text are often missed altogether by the search engines. That's because they don't have words that can be indexed easily. Most search engines look at the coding on a page and record the manner, file name and location details of the page, but not a whole lot else. So a page that consists of images, sound, video and no text is something the crawler can't handle. It falls into the "truly invisible web" category.

Other Invisible Web Characteristics

Another problem for crawlers is finding dynamically-generated web pages. When a database spits back the answer to your query, it generates a special results page on the fly, usually noted by cgi-bin contained in the URL. While most search crawlers could technically index this content, search engines are unwilling to index it and so this material also falls into the "invisible web."

This on-the-fly response page causes problems for search engines to index because the contents of those databases don't exist until you search for the information. To see an example, go to the Labor Department's Bureau of Labor Statistics web site (`http://stats.bls.gov`) and request the unemployment statistics for your hometown.

Some sites have both visible and invisible elements. For example, the U.S. Library of Congress site (`www.loc.gov`) maintains one of the largest Web collections in the entire world. Many of its pages are easily searchable in basic HTML pages. Huge portions of the Library's pages are in databases that are invisible to search engines. Often you can find the top-level page of an invisible web site using a search engine. But the material below the top-level page is not accessible. Think of it as being able to reach the front doors of a bookstore, but not being able to look inside at the books.

"Invisible web" resources tend to be more focused and often provide better and more specific results. This is especially true of government and academic institutions. They tend to be more comprehensive because they are pulled together by subject-specific knowledgeable people, who for the most part, don't have to worry about profits.

Another thing to remember, as Sherman and Price stress in their book, is when you have a choice between using a general purpose search engine or query-and-retrieval tools offered by a particular site, you are almost always better off using the site's tools. They will most likely be more focused on retrieving information from that particular site. So remember if you see a search tool available on a front-page of a web site that may be sitting on top of a database, use that search tool and not a general one to access much of the "invisible web content."

It's important to understand that no one is suggesting you abandon the search engines. The "invisible web" isn't always going to be your answer. But, once you understand when to use the "invisible web" and when to use other search tools, you can become considerably more efficient as a searcher.

Below is an excellent article, written by Sherman, that gives tips on searching the "invisible web."

Ten Tips for Searching the Invisible Web

By Chris Sherman

How does one go about finding information on the invisible web if we can't rely on our favorite search engines or directories? Here are ten tips for probing the vast reaches of the invisible web that Gary Price and I used when we were writing *The Invisible Web: Uncovering Information Sources Search Engines Can't See.*

1. Run Pre-Emptive Searches To Find Likely Invisible Web Content

The highest quality invisible web content is generally found in web accessible databases. Although they can't search engines can't penetrate and search databases, they can locate the home page or search form for many databases.

To search for databases, use your keyword together with the words "database," "repository," "archive" and so on in a Boolean query. For example:

> Census AND database
>
> "peanut farming" AND repository
>
> "widget manufacturing" AND 1998 AND archive

2. Use Reverse Link Searching

Once you've found a useful invisible web database, tap into the knowledge of other users who think highly of the resource to recommend other possible sites by doing reverse link searching. Reverse link searching is simply a request to the search engine to show all other pages on the Web that link to a particular page.

While all search engines use slightly different syntax, the "link" operator is generally used for this purpose. For example:

> `Link:http://www.janes.com/defence/glossary`
> (shows links to Jane's Defence Glossary database)
>
> `Link:http://www.24hourmuseum.org.uk/find_ft.htm`
> (shows links to the Museum Locator database)

3. Use Site Search Tools

Many databases are "hidden" in the reaches of larger sites. To find these, use the site search tools on large, authoritative sites such as the Library of Congress, the World Bank, and so on. Use the same strategies in Tip 1 to find invisible web resources using a site search tool.

4. Datamine Your Bookmarks

You may have already found good IW sites and bookmarked them. How do you tell if a bookmarked site is an invisible web resource? Use the "URL test" to find out. Simply put your cursor to the left of a question mark in a URL in your browsers address window, and erase everything to the right, including the question mark itself, then reload the page.

If you see an error message or a "page not found" message, you've probably discovered an invisible web site, since the data following the question mark was needed by the database to generate a meaningful page.

5. Monitor Content-Specific Mailing Lists and Forums.

Take advantage of experts in a field — they'll lead you to invisible web resources. A great way to do this is to track librarian and information professional mailing list discussions and forums. Discussion groups for journalists are also valuable to monitor: they're expert sleuths too!

To find discussion groups for your topic, check out the Directory of Scholarly and Professional E-Conferences at `www.kovacs.com/directory/`

6. Use Teoma's "Resources" Links For Datamining

The Teoma search engine has a unique capability to identify "hubs" and "authorities" that publish "link collections from experts and enthusiasts." While these resources are not often invisible web resources in themselves, they often point the way to them. And, since Teoma "discovers" these expert links pages for each query you run (rather than using precomputed relevance scores), you'll find that they serve as a great "mining" tool for finding invisible web content.

7. Use Invisible Web Pathfinders

Though there are no "pure" invisible web search engines, several pathfinders exist that point to a fair amount of excellent hidden content. These include:

Intelliseek Sites
`www.invisibleweb.com`
`http://beta.profusion.com`
A directory and meta search engine that both include invisible web content.

Invisible-web.net
`www.invisible-web.net`
The companion web site to our book, *The Invisible Web*.

Librarians' Index to the Internet
`www.lii.org`
A site created by professional librarians, categorized by the type of information resource. Search for "databases" when using this tool.

8. For "Difficult" File Types: Google: Filetype Operator

Google allows you to limit searches to "difficult" file types that aren't typically indexed by other search engines, including Microsoft Word, Excel, and PowerPoint documents.

```
filetype:doc "Alzheimer's research grants"

filetype:ppt "General Motors"
```

These two unusual file type examples will help find you word documents on Alzheimer's research grants, or powerpoints about or by people from General Motors.

9. Use Specialized Search Engines

Specialized search engines can often find invisible web content that general-purpose search engines can't find. For example:

Search PDF
http://searchpdf.adobe.com
Finds only PDF files containing your query terms.

Research Index
www.researchindex.com
An outstanding computer science academic paper search engine that can translate "hidden" file formats such as pdf, postscript and ghostscript on the fly and make them searchable.

10. Finding Images

Images are getting easier to find, with Google, FAST/AllTheWeb and AltaVista all offering good image search tools. Some other interesting image search tools include:

Google Catalogs
http://catalogs.google.com
Search the contents of mail order catalogs and get images as results.

Visoo
www.visoo.com
An image search engine that uses OCR techniques to "read" text contained in images.

Webseek @ Columbia University
www.ctr.columbia.edu/webseek/
A content-based image and video search and catalog tool for the Web.

-- Chris Sherman is co-author of *The Invisible Web: Uncovering Information Sources Search Engines Can't See*, with Gary Price. Chris Sherman email address: csherman@searchwise.com

To harness the "invisible web," you need to know where that information can be found ahead of time since you can't find it using general search engines. You need to ask yourself some framing-your-research strategic questions before you start looking for invisible web resources. (See Chapter 3, Framing Your Search.) Ask yourself what questions can this resource answer, what specifically am I looking for, and is this the best place to find that information.

Learning the difference between visible and "invisible web" resources is important because it will save time, and get you the best answer with the least effort.

The Best of the Invisible Web

Without a question, Sherman and Price's own collections of "invisible web" sites, found at www.invisible-web.net and Gary Price's longstanding Direct Search page at www.freepint.com/gary/direct.htm are pathfinder sites that will lead you to thousands of invisible web resources. What makes Direct Search so valuable is that Price links you directly to the search form offered, rather than making you click through several places to get there. Intelliseek's InvisibleWeb.com contains over 10,000 databases and searchable sources that are usually overlooked by the main search engines.

➔ *hot tip:* If you are looking to find invisible web material, one way you can use general search tools to jump start the process is to go to the advanced section of one of the major search engines and try doing a title search for a searchable database with specific sites, like .gov for government, .edu for education or a for geographic location like .jp for Japan or .ca for Canada.
Here are a few examples of that kind of search:

```
intitle: "searchable database" site:gov
intitle: "specialized database" site:edu
inurl: search intitle:database site:ca
```

Resources on Search Tools

There are some superb research tools to follow the latest news on search engines and some great books that provide details on how they work.

Must-Read Best Search Tool Resources

About.com - Websearch
www.websearch.about.com

This guide on the About.com site is a great way to keep up on the latest news on search tools.

Gary Price's Virtual Acquisition Shelf

http://resourceshelf.freepint.com

Another daily electronic newsletter that follows the industry's ups and downs.

ResearchBuzz.com

www.researchbuzz.com

Tara Calishain's terrific electronic newsletter keeps you up to speed on what's happening with search tools.

SearchEngineWatch.com

www.searchenginewatch.com

Danny Sullivan's excellent web site and subscription newsletter, now with the added bonus of Chris Sherman's daily *Search Day* newsletter.

Search Engine Showdown.com

www.searchengineshowdown.com

Greg Notess's analysis of how the search engines work and his daily blog.

Virtual Chase

www.virtualchase.com

Another superb site, pulled together by Genie Tyburski, a law librarian, offers up-to-date information on search terms, legal tools, and techniques for conducting online research.

Books:

- *The Extreme Web Search Engines* by Randolph Hock
- *The Invisible Web* by Gary Price and Chris Sherman

Both are available from CyberAge Press (www.infotoday.com).

Charts:

Regularly updated charts with the latest info on how search engines work.

- http://lisweb.curtin.edu.au/staff/gwpersonal/compare.html
- www.lib.berkeley.edu/TeachingLib/Guides/Internet/ToolsTables.html#Recommend7
- www.infopeople.org/search/chart.html
- www.searchengineshowdown.com

Additional Web Sites for General Search Tools

1Search
www.first-search.com
Collection of Vertical Search engines on specific topics like business, computers, pets, etc.

AllSearchEngines.com
www.allsearchengines.com
This has links to an incredible number of search tools.

AlphaSearch: Gateway to the "Academic" Web
www.calvin.edu/library/
Click on search resources. Gateway to the Academic Web links to internet "gateway" sites, all relevant sites related to a discipline, subject, or idea; instant access to hundreds of sites by entering just one gateway site.

ARCS Search
http://arc-s.search6.net/search/search/Search
Search engine with links to subject hubs.

Argus Clearinghouse
www.clearinghouse.net
Breaks material into 14 categories and hundreds of subcategories, such as "environmental."

Awesome Library
www.awesomelibrary.org
Excellent collection of Educational resources.

Best Search Tools Page
www.infopeople.org/search/tools.html
A superb starting page, with the search forms for the best search engines and subject directories all in one easy-to-use place. From the InfoPeople Project, it's a great place to compare the different search tools against one another.

C4 - Parallel Search Technology
www.c4.com
16 search engines, advanced queries, yellow pages, maps, directories, white pages and email. Formerly Cyber 411.

CIT Information Resource Guides
www.unc.edu/cit/guides/
Excellent guide to finding information on the Internet, particularly on education and technology.

Copernic
www.copernic.com
Fee-based site. Excellent tool for simultaneous searching of multiple engines.

E-Gineer
www.e-gineer.com
The "Domainator" database on this site helps find domain names, trademarks, definitions, synonyms, and more.

Highway 61
www.highway61.com
This meta-search tool allows you to adjust the level of response for sites, giving you control over your results.

IncyWincy
www.incywincy.com
IncyWincy provides access to all kinds of other search engines and invisible web resources. It has all kinds of flexibility in how to set up your results.

Lookle
www.lookle.com
Google-style knock-off search engine, but be aware that the search engine promotes its paid placement so your top results will likely have been bought and paid for.

Lookoff (multi-subject)
www.lookoff.com
Search engine site and tutorial site.

MetaEureka
www.metaeureka.com
Meta-search tool offers 27 search engines to choose from.

MetaSearch.com
http://7metasearch.com
Meta-search tool.

Moonmist
www.moonmist.co.uk
Meta search tool that chooses from almost 200 search engines to get your results.

Netsurfer Digest
www.netsurf.com/nsd
Netsurfer reviews web sites and evaluates them. Subscribe and get the electronic newsletter or browse the URL.

One2Seek MetaSearch

http://one2seek.com
Meta-search tool with strong international links.

Principles of Web Searching

http://mann77.mannlib.cornell.edu/refer
ence/workshops/WebSearching/
An excellent resource on explaining nuances of search tools
and how they work.

Research Index

www.researchindex.com
A computer science academic paper search engine that can
translate "hidden" file formats such as PDF, Postscript and
ghostscript on the fly and make them searchable.

Search Engine Colossus

www.searchenginecolossus.com
A worldwide collection of search tools.

Search Engine Watch's Search Engine Features Chart

http://searchenginewatch.com/webmasters
/features.html
Fee-based site. Shows how search engines rank pages – one
of the best sites on search engines and how they work.

Search Engines Galore

http://searchitall.hypermart.net
This has some excellent worldwide listings of search tools,
but the front page is very busy.

Search Idea

www.searchidea.com
Search engine and directory.

Search It All

www.search-it-all.com
Excellent, well-organized collection of search sites.

Search PDF

http://searchpdf.adobe.com
Finds only PDF files containing your query terms.

Search123

www.search123.com/
Good new search tool, small database, but solid accuracy.

SearchEngines.com (multi-subject)

www.searchengines.com
Collection of search engine sites from around the globe.

SearchOnline.info

www.searchonline.info
Free registration required. Excellent new meta-search tool.
Previously called Mywebhound, it is easily customized,
loaded with features and has a nice news feature as well.

Searchopolis

www.searchopolis.com
Filtered search engine geared to kids with content
restrictions, from N2H2 whose other product, Bess, is used
in schools all over the country to filter sites for kids.

SearchTurtle.com

www.searchturtle.com
New search tool, worth checking out. Small database.

Seek123

www.seek123.com
Meta search tool, but doesn't give control of which tools.

Suite 101

www.suite101.com
A member-based organization that recruits contributing
editors to create Web guides in their areas of expertise.

TheInfo.com

www.theinfo.com
Meta search tool, very useful to select tools you want.

Top Ten Links

www.toptenlinks.com
A collection of the best subject directories, based on votes
by those who use the site. Site reviewers pick the top ten
sites in each topic for content, style and visitors vote.

Tradeways Galaxy

www.einet.net
A subject-oriented site. It's deep, but spotty organization.

Webseek @ Columbia University

www.ctr.columbia.edu/webseek/
A content-based image and video search and catalog tool.

Where To Do Research

www.wheretodoresearch.com
A directory of research sites, not deep, but some useful
links. From Go Daddy Software.

Yahoo! Local Events

http://local.yahoo.com
Yahoo!'s list of local events, searchable by subject or
region.

Chapter 5

Specialized Tools

A Guide to Fact Finding, Document Finding, and People Finding Research Tools

People and Contact Information Finders — What Information Is Available? — Best People Finders — Reverse Phone Searches — Yellow Pages — Email Finders — Group and Affiliation Finders — College and Alumni Finders — Information Broker Finders — Legal Professional Finders — Medical Finders — Military Finders — Expert Finders — Genealogy & Personal History Tools — Adoption Tools, Biography-Finding Tools, Genealogy, Obits — Mapping Tools — Ready Reference Tools — Best Reference Tools — Specific Reference Tools: Calculators, Dictionaries, FAQs, Time — Quotation Finders — Networking and "Human Element" Tools — Usenet Newsgroups — A Newsgroup Primer — Searching Newsgroups — Abuse Of Usenet — Mailing Lists — Chat Rooms — Voice Chat — Instant Messaging — Conferencing — Videoconferencing — Online Audio Conferencing — Usenet: How It Works — Sidebars On Usenet Structure — Webrings — Blogs and Home Pages — Fee-Based Tools for Finding Specialized Information — Strategies for Using Fee-Based Services — How Do Fee-Based Tools Work? — The Tasini Decision's Impact on Fee-Based Tools — Best Fee-Based Tools; Comparing the Giants — Useful Fee-Based Tools — Additional Web Sites for Specialized Tools

As you already know, there are many, many types of research tools available online. Some are good at finding very specific facts, while others are better for more general topics. With 605.6 million people online, there are certain types of information that people look for again and again. Seeing the need for making this information easy to find, individuals and corporations have developed tools – what we call "specialized tools" – specifically for these searches. Now there are thousands and thousands of specialized web tools. As with everything else on the Internet, these tools are in a state of continuous improvement – their scope, depth, and targeting ability. Many of these specialized tools offer creative and innovative ways to find information.

For example, there are "people finders" that help find contact information — telephone, address, email — for individual people and businesses. Some help you find individuals and companies by professional or group affiliation. When you need specific information on a topic, expert finders locate people who claim expertise to be interviewed, testify, or teach a particular topic. A very common and growing use of the Internet is genealogical research and other forms of familial research, such as reuniting adopted children with their birth parents or siblings.

There are also many "print form" tools now available in web form, such as maps and reference tools. The online versions allow you to use these items in ways you never could in the traditional format — zooming in to a particular address on a map or finding a quote when you know only a couple of its words.

The Web also offers many ways to connect to others who may share your interests or may have that critical piece of information you are looking for. Through newsgroups, mailing lists, chat, blogs and many other means, it's easier and easier to find the "human" part of the Internet.

➜ *hot tip:*   **Always insist on original documentation. Never assume that online content is correct, since most online materials are, by definition, secondary source material that could have been input in error by a software program or by a human being. Try and find two authoritative sources for information, especially if your job depends upon it.**

Some specialized tools are free, and others cost money. A group of these fee-based tools are, in effect, supermarkets of information on all kinds of topics with incredible depth of information. Much like the search engines that also offer directories, some of these resources have several functions and fall into multiple categories.

Researchers use specialized tools for a variety of different reasons, including:

- to locate people
- as a pre-employment screening technique
- as a job-finding tool
- as a tenant or asset-screening tool
- for competitive intelligence about competing companies or businesses
- as a way of identifying potential customers and clients
- as a way to help you find people to raise money from, or
- as a way to find experts or people with knowledge on a subject that concerns or interests you.

Where do you start? Searching with specialized tools is like any kind of research; as shown in Chapter 3, Framing Your Search Strategy, you need to frame your question first and then figure out the best place to start looking. Ask yourself, am I looking for a phone number or for an expert? If you know the name of the person you are looking for and just want to know how to reach him or her, a people finder is the best place to start. If you are looking for a "type" of person – for example, a military professional – the affiliation or expert finders may help. If you are looking for someone to help you find more information, you may want to turn to a subject-specific site – for example, a genealogy site where you might find someone familiar with family histories in Oconomowoc, Wisconsin – or you may want to look for a professional information broker or a discussion group to uncover more resources.

This chapter is an overview of the most commonly used kinds of tools, and an introduction to the tools that are most useful. When backgrounding an individual or business, don't confine yourself to the specialized tools described in this chapter – use a combination of *all* the tools in this book

We can start this discussion of specialized tools by mentioning that people's home pages are a great resource for people-related information. If they have a web site, then more than likely you will find at least one way to contact them from there.

People finding is a very basic kind of online research but the procedures are like that of any other search: frame your research question first, then figure out the best place to start looking. Perhaps the person would be involved in discussion groups or might have a web site. Then, figure out which kind of specialized search tool might be the best starting point. Putting a name in quotes in a search engine will be helpful, but if you can pin down some additional details – like a college affiliation or something that ties this person to a job – you can focus the search more easily and go to the right topic-specific tools.

Contact Information and People-Finding Tools

For the most part, people finders are phone books or directories, providing publicly listed telephone numbers or other contact information to help you locate people. Using a people finder, you can do a local or national search in a matter of seconds. Keep in mind these tools vary considerably in accuracy and consistency. Some are free and available on the Web, while others cost money and are offered only through proprietary services.

→ *hot tip:* **Skilled researchers generally use a combination of free and fee-based services for people finding. The fee-based ones usually offer more extensive listings, with more accurate and more current information than the free sources.**

A critical question to ask yourself when using the free web-based people finders is, *how often are these tools updated?* The answer can vary widely, but there's an easy test for currency. Submit your own name or the name of someone with a *listed* phone number and see what information you find. If the results from this search are out-of-date, chances are other numbers will be as well. All people-finder databases originate from other vendors, so their information is, at best, third-hand. And since there's no official clearinghouse for processing email address changes – although there are some tools where you can list your change of email address – email addresses are even less reliable than phone numbers.

Where Does the Information Come From?

Nearly all the free phone books online gather their information from the same databases used by the regional phone companies as well as from public directories in the U.S. and in other countries. Some of them rely on self-reported information – the people listed submit and update their own listings.

The commercial people finders – sometimes called skiptracing tools – use a combination of different information resources to build profiles of individuals. Companies buy lists of information and all kinds of data from magazine companies, associations, and other groups then pull them all together into easily searchable databases. They're not restricted to listed phone numbers, so through their many resources, they gather unpublished phone numbers along the way. For example, many use credit headers to get phone numbers. Under U.S. law, companies are able to show you the header portion of credit reports, or identifying information, but are prohibited from selling you the personal financial information without the individual's permission. The header generally includes the consumer's name, address, age, year and date of birth, home telephone number, and previous address. Outside the U.S., credit information is rarely available, but it is gathered in many countries.

Not all of the fee-based specialty tools will be available to you. Some of them, like ChoicePoint's AutoTrackXP (www.choicepointonline.com), Merlin (www.merlindata.com), Accurint (www.accurint.com), and others restrict access to this skip-tracing information to safeguard you from harassment and violations of your privacy. For example, they may require that the researcher be in a particular profession such as law, insurance, law enforcement, or journalism, and can demonstrate a need for this particular information. However, without much effort, a lot of your personal information can be purchased online for a price. Some companies cast wide nets to gather this information and often pick up personal information from warranty forms, contests, and registration forms which you may fill out without ever thinking that someone might use them to gather information about you. Learn more about this in Chapter 14, Privacy and Protection.

What Information Is Available? How Far Can You Go?

Examples of specialized information available for sale include:

- Unlisted phone numbers, and even cell phone records at
  http://phone-number.batcave.net and www.discreetdata.com

- Driving record histories (these services seem to come and go online)

- Banking account records (www.tracerservices.com/bat.html)

There are many other web sites claiming to sell specialized information. For example, Techno-Max Pro (www.proto.inc2000.com/Techno-MAX.htm) advertises it will sell you software that will help you "Find out who that babe is driving that car" or "Find that girl you met in traffic or at the shopping center!" – and you get to do it while listening to the web site's version of the Mission Impossible theme.

Companies like Online Detective (www.onlinedetective.com) say they will sell the sources to obtain cell phone records, driver's license records, bank account records as well as Social

Security Numbers, probation records, arrest records, criminal records, restraining orders, tax records, credit records, and records of being in a mental hospital.

The original sources of this personal information, as well as the accuracy and legality of it, may all be questionable – so proceed with caution in this area of research. To learn more about what information is available about *you*, see Chapter 14 about privacy issues.

> ➜ *hot tip:*   **Portals like AOL, Yahoo! and MSN offer members the opportunity to view profiles of other members, which can be a great resource for locating people.**

Best People Finders (listed alphabetically)

Many of the top people-finding tools are U.S.-centric. But several really good ones cover multiple countries. This is a combined list of U.S. and non-U.S. tools.

All Nations Expatriates Telephone Search Engine

www.escapeartist.com/global/telephone.htm

This telephone search engine is a unique tool that will help you find the correct dialing prefix. It also tells you how much it should cost to make your call, and provides country-by-country phone books.

AnyWho

www.anywho.com

www.anywho.com/international.html

This outstanding site from AT&T is one of the best. It is thorough, claiming more than 98 million listings, and easy to use. It's divided into several categories, including people and businesses, and includes an excellent reverse directory to help you trace the name that belongs to a number.

AnyWho also brought a new component to free web search, something many of the fee-based tools have provided for years: the ability to search for neighbors online. This feature allows you to find anyone using a listed phone number for a specified block anywhere in specific countries. Reporters use this feature to locate and contact neighbors of people in the news. You can use it to locate the neighbor of someone you can't reach. AnyWho will also provide a map and directions to the neighborhood. Again, test its accuracy by submitting your own name. Only listed numbers are made available, and anyone can opt to be deleted. It has a separate file for non-U.S. searching.

Craig Ball's Phone Finder

www.craigball.com/phonefind.html

This is a good collection of phone finders pulled together in an easy-to-use form. Beware, it will result in multiple browsers opening.

InfoSpace.com

`www.infospace.com`

Like some others, InfoSpace.com offers maps, reverse directories and other tools. It recently purchased what remains of the portal and search engine site Excite. InfoSpace also features the phone books of several countries, including Canada and the U.K. It also has a good email finder that is strong for European and Canadian addresses (`http://www.infospace.com / 1 F74T930VPPH52 info/wp/email/index.htm`) and a reverse email finder (`http://www.infospace.com/ 1 F74T930VPPH52 info/wp/reverse.htm`)

It also has an international component, which is sorted by countries and territories, most listings link to a people finder, business finder, email search and even weather information (`www.infospace.com/info.netctr/index_int.htm`)

Nedsite

`www.nedsite.nl/search/people.htm`

A people-finding portal with links to many tools, including by country.

PeopleSearch.net

`www.peoplesearch.net`

You are either going to love this tool, or absolutely hate it. There will be no indifference on this one. It pulls together sixteen people finders and searches them at the same time. But you must use a fast-running computer. Here's why: the search takes longer to run and the results are like a meta-search tool for people finding. It covers phone books and search engines and is truly international in its searching. But it opens up sixteen browsers at the same time and gives you results in each of them. For many people, this will totally overwhelm your computer and could cause it to malfunction or freeze.

Switchboard

`www.switchboard.com`

This site has deep resources for phone directories as well as for email addresses, finding yellow pages information, maps, directions and a neat feature – what's nearby.

Teldir

`www.teldir.com`

This is a truly outstanding collection of phone finding tools from all over the world, broken down by global region. It also has a good collection of email finders.

Ultimate White Pages

`www.theultimates.com/white`

The Ultimate White Pages includes easy access to a centralized common interface to five phone books (Whitepages.com, WhoWhere.com, Switchboard.com, AnyWho.com, InfoSpace.com) which you can run in succession. It also offers reverse phone searching, maps and a pay search that offers a cleaner, easier way to search.

Whitepages.com
www.whitepages.com

An excellent U.S.-centric people-finding tool that has been around since 1996. It offers phone numbers, and also lets you locate area codes and Zip Codes for parts of the U.S.

WhoWhere?
www.whowhere.com

WhoWhere offers a powerful email address finder that works in English, French and Spanish. This Lycos-owned company also includes valuable business resources, like resume finders and a mortgage finder. One unique feature is its "people in the news," allowing you to find news stories from Lycos-partner HotBot on news-related topics. It also has a cool 3D feature that, when you run an address, will show you where on the globe it is, once you find the address, "zoom" into the globe to activate this feature. This doesn't help much with information, but is cool nonetheless.

WorldPages Global Find
www.worldpages.com/global

This international phone book provides access to white pages, government and business listings and phone books for more than 150 countries from Afghanistan to Zimbabwe. It is powered by Switchboard. Searching for individuals is limited based on which countries have online listings, but business and yellow page listings are plentiful.

Yahoo! People Search
http://people.yahoo.com

Yahoo! People Search is a good phone book but a much better email directory. It gathers profile information and links to that data when possible, which is very useful when you're trying to find one particular John Smith. But it usually does this through its business partners, like U.S. Search, which will cost you money. And in most cases, it is information you can find for free on your own if you know where to look. Yahoo! also offers email searching and excellent mapping tools through its partner – MapQuest.

Reverse Phone Searching (listed alphabetically)

These eight phone finders all offer reverse phone or reverse email capability, so if you have a phone number or an email address, but not a name, you can look it up and find out who it belongs to and possibly additional information about the person. Since I've already described most of these tools in the previous section, I am including only the direct URL here.

AnyWho – Reverse Phone
www.anywho.com/rl.html

ICQ – Reverse Email
http://web.icq.com/whitepages/search/

InfoSpace.com
http://www.infospace.com/ 1 F74T930VPPH52 info/wp/reverse.htm

Internet Address Finder - Reverse Email
www.iaf.net

Superpages.com - Reverse Phone
http://wp.superpages.com/wp/reverse.phtml?SRC=&STYPE=&WL=&WF=&T=&S=&A=&X=&P=&WES=&E=&WENum=

Also reverse yellow pages at http://yp.superpages.com/rform.phtml?A=&X=&P=&SRC=

White Pages - Reverse Phone or Address
http://whitepages.com/find_person.pl?fid=p

Yellow Page Finders

Yellow pages are another way to find specific people. There are dozens of good yellow page phone books online. Here are some of the better ones.

Infobel - International Directories
www.infobel.com/World/

This is one of the few truly international yellow pages.

Superpages
www.superpages.com

This yellow pages from Verizon, which has also taken over the web sites of two other excellent yellow pages, Bigbook.com and Bigyellow.com, is more than just the yellow pages of a phone book because of two features. One, called "The Nearest," (within its "Detailed Search" option) allows you to search for businesses by category and name simultaneously. The other, "Search Nearby," retrieves addresses within a specified radius of the business or address for which you're searching. You should have no trouble finding the 24-hour pharmacy closest to your mother's house. If you're contemplating a new business, you can also use it to find competitor locations.

Yahoo! Yellow Pages
http://yp.yahoo.com

You can search by category or business name for a city or near a specific address. The results can be sorted alphabetically or based on proximity. You can also link to a map or get directions.

Yellow Pages.com
www.yellowpages.com

A U.S.-focused yellow pages, but it also offers similar versions for regions of the world.

Email Finders

There is a lot of crossover of tools on the Web. So many of the phone finders already mentioned also include email finders. Below are tools that specialize in email addresses.

Remember, there is no central directory, so locating some email addresses could be like pulling a needle out of a haystack. You may find legitimate email addresses, but they can be years out-of-date. Again, check out your own address and name to see if yours is listed and accurate. (I checked almost all of these tools for my current email address, which I've had since 1996, and none of them had it indexed. Several still list the CompuServe address I haven't had since 1994).

While many of the phone books offer email-finding tools, there are others that are specifically geared to finding email addresses. They are:

FreshAddress.com
`www.freshaddress.com`

Want to update your own email address(es)? This site allows you to "register" your new email address and notify people of the change. In addition to publicizing your own change of email address, you can plug in the last known email address for someone else and if they are registered at FreshAddress.com, you will get the updated information, assuming that the person you are seeking hasn't set a privacy filter preventing you from doing so.

ICQ Email Directory
`www.icq.com/search/email.html`

An excellent people-finding tool – especially if you are looking for non-U.S. email addresses. This pulls information from the ICQ chat discussion database.

Internet Address Finder
`www.iaf.net`

This is one of the best email finders, with more than six million listings worldwide.

MESA (MetaEmailSearchAgent) - Email Finder
`http://mesa.rrzn.uni-hannover.de`

MESA, based in Germany, searches several web email directories simultaneously, then organizes the results by name and lists all known entries.

WED – The World Email Directory
`www.worldemail.com`

A huge database of email addresses, also an excellent phone book.

Worldemail.com
`www.worldemail.com`

A good tool for finding international email addresses.

Group and Affiliation Listing Finders

Sometimes you either don't know the specific name of the person you are looking for, or you do, and you can't find them through a phone or email lookup, and are hoping to find them through a professional or social affiliation. In either case, specialized group-finder tools may be the best route for your search. Also, trade associations are great ways to find specific people with specific knowledge. (See Chapter 9, Business Tools, for more information about finding associations.)

Often, linking a name to an activity or a job will help you pin down specific information. For example if you search for "Edward Egan" you will get references to several law professors and others who have the name of Egan. But if you were looking for the Cardinal of the New York Archdiocese, combining his name with "New York" or "cardinal" will move the sites you are looking for directly to the top of a search engine's results list. Sometimes what you are looking for can be found through specific job-related finding tools. Here are the better ones, listed alphabetically by category:

Accountant Finder

CPA Directory
`www.cpadirectory.com`

This is a searchable directory of certified accountants and firms.

Architect Finders

American Institute of Architects (AIAA)
`www.aiaaaccess.com`

This is a searchable site to find architects in the U.S.

Aviation Professional Finders

Landings.com
`www.landings.com`

`www.landings.com/_landings/pages/search/certs-pilot.html` (pilots)

`www.landings.com/_landings/pages/search/certs-ap.html` (mechanics)

`www.landings.com/_landings/pages/search/certs-me.html` (medical examiners)

Landings is more than just a people-finding tool, it is also a great way to locate pilots, mechanics and even aviation medical examiners.

College and Alumni Related Finders
Alumni.Net
www.alumni.net

This site is a good starting place for locating people connected to international universities and alumni associations. It has more than 85,000 colleges listed.

American Alumni Directory
www.aad.net

Another good alumni-finding tool, this one goes as far back as some elementary schools. But it only includes those who have already registered.

American Universities
www.clas.ufl.edu/CLAS/american-universities.html

Compiled by the University of Florida, this is an excellent starting point to find basic information about specific colleges and universities. Searching individually on each academic institution will point you to find directories for students, teachers, and employees.

ClassMates Online
www.classmates.com

This is a valuable people-finding tool for anyone who has attended a U.S. or Canadian school. But you must register first, which means that you can't search anonymously. Once you register, however, it is a great way to find someone, or at least people who may know where the person you are looking for may be now.

Colleges and Universities Web Site Links
www.mit.edu:8001/people/cdemello/geog.html

From the MIT main site you can access Christina DeMello's alphabetical listings of 3,000 colleges and universities from all over the world. Navigating this site is very difficult. If you are looking for worldwide sites, you will need language translation tools. (See Chapter 10, International Research for more information on translation tools.)

Colleges Email Finder
www.qucis.queensu.ca/FAQs/e-mail/college.html

This is an excellent collection of college email finders from around the world.

Friends Reunited
www.friendsreuinted.co.uk

A database of over 40,000 U.K. secondary and primary schools, colleges and universities with more than 4.5 million people registered. This site also allows you to search for workplace alumni.

Phonebook – Server Lookup
www.uiuc.edu/cgi-bin/ph/lookup

This site gives you access to hundreds of college campus phone books in the U.S..

School News
www.schoolnews.com

Another good tool for finding high school and college alumni associations. Like ClassMates, you must register to see the database.

UCSD Science and Engineering Library: People & Organizations
http://scilib.ucsd.edu/peopleorg/people.html#

A strong collection of science-related people-finding tools.

Universities.com
www.universities.com

This lists more than 4,500 colleges and universities around the world.

Information Broker Finders

The two sites below are places to locate information brokers – or researchers-for-hire – from all over the world. This is a great resource to help you locate people who can help you find not-easy-to-find information either online or elsewhere.

Association of Independent Information Professionals – AIIP
www.aiip.org/memberdirectoryhome.asp

The Association of Independent Information Professionals is made up of terrific researchers for hire, many with specific research strengths from like medical research, pharmaceutical to competitive intelligence.

Burwell's
www.burwellinc.com/bedirectory.html

Another fine collection of for-hire researchers.

Legal Profession Finders

AttorneyFind
www.attyfind.com/home.html

A great resource for locating lawyers; look-up by specialty and geographic area rather than name.

Federal Judicial Center
www.fjc.gov

U.S. government site contains biographies for all judges who have ever served in federal courts.

Martindale-Hubbell Lawyer Locator
www.martindale.com/maps/../locator/home.html

For lawyers and their bios, put up by long-time legal directory publisher Martindale-Hubbell.

Net Legal

www.netlegal.com

This is a great Canadian legal site that includes a good people-finding tool for lawyers in that country.

West Legal Directory

www.lawoffice.com/direct/direct.asp

Another excellent directory of lawyers put up by West Publishing of Westlaw Publications fame.

Medical Finders

Dentist Finders

American Dental Association

www.ada.org/public/directory/index.html

This is a searchable database from the American Dental Association – but a dentist must be a member to show up in the database.

Dentist Register and Rolls of Dental Auxiliaries U.K.

www.gdc-uk.org/search_ind.htm

The U.K. registry for dentists and dental staff.

Doctor Finders

ABMS Certified Database

www.abms.org

The American Board of Medical Specialties has a directory of credentialed medical specialists. It recognizes twenty-four medical specialty boards and is searchable, you must be a registered member to search for free.

AIM (Administrators in Medicine) DocFinder

www.docboard.org/search

A database of licensed physicians. Not all states are covered, but this site brings together the official licensing boards for many states.

American Medical Association Physician Select

www.ama-assn.org/aps/amahg.htm

This gives you the American Medical Association's Physician Select listing of licensed doctors. For their addresses and credentials, click on "AMA Health Insight."

Canadian Doctor Finder

`www.cpso.on.ca/Doctor_Search/dr_srch_hm.htm`

This is the Canadian College of Physicians and Surgeons of Ontario, and it can be searched by name or specialty.

ChoiceTrust

`www.choicetrust.com`

This is a free site from ChoicePoint that allows you to check the basic bio information on doctors, dentists, and chiropractors. For an additional US$9.95 you can get their medical credentials and see if they have ever been brought up for sanctions by the appropriate medical boards. Most of this material is available from different state agencies, but it is nicely pulled together in an easy-to-use web site.

Mental Health Finders

National Register of Health Service Providers in Psychology

`www.nationalregister.com`

This is the largest U.S. credentialing organization for psychologists in the U.S. Registration is required to search – you will have to send an email to the webmaster to start the process.

Health & Medicine Information Tools

By Susan M. Detwiler and John E. Levis

When you're sick, everyone has advice to offer. Your Aunt Tillie knows someone with your condition who ended up in the hospital; your friend's mother developed a severe rash all over her body because of it; your grandmother called to say she was sending over a "sure cure" — a pot of chicken soup made from her secret recipe. It's a fact of life that when you're sick, you're fair game for self-proclaimed experts.

The Internet has made your grandmother's secret chicken soup recipe available to everyone. Technology has made it possible for anyone with a few dollars and some spare time to set up a web sites hyping this cure and that, or offering up "what worked for me."

At the same time, the Internet has become a rich tapestry of scientific and medical truth, woven by truly knowledgeable people, cross-linked to each other by meta-sites and specialty search engines.

Avoid the personal web sites by avoiding the general search engines, and start instead with a good site specializing in health matters. One of the best is the U.S. Government's MedlinePlus at `www.medlineplus.gov`. This site lets you look for information by health topic or disease, lets you search by drug name, and offers dictionaries and directories. Its special section of other resources leads you to libraries and associations. For in-depth medical searching, MedlinePlus offers a link to Medline, the unparalleled repository of citations to clinical medical articles, sorted, categorized, abstracted, and indexed by our own U.S. government's National Library of Medicine (NLM). After decades of requiring the public to use a commercial vendor or dial direct for electronic access to this database (and its sister databases Toxline, Aidsline, Cancerlit, and Physicians Data Query, to name just a few), the government now makes Medline available almost everywhere. Using it through MedlinePlus brings you to PubMed, which links the results to full-text copies of many of the articles, with the opportunity to purchase articles that aren't available online.

For a more consumer friendly interface, or if you want to focus on one health topic on a regular basis, you might want to check out a commercial site.

One of our favorites is Medscape, at `www.medscape.com`. Written for the professional, Medscape requires registration but is free to use. It offers professional level coverage of medical specialties, and access to Medline and prescribing level drug information. If your interest is cardiovascular, you can opt to have the Cardiovascular home page show at each visit. Same for a number of other specialties. It doesn't ignore the layperson's understanding of health, either. Medscape provides well-written patient education materials which physicians – or you – can print out.

Medscape is owned by WebMD, which has a consumer level information site at `http://my.webmd.com`. While plastered with advertising, WebMD makes it clear which parts are supplied by their 'partners' and which come from the WebMD editorial staff. Information about diseases and conditions is easy to understand, and drug information is straightforward. There are also several discussion groups centering on different diseases, which act as online support groups for fellow sufferers. WebMD also recognizes that many of us take herbal medicines, by offering objective information about supplements such as melatonin or St. John's Wort.

Many medical centers and insurance companies have made it their mission to provide patient-friendly health information on their websites. A good example of this is the University of Texas M. D. Anderson Cancer Center at `www.mdanderson.org`. M. D. Anderson is an excellent resource for cancer patients. It provides basic information on understanding cancer, treatment research, cancer prevention and information on becoming a patient at M. D. Anderson. The insurance company Aetna created the subsidiary Intelihealth, at `www.intelihealth.com`, featuring information from Harvard Medical School and University of Pennsylvania School of Dental Medicine. Particularly useful on the Intelihealth site are descriptions of common diagnostic tests and procedures, a "symptom scout," and a searchable drug information database.

Another way to begin your quest is to find the professional association of specialists who treat your disease. Several professional medical associations have banded together to create Medem, a one-stop shop for consumer medical information at `www.medem.com`. The information in its library comes from organizations such as the American Medical Association, The Society of

Addiction Medicine, the American College of Obstetrics and Gynecology, and the American Academy of Facial and Plastic Reconstructive Surgery. The site also offers a way to find a specialist in your area, as participating societies make their member databases searchable.

The American Dental Association is another favorite site. You'll find it at `www.ada.org`. If you want to know about fluoridation, crowns, tooth brighteners or sealants, here's the place to start. For professionals, there is access to the *Journal of the American Dental Association* (*JADA*), which provides major articles from the current issue and a searchable archive.

You can also find associations devoted to coverage of the disease itself. The American Cancer Society, found at `www.cancer.org`, is a good example. This site offers extensive information to cancer patients and their families. It offers advice on finding a doctor, alternative treatments and links to other resources. The Crohn's & Colitis Foundation of America at `www.ccfa.org`, is another site with excellent credentials and up-to-date information.

To find the association you need, you can use MedlinePlus as a resource, or carefully use the search engine Google. Enter your health topic and add the word "association." If it rises to the top of the Google heap, it is likely to be a reputable site. The first result when entering "congestive heart failure association" is the American Heart Association's page for CHF, `www.americanheart.org/chf`.

The U.S. government has made a lot more than just Medline available as a dependable information source. One of the best sites for health care is the National Institutes of Health (NIH) at `www.nih.gov`. If you're not sure which government agency researches your disease interest, there's an alphabetical listing of diseases and which unit is responsible. If you're a research scientist, you can find out how to apply for NIH grants or open job postings. There's also a link to ClinicalTrials.gov, `http://clinicaltrials.gov`, which helps you find out if new research is underway, and whether you or your loved one is eligible to be included.

One of the best sources for information on conventional cancer treatment is the National Cancer Institute (NCI) at `www.cancer.gov`. There you'll find cancer information written from the perspectives of patients, the media, health care professionals and basic researchers. At the link to Cancer Information, there is access to the Cancerlit database, the Journal of the National Cancer Institute, articles on cancer screening, and NCI's extensive cancer statistics. If your interest lies in other diseases, then the Centers for Disease Control and Prevention (CDC) at `www.cdc.gov` will be of interest. Click on Health Topics A-Z and up comes a laundry list of communicable diseases and topics like pollution. You can use this site to find out what inoculations you'll need before your next vacation and what precautions you'll need to take once you get there. Like most government sites, you'll find excellent statistics. If you're doing basic research, there's information on CDC-funded grants.

Perhaps your perspective is more from the business side of health and medicine. There are many credible sources for drug-related information. When drug companies test drugs, they go through clinical trials. You can check ClinicalTrials.gov (above), or try Centerwatch at `www.centerwatch.com`. Centerwatch is a reliable resource for finding trials. It's divided into two sections, Patient Resources and Industry Resources. The patient section has a listing of available trials by therapeutic category, and an email notification system that lets you know when new trials begin. Under Drug Directories there is information about new Food & Drug Administration (FDA) approvals and a primer on clinical research. The industry information section profiles clinical research centers, companies that provide contract services to the clinical trials industry and industry news. Both sections have relevant links to other sites of interest to patients, their advocates and health care professionals.

Then there are the extensive FDA web sites at `www.fda.gov` which accesses information about drugs for human use, biologics, medical devices and radiology, toxicology, medical products reporting and more. In addition to a search engine, there are links to other government agencies and access to the Code of Federal Regulations.

Another place to look for credible information on scientific, medical and health care topics is on the meta-sites produced by universities and medical centers. An incredible resource provided by medical librarians around the country is HealthWeb, at `http://healthweb.org`. Each medical school takes responsibility for pulling together lists of sites that are specific to a particular medical subject. Starting with HealthWeb, you know that the information you link to will be credible.

What if you need information in a language other than English? According to the most recent U.S. Census, almost fourteen percent of the United States population speaks a language other than English language at home, and six percent do not consider themselves proficient English speakers. Several good websites address this need. The Centers for Disease Control and Prevention has a Spanish language version of its site at `www.cdc.gov/spanish`. The National Institutes of Health has `http://salud.nih.gov`. Through the National Library of Medicine, the University of Utah Health Sciences Center maintains a set of patient education materials in Spanish at `www.med.utah.edu/pated/handouts/indexspan.cfm`. More scarce are non-English, non-Spanish resources. Two of the best are the New South Wales Multicultural Health Communication Service in Australia, `http://mhcs.health.nsw.gov.au` and the United Kingdom's National Health Service site, `www.equip.nhs.uk/language.html`. Each of these have offerings in an amazing array of languages, from Arabic and Farsi to Urdu and Vietnamese.

The amount of credible information about complementary and alternative medicine (CAM) is also expanding. An excellent source for information about increasingly prevalent herbal supplements is HerbMed, at `www.herbmed.org`. Here is a side by side comparison of the chemical properties of the substance, what folklore has to say about it, and what scientific studies have been done on it. It's a great place to check out the latest herbal craze. A division of the National Institutes of Health, the National Center for Complementary and Alternative Medicine (NCCAM), offers fact sheets and consensus reports on various therapies at `http://nccam.nih.gov`. There is also a link to the PubMed CAM database.

Finally, if you have doubts about any given web site's credibility or the advice it gives you, ask your doctor. Despite everything that's available, it's wise to remember that when it comes to your own medical care, your best source of information is your personal physician. And, unless your doctor advises otherwise, you can still have that bowl of chicken soup while seeking out more information.

-- Susan M. Detwiler is president of The Detwiler Group, an information consulting firm that has long specialized in the business side of medicine and health. She has testified before the White House Commission on Complementary and Alternative Medicine Policy, and is author of *Super Searchers on Health & Medicine: The Online Secrets of Top Health & Medical Researchers*. Address: sdetwiler@detwiler.com and www.detwiler.com.

-- John E. Levis is president of John E. Levis Associates, a longtime specialist in primary and secondary market research in healthcare and medicine, and a past president of the Association of Independent Information Professionals (AIIP). Address: john@jelevisassoc.com and www.jelevisassoc.com

Military Finders

Military.com
www.military.com/Military/Locator/New/Splash/

A community of military members from all branches and all levels of status (active duty, reserve, retirees, veterans), defense workers, family members, and enthusiasts that helps you find current and former military personnel. Registration is required.

Military Public Records Finders
www.publicrecordfinder.com/military.html

This is a good mega-site of military-finding tools for current and former U.S. military personnel.

Military Search
www.military-search.com

An excellent starting point for all kinds of military-related searches, including message boards to help you find people.

Searchmil.com
www.searchmil.com

While not a direct people-finding tool, it is a wonderful clearinghouse of military information and can be used to direct you to find information about specific military facilities around the world.

➔*hot tip:* **Think outside the box when you are looking for information about people. In addition to the obvious kinds of people-searching tools, there are lots of other places that information about people may be found. For example:**

- If someone is an amateur ham radio buff, that hobby requires a Federal Communications Commission license. A database of those can be found at a site at the University of Arkansas at Little Rock at: `http://callsign.ualr.edu/callsign.shtml`

- If someone is an avid collector, they may have posted notes on the Usenet database asking for information about that subject, or may have tried to buy something on an auction site like eBay (`www.ebay.com`).

- If you are looking for an expert on a particular subject, an unusual but effective place to look can be in newspaper archives or on book web sites like Amazon.com, and Barnes & Noble (`www.b&n.com`) where bios and reviews are usually listed, or at the Library of Congress where you can check out an author: (`http://lcweb.loc.gov/catalog/browse/bks3subj.html`).

- Can't find someone and think they might have a web presence? Try using a search tool to sniff out a personal home page. Home pages – even of relatives – often contain a surprising amount of personal information.

Expert Finders

There are hundreds of lists of experts and methods of reaching and querying them. One way is to use specialized subject directories like those listed in the search engines section. But there are some excellent places online that will guide you to experts on specific subjects. Several of them have been compiled by journalism organizations to help their reporters and others in the media. Most are open to the public to use and several are excellent. Some are simply glorified yellow pages or classified ads where people can buy their listings. You must make a determination that the source of the database is credible and not paid in order to trust its listings. (See Chapter 12 for tips about assessing accuracy and credibility.)

Here are a few of the best and most respected expert-finding tools:

Facsnet: Sources Online
`http://facsnet.org`

This list of valuable sources – think tanks, advocacy groups, special interest organizations as well as government, academic and private sector experts – was developed by the Foundation for American Communications, a journalism group. At the Facsnet main page, click on "News Sources" or "Cardfile" – both require free registration.

IRE Beat Pages
`www.ire.org/resourcecenter/initial-search-beat.html`

IRE, Investigative Reporters and Editors, a collection of news reporters and editors, has pulled together a collective resource center of knowledgeable people on specific issues or, as journalists call them, "beats."

National Press Club Directory of News Sources
http://npc.press.org

This excellent database, compiled by the National Press Club library staff is another good collection of experts.

ProfNet
www.profnet.com

PR Newswire, a public relations company, offers a database of more than 8,000 information officers from universities, colleges, and think tanks. Their job includes getting their experts known to the media, but it is open to the public. You can request an expert by subject matter through an email and these spokespersons respond to your request or you can search the database without their help.

Sources & Experts
http://metalab.unc.edu/slanews/internet/experts.html

A directory of directories compiled by researcher Kitty Bennett, it is maintained by the Special Libraries Association's News Division – an invaluable resource.

Other Expert-Finding Tools

Allexperts.com
www.allexperts.com

This free question-and-answer service has pulled together more than 4,000 volunteers to answer questions on over 1,000 topics. Be prepared because if you can't find the information easily, you can write the "experts" and wait until they contact you by email.

Google
www.google.com

Google has a great advanced research tool for finding experts.

Newswise
www.newswise.com

Another research tool geared to reporters, for questions on medicine, science and business. Your requests are submitted to more than 350 universities and research centers.

Pitsco's Ask an Expert
www.askanexpert.com

A collection of links to over 300 addresses where you can send questions via email or through forms on web pages. It is also searchable and is very useful.

Reference Desk
www.refdesk.com/expert.html

This wonderful online reference tool also lists a large collection of expert sites. Be careful, some are very credible and others are collections of paid-for listings. But many are good. The best part of this site is a huge list of places where you can ask an expert questions on all kinds of subjects. Test them out on a subject you are familiar with or can verify their recommendations elsewhere before putting your own credibility on the line.

Genealogy and Personal History Tools

One of the most powerful examples of how the Web is used to share information is in the area of genealogy. In addition to making official records such as birth, marriage, and death certificates available without traveling miles to read them in person, people are now able to share familial information and take advantage of other people's research. Many distant cousins who might never have met in person can now, from the bits and pieces of information they have gathered or inherited individually, piece together entire family histories. Obituaries are also useful tools for filling in the gaps of family information.

Additionally, families that were separated by adoption are now reuniting via registries for children of adoption as well as for parents who gave children up for adoption.

Sometimes you may want to gather some information about a person you are about to enter into business negotiations with, or just someone you are interested in learning more about, such as a celebrity or historical figure. Online biographies and photos are a helpful tool in "getting to know" someone before ever meeting them in person. Here are just a few of the many specialized tools in the area of genealogy and personal history:

Adoption Tools

Many researchers try to locate their own personal history or try and find information for friends. There are a lot of state-specific adoption tools in the U.S. These are excellent starting points:

National Adoption Information Clearinghouse
`www.calib.com/naic/`

A comprehensive resource on all aspects of adoption. The clearinghouse is a service of the U.S. Government's Administration for Children, Youth and Families, a part of the U.S. Department of Health and Human Service.

WWW Library of Adoptee-Related Sites
`www.bastards.org/library/`

This is an excellent collection of adoption information. One part of this site is the best starting point for researching your own family if you are looking to find your birth parents.

Biography Sites

Biography.com
`www.biography.com`

This site allows you to browse biographies of more than 28,000 prominent individuals. Some of the material is drawn from the A&E cable television channel that provides bios to the Biography and History channels.

Biography Center
www.biography-center.com

Another good collection of bios, this one includes photos and provides extensive details.

Biography Dictionary
www.s9.com/biography/

Another extensive collection of biographies, this is easy-to-use and provides detailed bios.

Buscabiografias
http://buscabiografias.com

A Spanish-language biography site with a good collection of world leaders, entertainers, etc. – both present and past.

Internet Public Library - Biographies
www.ipl.org/ref/RR/static/ref15.00.00.html

Another excellent reference tool on many subjects, its deep collection offers of all kinds of biographical resources.

Lives, The Biography Resource
http://amillionlives.com

This is an excellent collection of biographies, but it has not been updated for some time. What makes it outstanding is its special collection pages – featuring the Civil War, Holocaust Survivors and other specific topics.

People Tracker
www.forbes.com/peopletracker/

This site, from *Forbes Magazine*, tracks more than 120,000 executives from major corporations around the world. Registration is free, but required.

World Biographical Index
www.biblio.tu-bs.de/wbi_en/

This is a great world collection of biographies with short, fact profiles.

xrefer
http://xrefer.com

This is actually a meta-search engine, but its database of reference books from many major publishers is extensive. As a result, it has a superb collection of bios. The search tool is simple, but what makes this really useful is the cross-referencing and adjacent entries to the right of your results. You will need to read the help page to get maximum use of this, but it is definitely worth the effort.

Genealogy Resources

There are thousands of excellent online resources for genealogical research. Here are a few that are simply a cut above the rest.

About.com – Genealogy Site

http://genealogy.about.com

Another of the excellent About.com sites, this one is a great starting point for beginners on genealogy and offers site reviews, newsletters, census resources, and a great collection of research sites for kids.

Ancestry.com

www.ancestry.com

Ancestry.com is a leading resource for family history online. The site offers over 1 billion names in over 3,000 unique databases. With a paid subscription base of over 500,000 Ancestry.com is the third largest paid subscription site on the Internet behind ConsumerReports.org and the Wall Street Journal's WSJ.com.

The American Family Immigration History Center

www.ellisislandrecords.org

Another incredible resource, this searchable database provides information on the twenty-two million immigrants and ship's crew who arrived at Ellis Island and the Port of New York between 1898 and 1924. Free registration allows searches to be saved and records to be annotated.

Census Online

www.census-online.com

Provides links to U.S. and Canadian census information broken down by county or province.

Cyndi's List of Genealogy Sites on the Internet

www.cyndislist.com

This is a staggering collection of resources – more than 123,000 links organized and cross-referenced into over 150 categories. It started as Cyndi Howell's personal collection and she's turned it into a profit-making and fun career. If you don't know anything about genealogy, this is the place to start. She started it in 1996, and over 2.6 million visitors have been to it since.

FamilySearch Internet Genealogy Service

http://familysearch.org

The Church of Jesus Christ of Latter-day Saints, also known as the Mormon Church, has built a truly worldwide collection of genealogical links. What makes this site so valuable is its easily searchable collection of 35 million names in its Ancestral File, and over 360 million names in the International Genealogical Index. It also has excellent instructions for beginners on how to conduct genealogy research for your own family.

Genealogy.com
`www.genealogy.com`

While this site is not as deep as Cindy's list or the Mormon church site, it is valuable for its how-to instructions and reference information on genealogy research. It also has a good family-finder search capability.

Olive Tree Genealogy – Ships' Passengers
`http://olivetreegenealogy.com/ships/toukp01.shtml`

If you know your ancestors traveled by ship from one country to another, you may be able to track down important information about them via ship passenger lists. This site also provides other databases of lists, such as church records and land deeds.

RootsWeb.com
`www.rootsweb.com/rootsweb/`

Another excellent searchable site with family trees, surname and genealogical mailing lists, and message boards. Ancestry.com now sponsors this site, although it is free to all users. Also tied to this site is an incredible discussion list, `www.rootsweb.com/roots-l/` that is also searchable and contains all kinds of tips from those who have already researched their own family's genealogy.

Social Security Death Index
`http://ssdi.rootsweb.com/`
`www.ancestry.com/search/rectype/vital/ssdi/main.htm`

These two sites offer free versions of the Social Security Death Index, a public record resource that is an incredible genealogy resource. It allows you to find obituaries, confirm that someone is dead, discover cemetery records and locate a death certificate or track down probate records –all important tools in researching genealogy.

Southern Quaker Genealogy
`www.geocities.com/Heartland/Plains/2064/squaker.htm`

Religious organizations usually kept good records about their members. This site is one example of the types of sites you can look for – it narrows the information to a religion (Quaker) and a region (Southern U.S.).

U.K. Family History Online
`www.familyrecords.gov.uk/`

This British-based site is another excellent collection of records for birth, death, marriage, military, adoption and other kinds of information.

USGenWeb Project
`www.usgenweb.org`

This one is U.S.-focused, but these are extensive worldwide resources – lots of them. It pulls together all of the state's genealogy web sites, but inevitably that leads to sites all over the world. Another terrific reference site for genealogy.

Obituaries

Obituaries can be a useful resource in people-finding research. They often lead you to other family members and past employers. Here are a few of the better obit-finding tools.

ObitFinder

www.legacy.com

This site contains more than a million recent obituaries from American and Canadian newspapers. To go back further, you will need to use one of the newspaper archives pay sites. (See the fee-based tools section later in this chapter as well as Chapter 8, News Resources.) Click on the search button to target your search..

Obituary Daily Times

www.rootsweb.com/~obituary/

Another site from the folks that bring you free access to the Social Security Death Index, this is a database of citations to published obituaries in newspaper from the U.S. and Canada.

Vital Records

See Chapter 7, Public Records for details and the best sites.

Mapping Tools

It is one thing to find a person; it is another to find a location. That's where mapping tools come in handy. The Internet is a terrific tool for maps; it easily handles graphics, and is more convenient to update than printed maps. Many map sites exist on the Web that give you directions, that tell you how to find biking routes in Algeria, or provide a view of the earth from outer space. Some companies have even developed special software that allow you to build your own map, while others offer features like notations of famous places.

Nearly all of the people-finding tools have a free mapping feature, which provide maps of and to the location of the person or business that you're seeking.

One thing to note, when you need to work with a large amount of map data, or need to be able to print out customized maps, you may decide to buy one of the many map software programs that you install on your hard drive, which you can supplement with downloads from the Internet. For example, the *Thomas Guide* (www.thomas.com) is a popular print and software map for many metropolitan areas in the U.S. The web product is further enhanced by the ability to download census information, such as median household income or median house price. Some of the best online mapping tools are:

All The World's Maps

www.embassyworld.com/maps/maps.html

This excellent site provides access to national maps for almost every country in the world. It also has a great collection of telephone directories, helps you find area codes, country codes for dialing, and embassy details for many countries. It is easily searchable, but be aware that cookies must be enabled to view all the map choices.

Atlas of Cyberspaces
www.cybergeography.org/atlas/atlas.html

This is an unusual collection of map-related information. It has all kinds of maps from artistic ones to geographic and topological. It's worth spending some time to roam around this site. Also available in Italian and Spanish, think of this site as the instructional site for how maps can be used.

DeLorme
www.delorme.com

By the creator of *The Street Atlas* software maps, this site generates door-to-door address routing and offers access to many of DeLorme's other products.

Expedia's Maps
www.expedia.com/pub/agent.dll?qscr=over&rfrr=357&&&&dchg=&&zz=10148
76791232&

Expedia, the Microsoft-owned travel network, has added an extensive collection of U.S. and European maps to its web site, allowing you to get point-to-point directions, find your hotels on the maps, and also save them to your profile for frequent use – a useful tool.

Goode's World Atlas
www.goodesatlas.com

To promote the 20th edition of *Goode's World Atlas*, Rand McNally offers thirty thematic maps and outline maps of the world, the fifty U.S. states, and the continents.

MapQuest
www.mapquest.com

Allows you to view an atlas, zoom in and out of a locality, locate specific addresses, get city-to-city or street-to-street driving information and locate convenience stores and automatic teller machines. In addition, the mapping feature gives user-friendly directions like "take a right" instead of "go northwest" – a real plus for the direction-impaired.

Maps On Us
www.mapsonus.com

A map, route and yellow pages service, when you enter a street address, a map of the area appears onscreen. Registration is required for some free, customized services.

MapBlast!
www.mapblast.com

Offers interactive mapping service using U.S. road maps. You can create maps of any vicinity and email them too, or download them to your handheld device.

National Atlas of the United States of America
www-atlas.usgs.gov

Offers official U.S. government maps – atlas style.

National Geographic
www.nationalgeographic.com

At the site index, click on Maps.

National Geologic Map Database
http://ngmdb.usgs.gov

The U.S. Geological Survey offers a great maps collection with the ability to search and find locations in many different ways. Very easy to use and useful.

Odden's Bookmarks:
The Fascinating World of Maps and Mapping
http://oddens.geog.uu.nl/index.html

Another extensive collection of links to maps, geographical societies and things cartographic.

Perry-Castaneda Library Map Collection
www.lib.utexas.edu/Libs/PCL/Map_collection/Map_collection.html

Another great collection of more than 230,000 maps.

Space Imaging
www.spaceimaging.com

This excellent site is particularly good for getting satellite images of any part of the world. The company operates a satellite that can see the entire earth. Its business is to sell those images, but you can view them for free. Its images have generated lots of news over the past couple of years, including providing the first independent confirmation of the status of the U.S. Navy EP-3 that was forced down on Hainan Island in China in 2001 and the first imagery from above of the World Trade Center destruction and the Pentagon after the September 11, 2001 attacks.

Teleatlas
www.teleatlas.com

Teleatlas' ETAK's SkyMap and geo-coding technology allows you to attach a global positioning (GPS) device to your laptop or wireless device, and helps find you anywhere on the planet. The company has added a very useful new capability – providing real-time traffic reports to your wireless or web device in sixty-five U.S. cities.

U.S. Census Bureau
www.census.gov

The Census Bureau has an incredible collection of maps, which you recreate to your own specifications by clicking on the Geography section of the main page. See Chapter 6, Government Resources for more information on the Census Bureau site.

USGS Geographic Names Information System
http://geonames.usgs.gov/gnisform.html

This is a terrific site that allows you to point a spot on the map and get all kinds of information like elevation, population, description, and history for the U.S. and also for worldwide sites. It is pulled together by the U.S. Geological Survey.

USGS National Mapping Information
http://mapping.usgs.gov

At the U.S. Geological Survey's site, in addition to mapping data, you can order maps.

Yahoo! Maps
http://maps.yahoo.com/py/maps/py

Putting directions in simple lefts and rights instead of northwest and southeast makes this a valuable tool for the directionally impaired.

Ready Reference Tools

When they need a quick fact or two, librarians reach over to a shelf of fact-finding tools known as "ready reference" – materials that include almanacs, encyclopedias, dictionaries, a thesaurus or two, and quotation sources. Not surprisingly, many of these are now available on the Internet.

There are also virtual libraries on the Internet – dozens of them, many of which are tied to universities. Plus, you can always try the enormous caverns of the virtual Library of Congress (www.loc.gov). Few, if any, libraries put complete texts online, but, many have made their catalogs searchable over the Internet and others are developing digital archives. Online listings tell you what library resources are available, and many web sites have Frequently Asked Questions (FAQ) summaries available on all kinds of subjects.

Acronym Dictionary
www.ucc.ie/info/net/acronyms/acro.html

This was the first acronym database on the Web and is extremely useful.

Britannica's Internet Guide (formerly Britannica)
www.britannica.com

The company behind the world-famous encyclopedia now offers the contents of the encyclopedia for free on the Web – and it's accurate and comprehensive. It now also offers a reasonably priced premium service (US$7.95/month, US$50 per year,) that offers much greater depth of resources. The company's literature used to call it the "thinking man's guide to the Web" because of its evaluations of web sites on a variety of subjects.

CIA World Factbook
www.cia.gov/cia/publications/factbook/index.html

The CIA compiles a thorough country-by-country index with details on governmental structure and geo-political impact regionally and globally. It also includes geographic and demographic detail.

Encyclopedia Smithsonian FAQs
www.si.edu/resource/faq/start.htm

The Smithsonian Institution receives a great many public inquiries covering a wide range of topics. As a result, they have compiled FAQs on many topics from aeronautics to zoology. This one is free and excellent.

Encyclopedia.com
www.encyclopedia.com

Based on *The Concise Columbia Electronic Encyclopedia*, now a part of the E-Library, the site provides current information available in all major fields of knowledge – from politics, law, art, and history to sports, literature, geography, science and medicine. More than 50,000 articles provide free, quick and useful information on almost any topic. Like many of the library sites, it does not provide full-text resources, but rather, short article summaries. Encyclopedia.com also provides links to a fee-based service, Electric Library, where users can find extensive full-text materials.

Information Please
www.infoplease.com

Another excellent encyclopedia comes from The Learning Network folks who make the *Information Please* almanacs. This site offers almanacs, dictionaries, encyclopedias and extensive educational tools for children, teenagers and students.

Internet Public Library (IPL) Ready Reference Collection
www.ipl.org/ref/RR/

Extremely thorough and wonderfully put together, the IPL is set up like a real building with a reading room and a reference center. The reference center is of particular value to researchers because of the well-organized way in which it has been constructed. Its ready reference section is worth spending some time on, so you know what's available when you need it in a pinch.

iTools
www.itools.com/research

A very useful collection of reference material, including full-text dictionaries and thesauruses as well as translations, acronyms, biographies and maps.

RefDesk
www.refdesk.com

An easy-to-use collection of links – including facts-at-a-glance and fact finders – an outstanding collection of sites.

St. Ambrose University – Best Information on the Internet – Online Reference Resources

http://library.sau.edu/bestinfo/Online/onlindex.htm

Best Information on the Internet is a wonderful collection from the librarians at St. Ambrose University in Iowa that links great collections of statistics from the census, political polling data, demographic information, universal currency converters and personal finance calculators.

U.S. Census Bureau

www.census.gov

The census is also a great resource for reference material. See Chapter 6, Government Resources for detailed descriptions.

Useless Facts

www.uselessfacts.net

You never know when you are going to need a reference site for useless facts. This one is loaded with good (but useless) material, like one year contains 31,557,600 seconds and the world record for rocking non-stop in a rocking chair is 440 hours. Essential information, right?

Virtual Reference Desk

www.lib.purdue.edu/vlibrary

This collection is a model for a well-organized, well-researched web site, courtesy of the librarians at Purdue University. It includes dictionaries, phone books, maps, science information, and other reference materials.

Specific Reference Tools

Calculators

Convert It

www.convertit.com/Go/ConvertIt/Measurement/Converter.ASP

An easy-to-use measurement conversion calculator.

Convert Me

www.convert-me.com/en

An interactive calculator with options such as converting measurements into metric and old Greek and Roman equivalents.

MegaConverter

www.megaconverter.com

This site has more than three dozen calculators, some easy-to-use, others not. Be aware that this site opens several windows so make sure your browser can handle it.

Online Conversions
www.onlineconversion.com

This site converts almost any measurement in any way possible – a good site to know about.

Dictionaries

Merriam-Webster Online
www.merriam-webster.com

This is most of the *Webster's Collegiate Dictionary* online – more than 160,000 entries as well as a thesaurus – an excellent reference tool.

WordReference.com
http://wordreference.com

An excellent, large bilingual dictionary for English to Spanish, and other languages. It allows you to translate one word at a time and also to install links so you can translate any work you select with your browser.

yourDictionary.com
www.yourdictionary.com

Think of this as the dictionary of dictionaries. It is an easy-to-use collection of more than 1800 dictionaries in more than 250 languages – maintained by Dr. Robert Beard of Bucknell University.

FAQs

FAQ (rhymes with shack) documents – acronym for Frequently Asked Questions – are excellent reference tools to get up to speed on a subject you don't know much about. They answer all of your frequently asked questions and are prepared in advance by those designing sites (who often get tired of answering the same questions over and over again).

There are several good FAQ indices on the Internet. Among the best ones are:

Internet FAQ Archives
www.faqs.org/faqs

Usenet FAQs
www.faqs.org/usenet

If you want to find a FAQ, try this search on a good search engine:

    +title:topic +faq

Or, substitute a one-word description of your interest in place of the word "topic." For example,

    +title:hepatitis +faq

Time Aids

Time and Date

`http://timeanddate.com`

This is a great reference tool – a guide to time, time zones, calendars and more. It helps you get the current time and date for more than 500 cities worldwide.

World Time Server

`www.worldtimeserver.com`

Another good resource to find the correct time anywhere in the world. It also allows you to download a free utility for Windows users that links you to the Atomic Clock and updates your clock to the exact time.

Worldtime

`www.worldtime.com`

Another time resource on the Web, this one is searchable by country name, and has some other cool interactive features.

Quotation Finders

Bartlett's Familiar Quotations

`www.bartleby.com/quotations`

Columbia University's Project Bartleby Archive provides a terrific collection of quotations, including the 1919 Bartlett version, as well as collections of ancient, biblical and Shakespearean quotes.

Creative Quotations

`http://creativequotations.com`

Another good searchable database of more than 25,000 quotations from almost 3,000 people – current and historic.

The Quotations Page

`www.quotationspage.com`

A searchable database of quotations compiled from quotation resources on the 'Net.

Yahoo! Reference: Quotations

`http://education.yahoo.com/reference/bartlett/`

Collection of sites where you can pin down quotations and who said them.

Networking and "Human Element" Tools

One of the greatest strengths of the Internet is the ability to find other people who can help you. You've already seen that if you've looked at the expert-finding section. But, in addition to academic and professional experts, there are people who have practical life experience with a subject.

You may need to identify people who've undergone certain experiences, or who possess a range of opinions. You can find them in the various types of interactive discussion forums. They all share one thing – opinions. Lots and lots of opinions – and experiences – about every subject imaginable. Some credible, some far from credible, so be on the alert.

The Internet is an ideal medium for accommodating and storing personal opinions. But, don't forget that people can and do lie, especially online where it's easy and convenient to create new online identities. This is especially true in chat rooms and newsgroups. It is not easy to ascertain if an online identity is genuine.

If you can't find something, somewhere on the 'Net is someone who knows about the subject you are looking for. Remember, among the reference interview questions to ask yourself is, "where do you find someone who knows about the subject or has real experience on that subject?" People are the hidden gems of the Internet, people will help a total stranger if you ask them nicely enough.

There are several types of discussion groups, chat rooms and other interactive resources. Many of them accommodate unconventional points of view and personal accounts. While you can find experts and knowledgeable people in all of them, you can also go on wild goose chases, so be skeptical until a "source" proves itself.

Usenet Newsgroups

Newsgroups are online discussion groups that have nothing to do with news. The beauty of newsgroups is that they accommodate everyone – *everyone*. Militia members, pornographers, and cultists of every stripe – they're all out there. So are, as Dave Barry likes to say, teenagers, poets, cat lovers, religious people, gays, gay teens who read religious poetry to cats and, of course, guys who have pointless arguments about sports. You can also find eyewitnesses to every experience imaginable. Newsgroup members talk to each other in groups, and you can read and respond, since newsgroups are public forums. You can "eavesdrop" on the discussion without participating, or respond privately to messages that interest you via email. All newsgroups comprise what is called the "Usenet" portion of the Internet.

Hands-down, the ultimate collection of Usenet postings is the former Deja News collection, now a part of Google (www.groups.google.com). It includes more than 800 million postings dating back to 1981, and is searchable on thousands of topics cataloged since the early 1990s.

➜ *hot tip:* **Consider the life span of newsgroup postings. Assume that anything you post to a newsgroup will be there forever unless you delete it using Google (http://groups.google.com). This goes for some mailing lists, too.**

So how do you use Usenet groups to find what you are looking for? First you need to understand how they are organized. Here's a primer on how it works.

A Newsgroup Primer

A newsgroup's address is its identity. For example, **alt.backrubs** is an address and a clear indication of topic. Newgroups belong to one of a growing number of subject categories, and are identified according to their addresses. Here's a primer:

alt is about alternative subjects and views, non-mainstream and is less categorically rigid than the other categories.

bionet is for biology and environmental-related newsgroups.

bit is an odd collection of mailing list groups that want to be cross-indexed within newsgroups, and runs the gamut from blues and bluegrass music to travel and transplants.

biz harbors mostly business-related discussions. A good place for company announcements and job leads, it is especially good for checking out competitors.

comp means computer-related.

k12 is geared to teachers and kids from kindergarten through high school.

misc is short for miscellaneous. This is a collection of things that don't fit elsewhere – "**misc**" is wide-ranging.

news is a misnomer. This is about updates and announcements concerning the newsgroups themselves, not about current news events.

newusers is for Usenet beginners. Lots of valuable tips and suggestions tend to appear here.

rec stands for recreation. For example, **rec.music.acapella** is one of more than forty other rec groups.

sci describes science-related discussion.

soc describes discussions of social and cultural topics, including country-by-country discussions at **soc.culture**.

talk denotes a group for opinions. Unsubstantiated rumors, absolute falsehoods and idle conjecture are here as well.

There are few newsgroup rules to begin with and virtually anyone can start a newsgroup. Some come and go quickly. "Alts" represent the widest cross-section of the Internet. When Tonya Harding and Nancy Kerrigan had their famous skating clash, the newsgroup **alt.kill.tonyaharding,die,die,die** popped up overnight. Currently there are similarly titled newsgroups about preschool icons Barney and the Teletubbies. More than thirty-five countries have their own newsgroups. Nearly every state in the U.S. has developed its own newsgroup, as have private companies. While the actual discussions may appear largely trivial, some groups, like `sci.med.diseases.cancer` and `alt.support.cancer` are great ways to find support and comfort for people and loved ones who are facing a disease.

Now that you understand the anatomy of newsgroups, here are some tips for searching them.

Searching Newsgroups

The golden key to searching newsgroups is Google (`http://groups.google.com`). Google – formerly Deja – is a free tool that catalogs the entire Usenet – or newsgroup – portion of the Internet. Google says it now consists of more than 800 million postings with over 35,000 categories, accounting for more than 500 gigabytes of disk space (the equivalent of about 500,000 400-page novels). And the volume is skyrocketing.

Another valuable way to research is Supernews (`www.supernews.com`), which offers a clean way to read Usenet postings. The only downside is that you can't easily search for specific messages as you can on Google. That's where Google shines. There are also several search engines that will hunt through newsgroups and retrieve postings – AltaVista and HotBot, for example. But Google is unquestionably the most thorough tool that monitors postings. Using Google is fairly simple – there's a "Basic Search," in which you submit a key term and wait. It will retrieve the most recent postings on that subject. To find a newsgroup about a subject of interest, click on the "Interest Finder." If you've already decided on a particular newsgroup, enter it through the "Browse Groups" option.

Search Options   help

Limit Search
these options help to further narrow your search

Organize Results
these options help to organize your search results

Match ⦿ all ○ any keywords

Language | any ▾ |

Example: FAQ or (frequently asked questions)

Subject | failure |

Results format
| tabular ▾ |

Example: alt.tv.x-files or "x-files"

Forum | alt.support.impotence |

Sort by
| confidence ▾ |

Example: demos@dejanews.com

Author | |

Results per page
| 25 ▾ |

Example: Apr 1 1997   Example: Apr 5 1997

Date | | | |
       from   to

There are also several more sophisticated search methods. By clicking on "Advanced Search," you can limit the number of postings by date; you can also isolate a particular posting. Say, for example, you wanted to locate someone who wasn't happy with Viagra. First you would use the Interest Finder to locate groups discussing Viagra. Most probably, your choice would be `alt.support.impotence`. Then click on "Power Search" and type "`alt.support.impotence`" into the space for Forum Name. Then submit the word "failure" in the subject field and run the query (see below). You'll get several postings.

You can also click on Author Profile to find other postings by that person. Smart users of Google use the "author profile" to get background information on people who have written about subjects of interest. To find the "author profile," go through "Advanced Search" on the front page.

You can take a poster's email address and put it through one or more people finder tools to come up with a name and address for that person – and other information. Of course, the reverse is also true. Keep that in mind before posting a message yourself.

Proper "netiquette" insists that before you post any kind of question, see if the subject has already been discussed in its FAQs archives. You can search the Google web site for a FAQ by inputting your subject of interest. Learn web manners from a netiquette primer maintained by Florida Atlantic University at `www.fau.edu/netiquette/net/`.

Case Study: Uncovering Government Abuse

By Dave Wickham

I am an electrician, and I often monitor Usenet newsgroups in search of timely information to include in a web page that I maintain covering fly-fishing on the Yakima River in Washington State. While browsing a fly-fishing newsgroup, an article caught my attention – not because of its content, but because the author used the same small local Internet provider I was using. The article, an offer to sell fishing tackle, asked respondents to contact an email address that was on a Washington state government server. He had posted this article from his home but was using his work account to receive requests for information.

I responded and the next day received three phone messages, as well as two emails originating from the Washington State Department of Social and Health Services. I began trying to track this person's activity on Usenet. The problem was that news servers usually only maintain postings for a few days. Google (`http://groups.google.com`), however, has archived Usenet articles for several years and provides search capabilities within this archive. I was able to retrieve all of this person's posts and discovered that, by using wildcards in the search string, I could retrieve Usenet posts originating from all Washington state government servers. For example, I could search for an individual at the Department of Social and Health Services (`user@dshs.wa.gov`) or I could use the asterisk wildcard to search for anyone posting from a Washington State government domain (`*.wa.gov`).

Browsing these retrieved postings, it was apparent that there were many state employees using the state system for personal use and pleasure at their offices. I compiled a portfolio of the worst examples of misuse and emailed a summary to every newspaper and television station in Washington that had an email address. I was sure that this information could lead to a great investigative story. The story would show government employees wasting time and would be easily verifiable.

But, only one media organization responded, and its reporter failed to follow up on a story. I was left with only one way to publicize the issue: the Internet. With help from my Internet Service Provider – which was willing to risk hosting a controversial and potentially high-volume site – the Public Servants' Internet Abuse Page was established at `www.adsnet.net/states.htm`. This page cites many of the examples I found, as well as a description of the method I used to acquire them.

The web page came to the attention of an Associated Press reporter in nearby Yakima, who used the web page and her own research to write an article about government employee Internet abuse that ran on the front pages of major newspapers in Washington and across the country. Since the article appeared, I have been contacted by hundreds of reporters, many of whom have used Google and similar archives to monitor Usenet activity by government employees on national, state, county and local levels. Stories uncovering similar abuses have appeared in the *Detroit News*, *Cleveland Plain Dealer*, *Portland Oregonian*, *Miami Herald* and several smaller papers. The web page was also described in *Editor and Publisher* magazine.

It is ironic that when I first placed the page on the Internet, I was trying to publicize an issue for which I'd been unable to get media coverage. These days, by far the majority of queries I receive are from reporters asking how to research a specific area or government agency. It's gratifying that these reporters then go on to write stories that are influencing how government employees are permitted to use the Internet during their working hours.

-- Dave Wickham is creator of the Public Servant's Internet Abuse Page.
Web Site: `www.adsnet.net/states.htm`   email: `davew@inlandnet.com`

To use `http://groups.google.com` and do the same kind of search Dave did, you need to go to the advanced groups file, put the "`*.wa.gov`" or whatever the subject is in the subject box and make sure you search by date or you will get results back to 1994.

Online Communities

Online communities are typically a hybrid of a content web site and message boards. Often they lure you in with useful articles, which you typically have found via a search engine, but hook you into coming back on a regular basis by connecting you to other people with similar interests through a message board section of the site. These message boards allow you to post messages and respond to posts, much like a newsgroup, but that do not use the Usenet structure of the Internet. Most of these sites are free, but some require registration or a user name.

The power of these sites is that they both offer "professional" content, usually written by staff members, as well as the personal experiences and tips from "regular people" on the message board. Often these do indeed become communities – a place where everyone "knows" everyone and communicate regularly both on the board and off the board.

There isn't a single catalog of all of these online communities, but you will often discover them as you research your topic. You may find that participating in these communities will bring you a wealth of information not available in the more formal sources of information on the Internet. They also help keep you entertained and may help you locate friends who have similar interests.

These online communities range from professional to personal. You can find an online community for virtually any topic that interests more than two people. Some examples are included below.

AllPM.com
www.allpm.com

A site for project managers that offers articles, templates, links and other tools for project managers. The "Forums" section provides multiple message boards to discuss topics such as career advancement and project management theory, and to ask for help with specific issues.

Beliefnet
www.beliefnet.com

Dedicated to discussing religions of all types, the content on this site ranges from the silly to the serious. Delve into the discussion areas and you will find message boards for dozens of religions, as well as topics such as death, prayer, spirituality, racism, and other heavy topics.

CruiseCritic
www.cruisecritic.com

If you are planning a cruise, you may want to stop by this site and check out the planning guides and other travel information, as well as the multiple message boards reviewing cruise lines, destinations, and debating every aspect of cruise life.

iVillage
www.ivillage.com

Intended to be an online community for women, iVillage has content and message boards for all aspects of life including health, home and garden, parenting, and more.

Organizedhome.com
www.organizedhome.com

A site for modern homemakers and neat freaks alike, the articles here range from pantry planning to using handheld computers for household management. The message boards section is divided into several categories such as decorating, holiday planning, cleaning techniques, cooking and kitchen planning, and money management.

Parent Soup
www.parentsoup.com

Kids don't come with manuals, so parents turn to sites like this for advice and guidance. In addition to its parenting guides – divided by age group – Parent Soup has message boards covering popular topics such as ADD, spanking, and daycare.

Scrapbookaddict.com
www.scrapbookaddict.com

The hobby of scrapbooking has seen a giant leap in popularity in recent years, and this site for the hardcore scrapbooker includes monthly tips, product reviews, and other related content. But core to the site is its community of "scrap addicts" who post scrapbook page layouts, tips on techniques, and general gossip on the Scrapper Talk and Mag Talk message boards.

ThirdAge
www.thirdage.com

A community for the aging baby boomer crowd – what the site calls "the best years of adulthood" – articles and discussion boards that deal with every day topics such as health and beauty, travel, and career.

TheWell.com
www.thewell.com

The very first online community, it's been around since the early 1990s. It is a cluster of electronic villages. Originally a free-for-all discussion on all kinds of political and social issues, it remains remarkably uninhibited, intelligent, and iconoclastic. It's now a subscriber-based service.

Mailing Lists

One of the most powerful ways of finding people with a particular interest (as opposed to finding an individual) is via electronic mailing lists. Mailing lists, like newsgroups, are large online discussion groups. There are more than 100,000 of them, each about a different subject, comprising every topic imaginable. According to Topica, one of the leading mailing list companies, it has twelve million subscribers.

Unlike newsgroups, you must subscribe to a list in order to receive the postings. All the messages on a subject are sent to a mailing list computer or majordomo computer and are forwarded to all the members of the subscribed group via email. None of the messages are private, but for the most part, they are not readable outside of the subscribed membership. Keep in mind that they can be forwarded outside the group, so you should still be careful about what you post. On rare occasions, they show up in search engines' databases, so you must remember to think of them as public mailing lists.

These lists give you access to people who care about a subject, sometimes passionately. Some have expertise and others don't, but to a researcher they offer access to a community of knowledge and a way to tap into great resources of information.

Mailing lists vary widely.

- Some are open to anyone who's interested.

- Some are restricted to members of a specified organization.

- Some are moderated while others are wide-ranging and freewheeling in their content

- And if it's a subject you care about, some are incredibly addicting and time consuming.

Moderators often use a screening mechanism to keep the postings on topic. With certain topics, moderators may have to calm emotions and ask participants to be civil.

To subscribe to a list, simply follow the instructions provided by the mailing list administrator. These instructions usually state that you should send a subscription request to the mailing list. Make sure you send it to the right place. Most mailing lists have two addresses:

- An administrative one that handles the subscribing/unsubscribing.

- Another administrator who routes all the postings.

To get on or off a list, send a note to the administrator, not the entire list. If you happen to err, you'll doubtless get a stack of angry email, called "flames." Your message should follow a standardized format, in which you leave the subject line blank and, in the body of the text, write "subscribe" followed by your first name and then last name with no punctuation. The server will send you a confirmation and a welcome note of rules and guidelines. Save and consult it if and when you decide to unsubscribe. This method works for most, but not all, mailing lists.

Free discussion being what it is, some mailing lists generate avalanches of postings daily. Be prepared. Some lists offer "digest" (all the posts are condensed to a single email) or "web only" options (see the posts on a private web site instead of email).

Make sure you know how to get off a list if it becomes overwhelming or useless. Always save the "welcome message," which will give you instructions on how to get off the list. Also, be aware that some of these archives are provided to search engines and so what you said in a discussion with other subscribers could end up showing up in a search engine's results.

The best list of web mailing lists, Topica (www.topica.com), is a comprehensive searchable directory of more than 100,000 live mailing lists worldwide. You can also use one of Topica's subject categories as a subject directory. Kovacs Consulting (www.kovacs.com) is another "must have" mailing list resource for monitoring personal-oriented mailing lists.

In addition to Topica, here are some other excellent mailing lists:

Cata-List

www.lsoft.com/lists/listref.html

This is a good collection of over 53,000 lists on all kinds of topics.

Cool List

www.coollist.com

This is another good, but small collection of lists. Like Yahoo!'s groups, this site will also let you set up your own discussion list.

Escribe

www.escribe.com

Another good collection of mailing lists, but a somewhat smaller universe of subjects.

International Federation of Library Associations and Institutions
www.ifla.org/I/training/listserv/lists.htm#4

This is a great collection full of all sorts of things including mailing lists, list etiquette, FAQs, and other general guides and resources.

Internet Scout - New List
http://scout.cs.wisc.edu/caservices/new-list/

This is not a search engine for mailing lists, but a mailing list about new lists or changes to existing lists and it is excellent. The archives are searchable.

ListUniverse.com
www.tile.net/lists/

One of the oldest and best collections of mailing lists.

The Mail Archive
www.mail-archive.com

This is a searchable archive of more than 5,000 lists.

The Mailing List Gurus Page
http://lists.gurus.com

One more strong collection of mailing lists.

Publicly Accessible Mailing Lists (PAML)
http://paml.net

This is another great collection of mailing lists and also has a terrific link to dozens of other collections of mailing lists (http://paml.net/sources.html).

Yahoo! Groups
http://groups.yahoo.com

Another huge collection of mailing lists, including the former Egroups database.

→*hot tip:* **When searching for a mailing list, think about what words or phrases might appear in the list's description. For example, if you want to talk about cats, you can search for "cats," but it may mean you won't bring up lists named "cat-lovers" or "felines." On the other hand, if you search for "cat," you'll find zillions of lists whose descriptions include the words "category" or "catalog." You could search for "cats" or "feline" but the best advice is to try and search several different ways if you don't find what you looking for immediately. Also, try reading several lists until you find the ones that will be most relevant to what you are looking for.**

Chat Rooms

Chat rooms are essentially free-for-alls in which large numbers of people monitor and converse in real time.

The word "chat" may be somewhat misleading because you are not really *talking* to anyone, just typing and reading text messages that other chat participants write. Once you enter a chat room, which is really just a web page, you can choose to only read the exchanges (that's known as "lurking") or you can join in by typing – called posting – your own messages.

Like the incredible proliferation of newsgroups, chat rooms focus on specific topics as well as general ones. They are more likely to be a waste of time than a valuable use of your resources.

You get what you pay for – and chatting is free, most of the time.

Chat room postings aren't officially archived, but people can and do freely copy and forward postings, and there is no assumption of privacy or ownership of your words.

The largest chat company in the world, which provides AOL's chat services as well as its own, is ICQ (http://web.icq.com).

Chat software can be used on the Web with your browser to conduct online discussions with one or as many as a thousand users simultaneously. While few people record chats, it can be done and some researchers at universities around the world have started to use chat discussions among faculty on specific subjects as a research tool. But to date there is no index of these "chats."

Where chatting can be most useful is as a tool to gather information about other people. This also works for Usenet groups and to a more limited extent, mailing lists. Remember what Canadian journalist Julian Sher, (www.journalismnet.com) calls one of his golden rules, "everything you say and do online can and will be held against you."

Many companies offer chat software and the best versions allow you to add images, video and audio to the discussions. One company, Webchat (www.webchat.org/index.shtml) uses the Internet browser with special software to let businesses do marketing, sales and educating consumers while chatting. Chat discussions are now used online to provide classes and technical support for web users.

America Online (AOL) has made its mark offering chat rooms of all kinds to its users. If you subscribe to AOL, all the software needed to participate in chat rooms comes with the AOL program. Examples of other online chat rooms include:

Meta Chats
www.ibiblio.org/dbarberi/links/chats/

World Wide Webchat
www.all-links.com/webchat

Yahoo!
http://dir.yahoo.com/Computers_and_Internet/Internet/Chats_and_Forums

One of the best collections of chat resources.

Voice Chat Resources

One of the hottest Internet trends is using your voice to deliver messages. Voice chat now has hundreds of thousands of users.

Some users gather in public chat rooms for free-form conferences; others conduct private conversations.

People have also figured out that chat technology can also save people money on long-distance phone calls. So many people have started adding computer speakers and microphones and using the Internet to avoid costly long-distance charges by letting it serve as their telephone.

Voice chat blends the sense of personality that comes through a phone conversation with the anonymity of online chat. So, people can still hide behind screen names while enjoying much more personalized interaction.

Sending voices over the Internet is not a new development. Internet telephony companies have been converting sound into data packets since the mid-1990s. With the right equipment, you can make a one-to-one call from a personal computer to a telephone, and the other way, or go from phone to phone. To cut costs and without us knowing it, many long-distance phone services now route calls over the Internet by using the same technology as voice chat. But, so far, voice chat does not yet match the quality of an actual telephone connection. Often, voice chat has silent gaps or the audio can fade in and out, just like when people use walkie-talkies or short wave radios.

With many of the voice chat services, typed communication is still a major component. People who talk to each other still have the option of typing messages to those in the chat room, allowing for simultaneous public and private conversations.

Although it is just starting to be used for business and as a research tool, consider the potential uses: business executives could conduct online conference calls to negotiate a deal, people could send private, privileged communications to lawyers, family members could gather together online for discussions. It is being used already as a customer service help tool for people buying software – you can reach a customer service representative without having to make a telephone call. Some universities are now using voice chat for group discussions. The Saddlebrook, New Jersey Police Department uses voice chat software to provide another communications channel between residents and police.

The most unusual use of this so far – and trust me, they're only just starting to figure this one out – is online karaoke. Of course, when you have that need to belt out Eric Clapton's *Layla*, go to www.vanbasco.com for song downloads and a karaoke player download.

To use voice chat, you must download software that places a voice chat window on the computer screen.

Following are some of the companies offering free services. Many of these package a voice player with their software so that those receiving the message can respond in kind.

Media Ring
www.mediaring.com

Media Ring offers voice chat rooms and individual chats as well – free demo available.

Paltalk

www.paltalk.com

> Paltalk, which recently purchased Hearme.com, enables instant voice-messaging between two people. It is now pushing into building multimedia communities, including audio, video, and PC-phone chatting.

Visitalk

www.visitalk.com

> Visitalk offers voice chat rooms, instant voice messages, and video email for US$4.95 a month.

Another hot trend is combined voice and video chat. It has become most popular for cyber-dating. A good example of this phenomenon is IFriends (www.ifriends.net)

Another video chat example is Eyeball Chat (www.eyeballchat.com), which provides video instant messaging. Looking to the cutting edge, Comet Video Technologies, (www.cometcam.com) is preparing to provide video and audio chatting capability via handheld devices in the near future.

Instant Messaging: Changing the Way People Communicate

When most of us think or first learn about Instant Messaging (IM), we think of teenagers in chat rooms screaming "Whassup?'" at each other over and over. And while that is definitely a part of this technology, there is a quiet revolution underway. If you are not part of the instant-message generation, you may be missing out. IM technology is changing the way we talk with each other and is starting to change the way we do business.

If you absolutely, positively need an answer now, you have two options – the telephone or instant messaging. For those that don't know, IM lets people carry on real-time one-on-one, small-group conversations – both text and voice (and soon video). It's becoming the new standard for fast communication, because it's easier in some cases and certainly cheaper than making a phone call, and quicker than email. In the U.S., more than half of the country's internet users, of those who use it, ninety percent say they use it every day.

Three of the biggest internet players – America Online, Microsoft and Yahoo! each have their own products. There is a bitter fight over which technology will dominate and ultimately generate big money for the winner.

Instant messaging got its start as an AOL feature in 1996. Now four programs handle the majority of the IM traffic. Two are owned by America Online: **AOL Instant Messenger** (www.aol.com), for both America Online Internet service users and nonusers, and **ICQ** (`www.icq.com`), which is used mostly for chat groups. Smartly AOL allows anyone – an AOL account member or not – to use the IM technology.

The other two are **Yahoo! Messenger** (`http://messenger.yahoo.com`) and **MSN Messenger** (`http://messenger.msn.com`).

What makes this technology so useful is that it works for Macs or PCs, laptops, handheld devices and even some cell phones. In Europe, a different technology – called SMS – is used for Instant Messaging on phones. A more advanced Instant Messaging technology, MMS is also being used in Europe and in Asia, where it enables users to send graphics, video, and sounds to and from mobile phones. With almost all of these technologies, all you have to do is add someone's name and email address to your list of friends or buddies, double-click, and you can start sending messages.

How popular is this new technology? Very. Each of the three companies makes huge claims about being the number one IM player in the world. But, their numbers are often like comparing apples to oranges. The most interesting numbers are these: Mobile Insights, a Mountain View, California-based consulting firm for the mobile computing and communications markets, predicted that by the end of 2002, the worldwide market for IM will be approximately 175 million users. And in Asia alone, a February 2002 study by Siemens found that sixty percent of mobile phone owners between the ages of 16 and 54 say they prefer to communicate using SMS or text messaging rather than email.

But there's a major hitch: the other person must use the same messaging program you do. Users on MSN Messenger can't chat with people on AOL's Instant Messenger (AIM) or Yahoo!'s Messenger.

So far, AOL seeing potential profits as the dominant technology, has kept its systems off limits to the others. Without a doubt, Instant Messaging would grow much faster if the major software companies ever reached an agreement that would allow their customers to message each other, regardless of which program they chose. But AOL has aggressively defended its network from any attempts by other companies to put users of the different systems in contact.

The AOL-Microsoft-Yahoo! rift goes back several years, when Microsoft and Yahoo! tried to build their instant messenger services on the back of AIM. Since then, the three companies have been slugging it out for years for dominance in the marketplace.

All of the major IM companies are using creative marketing pushes and developing new technologies to win this battle. For example, in October 2001, Yahoo! unveiled its latest version geared toward the broadband user. It offers users the ability to stream popular music, play games, and create cartoon backgrounds on the system.

AOL has offered its subscribers free Instant Messaging capability and opened up access to anyone who wants to download its AIM software. Microsoft's strategy has been to bundle its Instant Messaging client as part of its new XP operating system.

The battle has forced users to choose among the three different programs – or download three different services to their hard drive. Most people are deciding to install more than one program so they can talk with friends on different systems.

The important lesson is, as *Detroit Free Press* tech columnist Heather Newman points out, "just the fact that people are willing to go to that kind of trouble tells you how useful they've found the technology."

The best example of the value of Instant Messaging technology was during the September 11, 2001 terrorist attacks. People used the messaging applications to get in touch with family members when phone lines became jammed.

Already, the capabilities of most of these instant message programs have evolved to include the sending and receiving of photos and files, playing games and even phone calling on the Internet. It is where the technology goes next that is the most exciting part. IBM has already developed technology that will allow you to simultaneously send messages with instant language translation, which they call Sametime. So you can be writing in Korean to someone who only speaks Spanish and vice versa.

Most people use Instant Messaging as a quick text pager. But it has demonstrated some extraordinary uses. One woman communicated with a friend who was in hiding from an abusive husband. As she told Newman, they communicated through IM and "she was able to more clearly express her feelings, and the emotions were less traumatic, than if we had been discussing the same painful events on the phone. Sometimes it is better not to be able to hear the pain in someone's voice, and to be able to think before typing or more importantly, erase some typing before hitting the "send key."

For the deaf and hard of hearing population, Instant Messaging has been revolutionary. It has opened up a way of communicating with hearing people, through text paging or instant messaging. In addition to signed language (which may differ from country to country), deaf people can now IM one another with wireless devices. There is a signed language in each country. I have a deaf friend and when she came to visit, we were able to arrange to meet at the airport using text paging. We also regularly instant message – more often than we would touch base on the phone – because it is so easy to do. Some companies like Wyndtell.com, Skytel.com and Deafwireless are beginning to offer the capability to translate text into voice, allowing a hearing impaired person to communicate by simulated voice through these devices. Around the U.S., some teachers have started using IM to tutor students online, and academic researchers have been able to conduct tutorials and seminars for their colleagues at different colleges and universities.

But the greatest benefit is found in the business world.

The efficiency and ease of using IM has made it very popular at companies. What's even more useful to most IM users is that when you travel and you have a single phone line in a hotel and you are online with your computer, those you IM with can reach you because they see that you are online.

IBM has built encryption into its Instant Messaging program, allowing business executives to have confidential conversations. For e-commerce applications, IM may be the best and easiest way for a company to direct real-time service to a web site visitor who has a question, is lost or has special needs. It provides a flexible, comforting human touch to an otherwise automatic process.

Here are a few examples of how commercial businesses are having great success with IM. IGo Corporation (`www.igo.com`), a Reno, Nevada wireless phone and mobile computing accessories store uses it for customer service. You go to the web site, click on the "Live Help" button and customer service IMs you back to answer your questions.

Wingspan Bank, a Wilmington, Delaware online bank and investment service, offers IM for its customers. What makes it most helpful, they say, is that it has helped the company migrate from a self-service web site model to a people-oriented department store model. And for many of their customers, who only have one phone line, it has saved the frustration of having to get off the phone to call customer service. Like IBM, Wingspan uses encryption technology to conceal IM data from prying network eyes.

Already, the future of Instant Messaging is moving beyond the PC to voice and video. Expect a few years from now for the interface to most cell phones and wireless – personal digital assistants – to include a buddy list, which will help people communicate without having to make real-two way phone calls for simple communication.

Other Instant Messaging companies to watch:

CMGI (`www.cmgi.com`), owners of AltaVista and several other technology companies has purchased two of the innovators in Instant Messaging – Tribal Voice's PowWow and Icast's Icaster and are expecting to compete with the major players in the near future.

Odigo (`www.odigo.com`), whose SMS-Instant Messaging clients include several of the world's major phone companies, like British Telecom, Hungary Telecom, Austria Telecom and others like ESPN, Prodigy and computer giant NEC.

While it is not very expensive to install in a business environment, you need to set up a separate IM server and link it to your company directory. There is a genuine down side to using IM in this environment – the lack of an audit trail. You don't get a trail unless users print out a copy of each session. For those who need to keep records of every email and correspondence, IM is not the answer because there is no way to follow all the instant messages.

Conferencing

Using the Internet, you can communicate inexpensively around the world through the computer in real time. The technology has moved so quickly that conferencing is now an affordable way of doing business.

Conferencing can take many different forms, such as videoconferencing, audio conferencing, multimedia conferencing, screen-sharing, and to a lesser extent, chat discussion sessions.

Videoconferencing

Videoconferencing allows people in different locations to address educational, personal, and business issues more quickly, productively, and economically. It can be done one-on-one or one-on-many. It has great potential for reducing the costs of doing business and making small companies competitive.

The most popular form of Internet conferencing are two programs – CU-SeeMe, which allows people to use the Internet to see each other's faces in small windows on your computer screen and to hear their voices through computer speakers using digital cameras, and Microsoft's Net-Meeting (www.microsoft.com/windows/NetMeeting/default.ASP). To see what CU-SeeMe can do, take a look at www.rocketcharged.com/cu-seeme/.

For more details on how videoconferencing works, see:

Digital Connections - FAQ
www.dciglobal.com/faq.htm

Microsoft Windows - Media Technologies
www.microsoft.com/windows/windowsmedia/serve/faq.asp

Wire One - Videoconferencing Glossary
www.videoconference.com/glossary.htm

Online Audio Conferencing

Internet teleconferencing allows you to make calls around the world through the Internet for the cost of a local call. While the audio quality still leaves something to be desired, this technology is improving rapidly.

The software needed depends on your computer. Speak Freely for Windows (www.fourmilab.ch/speakfree/windows) for example, offers audio conferencing as well as voice mail – and it can be downloaded free.

Software programs like Net Meeting enable meetings and presentations in many locations simultaneously. You electronically raise your hands and when the moderator gives you the floor, you speak. Other software types allow you to conduct round-table meetings without a moderator.

Document conferencing software also exists, allowing people in remote locations to share work on projects via the Web.

To see how electronic conferencing is used in academia, see Diane Kovac's excellent Directory of Scholarly & Professional E-Conferences at www.kovacs.com/directory/.

Webrings

Webrings are a series of web pages linked together in a circle – all focused on the same or somewhat related subjects.

Instead of directories that allow you to look at links in a list form, a webring lets you move around a circle directly from one link to another. What makes them different from all the other mega-sites is that there are knowledgeable people all linked to one another and they tend to be less business-like and more social in their dealings. Pretty much, anyone who allows his site to be part of a webring is passionate about the subject matter and most of these people tend to be willing to help you if you want it.

The research advantage to you is this: webrings are focused and selective about specific topics.

One way to locate webrings is to use a general search engine with the search phrases "cats" and "webring" as the subjects if you are searching for a webring about cats, or use a web directory like Yahoo!, which lists more than 900 different webrings. For the most part, like discussion groups, you may need to join a webring to search it.

Here are a few good webring sites to start off with:

Google - Web Ring Systems
http://directory.google.com/Top/Computers/Internet/Web_Design_and_Developm ent/Web_Ring_Systems/

RingSurf
www.ringsurf.com

WebRing
http://dir.webring.com/rw

Blogs and Home Pages

"Blog" is short for "weblog," a web page made up of short, frequent posts arranged chronologically – an online news commentary. They range from very professional news about a company or person to diaries, photos, essays, poetry, even fiction. Many are the musings and emotional outbursts of the person writing the blog. Others are a collaboration of tips and tidbits on a particular topic, often rich in links. They are kind of like online journals on subjects the weblog's author, sometimes called a "blogger," find amusing or interesting. Ever since the Web developed in the early 1990s, people have posted their own home pages giving personal information and quirky observations. While lots of home pages still exist, many people have now turned to blogging instead of posting notes to keep up with constant changes on home pages. While many blogs are simply little more than online diaries, others are produced by people who are constantly scouring the web looking for useful sites and information. Like Usenet and discussion groups, these resources can be great for finding information about those who post them and also the subjects they write about.

Here's one from Boing Boing (`www.boingboing.net`).

"Disney and Kellogg's have launched 'Mickey's Magix,' a 'naturally sweetened toasted oat cereal with marshmallows.' According to the commercial, it turns the milk blue. Excuse me, I need to hit the grocery store."

One of the diary-style blogs is found at `www.indigohat.com/journal`. It is the journal of a woman named Carrie Ellis and it's most unusual and interesting.

Here's a typical paragraph from her site: "I have a very horrible fear of this thing that I have an inkling of. I'm afraid to find out one way or another and I don't know what I will do, whatever the outcome. I almost hope, in some sadistic way. Almost excited. At the same time, I totally dread the possibility."

Okay, so interesting observations, but how is this going to help me as a researcher?

A blog written by a specialist in a particular field can serve as excellent "radar" that can rival or even outdo expensive online alerting services. The most useful blogs allow you to keep up with the latest information on subjects you care about.

Three of my favorites are by veteran journalists with a lot of good information to impart. Jim Romenesko's MediaNews (`www.poynter.org/medianews/index.cfm`) tracks news about the news industry and adds his own commentary about them. It's become "must reading" for journalists to stay up on the latest gossip and news about the news business.

Dan Gillmor, respected technology columnist for *The San Jose Mercury News* publishes a daily weblog called ejournal:

`www.bayarea.com/mld/siliconvalley/business/columnists/dan_gillmor /ejournal/`

Steve Outing and Amy Gahran's daily e-media tidbits column covers the online content world, and regularly points to valuable web sites and articles for online journalists. Read them at `www.content-exchange.com/weblog/weblog.htm` or, if that doesn't work, `www.content-exchange.com` and click on "e-media tidbits."

What makes these sights so valuable is that the best ones often find material that is fresh and cutting edge. The trick is finding a blog written by someone who shares your own interests. The downside of blogs is they tend not to have much structure. But like webrings, bloggers tend to know about other bloggers with similar interests so you can use one site to get to another.

Many blogs are also useful for competitive intelligence research. Searching blogs for the names of companies or business people can often reveal some terrific gossip or even facts that you probably won't find anywhere else, at least for a while.

There are really two ways to find blogs. The first is to find a blog that interests you, and see which other blogs the author links to. The other way is to use a blog-specific search engine or directory. Search engine Daypop.com can search blogs.

Blogger.com
www.blogger.com

This is one of the biggest and most useful weblog sites. What really makes it valuable is this site will help you create your own blog.

BlogHop
www.bloghop.com

BlogHop is a directory of more than 8,700 blogs, rated for "quality" by other BlogHop users.

Eatonweb Portal
http://portal.eatonweb.com

A searchable directory of nearly 3,500 blogs, sortable by new additions – alphabetically or categorically – or filtered for non-English blogs only.

Bird on a Wire
http://www.birdonawire.org

A small blog directory, organized by geographic location, it offers all kinds of links, with U.S. links on the left side and the international ones on the right side. Site may be temporarily down.

Open Directory Project - Weblogs
http://dmoz.org/Computers/Internet/On the Web/Weblogs/

The Open Directory's list of blog directories, portals, and other sites is also a great starting point.

Blogdex
http://blogdex.media.mit.edu/

One of the first and most respected blog compilation pages.

The Diarist Registry
www.diarist.net/registry/

This is a collection of online journals and diaries. They tend to be more formal and less list-oriented than blogs.

Fee-Based Tools for Finding Specialized Information

There are hundreds of fee-based services or commercial online services that provide access to news and information records. Most of them are extremely good. Using them, you can find extensive background information about a person – name, Social Security Number, last five addresses, relatives' names, value of property owned or rented, all kinds of business records, information about neighbors, property records, vital records, voter registration and so forth.

The three big information supermarkets, Thomson's Dialog, Lexis-Nexis and Factiva (formerly Dow Jones), maintain virtual warehouses of information – extensive libraries of published information on a myriad of subjects, including full-text periodicals. Other fee-based tools contain public records derived from government entities, publishers' mailing lists, mail forwarding orders, real estate information, registered voter files, tax assessor and county recorder records, bankruptcy courts, and many other places. Through services like ChoicePoint, Merlin Data Systems, Search Systems and PublicData.com, you can "people search" by name using white pages, publishers' mailing lists, voter registration files, credit header files and property data.

Many of the proprietary services like Lexis-Nexis, Dialog and Factiva have developed easy-to-use point-and-click systems on the Web to expand their base market beyond librarians and professional researchers. Be warned, however, that there is so much content available that it still takes time to learn how to use each company's system effectively. All the supermarket databases claim to house more usable information than the entire Web. Dialog alone claims it has more than six billion pages of text in more than nine hundred databases. But what you will find remains the most sophisticated and thorough information available, far exceeding many web sites.

Strategies for Using Fee-Based Services

Mary Ellen Bates, a superb business search guru and the author of several books on searching – as well as a contributor to this book – often says that information may want to be free "but finding tools don't," and suggests you need to "get real" about what you are trying to accomplish and how you do it. She suggests that whether you are searching for yourself or for a client, your time is the most valuable resource you manage, and time and money are the major considerations in how you decide which tools to use.

One method is to start on the Web and pick off what she calls "low hanging fruit"– the obvious information you can find with quick searches of news articles, and keyword searching. If you ask yourself what is the source of the information or who is putting out the information, you will often find that you can get free information from advocacy groups, government agencies, and company press releases. But if you want high-value search tools that enable you to limit your sets, do field searching, limit by date and limit by language, those will usually be fee-based tools.

Where the fee-based tools really shine is in the value-added information they provide. For example, if you want to search the Securities and Exchange Commission's EDGAR database to get background information about a company, you can do it for free. But if you want to compare different businesses or use some of the special search and retrieval features, you are going to have to pay for it, by using fee-based services like EDGAR-online.com (`www.edgar-online.com`) or Hoover's (`www.hoovers.com`).

If you are looking for news archives, many news-based web sites will provide a few weeks for free. For more obscure or specialized trade publications, or anything more than six months back, you will have to use a fee-based database.

If you are doing a quick lookup of information, you can find most of what you need for free on the Web. Same goes for a few articles on the topic. But if you are looking for the comprehensive guide or doing what researchers like Bates call the "scorched earth" search, you are going to need to use a combination of free and fee-based tools and probably going to have to use them several times.

And if language is the determining factor, you are best to use a free web-based tool if you are fluent in the language you are searching in, but if you need it abstracted into English, a fee-based tool is probably your best bet.

Bates suggests a few tips that I completely agree with for determining how best to research using fee and free web-based tools. She suggests working from a checklist of formats like articles, white papers, statistics, and company web sites. Then, use the Web to identify ambiguities and help pin down the exact words, phrases, and parameters to do your fee-based search for the high value material. Then, she suggests doing an additional web search to double check for anything you may have missed the first time around.

How Do Fee-Based Tools Work?

Every company has a different fee structure. Some charge you for everything you download. Most of them have dropped the charges for your time online, charging a flat fee instead. But some charge for every document you look at.

Where you get a significant advantage is that the search engines on these tools are extremely robust and powerful. They allow you to conduct more precision searching. They also help you focus your results through refining techniques. They often offer material that is unique and not found on the Web, things like market research, doctoral theses and scholarly journals.

Fee-based services also allow you much more flexibility in defining your search. They provide a quality screening mechanism, determining on your behalf where the valuable resources might be found, centralizing them and letting you know where the resources come from. Fee-based services allow you to scour large numbers of resources simultaneously and run your search in one shot.

The tradeoff, as always, is time versus money. You spend more money to get an answer with a fee-based service, but you save time in the process.

➜ *hot tip:* **On fee-based services in particular, the structure of each database can be different, so if you are searching more than one database at a time, be careful to switch rules of operation when you switch databases. Even if you are searching on the same fee-based service, this happens.**

So, how do you choose between Dialog, Factiva and Lexis-Nexis or the thousands of other proprietary services online? Refer back to the questions from Chapter 3, Framing Your Search, and ask yourself:

- How much money do I need to spend?

- How much time do I have?

- Is what I need available when I need it?

- How comfortable am I with each of the different services?

- Most importantly, does a particular service have what I need?

→ *hot tip:* **Sign up for a free introductory trial with any fee-based service that interests you; sit at the controls and test-drive it.**

The Tasini Decision's Impact on Fee-Based Tools

A 2001 U.S. Supreme Court decision has jolted the world of online content providers. In *New York Times v. Tasini*, the Supreme Court ruled that *The New York Times* and other online database vendors violated the federal copyright act by publishing freelance materials in archival electronic databases without the writer's permission.

The ruling applies to all publishers who failed to obtain clearances from writers for digital rights. The court decision clearly gives the rights to reproduction of a freelance author's work to the author, not the publisher of the original print work, unless a contract exists between the author and the publisher that clearly spells out the transfer of those electronic rights.

What this means is that an unknown number of articles – hundreds of thousands for sure – licensed to database aggregators like Lexis-Nexis, Dialog, Dow Jones and many others are being sold without the owners' permission and either must be removed or some compensation must be worked out.

The hope of Jonathan Tasini and the National Writers Union, who sued the newspapers, was to get compensation for the electronic publishing of news stories for freelancers who had been compensated initially for the stories, but never for the electronic versions and to try to get additional future compensation for them.

It is almost a year later and it has not happened yet. *The New York Times* has in fact, removed 115,000 articles from Lexis-Nexis and others and tentatively shut down access to all *New York Times* book reviews on its own site. Other companies have also taken material that was indexed in these databases out of them, leaving holes in the content provided by these companies.

The most profound ramification of the decision is that libraries and the public – in particular researchers and scholars have lost access to complete archives of major newspapers, magazines, and other publications that accept contributions from freelancers. No longer can a researcher be confident, for instance, that he or she has exhaustively searched and found all the relevant material available in the online services. Instead, as Richard Wiggins, a computer technologist at Michigan State University suggests, even *The New York Times*, which for decades has billed itself as the "newspaper of record," now "becomes something like the ninety-two percent newspaper of record."

Different publications have reacted in different ways to the decision.

The Gale Group, now a part of Thomson, has a policy in light of Tasini that compensates the freelancer based on how often the article is requested, a sort of metered-compensation. Others have simply removed the articles completely, while still others have left a note indexing the article but saying it is no longer available as a result of the Tasini decision. The damage has been done, but as Barbara Quint, editor of *Searcher*, put it shortly after the decision, "searchers pay online commercial services top dollar not just for information, but for peace of mind about information. Now, not only will every search become a painful 'I wonder what I'm missing experience,' but searchers will never even know for sure when they are *not* missing anything or when a certain search strategy on a particular database did retrieve all the relevant material."

Since no genuine resolution of this dispute seems likely, the only hope for researchers, Quint suggests, is that libraries will continue to have CD and microfilm versions of the articles.

Best Fee-Based Tools

Here's a quick look at the three giant players in the commercial online database or fee-based online research tools and a snapshot look at several of the other tools that can be helpful for news, business and public records research.

Thomson Dialog
`www.dialogweb.com`

Dialog is like a supermarket because it has so many aisles with so many different varieties of products. The Dialog database says it contains five billion pages of information. Yes, five billion, which includes key categories such as news and media, medicine, pharmaceuticals, chemicals, reference, social sciences, business and finance, food and agriculture, intellectual property, government and regulations, science and technology, and energy and environment. Within each category are extensive collections of articles, journals and other written material. Dialog contains the full-text of over 7,500 publications stored in nearly 600 databases.

The key to using and understanding Dialog's depth is to read its "bluesheets," a detailed guide as to what is contained in the files, how best to search them and how far back they go.

Librarians all over the world have received extensive Dialog training and prefer to use the "Dialog Classic" version of the system. But for those who have not been schooled in the complicated search command language, Dialog has made an easy-to-use search method.

One of the Web's great frustrations in searching on the free Web is the duplication factor – finding the same thing several times. Dialog is especially good at eliminating the duplicates from the search results, allowing you to link different terms and rank the concepts you think will be most appropriate in doing your search.

Dialog's recent purchase by Thomson may ultimately make it a much, much stronger searching resource. You can already search Dialog for Profound, a high-cost database with information on markets, companies, country and economic data from around the world. It is available separately or as part of Dialog. Same goes for all the Gale Group resources, which include a series of excellent directories and reference resources.

Thomson's outstanding collection of business tools is still largely unavailable under Dialog, but officials say most of the resources will become available at some point. In the meantime, these Thomson resources are listed separately.

Pricing: There is a one-time sign up fee of US$295, an annual subscription of US$72-$144, but transaction-based pricing and flat-fee accounts are also available. Dialog also offers Open Access, which lets non-subscribers use the service and pay by credit card and you can still search Dialog Classic the old-fashioned way if you know how to. Dialog offers three versions of the program and a password on Dialog Classic or Dialog Web will get you free access to Dialog Select.

Factiva
www.factiva.com

Factiva's crown jewel is *The Wall Street Journal*, but Factiva owns an empire of media resources. There are differences between the Wall Street Journal Interactive Edition (www.wsj.com), Factiva (www.factiva.com) and Dow Jones Interactive (www.djinteractive.com). They all offer different resources and have different costs. The Wall Street Journal Interactive Edition provides an online version of the newspaper and access to the rest of Factiva for a monthly subscription fee. Factiva and Dow Jones Interactive (DJI) have significant other resources. Dow Jones has partnered with Reuters Worldwide News, one of the world's largest wire services, to form a series of very strong business-oriented research tool.

In addition to archives from *The Journal* and many other newspapers including *The New York Times, Los Angeles Times* and *The Washington Post*, Factiva and the other tools offer other information services, in-depth market research reports, company profiles, securities, dividends, and exchange rate information. It also has an extensive clippings file containing more than 8,000 sources from 118 countries and content in 22 languages. Its indexing capability allows it to universally index all types of content in many languages. Its "Publications" collection is quite extensive and its ability to compare companies' information and industry-wide information is top notch, allowing you to compare one industry's performance to another and get analysts' reports by region of the country. You can easily search by company, person and industry. You can also customize Factiva to get the clips and stories you want as well as receive specific subject-requested articles by email. One neat feature is that you can search it using pull-down menus to limit your search to lead paragraphs. This allows you to get the who, what, when, where, why and how of a news story without searching the entire story. It has several pricing options, but is relatively inexpensive compared to its Dialog and Lexis-Nexis counterparts. You can also work out different arrangements with its two related web sites www.djinteractive.com and www.business.reuters.com

Pricing: Factiva is free if you have a subscription with *The Wall Street Journal* for US$69/year plus per document charges. Transaction-based pricing and flat-fee accounts are available.

Lexis-Nexis
www.lexis-nexis.com

Lexis-Nexis started as an online service for the legal community, expanded to include case law from other countries, state law and public records, and then added the Nexis collection of full-text articles and abstracts of magazines, newspapers, and newsletters. Now owned by British-based

Reed Elsevier PLC, it has added a deep collection of financial information, market research reports, and country personality profiles and public records..

Lexis-Nexis now has four major product lines: legal, business, government and academic. Lexis' strongest suit is definitely legal. Its legal resources, available at `www.lexis.com` are better than anything you can find for free on the Web. It is expensive, but is certainly one of the best and most respected legal tools available.

Lexis-Nexis' business tools are vast and deep. They offer an extensive public records section and incredibly deep news resources – dating back to the late 1970s – with full-text articles and strong company backgrounding information. It also offers an excellent Company Dossier tool, providing information about individual companies, topically organized in a web-based point-and-click format. It covers public and private companies in the U.S. and outside, also topical reports like news, financial analysis, legal analysis and intellectual property analysis. Lexis-Nexis also has a special web tool for finding business web sites; and "task pages" on diverse topics such as "Recent Patents," "Joint Ventures," "Advertising Strategy," and "Expert Sources."

Lexis' government resources are also strong, offering access to political news resources. Its Academic Universe product works for students and universities.

Pricing: Subscription costs vary. Flat-fee and transaction-based pricing is available.

Comparing the Giants

The best researchers use all three – Lexis-Nexis, Dialog and Factiva – the way they use several search engines and other online search tools. On science and medicine, no doubt Dialog is tops. On news and breaking information, many find it is a toss-up between Lexis-Nexis and Factiva, and with Dialog's addition of many of the Thomson tools, including the Gale Group, it will certainly be competitive. Some prefer Factiva if the subject is business-related, with Dialog also strong but lean to Lexis-Nexis if it is more political or current-events oriented.

Useful Fee-Based Tools

Besides the three "supermarkets" there are hundreds of other useful and excellent fee-based tools. Here is a summary look at a few. See Chapter 9 - Business, Chapter 6 - Government, and Chapter 7 - Public Records, and the Vendor Profiles section for fee-based sites related to these topics.

➔ *hot tip:* **Don't forget to make use of your local library, which sometimes has access to these services and offers them to library visitors free or inexpensively.**

Countrywatch

`www.countrywatch.com`

Countrywatch provides reports on political structure, economics and news resources for about 191 countries to schools, libraries, and individuals. The basics are available for free, but the reports cost US$40 and you can subscribe to specific country newswires to monitor events abroad.

EBSCO
`www.ebsco.com`

EBSCO provides content for schools, and libraries based on a subscription basis. It has an extensive collection of academic-oriented resources.

EC Next
`www.ecnext.com`

This is an unusual fee-based tool. It serves publishers. It has developed a "family of malls" in which you can get reports from publishers about the business of publishing in different fields. What makes this useful to researchers is that its newsletter mall lets you purchase an issue or subscribe to over fifty professional or trade newsletters.

EIU - Economist Intelligence Unit
`www.eiu.com`

The online offering from the British magazine *The Economist*, this web site offers much more than just the magazine. It has analysis and political and economic forecasts and business background on more than 180 countries. EIU is available through other commercial services as well as by subscription on its web site.

Encyclopedia Britannica
`www.britannica.com`

See the description earlier found in the Ready Reference Tools section.

➜*hot tip:* **Web pages come and go, and they often change URLs. If the URL given in this book does not work, try shortening - truncating - lengthy URLs. Another trick is to search for the web site name in one of the larger search engines, such as Google. Remember, too, that search engines store the old pages and URLs, so eliminate hits that contain the non-working URL.**

H.W. Wilson
`www.hwwilson.com`

An academic and library-oriented biographical site, highlighting books and databases.

Leiden University
`www.leidenuniv.nl/ub/biv/specials.htm`

This site has free and fee-based tools. It contains links to all kinds of specialized search tools. This is a truly outstanding collection of sites on all kinds of subjects and is worth looking at. The fee-based tools are only a minor portion of this, but again, a good collection of sites.

Newsbank

www.newsbank.com

A strong database collection of newspapers, magazines and scholarly journals, geared to students and libraries. It is available by subscription.

Northern Light

www.northernlight.com

Access to free and "fee" news, analyst reports, and other market data. Its pay-per-view "Special Collection" includes hundreds of newsletters, magazines, and trade publications, and is ideal for the occasional searcher. Search results are conveniently organized into folders. Be careful, however, for fees on some documents, such as press releases.

Northern Light Search Alert Service (http://standard.northernlight.com /c/s.dll/cl_cliplist.pl) automatically scans its newswire feeds and special documents and sends a free email with news alerts. Special documents cost US$1-4.00 to retrieve. News feeds are free.

OCLC

www.oclc.com

OCLC is a nonprofit membership organization serving 41,000 libraries in 82 countries and territories around the world. Memberships are restricted to libraries of all kinds.

Ovid

www.ovid.com

Ovid provides a database of news and health information for medical, health, academic and corporate clients, available by subscription.

Phillips Publishing

www.phillips.com

Phillips, publisher of newsletters, magazines and directories, has put together industry intelligence web sites in several areas including the latest news on those subjects, email alerts, company profiles and market research as well.

ProQuest

www.proquest.com h

Proquest, part of UMI, the company that has provided archives newspapers on microfilm and CDs for decades, provides current and archived newspapers by subscription to its clients – mostly schools and libraries around the world, back to 1986.

Silverplatter

www.silverplatter.com

Another academic-oriented database which offers access to lots of other providers including EBSCO, Academic Press, Catchword, SwetsNet, and Ovid. It has over 250 different databases and is available for a free thirty days trial.

xrefer

www.xreferplus.com

This is an excellent reference search engine with subscriptions available primarily for libraries.

→ *hot tip:* A terrific resource of information on specialized tools is *Great Scouts: Cyberguides for Subject Search on the Web,* by Nora Paul and Margot Williams from Information Today's Cyberage books.

Additional Web Sites for Specialized Tools

192.com
www.192.com
Fees for some content. Infamous 'people finding' site. Has both telephone directories and electoral roll. You have to pay for more 'interesting' searches. But a good starting spot for British phone numbers.

555-1212.com
www.555-1212.com
Fee-based site. Phone books online. Better than many others because you can search several of the other web telephone services from this site.

Abuzz
www.abuzz.com
Ask *The New York Times* a question and they provide an answer.

AcqWeb's Directory of Book Reviews on the Web
www.library.vanderbilt.edu/law/acqs/boo krev.html
Part of the AcqWeb site, maintained by librarians, has great resources for book review sites on the Web.

Addresses.com
www.addresses.com
Thorough email finder for the U.S.

Advalas Zoeken
www.advalvas.be/
Email, chat, and SMS address finder from Belgium.

Air Force Biographies
www.af.mil/lib/bio/index.html
Air Force personal biographies, both active and retired.

Alberta.com
http://wp1.superpages.ca/people.phtml?S RC=alberta&STYPE=WS
Canadian people finder.

All About Colleges
www.allaboutcollege.com/colleges/united _states/usa.htm
College and university links.

AltaVista Photo Finder
http://image.altavista.com
Currently the most comprehensive database of images on the Internet, with the best searching capability. AltaVista has combined the Corbis photo database with indexed images from the Web to provide millions of images. Images not limited just to photos.

Amazing Environmental Organization WebDirectory
www.webdirectory.com
John Dickson's excellent site is the starting spot for all things environmental. It has more than 80,000 links in more than 100 countries.

American Veterans Confirmation Service
http://members.aol.com/veterans/warlib1 3.htm
Web site designed to help you identify if someone has served in the U.S. military -- any service branch. You will need special software to use this.

Ask A Science Question
www.newton.dep.anl.gov/aasquest.htm
10,000 questions on database.

Ask Dr. Science

www.ducksbreath.com
Ask Dr. Science, a syndicated radio program that is
searchable here.

Atomica reference search

www.gurunet.com/us/
Search a topic and get best news or biography/links, then
dictionary/encyclopedia/maps/quotes, etc.

Awesome Library

www.awesomelibrary.org
A comprehensive database of educational materials.
Includes only sites that have been reviewed and judged to
be of high quality by educators.

Beginner's Guide to Effective E-mail

www.webfoot.com/advice/email.top.html
A resource for how to use email more effectively. This
guide is also available in multiple languages at www.web
foot.com/advice/translations/index.html.

Bigfoot

www.bigfoot.com
This email search tool is one of the best. Includes email
listings by state and white page information by state and
city.

BookWire

www.bookwire.com
Home of the Boston Book Review, the Hungry Mind
Review, the Quarterly Black Review of Books and the
Computer Book Review, although searching is a little
unwieldy.

Bouvier Historical Law Dictionary

www.constitution.org/bouv/bouvier.htm
Bouvier's Law Dictionary was the pre-eminent legal
dictionary in the U.S. in from the 19th Century into the
1930's. This is a historical reference -- the 1856 Edition is
posted on the Internet.

British Ordnance Survey Maps

www.expedia.com/pub/agent.dll?qscr=over
&rfrr=-357
This site offers maps and driving directions for Europe and
North America.

BT Directory Enquiries

www.bt.com/index.jsp
British Telecom's phone books. Click on "Directory
Enquiries." You get 10 free per day.

Cameo

http://cameo.bvdep.com
Fee-based site. A source of British electoral roll
information, subscription-based and aimed more at the
professional market.

Canada411

http://canada411.sympatico.ca
A Canadian phone book for almost all provinces and
territories.

Canadian Information by Subject

www.nlc-bnc.ca/caninfo/ecaninfo.htm
Extensive subject listings from Canada by the National
Library of Canada.

Carroll's Government Directories & Charts

www.carrollpub.com
Government phone books and directories.

Chat Etiquette

www.stevegrossman.com/jargpge.htm#Cover
A guide to the jargon used in the world of chat.

Chronicle of Higher Education

http://chronicle.com
Academe This Week is the Chronicle's online news
service.

Clear Regulatory Boards and Colleges in North America

www.clearhq.org/boards.htm
Excellent collection of regulatory boards and professional
licenses in Canada and the U.S.

Commonplace Book, The

www.internetbookinfo.com/ibic/Commonpla
ce-Book.html
Internet Book Information Center provides a
comprehensive, opinionated source for information about
books.

Confering Software for the Web

http://thinkofit.com/webconf
David Woolley's excellent resource for learning about text-
based online conferencing.

Cybertown - 3DVR Community of the Future

www.cybertown.com
Cutting-edge 3-D technology with chat in a virtual environment.

Delorme's Earthamaps

www.earthamaps.com
Fine web map and route search tool.

Desk Ref

http://ansernet.rcls.org/deskref/
Good reference list of resources, organized by subject.

Dictionary of Phrase and Fable

www.bibliomania.com/Reference/PhraseAnd
Fable/index.html
Full text of E. Cobham Brewer's classic reference, which explains the origins of English phrases and characters from myths and fables.

Directories - Switzerland

www.directories.ch
Swiss email finder and phone books.

Directorio Global Net en Español

www.dirglobal.net
Spanish language subject directory.

Disinformation

www.disinfo.com
Calling itself the "subculture search engine," you will find things here on current affairs, politics and other subjects that you won't find elsewhere.

Dr. Felix's Free MEDLINE Page

www.beaker.iupui.edu/drfelix
A list of all the places on the 'Net that offer free Medline, the U.S. government's health-medical index.

Dun & Bradstreet Business Phone Address Finder

http://sbs.dnb.com/advFind.asp?bhcd2=10
15986283
Think of this as a buried treasure site. Designed as a service for small business owners looking for contact information, it does much more. A free and comprehensive database has names, links, executives etc and is sortable by DUNS number.

Edcuation Week on the Web

www.edweek.org
Education news and resources.

EDUCAUSE

www.educause.edu
The latest trends in education and technology.

Email Finder

www.emailfinder.com
The site offers a free and a fee-based email finder. It's mostly U.S.-based sites.

Email It Australia

www.email-it.net.au
Australian email finding tool.

Encarta Concise

http://encarta.msn.com
Searchable database of *Encarta Encyclopedia*.

Encyclopedia of the Orient

http://i-cias.com/e.o/
This site has a totally misleading title. It is actually a great encyclopedia for North Africa and the Middle East and is a wonderful starting point to learn about those complicated regions of the world.

E-search

www.esearch.ie
Irish email finder.

ETB

www.etb.at
Austrian email finder.

Everybody's Legal Dictionary by Nolo Press

www.nolo.com/dictionary/wordindex.cfm
Nolo's free legal dictionary.

Expedia

http://maps.expedia.com/QuickMaps.asp
Can find a topographic map showing location of any city/town worldwide. Not much detail for many countries but zooming in available in U.S., Canada, Mexico, Europe. These are nice maps, too.

ExpertSources NewsSource Center

www.businesswire.com/expertsource
This Business Wire service features company experts, except for the occasional expert on health care, biotech and

a few other topics. Fill out the detailed registration form, then send queries to the service, which will respond with a list of experts.

FAQ Finder
http://ps.superb.net/FAQ
A collection of FAQs on all kinds of subjects.

Find Me Mail
www.findmemail.com
This site lets you register your email or find old ones. Works for several countries.

FindLaw Directory of Experts
http://marketcenter.findlaw.com/experts_consultants.html
Considered by many in the legal profession to be the best expert witness directory.

Foreign Policy Experts
www.zianet.com/irc1/infocus/database/index.html
Foreign policy experts site.

Forté Free Agent Newsreader
www.forteinc.com
Fee-based site. Tools for searching Usenet.

Getty Thesaurus of Geographic Names
www.getty.edu/research/tools/vocabulary/tgn/index.html
Locate the longitude and latitude details for any North or Central American County.

Good Stuff
www.netins.net/showcase/trhalvorson/g-stuff/index.html
TR Halvorson's collection of links to legal and business sites.

Government Records.com
www.governmentrecords.com
Aristotle Industries' new web site with extensive voter records and other public records-oriented databases for sale.

Go Gettum
www.gogettem.com
Meta-search tool with access to lots of search tools and 2,600 specialized directories.

GreekPages University
www.greekpages.com
This collection of resources lets you find folks in sororities and fraternities.

Greekspot.com
www.greekspot.com/directory.htm
A master directory of fraternities and sororities.

Grolier
http://go.grolier.com/
Fee-based site. *Grolier encyclopedia.*

Harris County Appraisal District
www.hcad.org
Example of property records on the Web.

Harvard
www.law.harvard.edu/Library/
Harvard University Law School Library - excellent academic resource.

HealthAtoZ
www.healthatoz.com
Quick access to medical information on the Web.

IBM-Israel
www.ibm.net.il/WebPh
Israeli email and phone finder.

ICQ: World's Largest Internet Online Communication Network
www.mirabilis.com
A chat service tool – allows you to know when others are online.

Indo.com - How far is it?
www.indo.com/distance
Put in two place names if you have them (anywhere in the U.S. and most cities of the world), or a place name and coordinates, or two locations (latitude & longitude).

Information & Privacy, The Office of
www.usdoj.gov/oip/oip.html#
Various filtering agents and bots.

INFO-USA
www.infousa.com
Another excellent reverse phone book.

International Association of Assessing Officers (IAAO)

www.iaao.org
Education and trade arm for tax assessors worldwide; also, web site links.

International Research Center

www.researchedge.com
Mark Goldstein's strong collection of research links.

Internet File Converter for the Palm

http://pilot.screwdriver.net
Found something on the Internet you'd like to carry around in your Palm? Put the URL of the page into this page and it will convert it to PalmDOC format to import. (You need to have a DOC reader installed on your Palm).

Internet Movie Database, The

www.imdb.com
Two thumbs up as the best movie site. It's so good that reporters who cover Hollywood use it as a bible.

IQ DATA Systems

www.iqdata.com
Fee-based site. Commercial service indexing real estate and assessor information.

I-Ring.com

www.I-ring.com/find/
Another good email finder, uses four others and lets you search them simultaneously.

Jump City

www.jumpcity.com/start.shtml
Another great collection of specialized search engines.

Keen.com

www.keen.com
Advice site on the Web, interesting way to find experts.

KidsClick!

http://sunsite.berkeley.edu/KidsClick!
KidsClick! is a searchable and browsable directory of close to 4,000 Web resources of use to kids and those who work with them.

Latitude and Longitude Lists

www.bcca.org/misc/qiblih/latlong.html
A site to locate latitude and longitude of specific places.

Le Gratuit

www.legratuit.com/Outils_de_recherche/Annuaire_telephonique/
French portal site.

List of Usenet FAQs

www.cis.ohio-state.edu/hypertext/faq/usenet/top.html
Lets you search for FAQs on Usenet newsgroups by subject or keyword.

List Tool

www.listtool.com/
Web site that helps you subscribe to and unsubscribe from hundreds of mailing lists.

Look4U (China)

www.look4u.com
A people finding tool specifically geared for finding Chinese people all over the world.

Maple Square

http://maplesquare.com
Searchable and browsable Canadian Internet subject directory.

Maporama International

www.maporama.com/share
Detailed Maps of 14 European countries, Canada and the U.S., maps of countries worldwide, and driving instructions for 18 European countries. Downloadable to your Palm Pilot or mobile phone, too.

Mappy.com

www.mappy.com
Get maps and driving directions for the U.K. and much of Europe.

MG's House of News Knowledge

www.duke.edu/~mg/usenet
Directory of Usenet tools.

Military.com: Personnel Locator

www.military.com/Military/Locator/New/Splash/0,11988,00.html
Military locator site, including Coast Guard, but you must register.

Mit Opasia

www.epost.dk
Danish email finder.

Mobile Phone Numbers
www.mobilephoneno.com
Searchable database of cell phone numbers, also can search by occupation in some cases. Limited database since you need to register to be included.

Montgomery Central Appraisal District
www.mcad-tx.org
Example of property records on the Web.

National Expertise Index Homepage
http://strategis.ic.gc.ca/sc_innov/cite/engdoc/search.html
An excellent Canadian research, technology and innovation expert finder.

National Obituary Archive
www.arrangeonline.com
Has short notices from the Social Security Administration for most people and more substantial write-ups for the famous obituary databases on Lexis.

National Personnel Records Center
www.nara.gov/regional/mpr.html
Military forms to get records from the National Personnel Records Center.

Navy Personnel Finder
www.navydirectory.smartlink.navy.mil
Navy personnel finder.

Newstream
www.newstream.com
a collection of American news and experts gather and organized by a Medialink, a public relations firm. They also offer a European and U.K. collection.

NIC 0Top - Top Level Heritage
http://sunsite.unc.edu/usenet-i/hiers/top.html
Description of various Usenet newsgroups.

NRC Expertise Database
www.nrc.ca/expertise
Science experts from a Canadian government database.

OneLook Dictionaries
www.onelook.com
Access to more than 80 specialized dictionaries on business, medicine, science, etc. You can search them simultaneously.

Online Athens: Police Blotter
www.onlineathens.com/news/blotter.shtml#
Athens Daily News (Georgia) police blotter.

Open Market - The Internet Index
www.openmarket.com/intindex/index.cfm
Monthly set of Internet stats and strange facts about online usage.

PEAK Mailing Lists
www.peak.org/peak_info/mlists/
Excellent collection of mailing lists.

People Finding Service (Yugoslavia)
www.kakarigi.net/people
A message site to help reunited lost relatives, friend separated during the wars in Yugoslavia.

People Site
www.peoplesite.com
Some fee-based content. Basically a lost/found message board site for several categories and front end to a commercial investigation service as well. Categories: adoptions, former spouse, friends, lost loves, runaways, missing persons, relatives, genealogy, strangers, etc.

PeopleFind
www.peoplefind.com
Fees for some content. Public records provider focused on people searching.

PeopleSpot.com
www.peoplespot.com
Think of this as a people-finding starting point. It's got an unusual collection of biographies, people finders, email finders, reverse directories, chat groups and genealogy.

Personal Pages Worldwide
www.utexas.edu/world/personal/index.html#university
Another good collection of college sites which will point you to people and staff finding tools.

Phonenumbers.net
www.phonenumbers.net
Links to international phone directories from many countries.

Planet Alumni
www.planetalumni.com
Will help you find former classmates for high school college and military. First, you must register.

Poultrynet
http://poultrynet.gatech.edu
Looking for an unusual search engine -- here it is -- a searchable subject index devoted to chickens and poultry in general.

Public Interest Research Groups (PIRG)
www.pirg.org/reports
Click on Consumer to find reports about consumer protection information, environmental concerns, dangerous toys, tobacco, etc.

Quickmaps
www.esri.com/data/online/quickmap.html
From ESRI, the people who produce ArcData mapping software. These are the only maps I've found that can give you pretty good detail on most of the world. I've been impressed with the views it has of Cuba, more than any other online map.

Quotations Page, The
www.starlingtech.com/quotes
Eclectic collection of modern quotations.

Researchpaper.com
www.researchpaper.com
Huge collection of school-related research papers. Once in a while you may find something you need.

Reunions Online
www.reunionsworld.com
This site is not searchable, but you can post an ad looking for someone.

Rominger Legal People Finder
www.romingerlegal.com/finder.htm
A people finding collection of tools, all brought together in one place. Easy to use. You can enter a name and use checkboxes to search in email finders, white pages, celebrity files, home page searches and more.

Search Mailbase
www.mailbase.ac.uk/search.html
Search academic mailing lists by topic or name/email address of list members. Message content can be searched for each group.

Shipmates
www.shipmates.com/shipmates
(Site may forward) Shipping industry people finding tool.

SkyEx
www.skyex.com/default1.htm
Locate Hungarians around the world.

Sofcom
http://www2.sofcom.com.au/Directories/EMAIL.AUmain.html
Australian email finder.

Sources Select Online
www.sources.com
If you need an expert in Canada, this long-trusted Canadian directory is online and searchable. People pay to be listed here, however.

Specialist Email Directories
www.emailaddresses.com/email_lookup_specialist.htm
Good collection of email address finders and free email tools.

Suchen.de
www.suchen.de
German email finder and other tools.

Symbols.com
www.symbols.com/contents.html
Posts a dictionary of symbols.

The Canadian Encyclopedia
www.thecanadianencyclopedia.com/
If you want to learn about Canada, this is a great starting point. But you will need some advanced internet tools plug-ins.

The Lawyer Pages
www.thelawyerpages.com
Provides consumers with a way to find attorneys by specialty and locale.

Top of the Web
www.december.com/web/top.html
An excellent collection of links on a variety of subjects. Including searchable indices and directories. From Internet guru John December.

TopoZone
www.topozone.com
Provides U.S. topographical maps from the Web. You can search by place name or longitude and latitude, and see the map in up to four resolutions, and full screen display.

Travelangs
http://dictionaries.travlang.com/
Posts dozens of dictionaries for translating words from one foreign language to another.

U.K. Streetmaps
www.streetmap.co.uk
Has detailed maps of London streets, roadmaps for rest of mainland Great Britain.

U.S. Geographic Names Server
http://mapping.usgs.gov/www/gnis
Find any geographic feature in the U.S. (creek, mountain, church, canal, shopping center, etc.) ia this site from the U.S. Geological Survey.

UT Austin Search: Searching for People
www.utexas.edu/search/email.html
Good collection of email address finders.

Videoconferencing
http://disc.cba.uh.edu/~rhirsch/spring97/rappold1.htm
Scholarly site for videoconferencing information.

Virtual Library -International Affairs Resources
www.etown.edu/vl
International affairs experts with thousands of links in many categories.

Virtual Search Engines
www.dreamscape.com/frankvad/search.html
Excellent guide to specialized search engines.

Weather Information Sites
www.wrcc.dri.edu/ams/wxsites.html
The definitive weather site, with thousands of links.

webCATS
www.lights.com/webcats/#
A research tool for locating library catalogs on the Web, searchable geographically.

What is Usenet
www.faqs.org/faqs/usenet/what-is/part1/
Frequently asked questions about UseNet.

Whereis Online
www.whereis.com.au
Street map atlas for Australia. Put in an address and get a map, also has phone directories.

White Pages
www.whitepages.com
U.S. and Canadian phone finding tool.

World Biographical Index
www.biblio.tu%2Dbs.de/
Based on the 5th edition of the *World Biographical Index*, this site containing about 2.4 million short biographical entries of prominent individuals.

Worldwide Map Collection from UT Library
www.lib.utexas.edu/Libs/PCL/Map_collection/Map_collection.html
Has scanned maps from everywhere, old and new.

WWWomen
www.wwwomen.com
What distinguishes this from other women-oriented sites? It's incredibly comprehensive, with more than 20,000 links to all things related to women.

Yahoo! - Dictionaries
http://dir.yahoo.com/Reference/Dictionaries
Thorough list of online directories.

Yahoo! - Dictionaries (Foreign Languages)
http://dir.yahoo.com/Reference/Dictionaries/Language/
Yahoo! listing for international language dictionaries.

Chapter 6

Government Resources

U.S. and International

U.S. Government Gateways — Best Government Gateways — Best Online Government Resources — State And Regional Resources — Best Sites For U.S. And International Government Statistics — Best International Resources — Foreign Governments And Inter-government Organizations — For Finding Non-U.S. Government Sites — Finding International And Inter-government Agencies — Finding Other International Legal Information — Legal And Legislative Resources — Free Legal Resources On The Internet — Additional Congressional Sites — Top Political Sites — Political Resources — Law Enforcement Sites

Government archives can be excellent tools for researching a subject, tracking government actions, or finding data about specific people, companies, or organizations. This chapter will focus on sources for researching general subjects and tracking government activities; the following chapter – Chapter 7, Public Records – will discuss researching specific people or entities using the public records collected and provided by governments and other agencies.

While the Web is a global information place, one area where the difference between regions and countries is overwhelmingly clear is in the area of online government resources. Not all governments collect and distribute the same information, and not all governments embrace online access to information equally.

The governments in the U.S. – federal, state, and local – tend to collect and disseminate more information than most governments and also tend to use the Web to make this information available. This probably began with the U.S. federal government's early determination that the Internet solved a big democratic predicament by providing open and easy access to governmental information resources.

As the Internet has developed, federal, state and local governments have moved online and their presence has matured. Most federal agencies have progressed from simply posting mission statements and public relations materials to organizing and archiving valuable resources. The Electronic Freedom of Information Act (EFOIA), approved by Congress, requires all federal agencies to put all forms, documents and data online – a step that has continued their evolution.

The quantity and availability of information from government sites probably explains why they are some of the most popular sites on the Web.

Because U.S. government sites comprise the largest portion of government sites online, much of this chapter focuses on U.S. government resources, although there are non-U.S. resources mentioned, and many U.S. sites include non-U.S. information.

Much like the Web itself, the U.S. government's online presence is great in some places, good in others, and poor elsewhere. State and local governments generally have a strong presence on the Internet – largely for free – and many states provide excellent public access to records and information.

You should also keep in mind that the U.S. government is also the biggest wholesaler of private information. Federal and state government agencies routinely sell databases to marketing companies and other interested buyers. However, there is a viable trend of federal and state legislation to prohibit the government from making a profit from selling certain records – such as the Federal Driver's Privacy Protection Act.

U.S. Government Gateways

In the U.S., almost every federal government agency is online. There's a nationwide network of depository libraries, including the enormous resources of the National Archives (www.nara.gov), the twelve presidential libraries, and four national libraries (the Library of Congress, the National Agricultural Library, the National Library of Education and the National Library of Medicine). There are almost 5,000 government web sites from more than forty-two U.S. departments and agencies.

Because there are so many government web sites, you may need to turn to the hundreds of web sites, called government gateways, that organize and link government sites, in order to find the starting point for your research. Some gateways are simply collections of links. Others provide access to bulletin boards of specific government agencies so that you find and contact employees with specific knowledge. Guides are becoming increasingly important in light of the growing number of reports and publications that aren't printed any more, but simply posted online.

Best Government Gateways (listed alphabetically)

Unless otherwise noted, these gateways are primarily for U.S. federal governments.

Documents Center
www.lib.umich.edu/govdocs/index.html

Documents Center is a clearinghouse for local, state, federal, foreign, and international government information. It is one of the more comprehensive online searching aids for all kinds of government information on the Internet. It's especially useful as a meta-site of meta-sites.

Federal Web Locators
www.infoctr.edu/fwl/

This web locator is really two sites in one: a federal government web site
(`www.infoctr.edu/fwl`) and a separate site that tracks federal courts
(`www.infoctr.edu/fwl/fedweb.juris.htm`), both of which are browsable by category or
by keyword. Together they provide links to thousands of government agencies and departments.

FedLaw

`http://fedlaw.gsa.gov`

FedLaw is an extremely broad resource for federal legal and regulatory research containing
1,600+ links to law-related information. It has very good topical and title indices that group web
links into hundreds of subjects. It is operated by the General Services Administration (GSA).

Fedstats

`www.fedstats.gov`

A terrific collection of statistical sites from the federal government and a good central
clearinghouse for other federal statistics sites.

FedWorld Information Network

`www.fedworld.gov`

FedWorld helps you search over thirty million U.S. government pages. It is a massive collection
of 15,000 files and databases of government sites, including bulletin boards that can help you
identify government employees with expertise in a broad range of subjects. A surprising number
of these experts will take the time to discuss questions from the general public.

FirstGov

`www.firstgov.gov`

Responding to the need for a central clearinghouse of U.S. federal government sites, the U.S.
government developed FirstGov and linked every federal agency to its site as well as every state
government. It has an easy-to-use search tool, allowing you to specify if you want federal or state
agencies and to easily locate business regulations and vital records. It also lets you look for
federal government phone numbers and email addresses. This is an easy-to-use starting point,
powered by the FAST/AllTheWeb search engine. Also, check out the FAQs of the U.S.
government for questions and answers about the U.S. government (`www.faq.gov`).

Google's Uncle Sam

`www.google.com/unclesam`

Google's Uncle Sam site is a search engine geared to looking at U.S. government sites. It's an
easy-to-use tool if you know what you are looking for.

Govbot – Government Search Engine

`http://ciir.cs.umass.edu/ciirdemo/Govbot`

Developed by the Center for Intelligent Information Retrieval, Govbot's searchable keyword index of government web sites is limited to sites with a top-level domain name ending in `.gov` or `.mil`.

Healthfinder

`www.healthfinder.gov`

This is a great starting point for health-related government information. See the Susan Detwiler sidebar in Chapter 5, Specialized Tools, for more health sites.

InfoMine: Scholarly Internet Resource Collections

`http://lib-www.ucr.edu`

InfoMine provides collections of scholarly Internet resources, best for academics. It is one of the best academic resources anywhere, from the librarians at the University of California Riverside. Its Government Information section is easily searchable by subject. It has detailed headings and its resource listings are very specific. Since it's run by a university, some of its references are limited to student use only.

SearchGov.com

`www.searchgov.com`

A private company that has an effective search for U.S. government sites.

Speech & Transcript Center

`www.freepint.com/gary/speech.htm`

This site links directly to web sites containing transcripts of speeches. Pulled together by former George Washington University reference librarian and *Invisible Web* author Gary Price, it encompasses government resources, business leaders, and real audio. A large section is devoted to U.S. and international government speech transcripts – including Congressional hearings, testimony and transcripts.

U.S. Federal Government Agencies Directory

`www.lib.lsu.edu/gov/fedgov.html`

This directory of federal agencies is maintained by Louisiana State University and links to hundreds of federal government Internet sites. It's divided by branch and agency and is very thorough, but focus on your target because it's easy to lose your way or become overwhelmed en route.

U.S. Government Information

`www-libraries.colorado.edu/ps/gov/us/federal.htm`

This is a gem of a site from the University of Colorado and a good starting point. It's not as thorough as the LSU site above, but still very valuable.

Best U.S. Federal Government Web Sites

U.S. tax dollars are put to good and visible use here. A few of the government's web pages are excellent. Some can be used in lieu of commercial tools, but only if you have the time to invest.

A few of the top government sites – the Census and the Securities and Exchange Commission – are models of content and presentation. They are very deep, very thorough, and easy to use. If only the rest of the federal government would follow suit. Unfortunately, the best of the federal government is just that: the best. Not all agencies maintain such detailed and relevant resources.

Following are the crown jewels of the government's collection, in ranked order:

U.S. Census Bureau

www.census.gov

Without question, this is the U.S. government's top site. It's saturated with information and census publications – at times overwhelmingly so – but worth every minute of your time. A few hours spent here is a worthwhile investment for almost anyone seeking to background a community, learn about business, or find any kind of demographic information. You can search several ways: alphabetically by subject, by word, by location, and by geographic map. The only problem is the sheer volume of data.

One feature, the Thematic Mapping System, allows users to extract data from Census CD-ROMs and display them in maps by state or county. You can create maps on all kinds of subjects – for example, tracking violent crime to farm income by region. The site also features the Statistical Abstract of the U.S. with a searchable index at www.census.gov/statab/www/stateabs.html.

The potential uses of census data are infinite. Marketers use it to find community information. Reporters search out trends by block, neighborhood or region. Educators conduct research. Businesses evaluate new business prospects. Genealogists trace family trees – though full census data isn't available for seventy-two years from the date the census is taken. You can even use it to identify ideal communities in which to raise a family. Jennifer LaFleur, now at *The St. Louis Post-Dispatch* did a story while at *The San Jose Mercury News* using the census site to find eligible bachelors in specific areas of San Jose. Additional census resources include:

1990 U.S. Census LOOKUP

http://venus.census.gov/cdrom/lookup/

This site provides detailed census data down to the county level.

Census Tract Street Locator

http://tier2.census.gov/ctsl/ctsl.htm

This site provides 1990 census data searchable by street name or Zip Code.

State and County QuickFacts

http://quickfacts.census.gov/qfd/

At all its levels, this site has very easy-to-use census information.

And one other census-related site that is superb is the University of Virginia's Fisher Library's historical census data browser, going all the way back to 1790. It can be found at http://fisher.lib.Virginia.EDU/census/.

Census FactFinder

http://factfinder.census.gov

An easy way to find quickie facts from within the Census' huge web site.

Census Industry Statistics

www.censusgov/main/www/industries.html

Industry-by-industry statistics.

U.S. Securities and Exchange Commission (SEC)

www.sec.gov

Only the Census site is better than the SEC site, which is a first-rate, must-stop place for information shopping on U.S. companies. Its EDGAR database search site (www.sec.gov/edaux/searches.htm) is easy to use and provides access to documents that companies and corporations are required to file under regulatory laws.

The SEC site is a great starting point for information about specific companies and industry trends. The SEC requires all publicly-held corporations and some large privately-held corporations to disclose detailed financial information about their activities, plans, holdings, executives' salaries and stakes, legal problems and so forth. For more details, see Chapter 9, Business Tools.

Library of Congress (LOC)

www.loc.gov

This site is an extraordinary collection of documents. Thomas, the Library's Congressional online center site (http://thomas.loc.gov/home) provides an exhaustive collection of congressional documents, including bill summaries, voting records and the full Congressional Record, which is the official record of Congressional action. This LOC site also links to many international, federal, state and local government sites. You can also access the library's more than five million records online, some versions in full-text and some in abstract form. Though the library's entire 121 million item collection is not yet available online, the amount online increases daily. In addition to books and papers, it includes an extensive images collection ranging from Frank Lloyd Wright's designs to the Dead Sea Scrolls to the world's largest online collection of baseball cards. The Library of Congress also has a terrific collection of international information on its web site at www.loc.gov/rr/international/portals.html.

Superintendent of Documents Home Page (GPO)

`www.access.gpo.gov/su_docs`

The GPO is the federal government's primary information printer and distributor. All federally funded information from every agency is sent here, which makes the GPO's holdings priceless. Luckily, the GPO site is well-constructed and easy to use. For example, it has the full text of the *Federal Register*, which lists all federal regulations and proposals, and full-text access to the *Congressional Record*. The GPO also produces an online version of the *Congressional Directory*, providing details on every congressional district, profiles of members, staff profiles, maps of every district and historical documents about Congress. This site will expand exponentially over the next few years, as the number of materials go out of print and online. GPO Access also allows you to electronically retrieve much of the bureaucratic paper in Washington, electronically, from the Government Printing Office including searching more than seventy databases and indices. If you need some help finding things, use the topic-specific finder at this site.

National Technical Information Service (NTIS)

`www.ntis.gov`

The best place to find federal government reports related to technology and science. NTIS is the nation's clearinghouse for unclassified technical reports of government-sponsored research. NTIS collects, indexes, abstracts, and sells U.S. and foreign research – mostly in science, technology, behavioral, and social science data.

IGnet

`www.ignet.gov`

This is a truly marvelous collection of reports and information from the Inspector Generals of about sixty federal agency departments. They find waste and abuse within government agencies. It is well worth checking when starting research on government-related matters.

General Accounting Office GAO Reports

`www.gao.gov/decisions/decision.htm`

The Comptroller General Opinions from the last sixty days are posted on this GAO web site. These reports and opinions are excellent references. For historical opinions back to 1996 go to `www.access.gpo.gov/su_docs/aces/aces170.shtml`.

White House

`www.whitehouse.gov`

This site wouldn't make this list if not for its economic statistics page and the transcript of every official action the U.S. President takes (`www.whitehouse.gov/news/`). Unfortunately, as with many government sites, its primary focus is in promoting itself.

DefenseLINK – U.S. Department of Defense (DOD)

`www.defenselink.mil`

This is the brand-name site for Pentagon-related information. There's a tremendous amount of data here – categorized by branch of service – including U.S. troop deployments worldwide. And to the Pentagon's credit, they've made this a very easy site to use.

Defense Technical Information Center (DTIC)

www.dtic.mil

The DTIC site is loaded with links and defense information – everything from contractors to weapon systems. It even includes de-classified information about the Gulf War. It is the best place to start for defense information. You can even find a list of all military-related contracts, including beneficiary communities and the kinds of contracts awarded. The only problem with the site is there's no search engine to make it easy to find information.

Bureau of Transportation Statistics

www.bts.gov

The U.S. Department of Transportation's enormous collection of information about every facet of transportation. There's a lot of valuable material here including the Transportation Statistics Annual Report. It also holds financial data for airlines and searchable databases containing information about fatal accidents and on-time statistics for airlines, which can be narrowed to your local airport.

National Archives And Records Administration

www.nara.gov

A breathtaking collection of research online, for example the National Archives has descriptions of more than 170,000 documents related to the Kennedy assassination. It also contains a world-class database holding descriptions of more than 95,000 records held by the Still Picture and Motion Picture, Sound and Video Branches. This site also links to the twelve Presidential Archives with their records of every person ever mentioned in Executive Branch correspondence. You can view an image of the original document. The Archives Research Center Online has great collections of family history/genealogy research and veteran's service records.

FedWorld.gov

http://www.fedworld.gov

This thorough government clearinghouse site, run by the Commerce Department's National Technical Information Service, offers access to Firstgov, the U.S. Government's comprehensive site, but also allows you to search government publications, U.S. Supreme Court decisions and helps you find government jobs.

Federal Consumer Information Center National Contact Center

www.info.gov

While this is largely a telephone service that gets more than a million calls a year, this web site tries to provide a way through the maze of federal agencies. It includes a clearinghouse of phone numbers for all federal agencies, state, and local government sites as well.

SciTechResources.gov

www.scitechresources.gov

This is a tremendous directory of about 700 science and technology resources on U.S. government sites from the U.S. Department of Commerce, National Technical and Information Service.

Bureau of National Affairs, The

www.bna.com

An expensive but useful group of topic-focused newsletters providing details on U.S. government action at different federal agencies like the Daily Labor Report, Bankruptcy Law Daily, and the Biotech Watch. This private company has hundreds of newsletters you won't find elsewhere.

Best Sites for U.S. Government Statistics
(listed alphabetically)

For many people, the U.S. federal government is most useful at providing current and reliable statistics on trade, the economy or immigration. Here are some of the best sites for that purpose.

Bureau of Economic Analysis (BEA)

www.bea.doc.gov

As part of the Commerce Department, BEA covers national, regional, and international topics such as gross domestic product, personal income, population, employment, balance of payments, investment abroad, and foreign investments in the U.S.

Bureau of Justice Statistics (BJS)

www.ojp.usdoj.gov

A terrific U.S. Department of Justice site for statistics on crimes, victims, drugs, criminal offenders, law enforcement prosecution, courts and sentencing.

Bureau of Labor Statistics (BLS)

http://stats.bls.gov

The Labor Department's statistical shop – BLS – houses information on everything about U.S. labor, employment, earnings, prices, the economy in general, and even foreign labor statistics.

CIA World Factbook

www.odci.gov/cia/publications/factbook/index.html

The Central Intelligence Agency's publication resource about international statistics and reliable background information about other countries.

Congressional Research Service Reports

www.house.gov/markgreen/crs.htm
www.house.gov/shays/CRS/CRSProducts.htm

The Congressional Research Service, a research library for Members of Congress, releases comprehensive and reliable legislative research and analysis reports. They are not officially available for the public, but two lawmakers, Representatives Chris Shays, R-Conn. and Mark Green, R-Wisc., have posted many of them on their websites. These are excellent places for background information on legislative issues.

Fedstats

www.fedstats.gov

This site is the central locator for U.S. government statistics supplied by more than seventy federal agencies.

Fedstats - Mapstats

www.fedstats.gov/mapstats/

A one-stop shop for U.S. government statistics – broad ones, anyway – organized by state and county. Gives basic info on agriculture, population, business, crime, education, energy, and miscellaneous information.

St. Ambrose University - Statistical Sources

http://library.sau.edu/bestinfo/Online/onlindex.htm

http://library.sau.edu/bestinfo/Online/statistic.htm

Theses two sites, by Iowa's St. Ambrose University, contain some good information in useful categories – including Business and Economic Statistics, Social and Demographic Data, Public Opinion Data, and Useful Data and Formulas, which includes personal finance calculators and mortgage relocation cost estimators.

STAT-USA Internet

www.stat-usa.gov

STAT-USA is a U.S. Census Bureau-sponsored site with great statistics and good regional information. However, be aware that STAT-USA and the National Trade Data Bank, also available on this site and at Census, are excellent fee-based services.

Statistical Resources on the Web

www.lib.umich.edu/govdocs/stats.html

This is a phenomenal collection of statistical information by subject, including regional information. Its International collection (www.lib.umich.edu/govdocs/stats.html) is also outstanding and an example of how you can find so much non-U.S. information inside the U.S.

White House - Economic Statistics Briefing Room
`www.whitehouse.gov/fsbr/esbr.html`

This site is one of the most valuable clearinghouses of government statistical resources.

In addition, Paula Berinstein's *Finding Statistics Online* from Cyberage Books is an excellent book on how to locate the elusive numbers you need.

U.S. State and Regional Resources

The federal government isn't the only government entity with valuable information online. Each of the fifty state governments and six U.S. territories have a web presence. Some are top quality, like Texas and Florida. Others aren't as good. Some of these sites were recommended by Greg Notess, author of *Government Information on the Internet*.

➡ *hot tip:* To find state, county and city governments, you can use search engines to locate specific sites. Here's another way to find a localized site. They will work on most major search engines.

State: Try the URL `www.???.state??us` with the first set of question marks representing the agency's abbreviation and the second set represents the two-initial state abbreviation. For example, to find the Ohio Department of Transportation you would type `www.dot.state.oh.us`

County Governments: Many (but not all) county governments can be found at a URL like `www.co.???.??.us` where the first question marks represent the county name and the second set represents the state abbreviation. For instance, `www.co.fairfax.va.us` is Fairfax County, Virginia.

City Governments: Most, but not all, city governments can be found at `www.ci.???.??.us` where the first set of question marks represents the name of the city and the second set represents the two-initial abbreviation for the state. For example, `www.ci.milwaukee.wi.us` is the address for Milwaukee, Wisconsin.

Best Regional Gateway Sites (listed alphabetically)

Global Computing
`www.globalcomputing.com/states.html`

A solid collection of links on a variety of topics, this site is especially strong on state and local government topics.

Government Information Sharing Project
`http://govinfo.kerr.orst.edu`

This site, from the Oregon State University Library, is a great collection of online databases about everything from economics to demographics. It's particularly valuable because it has regional information on the economy and demographic breakdowns all the way down to the county level. Its content is sometimes outdated. Still, it's worthwhile for finding how federal money trickles down to localities and where state and local agencies spend tax dollars.

National Association of State Information Resource Executives (NASIRE)

www.nascio.org

This site from the National Association of State Information Resource Executives represents chief information officers and managers from the fifty states, six U.S. territories and the District of Columbia. It provides state-specific information on state-government innovations. Its companion site https://www.nascio.org/textonly/statesearch/index.cfm provides a directory for state government information by subject areas such as education, revenue, treasurers and state legislatures. It can be used to find state agencies and administrative departments grouped by function, rather than just listed by state. While not completely comprehensive, it's updated frequently and appears fairly accurate.

State and Local Governments on the Net

www.statelocalgov.net/index.cfm

Each state's resources are categorized by State Home Page, Statewide Offices, Legislative Branch, Judicial Branch, Executive Branch, Boards and Commissions, Counties and Cities. In addition, the site features some other state-oriented categories such as Multi-State Sites, Federal Resources, National Organizations, and Other Links.

It's an excellent finding aid for state and local government resources. The categorizations of each state's listings enable quick identification of pertinent web sites.

State Web Locator

www.infoctr.edu/swl/

http://vls.law.vill.edu/Locator/statecourt/

The state web locator, another site from the folks at Villanova Law School, includes links for all fifty states and a few territories and possessions. Under each state, the sites are categorized by headings such as State Home Page, Executive Branch, Legislative Branch, Departments, Agencies and Judicial Branch. It's not quite as up-to-date as some of the other sites, but it is still useful. Its sister site, the...

State Court Locator

http://vls.law.vill.edu/Locator/statecourt

...provides links to the sites of state and local courts. It includes sites with state court opinions, rules of court, and county court links. The page is arranged alphabetically by state. These two state resources, and the two federal ones from the same law school are top-notch resources.

Stateline.org

www.stateline.org

The Pew Center on the States offers useful state-specific information of all kinds – a useful site.

WWW Virtual Library: Law: State Government

www.law.indiana.edu/law/v-lib/states.html

This listing, part of the World Wide Web Consortium's Virtual Library, is a list of links to state government sites arranged alphabetically by state. Within each state section, there is no obvious order to the listed links. It links primarily but not exclusively to state legal web sites.

This site is not as useful as the State and Local Governments site because it doesn't categorize by function the links under each state heading. However, it can supplement the other site.

Yahoo! Government: U.S. Government: U.S. States

http://dir.yahoo.com/Government/U_S__Government/State_Government/

This section of the well-known Yahoo! directory includes links to governmental sites in all fifty states. It also features some multi-state categories such as Organizations and State Government Jobs. Within each state's section, it lists the main government page first, then any subcategories that might be available and then an alphabetical list of other government sites.

This site has much broader coverage of state government than some of the other finding aids.

Best International Resources (listed alphabetically by category)

While the U.S. government sites are certainly the majority of the government sites online, there are certainly several resources for non-U.S. information. Unfortunately, many of them also tend to have a transitory presence on the Web – coming and going as the various governments are able to support them. A few of the more reliable ones are listed here. You may find additional resources in Chapter 10, International Research. Many of these sites were recommended by Greg Notess, author of *Government Information on the Internet*.

International and Inter-Governmental Agencies Finders

Geneva International Forum

http://geneva.intl.ch/gi/egimain/edir.htm

Geneva International focuses on international organizations located in Geneva. This site is a directory of international institutions, missions, consulates and foreign companies. You can access the database by theme, keyword, and geography as well as by type of organization (for example, United Nations agency intergovernmental organization, non-governmental organization, and permanent mission). The institutions listed here cover a wide range of social, technical and scientific themes.

International Agencies and Information
www.lib.umich.edu/govdocs/intl.html

This site, referred to previously, is a wonderful starting point for international sites and several other government-related information. It can be searched two ways – frames and non-frames. The frames version (see the site's glossary page for more information on frames) of the University of Michigan Document Center web site is easier to navigate than the no-frames version. It directs the user to many other lists of international and inter-governmental web site via pointers. The frames version provides access via agencies, related sites and subject. The Inter-Governmental Agencies section is an alphabetical listing by acronym in the frame or by agency in the full-window version of the site. Make sure to check the international, U.S. and "foreign" resources sections; they are loaded with good resources.

International Government Publications
www.library.northwestern.edu/govpub/resource/internat/igo.html

This site from Northwestern University has listings of internet resources from non-U.S. governments and for inter-governmental organizations are one of the best starting points for international governmental sites. Think of it as a finding aid for international organizations.

Inter-Parliamentary Union (IPU)
www.ipu.org

The IPU is an international organization of parliaments. The IPU web site features two databases and links to parliamentary web sites around the world. The two databases are PARLINE and PARLIT. For all countries with a national legislature, the PARLINE database provides general information on each parliament's chambers, a description of the electoral system, the results of the most recent elections, and information on the working of the presidency of each chamber. PARLIT is a bibliographical database covering parliamentary law and legislative elections throughout the world from 1992. Other sections include Functioning and Documents, Main Areas of Activity, Publications, Women in Parliaments, and Press Releases.

This is an information-rich site, and the two databases are especially valuable.

United Nations System of Organizations
www.unsystem.org

This site is the official web site locator for the United Nations System of Organizations. It includes an alphabetic index of all United Nations Organizations (UNOs) with their abbreviations as well as the city where the headquarters is located. The other option is the official classification of the United Nations System of Organizations with its explanation of the various categories of UNOs, including program, specialized agencies, autonomous organizations, and inter-agency bodies. Under Frequently Requested Information, the site gives a listing of UNOs that provide online information for frequently requested items. System-wide searching is available across all the United Nations web sites.

This site should be your first stop if you are looking for web sites of component United Nations organizations. The listings are easy to browse, and they clearly indicate agencies that have Internet presence.

Another United Nations-related site `www.un.org/Pubs/CyberSchoolBus/` is an excellent educational site for school kids, but it is also a wonderful starting point for country-specific information and links to governments and their relations to the United Nations.

University of Minnesota: Web Sites on National Parliaments
`www.polisci.umn.edu/information/parliaments/index.html`

This page presents a simple list of links to web sites by or about parliamentary bodies from different countries. The entries range from the Estonian Riigikogu to the Nicaraguan National Assembly and the Israeli Knesset. Toward the bottom of the page is a short list of international and regional parliamentary institutions.

This is an excellent searching aid. Though simple in design, it is an effective tool for locating parliamentary web pages.

International Government Site Finders

Governments on the WWW
`www.gksoft.com/govt/`

This is quite an extensive list of international, national, regional and local governmental and government-related web servers. Its database covers many governmental institutions – including parliaments, ministries, offices, law courts, embassies, city councils, public broadcasting corporations, central banks, multinational organizations and political parties. More than 17,000 entries from 220 countries and territories are listed. Available in English and German, it is arranged in a hierarchical index organized by continent, country, then by smaller divisions. It also provides thematic groupings by categories, such as head of state, parliament, political parties, elections and currency. Also make sure to look at the regional sites for extensive links to different countries.

Yahoo Government: Countries
`www.yahoo.com/Government/Countries`

This section of the well-known Yahoo! Directory of Internet Resources covers government sites from over 1,400 other countries. Under a country's name, the links may include sections such as Agencies, Elected Officials, Embassies and Consulates, Executive Branch, Law, Legislative Branch, Military, Ministries, and Politics.

While this site is not as comprehensive as Governments on the WWW, it is a useful adjunct that occasionally has links not found there.

Legal Information

Country Studies

http://lcweb2.loc.gov/frd/cs/cshome.html

Another outstanding site from the Library of Congress, this is a series of books that contains studies of more than 100 countries. You can search all countries, any combination of countries or any combination.

Economagic

www.economagic.com

This is a great site for more than 100,000 economic charts and spreadsheets from the U.S. and Japan, as well as Asia and Europe.

LawRunner - Global Index

www.ilrg.com/nations

LawRunner functions as an international finding aid in a number of ways. It links to central government, legislative, judicial, and other legal web sites of a long list of countries. In addition, it provides a scripted interface to AltaVista that limits the search to results from top-level domain web sites.

Statistical and Economic Information

ELDIS

www.eldis.org/country/

This is a terrific country-specific guide to agriculture, environment, economics, education, gender, politics, health, and tourist info.

International Documents

www.library.northwestern.edu/govpub/resource/internat/foreign.html

This is a good starting point for finding government resources around the world. Pulled together by the library at Northwestern University.

Countries and Regions (Information)

www.trade.gov/td/tic

The Commerce Department's International Trade Administration site has some excellent background information on trade issues organized by world region.

TradStat

www.tradstatweb.com

TradStat – available on Thomson's Dialog, a commercial service – provides detailed numbers, statistics and industry-by-industry breakdowns, including tables and charts.

U.S. State Department: Regions

`www.state.gov/www/regions.html`

This is a U.S. government web site, but it provides good country descriptions accompanied by geopolitical, contextual analysis for non-U.S. countries.

CIA World Factbook

`www.odci.gov/cia/publications/factbook/index.html`

Another U.S. site, the Central Intelligence Agency's publication resource about international statistics and reliable background information about other countries is a terrific place to get background information.

U.S. Political Sites

Political sites tend to come and go with the election cycles, but the handful of top political sites listed here are consistently excellent.

Best Political News Sites (listed alphabetically)

There are several must-read publications when it comes to U.S. politics. All Politics is a free site, the rest are subscription-based.

Congressional Quarterly

`www.cq.com`

Congressional Quarterly (CQ), one of the two best news magazines covering Congress, offers some content for free and the rest by subscription. It also offers several daily newsletters, and a series of books. *Congressional Quarterly's* web site is strong for finding information about candidates at the federal and state levels, but it is expensive. They also own the *Campaigns and Elections* magazine, which is useful reading for insiders. CQ also partners with C-SPAN and puts up a lot of content for free.

CNN All Politics

`www.cnn.com/ALLPOLITICS/`

This is definitely the first place to start when you want the latest political news. It is free and CNN also offers a free weekly political briefing by email.

The Hill

`www.hillnews.com`

A twice-weekly news page on Congressional activity.

National Journal
http://nationaljournal.com/

National Journal is the other must-read news magazine covering Congress. It offers *Hotline*, the political junkies' must-read daily newsletter on politics. *National Journal* has incredibly deep resources, including polling data and information on every House and Senate race.

Roll Call
www.rollcall.com

Another twice-weekly newspaper devoted to Congressional activities.

Best Political Resources (listed alphabetically)

Almanac of Politics and Government
www.polisci.com

An annual compilation of facts and figures on American government and political figures.

Center for Responsive Politics
www.opensecrets.org

The most aggressive and accurate site where money and politics collide. It allows you to track donations and contributions for most political races. Be aware, these folks are advocates, but they tell you so. Check their extensive databases.

Elections around the World
www.electionworld.org

A comprehensive guide to elections in every independent country and autonomous overseas dependency in the world. It's also a terrific collection of links to other political databases.

The Jefferson Project
http://solstice.stardot.com/jefferson

Outstanding Jefferson Project is a great starting point for finding all types of political sites. It's free and also has links to all the presidential candidate web sites.

Political Information
www.politicalinformation.com

This is a terrific searchable collection with more than 5,000 documents on U.S. politics.

Political Moneyline
www.tray.com/FECINFO

Former FEC official Tony Raymond's site is excellent for locating contribution information and tracking money and politics. It's better and easier to use than the Federal Election Commission's site.

Politics Online

www.politicsonline.com

Politics Online is a good site for keeping current on insider trends. It is compiled by democratic consultant Phil Noble. The site is balanced, regularly updated and free.

Project Vote Smart

www.vote-smart.org

This non-profit group aggressively monitors election campaigns and gives the voter information to help them make informed decisions. An outstanding feature for researchers are transcripts of candidates' political statements.

Political Resources on the Net

www.politicalresources.net

This is a very thorough directory of international political sites available on the Internet, searchable and sorted by country, with extensive links to all kinds of political sites.

Votenet

www.capweb.net

Votenet is a good collection of political sites for details on how to raise money, vote electronically and all kinds of political resources. Some of it is fee-based.

Legal/Legislative Resources

Legal research involves figuring out how a judge in a court of law would deal with a given issue. Can you use the Web to do traditional legal research? Yes, but it will be expensive. In the United States, many of the valuable primary law materials necessary for legal research include recent federal and state court opinions, state statutes (for most, but not all, states), federal statutes, federal regulations and, in some states, administrative regulations.

In legal research, finding information is only the beginning. You must also find out how courts have interpreted existing facts, whether the opinion still stands or has been over-ruled by a higher court, and what legal scholars think of the issues.

Many of the great legal tools are now available on the Web, and the tools for analyzing the law and accuracy are online – it's just that they aren't free. There are some fine legal sites on the Internet. If you're going to court, you'll want complete reliability, which means comprehensive research. First, let's discuss where you can do legal research on some fee-based tools.

Best Fee-Based Legal/Legislative Resources

Lexis-Nexis
www.lexis.com

Lexis-Nexis is part of the European publishing conglomerate Reed Elsevier. Lexis' legal section is one of its strongest points, providing one of the few places where lawyers can get accurate and thorough information to take to court. But, it is expensive. Lexis recently purchased another of the best legal tools on the web, CourtLink (www.courtlink.com), which offers data from federal circuit courts of appeal, bankruptcy courts and U.S. District Courts, in addition to a small collection of state documents. Most of the online services begin keeping files only after lawyers have filed paperwork, but CourtLink gets in a step earlier. CourtLink includes charges made against someone.

See the Fee-Based Tools section in Chapter 5 for more information on Lexis-Nexis.

PACER
http://pacer.psc.uscourts.gov

PACER is an electronic bulletin board providing docket numbers, thorough case summaries and texts of opinions from most of the country's federal courts. It is the federal government's central courts system made available to the public. It's searchable by case number, defendant and plaintiff, and you can download – even print – the indices and summaries. It is inexpensive (relative to Lexis and Westlaw) – at well under a dollar per minute. Register for PACER at 1-800-676-6856.

Westlaw
www.westgroup.com

In their collections, Westlaw and Lexis-Nexis have large sections of primary law sources – including statutes, court cases, secondary sources and opinions, legal encyclopedias, periodicals and law journals. They are, in effect, a law library online and almost as thorough as an actual law library. Both database vendors have added natural language search features, and both provide variable pricing structures, but there's no way around the fact that they are expensive. Westlaw is now part of the Thomson group.

Best Free Legal Resources

There are some very valuable primary sources on the Internet. At the federal level, online materials include complete collections of federal statutes (known as the U.S. Code), federal court rulings, many state rulings, collections of federal and state laws as well as historical documents like the Constitution and the Declaration of Independence. Four sites stand out above the others – FindLaw, the Virtual Chase, The Law Engine, and LLRX. They are truly outstanding sites for legal information and other subjects.

All Law
www.alllaw.com

A law-focused search engine and legal directory, including state resources.

CataLaw
www.catalaw.com

This is a catalog of catalogs for legal-related information. It's a good starting point for legal information.

Counsel.net
www.counsel.net

This is a collection of chat rooms and discussion groups for lawyers, legal resources and job boards.

eLawCentral
www.elawcentral.com

Another good collection of legal tools on all aspects of practicing law.

The Law Engine
www.thelawengine.com

A super site with loads of resources on all aspects of the law. This site is a close second to FindLaw for the best of free sites.

FindLaw
www.findlaw.com

FindLaw is truly outstanding – one of the top free web sites for legal resources. It includes statutes, laws, law schools, judicial opinions, law journals and reviews, and a vast array of other searchable resources.

GigaLaw.com
www.gigalaw.com

A legal site with interpretations of the latest court rulings worldwide, changes in laws and legal research, discussion lists, newsletters, and a strong search capability.

Global Legal Information Network
www.loc.gov/law/glin/GLINv1/

This site, part of the extensive Library of Congress site, is an excellent starting point for worldwide legal resources.

Hieros Gamos
www.hg.org

This is an incredible site for international legal resources.

The Internet Law Library
www.lawguru.com/ilawlib/index.html

This site will point you to other U.S. and international legal resources.

Law Library Resource Xchange
www.LLRX.com

This site, pulled together by a group of law librarians, is a wonderful collection of legal information and other topics on government, public records and reference, among others.

Law.com (formerly Counsel Connect)
www.law.com/resources

Counsel Connect, now Law.com, is owned by investment bankers, and is closely affiliated with American Lawyer Media and its collection of legal newspapers. Law.com is an extensive legal site with a great collection of legal resources.

Legal Information Institute
www.law.cornell.edu

One of the best legal libraries online, this has an extensive online legal database, which includes Supreme Court decisions going back to the 1930s, and the U.S. Code. It also has a terrific collection of secondary sources, such as lists and biographies of legal experts as well as lists of law journals. This site also has a searchable version of the Code of Federal Regulations, the formal version of U.S. laws, at http://cfr.law.cornell.edu/cfr/.

Legal Research.org
www.legalresearch.org

This is the "best" site to reach Canadian legal resources – Catherine Best's – and it is good too.

Meta-Index for U.S. Legal Research
http://gsulaw.gsu.edu/metaindex

This site, built by the Georgia State University College of Law, provides a simple searchable database of federal legal information. From it, you can access Supreme Court opinions all the way back to 1937, every federal court of appeals decision, and the *Congressional Record*.

Thomas – U.S. Congress on the Internet
http://thomas.loc.gov

If you're tracking a bill that's moving through Congress, visit this site for official Congressional information, including voting history and committee membership. It also has full-text versions of the *Congressional Record* and the *Federal Register*. For more details and resources go to `http://thomas.loc.gov/home/legbranch/legbranch.html.`

U.S. Courts Site
`www.uscourts.gov`

This site also offers all kinds of other excellent court resources for the U.S. federal government. Including the U.S. Supreme Court, the Court of Appeals, the U.S. District Courts and the Bankruptcy Courts.

The Virtual Chase
`www.virtualchase.com/resources/contents.shtml`

This site is so good that you need to spend some time on it. It links to all kinds of legal and other information. See also the "other legal information guides" page on the Virtual Chase site.

Congressional Sites

In addition to the U.S. House and Senate sites mentioned throughout this chapter, here are sites on the various aspects of the U.S. Congress.

Congressional Record Filter
`http://ils.unc.edu/crfilter/`

As an alternative to the Library of Congress' Thomas site, you can search the *Congressional Record*, the official record of Congressional action, back to 1993. But you must fill out a questionnaire to use it. It also requires a Netscape browser.

Congressional Email Directory
`www.webslingerz.com/jhoffman/congress-email.html`

This is an email directory searchable by state or lawmaker name.

Federal Register
`www.access.gpo.gov/su_docs/aces/aces140.html`

This site offers up-to-date, full text access to the *Federal Register* the official daily publication of federal regulations: rules, proposed rules, and notices of federal agencies. It also lists all presidential executive orders and official presidential documents.

U.S. House of Representatives
`www.house.gov`

The official site for the House of Representatives. All members sites are linked directly from this site. Also linked are upcoming committee hearings and contact points for all staff and congressional committees.

U.S. Senate

www.senate.gov

The official site for the U.S. Senate. All members sites are linked directly from this site as well. Also linked are upcoming committee hearings and contact points for all staff and Senate committees.

Law Enforcement Sites

AJAX - U.S. & International Government, Military & Intelligence Agency Access

www.sagal.com/ajax/ajax.htm

A thorough set of links to establishments of the United States and international military, police and intelligence community.

Coplink.com

www.coplink.com

This is a terrific collection of over 10,000 links to other law-enforcement related sites and also has a terrific jobs database for law enforcement jobs.

Cops Online

www.copsonline.com

This site is strong for the community networking you can do through chat discussions and bulletin boards. It also has a jobs discussion board.

Fugitive Watch

www.Fugitive.com

Fugitives and missing people site that also has news and search capability.

INTERPOL

www.interpol.int

This official site of the International Police Organization provides basic information about the structure and purpose of INTERPOL. It's also helpful for background information on DNA profiling, counterfeiting, fingerprinting, and other legal-related information.

The Official Directory of State Patrol & State Police

www.statetroopersdirectory.com

This site contains a directory of state trooper and sheriff-related web sites for each of the fifty United States. It also has links to other law enforcement related sites.

Transactional Records Access Clearinghouse (TRAC)

http://trac.syr.edu

TRAC is an incredible site geared to providing statistics on U.S. federal law enforcement. It provides data on all kinds of things from employee numbers to prosecutions to sentencing details. The information is gathered using the Freedom of Information Act (FOIA), and there are separate sites on all the major law enforcement agencies – ATF, Customs, DEA, FBI, INS, IRS – which are excellent.

Additional Web Sites for Government Resources

Campaigns & Elections Magazine

www.campaignline.com
Fee-based site. Nuts and bolts magazine for campaign strategy from *Congressional Quarterly*.

Center for Public Integrity

www.publicintegrity.org
Chuck Lewis' excellent site for tracking where money and politics collide.

Commerce Business Daily

http://cbdnet.gpo.gov
Commerce Business Daily is the government's list of all bids and contracts and announcement awards. Essential reading for anyone wanting to do business with the government.

DEA Drug Data

http://www.ojp.usdoj.gov/bjs/dcf/contents.htm
Drug use statistics from the Drug Enforcement Agency.

Dept. of Education: Topics A to Z

http://ed.gov/topicsaz.html
U.S. Education Department's links to the best starting points on a variety of educational topics.

Emergency Response Notification System Data & Documentation

http://epa.gov/ERNS/
Environmental Protection Agency Emergency Response reports. You may report spills to the Coast Guard's response center at www.nrc.uscg.mil/nrchp.html

Endangered Species Database: U.S. Fish & Wildlife Service

http://endangered.fws.gov/listdata.html
Lists of endangered species compiled by the U.S. government.

EPA's Toxic Release Inventory TRI Query Form

www.epa.gov/enviro/html/tris/tris_query.html
Environmental Protection Agency's database of company toxic filings.

Establishment Search in Occupational Safety & Health Administration (OSHA)

www.osha.gov/cgi-bin/est/est1
Database of health inspection reports.

European Patent Office

www.european-patent-office.org
European patent and trademark information.

FAA Office of System Safety, Safety Data

http://nasdac.faa.gov/
Federal Aviation Administration safety data site, including "Excel" and Bureau of Transportation statistics.

Governing Magazine
www.governing.com
Fee-based site. Congressional Quarterly's magazine for state and local political campaign information.

Governments of the 100 Largest American Cities/Counties
www.wheretodoresearch.com/Govt_Local.htm
Useful site for finding U.S. government sites.

International Documents Task Force (IDTF)
www.indiana.edu/%7Elibgpd/idtf/
Documents from international organizations and governments, with links.

Litigator's Internet Resource Guide
www.llrx.com/courtrules/
A tremendous collection of federal, state and local court rules online, This site is loaded with all kinds of great legal research. This specific site gives you the court rules for courts all over the U.S.

Monthly Estimates of the U.S. Population
www.census.gov/population/estimates/nation/intfile1-1.txt
Downloadable text files of population estimate information.

National Center for Health Statistics
www.cdc.gov/nchs/
Center for Disease Control statistics collection.

National Council of State Legislators
www.ncsl.org/public/sitesleg.htm
Search for state legislation by clicking on public user. Outstanding set of resources.

National Science Foundation
www.nsf.gov
This site is focused mainly on the bureaucratic structure of this government agency; but on the interior pages you'll find a wealth of scientific information.

NTSB (National Traffic Safety Board) Aviation Accident/Incident Database
http://nasdac.faa.gov/asp/asy_ntsb.asp
Transportation Safety Board's database of aircraft accidents. More details can also be found at
https://www.nasdac.faa.gov.

Oyez Oyez Oyez
http://oyez.nwu.edu
Information about Supreme Court cases, including some actual proceedings in Real Audio format.

President's Historical Site
www.ipl.org/ref/POTUS/
This is a terrific collection of resources about U.S. presidents.

Right Site, The
www.easidemographics.com
This site takes Census data and repackages it into regional information and is a great resource for numbers and info about communities.

Social Law Library
www.socialaw.com
A great legal research site including international law sites.

State Poverty Rates
www.census.gov/hhes/poverty/poverty96/pv96state.html
HTML tables of U.S. Census information.

StateLaw - State & Local Government - Executive, Legislative & Judicial Information
www.washlaw.edu
State Internet resources, legislation, courts, statutes, etc.

TaxWeb
www.taxweb.com
Consumer-oriented directory for federal and state information.

U.S. Government Information on the Web Subject Index
http://library.stmarytx.edu/acadlib/doc/us/subjects/submain.htm
Links to U.S. government information searchable by subject.

Web sites on National Parliaments
http://www.polisci.umn.edu/information/parliaments/index.html
Resource of foreign government sites.

Chapter 7

Public Records

The Information Trail

Government Records vs. Public Records — The Changing Landscape of Public Records: 9-11 Fallout — Types of Public Records — Bankruptcy Court Records — Corporate Records — Court Records — Probate, Tax Court, Naturalization Court Records — Courthouse and State Agency Records — Fictitious Business Name Statements, Grantor/Grantee Indices, Property, UCC, Vital Records, Voter Registrations, Useful Records From Law Enforcement Agencies — Missing Children, DMV, Consumer Affairs Records — Public Records Databases Fee-Based Tools — Document Access and Retrieval — Free Public Records Tools — Non-U.S. Public Records and Other Sources of Information — Aircraft, Ship Operations — Data Sources for Asset Searches — Pre-Employment Background Checks — Thinking Outside the eBox — Additional Web Sites for Public Records

Public records are public treasures. They oil the wheels of U.S. democracy.

- They tell us if the guy living next door, who happens to be the tax assessor's brother, is assessed at the same rate as we are and if he is paying his taxes.

- They reveal whether the poor folks in town are getting the same treatment in court as the rich folks.

- They disclose when the mayor has received big campaign contributions from the contractor who's chosen to build the new city hall.

- They enable us to make certain everyone has voted only once.

- They assure us that the company selling public stocks has an adequate financial base; and that the man you're marrying isn't already married to three other women.

It's not overstating matters to say that democracy depends on public access to public records. You have the right to use them, and you can use them for any reason you wish.

- Journalists, private investigators, reunion organizers and skip tracers use them to locate people.

- Realtors use them to price property, and then hunt for buyers by combining change of address forms and marriage notices.

- Diaper-makers use them to locate and market to parents of newborns.

- Political activists use them to profile potential voters.

- Investors use them to research a corporation's board of directors.

- Employers and lenders use them to verify information on applications.

- Attorneys and paralegals use them to identify the assets of a company or a person before they decide to sue.

Lists of people, lists of companies, assets, transgressions, lists of things – nearly everything the government regulates, licenses, inspects or taxes – are available through public records. Unfortunately, public records also tend to be an American thing. Most other countries do not have extensive public records, so this chapter will focus primarily on U.S. public records.

What are the differences between government records and public records?

Government Records vs. Public Records

Government information is information the government keeps, compiles, and generates. Technically, every piece of paper in every government agency is government information – everything typed, computerized, recorded, photographed, filmed, videotaped, etched in stone or even encrypted. However, not all of it is available to us. For example, the Internal Revenue Service collects your tax return, but federal law forbids its disclosure. Thus, your tax return isn't made public and isn't a public record. Rather, a public record is government information that we, the American public, have a right to access, view and copy as a result of the federal Freedom of Information Act (FOIA). You can read the FOIA for yourself at the U.S. Department of Justice's Office of Information and Privacy under "Significant New Decisions" at `www.usdoj.gov/oip/foia_updates/Vol_XVIII_4/page2.htm`.

The Changing Landscape of Public Records: 9-11 Fallout

What was once public information may later become private. Many times, tragedies cause legislators to reconsider what information is available and how it is used. For example, after a stalker used driver's license information to locate, attack, and kill a young actress, the state of California limited access to driver's license information.

In the U.S., the decision about which records are made public is made on a state-by-state basis. So far, Florida is the most aggressive about putting records online. Texas, Kentucky and New York also have many records online. As a result of the September 11, 2001 terrorist attacks on the U.S., already there are changes in what each state is making available. Many states are removing public records from their online resources out of fear that the information may be used for future attacks.

For example, because of privacy concerns and fear of identity fraud in Texas – one of the better public record sites – the names, dates, and places of birth and death – critical facts in genealogy research – have been removed from the Texas Department of Health web site at `www.tdh.state.tx.us/bvs/registra/bdindx.htm`. That agency has decided to permanently keep the records off its web site. The records are accessible by microfiche, however, and state officials say they hope that removing records from the easily accessible Web will keep people from using the information illegally. The microfiches will still enable legitimate use.

Texas, one of fourteen states that has open birth records, is not alone in placing restrictions. California Governor Gray Davis suspended the state release of birth and death data, also because of identity fraud concerns. The state of New Jersey (`www.newjersey.gov`) has removed chemical information from its web site. New Jersey is now withholding Internet access to information – collected under its Community Right-to-Know Survey – on 30,000 private sector facilities that must report on chemical storage, including quantities and types of containers, for about 1,000 to 1,200 different chemicals. This information had been available online for about eighteen months. Firefighters were increasingly using this data, accessing it on the way to fires.

Even some of the for-profit genealogy sites, which has become a big business with the advent of such information, have taken down information. One web site, RootsWeb (`www.rootsweb.com`), reportedly removed index information on Texas and California.

The same problem has occurred at the federal level. OMB Watch (`www.ombwatch.org`), an advocacy group that monitors what information is being removed from government web sites, points to several actions that it argues is undermining information the public needs to protect its own safety.

Among the many federal web sites that have removed information are:

- The Environmental Protection Agency (EPA) (`www.epa.gov`), which no longer allows direct access to the Envirofacts databases, which explain what toxic chemicals are found in water, hazardous waste, toxic waste, and Superfund sites, and is broken down by community. The EPA had originally created the database to provide the public with direct access to the wealth of information contained in its databases. The public is no longer able to access the information.

- The Department of Energy (`www.energy.gov`) removed from its web site detailed maps and descriptions of all ten nuclear facilities with weapons-grade plutonium and highly-enriched uranium.

- The U.S. Geological Survey (`www.usgs.gov/`) has removed a number of its reports on water resources.

- The International Nuclear Safety Center (`www.insc.anl.gov`) has removed interactive maps from its site.

For more information on what has been removed, the issues surrounding their removal, and the government responsibility versus the publics right to know debate, search the OMB Watch.org web site.

> → *hot tip:* Government entities can wear multiple hats. Take the time to ascertain an agency's mission and its agency functions; you'll have a clear perspective of what data exists and the agency's goals in obtaining the information. It will put you ahead of others who may not get certain public records because their requests aren't specific.

Types of Public Records

There are many, many types of public records. Familiarize yourself with all of them because you may find that records that seeming unrelated to your search may actually contain that one kernel of information that will lead you to a major breakthrough. By stringing together multiple pieces of information, you may end up exactly where you want to be.

Bankruptcy Court Records

Here you'll find the names and addresses of all the creditors owed by the debtor, as well as the amounts claimed. In addition, you'll find a listing of the assets the person had at the time the case was filed and how much each creditor might actually get.

These records contain lots of detail – sometimes down to numbers of T-shirts owned. Bankruptcy proceedings can tip you off to other court records for details like alimony and child support.

Through PACER (http://pacer.psc.uscourts.gov/), a government-sanctioned fee-based service, every bankruptcy court is now online, A few bankruptcy courts offer information online for free. One example is in the Eastern District of Virginia where the index of every bankruptcy in that region prior to January 1, 2002 is available online and searchable at http://vaeb.uscourts.gov/home/SearchNM.html.

Several companies offer nationwide bankruptcy indices, including Lexis-Nexis (www.lexis-nexis.com), Banko (www.banko.com), ChoicePoint (www.choicepointonline.com) and Merlin Data Systems (www.merlindata.com). For additional companies, see the Appendix for The Private Online Sources of Public Records Index.

Corporate Records

To do business in your state, a corporation must register with the Secretary of State's Office, which in most states collects and maintains extensive information on corporations, other business entities, and some political contribution records, depending on the state. Most offices have some sort of an online presence, but actual availability varies by state. Commercial vendors like Merlin Data, for example, offer much easier access and indexing of the information than does the state government. Many state offices will tell you over the phone if a commercial provider exists.

In addition, two kinds of business entity records can prove valuable: limited liability company (LLC) or limited liability partnerships (LLP).

- LLCs provide the benefits of a corporation but also some of the legal protections of a limited partnership. In many states, the papers are open for inspection.

- LLPs provide varying amounts of detail.

Both kinds of documents will identify the company's officers and locations. Some states have family limited liability companies, which help families reduce their tax burdens when a business is transferred to offspring. Few of these records are free on the Internet, but many fee-based services offer indices of partnership records.

Court Records

You can find valuable data in criminal court, civil court, family court, bankruptcy court, probate court, and U.S. district courts, which are discussed, in turn, below. Court records are loaded with good information and are invaluable for backgrounding individuals and companies. Naturalization court, tax court and most other court and hearing boards are also valuable resources for information, though they're just starting to come online.

Online searching is generally limited to a copy of the courts' docket sheets. The docket sheet contains the basics of the case: name of court, including location (division) and the judge assigned; case number and case name; names of all plaintiffs and defendants/debtors; names and addresses of attorneys; and nature and cause of action. Information from cover sheets and from documents filed as a case goes forward is also recorded on the docket sheet. While docket sheets differ somewhat in format, basic information contained on a docket sheet is consistent from court to court. Docket sheets are used in both the state court systems and the federal court system.

Some state courts provide electronic access to their records. In Alabama, Iowa, Maryland, Minnesota, New Mexico, Oregon, Utah, Washington, and Wisconsin, where "statewide" online systems are available, you still need to understand (1) the court structure in that state, (2) which particular courts are included in their online system, and (3) what types of cases are included. Without proper consideration of these variables, these online systems are subject to misuse, which can lead to disastrous consequences like failing to discover that an applicant for a security guard position is a convicted burglar.

For an in depth analysis of free and fee-based court records nationwide, turn to *Public Records Online* by Facts on Demand Press. To find links to the state and municipal courts that offer free online access, visit `www.publicrecordsources.com`.

Criminal Court Records

These records show convictions ranging from felonies such as murder, rape, robbery and kidnapping all the way down to misdemeanors such as minor traffic violations, petty theft, city code violations, drunk driving, and drug possession/use. Nearly every court has a name index, but little of this is currently online. You can find an index indicating that a particular criminal court record exists, but that's about it. If you can't look it up yourself, a friendly clerk should be able to help you view at least part of the case file without charge. A friendly telephone manner never hurts. In a criminal court case, the key is to find the document called the complaint, which usually indicates the charge or charges against the defendant. It will often include the arrest report, with identifying information about the defendant and the reason for the arrest.

Civil Court Records

Civil court cases arise when someone – a person, a company, an association or a government agency – sues another person or entity. The suing party claims damage and seeks financial restitution. Civil cases can be a treasure trove because they're prompted by anger – the same anger that prompts the airing of dirty laundry. That's why divorce cases are such a valuable source of personal information.

The type of court depends on the amount of damages requested. Investigative reporter Don Ray notes that, interestingly, anger levels and court levels tend to be proportionately reversed, so that small claims court should be your first destination. In small claims court, the plaintiff might win, but learns that the defendant can hide and protect his assets, which can make actual collection impossible. The result is a victorious, but angry, plaintiff. Find that person and you'll find an oft-times juicy source of information.

Divorce Cases

Divorce documents can be great sources of personal information. In a divorce proceeding, much of what's written is fiction created to get money from the opposing side. Figure that about half of what is said is true.

Probate Court

Depending on the state, probate court is sometimes part of county's main jurisdictional court and sometimes on its own. Probate court exists to resolve disputes over who gets what when someone with assets dies. As Don Ray likes to say, "where there's a will, there's a family." And, "when there's a will, there's a fight" – because where there's a will, there's someone who feels cheated. And, when there's someone who feels cheated, there's a probate judge who'll settle the dispute and make certain things are fairly distributed, or at least as the deceased meant for it to be.

Probate court is a good place to check asset distributions to relatives. Remember the friends and enemies rule: look for a relative who may have been slighted and is willing to talk about it.

Tax Court Records

As with divorce records, tax cases sometimes involve proceedings that cause individual tax filings to be made public. Tax cases are heard primarily in Washington, D.C., but the court travels to regional offices around the country every year and conducts field hearings. Few, if any, tax court records are available online, though occasional news stories about significant tax cases are available.

Naturalization Court Records

These documents result from the process of petitioning for citizenship. Every applicant must fill out a lengthy questionnaire about his or her life in both countries and provide character references. These records are not yet online, but efforts are being made to computerize them in California and Texas. You can expect to see them online in the near future.

Recorder's Office and State Agency Records

A multitude of information can be found on recorded documents at the county, parish or city recorders' offices and at various state agencies.

Fictitious Business Name Statements

In many states, fictitious business name statements are called "doing business as" (also referred to as "d/b/a" or "dba") or "assumed names" filings. When a person, partnership, corporation or some legal entity uses another name, it's required to publish the names of the true owners. These records can usually be found for free at the Secretary of State's office, or at local government offices. Some states put them on the Web for free. They are usually available from fee-based services as well.

Property Records

You'll find some of the best information about people in property records – if the person you are investigating is a property owner.

Property records are divided into two major categories:

- Records related to property taxes, usually found at the assessor's office.

- Records related to property ownership, usually found at the recorder's office.

According to BRB Publications, property records are the fastest growing category of freely accessible records on the Internet. Most likely you'll find them at county or city level sites.

The assessor's records are updated annually and generally searchable up to five different ways – by name, property address, legal description, file number issued, or physical location (point to it on the assessor's map). The file will likely refer to the property deed on file at the recorder's office, so it makes sense to visit the assessor first. The assessor will have fairly current information about the physical property, buildings on the property, its value and the billing name and address of the taxpayer, usually the owner, but not always.

The recorder has a completely different job: to keep copies of important documents so that no one will alter them. It's important to understand this distinction. The recorder doesn't care about the contents of the document or, for that matter, whether the seller even owned the property in the first place as long as the signature is real. The assessor, on the other hand, doesn't care who owns the property as long as someone receives the tax bill.

Online commercial services index assessor information for nearly the whole country. Companies like DataQuick (www.dataquick.com) and IQ DATA Systems (www.iqdata.com) sell real estate information online. Some companies, such as KnowX (www.knowx.com), a ChoicePoint company geared to consumers, provide real estate assessor and recorder information on the Web for a fee. Many other companies are starting to move toward offering web-based access to this information.

A good free resource for finding property information on the Internet is BRB Publications' www.publicrecordsources.com. IAAO, the International Association of Assessing Officers (www.iaao.org), is the trade organization and education arm for the various tax assessors across the world. While it doesn't offer property records, you can find someone who might be able to help you locate a particular record quickly if you can't find it online.

Uniform Commercial Code

UCC filings are to personal property what mortgages are to real property. UCC filings are used to record liens in financing transactions such as equipment loans, leases, inventory loans, and accounts receivable financing. They are in the category of financial records that must be fully open to public scrutiny so potential lenders are given notice about which assets of the borrower have been pledged. Lenders usually receive some kind of collateral when they lend money, and UCC filings can help identify both parties and their assets.

Uniform Commercial Code (UCC) recordings are filed either at the state or county level, according to each state's law. Some states require dual filing.

States that offer online access to corporation records generally put the lien records online as well. There's less likelihood of finding this information online at the local government level, where private companies compete to obtain and offer access.

A number of private companies have created their own databases for commercial resale. As with tax liens, this is a very competitive arena. There are several nationwide commercial databases available, like Lexis-Nexis and ChoicePoint, as well as strong regionally-focused companies like Superior Online (www.superiorinfo.com) and Commercial Information Systems (www.cis-usa.com).

Tax Liens

The federal government and every state has some sort of taxes, such as those associated with sales, income, withholding, unemployment, and/or personal property. When these taxes go unpaid, the appropriate state agency can file a lien on the real or personal property of the subject. Normally, the state agency that maintains UCC records also maintains tax liens.

Individuals vs. Businesses

Tax liens filed against individuals are frequently maintained at separate locations from those liens filed against businesses. For example, a large number of states require liens filed against businesses to be filed at a central state location, i.e., Secretary of State's office, and liens against individuals to be filed at the county level, i.e., Recorder, Register of Deeds, Clerk of Court, etc.

State vs. Federal Liens

Liens on a company may not all be filed in the same location. A federal tax lien will not necessarily be filed at the same location/jurisdiction as a lien filed by the state. This holds true for both individual liens and as well as business liens filed against personal property. Typically, state tax liens on personal property will be found where UCCs are filed. Tax liens on real property will be found where real property deeds are recorded, with few exceptions. Unsatisfied state and federal tax liens may be renewed if prescribed by individual state statutes. However, once satisfied, the time the record will remain in the repository before removal varies by jurisdiction.

Grantor/Grantee Indices

Sometimes the recording offices refer to their records as "Grantor/Grantee" records. This term is a catch-all for a wide assortment of public records. You can find judgments, property transfers, financing statements, liens, notices of default, powers of attorney – about one-hundred document types.

If you can find them free online, it'll be at the county level. Commercial services harvest this information and sell it. Superior has put up most of New York City's real property, deed/mortgage and other property records. Many of the larger data providers, such as Lexis-Nexis, have much of this grantor-grantee information as well.

Vital Records

Birth, death, marriage and divorce documents are all vital records. They are required documents, but, in many states, access is restricted.

Birth Certificates

Birth certificates are loaded with information. You'll find names of parents, mother's maiden name and previous births, place of birth, address, profession, place of employment and obstetrician. They're a great way to find the parents' places of employment and their birthplaces as well.

Marriage Certificates

Marriage certificates are also filled with information. They give the bride's maiden name, home and work addresses of both parties involved and the witnesses at the time. Most states require two witnesses at a wedding (typically, the best man and the maid of honor), who are usually great leads for tracking information about a divorce or good background about the husband or wife.

Divorce Records

Divorce records can be found in the civil court indices or sometimes contained in separate databases. The actual records often include much detail about the divorcing couple – everything from assets to pet custody.

Death Certificates

Death certificates lead you to the existence of possible probate court filings. Probate court records, in turn, might provide the names of relatives and other family members, as well as lists of liabilities and assets.

Two genealogy sites from Ancestry.com (`www.ancestry.com`) and Rootsweb.com (click on SSDI at the Rootsweb site) offer the Social Security Death Index for free on the Web. Other services offer that same database, but at a cost.

Online death record indices can include the deceased's name, date of death, date of birth, destination of Social Security benefits, Social Security Number, location of the Social Security Number issuance, and last residence. But only the actual death certificate – available at the county level and not yet online – includes cause of death, place of death, and next of kin.

Using Vital Records

Are these records online? Yes, but usually it costs money to access them. The Internet is particularly weak for public records like birth and marriage certificates. Kentucky (http://ukcc.uky.edu/~vitalrec) offers online indices of marriage, divorce and death records, and is the first state to do so. One company, VitalChek, has a voice and fax network program through which, for a fee, they'll find certified copies of vital records. Its web site (www.vitalchek.com) lists accessible vital records. Indices to state vital records can also be found through Vital Records Information, (http://vitalrec.com/index.html). Both indices are free, but record orders cost money.

Several non-U.S. countries post vital records online, including Australia, Austria, Canada, England, Finland, France, Germany, Hungary, Ireland, Italy, New Zealand, Poland, Portugal, Scotland, and Slovakia. For list of links, go to http://vitalrec.com/links2.html

Other vital records are available from fee-based vendors. DCS Information Systems (www.dnis.com), a Texas-based company, offers many states' birth records, Merlin Data Systems offers marriage records for California. Legal database companies, like Lexis-Nexis and Thomson's Westlaw offer death records and indices to many of these records, but not death certificates. Some states also offer death records online including California, Kentucky, Maine and Texas.

Voter Records

If you're trying to locate someone, a useful public record is a voter registration record. Most adults register to vote, and the records are almost always public. Every state has a central election agency or commission, and most have a central repository of voter information. The degree or level of accessibility to these records varies widely from state to state. Over half of the states will sell portions of the registered voter database, but only ten states permit individual searching by name. Most states only allow access for political purposes such as "Get Out the Vote" campaigns or compilation of campaign contribution lists.

Voter Registration records are a good place to find addresses and voting history. Nearly every state blocks the release of Social Security Numbers and telephone numbers found on these records. However, the records can generally be viewed in-person at the local level.

There are some vendors that sell voter records – of course paying strict attention to the state access laws. One company is worth mentioning here, Aristotle (www.aristotle.com). They offer nationwide voter information as a fee-based service that can be purchased on a state-by-state basis.

Useful Records from Law Enforcement Agencies

There are a number of state agencies that maintain record databases for law enforcement purposes. This category includes, criminal records, incarceration records, motor vehicle records, and consumer licensing records. They are useful resources in this context.

Some records make their way into the public view because they become part of news stories, are published in phone books or other ways. These are technically not public records, as the public has no rights to this information. But they become public anyway.

Arrest and Incarceration Records

Arrest records have been openly available for decades from most local police stations in the form of the "booking log." They're usually not available from public record vendors (remember: arrests don't always result in convictions), but some communities and community newspapers have begun to post arrest records. Many states and cities have posted inmate records and lists of who is in the local jails. Florida, for example, has a searchable directory of its statewide inmate population at `http://www6.myflorida.com/activeinmates/search.asp`.

Prisoner locator services are available free from the states' corrections or prisons departments, and online inmate locator searches for several states can be found at the Corrections Connections Inmate Locator site (`www.corrections.com/links/inmate.html`) or from the Bureau of Prisons at (`www.bop.gov/inmate.html`).

Criminal Records

Every state has a central repository of major misdemeanor, felony arrest records and convictions. States submit criminal record activity to the National Crime Information Center, which is not open to the public. Not all states open their criminal records to the public. Of those states that will release records to the public, many require fingerprints or signed release forms. The information that could be disclosed on the report includes the arrest record, criminal charges, fines, sentencing and incarceration information.

In states where records are not released, the best places to search for criminal record activity is at the city or county level with the county or district court clerk. In some counties, felony and misdemeanor records are maintained in a combined index, in others felonies and misdemeanor records must be checked separately. Many of these searches can be done with a phone call.

For detailed information about criminal records, see *The Criminal Records Book* by Facts on Demand Press. The *Public Record Research System (PRRS)* from BRB Publications provides detailed descriptions of each criminal record related jurisdiction – and 20,000 others – which can be extremely helpful in determining which court or courts should be checked for felonies and misdemeanors. It is available at `www.publicrecordsources.com` as an online subscription. It is also available in book form and as a CD.

A few local governments and some state-related agencies post criminal records. Here are some examples:

- Eight Oklahoma counties have posted criminal records for free at `www.oscn.net/applications/oscn/casesearch.asp`. But while the Oklahoma site includes defendant identifiers, most of the free sites do not.

- The Marion County Sheriff's Department and the Indianapolis Police Department make criminal histories available at a low fee. Civil records are available for free at `www.civicnet.net`

- In South Carolina, a statewide criminal check is available for US$25 per name from the South Carolina Law Enforcement Division at: `www.sled.state.sc.us/SLED/default.asp?Category=SLEDCRC&Service=CRC`

Sexual Predator Databases

At last count, forty-some states have made available on the Internet portions of their databases of people convicted of sex crimes. Many of these sites offer searches of prior inmates and will show those individuals on probation.

An example of Florida's is `www.fdle.state.fl.us/sexual_predators/`.

A national state-by-state list showing online sites and detailing when written searches are required can be found at `www.stopsexoffenders.com/statelistings.shtml`. Search tools will readily turn up other such lists.

Missing Children Information

Databases of missing children are readily available on the Internet. Search under "missing children."

Driver and Motor Vehicle Records

The retrieval industry often refers to driving records as "MVRs." Typical information on an MVR includes full name, address, Social Security Number, physical description and date of birth along with the conviction and accident history. Also, the license type, restrictions and/or endorsements can provide background data on an individual.

Vehicle registration records have an edge over driver's license records as an information source because they're updated yearly. They can provide you with the owner's name (sometimes both husband's and wife's), address, name and address of the bank or title-holder, usually a credit union or finance company. Of course, there's also the make, model and year of the car, its license number and even its vehicle identification number (VIN). Some registration data is available from fee-based services. Due to privacy concerns, none is freely accessible on the Internet.

In recent years there have been major changes regarding the release of motor vehicle data to the public. This is the result of the Driver's Privacy Protection Act (DPPA). States differentiate between permissible uses – fourteen are designated in DPPA – and casual requesters to determine who may receive a record and/or how much personal information is reported on the record. Effective June 2000, if a state DMV chooses to sell a record to a "casual requester," the record can contain personal information (address, etc.) only with the consent of the subject. Some states even block certain personal information to those with a "permissible use." Further, many state DMVs no longer sell lists of drivers or vehicle owners to commercial vendors and marketers.

Ironically, as states are closing the door to many users, states are also moving towards making data readily available electronically to those with a permissible use. The Private Online Sources of Public Records section at the back of this book profiles a number of commercial vendors that specialize in supplying motor vehicle related records. Those interested in further information about either driver or vehicle records and individual state restrictions should obtain BRB Publications' *The MVR Book*.

Consumer Affairs Records and Licenses

Most states license, certify, or register professionals such as contractors, hair dressers, doctors, psychologists, private investigators, automobile repairers, accountants, electricians, funeral directors, and so forth.

The information available, however, is likely to be limited. Usually you can find out the date of licensing, a work address, date of birth and, in some cases, pertinent education. Few listings are online for free, though fee-based services offer licensing information for many states. Some states do post professional license lists – for example the New York State Education Department Online License Verification at `www.op.nysed.gov/opsearches.htm` and the Utah Department of Commerce Division of Occupational and Professional Licensing at `www.commerce.utah.gov/opl/index.html`. Commercial vendors provide regionally focused information on licensing boards. Merlin specializes in California and KnowX focuses on Georgia. Therefore, they are particularly good sources for this kind of information.

Public Records Databases Fee-Based Tools
(listed alphabetically)

A Note About Public Record Vendors Online

There are five main categories of public record professionals: distributors and gateways; search firms; local document retrievers; investigative firms; and information brokers. The Private Online Public Record Sources Indices and Profiles sections of this book contain information on over 170 of the primary distributors and gateways who offer online information of some type.

Distributors are automated public record firms who combine public sources of bulk data or online access to develop their own database products. Primary distributors include companies that collect or buy public record information from its source and reformat the information in some useful way. They tend to focus on one or a limited number of types of information, although a few firms have branched into multiple information categories.

Gateways are companies that either compile data from or provide an automated gateway to primary distributors. Gateways thus provide "one-stop shopping" for multiple geographic areas or categories of information.

Companies can be both primary distributors and gateways. For example, a number of online database companies are both primary distributors of corporate information and also gateways to real estate information from other primary distributors.

Search Firms. All over the Internet, public records vendors are easily found. These vendors are generally referred to as search firms. These companies furnish public record search and document retrieval services through outside online services or through a network of specialists, including their own employees or correspondents.

➜ *hot tip:* **Keep in mind is that some "search firms" are legit, some are not. If a vendor offers a "national criminal record search" or offers access to a driving record without asking for the use or purpose of the request, then beware! Many states have restrictions on what can be released; companies who offer you records for a purpose you are not eligible for could later cause some very serious legal or ethical problems for you.**

Listed below are a few other favorite public record database sources. Again, a complete list of the nation's leading public record distributors and companies can be found in the Private Online Public Record Sources section in the back of this book.

Accurint
www.accurint.com

Accurint is a strong database of public records available for a fee.

ChoicePoint
www.choicepointonline.com
www.knowx.com
www.dbtonline.com

ChoicePoint is the major player in letting you search county, state and federal public records information, including UCC filings and other corporate documents. These tools are used by lawyers, private investigators, law enforcement, and insurance companies to conduct searches for locating people and verifying business information and assets. They have purchased and merged several large public records companies – CDB Infotek, KnowX, IRSC, and DBT Autotrack among others – and now offer all of them as part of the ChoicePoint suite of tools.

Dataquick
www.dataquick.com

Fee-based real property information center.

IQ Data Systems
www.iqdata.com

Real estate information and full document retrieval from every U.S. jurisdiction.

Superior Information Services
www.superiorinfo.com

This is a regionally-focused, fee-based business search for retrieving court documents and corporate filings from several East Coast states.

Netronline
www.netronline.com

Parts of the web site are free; the deeper information is fee-based. See the free section below.

Rapsheets
www.rapsheets.com

Rapsheets provides two pricing options, a membership fee that gives you limited access to criminal searches and social security traces, of course, within the limits of the Fair Credit Reporting Act – and also has a non-members instant criminal search available as well.

Document Access and Retrieval

Local document retrievers search specific requested categories of public records usually in order to obtain documentation for legal compliance (e.g., incorporations), for lending, and for litigation. They do not usually review or interpret the results or issue reports in the sense that investigators do, but rather return documents with the results of searches. They tend to be localized, but there are companies that offer a national network of retrievers or correspondents. The retriever or their personnel go directly to the agency to look up the information. A retriever may be relied upon for strong knowledge in a local area, whereas a search generalist has a breadth of knowledge and experience in a wider geographic range.

The 725+ members of the Public Record Retriever Network (PRRN) can be found, by state and counties served, at www.brbpub.com/PRRN. This organization has set industry standards for the retrieval of public record documents and operates under a Code of Professional Conduct. Using one of these record retrievers is an excellent way to access records in those jurisdictions that do not offer online access.

Free Public Records Tools (listed alphabetically)

The following sites are excellent sources of public record resource lists and tools.

Black Book Online
www.crimetime.com/online.html

Robert Scott's site is geared to private investigators, and therefore has a terrific collection of links for public records research.

BRB Public Records Online
www.brbpub.com

A strong collection of free public records resources from the publisher of *Find It Online*. Their articles and newsletters are cutting edge.

National Association of Secretaries of State: Corporate Backgrounders
www.nass.org/busreg/corpreg.html

A good starting spot for basic corporate filings searching at the state sites.

Netronline
www.netronline.com

Netronline is a real estate and public records site. The public records portion links you to different states' official sites, and the property records portion is available on a per-piece basis after you register. Parts of the web site are free; the deeper information is fee-based.

Portico
http://indorgs.virginia.edu/portico/home.html

An outstanding collection of public records links.

PublicRecordFinder
www.publicrecordfinder.com

A list of thousands of free public records sites.

Searchsystems.net
www.searchsystems.net

It is one of the largest free collections of public records databases on the Web. Formerly the PAC-Info site, just click on a state and you'll get a list of all free public record collections for that state.

Non-U.S. Public Records and Other Sources of Information

First are two examples of sites that specialize in general information about a nation or region:

Cerved
www.cerved.com

This is an Italian public records and company information site. Content is primarily in Italian, with search capability in English and Italian.

United Kingdom Public Records Office
www.pro.gov.uk

The official records site for British public records.

Aircraft Registration

Aircraft registration is available in several countries – some are official government records, others are private companies. Among the countries available are Australia, Austria, the Bahamas, Brazil, Croatia, Denmark Ireland, Japan, the Netherlands, New Zealand, Norway, South Africa, Sweden, Thailand, U.K., and Venezuela. Landings.com is the best place to find this information:

- www.landings.com/_landings/pages/search/search_namd_full.html (U.S.)
- www.landings.com/_landings/pages/search/reg-world.html (World)

Legal Information

Every country in the world has laws and figuring out what the local laws are can be difficult. World Law, an Australian site (`www.austlii.edu.au/links/`), has a terrific database of what the laws are in different countries, and it provides a convenient link to AltaVista's Babelfish in case a translation is needed.

Ship Operators

Since the shipping industry is worldwide, there are some shipping registries available around the world. A good starting point for information on this is the World Shipping Directory at `www.wsdonline.com`.

Data Sources for Asset Searches

By Lynn Peterson

Asset searches are conducted by potential lenders, business partners and people considering initiating a lawsuit, among others. Components of an asset search include:

Liabilities

If there are no significant liabilities then the way is cleared for a full asset investigation. One good way to assess liabilities is to search for bankruptcies, liens, judgments and notices of default or foreclosures – generally through commercial vendors. Also, bankruptcy case files contain detailed records of both assets and liabilities, as do pending civil litigation.

Real Property

A home is usually a person's largest single asset. Most public record vendors offer statewide databases searchable by owner name. Don't forget that ownership may be recorded under someone else's name (often a relative), or as a family trust.

Vehicles, Boats and Aircraft

Motor vehicle records, searchable via many vendors, include cars, trailers, buses, RVs, and motorcycles. In some states, such as California, it's not possible to search the whole state by name of individual; rather, vehicles are registered by address. Smaller boats can be found via DMV searches in several states. (Boat registrations in some states may be handled by the Department of Fish and Game, the Department of Natural Resources, Parks and Wildlife, or a myriad of other state agencies and are not available online.) Larger vessels (those over 27 feet) are registered with the U.S. Coast Guard, and can be searched through commercial vendors.

Similarly, the Federal Aviation Administration's aircraft ownership records are also commercially available. You can also check state governments for what is publicly available.

Credit Reports

Credit reports can provide clues to real property held in someone else's name. As an example, when no property is found, the credit report might list a mortgage or a car loan. They can also point to hidden assets by indicating many credit cards or large credit card balances. Non-header credit report information is accessible only with the written consent of the creditee, or when the creditor possesses a judgment against the creditee. And, as noted elsewhere in this chapter, credit reports are error-prone and unreliable as sole sources of data.

Business Records

Look for businesses in which the subject is an owner or financial participant. Numerous online databases of company affiliations are available. Also, search for corporations, partnerships and fictitious name filings (such as DBAs). Uniform Commercial Code (UCC) filings may also indicate assets. Sales tax permits can point to retail businesses owned by an individual. ChoicePoint offers sales tax information from Texas and California, for example.

Court Records and Judgments

Court records can contain detailed financial data – especially divorce, probate and small claims. See earlier in this chapter for more detail.

Stocks

Stock ownership is available online for individuals who own more than five percent of a publicly-held company through the SEC's EDGAR database and other free and commercial sources. The same is true of stock ownership data of officers, directors, and shareholders that own ten percent of the stock of a public company and those who intend to sell a specified amount of a restricted stock. (For more detail, see Chapter 9, Business Tools.)

Bank Accounts and Insurance Policies

Although public records, such as court cases, can point to the existence of bank accounts and insurance policies, the information isn't usually searchable online. Private investigators sometimes provide bank account or insurance information, but old-fashioned phone work involving the use of pretexts is how this information is usually obtained. Bank loans listed on credit reports can indicate an individual's relationship with a particular bank; however, credit reports don't contain bank account information (although UCC filings may).

--- Lynn Peterson, President of PFC Information Services, Inc. in Oakland, California, is a well-known expert in public record research and retrieval. Lynn's web address: www.pfcinformation.com
email: lpeterson@pfcinformation.com

Pre-Employment Background Checks

By Lynn Peterson

Pre-employment background screenings can be conducted only with written permission from the applicant. They vary widely, depending on the nature of the job. If the employment is denied due to information discovered with the background check, the applicant is entitled to a copy of the report. Here are some common data sources.

Understanding Credit Reports

Credit reports are divided into three sections. The first, known as the header, includes formal names, former names, addresses, former addresses and, sometimes, employment history. Thus, credit reports are a good way to verify the information provided on the application or resume. Also, this information may point to other geographic areas or previous names that should be checked.

The next section contains public records, such as bankruptcies, tax liens and judgments – and, sometimes, collection accounts.

The third section is about the applicant's accounts and payment history – of interest if the job entails money-handling, or if amounts owed are disproportionate to salary level. Also listed: creditors that report data, such as amounts owed, monthly payments due and payment histories.

While credit reports can be obtained online, they are restricted. Small employers usually obtain this information through a smaller credit reporting agency or broker.

Keep in mind, however, that credit reports are notoriously unreliable. An old study from 1998 by the Public Interest Research Group found, for example that about seventy percent contained some type of error, and twenty-nine percent contained errors serious enough to result in a denial of credit.

Social Security Numbers

Social Security Numbers (SSNs) can be verified via direct access to credit bureau databases or through most of the large commercial public record vendors. The information available from Social Security verification is essentially the credit header and nothing else. Input the Social Security Number and out comes verification, as well as header information for any names associated with that SSN as reported by creditors to the credit bureaus.

For example, a potential employer might seek to verify a Social Security Number provided by applicant Susie Smith, born in 1972 only to find that the Social Security Number was issued in 1965 under the name of Gordon Jones. It could be that the Social Security Number itself was mistakenly transcribed, or perhaps the actual card has been altered in some way. Often identity thieves will use Social Security Numbers of people who are dead.

Criminal Records

There's no national criminal records database, except for the FBI's NCIC (National Crime Information Center) database, which isn't public and is accessible only by criminal justice agencies. There are literally thousands of separate criminal indices maintained at the counties, parishes, cities and townships nationwide, and most are not available online.

At the state level, more than half the states have designated their statewide criminal records repositories as public records, but only a handful allow online access (including Alabama, Colorado, Florida, Hawaii, Maryland, Mississippi, Oregon, Texas, and Washington), often at a cost. But the records may not be complete. For example, Maryland's records include state district court records from all counties, but only three circuit courts – even though all felonies are tried at the circuit levels.

The Texas Department of Public Safety Criminal Records database at http://records.txdps.state.tx.us/dps/default.cfm allows anyone to search statewide for criminal histories and sex offender information – the first state to allow Internet access to criminal data. However, the courts and agencies don't always report their data in a timely fashion, and don't always include dates, locations and other details. Similarly, Ohio and Michigan offer online access to statewide arrest (not conviction) records via a subscriber-based service called OPEN - Online Professional Electronic Network. Bear in mind also that criminal records are indexed by defendant name, not Social Security Number.

Commercial vendors offer online criminal court records for parts of Arizona, California, and Texas but the information is usually limited to defendant name, case number, and date. The actual documents cannot be retrieved online . Numerous vendors will retrieve criminal records (with a delay of up to ten days) – including Adrem Profiles (www.adpro.com) and AVERT (www.avert.com). It links to its parent company, ADP. Through PACER (the source for Federal Court and Bankruptcy records described previously in this chapter), many federal courts are searchable online by defendant name, with no other data available online. Many of the federal courts allow access to criminal cases. However, records are searched by name of defendant and no identifying information pertaining to the subject is available online. One company, Court Express, offers software to make it easier to search PACER at www.courtexpress.com.

One more note about criminal records checks. Numerous services on the Internet advertise "nationwide criminal records checks." The adage that "if something sounds too good to good to be true, it usually is" clearly applies. These so-called "national criminal records" usually consist of a search of online newspapers and magazines. The gaps are obvious since usually only the most serious and bizarre crimes are reported in the newspaper, and online searches of newspapers don't include every newspaper in the country.

Civil Court Records

In general, civil court records are more widely available online than criminal court records. In fact, PACER provides online access to civil records from most U.S. District Courts. However, as with online criminal records, once an applicant's name is matched, the actual records must be pulled. Some of the larger vendors that provide immediate access to civil court records are Lexis-Nexis, ChoicePoint, Merlin and Superior Online.

DMV Reports

As noted earlier in this chapter, DMV information access is restricted, though many states sell the data to large "middle man" firms that, in turn, sell the data to third-party vendors. Large commercial vendors such as ChoicePoint's DBT allow for delayed retrieval of DMV information in most states. Among notable gateways, TML (www.tml.com) stands out because it provides immediate online access to DMV data from approximately thirty states. But this data is severely restricted as to who can get this information. For more information about DMV data restrictions, consult the Driver's Privacy Protection Act and the Federal Fair Credit Reporting Act.

Bankruptcies, Liens and Judgments

Information about bankruptcies, liens, and judgments is included in credit reports, although credit reports are notoriously inaccurate. For example, judgment data may not be listed if, say, a Social Security Number isn't listed when the judgment is recorded at the county, or if the address doesn't match. All of the major online commercial public records vendors offer a combined index of bankruptcies, liens and judgments, but availability varies from state to state. Bankruptcies can also be searched online via PACER.

Professional Licenses

Professional license information is just beginning to appear on the Internet. Commercial vendors offer online data for more than a dozen states. Utah offers online searches on the Internet, and Nebraska provides Internet access to private investigators and collection agency licenses. The American Board of Medical Specialties (ABMS) Public Education Program's physician locator and information service offers Internet access to physicians' specialty certification records. (For more about specialty people finders, please consult Chapter 5, Specialized Tools.)

Academic Records

University registrars can verify academic credentials over the telephone. Also, many alumni associations have web sites that include biographical information about alumni. A good starting point is Christina DeMello's section of the Colleges and Universities Web Site Links `www.mit.edu:8001/people/cdemello/geog.html`). Other resources are listed in Chapter 5, Specialized Tools, in the people finder tools.

Workers' Compensation Records

These records are public in some states, but are obtainable only via subpoena in others. The Americans with Disabilities Act (ADA), which specifies access, states that employers (with fifteen or more employees) can access Workers' Compensation claims only in cases of a clear, conditional offer of employment.

Most frequently, Worker's Compensation records are obtained from employment screening firms and third party commercial vendors that maintain proprietary databases, such as AVERT, U.S. Datalink (`www.usdatalink.com`) and Informus (`www.informus.com`). California allows public access to EDEX, its database of adjudicated claims. Information about California's Workers' Compensation EDEX is available via CompData (`http://wcab.net`). Other states are expected to follow suit.

--- Lynn Peterson, President of PFC Information Services, Inc. in Oakland, California, is a well-known expert in public record research and retrieval. Lynn's email address: `lpeterson@pfcinformation.com` Web site: `www.pfcinformation.com.`

Here is an interesting article written by Don Ray.

Thinking Outside the eBox

By Don Ray

If you're one of millions of World Wide Web searchers who has made a major search engine your home page, you may have fallen into an easy trap. You may have been lulled into the one of two beliefs – that you can find everything you could possible want on their site and that everything of any importance to anyone is already online somewhere. Both of these beliefs are false. The most successful searchers of information use very specialized tools on the Internet – tools to suit the needs of their particular searches. And the best searchers are ready to jump off the Net at any moment when it leads them to off-line sources and people.

A good example is when I decided to track down the criminal records of my stepfather who died in 1974. Aside from knowing his name and date of birth, I knew he had spent a lot of time in Peoria, Illinois, and that he had gone to prison when he was a very young man. Although I wasn't sure which state he had served time in, Illinois was the logical place to start.

As much as I might have wished, I knew from experience that my late stepfather's prison record would not be accessible on the Internet. Why? Because people post the vast majority of the information on the Internet with the assumption that there will be a sizable number of people desiring to gather the information. The demand for prison records of more recent inmates would certainly be a thousand times greater than records from the 1920s and 1930s. So did I skip the Internet altogether? Absolutely not.

I went straight to the web site of the Illinois Secretary of State – knowing that, in most states, that's the office that maintains very old records, the state's archives. It took only a few minutes to find that, indeed, the types of records I was seeking existed and, even better, appeared to be thorough, detailed and well indexed.

Score one for the Internet.

I also knew from experience that, in many cases, the records stored at the state archives are not accessible without the blessing – okay, approval – of the agency that generated the records. So I jumped off-line and called the Secretary of State's office to find out the name and phone number of the person at the Illinois Department of Corrections who had the power to grant me permission to get information from their files.

As I suspected, he referred me right back to the Secretary of State's office, but he gave me the name and phone extension of the woman who could look the name up. When I told her I'd already talked with the man from Corrections, she was happy to run my stepfather's name through her computer index. But I didn't just give her a name – I told her all about how my stepfather had first revealed to me that he'd been in prison. My excitement rubbed off on her and she went out of her way to help me solve my personal mystery. In essence, I deputized her.

She was tickled to tell me that there were, indeed, documents on file regarding my stepfather. I still didn't know what part of the files were available for public inspection, so I kept quiet while she read me everything on her computer screen. Only after I learned that he had served eleven years for armed robbery and another year in federal prison for embezzling did I ask her if I could buy a copy of the file. Fortunately, she was able to send me the files.

When I received them, I pored over every page and digested the gravity of my stepfather's crimes – how he and three others had tied up all three generations of a farm family and stolen $40,000 in negotiable bonds. My stepfather had held the gun on them.

This was not information available on the Internet.

Toward the back of the file I was surprised to find reference to two wives he had had before my Mom and reference to two sons generated by those marriages – one from each wife.

Armed with the boys' names and years of birth, I went back on the Internet again and found the phone numbers for the courthouses in the cities in which I believed the boys were born. I used email to contact a friend of mine on the East Coast – a young woman who has a wonderful knack for making clerks want to trek down to the dusty basements and manually pull the old divorce files. Then she encouraged the clerks to read to her the vital information she needed – the boys' full names and birth years.

Back to the Internet to a fee-based database, DBT's Autotrack (now a part of ChoicePoint), that enabled me to search the entire United States for the two boys. I found one in a small town in Texas and the other in North Dakota. A free phone directory database on the Internet helped me find phone numbers for both of them.

No, I didn't contact them using email – nothing is more effective and dramatic than a phone call from someone who grew up with their dad. They were both happy to learn things about the father they had hardly known – and they were even more thrilled to get to meet each other – half brothers. And I should add that they both adopted me as a full-fledged brother. They're now a permanent part of my life – all made possible because of the Internet as well as the telephone and some wonderful, helpful people.

When you need to find any type of information, keep in mind that what you're seeking may not exist on the Internet – or it may not exist where you think it is or should be. But there's almost always a file or a document out there that has the information you want within it and there's almost always a person out there who knows where it is. Find the person and you find the rest.

The Internet has enabled most anyone to find old friends, school mates or military buddies. But some people make the mistake of limiting their search to national telephone directories. Or often they post on various web sites the names of the people they're seeking – in the hope the person they're searching for will see their names.

Savvy searchers of people – or searchers of information a particular person may have – think in wide angles. They know that there are thousands of places on the Internet that list the names of people – or thousands of sites with searchable databases.

You should look for names in databases made accessible by local, state and federal databases – such as county recorders and assessors who allow searches of their property records, county sheriffs who allow the public to search the jail records for inmates, courts that allow searches of their civil indices, state controllers who allow people to look for unclaimed moneys, state attorneys general who offer up listings of convicted sex offenders, secretaries of states who allow anyone to search records of corporations or partnerships or campaign contributors and the Securities and Exchange Commission (`www.sec.gov/edgar/search/webusers.htm`) that allows anyone to find astoundingly detailed information about corporations and the people behind them.

Determined investigators don't stop at government web sites – they use search engines such as AltaVista (`www.altavista.com`) to search for people's online resumes and, armed with key pieced of information, search fee-based databases such as Merlin Data Systems (`www.merlindata.com`) to obtain dates of birth, Social Security Numbers, names of spouses and key addresses. With that information they can access the unofficial transcripts from some colleges and universities their targets attended.

Type the names and email addresses of the people you're investigating into databases that maintain full-text records of messages people have posted on Usenet bulletin boards such as (`http://groups.google.com`). If you're really feeling clever and determined, try searching the online auction sites such as eBay (`www.ebay.com`) for the names and email addresses of the people you're investigating. Some people on the lam support themselves by selling things on Internet auction sites. The sites allow any subscriber to get a listing of all of the people who bought items from any particular seller. By contacting the buyer, an investigator can sometimes learn the exact address where the buyer sent the money for the item he or she bought.

And then there are the genealogy sites (`www.familysearch.org`), alumni sites (`www.classmates.com`) and military association sites that often list detailed information – information people voluntarily submitted about themselves or their family members.

Remember, a search on the best search engine will not usually hit on these entries – you must do the search on the particular site in question. One of my favorites contains the names, photographs and service information of thousands of former members of the U.S. Navy, U.S. Marine Corps, U.S. Coast Guard and Merchant Marines: `www.lonesailor.org/log.php`

Ignore everything you're hearing or reading about privacy promoters seeking to limit access to information on the Internet – profits and capitalism will always win in the end. The very government that may enforce the new Internet privacy laws are the very folks who are putting information on the World Wide Web at the fastest pace. And right behind them are corporations, associations, and smart businessmen who are more than happy to provide information to a public with an insatiable appetite for information.

To be a successful researcher, I suggest you keep up with these wonderful resources as they blossom and be wise enough to jump off the 'Net and communicate with the people who have the answers – not on their web sites, but in their brains.

--- Don Ray is a multimedia investigative journalist and a sought-after speaker in information gathering, privacy and public records. He has written books on sources of information, interviewing, checking out lawyers and on document interpretation. You can reach him at `donray@donray.com`

Additional Web Sites for Public Records

Also see the Vendor Profiles Section for public record companies that offer database and online services

California Sex Offenders

www.sexoffenders.net
Site that tracks sex offenders who have been released into communities.

CompletePlanet

www.completeplanet.com
Bright Planet offers a directory of public databases and specialty search engines has been expanded – not very focused, but worth a look.

Find an Eye M.D.

www.aao.org/aaoweb1/findeyemd/index.cfm
Searchable database from the American Academy of Ophthalmology.

Government Records.com

www.governmentrecords.com
Aristotle Industries' new web site with extensive voter records and other public records-oriented databases for sale.

Harris County Appraisal District

www.hcad.org
Example of property records on the Web.

Health Pages

www.thehealthpages.com
Nationwide database of physicians and dentists and other health related professionals.

Information & Privacy, The Office of

www.usdoj.gov/oip/oip.html
Various filtering agents and bots.

Montgomery Central Appraisal District

www.mcad-tx.org
Example of property records on the Web.

NASD Public Disclosure for Brokers

www.nasdr.com/2000.asp
Database on member brokers, includes current and previous employment.

Online Athens: Police Blotter

www.onlineathens.com/news/blotter.shtml
Athens Daily News (Georgia) police blotter.

Online Death Records

http://home.att.net/~wee-monster/deathrecords.html
Online searchable death records including SSDI and database of obituaries.

Public Interest Research Groups (PIRG)

www.pirg.org/reports
Consumer protection information, environmental concerns, dangerous toys, tobacco, etc.

Stockbrokers.com

www.stockbrokers.com
Stock brokers and other financial professionals by name. Registration required, no fee.

Tracers

www.tracersinfo.com
Fee-based site. They offer access to county, state and federal public records information.

U.S. Bankruptcy Court for the Western District of North Carolina

www.ncwb.uscourts.gov
North Carolina bankruptcy court.

WebDental

www.webdental.com
Database of practicing dentists.

Chapter 8

News Resources Online

It spread like a wildfire. Everyone was talking about it – the most candid, honest, refreshing graduation speech they'd ever heard. It was allegedly an 850-word commencement address given by author Kurt Vonnegut to the graduating class of 1997 at the Massachusetts Institute of Technology. The speech was spiced with pithy life advice such as "Wear sunscreen," and "Be kind to your knees. You'll miss them when they're gone."

In journalism, there is an expression – "If your mother tells you she loves you, check it out." Perhaps this Vonnegut story is fictitious. What could be done to check it?

You could check the MIT web site to see if there was a published commencement address or a mention of Vonnegut as the speaker. You could attempt to contact Vonnegut. You could look for newspapers from the alleged day of the speech and see what had been written about it.

Using Lexis-Nexis and Dialog, a check of the *Boston Globe* and *Boston Herald* reveals nothing. Typing "be kind to your knees" on a search engine results in no hits. In addition, the MIT web site claims that U.N. General Secretary Kofi Annan gave the commencement address for the 1997 graduating class.

Here's what really happened:

The "sunscreen speech" was never given. It had actually been part of a column by Mary Schmich, a self-deprecating *Chicago Tribune* columnist, best known as the text writer of the cartoon *Brenda Starr*. As a result of the email and subsequent controversy, she was interviewed on ABC's *Nightline* and by *People Magazine*. Vonnegut heard about the "sunscreen speech" from his wife after someone sent her a copy of the email.

At MIT, an editorial assistant started getting a lot of phone calls from journalists about the "speech." After checking a copy of Annan's speech, the assistant got an email suggesting that the "Vonnegut speech" sounded remarkably similar to a column in the *Chicago Tribune*. She searched the *Tribune*'s web site and found Schmich's "Sunscreen" column. To confirm her findings, she visited MIT's library and viewed a two-month old paper copy of the issue of the *Tribune* that contained the column. That day, she told a reporter, "You can't believe everything you read on the Internet."

What started as a rumor and mushroomed overnight into an "email classic" was able to be disproved quickly and efficiently using online resources. As evidenced by this anecdote, the Internet is powerful. Using the Internet, rumor and innuendo can spread like a brush fire. At the same time, the Internet can be used to uncover the truth.

Go to `www.wesselenyi.com/speech.htm` to view the full text of the fictitious "Sunscreen" speech.

A similar situation occurred after September 11, 2001 when people were overwhelmed by an email titled "America–Good Neighbor" that proclaimed that America was a great neighbor and friend to the world. It had originally been written in 1973 by Canadian broadcaster Gordon Sinclair but appeared to be new and wonderfully patriotic in light of the September 11 terrorism.

You don't have to be as prominent as Kurt Vonnegut or as pro-American as Gordon Sinclair to find information about you mentioned in the news or for references to show up on the Internet. If your name was mentioned in a newspaper, chances are good that it can be found – either on the Internet or through the fee-based databases discussed in Chapter 5, Specialized Tools.

The Internet has dramatically increased the pace of daily journalism. Distribution online has turned once-a-day newspapers into 24-hour operations, increasing the pressure on television and radio broadcast news operations to meet continuously rolling deadlines. It has also dramatically changed how news is archived – no longer is old news only relegated to microfilms in the library. In fact, "old news" – as long as it is less than a decade old – is sometimes as readily available on the Internet as today's headlines.

The Internet has enabled just about anyone to be a reporter and a publisher. With the capability for frequent updates and unlimited archive space, there's enough free news coverage available on the Web to satisfy any news junkie.

There are general news tools, regional news tools, specialized news tools based on topics, and different kinds of news tools depending on the part of the world you are looking in. Some are highly credible and some are simply gossip or public-relations "spin" trying to persuade you of something. And like the Internet, the technology is changing rapidly. News is now delivered wireless to your pager, cell-phone or hand-held device. Video-satellite phones are now broadcasting images from remote war-torn parts of the world right into your living room. Streaming video images are available in some countries directly to your cellular phone.

And, if you know what you are looking for and have the resources and tools to get it, you can have customized news delivered to you almost any time, anywhere.

So how can you use this world of online news to your advantage? Online news sources can help you find an expert, learn about a medical condition, locate someone you once knew or provide background information on a particular topic. Whether you are following an election, checking on the political climate in the Middle East, searching for information on a recent school board meeting, or trying to find a weather forecast for a city you are going to visit, you can find the latest information online through news sources.

What Kind of News Are You Looking For?

Just as you don't use an electric drill to put a nail in a wall, you need to use right kind of information resource to find the right kind of information. It's an important lesson to learn that applies to all kinds of searching.

Online Versions of Stories from Print, Radio, or TV

If you are just looking for a copy of a story already published or broadcast, often the original publication's web site is a good place to start. Television stations have started to provide video clips and archives of video and text materials for free or inexpensively. Public Broadcasting's *News Hour with Jim Lehrer* (`www.pbs.org/newshour`) goes so far as giving you audio and text transcripts of the nightly news program. CNN (`www.cnn.com`) provides transcripts of most of its programs as well as video streaming. Search engines AltaVista (`www.altavista.com`) and Lycos (`www.lycos.com`) are among several search engines that now offer video clips that are searchable by keyword. Most transcripts are searchable by keyword.

Many newspapers and magazines provide free access, but force you to register so they can gather marketing information about you and/or for you. Others require passwords or payment. Some publications provide access to one or two stories to encourage you to purchase the hard copy of the magazine, and still others provide free access to that day's news, but make money by selling copies of archived material for a modest fee.

See the lists of news wires, newspapers, magazines, newsletters, television stations, radio stations, e-zines and other publications later in this chapter.

More In-depth Coverage of a Subject

Generally speaking, the free news resources don't come anywhere close to replacing commercial online news databases like Lexis-Nexis (`www.lexis-nexis.com`), Factiva (`www.factiva.com`) and Thomson's Dialog (`www.dialog.com`). The fee-based services offer unmatched depth of coverage. At best, the Internet's leading free resources offer a two weeks' worth of coverage or a few dozen stories about a subject; the commercial services add thousands of new articles every day and maintain deep archives that are available on demand. In addition, the commercial services offer a full range of searching options, like field searching and Boolean capabilities. For a much more extensive discussion of this, see *USA Today* Librarian Bruce Rosenstein's article in *Online Magazine*, July, 2001 at: `www.infotoday.com/online/OL2001/rosenstein7_01.html`.

Archived Stories Not Available Elsewhere

As discussed in the Chapter 5, Specialized Tools, the giant supermarkets of information for news are Lexis-Nexis, Factiva, the Dow Jones/Reuters combination, and Thomson's Dialog. These are without a doubt the best tools for finding archived newspaper and magazine material on the Internet – but they cost money. All three require a subscription, although Factiva does allow you to purchase articles on a per-article basis. The cheapest is Factiva, you can access their entire database by getting a *Wall Street Journal* subscription for US$59.00 plus the per-article fee..

What makes all of these tools so valuable is the depth of their resources. Lexis-Nexis, for example, has full-text newspaper files going back to the 1970s. And each of these tools offer different newspaper collections, regional search capability and different dates of coverage.

Breaking News

Breaking news is news that is happening *now*. Which means that you need to find an online resource that is constantly updated. This is the area of news research most people are unfamiliar with. When the terrorist attacks on the U.S. happened September 11, 2001, millions of people turned to the Web to find the latest information. But so many of them turned to the wrong tools – using search engines instead of news tools.

If you went to a general search engine and put in the phrase "world trade center" as many tried to, you didn't get the most recent news about the planes crashing into New York's Twin Towers. For the most part, you saw old photos of the still-standing World Trade Center. That's because general search engines only search for what is already contained in their databases and don't search for news. It took most of the search engines between four to six hours to post special pages including the latest headlines.

If you had looked at AltaVista, you would have found information with the latest news quickly. That's because they have a partnership with a genuine news search tool, Moreover (`www.moreover.com`), which provides the latest headlines, scouring only news-related sources for information. Another news-related site, NorthernLight's current news page, also had the information shortly after the event.

News sources like news wires (Associated Press, Reuters, and United Press International), TV networks, the major well-respected newspapers, or magazines had the latest news about September 11 on their sites as fast as their reporters could gather the news. You could also have checked any of the news-only search tools (also known as focused crawlers) and quickly found the latest wires and news information on the breaking story.

These kinds of tools give you several advantages over other web resources. They get you the most current information because they can avoid the time lag issue faced by search engines having to index material, and they get you to deeper, more focused content. Each news tool is unique so spend some time with many of these before you need them for breaking news information. How do you figure out the best or most reliable? The best answer is to go with the brand you trust. The Web gives you an opportunity to experience many news options. Thousands of news outlets all over the world post extensive information on their web sites for free. Many let you search archives, but a great many see news as another potential revenue stream and charge for access to their archives. I list the best of each category of these tools later in the chapter.

> ➜ *hot tip:* Be aware of two important things – with the consolidation of many journalism organizations, some newspapers now own TV stations and the reverse. The same holds true for magazines and newsletters. So a great trick to finding excellent journalism sites is to look at which sites are linked to the good journalism sites you like. Also, if you find news on a web site, you also need to be aware of copyright issues before you can use the information.

Free vs. Fee News Sites

With so many free and fee-based options out there, how do you know which source to turn to? The answer is if possible, you use both. Always use a combination of web resources and traditional online services to get the maximum, most thorough results. If you are just looking for a quick piece of information, you can use the Web and find what you want. If you want to find great depths of information about a topic, you will need a combination of the free and fee-based tools to get it.

Another major benefit of using the traditional online services is the ability to search across multiple publications. They each have a standardized form, allowing you to pick and choose the resources you want to look at. All three of these resources also offer extensive Boolean and field searching, allowing you to pin down the specific information you are looking for.

The Web has several strengths over commercial online services, including:

- Latest material
- Easiest way to find photos, graphics and video
- Especially valuable for those on tight budgets
- Easier to use for the spontaneous search
- Easier for general searches, browsing, finding additional links
- Online chats and discussion groups can point you to more resources, experts – only available on Web
- Some discussion groups are archived

Traditional commercial database also have some strengths over the Web, including:

- Availability of older material and anything archived
- Much easier to search hundreds of files simultaneously
- Ability to use sophisticated Boolean searching, field searching like dates
- Cleaner search environment (knowing what files you choose from)
- Reduced risk of viruses

- Access to easily indexed categories

- Absence of advertising

- Reliability of finding what you need when you need it

- Accuracy – commercial companies stake their well-deserved outstanding reputations on it

→ *hot tip:* **Time is money. If time is the over-riding factor in your research, go with a fee-based service. Unless you know specifically where to look on the Web, you can search hundreds of publications simultaneously and restrict your search by date or subject.**

Types of News Resources

Just as there are many types of news searches, there are many types of news sources. Like all the other research tools, some of these sites fall into many categories. They are listed them below by the category they are best known for. Be sure to use a mix of each of these tools in your news research, following the guidelines covered above.

News Wires

While news wire services have always been crucial information sources in newsrooms, they've become more influential as the Internet has expanded. The Internet's strength is its ability to accommodate immediacy of breaking news – which the news wires deliver. One example is the relaying of Federal Reserve Board announcements that influence the world markets. News wires are staples of online news services and key components of news filtering tools.

There are five types of wire services:

International news wires all operate differently and have varying standards of editorial quality, journalistic integrity, and credibility. The two dominant international wire services – The Associated Press (AP) and Reuters – are credible, reliable, journalistically-independent operations with thousands of bureaus worldwide. They cover everything from general interest to politics to business to crime for their local, national and international services. The AP is dominant in the U.S., but Reuters is more well-known around the world and has a much bigger online presence. That's because AP is a cooperative organization available to member organizations only, while Reuters offers its menu of wire service products to any interested consumer.

National news wires represent their home countries but are largely unknown elsewhere. Examples include Notimex in Mexico, Xinhua of China, Jiji and Kyodo in Japan, and PA in England. Some are credible news organizations and others are publicity vehicles for their governments. Notimex, the Mexican news service, for example, is a reliable, largely credible news service covering issues related to Mexico, but it is funded by the Mexican government and its coverage must be regarded with reservations.

Specialty wires are geared to specific topics, like business, telecommunications or health care. Examples include Dow Jones and Bloomberg Business News, both of which offer business-focused coverage that is journalistically strong and credible.

Re-packagers are wire services that are efforts by existing news organizations to sell their coverage to other news outlets. The *Washington Post* and the *Los Angeles Times* sell their combined products as one wire service. Another, the Knight-Ridder-Tribune wire, consists of news from papers owned by the Knight-Ridder newspaper group (including the *Philadelphia Inquirer* and *Miami Herald*) and the Tribune papers (which include the *Chicago Tribune*, *Los Angeles Times*, and the *Orlando Sentinel*). The repackaged products are considered as credible as the newspapers they represent.

Corporate press release services like PR Newswire, Internet Wire, Business Wire, and U.S. Newswire are publicity machines for companies. They aren't objective news tools, but rather, relayers of company press releases and corporate messages with no editorial or journalistic credibility. That said, they're still valuable for information that issuing companies want you to have – but you must not mistake them for unbiased sources.

Best Online News Wires (listed alphabetically)

Many other companies offer access to wires. America Online, CompuServe and Prodigy all offer varying clusters of wire services. AOL offers the strongest collection of wires of those three. Nearly all of the portal sites now offer news wires of some form or another.

The Associated Press (AP)

http://wire.ap.org

From this web site, you can access the AP's regional and national wires.

Reuters

www.reuters.com

You also can get Reuters' key headlines and the top stories at Yahoo!

United Press International (UPI)

www.upi.com

United Press International, another wire service, recently moved to the Web.

Newspapers

There are more than 5,000 newspapers online, according to two of the best journalism news web sites, Newlink and *Editor & Publisher* (www.editorandpublisher.com/editorand publisher/business_resources/medialinks.jsp). Both provide online links to thousands of newspapers as well as TV, radio and other media. The top international news link site is Kiosken, which links to more than 15,500 sites (http://www.esperanto.se/

kiosk/engindex.html). As far as newspapers, not all provide full-text and even fewer provide archives of past issues. Interestingly, more than forty percent of all online newspapers are now based outside the U.S. Many sites make their money from advertising and provide the online versions of the newspapers for free as publicity and a public service. Some make money by providing interview transcripts and other reports for a fee. Still others charge only for access to archived content older than a few days.

The best online newspapers are taking full and creative advantage of the Internet's unlimited storage space and interactivity. For example, you may be able to input your Zip Code and find out how your local schools rank statewide, your lawmaker's Congressional voting record, or the local crime rate relative to similar neighborhoods.

Archive holdings vary. Some newspapers – such as the *Los Angeles Times* and the *San Jose Mercury News* – charge readers per story read or downloaded. Some newspapers archive only their web site postings; others, only the print publication; still others archive both. For example, you can search the *Washington Post*'s two-week web archive for free, and its full-text newspaper archive (dating back to the 1980s) from commercial vendors. Unfortunately, most online newspapers do not offer access to their archives at all.

Best Online Newspapers

Here are some of the better and bigger online newspapers, listed in alphabetical order.

Chicago Tribune

www.chicagotribune.com

This award-winning site is cleanly designed and easy-to-use: the home page connects you to splash screens that rotate new content every twenty seconds. Click on items of interest; then click on the *Tribune* logo to return to the main page. Because the *Tribune* is a multimedia company, it often offers multimedia content that includes video clips, sound clips and photo images. The archives, however, aren't free. It provides seven days free if you register.

International Herald Tribune

www.iht.com/frontpage.html

The *International Herald Tribune* is a joint project of the *New York Times* and *Washington Post* and is printed in Europe. It has some tremendous access to wires of all kinds and is internationally focused so it can be a great resource.

Los Angeles Times

www.latimes.com

The *Los Angeles Times* has put its stellar newspaper online with a fee-based archive and a free retrieval feature. The *Los Angeles Times* site is deep and offers extra features to online users. Incorporated into the online stories are links; for example, a business story from the print version may contain links to current stock quotes and corporate profiles of companies mentioned in the article. Its archive is relatively inexpensive and easy-to-use. Note: only same day articles are free.

Le Monde

`www.lemonde.fr`

Excellent French daily newspaper -- an international newspaper for the French-speaking world.

New York Times

`www.nytimes.com`

The *New York Times* site is, like the newspaper, almost in a class by itself.

Posted is most (but not all) of the national edition (the Sunday magazine, for example, isn't online). There are a few online-only sections like its terrific, state-of-the-art articles about cyberspace news. You can also contact reporters, debate with fellow readers and obtain details that didn't make it into the edited versions of the stories. The *Times* site requires registration, and they sell their subscriber lists to advertisers. They also sell their archives to subscribers at a substantial discount compared to nonsubscribers.

One of the most creative uses of the *Times* online is the "Book Review Section" and the "Books on the Web Section," which provide books reviews going back to 1980.

USA Today

`www.usatoday.com`

Another terrific web site, loaded with much of the newspaper's contents and many more developed just for the web site. It's interactive with chat groups and shopping deals. Unfortunately, it does not include much of the reporting of its sister, the Gannett News Service, which carries local reporting from many newspapers around the country. For that you need to go to the many national Gannett-newspaper sites.

One of its best features is in the "Life" section and is a "Hot Sites" web guide – Sam Meddis' not-to-be-missed column once you are hooked on searching online. The newspaper's "Technology" section is also top-notch.

Wall Street Journal

`www.wsj.com`

The Journal Interactive edition costs US$29 a year if you subscribe to the print version and $59 if you don't – a real bargain. It contains nearly everything printed in *The Journal*, plus special online reports, a sports section and access to the Personal Finance Library — which includes the Dow Jones Business Directory, a guide with reviews and links to more than 350 useful business sites. You also get access to the extensive Dow Jones Publications Library. Searching the more than 3,500 newspapers, magazines and newsletters costs nothing; headline viewing is also free. The first ten articles are free; subsequent ones are about US$3. each.

Washington Post

`www.washingtonpost.com`

One of the most exhaustive news web sites – there are two weeks' worth of the entire newspaper there – easily searchable, and also most of the Associated Press wire for that same two week period. The *Washington Post* does a good job of regularly updating its news site, especially when major news is breaking. It also offers all kinds of special databases, including access to the Hoover's Corporate Directory of more than 10,000 companies in more than thirty-six countries (see Chapter 9, Business Tools, for more about Hoover's), news links and reference material for more than 200 countries and news wires about all fifty states. Like the *Los Angeles Times* online, you must register to use *The Washington Post*.

Magazines & Newsletters

The magazine world has jumped onto the Internet as a way to disseminate information for current and potential subscribers, offer corporate information, and advertise other products. It has made once-weekly magazines into daily and regularly updated news publications, greatly increasing the value of their product.

The Internet makes niche publications easily accessible. For a publisher, the problem is finding the appropriate balance between giving enough and giving too much information for free on the Internet. Publishers want to provide enough online material to gather interest, but they don't want to provide so much that a print subscription becomes unnecessary. Some see the online access as a way to supplement print subscriptions and others see it as an alternative to print subscriptions. As a result, there are all kinds of resources, ranging from bibliographic information like tables of contents, abstracts, and some full-text articles to some entire magazines and newsletters.

Many magazine sites also require user registration even if there is no access fee. Few magazines post the full contents of their publications. Most simply offer a few, selected "hot articles" from the issue in full text.

Magazines like *Advertising Age*, when posting key articles on their sites, change the titles and often omit other citation information for the web site editions, making research difficult. On the other hand, *Advertising Age* does put additional supporting information on the web site (`www.adage.com`) that does not find its way into the print addition.

Some of the best magazines in the world offer excellent sites on the Internet. AOL Time Warner, for example, owns *Time Magazine*, *Money*, *People* and many of these sites offer more content than is contained in the weekly magazines. *Business Week*, for example, puts out special technology sections regularly on its outstanding web site (`www.businessweek.com`). *Atlantic Magazine's* (`www.theatlantic.com`) Atlantic Unbound combines the magazine's print edition with web-only resources including audio files with poets reading their poems, while *National Geographic* (`www.nationalgeographic.com`) offers amazing graphics in its archived "Features" section and an archive that dates back to 1888. Some web sites go even further than their magazine counterparts. One good example of this is *Smithsonian Magazine* (`www.smithsonianmag.si.edu`), which offers articles back to 1995 features not available in the printed magazine such as a gallery of photographs by Smithsonian photographers.

Best Magazines & Newsletters (listed alphabetically)

With so many excellent quality magazines, what is most useful to a researcher are the tools to help you find magazines. There are several outstanding magazine finding tools online.

FindArticles.com
www.findarticles.com/PI/index.jhtml

This site features an archive of hundreds of magazine articles from more than 300 magazines since 1998. It is searchable by subject or by magazine and what makes this site unique is that it is the first traditional periodical aggregator to release its material on the Web with ad revenues as the sole funding mechanism. It's a joint project of the LookSmart search directory and the Gale Group, now a Thomson company.

Ingenta
www.ingenta.com

This is a searchable online database that gives you a summary and also provides an article delivery service for more than 26,000 magazines and journals – mostly academic ones. It is a huge collection and a terrific place to find academic bibliographic citations or see what kind of educational, scientific, legal and medical journals may have information on the subject you are researching. This used to be called Uncoverweb and was originally part of the Colorado-based CARL library network.

MagPortal.com
http://magportal.com

This is another excellent aggregator of magazine articles. It features more than 150 periodicals, and when you search, you get an abstract of what's available and a link to the full-text. It is also keyword searchable. By logging in, you can have searches done for you based on keyword selection with results held for you until you log on again. The only downside is that the archive only goes back about to 2000.

Media Finder
www.mediafinder.com

This fee-based site has a phenomenally deep collection of newsletter listings, which are keyword searchable. It has a national directory of magazines and another of directories and catalogs. You must subscribe to access.

NewJour
http://gort.ucsd.edu/newjour/

This is a searchable archive for NewJour, the Internet mailing list for announcing new electronic journals and newsletters. This is a great place to find out if a newsletter exists online with data about a subject you are researching.

PubList
www.publist.com

This is a clearinghouse of more than 150,000 of the world's periodicals. It contains hyperlinks to some of the publishers and in some cases you can purchase the article. It's searchable by keyword or browsable by publisher, title, and subject. However, its primary purpose is to get you to buy subscriptions to these periodicals and buy some articles on a per-piece basis.

Slate
`www.slate.com`

Slate is an excellent political and pop-culture-focused online magazine. Its daily political updates are opinion, but guaranteed to spur an argument.

Television & Radio

As brands and known commodities, the networks are trying to be bold and innovative on the Internet, but also maintain the look and feel that appeals to their TV viewers. ABC, NBC, CBS, CNN, FOX, Canadian Broadcasting Corp (CBC), and the BBC are excellent resources for news information. Several of them also have superb radio networks and strong web sites as well.

Best Television & Radio Sites (listed alphabetically)

ABC News
`www.abcnews.go.com`

Like the other networks, ABC offers breaking news headlines, and in-depth features at its site. Its web site is rich with content and lets you search for video clips from the multimedia archives. In addition, ABC has put considerable effort into discussion groups about breaking news. It is one of the stronger news sites online. ABC News is part of Disney Corporation (`www.go.com`).

ABC Radio, working with Real Audio technology, regularly puts breaking news online at `www.abcradio.com`.

BBC News
`http://news.bbc.co.uk/`

BBC News and BBC Radio are respected worldwide and are available on this excellent web site. This site offers access to all kinds of BBC content and is worth spending some time on to help you customize what you are looking for. It offers world and U.K. news and is also available in many languages. It also offers a news ticker, which you can place on your computer for the latest headlines, and email alerts for breaking news as well as a wireless version for your hand-held.

One more note, BBC News' "advanced search" lets you limit by publication date so it can be incredibly useful (`http://newssearch.bbc.co.uk/ksenglish/query.htm`).

CBC News
`www.cbc.ca/news/`

Canada's flagship news operation is an excellent news web site with world-wide information. It is easily searchable, downloadable to your handheld-wireless device and provides email alerts sent on key topics. It also offers Canadian radio news and a French-speaking version.

CBS News
`www.cbsnews.com/sections/home/main100.shtml`

The CBS News site is one of three CBS sites. Its hard news site offers news, video and sound clips, and is updated frequently – especially when major breaking stories occur. Its other sites,

CBS Sportsline and CBS Market Watch are linked at the bottom of the site. They are excellent resources for sports and business news. CBS Radio, partnered with the Westwood One Radio Network and Infinity Broadcasting, offers a full complement of news at www.cbsradio.com.

CNN Interactive
www.cnn.com

CNN Interactive offers breaking stories, as well as easy-to-download video clips with sound. CNN does graphics well, and most coverage is graphics-rich, so when a new story breaks in a distant part of the world, you'll get maps and background as well as the news. One of its strengths is that the current coverage is cross-referenced with previous stories about the same topic.

The CNN site maintains about a month's worth of content on the site as a free searchable news database, which is much more extensive than other news sites. CNN also provides extensive access to video archives and live video from that day's news.

Fox News
www.foxnews.com

Fox News has emerged as one of the largest cable networks in the United States and it is a part of Rupert Murdoch's efforts to build a worldwide cable TV network. It has built a useful web site loaded with content including video segments. It also links to Fox Sports. One unique feature, which is excellent for researchers, is the site posts a rolling transcript of its current news report.

MSNBC News
www.msnbc.com

MSNBC is the web outlet for the resources of NBC, MSNBC and sister network, CNBC. NBC was the first TV network to launch a major presence on the web, and it is a very strong site. NBC has intelligently tied all its local affiliates to the web site, enabling you to choose a region from a country map on the site and access local news.

National Public Radio (NPR)
www.npr.org

If you are a fan of *Morning Edition, All Things Considered* or other wonderful programs, you can now go to NPR's web site and find the programs you missed. Regional programming is available.

Video Images
Want the latest video images on your computer, here are some of the best places to go:

ABC
http://abcnews.go.com/sections/us/video_index/video_index.html

AP/Washington Post
http://a188.g.akamaitech.net/f/188/920/1m/www.washingtonpost.com/wp-srv/mmedia/aplive.htm

Trend Stories (not breaking dailies)

BBC
www.bbc.co.uk/newsa/n5ctrl/live/now1.ram

CNN
www.cnn.com/video/netshow/

C-SPAN
www.c-span.org/terrorism/

MSNBC
www.msnbc.com/m/v/video_news.asp

PBS
www.pbs.org/newshour/video/index.html

Price's Video List
www.freepint.com/gary/audio.htm

E-Zines

One of the Internet's most unusual creations is e-zines – magazines developed online that do not have companion printed versions. Like blogs, they tend to be opinionated, hip, irreverent and sometimes bizarre publications, often produced by one person or a small group of people. Many are done for fun or personal reasons. Most don't contain advertisements, and are not really geared for a mass audience.

E-zines and online publications appear, disappear and reappear as quickly as mouse clicks, but here is one good starting point to help you uncover the unique world of online-only publications:

Doug Millison's Kiosk of Online Journalism
www.online-journalist.com/resources2.html#Online

News Search Tools

The latest – and most useful trend – has been the increase in news-specific search tools. They are focused crawlers that search news-only or news-focused sites. Several of these tend to be excellent sources for breaking news, but also provide great depth in finding information. Several of these are also journalism collections or sites with lots of links. Be aware they fit in multiple categories.

➡ hot tip: Use several news search tools simultaneously on a regular basis so you can find the information immediately when you hit your "I need it now" deadline.

Best News Search Tools (listed alphabetically)

ABYZ
www.abyznewslinks.com

This is a truly international news search tool. You can look by country, region of the world or keyword search – an outstanding collection of news resources.

Ananova
www.ananova.com

This U.K.-focused news search tool is a good one. It is useful for non-U.S. news and includes your own personal video feed from Ananova, the video news reader.

Daypop
www.daypop.com

This is a terrific news search tool. It searches news, blogs and also has an additional tool – it brings up "cached" links for each listing, which gives you a copy of the page as seen by the Daypop crawler. This helps in case the original page no longer exists or can't be reached. It also allows you to limit your search to a variety of date ranges.

Infojunkie
www.infojunkie.com

This is another good news search tool. It draws from places like CNN, MSNBC and other U.S.-based publications. It also draws heavily from entertainment and sports sites, like "ain't-it-cool news" and "E-Online" so be ready for an unusual mix of news, sports and entertainment. Useful if you are looking for pop-culture.

Moreover
www.moreover.com

This is truly one of the best sites for breaking news on the web. It is a one-stop shop, gathering headlines from 1,800 news sources. It allows keyword searching and if you sign up (which gets you access to the professional version – and 3,000 news resources) it will email you results of your personalized searches. It also powers the AltaVista news site (www.news.altavista.com), but the latest information can always be found first at Moreover's site.

Net2one
www.net2one.com

Like Moreover, Net2One provides news feed and keyword searching of news content. It provides several versions – U.S., U.K. and a few others which tailors the search to primarily those countries. And it delivers the information as email alerts.

News Edge
www.newsedge.com

This Thomson company's news resource allows customization, especially for business applications.

News Index
`www.newsindex.com`

A terrific collection of international news resources, it is especially good for non-U.S. information. You can customize it to show specific subjects daily. One problem is it does not distinguish between PR wires like U.S. Newswire and real news wires like the AP, so be aware of this distinction when you look at results.

NewsNow
`http://newsnow.co.uk`

This British-based search tool is another excellent collection of news resources. It offers up to thirty days worth of searchable news content. It can be customized to fit your needs and is constantly updated and drop down menus are very easy-to-use.

NewsTrawler
`www.newstrawler.com`

This is another good international news search tool that you can customize to suit your needs. It is more of a meta-search tool, allowing you to search one or several sites of your choosing to find the subject you need. Its web-based news sources are not all top-flight ones, and it's a bit tougher to use than some of the ones listed above, but as a secondary tool it does offer options others don't, especially for searching by country.

Northern Light's Current News
`www.northernlight.com/news.html`

This search engine's recent purchase by Divine Inc. and their subsequent decision to abandon the public search engine makes you wonder if it will continue to service this outstanding current news tool. Let's hope so. It gathers news from hundreds of top-quality sources and has sixty-two newswires that are constantly updated. So, it's a great tool when you are looking for the latest news. It also allows you to search for news from the last fourteen days. In addition, you can purchase articles from its special collection, a huge index of news resources, for between US$1-4 per article.

Pandia
`www.pandia.com/news/index.html`

If you are looking for international news, this is one of the best news finders. This site also offers a radio-only search tool, which allows you to listen to news and talk stations from all over the world, a great way to spot trends. It's part of an excellent search engine. *In the interests of fair disclosure, I should mention Pandia awarded the previous edition of this book its 2000 Pandia "Best Internet Book" award.*

Rocket News
`www.rocketnews.com`

This keyword searchable news tool is another excellent collection of news tools. You can also choose news topics and get a headline list, but it only goes back five days.

Total News
www.totalnews.com

This one is U.S.-focused. It features channels of news, allowing you to search by keyword or topic or also to look at specific news wires and networks.

The Better News Gathering Tools (listed alphabetically)

A few words about general search engines and news. Several of the major search engines, rising to the demand for the latest news and the inability of their crawlers to stay current enough to handle breaking news, have launched news-gathering search tools, separate from their search engines. Many of these are excellent tools, and are listed below:

AllTheWeb/Fast News
www.alltheweb.com/?c=news

This site lets you keyword search against many news sites and is regularly refreshed. It has added extensive foreign news in its current news archive – much deeper than others.

AltaVista News
www.news.altavista.com

This is an excellent news search powered by Moreover (see above). It is actually better than using Moreover for keyword searching because of its relevancy ranking, but not as good as Moreover for the latest news.

Google Headline News
http://google.com/news/newsheadlines.html

This site grabs news headlines from more than 100 leading newspapers into a single page. It draws from many of the best news tools online, including CNN, *The Washington Post, The Boston Globe*, *The San Jose Mercury*, and international tools as well.

Lycos News
http://news.lycos.com

Lycos recently added a news tool to its web site with a cool "newsmine scrollover feature." When you get a story, it will say it is "newsmine enabled" on the top of the story and certain words in a news story are hyperlinked with a small magnifying glass icon next to them. If you move your mouse over the link it will pop up links to additional information about that word, including Lycos' business partners who are trying to sell products, and some useful web sites.

Yahoo! News
http://news.yahoo.com

Yahoo! gathers most of is breaking news tools from the wires services, in particular AP and Reuters, so it's excellent for breaking news. It also offers other news resources.

Journalism Collections

Many of the best journalism sites on the Web are collections of other news-related sites. To varying degrees, they include very thorough collections of links of great research sites geared to other journalists. Although many come from mainstream journalists some are from the most unexpected places. Many of these sites are geared to journalists; if you are looking for information, they are incredibly valuable. My own web site, Deadline Online (`www.deadlineonline.com`), has links to hundreds of valuable news resources and many of this book's key sites.

Best Journalism Collections (listed alphabetically)

AILEENA
`www.aileena.ch`

Another outstanding site, from Switzerland, with 5,500 links to newspapers, radio and TV stations in an amazing 174 countries. A superb place to find local news for almost any country that has news online.

Assignment Editor.com
`www.assignmenteditor.com`

This site offers some free and some fee-based tools and is an extensive collection of sites, useful information and resources for finding information quickly. This is a wonderful starting point.

Cyberjournalist.net
`www.cyberjournalist.net/supersearch/`

Jonathan Dube, the technology editor for MSNBC, has developed a terrific collection of news-related search tools and resources. It offers many of the best ones on the opening page with easy search capability.

Editor & Publisher Interactive
`www.editorandpublisher.com/editorandpublisher/business_resources/medialinks.jsp`

Editor & Publisher Magazine's outstanding collection of U.S. and Canadian links to large collection of newspapers, as well as TV stations, radio stations and magazines is another great place to start.

Electronic Library
`www.elibrary.com`

This is a fee-based collection of more than a million newspaper articles and hundreds of thousands of magazine articles and book chapters. It also includes TV and radio transcripts. The first thirty days are free.

Gary Price's News Sites

One of the areas that the *Invisible Web* guru has focused on is news-gathering tools. He has pulled together a collection of them that should be your starting point for news-related information.

Specifically his news center is one of the most comprehensive for print news resources. His Audio/Video Search collection is top-notch for TV and Radio sites and his speech and transcript center is also a great news-finding tool. These are "must-see" tools.

News Center (print)
www.freepint.com/gary/newscenter.htm

Audio/Video Search
www.freepint.com/gary/audio.htm

Speech and Transcript Center (U.S. and world)
www.freepint.com/gary/speech.htm

Information Today's Fulltext Sources Online (FSO)
www.infotoday.com/fso/default.htm

This is not a search tool at all, but a wonderful collection of what news resources exist on the Internet. It directs users to full-text magazines, newspapers, newsletters, wires and broadcast transcripts. Unlike many of the other entries in this list, FSO – based on a book of the same name – is a fee-based service that's accurate, invaluable and updated twice yearly. Buy the book and get free online access to the password-restricted portions of the web site.

Journalism Net
www.journalismnet.com

This is Julian Sher's list for investigative reporters with special sites for Canadian journalists. Both this site and Megasources, while serving Canadian journalists well, extend deeply into international sources and resources as well. This also has some excellent training resources.

Journalist Express
www.journalistexpress.com

Another excellent starting point for researchers – with easy access to all kinds of news tools, search tools, reference tools, phone books and even has gossip sites and stock markets.

Journalist Toolbox
www.journaliststoolbox.com

This is a superb collection of journalism-related sites. It is so deep that it is more than just a journalism site, it's a researcher's delight. Pulled together by Mike Reilley, a former *LA Times* and *Chicago Tribune* editor.

Mario Profaci's Cyberspace Station
http://mprofaca.cro.net

This site, by a Croatian journalist, while a bit unorthodox, is loaded with information about spying and terrorism and other subjects. It is also filled with more than 400 pages of materials and links, and excellent news tools for war-torn regions like the Balkans.

Megasources
www.ryerson.ca/journal/megasources.html

A truly staggering collection of online resources compiled by Ryerson Polytech professor Dean Tudor. Though it has especially good Canadian resources, it's loaded with international resources.

National Press Club
http://npc.press.org/library/reporter.shtml

Washington D.C.-based National Press Club has a tremendous collection of news resources. Its Directory of News Sources is a great "experts" list. There is also a strong collection of journalism links. Search by category – there are hundreds – from abortion to workplace issues, organization or name, and keyword. There are other resources on the press club's main site at http://npc.press.org.

NewsDirectory
www.newsd.com

This site just keeps growing. A comprehensive guide to the world's English-language online media, NewsDirectory has more than 7,000 newspapers and magazines as well as over 1,000 U.S. television broadcasters. It's easily searchable; locate newspapers by geographic region or subject. It used to be known as the Ecola Newsstand.

Best News Collections: Print & Broadcast

NewsLink
www.newslink.org

This site is a clearinghouse for one of the most comprehensive online list of domestic and international newspapers – well over 4,000. With links to broadcast sites, magazines and surveys, this site is carefully organized and easily maneuverable.

Newspaper Association of America
www.naa.org

Another excellent collection of North American newspapers. The site has several additional useful links besides newspapers.

Newspapers Online
www.newspapers.com

This is a tremendous collection of newspapers from all over the world. It is especially deep and you can find resources here that you won't find anywhere else.

Poynter Institute's Research Center
www.poynter.org/research/

This terrific site amasses valuable web resources for journalists. It is part of the Poynter Institute's site, and this collection is excellent.

Reporter's Desktop
www.reporter.org/desktop

A gem. This awe-inspiring site by *Seattle Times* Pulitzer prize-winning reporter Duff Wilson is an excellent starting point, with direct links to useful news tracking tools. The site is now hosted by Reporter.org, a collection of non-profit journalism organizations. The site is loaded with journalism-resources and is worth looking at.

Sources & Experts
www.ibiblio.org/slanews/internet/experts.html

An outstanding collection of experts lists compiled by *St. Petersburg Times* news researcher Kitty Bennett and posted on the SLA News Division web site.

Special Libraries Association (SLA) News Division
www.ibiblio.org/slanews/

The Special Libraries Association News Division is an international organization for news librarians and researchers. The site has a goldmine of valuable tools for any researcher.

Ultimate Collection of News Links
http://pppp.net/links/news/

This is a terrific collection of more than 8,000 links to online newspapers and magazines around the world. The directory is organized geographically.

World News Connection
http://wnc.fedworld.gov

This news tool, pulled together by the U.S. government, is an excellent source of material pulled from thousands of non-U.S. news sources including newspapers, "gray" literature such as conference proceedings, and non-classified technical reports, translated into English. It is available at a cost of US$65 per month for a single user and considerably more for multiple users.

Worldnews
www.worldnews.com

This easily searchable news resource has links to thousands of resources for hundreds of different countries. This is a superb place to find news from all around the world, and it offers you the opportunity to read it in dozens of languages.

Yahoo! News Collection
www.yahoo.com

Go to the site and click on "News & Media." This collection is especially strong because you can search by subject or region. It is also a great starting place for finding a quick overview; you can search by media outlet's name, by municipality name or by geographic region.

Archives and Transcripts

Most journalism sites keep material online for only one to three days. For news older than, say, a week or two, you'll have to refer to an archive and that's where the charges start to add up because most of these cost money.

To date, very few newspaper archives have developed a successful business model for making money on the Web. Other fee-based services have long archived news stories and have been quite successful in housing and storing huge amounts of news information.

On the Web, storage space (a hard drive) costs money to maintain, and demand for the past is low. On the free web, few news archives date back several years. Some small and regional newspapers around the U.S. have free news archives, including *The Detroit News*, *The New York Daily News*, *The Raleigh (NC) News & Observer*, *The Seattle Times*, and *The San Francisco Chronicle* and *San Francisco Examiner*. Among the international free archives are *The London Daily Telegraph* (you must register), *The Guardian*, *The Kenyan Daily Nation*, *The Zambia Times*, and *The Bangkok Post* among others. Links to all of these can be found on the SLA link listed below.

Other good sources for archives are:

FT Global Archive
http://globalarchive.ft.com

The Financial Times site is a strong searchable archive of over 100 leading news and business sources from around the world. In May, 2002, FT announced they would begin charging a fee for access to archives.

jake
www.jake-db.org

Jake (which stands for Jointly Administered Knowledge Environment) is an online archive offered by librarians originally at Yale University and now hosted by other libraries. It is particularly helpful in figuring out periodicals available online. It has extensive academic journals and more than 195 databases in its collection.

SLA News Division - Main Archives
www.ibiblio.org/slanews/internet/archives.html

SLA News Division - Archives
www.ibiblio.org/slanews/internet/ForArchivesnopara.html

The best collection belongs to the Special Libraries Association's News Division, which is a group of news librarians from media companies. Originally it was compiled by Margot Williams of *The Washington Post*. It links to all kinds of archives and describes costs and geographic coverage. It also has a terrific new site for foreign newspaper. This is the key site to help you find out what archives are online and available. There's a great collection of related links.

Value-Added Journalism Sites

These are fee-based journalism tools that have thorough news resources available at reasonable prices. They are good alternatives to the major supermarket-style tools like Lexis-Nexis, Factiva and Dialog.

Best Value-Added Journalism Sites (listed alphabetically)

E-Library
http://ask.elibrary.com

Subscription required, although searching is free. There are brief abstracts on the web site, geared mostly toward students at schools and libraries. But it offers material not found elsewhere.

NewsLibrary
www.newslibrary.com

Per-article charges, or buy in groups of three, ten, twenty-five, forty, etc.

Northern Light
www.northernlight.com

It's excellent special collection is still online and available on a per article basis. It is a deep database filled with thousands of articles that cost between US$1-4 per article.

Quickbrowse
www.quickbrowse.com

Tired of culling through dozens of newspapers before you've had your morning coffee? German reporter Marc Fest may have an answer in his new aggregation tool, Quickbrowse. This fee-based web service allows you to decide what newspapers or web sites you want to read. These are then downloaded in one browser window. Then, as you scroll down, click on the headlines that interest you; your selections are loaded on another page, in the background. When finished browsing, click over to this new page, read the stories, each retaining the look and feel of its original publication. This is a major timesaver and is one of the best new innovations.

Additional Web Sites for News Resources

1st Headlines
www.1stheadlines.com
Excellent new tool for finding breaking news.

7@m International News Wires
www.7am.com
Posts updated headlines from Nando Times, CNN, Fox News, Reuters/Yahoo!, and AP.

A Journalist's Guide to the Internet
http://reporter.umd.edu
Excellent starting point for journalists, the site is maintained by Chris Callahan, assistant dean at the University of Maryland College of Journalism and author of a book of the same title.

NewsLink
http://newslink.org
Compilation site for thousands of newspapers, magazines and TV and radio stations, pulled together by NewsLink.

AltaVista Canada - Canada News Index
www.altavistacanada.com
The Canadian News Index gathers information from over 300 Canadian news sources daily. To use the service, simply select the appropriate option on the AltaVista Canada homepage. It appears just above the search box.

Artigen Newswire: Information Technology
www.artigen.com/newswire/infotech.html
Info-tech filtering tool for tech news.

AudioNet
www.audionet.com
An extensive directory of radio stations broadcasting live over the Internet. Tune into live audio from around the world. Requires free Real Audio software, a sound card, and at least a 14.4 modem.

Barbara's News Researcher's Page.
www.gate.net/~barbara/index.html
Barbara Gellis Shapiro's collection of internet resources.

BiblioData's Full-Text Sources Online (FTSO)
www.bibliodata.com
Fee-based site. Offers lists of full-text newspapers or magazines online; however, a subscription is required to access site details.

Burrelle's
www.burrelles.com
Fee-based site. Press clippings, media monitoring, broadcast transcripts.

C4.com
www.c4.com
Mega-search site, which has excellent news research tools. Register and you can customize it for more precision.

Canada Newswire
www.newswire.ca
Canadian news wires.

CANOE
www.canoe.com
Another Canadian wire service.

CBS News
www.cbs.com
Site asks you to type in your zip code, and then it provides local news for you every time you go to the main page.

CEOTrack News page
www.ceotrak.com/news_information.asp
Another good journalism collection, this site has good directories online on several subjects and strong business news resources.

Christian Science Monitor
www.csmonitor.com
One of the few national newspapers with a free full-text archive going back decades.

CJR Journalism Resources
www.cjr.org/html/resources.html
Columbia Journalism Review Magazine has compiled a page of good links, valuable resource guides and source lists on subjects like covering mental health issues, crime, tobacco and AIDS.

CNN QuickNews
www.cnn.com/QUICKNEWS/
A morning email from CNN Interactive. CNN also has a personalized news tool now that caters to your selections when you visit their pages.

Columbia Missourian Newsroom Web Resources

www.missouri.edu/~jschool/missourian
Collection of journalism links compiled by *Missourian* editor Stan Ketterer.

CRAYON (Create Your Own Newspaper)

www.crayon.net
This site allows you to create your "own" newspaper by signing up for a free account and then selecting the subjects you want, with news feeds from hundreds of resources.

C-SPAN

www.cspan.org
C-SPAN is unvarnished coverage of Congress. The web site has news, video and sound clips and is terrific.

CyberSkeptic's Guide to Internet Research

www.bibliodata.com/skeptic/skepdata.html
Fee-based site. Ruth Orenstein's newsletter, CyberSkeptic, which is geared to professional researchers of all stripes, now published by Information Today.

Drew Sullivan's Homepage

www.drewsullivan.com
Excellent resource of databases on the Web.

Drudge

www.drudge.com
Journalism gossip site - its strength is its links, not the gossip.

Enews.com

www.enews.com
Search for magazines by subject – and links you to help you buy magazine subscriptions – no articles available.

ESPN.com

http://espn.go.com
One-stop shopping for sports of all kinds.

Essential Links

www.el.com
Essential Links is a portal with a collection of news links.

European Journalism Page

www.demon.co.uk/eurojournalism/media.html
Resources of interest to journalists covering Europe.

Ewatch

www.ewatch.com
Fee-based site. PR Newswire's electronic clipping and monitoring service.

E-Zine list

www.meer.net/~johnl/e-zine-list
Collection of E-zines from John Labovitz.

FACSNET

www.facsnet.org
This site, funded by the Foundation for American Communications, has a tremendous set of resources including a top-notch experts list and background material on a wide range of public policy issues.

FindLinks

www.findlinks.com
Phone finder and yellow pages phone finder.

Focus Best

www.focusbest.net/journalism/
A collection of news headlines and assorted journalism-related sites.

Gebbie, Inc

www.gebbieinc.com/dailyint.htm
Good collection of U.S.-based TV, radio, and newspapers, including small community dailies, weeklies and trade journals.

Guide to Electronic & Print Resources

www.cio.com/central/journalism.html
Good list of tools for writers compiled by Anne Stuart, editor of CIO Magazine.

Headline Spot

www.HeadlineSpot.com
Links to hundreds of sources of news and information. Also has some innovative features like cool tools for journalists and a behind the news section.

Headlinespot.com

www.headlinespot.com
Another excellent news research.

IDG

www.idg.net
Some trade publishers, such as provide online searches of their publications.

iMente
www.imente.com
A Spanish news headline service that draws from a deep database of resources.

InfoBeat
www.infobeat.com
This service allows you to select customized news summaries and headline reports.

Integrated NewsWire
www.artigen.com/start.html
Lists current headlines from various sources in these categories: Information Technology, World, Far East, MidEast, SciTech, Health, Biz, Music, Humor and Cool Sites.

Interlope News
www.interlope.com
Interlope News provides continuously updated headline news linked to full-text stories from around the world. Extremely diverse group of resources.

Internet Archive, The
www.archive.org
Extremely useful web archive tool called the "Wayback Machine." It saves copies of most web pages. Sponsored by Brewster Kahle, founder of Alexa; this is the best resource to find old web pages.

Internet Hourly News - ABC
www.realaudio.com/contentp/abc.html
Plays audio feeds from ABC News live on your computer.

Internet Resources for Journalism
www.mnstate.edu/gunarat/ijr/
Minnesota State University Moorhead Journalism professor Shelton Gunaratne's list of resources and tools for journalism researchers.

Izvestia
www.online.ru/mlists/izvestia/izvestia-izvestia
Russia's Izvestia news service.

Journal of Commerce
www.joc.com
With free registration, you can read the articles and review the archives of this business publication and it links to all kinds of business resources.

Journalistic Resources Page
www.it-kompetens.com/journ.html
Excellent site for European publications.

Kidon Media-Link
www.kidon.com/media-link/index.shtml
This Netherlands-based site is a comprehensive directory of online news media including links to news agencies, magazines, internet, newspapers, radio and TV. Searchable by keyword and by foreign language.

Kiosk
www.online-journalist.com/resources2.html
Good collection of web-published zines, but may be somewhat out of date.

Magazine CyberCenter
www.magamall.com
Fee-based site. This Canadian-based site is a very good place to locate magazines online, but you will have to buy subscriptions.

Meating Place
www.meatingplace.com
Free services can be found in trade group publications that track industry news, such as which tracks stories in the meat and poultry industry.

Mercury Center
www.mercurycenter.com
One of the top news resources online – especially Silicon Valley coverage. Also use www.sjmercury.com.

Metagrid - English
www.metagrid.de/usa/
This is a German-based search tool that provides access to magazines around the world -USA version.

Metagrid - German
www.metagrid.de/
This is a German-based search tool that provides access to magazines around the world - German version.

MIT List of Radio Stations on the Internet
http://wmbr.mit.edu/stations/list.html
To date, this is the best list of radio stations assembled on the web. It is constantly updated and easily searchable by call letters or geographic region. It's primarily U.S.-focused, but has a good collection of stations from around the world as well.

MSNBC News

www.nbcnews.com
A news site that has ties to all its local affiliates, enabling you to get regional news as well.

My Yahoo!

http://my.yahoo.com
News that can be personalized to the issues you care about.

Nando Times

www.nandotimes.com
Published by *The Raleigh News and Observer* contains that newspaper and a collection of wires including AP, Reuters and *New York Times* News Service.

Navigator

www.nytimes.com/library/cyber/reference
/cynavi.html
Rich Meislin maintains this reference home page for reporters at *The New York Times*. Good for anyone, though.

New York Times Direct

www.nytimes.com/info/contents/services.
html
Get *The Times* or specific sections delivered to you daily electronically.

New York Times: Books

www.nytimes.com/pages/books/index.html
New York Times' Book Review section - good way to find experts and knowledgeable authors.

NewsBank, Inc.

www.newsbank.com
A news tool, geared toward schools and academics.

NewsCenter

www.freepint.com/gary/newscenter.htm
Gary Price's outstanding collection of news resources.

NewsDirectory.Com

www.ecola.com
Covers newspapers, magazines and TV stations – extensive magazine collection of links.

Newshub

www.newshub.com
Updated every fifteen minutes with headlines in these various areas, including Technical, Financial, World, U.S., Science, Health and Entertainment.

Newsisfree

www.newsisfree.com
Scans news sites and weblogs and lets you customize a page from the materials available. A rich site summary resource.

Newslab

www.newslab.org
Newslab is a TV journalism site that is strong on criticism and deep on resources.

NewsLinx Headlines

www.newslinx.com
Offers a daily compilation of headlines, with links to articles, mostly on Internet and computer-related subjects.

NewspaperLinks

www.newspaperlinks.com
The Newspaper Association of America's site has links to many newspapers and newspaper industry news.

Driving a Newspaper on the Data Highway!

www.well.com/user/mmcadams/online.newsp
apers.html
Mindy McAdams' page about news online. Good historical page.

NewsPlace for News & Sources

www.niu.edu/newsplace
Professor Avi Bass from Northern Illinois University maintains this collection of news research tools and sources. It is especially strong if you are looking for political resources.

Newstrove

www.newstrove.com
Subject-focused news search tool. Good for major news subjects; internationally focused.

Paperball

http://paperball.fireball.de/
This is a German-based search engine company that allows you to search German news.

Reporter.org

http://reporter.org
One of several sites maintained by Investigative Reporters and Editors and the National Institute of Computer Assisted Reporting.

Scoop Cybersleuth's Internet Guide

http://scoop.evansville.net

Collection of journalism resources by James Derk, computer whiz of the *Evansville Courier-Journal*.

SLA News Division

www.ibiblio.org/slanews/

The Special Libraries Association News Division is an international organization for news librarians and researchers.

Speech & Transcript Center

www.freepint.com/gary/speech.htm

Speech and transcript clearinghouse.

SuperSeek

www.superseek.com

Over 1,200 search engines and directories, and over 6,000 media-related web sites.

The Onion

www.theonion.com

Excellent satire of news, just in case you need a laugh.

The Smoking Gun

www.thesmokinggun.com

The Smoking Gun is a gossip-news site, that often comes up with insider stories and occasionally breaks real news.

The WIRE - Breaking News from the Associated Press

http://wire.ap.org

Access to the regional AP wires and also the national wires.

Tribnet.com, The Tacoma News Tribune

www.tribnet.com

Tacoma News Tribune and access to wires.

U.S. News & World Report Online

www.usnews.com

Offers its contents online and has several other non-print sections, like a college and careers section, an email newsletter and discussion forums.

U.S. Newspapers

www.usnpl.com

Good list of news sites – newspapers, TV and radio.

USA CityLink Home Page

www.usacitylink.com

Collection of links to regional cities with travel, tourism and relocation information.

Vanderbuilt Television News Archive

http://tvnews.vanderbilt.edu

Collection of the evening news broadcasts of the three major networks, ABC, CBS, and NBC, since 1968. It is searchable and browsable; includes abstracts/descriptions.

Virtual Tuner

www.virtualtuner.com

Fast way to find radio stations around the world by country or by news category.

Weather Channel

www.weather.com

Storms, hurricanes and earthquakes details as well as allows you to program it to give you your local weather whenever you log on.

WebClipping.com

www.webclipping.com

Fee-based site. Clipping service available to track businesses, news.

WebWatcher Project

www.cs.cmu.edu/afs/cs.cmu.edu/project/theo-6/web-agent/www/webagent-plus/webagent-plus.html

WebWatcher is a World Wide Web filtering system developed at the Carnegie Mellon University Learning Lab learns your preferences and highlights interesting links on web pages you visit.

WWW News Resource Page

http://sun3.lib.uci.edu/~dtsang/netnews1.htm

Good collection of mainstream and alternative news sources. You can find campus newspapers, also extremist and ethnic news resources.

Chapter 9

Business Tools

Business Resources

Business Resources in General — Backgrounding a Company — Company Directories; How to Find Basic Information — Financial Backgrounding and Research — Should You Pay for SEC Documents? — Company Information from News Sources and Public Relations News Wires — Free Web-Based Business Backgrounding Tools — Fee-Based Business-Focused Tools — Assortment of Fee-Based Business Tools — Credit Companies — Conducting Market Research — Market Research Data Vendors and Brokerage Reports — Business Valuation: An Example — Sales Prospecting — Competitive Intelligence — Quick, Effective and Free Competitive Intelligence — Patents and Trademarks — Personal Financial Information — Investment Research — Stock and Bonds — International Trade — Non-Profits and Charities — Additional Web Sites for Business Tools

Information is the lifeblood of business. The Internet enables smaller firms to compete with larger ones and large ones to diversify. Business resources on the Web are plentiful. You can find company profiles, trade data, business news, corporate tax and legal advice, management strategies, small business information, executives' biographical data, financial reports, and much more. The Web's free resources are a good starting point, but the most detailed information and sophisticated analyses are available through fee-based companies.

Savvy business researchers often use a collection of different tools to get the information they need, including the Web, fee-based databases, CD-roms, and print resources. One of the interesting trends for most businesses has been an acceptance that the Web is a useful tool. Some industries have reluctantly resisted change, but most business people have quickly taken to technology. Four years ago, realtors were fearful of the new technologies and resisted. Then some began to use it. Now, with online 360-degree video views of homes, realtors no longer have to do labor-intensive introductory walkthroughs. It has revolutionized their business.

Now, most professional businessmen and women demand and have web access to information tools at their desktop. Many are also pushing for wireless access to information tools. The result is more and better information available on the "open" Web, But to be thorough and exhaustive in business, you must use a combination of free and fee-based tools.

Company research is a good starting point for business. In addition, you can often find out about businesses by looking at what they say about themselves on their web sites, through their press releases and of course, through what their competitors say about them. Then it's always a good idea to look at what they tell their regulators. In the U.S., that means the Securities and Exchange Commission or another federal government agency.

Industry and trade associations are good resources for information mostly found on web sites or purchased. There is an abundance of this kind of information in the United States, not as much in the rest of the world.

Many U.S. companies analyze trade sectors worldwide, so information can often be found about non-U.S. companies using U.S. resources.

U.S. information is plentiful for several reasons. Market research reports can be purchased and where there's money involved, there's usually a company or an entire industry trying to capitalize on it. You can use that to your advantage. Also, with nearly every aspect of business, there is usually an academic resource that studies that field or has developed an expertise in that field.

For example, as a reporter covering the U.S.-Mexico border for a group of Texas-based newspapers, one of the most useful places to find information was from the U.S. Government, which regularly monitored different business sectors and required extensive government reports. Whether it was the U.S. Department of Agriculture, the Environmental Protection Agency, or the U.S. State Department, or private associations, the more federal government regulations, the more reports you could find and therefore the more information available about a region. As a reporter, I was often able to use U.S.-based trade group reports to monitor the activities of the joint U.S.-Mexico "maquiladora" plants operating on both sides of the border. The trick is that you need to think about where information might be available outside the local country or origin.

Backgrounding a Company

There are a number of reasons to background a company. Information about a company's hiring practices and material can help you prepare for an interview, a sales call, or provide the background material needed to evaluate potential vendors, suppliers, or takeover targets. A basic overview, for example, might include:

- Company's formal name
- Address and telephone numbers of the company's main offices and major facilities
- Activities of the parent company, divisions and subsidiaries
- Executives' names, titles and salaries
- Board members' names, affiliations and backgrounds
- Number of employees
- Company history
- Assessments of the company by creditors, investors, analysts and competitors
- Company and industry analyses
- News reports

Where Do You Start?

First, pin down exactly the kind of information you really want. Ask yourself how thorough you need to be and how much you need to know to answer your questions. Narrow your focus and then, when you do go online, whether via the Web or proprietary services, select the tool most likely to hold the answer to your focused request.

A critical question is whether a company is privately owned or publicly held. It's the biggest factor in determining how much information is available to the public. Remember that there is a lot of information about non-U.S. companies and countries from U.S. resources if you know where and how to look. Under U.S. federal law, publicly-owned companies are required to disclose certain information about their operations – including many of the details mentioned above – to shareholders and also to the U.S. Securities Exchange Commission (SEC) and other federal and state regulatory agencies.

The SEC web site is usually the best starting point for research on a publicly-held business. If the company is publicly-held, you can count on finding a great deal of information, including:

- Profiles of the company

- Company history

- Market information

- Facility locations

- Names and positions of top executives

- Financial statements

- Ratings and possibly credit information

On the other hand, private companies are subject to much looser requirements; their public profiles tend to be less distinct, and therefore, your data-gathering strategy must be different. A company's web site isn't a bad place to start, but keep in mind that the information on their site is what the company wants you to know. That information is often an "exaggerated" perspective rather than an honest one.

For private companies, you may have to use less conventional means to get meaningful information – such as news clippings, state tax office and Secretary of State registrations, rival companies' web pages, and fee-based services. You can consult business directories, industry analyst and broker reports, newspapers, magazines, newsletters and former employees and vendors. Some data can be found from fee-based sites like Dun & Bradstreet, Hoover's, Dow Jones, and others or on the company's web site, some from a company's or an individual's credit report. Another source is companies that specialize in corporate research.

Also, just about every company in America strives to maintain a web presence; their web sites contain company-generated information.

Outside North America, some countries do have public company reporting requirements, but many do not make the information available to the public. Others make it available, but it is extremely costly to get.

Company Directories: How to Find Basic Information

Company directories are plentiful. A few resources stand out above the rest. Each offers information with varying degrees of reliability, and it pays to take the time to try several. You'll be surprised at the range of difference in the results.

Company Research from Lycos

http://business.lycos.com/companyresearch/crtop.asp

The information on this valuable site comes from Dun & Bradstreet, which houses one of the largest business databases, and from its partner Lycos. The data here is reliable and includes company name, mailing address, phone number, CEO's name, annual sales, number of employees and other basic information. The free information is merely *a fraction* of the data that Dun & Bradstreet has.

Corporate Information

www.corporateinformation.com

This site is a good starting point to find companies and corporate data from around the world. Organized by country, it offers links to corporate directories and other useful sites.

Hoover's Online

www.hoovers.com

Like its major competitor Dun & Bradstreet, Hoover's has a free site of information capsules that include company descriptions, information about key competitors, rankings, and subsidiaries as well as current news related to the company. It is geared toward public companies. What distinguishes Hoover's from the others – whether free or fee-based – is the Business Boneyard, a recent addition to the already-strong Hoover's site where you can find out what happened to now-defunct business listings that vanished from the corporate landscape. Hoover's is also available on AOL using the keyword "hoovers." It also offers a superb sales-lead finding tool.

PRARS (Public Register's Annual Report Service)

www.prars.com

This service lets U.S.-based investors order annual reports free via the Web. PRARS also has a second web site with annual reports available at www.annualreportservice.com.

Additional sites for finding free annual reports are www.reportgallery.com and www.carol.co.uk for company annual reports from around the world.

Thomas Global Register

www.tgrnet.com

The Thomas Global Register allows you to search from among 500,000 manufacturers and distributors organized by 10,500 industrial product classifications, in nine languages and from twenty-six countries. You must register, but the links are extensive. It also offers the Thomas Register of American Manufacturers at www.thomasregister.com, a directory of 170,000

U.S. and Canadian companies. There is also a register of European manufacturers, and the site is entirely free.

Europages, the European Business Directory

www.europages.com

This site catalogs more than 500,000 businesses in Europe with contact information. You can search it by company, industry or for products. It also has a business information section that provides business news and trends. It is searchable in seven European languages.

Internet-Prospector

www.internet-prospector.org

This site, part of the Internet Prospector site, provides contact information and links to Secretary of State, and Corporation Databases (when available) for U.S. states. The main site is geared for research for non-profit fundraisers and it has a great archive. It's charities listings can be found at www.internet-prospector.org/charities.htm (see the non-profits section later in this chapter).

SEDAR

www.sedar.com

This is the Canadian-version of the Edgar system – the System for Electronic Document Analysis and Retrieval database provides easy access to public financial information for Canadian businesses.

TradePort

www.tradeport.org/ts/

This is a strong site for international trade. It has thorough information on countries, as well as a California companies database.

Who Owns What

www.cjr.org/owners

This list, compiled for journalists by one of the leading journalism magazines, shows who owns what magazines, newspapers, radio stations, television stations, cable companies and book publishers, and what subsidiaries they own.

Big Charts

http://bigcharts.marketwatch.com

Big Charts is a part of the CBS Marketwatch site. It includes stock quotes, and charts with links to news, SEC filings and market research. Historical quotes go back as far as 1970. Comparison charts are also available.

Global Edge

http://globaledge.msu.edu/ibrd/ibrd.asp

This site, maintained by Michigan State University, provides news, statistics, directories, government, trade and banking information for countries and regions of the world.

Marketguide Screening

http://marketguide.com/screen/Sscreen.asp

Market Guide Screening, from Multex, is a site that lets you identify companies by a very specific type of criteria; e.g., their earnings or valuation or other factors.

Market Search Directory
`www.marketsearch-dir.com`

Free information on 20,000 market research reports from 700 firms. It offers you a summary and a contact on where to get the detailed information, and it is searchable by industry.

CEOexpress
`www.ceoexpress.com`

An incredibly strong page of links to news, business research, both U.S. and non-U.S., and office tools. A great starting page for business research and can also be used as a company finding page.

Financials
`www.financials.com`

Financials gives you information on over 10,000 public companies pulled from other sources for free. The company data, provided by Zacks, Marketguide, and Stock Smart, includes contact information, quotes, financial snapshots, and links to company homepages, news articles and corporate filings.

➜*hot tip:*   In addition to their free services, Dun & Bradstreet, NewsPage.com, Hoover's and other companies also offer much more extensive company profile information for a fee. See the fee-based section later in this chapter.

➜*hot tip:*   Sometimes researchers don't "know" the industry they need to research — the right terms or proper jargon to look for. Amelia Kassel, a super business researcher who runs her own firm, Marketingbase.com, uses what she calls a "pearl-building" technique with a very useful site called Guidebeam.com. The site — an Australian one — generates a list of terms and concepts and then creates a thesaurus of related concepts, based on Google and Yahoo!'s databases. It lists how many sites it finds related to your terms and that helps you rank the most useful terms. It's a creative way to get ideas for terminology in a field you are not familiar with.

Financial Backgrounding and Research

Securities and Exchange Commission
`www.sec.gov/edgarhp.htm`

The single most important – and most impressive – business resource is the Securities and Exchange Commission's EDGAR web site. EDGAR, which stands for Electronic Data

Gathering, Analysis and Retrieval, is a resource of unparalleled depth and breadth. Visit it first regardless of the size of your research budget.

Its holdings are vast, but not totally comprehensive, and it's important to know what they comprise. Since May 1996, all public domestic companies have been required to file all their mandatory statements electronically. These documents are available on EDGAR. Electronic filing was optional during the 1994-1995 phase-in period, and online document availability for that period is inconsistent. You can search and/or request manually-filed documentation in person or by phone, however. Also, keep in mind that some SEC-related documents are not made public, and consequently these are unavailable on EDGAR.

Needless to say, the information found within EDGAR is likely to be more detailed and more reliable than a company's own web site because the company is reporting to its federal regulator.

It's well worth spending the time to familiarize yourself with the myriad of SEC forms that companies are required to file. From the SEC's Home Page, one may click on "Quick Forms Lookup" for descriptions of these forms. For example, a 10-K form will give you an overview of a company's future plans. Knowing what's been filed can give you a good idea of the company itself. Form 13-F is a quarterly report of equity holdings by institutional managers holding equity assets of US$100 million or more.

The SEC has recently added access to 13-G filings, which declare when a stockholder sells five percent or more of their shares. It's a required filing and they are a welcome addition to the web site. Several fee-based services also provide access to them.

EDGAR contains other valuable information, such as the SEC Digest, which chronicles daily agency activities and enforcement actions. The main SEC site also describes enforcement activities. Currently, neither is searchable, but that may change soon.

Here are some of the many web sites that harvest and enhance SEC data:

10-K Wizard
www.tenkwizard.com

With free access to SEC data, 10-K Wizard stands out due to its exceptional search capabilities. It also offers several fee-based subscription products including real-time SEC data for a fee. The web site also adds company snapshots and key financial indicators.

EDGAR Scan
http://edgarscan.tc.pw.com

PricewaterhouseCoopers' version of the EDGAR database, it isn't as up-to-date as Free EDGAR or as easily searchable as 10-K Wizard, but its simplicity allows easy access to SEC filings.

EDGAR Online People
http://people.edgar-online.com/people

This service allows users to search SEC filings using executives' names. Information is available from the last six months of proxy statements and includes company position, corporate board memberships, stock ownership, options, sales and executive compensation. You can register and run the index for free, but you must subscribe to the pay service for more detail. The main site, `www.edgar-online.com` is a terrific company finder with the best and easiest-to-use interface in looking at SEC documents.

Free EDGAR

`www.freeedgar.com`

This free resource, now owned by the EDGAR Online company, offers the most timely and convenient access to SEC filings of any of the free sites. It is easily searchable and has the full EDGAR database. But it is no longer all free. Watchlist Alerting, RTF and Excel Downloading, and Full Text Search are now part of the subscription price. There are individual and group subscriptions.

Global Securities Information

`www.gsionline.com`

Global Securities Information, which runs LiveEDGAR and the Mergers and Acquisitions Database on a subscription basis, follows the securities industry and provides up-to-the-minute information from the Securities and Exchange Commission and makes it easy-to-use and searchable. It has an extensive lineup of other business tools that are used by law firms, investment banks, news organizations, accounting firms and Fortune 500 corporations.

SEDAR (System for Electronic Document Analysis and Retrieval)

`www.sedar.com`

Canada's version of the EDGAR system is similar to EDGAR in structure. It is bilingual, free and includes most filings required of public companies.

Should You Pay for SEC Documents?

Many of the major business resource companies – such as Standard & Poors, Moody's, Dun & Bradstreet and others – also offer SEC data — for a fee. When does it make sense to pay for SEC documents? It generally comes down to time versus money. When saving time is more worthwhile than worrying about the money, fee-based tools are irreplaceable.

Jan Davis Tudor, who runs Portland, Oregon-based JT Research specializing in business research, often uses SEC documents to get information. She doesn't always get them from EDGAR: "If I need just one document, chances are I'll obtain it from one of the non-SEC web sites," she says. But if she has a specific question, she prefers to visit Global Securities Information at `www.gsionline.com` which is also available via dial-up connection and dedicated line. It provides enough value-added features, she says, to justify paying for the documents. What she really likes is its ability to search across the entire EDGAR database using keywords, SIC (standard industry code) or form type. Pricing is fair — pay as you go, on a per-minute basis — and documents are preformatted so they're predictable and easy to use.

Company Information from News Sources and Public Relations News Wires

News tools are great sources of corporate information, and so are public relations wire services. Four particularly valuable sites mentioned below are great sources of company-generated information, such as new product announcements, joint ventures, management changes, dividends distributions, mergers and acquisitions. As with company web sites, however, the information reflects the company's interests. While there are many of these so-called "wires," these are the ones that tend to have the most useful information:

Business Wire
www.businesswire.com

USNewswire
www.usnewswire.com

PR Newswire
www.prnewswire.com

Internet Wire
www1.internetwire.com/iwire/home

The Additional Sites section at the end of this chapter lists many more as does Chapter 8, News Resources. Many others can be found at Yahoo!'s press release page:

http://dir.yahoo.com/Business_and_Economy/Business_to_Business/News_and_Media/News_Services/Press_Releases/

You can also receive them through some of the free search engines or through fee-based vendors like America Online and Dialog.

In the U.S., another way to look at business news is by region. Here are the more outstanding tools for business news.

Business News

CBS MarketWatch
www.cbsmarketwatch.com

CNNfn (CNNmoney)
http://money.cnn.com

These free sites are standouts. Both deliver timely, reliable news and market information, along with stock quotes, charts, and other data. Investors can use tools on either site to track their personal portfolios. Both draw content from their own staffs of reporters. Also check out CNN's sister sites.

The Motley Fool
www.fool.com

Another free site that specializes in financial news and opinion, it is particularly good because of its message boards and discussion groups, which are notorious for their rumor-slinging. You can get some good tips, but you must realize these are often unconfirmed rumors.

Bloomberg Business News
www.bloomberg.com

This is a particularly strong business news wire service, available by subscription. It provides real-time financial and investment information. It delivers news on world markets, financial data.

It also covers business segments extensively. The news section – including top daily headline stories from papers around the world – mutual funds, stocks, etc. can be accessed without charge.

BusinessWeek
www.businessweek.com

Magazine subscribers get full access to the articles and special reports at the web site. You can read the current issue online, but for past articles you will need to subscribe to the web sites. It's international coverage and technology coverage are excellent and it is part of the McGraw-Hill family of magazines and newsletters.

The Wall Street Journal
www.wsj.com

It is fee-based and also available through its partner, Factiva. It is exceptionally good for business information.

The Financial Times of London
www.ft.com

Another wonderful business news resource, it has recently changed to a subscription model. Its archives goes back decades.

The Street.com
www.street.com

It offers free news, but you must subscribe at US$9.95 per month or US$99.95 a year to get its insights and commentaries. If you are tracking stocks and the markets, you will want to subscribe.

➜*hot tip:* **Don't forget to check general news outlets when searching for business information.**

Here are two other regional U.S.-based sites:

Bizjournals
www.bizjournals.com

Published by the American City Business Journals, it's a free site where more than forty-one local business publications have pooled their coverage. They provide in-depth reporting about companies headquartered in their regions. You can limit your search to a specific city or search across the entire web site. It's especially valuable because it gives you a community perspective.

Crain's Business Publications
www.crainsny.com

Additionally, there are the Crain's business publications online. Crain's has several publications but no centralized site, so to find the regional information for business news from Detroit, Chicago, or Cleveland, go to the Crain's New York site and navigate to sites you need.

Free Web-Based Business Backgrounding Tools

Brint
`www.brint.com`

> The Biz Tech Network (BRINT), started at the University of Pittsburgh, but has turned into a strong topical resource on information technology and business. Register for free access.

Europages
`www.europages.com`

> Discussed in the international section, it bears repeating in this business chapter as a starting point for finding out information about 500,000 public and private businesses in Europe. It's a yellow pages with much more detail and is available in most European languages.

Virtual International Business & Economic Sources (VIBES)
`http://libweb.uncc.edu/ref-bus/vibehome.htm`

> Another U.S.-based academic resource, this one provides global, regional, and U.S. listings for international business and economic information, including full-text articles, statistics, and links to other strong sites.

Business 2.0
`www.business2.com/webguide`

> *Business 2.0*, one of the AOL-Time Warner family of magazines, offers way more than a magazine. It has an excellent collection of business-related sites. This web guide is a great starting point for getting the business basics. The site, tied to the magazine *Business 2.0* also has links to companies, profiles of business leaders and even allows you to ask questions of its research staff.

Fee-Based Business-Focused Tools

There is an amazing amount of business information on the free part of the Internet and, as with news information, you can find most of what you are looking for, if you are patient. But, if time, depth, and exactness are considerations, then fee-based tools are more desirable. Overall, the supermarket-style fee-based services are superb research tools. These commercial services can give you an edge on the competition if history is an important factor in your decision-making.

The impact of business-to-business e-commerce is now having a profound effect on information providers. Giant supermarket-style companies like Lexis-Nexis, Dialog, and Factiva-Dow Jones are now making efforts to attract the large numbers of consumers using the Yahoo!s and AOLs to find business information. The inevitable result will be the convergence of vendors, partnering, and alliances to better supply business information to the end user.

Paying for your research is especially important for business research, because in most cases, the decisions you make for research affect your company's bottom line, or failure to find the information you need could cost you your job. How do you figure out which tool to use? Several factors play into that decision, but the scope of the products – how easy is it to use, and what it offers in comparison to others – are some of the things to consider.

➜*hot tip:* **Think of business research as building a big jigsaw puzzle. Everything you find comes in pieces and you are the person who needs to build the whole out of the different pieces. If you want to get definitive business information on a company, you cannot survive without the major fee-based databases.**

Here are some of the strengths and weaknesses of Dialog, Dow Jones-Factiva, Lexis-Nexis, and Thomson Financial as business research tools.

Dialog
www.dialog.com

Dialog features almost 600 different databases and brings them all together in one searching language. If you know how to search it using what they call command language, you can be incredibly efficient at finding what you want. It has extensive business resources, including access to 280,000 U.S. company profiles – mostly private companies. It also offers company details all over the world. But so far, the information is hit or miss, according to search experts especially when compared to Lexis-Nexis. If you are looking for S&P 500 companies, Dialog's company profiles, available for US$100 per report, are deep and quick and regularly updated. Dialog is getting ready to offer a new "newsroom" building on its acquisition of NewsEdge and integrating sources from Dialog, Datastar, and Profound.

It offers unusually inexpensive access to Proquest graphics and images, a new feature, and easy access to the high-end analyst reports from Investext. Be aware, however, that if you use Dialog Select, you only get about thirty percent of what's available through Dialog's other products of Investext reports. It now offers transaction- based pricing.

While Dialog's business tools are strong, its owner, Thomson, has a series of stellar business tools so far not available on Dialog. They are listed as a group directly – but are only available individually.

Factiva - Dow Jones Interactive
www.djinteractive.com

www.factiva.com

This alliance between Dow Jones and Reuters is a global one. Their combined Business Briefing pulls information from nearly 8,000 sources. So far, not all of the Reuters International business resources are available. But, it's very easy to use, there's no cost for searching, and it is a superb tool for quick reference.

Factiva - Dow Jones is especially good at specific industry information. For business information, the Dow Jones Web Center is a tremendous place to start.

Lexis-Nexis
`www.nexis.com`

The Lexis-Nexis business tools are very deep when it comes to backgrounding a company. Part of that is because it has a strong collection of court records and public records – like secretary of state doing-business-as reports in most U.S. states. It has a lot more content than Dialog, but that will change if the Thomson products become available on Dialog. You can access Nexis directly or through "Classic Lexis-Nexis" Be aware that when using these tools, you are charged for every search, and results – whereas Classic has cost-saving features. You do want to learn the differences as they will save you considerable money.

Thomson Financial
`www.thomsonfinancial.com`

The latest major player in the business sector, Canada-based Thomson Financial, has combined several prominent business companies, including Investext, Securities Data System, CDA/Spectrum, American Banker/ Bond Buyer, Research Bank, Tower Group, First Call, Nelson Information, Sheshunoff Information, Disclosure, and the Faulkner & Gray newsletters into a powerhouse business finance publisher. These resources are geared primarily for business and are very expensive, but incredibly valuable. Their individual listings follow:

The Thomson Financial Group:

Alacra
`www.xls.com`

Formerly known as Portal B, XLS.com and Data Download, this Thomson company integrates business web sources with eighty databases in one interface. Some of these databases are quite unique – for example, it offers the leading thinking on business through databases on business schools and in-depth case studies. One real bonus is that it lets you download information directly into your spreadsheet, saving hours of typing and data conversion. It does not include some of the Gale databases like Prompt and Trade and Industry, which are owned by the same company.

Datastar
`www.datastarweb.com`

Another Thomson-owned company, this is one of the big commercial databases, which is focused on Europe and the world, rather than the U.S. It is an excellent tool that is particularly good on company information. It also provides access to TradStat Web, a superb trade database.

Derwent
`www.derwent.com`

A searchable patent and trademark database.

First Call
`www.firstcall.com`

First Call is one of several Thomson Financial tools that are available individually or as part of Dialog. This is a high-end tool that provides extensive quantitative data and research analyses on stocks and corporate performance. You can also get First Call through other online vendors.

IAC InSite
www.iac-insite.com

A subscription service run by Intelligence Data (who also operates Intelliscope), InSite offers customers the ability to search more than 1,000 trade and industry publications, regional business journals, management journals, newswires, and business magazines on dozens of industries.

Intelliscope
www.intelliscope.com

Intelliscope is a subscription-based service that provides company information on more than 45,000 companies in 200 countries. Quantitative and analytical data from hundreds of banks, brokerages, trade associations, and market research and consulting companies.

Mark Intel
www.tfsd.com

Mark Intel does the marketing research reports for Thomson Financial – another excellent tool.

NewsEdge
www.newsedge.com

NewsEdge is a business news database recently purchased by Thomson. It pulls from over 2,000 news sources, providing personalized news to your business or corporate intranet.

Profound
www.profound.com

Profound, a high cost business market information providers is currently available as a separate tool or as part of Thomson Dialog

Prompt
www.Galegroup.com

Prompt is a database of business, industry and trade information, formerly available from the Gale Group and now a part of Dialog.

SAEGIS
www.thomson-thomson.com

SAEGIS is the Thomson-Thomson site for global trademarks and domain names. Use it to search for information on trademarks and copyrights. Pricing varies, from US$.50 for "hits" with basic trademark information to usage fees for databases. There's background info on trademarks and copyright as well, and links to organizations, government agencies, and legal materials related to intellectual property issues. The directory of intellectual property law firms may also be helpful.

Thomson Financial Securities Data (formerly Investext)
www.investext.com

The grandparent of investment research now has a web site. This is a very expensive tool, but it offers more than 2.5 million reports from 800 investment banks, market research firms, and trade associations worldwide. Another part of this group is www.sdponline.com/index.html – a merger and acquisitions database.

Shareworld
www.shareworld.tfsd.com

Provices shareholder information for many companies around the world.

Other notable Thomson web sites are www.thomsondirect.com and www.tfibcm.com.

➔ *hot tip:* **Both Gary Price and Amelia Kassel, two excellent searchers, strongly recommend you make sure you have a local library card. Many public libraries offer free or low-cost access to several high-end databases like Ebsco and OCLC's First Search and you can save time and money – and support your local library in the process. Many libraries allow remote dialup access as well, letting you work from your own home.**

Assortment of Fee-Based Business Tools

Being a mixture of business tools, services, and products – and always seeming to change their content – many useful business-related internet sites cannot be categorized. Here is a selection of the more popular ones, from the U.S. and abroad. Additional market-research specific sites are listed under the Market Research section.

10-K Wizard
www.10kwizard.com

This is a fee-based way to look quickly and easily at the U.S. Securities and Exchange Commission data. The company will email you with alerts. You can search company's proxy statement, and it will search public companies.

Annual Report Gallery
www.reportgallery.com

This site is a place to get annual reports from global companies for free. You can also pay and get broker research reports from more than 200 U.S. and Canadian brokerage houses. This is a very important business resource that many of the major business players offer as well for an added fee.

BankruptcyData.Com
www.bankruptcydata.com

BankruptcyData.Com is a subscription-based web site that follows and monitors business bankruptcy filings from U.S. federal bankruptcy districts on a daily basis.

Best Practices Database.com
www.bestpracticesdatabase.com

This is a terrific new resource that follows "best practices" for business in several fields, like Internet and E-business, knowledge-management, and sales and marketing. It provides free searching and pay-as-you-go or fee-per-document pricing.

Bureau Van Dijk

www.bvdep.com

Bureau Van Dijk Electronic Publishing is one of the leading sources of online business information in Europe. Its database focuses on the financial information of public and private businesses. It also offers several other databases, including Amadeus, which offers financial information on four million European companies, Global Researcher, which contains financial information on 25,000 public companies worldwide and BankScope, which provides bank information on 11,000 banks worldwide.

BusinessCredit USA

www.businesscreditusa.com

This site provides basic business backgrounding information on 1.2 million U.S. businesses.

Cambridge Scientific Abstracts (CSA)

www.csa.com

CSA has been publishing abstracts and indices to scientific and technical research literature for over thirty years. Its fee-based web site offers access to more than seventy scientific databases.

CCH

www.cch.com

This company compiles tax and business law information as well as provides software for insurance, legal, accounting and other businesses. Its well-respected resources include the Standard Federal Tax Report, which details all tax changes in the U.S. and is a bible to the accounting industry and anyone who monitors tax information. It has a similar product for the legal world, monitoring court dockets in the U.S.

CompaniesOnline

www.companiesonline.com

This is a great starting point for getting basic profiles of almost a million companies – both private and public – tracked by Dun & Bradstreet. In addition to the basics, you can order additional credit and background information from Dun & Bradstreet's databases via credit card.

CorporateInformation

www.corporateinformation.com

This excellent site provides information on more than 350,000 companies worldwide and several industries. It also ties company profiles to the latest news headlines.

CorpTech

www.corptech.com

CorpTech provides thumbnail sketches on more than 50,000 high-tech companies, and the ability to search for names of executives – a good people-finding tool. In addition, you can purchase more extensive detail about sales and executives.

Datamonitor

www.datamonitor.com

Datamonitor is a business intelligence monitoring company for businesses, Datamonitor provides strategic planning, reports, briefing, and profiles of thousands of companies, industries and countries. It is available on a subscription basis, but also provides news and other information for free. It is an excellent international resource.

Dun & Bradstreet

`www.dnb.com`

One of the best web sites for monitoring company information worldwide, it offers a wide range of services and products, including corporate linking, as well as business information and country reports. Many of DnB's resources are available on other fee-based databases including the Million Dollar Directory (`www.dnbmdd.com`).

Euromonitor

`www.euromonitor.com`

This global market research companies sells marketing information on its own web site and through commercial providers. It has a very strong database of information.

FIS Online

`www.fisonline.com`

FIS is a subscription-based service offering company backgrounds on thousands of public and private U.S.-based companies. It is part of Mergent, and is formerly known as the Moody's Financial Information Service. There are several great business research tools, you can find bond ratings in your area and be sure to check each agency's "watchlist."

Hoover's Online

`www.hoovers.com`

Hoover's offers a free service that gives you thumbnail profiles on thousands of companies. Its fee-based tool provides much more detail. It will allow you to identify competitors and profile them, and lets you to do baseline benchmarking of finances for public companies. The site also includes summary financials for public companies, links to current news stories, analyst reports and all kinds of other information and is easily searchable. It has recently added country-by-country financial information for many countries in Europe and a top-shelf sales-lead locating tool.

InfoUSA (formerly ABII)

`www.infoUSA.com`

InfoUSA, formerly American Business Info offers a fee-based white pages and yellow pages where you can get details on top executives, ranges of sales for businesses and details on different industries in geographic areas. This information is available through other fee-based providers.

ISI Emerging Markets

`www.securities.com`

The ISI Emerging Markets page is a terrific international databases on emerging markets in Asia, Latin America and Central and Eastern Europe, with extensive free information and additional information for a fee. It offers multiple languages and translations. It is extremely costly and geared to high-end corporate customers; however, it is a great place to find out about the business of the world.

Key Note

www.keynote.co.uk/

One of the U.K.'s leading supplies of market information, it is available on a subscription basis.

Kompass

www.kompass.com

Kompass is one of the best worldwide business resources. It offers background information for free – and even more for a fee – about 1.6 million companies (and 3.2 million executives). It has more than 50,000 products and has databases of more than 744,000 trade and brand names.

Medline Public Search

www.medportal.com

This is a searchable version of the National Library of Medicine's Medline database. Several other versions of Medline are available on different fee-databases. You can also search it for free on some databases. Two of the government versions are:

> www.nlm.nih.gov
> http://medlineplus.gov

Multex

www.multex.com

Multex collects analyst reports from dozens of banks, brokerages and market research firms around the world. You can purchase their reports on a per-piece basis or via subscription. It is a useful tool and an inexpensive way to get some of these analyst reports. Be aware that Merrill Lynch is one of their investors, so their reports tend to be the most recent available.

OneSource

www.onesource.com

OneSource is a worldwide provider of information, primarily to the intranets of many of the nation's largest corporations. It provides financial news, statistics, business and industry information on more than a million public and private companies from more than 2,500 sources of content.

Primark Financial

www.primark.com

Primark is the owner of several magazine companies, the excellent About.com subject directory and a series of financial sites, including what used to be known as Disclosure, Inc. Primark Financial offers all of those plus access to a combination of a dozen databases including an easy-to-use database of SEC filings, investment analyst reports, and three international databases – Global Access, Datastream and Worldscope. It's worth a look when you are searching internationally, but is stronger for U.S. information.

Questel/Orbit

www.questel.orbit.com

Questel/Orbit focuses on searching for patent and trademark information in the U.S. and overseas. It has an extensive easy-to-use database.

Selectory Online
www.selectoryonline.com

This is a fee-based manufacturing database, compiled by Harris InfoSources. It includes more than 360,000 companies and is easily searchable in a variety of ways. You must subscribe or pay on a per-use basis. It is a paid alternative to using the Thomas Register for locating manufacturing companies in the U.S.

Skyminder
www.skyminder.com

This site, from a European-based company, provides business information on millions of private companies worldwide. It provides full-text articles as well and is available by subscription or on a pay-per-view basis.

Standard and Poor's
www.standardandpoors.com

This division of publishing giant McGraw Hill provides valuation services, financial reporting, tax data, business combinations, corporate restructurings, capital allocation and project investment. Another good site for finding bond ratings, it provides objective financial information, credit ratings, and risk analysis to the global financial community. Its reports are available by subscription.

STN
http://stnweb.cas.org

This is a fee-based database that excels as a collection of scientific materials including chemistry, patents, and technology items.

Tech Savvy
www.industry.net

Looking for an engineer or manufacturing firm, this is another fee-based database designed to help procurement professionals and others identify companies, products, and current manufacturing standards. It also offers company profiles. It is available by subscription.

Teikoku Databank
www.tdb.co.jp

This is one of the largest Japanese credit reporting companies, providing financial and corporate information databases on Japanese companies. It is also available on commercial databases like Lexis-Nexis and Dialog.

Wall Street Transcript
www.twst.com

These are searchable interviews with CEOs, CFOs, other senior management of public companies, and securities analysts. You search for what you want, then talk to someone at a phone center who helps you are get what you need. TWST also provides industry reports and your subscription fee is based on the number of sectors and length of time.

Credit Companies

There are three major U.S.-based credit companies. Here you can get your own credit report, or if you qualify (lawyers, investigators, law enforcement, etc.) you can get access to other people. It is also where you can attempt to fix problems on your credit report.

Equifax
www.equifax.com

Experian
www.experian.com

TransUnion
www.transunion.com

Conducting Market Research

Market research is information that helps you decide if you have a viable product or service (whether new or existing) and how you can sell it. It includes any and all information about companies and their products – including product reviews, launch plans, campaign strategies, company rankings, market size and share – that can identify new opportunities and influence existing plans. It's not just about what competitors and markets are doing. It's also about understanding markets and predicting how they will evolve and change.

Usually, market analysis includes extensive chart comparisons, analyst recommendations, income estimates, equity return calculations, risk profiles and an overall assessment as well as continuous monitoring and appraisal of ongoing developments. Market research is critical to funding decisions made by venture capitalists and other potential investors. The Internet is an excellent platform for doing market research, and many companies use it to research and develop market reports. Market research is about developing marketing strategies, anticipating changes and monitoring markets, identifying new sources of competitive advantage, helping sales staff's win new business and prioritizing research and development spending.

Free Sources of Market Research Data

Market research is quite lucrative and most reputable research companies charge enormous prices for their work. You can assume that nothing in this field is even close to free. However, research companies often release their best, most interesting reports or portions thereof to the press to generate publicity. As a result, many of the most valuable market research reports are summarized in trade publications and general business publications online, and you can read these news articles in lieu of paying for the actual high-priced reports.

The U.S. federal government also has terrific free resources for marketing information. If you're looking for marketing statistics or demographic information about a city or community, the best starting point is the U.S. Census Bureau web site at www.census.gov. It's searchable by city, state, Zip Code or industry. For outside the U.S., the U.S. Census also has a terrific site linking you to statistics in hundreds of other countries.

FirstGov.gov (www.firstgov.gov) will connect you to hundreds of U.S. government agencies that offer market and statistical research data, as will FedWorld (www.fedworld.gov) and FedStats (www.fedstats.gov). The Labor Department's Bureau of Labor Statistics (BLS) site at www.bls.gov is valuable, with detailed occupational employment and wage estimates for 334 metropolitan areas.

The Commerce Department's Bureau of Economic Analysis (BEA) at www.bea.doc.gov handles most of the key economic indicators for the U.S. Government. BLS focuses on labor, employment and those types of statistics, while BEA takes a more global, market-oriented perspective. Both sites have mountains of good information.

Another valuable repository of federal data is STAT-USA at www.stat-usa.gov. STAT-USA's statistics, based on the U.S. Census, cover most economic sectors, all the way down to the regional and community level. This data is critical to market research because it gives you demographic profiles of specific communities.

For international statistics, there is a terrific collection of global official statistics sources from the Library of Statistics of Finland at http://seitti.funet.fi:5000/etusivu_en.html.

➔ hot tip: One good search strategy to find statistics is to list search terms in a string. If you are looking for energy statistics, you should try and string together words like energy, facts, and association or if that doesn't work, use words like statistics, FAQ and numbers.

Trade associations are also valuable resources for information on industries. The central clearinghouse for the thousands of trade associations is the American Society of Association Executives (www.asaenet.org) based in Washington, D.C. This links to more than 1,700 associations, all searchable by name.

Another site for finding associations is the Internet Public Library's Associations on the 'Net list at www.ipl.org/ref/AON also Association Central at www.associationcentral.com

If you can't find what you are looking for from an association or through research, another option is to choose from among the hundreds of firms that offer specialty market research.

➔ hot tip: In considering marketing information sources, ask yourself:
who would care passionately about this information?
Those with an interest or stake in the information
you seek will be more likely to have the data.

Market Research Data Vendors and Brokerage Reports

There are many market research data vendors, and they are costly. What is available on their web sites tends to be only the summary or a minor portion of the information that companies pay for costly subscriptions One excellent way to discover what different companies are following is to watch the commercial press for the summaries they publish or to track the web sites of market research companies, which tend to publicize their findings. Dialog's Findex file offers abstracts with the latest market research summaries. Below are four excellent free resources followed by several valuable commercial companies:

Research Edge
www.researchedge.com

Mark Goldstein's collection of market-related and business-related tools is a good starting point for finding sales and market information about companies and products.

Web Digest for Marketers
http://wdfm.com

Larry Chase's excellent newsletter about developments in marketing is a must-read if marketing is your business. It is also a useful tool to background new and innovative companies, and for finding places where marketing research is available.

The USA Market Research Association
www.bluebook.org

This trade association's membership list is an outstanding resource, organized both geographically and by research specialty, with more than 1,200 company listings. A great starting place for market research information.

Infotech Trends
www.infotechtrends.com

This is a web-business database that offers tabular data and statistics from sixty computer journals. It is subscription based or pay as you go by credit card. It is a great place to find marketing data in the media.

Datamonitor
www.datamonitor.com

Datamonitor provides another extensive database, this one considerably more international than the others listed here.

FIND/SVP
www.findsvp.com

Like others, FIND/SVP offers a thorough database. It also provides considerable information for free, including responses to non-client questions from previously published materials.

First Call
www.firstcall.com

See Thomson section, earlier in this chapter.

Frost & Sullivan
www.frost.com

This marketing company has an extensive research database, but only accessible to paying clients.

Investext Group
www.investext.com

See Thomson section, earlier this chapter.

Jupiter Communications
www.jup.com/home.jsp

This site contains reports of this industry leader, which are reserved and password-protected for its top-dollar-paying clients. It has merged with Media Matrix, and carefully follows consumer and media companies.

Piper Jaffray
www.piperjaffray.com

Piper Jaffray, now a part of U.S. Bancorp, offers a free and very helpful web site that will point you to studies and press releases about market companies.

MarketResearch
www.marketresearch.com

This mega-store for market research information has more than 350 companies. Searching is free, then you purchase sections of the desired market reports. These reports tend to be expensive so it helps when you can do comparisons for nothing. It is a cheaper alternative to Dialog's Profound. It also offers email alerts by topic.

Multex
www.Multexinvestor.com

Multex is another aggregator of market research information. It offers analyst reports for as little as US$5-$20 dollars.

First Research
www.1stresearch.com

This is another good market research aggregator with reports at affordable prices

Zacks
www.zacks.com

Zacks specializes in market analysis with analyst recommendations on many industries and companies. Zacks offers lots of good free material and more extensive information if you're willing to pay for it.

EMarketer
www.emarketer.com

This company specializes in Internet analysis and online demographics. Reports are purchased on a per-report basis.

IMR

`www.imrmall.com`

This web site pulls together market research reports from more than forty sites. You can search the reports for free, but you have to buy all or part of the report.

➜ *hot tip:* **Expertise counts! Since market research is very expensive, it's best to enlist the aid of someone familiar with the field and its resources. If you plan to go directly to a pay service, study the online help files carefully and thoroughly beforehand in order to familiarize yourself and avoid paying hundreds of unnecessary dollars.**

Business Valuation: An Example

By Eva M. Lang

One of the fastest-growing areas in the accounting/financial consulting industry is the business valuation sector. Business appraisers, also referred to as private equity analysts, determine the value of privately-held companies for a variety of purposes including mergers, estate tax planning and marital dissolution.

The IRS requires appraisers to consider the economic and industry conditions in which the client operates and to compare the subject company to other similar companies. Performing the requisite industry, economic and market analyses requires significant research. Recently, I prepared to value a small chain of restaurants in the upper Midwest. I set out to obtain information on the restaurant industry, including publicly-traded restaurant companies, and on economic conditions of the regional market. Normally, I check the Internet first, and then move on to commercial data vendors such as Dialog.

Business appraisers use a variety of sources to gather information for an industry analysis. I started my search at Hoover's Online at `www.hoovers.com`, which provides both an industry snapshot and a list of public companies in the industry. The Hoover's Industry Snapshot provides information on industry structure, trends and major players. For example, the Hoover's Restaurant Industry Snapshot is five pages long and includes a chart detailing industry sales by sector, links to major players in the industry, a glossary of industry terms, links to related sites, and current industry news stories.

My next stop was the American Society of Association Executives at `www.asaenet.org`. This site is a searchable directory of more than 1,000 trade associations currently operating on the Web. The ASAE site pointed me to the web site of the National Restaurant Association, a site rich with data on both the restaurant industry and market conditions in selected areas.

After gathering the Hoover's data and trade association data, I wanted to find out what Wall Street analysts think of the restaurant industry. For this, I turned to the Multex web site (`www.multexnet.com`), where I was able to purchase analyst reports on the restaurant industry. I find that the Multex site, with pricing based by report, is often cheaper than other similar databases, such as Investext, which charges on a per-page basis.

To round out the industry analysis, I moved on to the many sites that offer articles from trade and industry publications. Options include the Electric Library (`www.elibrary.com`), the Dow Jones Publications Library (accessible with a subscription to Wall Street Journal Interactive at `www.wsj.com`, through Factiva at `www.factiva` or Dow Jones Interactive at `www.djinteractive.com`) and databases accessible through the Dialog or Lexis-Nexis information services. For my restaurant industry research, I was able to locate a number of useful articles from the Dow Jones Publications Library.

The industry research turned up names of some of the public companies in the industry. To get a comprehensive list of companies in a particular industry, I did a search by SIC in several different databases because not all contain the same universe of public companies or classify them in the same way. Disclosure's company database (now part of Primark), Moody's Corporate Records, and Media General Financial Services (`www.mgfs.com`) all allow searches by SIC. For a quick and cheap list of companies by industry, I also looked at the FreeEdgar site (`www.freeedgar.com`). Choosing the "Search Filings" option on its home page will take you to a search screen that allows you to search by company name, ticker or SIC Code. If you enter a SIC, you will get a list of the companies in that industry that file with the SEC.

Finally, I assembled the data for an economic analysis. For national economic data, I usually go first to the to the federal government sites, such as the U.S. Census Bureau (`www.census.gov`), the Bureau of Economic Analysis (`www.bea.doc.gov`) or the Bureau of Labor Statistics (`http://stats.bls.gov`). For my restaurant client, I needed regional information. I found the Federal Reserve Bank system to be helpful in this regard. Federal Reserve District sites, including the Minneapolis bank, are accessible from `www.federalreserve.gov` (Federal Reserve Bank map with links). I found the most helpful information in the Federal Reserve Bank Beige Book at `www.federalreserve.gov/FOMC/BeigeBook/2001/`.

At this point, I had looked at the subject company in the context of its economic and industry environment and in comparison to other companies. The information provided a solid foundation from which to assess whether the company is more or less valuable than others operating in similar conditions.

-- Eva M. Lang is an authority on electronic research for business and litigation support services. She is also technology columnist for *CPA* Expert Newsletter. Her email address is: `lemay_lang@csi.com`

Sales Prospecting

Sales research is the process of identifying potential consumers who possess characteristics of interest to you. Screening that pool of potential customers and finding potential leads who may buy is known to professionals as "sales prospecting."

Dozens of companies gather and sell mailing lists on and off the Internet. They include companies like:

Centrus Online
www.centrusonline.com

Acxiom Direct Media
www.directmedia.com

Direct Channel
www.directchannel.com

All charge for their services. Dun & Bradstreet is also in the direct mail business.

Hunting for potential customers online by contacting them indiscriminately is feasible but tacky, and invites irate responses called flames. Most mailing lists and newsgroups are very sensitive to unsolicited email that is not relevant to their main focus. Just because 1,500 avid viewers of the TV show The Sopranos belong to a newsgroup doesn't mean they'll be happy to read your solicitation for, say, insurance premiums. You may get a warmer reception if you target a specific group with information of interest – for example, if you send a message about your new screenwriting software to misc.writing.screenplay or alt.writing. The trick is to make your posting relevant to the common interest.

On the other hand, companies don't seem to mind if you send a blanket posting to them about the gizmo for which you're seeking distribution. In that case, one of your best stops should be the online business directories like Superpages (www.superpages.com) and others phone finding tools. (See Specialized Tools, Chapter 5.) Superpages is especially good because it allows you to determine competitors by location. It can be searched by area code, company name or by category. For example, if you're thinking of opening a car dealership, Superpages enables you to find the locations of all your potential competitors.

One of the fee-based tools, Hoover's (www.hoovers.com) can also help you identify potential customers by industry and/or region. It has a new lead-finding tool that targets 86,000 decision makers by location, industry, sales, and growth rates. Information is drawn from Hoover's proprietary database of more than 18,000 public and private companies.

Competitive Intelligence

Competitive intelligence (CI) is the collecting and using of public information about rival companies' activities and plans. The best CI work allows companies to predict their competitors' activities and strategies. There are several types of competitive information. Trade journals, online databases, paper documents, employee information, industry experts, and trade organizations are the most common uses of competitive intelligence information. Information from sales representatives, customers, internal documents, databases, telephone interviews, government records, direct observations, clipping services, security analysis, direct contact with competitors, personal interviews, and suppliers all provide other forms of competitive intelligence information.

CI involves detailed analysis of all or some of these resources.

CI Example

Suppose you hear a rumor that a global insurance company is planning a major relocation and you want to know more. CI specialist Melissa Pankove, of the New Jersey-based research company InSearch, recommends the following:

- Search online databases for press releases about relocation plans.

- Visit web sites that specialize in insurance news and information, including rating agencies that provide qualitative analysis on insurance companies and those of local insurance companies.

- Check rival companies' web sites, which are likely to offer extensive corporate information.

- Then go to the SEC's EDGAR database to glean information that may not be on the company's site.

- Research news resources. In this case, it's possible that a local newspaper reporter may have gotten wind of a relocation.

- Call local government officials to ask about a relocation. Chances are that if a relocation has been given the green light, someone at the local government will know about it.

Best Competitive Intelligence Sites

Competitive Intelligence Resource Index
www.bidigital.com/ci/

This site offers a variety of resources for the business and competitive intelligence professional. It contains links grouped by the kind of information they provide (statistics, news, company information). It also offers links to publications and professional associations.

FIND/SVP
www.findsvp.com

This site provides business research reports, including market research, on many subjects, as well as customized research services. One of its best resources is Robert Berkman's excellent *Information Advisor* newsletter.

Fuld & Company, Inc
www.fuld.com

This is an extensive site by a leading consultant. It offers Intelligence Pyramid, also a CI primer at www.fuld.com/i3/index.html and an extensive internet index. Fuld & Company also publishes *The Competitive Intelligence Guide*.

Montague Institute
www.montague.com

Montague Institute is a newsletter company that focuses on intellectual capital, knowledge-based publishing and business intelligence. It generates a free newsletter that contains good researching tips.

OneSource
www.onesource.com

See the Business Section earlier in this chapter.

Open Source Solutions
www.oss.net

Washington Researchers, a directory publisher, has compiled a list of tips for locating competitor facilities, researching emerging technologies and locating competitor information. It offers many CI-related books, including an essential US$885 three-volume set called *How to Find Information About Any Company*.

Society of Competitive Intelligence Professionals
www.scip.org

The site for the trade association for CI professionals includes online forums and an online library of publications designed for CI professionals, and useful for everyone. It has a searchable database of professionals with CI expertise.

Washington Researchers
www.washingtonresearchers.com

This company, which conducts private training and public seminars, offers a free weekly newsletter and a good, although somewhat out-of-date, resource guide to CI sources.

Trade Show Central
www.tscentral.com

This site is searchable by industry, type of gathering, keywords, geographic range and date – but not by company name. It covers more than 30,000 trade shows, conferences and seminars worldwide.

Other trade show sites that can be useful for competitive intelligence include:

Conferenza
www.conferenza.com

TechCalendar
www.techweb.com/calendar/

➜ *hot tip:* Check for contracts awarded and researchers' presentations posted at conference web sites. Helene Kassler, a competitive intelligence specialist, recommends visiting a search engine and submitting the company name followed by words like conference, speaker, contract, project, client, customer vendor, alliance or joint venture.

➜ *hot tip:* Don't forget the commercial data vendors – the large supermarket databases as well as smaller providers of tools. They may offer company and personal information about company officials that can be helpful as competitive intelligence data.

Quick, Effective & Free Competitive Intelligence Using AltaVista's Link Feature

By Jennifer Kaplan

Let's say you're launching a web business targeting business travelers. It's common knowledge that Biztravel.com (www.biztravel.com) is a player in this market and therefore a major competitor. Let's check them out. Typing in "biztravel.com" in the browser leads us nowhere, but submitting "www.biztravel.com" brings us to the site. Here's our first valuable piece of data: our rival is a web-based business, but someone there hasn't yet figured out how to get us to the site without the "www" and nobody else there has noticed. Any commercial site, particularly one that has invested heavily to build brand recognition of its own domain name, or URL – should be reachable with and without the "www." If we weren't persistent, Biztravel.com would have just lost a prospective customer.

With URL in hand, we then go to AltaVista at http://altavista.com and click on "Advanced Search." I prefer the "Advanced Search" function because it lets me narrow my searches by date. Many of the other advanced search features are available in the ordinary search mode, however. A "Link" feature is available on some other major search engines including HotBot, AllTheWeb, and Google, but AltaVista is our search engine of choice here.

The Link Feature

The "Link" feature is a powerful way to investigate your category and your competitors. It can be a great tool for uncovering promotion, advertising and sales opportunities.

Using the Link feature, we can learn a lot about our competitors. In the advanced search's Boolean expression box, type the following: `link:www.biztravel.com`. About 2,494 matches are found. These are sites that link to the Biztravel.com site. By the time you read this, these numbers will have increased considerably because the Web – as well as AltaVista's index – is expanding so quickly.

This information is quite valuable. Most of the time, people get to web sites by linking from another site. So the number and quality of sites pointing to your site is very important. If you think of sites that point in as sales leads, you'll understand that while quantity matters, quality is really more important. A hundred promising leads are always better than thousands of unqualified leads.

The Importance of Linked Sites

Although the number of sites linked to the site may not seem important, it can tell us a lot in context. For instance, how does the number compare to that of a similar site? Let's take a look at another travel site. Microsoft Expedia Travel is very popular, and it's backed by the Microsoft name, marketing prowess and dollars. By using the link command for the Microsoft Expedia Travel site (`www.expedia.com`), we find about 1,818 sites linked.

Before we draw any quick conclusions, we must first understand that Expedia has multiple entry points. If, for example, we try: `link:expedia.msn.com`, we get about 10,470 sites pointing in, and if we try `link:expedia.com`, we'll get only about 4,468 matches. Let's keep in mind that Expedia appeals to a broader travel audience – not just business travelers – and it's been around longer than `Biztravel.com`, so we would expect it to have more sites pointing in. Still, this is the type of competitive intelligence of which Biztravel should be aware.

Another way to use the link command count is to watch it over time. Noting the results before and after an online promotion campaign is a quick, easy, free way to measure the campaign's effectiveness.

While you're researching online, don't forget to keep your eyes open for other valuable nuggets of marketing information. For example, advertising can provide us with good data. AltaVista – like most of the big search engines – sells keywords to advertisers. That means any time a visitor searches a word, or set of words, that has been purchased, a banner advertisement pops up. Travel is a very popular category – one of the biggest on the Internet – so each time we try one of these searches, a travel-related banner comes on screen. From this we can quickly see whose spending money to target particular audiences. You may even want to type some of your own keywords into the search box just to see what words have already been purchased and how competitors' advertising messages are focused.

Whatever your field of business, try using the "Link" feature on your site and on your competitors' sites. You'll be able to learn a lot. If you have an extra twenty minutes, make an excellent investment by reading through AltaVista's help section. AltaVista is a powerful search engine that's continuously improving and innovating. By learning its features and functions, you can add its power to your creativity and your business judgment for just a little time – no money needed. That's good business.

-- Jennifer Kaplan is CEO of Jkreative. Her email address is `Jennifer@jkreative.com`. She has no personal stake in AltaVista.

Patents and Trademarks

Patents are documents that give an inventor or employer the right to manufacture and market an invention. They are important because the holder of a patent or trademark *controls* the rights to it – rights that can be licensed or sold. To be patentable, the process, design, or device has to be useful, which means that it works and is unique or different from what others have done. Patent research is complex work and a true specialty.

In addition to looking up the actual patent, most researchers will consult scientific journals, popular magazines, conference papers and trade shows.

Here are some of the best patent research web sites:

U.S. Patent and Trademark Office
`www.uspto.gov/patft/`

The U.S. Patent and Trademark Office is the mother lode of patent data. This government site is excellent for searching patent citations by company name, inventor, keyword, and/or patent class. It's free, dates back to 1976 and is your best starting place. The search site is at `http://patents.uspto.gov`. The Patent Office also offers links to non-U.S. patent resources at `www.uspto.gov/web/menu/other.html`.

Derwent
`www.derwent.co.uk`

Derwent, now a Thomson company, is a site that many professional patent searchers use. It is fee-based, searchable and can be tailored to your specific needs.

European Patent Office
`www.european-patent-office.org`

The European Patent office recently began offering free patent information for Europe.

Patent Café
`www.patentcafe.com`

This is a searchable and thorough site for patents, intellectual property and invention resources.

Micropatent

`www.micropat.com`

Micropatent offers the U.S. patent database in abstract form and in full-text for a fee. It also offers a subscription alert service for European, Japanese, and other patent/intellectual property application filings, which is important because the U.S. Patent Office doesn't publish patent information until patents are actually granted (up to two years later).

Questel-Orbit

`www.questel.orbit.com`

This is a fee-based science database that also offers extensive patent research.

➡ *hot tip:* **Patent research is best left to professionals. For a list of some of the best researchers in the business, contact the Association of Independent Information Professionals (`www.aiip.org`), which maintains a membership list searchable by subject specialty.**

Patents do not generally denote humor, but if you need a laugh while doing patent research, here is a very funny patent-related sites worth taking a glance at.

Patently Absurd! Weird Patents

`www.patent.freeserve.co.uk/`

This is another humorous collection of strange patents. It also contains links to serious patents in the U.K., Europe and around the world.

Personal Financial Information

Personal finance resources abound on the Internet. You can spend a lifetime exploring the swelling number of resources, checking leads and evaluating tips. Among the most valuable for getting up to speed on the art of investing are Quicken (`www.quicken.com`), Yahoo! (`http://quote.yahoo.com`), Microsoft (`http://moneycentral.msn.com`), and the terrific collection at About.com (`www.about.com` — look under "Business"). In addition, some Internet gateways such as America Online and MSN offer extensive personal finance and business resources.

BANK Rate Monitor Infobank

`www.bankrate.com`

This site has very good how-to information for consumers and lenders. Includes the latest survey of the best deals in about seventy cities for mortgages, loans, home equity lines and money-market accounts.

Financenter

`www.financenter.com`

Got a financial situation you want to analyze? This is the site for you. It has more than twenty financial calculators that apply to household-related situations — refinancing a house, buying or leasing a car, etc.

INVESTools
www.investools.com

INVESTools is a "supermarket" of more than thirty financial newsletters and publications that you can buy piecemeal. There is a charge, but it's quite reasonable. Submit the company's name, symbol or other information and your hits will be displayed complete with hypertext links to the periodicals and pricing options. It also offers personalized email updates on subjects you've selected.

Mutual Funds Interactive
www.brill.com

This free newsletter offers the inside scoop on mutual funds – lots of experts' commentaries, fund-manager profiles, basics of fund investing, etc. It also offers links to home pages of mutual funds and to fund-related web sites, such as the "Money Talks" site of investment columnists.

Quicken Investments (formerly NETworth)
www.quicken.com/investments/quotes

This is an all-in-one web site for investment research that searches the top twenty-five mutual funds by category or time period, then links directly to their Morningstar reports. Its database of 200 funds is searchable by total return, size, sales fees and other criteria. There's a great deal of useful information here. It's free, but you'll have to register for a password to access some sites. Also, skip the financial planning forum, where companies hawk their services.

RAM Research Group
www.ramresearch.com

This unusual site hosts the "Payment Card Planet of Cyberspace," which has some lists of good no-fee and low-rate credit cards, rebate cards, secured cards, and even some credit union cards. You can apply online.

BanxQuote: The Financial Supermarket
www.banx.com

This site provides mortgage, personal loan, credit card, and CD rates in the fifty U.S. states. It also offers daily market quotes, bank rates etc.

Investment FAQ
www.invest-faq.com

This is a useful frequently asked questions list about investments, stocks, bonds, and other personal finance options.

InvestorGuide
www.investorguide.com

This is an excellent and thorough source of information for the investor with a detailed list of frequently asked questions.

Investment Research

Investment research is well-represented on the Web. You can easily gather current and historical stock quotes, find investment advice, research companies and even buy, sell and manage your investments online. So much business information is available online that a number of Internet companies that specialize in personal finance matters are creating free gateway web sites as resource guides.

For more extensive information, please refer to the earlier sections of this chapter – in particular the sub-sections on backgrounding companies, the SEC's EDGAR database, marketing information, and competitive intelligence. Also, note the extensive list at the end of this chapter.

Stocks and Bonds

There are hundreds of sites to help you with investing stocks and bonds. Investors who want to trade stocks online will find that e-trading is inexpensive and no-frills. Online brokers do not provide individualized investment advice since and commissions are approximately US$7.95-$29.95 per trade. Some noteworthy sites are:

Schwab.com

www.schwab.com

The online arm of Charles Schwab & Co., Inc. is one of the more expensive ones for trades, but offers a well-organized, easy to use tool to follow your sticks and track industries. It also offers news, quotes, charts and some limited financial reports.

Datek Online

www.datek.com

This company is less expensive than Schwab and also features news, charts from Big Charts, and other resources, but not as extensively as Schwab.

CBS MarketWatch

http://cbs.marketwatch.com/news

Another excellent site to use for tracking stocks and bonds is actually a news site. This site is a tremendous financial site, allowing you to track or buy stocks, bonds and mutual funds in addition to following business news. It also links to Hoover's and Zacks and has more resources available by registering.

International Trade

International trade is a major area of business and there are a group of excellent resources available – free and fee-based. Here are a few valuable places to get you started on international trade research.

Tradstat

Available through Dialog; see the Fee-based Focused Business Tools section earlier this chapter.

Tradeport

www.tradeport.org/ts

The site, put together by some California trade groups, offers an excellent place to learn about trade information and market reports. It gets much of its statistical information from STAT-USA. The most useful information is definitely the market research reports, which assess specific industries and countries. Couple those with newspapers from the region – particularly business ones like *The Wall Street Journal* or *Financial Times* and you can get up to speed pretty quickly.

International Trade Web Resources

www.fita.org/webindex/

This site, compiled by the Federation of International Trade Associations (FITA), has all kinds of links to international trade resources.

U.S. International Trade Commission

www.usitc.gov

Another U.S. government site that has information about all kinds of countries and import and export information as it relates to the U.S. The trick to finding out about non-U.S. countries is to use the information available about the U.S. exports and imports as a starting point.

Non-Profits and Charities

Charities and non-profits are a huge industry in the United States. There are more than 850,000 registered non-profit organizations that get special tax status from the U.S. government, allowing them to accept tax-deductible contributions. Some are small groups that rescue feral cats and others are large enough to be considered multi-billion dollar corporations. Most charities and non-profits have boards of directors and those tend to come from a mix of local community activists and corporations. There are also thousands of groups like these all over the world. They can be a great way to find information about people as well.

There are some excellent resources for tracking charities and non-profits. Here are a few:

Action Without Borders

www.idealist.org

A terrific place to start when dealing with non-profits around the world, this is a searchable directory of over 20,000 nonprofit web sites in 150 countries.

BBB Wise Giving Alliance

www.give.org

This is the merger of the National Charities Information Bureau and Philanthropic Advisory Service of the Council of Better Business Bureaus' Foundation. It compiles data based on IRS Form 990s. It is a very strong resource.

The Chronicle of Philanthropy

www.philanthropy.com

The Chronicle of Philanthropy is the major newspaper covering the non-profit world. Its site features the newspaper content and a terrific set of links to all forms of non-profit information.

Foundation Center

http://fdncenter.org

The Foundation Center is the largest and deepest library on the non-profit world. It has an extensive collection and is easily searchable with more than 20,000 bibliographic citations. This is a terrific starting point.

GuideStar Donor's Guide to Charities and Nonprofit Organizations

www.guidestar.org

GuideStar is one of the best sites for non-profits. With information on more than 850,000 American charities and non-profit organizations, it is easily searchable and particularly good to find out who it is asking you for money. It assembles its data from the two primary sources available — the Internal Revenue Service Business Master File of 501(C)(3) nonprofits, and IRS Form 990 filed by nonprofits with more than US$25,000 in annual revenue. GuideStar also obtains information from the organizations and includes it whenever possible.

Internet Nonprofit Center: The Nonprofit FAQ

www.nonprofits.org/npofaq/

This is a frequently asked question page for the internet newsgroup soc.org.nonprofit. It is required reading for anyone interested in the non-profit world.

Internet Prospector

www.internet-prospector.org/secstate.html

This site is great for finding contacts to Secretary of State offices and for tracking corporations and non-profits. It also has a reference desk, which provides links to non-profit research.

National Center for Charitable Statistics

http://nccs.urban.org

NCCS is part of the Urban Institute's efforts to disseminate information on non-profit organizations and their activities in the United States.

Urban Legends Research Center

www.ulrc.com.au/html/report.asp?CaseFile=ULRR0087&Page=1&View=Request

This Australian site explains bogus charities.

Additional Web Sites for Business Tools

About.com: Industry & Business

http://about.com/industry/

Gathers and packages business information for users. Formerly The Mining Company. Also see About.com: Stocks

American City Business Journals

www.amcity.com

More than 35 local business publications pooled together. Includes details about companies headquartered by region.

Amer. Demographics/Marketing Tools

www.demographics.com

The nationally-renown magazine company offers access to the magazine's archives and also marketing tools.

ASI Market Research Center

www.asiresearch.com

ASI Market Research, a firm that specializes in television advertising research has a lot of free market-oriented information on its web site.

Association Central
www.associationcentral.com
Trade association clearinghouse site.

B&E DataLinks
www.econ-datalinks.org
The American Statistical Association's searchable index.

Bank Rate Monitor
www.bankrate.com/brm/default.asp
Banking site with international information, newsletters includes calculators for mortgage rates and other things to help you customize to your needs.

BANK Rate Monitor Infobank
www.bankrate.com
This site has very good how-to information for consumers and lenders. Includes the latest survey of the best deals in about seventy cities for mortgages, loans and home equity lines and money-market accounts.

Barron's
www.barrons.com
Published weekly by Dow Jones. Provides investment information and analysis to both individuals and institutional investors.

Biz Web
www.bizweb.com
This web business index has more than 43,000 companies listed in 192 categories. Has some evaluative references.

BizTravel.com
www.biztravel.com
Travel site geared to the business person.

BizWiz
www.clickit.com/touch/bizwiz.htm
A business supersite.

Bond Market Association
www.investinginbonds.com
Get up to speed on the bond industry, and much more.

Briefings.com
www.briefings.com
Fees for some content. Business newsletters and magazines.

Bureau of Economic Analysis in the Commerce Department
www.bea.doc.gov
Handles most of the key economic indicators for the U.S. Government.

Business Advisor - Deloitte & Touche
www.dtonline.com
Deloitte & Touche business adviser.

CARL Corporation
www.carl.org
Fee-based site. Click on Search CARL or Search UnCover. CARL provides an article delivery service with a table of contents database and an index to nearly 18,000 periodicals.

CBS MarketWatch - Market Data
http://cbs.marketwatch.com/data/marketdata.htx
Extensive market data pages and set of links.

Centigram Home
www.centigram.com
Fee-based site. Provides revenue-generating, integrated and enhanced services to providers in emerging markets.

Cents Financial Journal
http://lp-llc.com/cents/current/home.htm
A financial journal for online business traders.

Company News On Call
www.prnewswire.com/cnoc/cnoc.html
PR Newswire's company research database, allows you to search for news or PR stories about specific companies.

Company Research
http://iws.ohiolink.edu/companies
"How-to" guides for company and industry research projects - also has a good list of recommended sources.

Cornell University
www.ilr.cornell.edu
Resources for workplace issues.

Corporate Watch: Researching Corporations
www.corpwatch.org/trac/resrch/resrch.html
Corporate Watch's "How to Research a Transnational Company." Contains valuable tips.

Daily Stocks

www.dailystocks.com
One of the best sites online for information on investing.

Direct Marketing Association

www.the-dma.org
Trade association for direct marketing industry.

E*TRADE

www.etrade.com
E-trade's online resource center.

EBN Interactive

http://gretel.econ.surrey.ac.uk/~ivan/WebDoc/ebn-inde.htm
European business resource.

Economics Indicators Site

www.methodist.edu/business/tracking.htm
A good research guide on where to find key economic data.

Edward Lowe Foundation

www.lowe.org
Extensive small business resource center.

European Research Gateway Online

www.cordis.lu/ergo/home.html
More than 94,000 records from R&D projects currently in progress in European Union states and associated countries.

Export Hotline

www.exporthotline.com
Great starting place for information on U.S. imports and exports.

Export@ll.net

www.exportall.net
Site with strong international links for export-related and country-specific info.

Family Business

www.smartbiz.com/sbs/cats/family.htm
Small business supersite from Smart Biz.

Fed World

www.fedworld.gov
A central clearinghouse for U.S. government information.

Federal Reserve Bank Beige Book

www.federalreserve.gov/FOMC/BeigeBook/2001/
Federal Reserve's economic conditions of different geographic regions of the U.S.

Firstgov.gov

www.firstgov.gov
Will connect you to hundreds of U.S. government agencies that offer market and statistical research data as well.

Fuld & Company, Inc: CI Strategies & Tools

www.fuld.com/i3
Competitive intelligence tools.

Global Business Web

www.gbw.net
International business resources.

Gomez Advisors

www.gomez.com
Independent rating of top online stockbrokers.

Green Book, The

www.greenbook.org
The New York Chapter of the American Marketing Association publishes a free directory of market research firms. This is a valuable free source to identify companies in specific industries.

GT Online

www.gt.com
GT Online resources page for Grant Thornton LLP international management and consulting firm.

IBM Patent Server Home Page

www.patents.ibm.com
Search patent and trademark records.

IDS: Market Research

www.csa.com/csa/journals/journals-main.shtml
Summaries of market research reports and related publications from over 900 publishers worldwide.

IDS: The Internet Database Service

www.csa.com/csa/ids/ids-main.shtml
Password required Cambridge Information Group publishes *The Worldwide Directory of Market Research Reports, Studies and Surveys*, which can be located on Dialog, also at Cambridge Scientific Abstracts Internet DB Service.

Inc.'s Resources for Growing Small Business

www.inc.com
Inc. Magazine's online resources.

Industry Link

www.industrylink.com
A directory of industry-related web sites, organized by industry and categorized as "resource" or "commercial."

Industry.net Buying Guide

www.industry.net/home/search-pc.html
One of the easiest and best places to find a free searchable directory of more than 20,000 manufacturers and distributors of more than 10 million products.

Integra Information

www.integrainfo.com
Fee-based site. Excellent but costly database of benchmarking data on privately-held companies. View industry snapshot reports with financial data.

Intellifact.com

www.intellifact.com
An incredible collection of business information including more than 340,000 company profiles and in-depth financial information.

InterNet Bankruptcy Library

www.bankrupt.com
Worldwide Troubled Company Resources has news, discussion groups, resources, and alphabetical listing of U.S. companies filing for bankruptcy.

Investor Access

www.investoraccess.com
A country-by-country list of links to investor information from the Euromoney Institutional Investor Group.

Invest-o-rama!

www.investorama.com
Exhaustive directory of investment sites online.

IPO Central

www.ipocentral.com
Current list of initial public offerings. This site also has a comprehensive list of all U.S. IPOs filed since mid-1996. It also provides some news and analysis on a weekly basis.

IPO Express

www.edgar-online.com/ipoexpress
Database of more than 2,500 initial public offerings.

IRIN

www.irin.com
This free resource provides a full image format of online annual reports, quarterlies, fact books and press releases for over 2,000 companies.

Knowledge Express

www.knowledgeexpress.com
Fee-based site. A search will yield key contacts, potential partners, market information, patent information, new products concepts and more. Copyrighted DB services.

Marketing with Technology News

www.mwt.com
Web resource for web marketing articles and information.

McKinsey & Company, Inc.

www.mckinseyquarterly.com
Database of more than 400 articles that have appeared in the excellent *McKinsey Quarterly*.

Merrill Lynch Financial News & Research Center

www.merrill-lynch.ml.com/financial/res.html
Fees for some content. Free investment research from Merrill Lynch.

Microsoft Expedia Travel

http://expedia.msn.com
Another extensive travel site, geared to business.

Money Page

www.moneypage.com
Comprehensive guide to banking and finance; has resource lists on bank technology, electronic money, news, regulations and others.

NASD Regulation

www.nasdr.com
This is the regulatory arm of the National Association of Securities Dealers, the organization that separately runs the Nasdaq Stock Market. Its public disclosure program helps investors to select brokers or securities firms.

National Assoc. for the Self Employed

http://www.nase.org/benefits.asp
Nat'l Assoc. for the Self-Employed's benefits list - Internet links for small business.

NetPartners Internet Solutions: Company Locator

www.netpartners.com/resources/search.html
Searches a database of web addresses from InterNIC, an organization that provides Internet registration services. The database primarily contains American companies.

NVST Private Equity Network

www.nvst.com/pnvHome.asp
Venture capitol, mergers and acquisition resources.

Office.com Business InfoCenter

www.office.telebase.com/cgi-bin/scribe.cgi/index.htm
Registration required. Formerly from NewsPage, then Individual.com, it provides industry news through its Business Info Center databases. Registration also entitles you to information about competitors.

Patent Portal

www.patitia.de
Patent Portal features annotated and graded links to patent resources on the Web, patent news, and discussions of issues shaping patent law.

Planet Business

www.planetbiz.com
An aid for finding business sites worldwide.

PRWeb

www.prweb.com
Thousands of press releases from a full spectrum of business and industry, released online within 90 days.

Princeton University Survey Research Center

www.princeton.edu/~abelson/index.html
Links to a lot of survey and polling information, including the Gallup and Pew Research Centers.

QPAT-US

www.qpat.com
Fee-based site. Patent information.

Red Chip Review

www.redchip.com
Fees for some content. A magazine on small cap stocks.

Silicon Investor

www.siliconinvestor.com/index.gsp
Fees for some content. Financial information, stock quotes, financial data, technical charts and message boards.

SilverPlatter

www.silverplatter.com
Fee-based site. Proprietary site with organization and special business listings.

Small Business Journal

www.tsbj.com
Small Business Journal magazine.

TechNews.com

http://www.washingtonpost.com/wp-dyn/technology/
Fee-based site. Telecommunications business resource from *The Waashington Post*. Formerly Newsbytes.

USADATA

www.usadata.com/usadata/market
Market data by community and region.

Verity

www.verity.com
Verity provides business software for Intranets including searching and indexing capability.

Worldbox

www.worldbox.com
Fee for additional content. Information on more than 50 million businesses worldwide. Basic info is free. Additional is fee based.

XLS.com

www.xls.com
Fee-based site. Data Dowlink is a great collection of more than 70 databases, it lets you download information directly into your spreadsheet, saving hours of typing & conversion.

Chapter 10

International Research

Often, what you research on the Web takes you no further than a server on the other side of your country. But sometimes you find that you need information in another country – and the Web is certainly an easy, inexpensive way to get that information, if it's available.

If you think that you'll rarely need to perform an "international" search, then stop to consider these "worldly" search examples:

- You are planning a vacation in Asia, but need to know which countries are in political turmoil and which ones are safe to visit.

- Your friend wants you to help him find a phone number for his cousin from Mexico..

- You need to know what the banking laws are for transferring money from the country of the Solomon Islands, but you don't speak or understand Melanesian or any of the 120 indigenous languages spoken there.

- Your company is interested in taking its product to Latin America, but you need to find out which country will create the most lucrative opportunity.

- You need to find out who is the largest employer is in Goma, Congo.

While the Web certainly makes information in other countries easier to find, dealing with something "foreign" is still a culture shock for most people. The Internet does make the world smaller, but it doesn't eliminate the major hurdles you have to face when seeking information in countries where record keeping or information laws may be very different from what you are accustomed to.

Before searching for information in other countries, your first task should be to answer the question "is this information available?" It is easy to assume that the same information we find in our country can be found in other countries – you just need to know where to look for it. This is not the case. For example, if you were searching Pakistan to find birthday party favors like balloons, whistles, streamers, and candles, you would be unable to locate them – on the Internet or in a store – because Pakistani children don't tend to have birthday parties the way children in other countries do. It's not a ritual that is celebrated there.

➜ *hot tip:* It is true: every country has its own unique resources, different laws and customs that you need to understand to successfully find what you need. What's available in one country may be prohibited from being disclosed in other countries. Therefore, it is helpful to know whether the information you seek is collected and made available before banging your head against the keyboard because you can't find it.

Even if you overcome these regulatory and cultural barriers, sometimes you may need to use a translation tool or service to better understand your results. Be sure to read the comprehensive section on these translation tools later in the chapter.

Information Barriers

One of the biggest challenges in doing country-to-country or regional comparisons is finding reliable standardized information. The United States and the European Union have made great strides in establishing standards for information. But the kind of information available and how often it is updated varies from state to state and country to country. No standards whatsoever are available for Africa or Latin America.

Regulatory Barriers

Here's an example. In the U.S., publicly-traded companies are required to gather financial statements and publicize the information quarterly, and provide an annual report within ninety days of the fiscal year end. Private companies, however, are not required to release any information. In the U.K., financial reporting requirements are extensive, providing pretty much everything about a company. Even if the company is privately held, they have to make their financial statements public. How current are those reports? In the U.K., companies have up to a year after the fiscal year ends to file their annual reports. In Asia, about the only places you can get private company information is from Dun & Bradstreet or a local regulatory commission. It's rare to find it computerized. Getting the info from D&B will cost you money, and the local commissions may be unreliable, often requiring you to find someone locally who can provide the information. In China, researchers say, the government doesn't want people to know details about China's economy. The best you might get is a press release through the Chinese news agency Xinhua. But, this has begun to change as companies like *The Financial Times* (*FT*), America Online, and others develop joint ventures there.

But none of these countries require public disclosure of information on the Web. It gets even more confusing when it comes to personal information. In the U.S., availability of public records varies from state to state. The European Union has strict privacy rules governing what information can and can't be made public. Italy, a member of the E.U., has an even more stringent privacy law, putting strict restrictions on how you collect, store, and distribute "personal data." They define this as all information that can be associated with a person, company, or organization. Before releasing data, that law requires the written consent of the subject. Italian researchers suggest the law is seriously impeding all information gathering as people are simply afraid to give out any information.

In the United States, most federal or state agencies gather and release all kinds of public records. For example, how much money you paid for your home or condominium is information easily obtained. This helps the individual who is trying to buy property because they can get an accurate value of the house next door. Most countries outside the U.S. consider this private, not public information, so property information is not made available. When Americans look outside the United States, they wrongfully assume that similar information is available and are surprised to find it is not.

Another area where you will see significant variance in what's available involves legal cases. U.S. laws and regulations and many court records are easily accessible, and are increasingly published online, but that's not the case, for example, in most Asian countries. Finding out if a company has been involved in legal cases in the U.S. is easy, but similar information is not generally disclosed in countries like Japan. On the other hand, market shares of consumer products are easily found for a price in Japan, while that information is considerably more difficult to find in Latin America.

Cultural Barriers

Sometimes lack of access to information is not based on local laws, but on local customs. For example, nearly everyone in the United States has a telephone number and unless they specifically request it to be unlisted, those phone numbers are available to be searched on the Internet. While most countries have phone books and centralized phone information, that information is not even collected in parts of Mexico and Africa. While most of Latin America does not have reliable company directories, they are plentiful in Europe.

Another cultural difference is online access to media. Huge collections of newspapers, magazines and other published materials are available in the United States, much less so in other countries.

There are also cultural nuances that can hamper your search. For example, in doing research in Mexico, people prefer to meet you in person, not to talk electronically or on the phone. In Japan, a phone call is preferable to an email or a fax. Unless you understand these cultural distinctions, you can violate accepted protocols that prevent you from getting to important information.

➔*hot tip:* **Sometimes you may find that you need the assistance of a "guide" who works in that country. To help you find that special guide, see the "Importance of People" Section late in this chapter — it may be the shortcut you need.**

Technical Barriers

When cultures and regulations don't restrict information online, sometimes it comes down to technical ability. There's often an assumption that every country has the infrastructure to collect and publish data. But in countries where they don't have roads, telephones, or even running water, it's unlikely they would have cutting edge data collecting capabilities. Still, most of the major countries have lots of resources available on the Internet. Some small countries also have surprisingly valuable resources; the Czech Republic posts extensive detail about its country on the Internet.

Cost Barriers

In the U.S., phone lines and flat-rate Internet access is readily available. In other countries you may be paying more for Internet access or even phone access on a minute-by-minute charge. With unlimited access, you can take the time to research, but if you are paying by the minute, you may want to consider whether it is cheaper to research online, or to make a few well-placed phone calls. Additionally, in planning your research budget, you may want to determine if the information you need is available online at little or no cost, or if you will have to subscribe to an online database. For those with limited access or blocked by pay-per-minute charges, experienced researchers suggest you spend your time trying to find a knowledgeable person who can help you.

Bias Barriers

The Internet is often a tool to express a point of view. What one person finds to be objective, unbiased information is a loaded weapon to someone with a strong opinion on that subject. As a result, in critiquing sites, you must ask yourself what is the message they're trying to get across and how much bias spills onto their site. When searching a subject that is politically charged, be especially aware for the subtle and sometimes not-so-subtle efforts to persuade. See Chapter 12, Evaluating Accuracy for more on this.

Language Barriers

Once you know the information is available, will you be able to understand it? The next big barrier to overcome is the language barrier. Two recent studies[1] show that between 44-50% of today's Internet users speak English, yet 70-86% of Internet pages are in English. In contrast, it is estimated that by the end of 2003, only a third of Internet business will use English. Worldwide, native Spanish speakers outnumber native English speakers and the number of native Chinese speakers more than equals both groups combined.

English is the dominant language, the studies found, because it was established early as the language of the wired world. That is changing as more non-English-speaking countries build out the infrastructure to allow their citizens greater web access. So soon, to really benefit from all that is on the Internet, you will either have to understand other languages or use the tools that can help translate foreign languages into your own.

---

[1] A Forrester Research study in 2000, and an academic study by researchers at Tel Aviv University, Israel, and the University of California at Berkeley, California, U.S.

➜*hot tip:* **Before you begin your international information hunt, remember that it is often like a soccer match – you must understand the rules, know where the goals are, and identify who's on your team. Knowledge and flexibility are absolute musts.**

Translation Services

There are already valuable free or fee-based translation services available online. Their features and accuracy vary as widely as their language and subject matter. Some translators can translate phrases into many languages, or can translate an entire web site into another language. Some give you the essence of what's on a page, and others give you literal translations.

Most of the translators listed below work in a similar manner. What differs is what languages they offer. Most offer languages in and out of English. But, if you need to translate from French to German and German to French, then only one listed tool, Systran, will help you.

Two of the major search engines — AltaVista and Google — offer excellent translation capabilities. Point these tools to a particular web page and they will quickly translate it for you.

Babelfish, from AltaVista
`www.babelfish.altavista.com`

...offers twenty-five languages.

Google's Language Tools
`www.google.com/language_tools`

...currently translates five European languages, and more languages are being added.

Other good tools include:

SDL International FreeTranslation
`www.freetranslation.com`

...allows you to translate six languages to/from English. The company also offers a more sophisticated level of translation product for a fee.

Systran
`www.systransoft.com`

...offers five languages in and out of English, also French to German and German to French.

World Lingo
`www.worldlingo.com/products_services/worldlingo_translator.html`

...provides free translation from and into Japanese, Chinese, Korean, and other languages.

Intertran Translator
`www.toad.net/~royfc/dicts.html`

One of the most versatile translation tools for free on the Web, it offers all kinds of combinations of more than twenty-five languages including Russian, Croatian, Greek, Polish, and other Slavic languages.

Two excellent collections of language tools are:

www.resourcehelp.com/qsertranslate.htm

http://translation-guide.com

Aids to Understanding

Whatever language you are researching in, sometimes you need a little extra help understanding what is being said. Fortunately, the Internet is rife with dictionaries, thesauruses, and other reference tools. Most of these are available in English (see Chapter 5, Specialized Tools), but some terms are particular to a country or region and require a local explanation. Eurodicautom (http://europa.eu.int/eurodicautom/login.jsp) is an online version of the European Commission's Translation Service, giving translations of technical terms, abbreviations, acronyms, and phraseology in most European languages.

It is possible you may need to read characters other than the ones on your keyboard. For example, you would need to enable different character fonts to see Chinese or Korean. The latest browser versions of Internet Explorer and Netscape now have the capability to handle these characters. Starting with Internet Explorer 5.0 and Netscape 6.0, language fonts were added.

Internet Explorer's Auto-Encoding feature works with the coding of web pages to determine which character sets to display. To take advantage of this, go to "View," then "Encoding," then select "Auto Select." If you want to change it to display a particular character set, then select "More" instead of "Auto Select" and choose the language you wish to display. If the character set a web page requires is not already loaded onto your machine, you may be need to download additional software from IE. To make sure you receive a prompt when additional software is needed, go to "Tools," then "Internet Options," click the "Advanced" tab, then select the "Enable Install on Demand" check box. In Netscape, simply go to "View," then "Character Set," and select the appropriate language.

Where to Find the Information

In learning a part of the world you are unfamiliar with, you will need to use multiple tools to get a good understanding of that region. There are literally thousands of potential resources online. Several of the best resources are listed in this chapter. As always, remember to first plan a search strategy for finding the information you need.

➜*hot tip:*   **Knowing the country codes at the end of a foreign web site helps you identify the source, the language, and something about the culture. See Chapter 2, The Basics, for the country codes.**

On almost any international search, there are four good places to start.

- **Government sites** – Many countries have very useful governmental sites that often point to other sites. Searching for the main governmental site may be a good place to start for information about a company or business. Even if you are searching for information about another country, the U.S. government is a great starting point because undoubtedly some part of the U.S. government is monitoring whatever is going on there. This means you can usually find information about almost any subject somewhere in the U.S.

- **Educational sites** – Name a topic and somewhere, some academic has made that his specialty, presenting their findings online — in higher education it is "publish or perish." You can find a lot of useful information by looking for a professor or PhD who knows your area of interest inside and out. There are some educational links later in this chapter, but keep in mind you can begin with your own local university and then expand your search from there.

- **Media sites** – Try looking through the archives of the local media for information and resources in that nation or region. Even if an article doesn't have all the details, it may list a web site or person you can contact for more information – take close note of the sources an article cites. You can contact these sources, too!

- **Search tools** – Search engines and subject directories can be valuable if you know what you are looking for. Of particular use are specialized search tools focused on particular regions or topics. (These search engines/subject directories are featured later in this chapter.)

General, Statistical and Economic Information for a Country or Region

Let's look at some more specific starting points for popular areas of research.

If you are just getting started on finding basic information about a country but know absolutely nothing about it, then you should start with basic country backgrounding tools like encyclopedias and country profiles. The U.S. government has country-specific and regional profiles on its State Department page and also the U.S. Central Intelligence Agency's Factbook is a terrific starting point. Each provides extensive, up-to-date background information about most countries and regions of the world.

The CIA Country Profile (www.odci.gov/cia/publications/factbook/ind.html) includes maps, statistics, population details, and overviews of the economy, the political situation in that country and the region, and other pertinent information. The U.S. State Department site (www.state.gov/r/pa/bgn) goes a step further by providing the basics about the government, economy, history of the region, political leaders, how the judicial system works, and if it's safe to travel there. If you are looking for the basics on a nation, without encountering much political cheerleading, these two sites are superb starting points.

Say you want to find out about specific industries and how they compare to the same industries in your country. An excellent resource to begin with is the World Bank (www.worldbank.org/data/countrydata/countrydata.html), which has snapshots of the business profile of different countries and specific industries as well as comparisons, maps, data, development details, etc.

Where the U.S. government is particularly strong in providing details about other countries is in the import/export and trade areas. The Commerce Department site (`http://home2.doc.gov`) is loaded with good material – the best stuff is at the Commerce Department's International Trade Administration (`www.ita.doc.gov`). Particularly good are country commercial guides available at `www.usatrade.gov/website/ccg.nsf/ccghomepage?openform`. Much of the information has been merged with the U.S. federal government's primary site FirstGov at `www.firstgov.gov`. Its links will help route you to other U.S. government sites.

→ **hot tip:** **Where the U.S. government is particularly strong in providing details about other countries is in the import/export and trade areas. The Commerce Department site (`http://home2.doc.gov`) is loaded with good material – the best stuff is at the Commerce Department's International Trade Administration (`www.ita.doc.gov`). Particularly good are country commercial guides available at `www.usatrade.gov/website/ccg.nsf/ccghomepage?openform`. Much of the information has been merged with the U.S. federal government's primary site FirstGov at `www.firstgov.gov`. Its links will help route you to other U.S. government sites on topics that can include foreign nations.**

Another incredibly valuable site on the Commerce Department's web site is the statistics area (`www.stat-usa.gov`). The U.S. government charges US$175 per year for unlimited access to all of these reports, however, some of the material can be found for free on other American government web sites. Stat-USA's Globus and NDTB section includes global business opportunities with details on trade leads from the Commerce Department, Agriculture Department. and also procurement activity from the Defense Department and the United Nations, among others. One of the best free resources anywhere is the U.S. government's central clearinghouse for statistics, FedStats (`www.fedstats.gov`). It provides links to statistics from hundreds of government agencies.

Some U.S.-based fee-based commercial online services also offer incredibly detailed trade-related information. Two of the best are Data Downlink's XLS site at `www.xls.com` and Dun & Bradstreet's Worldbase database at `www.dnb.com` which provides detailed reports on companies around the world.

Most countries have statistical offices or central banks that regulate their commerce. Many countries release that information, but others hold it closely. Some, like the Bank of Poland, maintain excellent records and release much of their information. Some countries sell that information. Efforts to standardize how banks and governments record and report their data are being made by the International Monetary Fund, and added pressure from the American Depository Receipts – the publicly-traded stocks that represent shares in non-U.S. stock – is leading to more reliable consistent information. So, for financial data, an excellent starting point in most countries is that country's central bank. Some standardization is now available on gross domestic product, unemployment rates, export/imports, and deficits.

No such effort has begun for demographic data. In the United States, the U.S. Census at `www.census.gov` is a goldmine of data about American culture. The census compiles information about everything from the unemployment rates in local communities to national economic indicators to the country's divorce rates. (See Chapter 6 - Government Resources.) However, many of the questions asked by the U.S. Census are cultural in nature and are not applicable to other nations and other cultures. Some questions simply don't apply outside a particular country, like the number of televisions or the number of bathrooms in your house. In some countries, television as we know it doesn't exist. Some communities do not have running water, much less private bathrooms.

Embassies – A Valuable Resource

Embassies are another valuable resource – find out if your country has a foreign embassy and how to contact it. The job of most embassies is to represent its country in the foreign nation. In doing so, embassy staff are always looking for any opportunity to help promote their country. You can benefit from their expertise. Now, while you won't get unbiased information there, you will get lots of information and often that embassy can put you in touch with experts in the field.

Where this can be especially useful is if you are researching a remote country like Swaziland, a kingdom near South Africa. If you've already done the country background, then you probably want to make contact with someone who can guide you to the experts you need. Seek that contact through official channels, checking its embassies around the world. You could contact their representative at the United Nations, but chances are that you won't get a quick response.

Usually, if you are looking for the foreign embassy in the United States, the best place to start is in Washington, D.C., where most embassies are located. If you are not sure how to contact the appropriate embassy, prior to 9/11/2001 you could go to The Embassy Web (`www.embpage.org`), a searchable database of thousands of email addresses, phone numbers and names of American personnel listed in that embassy, pulled together by Norbert Marrale. It linked to non-American embassy personnel and tells where diplomats from that country were stationed around the world. It also listed links to books and offers useful background news from the region as well.

Online, the Electronic Embassy (`www.embassy.org/embassies/`) is another good place to find contact information. Like the United Nations, the staffs are small, so email may not be answered.

Another resource that seems to be worldwide and surprisingly useful is Chambers of Commerce. Because they are all locally-based, their usefulness and the quality of their information will vary. There are local chambers of commerce, for little communities within countries, to the large ones like the U.S. Chamber of Commerce, a national organization that acts as a clearinghouse for hundreds of smaller groups. Several chambers have useful information about their communities posted on their web sites.

American Chambers of Commerce Abroad
`www.uschamber.com/chambers/international/international directory.asp`

Sheri Lanza, in her excellent book, *International Business on the Web*, suggests that the Am Chams, or American Chambers of Commerce Abroad, is a particularly helpful group because it is comprised of associations of business executives interested in U.S. foreign trade and investment.

World Chambers

www.worldchambers.com

World Chambers is a collection of over 10,000 chambers of commerce from all over the world.

China Chamber of International Commerce

www.ccpit.org/chiVersion/indexCh.html (Chinese version)
www.ccpit.org/engVersion/indexEn.html (English version)

Asian researchers agree: the China Chamber of International Commerce is a valuable site for business information about China.

Searching For Foreign Companies

Researching a company that is U.S.-based is relatively easy. If it is a publicly-held company, it is required to report in excruciating detail about business activities to specific federal agencies. If it is privately held, no such requirement exists. For these, many pay services like Hoover's (www.hoovers.com) and Dun & Bradstreet (www.dnb.com) will usually have some valuable information. (See Chapter 9, Business Resources for considerably more detail.)

Sometimes you can find valuable information about non-U.S. companies by tapping resources in the U.S. A good starting point is often the U.S. government itself. A global company like Microsoft – which has operations in 118 countries – must report about the profitability or liability of all of those operations to the U.S.-based Securities and Exchange Commission. So, one of the obvious options in starting to trace information about international businesses is to see if they do business in the U.S. For details, look at whatever American government agency regulates them or monitors their industry.

Region by Region and Country-Focused Tools

Most of the tools for international searching tend to be focused on particular regions and specific countries. Many of the more useful tools are presented below. While the Internet is too large to give you anything close to a comprehensive look at the search tools, these regional and country-specific tools will get you pointed toward resources in every part of the world. In addition to pointing you to search engines, there are a lot of excellent government, news, and business sites worth recommending. Again, these are just *some* of the best sites. Also see the topic-specific finders in the other chapters and in the appendix.

➜**hot tip:** Remember to look at which sites are linked to these to find other valuable ones. To do that you can go to a search engine like AltaVista and type in "link:africaonline.com" and you'll find more than 30,000 sites linked. That should get you started on African sources.

An excellent place for English-speaking researchers to start:

Portals to the World
www.loc.gov/rr/international

This site, from the Library of Congress, is a superb starting point for finding information about different countries of the world. It uses and relies on Library of Congress sites and resources to provide extensive country-specific information about the world. It shows off the incredible value of a great library.

Africa

Africa Online
www.africaonline.com

An excellent collection of resources for all of Africa. Links to news, business, and education.

Woyaa
www.woyaa.com

A combination search engine/directory, this site has an excellent directory — available in French and English — and resources for all of Africa.

Africa South of the Sahara
www-sul.stanford.edu/depts/ssrg/africa/

Remember the suggestion earlier in this chapter that some academic somewhere is studying your subject? This site is proof of how excellent academic resources can be. A superb directory.

Africa Index
www.africaindex.africainfo.no/

This is another excellent directory to African resources.

African Guide
www.africanguide.com

Another good starting point, especially if travel is your interest.

South Africa

Ananzi
www.ananzi.co.za

This is an excellent subject directory searchable for links throughout South Africa and neighboring countries. What makes it most useful is it indexes news stories, so you can easily find up-to-date information.

Congo
www.brazzaville-adiac.com

This is a good starting point for news and directory resources in the Congo.

North Africa

Egypt

See The Middle East section, below.

Kenya

`www.kenyaweb.com`

This is an excellent directory for Kenyan resources.

Libya Resources on the Internet

`www.geocities.com/Libyapage`

This is a good starting point for information about Libya.

Morocco

`www.marweb.com`

This site provides useful links related to Morocco and Mauritania.

Somalia

`www.banadir.com/links.shtml`

A collection of useful links about Somalia.

Tunisia

`www.winoo.com`

A good directory of Tunisian resources.

Middle East

Middle East Pages

`www.middle-east-pages.com/me.html`

You could call it the Yahoo! of the Middle East. A good starting point.

Arab Search

`www.arab.net (news stories)`
`www.arab.net/search/welcome.html (search engine)`

A good starting point for Arab resources, with excellent country background information.

1001 Sites

`www.1001sites.com`

This is an excellent clearinghouse for information about the Middle East, including daily English translations of the Middle Eastern press. It is a project of Arab World Online and has superb country profiles.

Arabist

`www.arabist.com`

A guide site to Middle Eastern and Arabic subjects.

Iran Mania

`www.iranmania.com`

A searchable directory of Iran-related information.

SearchIR

www.searchir.com

SearchIR is a good international web site in English for Iran-related information. This is a huge database of Islam-related material.

Walla

www.walla.co.il/

An Israeli site guide and search engine.

ArabBay.com

www.arabbay.com

This is a directory for the Arab world, with an area for each major Arabic country.

HyeGuide.com

www.hyguide.com

An Armenian directory of web sites.

Egypt

Egypt Search

www.egyptsearch.com

A good Egyptian search engine and directory.

Turkey

Dost.net

www.dost.net

This is a Turkish and English business directory.

EGENET

www.egenet.com.tr

A Turkish web search tool with English translation.

Europe

European Search Engines

www.netmasters.co.uk/european_search_engines/

This is a thorough list of European search sites broken down by country. There are no details on which sites work or how effective they are, so you are on your own.

Euroseek.Net

www.euroseek.net

Recently bought by Worldlight.com, this is an excellent European-based search engine in which you can read instructions in over forty languages. It doesn't translate the results, however.

Diabolos
www.diabolos.com

This European-oriented search engine has strong global coverage. It is available in Italian and a few other languages, but you'll have to know some Italian to work this site.

Euroguide
www.euroguide.org/euroguide/subject-listing/

This site guides you through the maze of European information on the 'Net. It is easily searched.

WebWatch
www.webwatch.be/Search-engines.html

This Belgium-search engine can search all of Europe, and does it in multiple languages.

France

Abondance
www.abondance.com

This is an excellent search engine for France and French speakers. C'est tres bien.

Voila France
www.voila.fr

The flagship of the Voila Search Engine that indexes over 100 million pages.

Germany

Klug Suchen
www.klug-suchen.de

This is an excellent guide to German-oriented search engines and directories. It will link you to all the other German search sites.

Fireball.de
www.fireball.de

This is one of the largest search engines in Germany. It also has links to all kinds of German-language sites all over the world.

Greece

Hellenic - Greece
http://www.robby.gr/

A combination search engine and directory that focuses on Greek domains.

Ireland

Ask Paddy
www.askpaddy.com

This Irish-focused web directory allows you to search by county.

Searching Ireland
`www.searchingireland.com`

A search directory of Irish sites, it also compiles search results from other Irish search engines.

Italy

Arianna
`http://arianna.iol.it`

This huge Italian web directory has almost one-hundred categories and also provides MP3 music searching by artist, title and song. It also lets you search all of Italy's Usenet newsgroups.

Virgilio
`www.virgilio.it/home/index.html`

A directory of more than 4.5 million Italian web sites, Virgilio has advanced search capabilities.

Super Eva
`www.supereva.com`

A terrific Italian search engine.

Netherlands

WWWIJZER
`wwwijzer.nl`

This is a Dutch search engine and human-compiled directory of web sites.

NL-Menu
`www.nl-menu.nl`

This search engine and directory, available in Dutch and English, is maintained by the National Library of the Netherlands. It is particularly focused on science and education, but also offers resources on other subjects.

DutchESS: Dutch Electronic Subject Service
`www.kb.nl:88/dutchess/`

This is a Dutch search engine, from the Dutch National Library. It is geared to find free international resources from the academic perspective.

Poland

Wirtualna Polska
`www.wp.pl/`

Virtual Poland is a good directory of Polish sites.

Spain and Portugal

BIWE Buscador en Internet de Webs Espanoles
`www.biwe.es/`

This is a directory of Spanish-language web sites geared to Spain.

OZU
www.ozu.es/index.htm

OZU is a Spanish search engine and directory.

AEIOU
www.aeiou.pt

AEIOU is a Portuguese search engine.

Portugal Info
http://portugal-info.com

A subject directory for Portugal.

Switzerland

Search.ch
www.search.ch/

A combination search engine and subject directory, this site searches Switzerland resources and also sites in neighboring Liechtenstein.

Yugoslavia

Beocity
www.beocity.com

A Yugoslavian portal that combines search capability and a subject directory.

YuSearch
www.yusearch.com (in English)
www.yusearch.com/indexs.html (in native language)

This is an excellent directory and search engine covering Yugoslavia and the Balkans.

Other Central European Sites

Croation Directory   (Croatia)
www.iskon.hr/

This is a good Croation internet directory.

Superzoznam.Sk   (Slovak)
http://szm.sk/

A search engine and directory for Slovak sites.

HuDir   (Hungary)
http://hudir.hungary.com

HuDir is a web directory of thousands of Hungarian sites.

Scandinavian Countries

Denmark

Kvasir.dk
www.kvasir.dk

An excellent search tool for Danish and Scandinavian resources.

Jubii
www.jubii.dk

A search engine and directory combination for Denmark and Danish sites.

Finland

Evreka
www.suomi24.fi/

This Finnish edition of the Evreka search engine can be searched for all of Scandinavia.

Haku.net

This is a Finland-specific search engine and directory.

Iceland

The Web Collection
www.hugmot.is/

A strong collection of Icelandic sites.

Norway

Scandanavia Online - Norway
www.sol.no/

This is an excellent portal site, combining the Kvasir search engine with a good directory.

Gulesider
www.gulesider.no/index.jsp

Gulesider is another good Norwegian subject directory.

Sweden

Evreka
http://evreka.passagen.se/

This site is a directory covering Sweden. It also offers search engine capability and links to the rest of Scandinavia.

ALLT.com
www.allt.com

A directory of Swedish sites.

United Kingdom

BUBL LINK
http://bubl.ac.uk/link/

This is truly an outstanding subject directory. It's large and well-organized.

SearchUK
www.searchuk.com

This excellent, large search engine looks for U.K.-related domains.

UK Plus
www.ukplus.co.uk/ukplus/SilverStream/Pages/pgUKPlusHome.html

This site searches U.K. sites and is prepared by a team of journalists, so the subjects tend to be carefully selected.

Russian Regions - Former Soviet Countries

Russian Search Engines
www.zhurnal.ru/search/engines.shtml

These are pointers to Russian guides on the Web.

Azerbaijan Search
www.search.az

This site offers everything from news to energy resources to love and dating resources.

Activist   (Estonia)
www.aktivist.ee

This is a terrific Estonian directory.

Ex USSR Search Engines
www.zodchiy.ru/links/search

This is a good collection of search engines, directories and link-pages for former USSR countries.

RUCITY.Com
www.rucity.com

A good directory of sites related to former Soviet countries.

APORT
www.aport.ru

This huge Russian search engine has more than a million documents.

Russian Internet Guide
www.neystadt.org/russia

Russian search engine from John Neystadt has a unique feature: a postal address lookup.

Australia and the Far Pacific

South Pacific Directory
www.emaxia.com

The web directory for Samoa and other far off paradises.

Australia

Anzwers
www.anzwers.com.au/

This is a well-known and popular guide to Australian and New Zealand web sites.

Go Eureka
www.goeureka.com.au/standard.php

The super search capability of this search tool makes it excellent — you can field search for links, dates, titles and URLs. Search it regionally, by country, or globally.

Black Stump Australiana
www.blackstump.com.au/aussie.htm

This is a good directory of Australian web sites categorized by topic and maintained by Peter Garriga, who is very selective.

Oz Search Internet Guide
www.Ozsearch.com.au

A subject directory of Australian sites.

Philippines

See the Asia Section, which follows.

Asia

Asiaco
www.asiaco.com

This is a country-by-country directory with thousands of web sites for over thirty Asian countries. It also offers a helpful map of Asia.

AsiaDragons
www.asiadragons.com

This is a searchable directory for most Asian countries.

AsiaNet
www.asianet.com

This is a central clearinghouse for directories from all over Asia as well as a few from other regions of the world.

SAARC – The South Asian Search Engine
www.southasia.net

Search engine and directory of Southeast Asian resources. It's browsable by subject and country.

Afghanistan

Afghan Web
www.afghan-web.com

This is geared to non-Afghans; written in English. It offers news resources in addition to search capabilities.

Kabul Search
www.kabulsearch.com

This site is geared toward the people of Afghanistan as well as the rest of the world. It is easily searched and offers a directory.

China

Yahoo! China
http://chinese.yahoo.com

This is Yahoo!'s web site for China, in Chinese.

Asiaco-China
http://china.asiaco.com

Asiaco's directory of Chinese web sites.

Chinascape
www.chinascape.org

This site is a search engine focused on Chinese culture, searchable in English.

India

Jadoo
www.jadoo.com

Jadoo is a major directory of Indian web sites.

India Spider
www.indiaspider.com

A good computer-generated search engine and directory that also offers discussion forums.

Indiatimes.com

This is a portal site from the *India Times* newspaper. It includes an extremely thorough web directory, search engine and all kinds of interactive chats, photo galleries, and news headlines.

KHOJ India Directory
www.khoj.com

This is a huge searchable directory. It also has a directory of top-quality links.

Japan

Japanese Search Engines
www.atrium.com/cgi-bin/banner/display.pl?h=search

This is definitely the first place to start on Japanese sites. It's a compilation site of all the Japanese search engines and how to use them, with links to Japanese and English versions.

Goo
`www.goo.ne.jp`

This Japanese search engine is backed by Inktomi and the big Japanese phone company, NTT. It's a strong, easy-to-use search tool.

Malaysia

Cari
`www.cari.com.my/`

This is a guide to Malaysian sites. You can search for Malaysian-only sites and global sites in English or Malaysian.

Philippines

Yehey
`www.yehey.com`

This is a large directory of Philippine resources.

Ask Jose
`www.askjose.com`

This is not a question-and-answer search tool like Ask Jeeves, but a search engine and portal site that offers Philippine resources. It's also country-specific for Hong Kong, Singapore, and Taiwan.

Thailand

Thailand
`www.siamguru.com`

This excellent site offers a search engine, news, music and images as well as a directory for Thailand-related sites.

Latin America

LatinWorld.com
`www.latinworld.com`

This search engine works for countries all over Latin America.

Yupi
`www.yupimsn.com`

This is a Latin American-focused, Spanish-speaking web site, now owned by MSN.

En Espanol
`www.enespanol.com/home.html`

While most sites are geared toward regions of the world, some are geared to ethnicities. This is a site geared to the Spanish-speaking world. This site has extensive links to Spanish sites and cultural related information.

Ugabula.com
www.ugabula.com

Their slogan is "It's a jungle out there. Trust the beast." The web site's logo is a gorilla, but the search engine is far from unruly. It's easy to use and covers all Latin American countries.

LANIC Latin American Network Information Center
http://lanic.utexas.edu

This is a searchable directory pulled together as part of the Latin American Network Information Center at the University of Texas. It is a good compilation and easy to use in English, Spanish and Portugese.

Star Media
www.starmedia.com

Geared toward pop culture, this is a very popular Latin American search site. It is a portal offering news, email, chat, and all kinds of interactive polling.

Terra
www.terra.es/

This is a directory of Spanish-language web sites, from the folks that own Lycos. You can search the web or look at regional editions for Argentina, Brazil, Chile, Colombia, Costa Rica, Dominican Republic, El Salvador, Guatemala, Honduras, Mexico, Nicaragua, Panama, Peru, Spain, Uruguay, and Venezuela. Use Terra and add the country code, i.e., Terra Argentine can be found at www.terra.ar. The U.S. version (in Spanish) is found at www.terra.com

El Salvador

Buscaniguas
www.buscaniguas.com.sv/

A good Salvadoran search engine.

Brazil

Radar UOL
http://radaruol.uol.com.br/

This Google-style Brazilian search engine is easy to use.

Cade
www.cade.com.br

Modeled after Yahoo!, this is a strong directory of Brazilian resources.

Mexico

Mexico Online
www.mexonline.com

This independent, easy-to-use site is great for finding information related to Mexico.

Mexico Global
www.mexicoglobal.com

A Mexican directory with links to a wide variety of subjects.

Nicaragua

Xolo
www.xolo.com.ni/

This is a good place to start on Nicaraguan resources.

The Caribbean

Caribseek
www.caribseek.com

A terrific starting point for Caribbean resources with links to sites on every island in the region.

Canada

Maple Square
http://maplesquare.com

This Canadian subject directory is searchable and easily browsed.

AltaVista Canada
http://ca.altavista.com

This is the Canadian version of AltaVista, with access to millions of Canadian-specific web pages. It also has a directory from LookSmart, also Canada-focused. You will also find specialized government, news, and health searches produced by Telus, one of Canada's largest telecommunications companies.

World Educational Resources

Educational resources are especially valuable for international research because academics tend to focus on particular regions and countries. thus many get to know an area well. In her book *International Business Information on the Web*[2], Sheri Lanza has identified some wonderful academic resources.

- The Andersonian Library at the University of Strathclyde runs the Bulletin Board for Libraries (BUBL) at http://bubl.ac.uk/link/countries.html that contains links about nearly every country in the world.

- Everything International (http://faculty.philau.edu/russowl/russow.html) is another excellent collection of links by Professor Lloyd Russow at Philadelphia University in

---

[2] *International Business Information on the Web*, by Sheri Lanza from Cyberage Books, 2001

the U.S. The site has lots of country and regional data as well as links to hundreds of international organizations.

- Statistical Data Locators (`http://ntu.edu.sg/library/stat/statdata.htm`) organized by region, from the Nanyang Technological University Library in Singapore.

Global Search Tools

Most of the general search engines (see Chapter 4 - General Search Tools) have international resources included in their indexes. Google, Altavista and Alltheweb are particularly strong for international links. But a few search tools focus intentionally on scoping out international information. These can make useful starting points for global research.

All Searchengines
www.allsearchengines.com/foreign.html

A good combination of search tools around the world.

Geographic Name Server
http://164.214.2.59/gns/html/index.html

Look up servers across the globe. Scroll to the bottom of the page and hit the "access Geonet" button. Also provides maps for all over the globe.

International Search Engines
www.arnoldit.com/lists/intlsearch.asp

An excellent collection of international search engines from Stephen Arnold, a long-time search trend watcher. Unfortunately there's no description about the sites, but if you need to find resources in places like Myanmar, this is another useful tool.

International Search Engine links
http://www.anancyweb.com/international_search.html

Another good set of international search links

Ithaki
http://www.ithaki.net/indexu.htm

Ithaki is a multi-lingual metasearch engine that searches more than 200 selected tools worldwide. It also allows you to limit your search to specific categories, like image searching or book searching. As a cutting edge tool, it also now offers a WAP search tool for searching through your wireless device at `http://ithaki.net/wap.html`.

One World Nation's Online
http://www.nationsonline.org/oneworld/

Has seemingly objective links to information, news and politics throughout the world, but seems to be more of an activist's site. Still, valuable information is found throughout the site.

Orientation
www.orientation.com

Another globally-oriented site with separated areas for: Asia, Africa, Central & Eastern Europe, Middle East and Oceania. These sites are excellent and they have individual sites for most every country in the world. Very comprehensive, not particularly selective.

Search Engine Colossus
www.searchenginecolossus.com

It contains listing for almost 100 countries, each showing the search tool and what languages it can search in.

Search Engines Worldwide
www.twics.com/~takakuwa/search/search.html

While this tool does not explain the languages it can search in, it contains links to 1500 search tools in almost 180 countries. Unfortunately, while the links are great, some explanation of which ones are most useful for what topics, would be worthwhile. At least it gives you a beginning point. Keep your list of translation tools nearby. You will need them in working with this site.

Virtual International Search
http://www.dreamscape.com/frankvad/search.international.html

Another combination of international search tools. It promises more than it delivers, but it does have some good starting points.

World Skip
www.worldskip.com

This search tool has news, products, travel etc, but what distinguishes it is that is has separate portals for more than 200 countries and resources for each one of them. This site is really strong when you need to drill down to country-specific details.

Voila
www.voila.com

This French site allows you to search in several languages including Denmark, France, Italy, the Netherlands, Portugal, Spain. Its advanced search allows all kinds of tools to focus searches. They proclaim: Le moteur de recherche *pour les geeks,* or the search engine geared for the geeks.

Global Subject Directories

Many of the better subject directories like Yahoo.com, About.com and the Librarians Index to the Internet (www.lii.org) offer excellent international resources. But like the search engines, a few directories focus primarily on international resources. Here are some of the best.

KOMPASS
www.kompass.com

This is a great business tool, a global directory of 1.5 million companies. Some information is free, others require a subscription. Much of this information can be obtained from other online subscription databases. It has a major weakness – it doesn't have information on Japan or most of Latin America.

Fossick
www.fossick.com

Fossick is a central clearinghouse for more than 3,000 subject-specific search engines. What makes it so useful is the "everywhere" section, which connects you to thousands of search tools in countries all over the world.

World Regional Subject Directories

With the Internet covering so many resources around the world, a quickie search on a search engine can overwhelm you. Instead, when searching international sites, the first thing to do is find specific regional resources that can help you. And if you begin in a region you are largely unfamiliar with, then a subject directory will be a much more useful first tool than a search engine. A subject directory will allow you to browse categories and gain a much better overview of what information might be available. And, as was talked about in Chapter 3, when you search, you need to be as precise about what you are looking for as where you look for it.

Here are a few good regional subject directories to get your started.

Asiaco   (Asia)
www.asiaco.com

BUBL LINK   (United Kingdom)
http://bubl.ac.uk/link/

This is truly an outstanding subject directory. It's large and well-organized

European Search Engines
www.netmasters.co.uk/european_search_engines/

LatinWorld.com
www.latinworld.com

Middle East Pages
www.middle-east-pages.com/me.html

Portals to the World -- International Resources of the Library of Congress
www.loc.gov/rr/international

Russian Search Engines
www.zhurnal.ru/search/engines.shtml

Woyaa
www.woyaa.com

World News Tools

Whether you are trying to get up to speed on a region or a specific place, news tools can be vital ingredients in your research. Remember: the quality of information may vary dramatically from what you are used to in the U.S. One remedy is to search at several levels: focus on finding the most recent information, information from geographically local publications, and of course, reporting from internationally respected news organizations. All can be useful, with reliability being one of your concerns.

There are excellent international resources that cover the world – everything from the Reuters and Associated Press wire services to newspapers like the *International Herald Tribune* and the London-based *Financial Times*. The *FT* is particularly useful for information because its entire archive is online and easily searchable for free. Unfortunately, not many local newspapers are available on the Internet as searchable texts. Even the major fee-based services have limited access to newspapers from around the world. The problem seems to be that most local newspapers are simply not online.

Another potential source of information are the annual lists of the biggest and best companies, which are put out annually by journalism companies. Several business publications, including *Forbes Magazine*, *Fortune Magazine,* and *Industry Week Magazine,* publish annual business lists. But the most useful collection of these lists is Gary Price's Excellent List of Lists, found at `http://gwis2.circ.gwu.edu/~gprice/listof.htm`. It is always worth checking.

A few international news resources are listed here. See Chapter 8, News Resources for additional international news resources.

World Online News

International Herald Tribune
`www.iht.com/frontpage.html`

A great resource due to its international focus, the *International Herald Tribune* is printed in Europe as a joint project of the *New York Times* and *Washington Post*. It has some tremendous access to wire services of all kinds.

News Search Tools

ABYZ
`www.abyznewslinks.com`

This is a truly international news search tool — an outstanding collection of news resources. You can search by country, region, or keyword.

Ananova
`www.ananova.com`

This U.K.-focused news search tool is a good one. It is useful for non-U.S. news searching and includes your own personal video feed from Ananova, the video news reader.

Pandia
`www.pandia.com/news/index.html`

If you are looking for international news, this is one of the best news finders. This site also offers a radio-only search tool, which allows you to listen to news and talk stations from all over the world — a great way to spot trends. It's part of an excellent search engine.

Robert Nile.com
`www.robertniles.com/stats/`

Statistics page for those not-prone toward math, from journalist Robert Niles.

International Journalism Collections

AILEENA
www.aileena.ch

An outstanding site from Switzerland with 5,500 links to newspapers, radio, and TV stations in 174 countries. It is a superb place to find local news for almost any country that has news online.

Ultimate Collection of News Links
http://pppp.net/links/news/

This site offers a collection of more than 8,000 links to online newspapers and magazines around the world. The directory is organized geographically.

Worldnews
www.worldnews.com

Worldnews is an easily searchable news resource with links to thousands of resources to hundreds of different countries. This is a superb place to find news from all around the world. It offers you the opportunity to read it in dozens of languages.

Kiosken International Publications Link (Sweden)
www.esperanto.se/kiosk/enplena.html

This is a superb collection of international newspapers sites.

A Plug for the Fee-Based Services

Most of the resources discussed in this chapter are free sites. However, some of the best sites on international resources cost money. Many of these companies are European or Asian-based and being local, they are able to gather and input information that never finds its way to the free Internet. Companies like Bureau Van Dijk, a European-based company at www.bvdep.com, offer extensive business information on that continent for a fee. The Nikkei Net Interactive www.nni.nikkei.co.jp offers extensive Japanese records.

You may also want to check out the three major U.S. commercial services – Factiva (formerly Dow Jones/Reuters), Lexis-Nexis, and Dialog – who have seriously beefed up their international offerings and have begun adding non-English content to their indices.

➜ *hot tip:*   One excellent tip in juggling the expense of pay services (and their easy-to-use structure) versus the free-wheeling Internet is to locate the sources you need on the pay services, then go directly to the source on the Internet to gather your information. While this may be a way to save money and get your material directly from the initial source, be aware that valuable detailed information that is available on the pay services may not be easily obtained for free on the Internet, if at all.

See Chapter 5, Specialized Tools and Chapter 9, Business Resources for other good fee-based services.

More Tricks For Global Research

If one web site is particularly useful, chances are other sites that choose to link to that page will be useful as well. If you cannot find a "related links" section of the web site, you can use AltaVista and a few of the major search engines and run a "link:domainname" search, putting the company name after the "link:" to see which sites are linked to that web site.

It's also a great check to see if the site has credibility within its field. Take www.swazi.com, the internet service provider for most of the country of Swaziland. If you didn't know that it was an excellent resource for information on the country of Swaziland, you could go to AltaVista and put in the search "link:swazi.com" You would see that www.swazi.com has more than 600 links to it, including most of the government sites for Africa, plus credible trade, government, legal, and tourism sites. That gives you some indication that the information contained on the page can be useful, and should be at least somewhat credible. For example, if you "link test" The Dancing Paul Page (www.dancingpaul.com), it has over 800 links, but most of them are to humorous, quirky, or self-proclaimed "useless" pages.

Many companies and organizations link or post reports about themselves written by third parties, i.e., news articles, analyst reports, financial news, etc. While these obviously wouldn't be posted if they didn't show the organization in a positive light, at least some of the information provided is coming from an external source. Additionally, some of these reports will mention competitors, which may lead you to more information about the specific company or industry you are researching.

Another trick that researchers have learned from their own mistakes is not to assume you know the correct term for the word you are looking for. For example, in the English-speaking world, it's called *insurance*, but in Germany it's called *versicherung*. So looking for the word *insurance* on a German site might not get you as many results as using the keyword *verischerung*.

➜ *hot tip:* **If you know you are looking for topic-specific information, you may be better off searching for pages on that specific subject than searching on a country-by-country basis. If, for example, you wanted to know how the ski resorts compare between the Swiss Alps and the peaks of Colorado, a comprehensive skiing web site would more likely provide that comparison than country-focused search tools.**

The Importance of People

There may be times when you simply can't locate the information you want, or you don't know enough about the country to find what you need. Since finding someone who knows the subject matter can be a major benefit to finding information quickly, the top international researchers have figured out the trick to overcoming international online roadblocks – looking for people.

Ask yourself: who would be knowledgeable and interested in the issue you are searching about, what agency or group might monitor that subject? Who might collect information about it? Follow the primary rule journalists researching a new subject ask: "who would know?" Then ask the follow-up – *who else* might have this information?

People tend to be very friendly on the Internet. The language barrier aside, the technique used by online researchers is to find a discussion group or a mailing list with people familiar with the subject, then tap their collective or individual knowledge. Email them. Chat with them.

For research that begins in a foreign country, often in a foreign language, a reference librarian from that country can be a tremendous asset to you, not only because of what kind of online information they could point you toward, but their ability to locate and speak with people in their community.

If you don't know anyone in a region and need to make some contacts to get that cultural understanding, the attaches at your country's embassy will usually be helpful. And, chambers of commerce in your country may be monitoring the country you are targeting, and may be able to point you to contacts there. People from local universities and trade associations are also potential sources of valuable information.

See the Human Element section of Chapter 5 for more about using people as your research tools.

Going Global

By Mary Ellen Bates

The Web has, of course, revolutionized how we find information. But one of the unexpected effects of the Web has been to raise the awareness about the information sources that lie beyond our own borders. Type in the word "astronomy" in a search engine, for example, and you're likely to find web sites from all over the world, and from groups as varied as NASA, Bonn University, the Canada-France-Hawaii Telescope Corporation, and the U.K.'s Particle Physics and Astronomy Research Council. Those are just a few of the English-language sites.

Researchers can no longer think that they have covered all the bases by throwing a few words into a general search engine and using one of the value-added online services. The information world outside the U.S. isn't as tidy – the online databases aren't comprehensive – much government information isn't in electronic format at all. As we become more aware of the need to expand our research beyond our borders, we're also learning that the research techniques that worked for finding U.S. information often don't apply when we're doing global research.

I am the author of *Super Searchers Cover the World: the Online Secrets of International Business Researchers*[3], and I picked up some invaluable tips while interviewing twenty global super searchers. Among the lessons I learned were:

It's not who you know, it's who will talk to you. Use the Web to find people to talk to. In many countries, the information you need is more likely to be in someone's desk drawer than on the open Web. And you have to establish a relationship with that one expert before you can get a hold of the information you're looking for.

Use your peripheral vision. The information may not be where you expect it, but it might turn up somewhere else. A government report might not be on that agency's web site; look for it at association or NGO (non-governmental organizations) web sites.

Embassies are your friends. If you're an American doing research on an industry in Italy, email the U.S. Embassy in Italy and ask for their help. Then contact the Italian Embassy in the U.S. and find out who is assigned to help facilitate trade between the two countries. Embassy support staff are often great resources for hidden information.

Check your spelling. It seems like such a small thing, but you'll miss half of the information out there if you only look for *aluminum* and not *aluminIum,* or *labor* and not *labour.* Also watch for synonyms – America's *retirement* is Australia's *superannuation.*

If you want information from a particular state, country, or region, start with a directory or country-specific search engine. When you eliminate "the rest of the world" you can construct a broader search and still get targeted results.

Make sure your question makes sense in the region you're researching. One of the super searchers I interviewed described looking for information on consumer preferences for washing machines in Latin America. It turns out that most people were happy to have any functioning washing machine, and didn't care whether it was new or used, front-loading or top-loading, with or without an automatic fabric softener dispenser. The bigger problems were finding the money to purchase such a luxury item and having reliable electricity with which to run it!

Don't expect to find information consistency across borders. The European Union has done a good job of collecting standardized data, but don't expect that consistency to show up elsewhere. You might want to see a comparison of tungsten powder use in China, Russia, Bolivia, and South Korea, but you can't be assured that the numbers from each country are accurate, up-to-date, and based on the same underlying assumptions.

Don't expect to find local newspapers online. The major value-added information providers such as Dialog and Lexis-Nexis don't have many non-English language newspapers. The web-based aggregators don't either. And newspaper articles are generally part of the invisible web – inaccessible to search engine spiders, thus not found through a search engine. Instead, use a country-specific directory or portal to identify the local newspaper, then go to that site directly.

---

[3] *Super Searchers Cover the World: the Online Secrets of International Business Researchers*, Information Today, 2001

Replace your "assumptions cache" every six months. Your old favorites of a few months ago may not be the best information sources now, particularly when information services are shutting down, moving from free to fee-based, and getting swallowed up by other vendors. Keep an eye out for new resources. Read the information industry publications to learn about changes in the existing online services. Subscribe to email discussion groups that cover whatever subject area you research the most.

As a start to recalibrating your "assumptions cache," you can check out www.infotoday.com/supersearchers/sscw.htm, which is an annotated list of all the resources mentioned by the super searchers in my book.

-- Mary Ellen Bates is the owner of Bates Information Services, providing business research to business professionals and consulting services to the online industry. She is the author of five books, including *Super Searchers Cover the World*, *Researching Online For Dummies, 2nd Edition*, and *Mining For Gold on the Internet*. Prior to starting her business in 1991, she worked in specialized libraries for a number of years, and has been online since the late 1970s.

Email address: mbates@batesinfo.com — Web address: www.batesinfo.com

Additional Favorite International Resources

Here are two books an international researcher shouldn't be without: Sheri Lanza's *International Business Information on the Web* and Mary Ellen Bates' *Super Searchers Cover the World*, both from Cyberage Books.

Additional Web Sites for International Research

Australian White Pages
www.whitepages.com.au
Australian white pages and phone finder.

British Government Publications BOPCRIS
www.bopcris.ac.uk/
Search British government publications from 1688-1995 from the stands for British Official Publications Collaborative Reader Information Service. You can also browse by subject or date.

Chiefs of State and Cabinet Members of Foreign Governments
www.cia.gov/cia/publications/chiefs
Latest update of this CIA list, dated 1/9/02.

European Union Statistics
http://europa.eu.int/comm/eurostat/
European Union web site with emphasis on statistics.

Great Britain Historic Database Online
http://hds.essex.ac.uk/gbh.asp
British Historical database from the University of Essex.

India Mart
www.indiamart.com
This is most like a yellow-pages phone book for Indian companies, searchable by subject.

International Salary Calculator
www.homefair.com/homefair/calc/salcalc.html
Calculator which helps people determine how much it will cost to relocate to another city.

Robert Niles.com
www.robertniles.com/stats/
Statistics page for those not-prone toward math from journalist Robert Niles.

Chapter 11

Managing & Filtering Information

Keeping-Up Tools

Managing Incoming Information — Managing Email — Managing Web Sites Using Bookmark Folders — Managing Downloads — Managing Your Twinkie Time — Managing Your Offline Life — Unifiers: Helpful Hard-Drive Organizers – Filtering: Controlling the Deluge — Filtering For Kids — Best Filtering Tools — Bots as Personal Search Tools – Best Bots — Push Technology — Push: The Downside — Alert Services – Computer Virus Alerts — Competitive Intelligence Alerts — Table of Contents Alerts — News Alerts — Keeping-Up Tools

Do you feel oppressed by the sheer volume of phone calls from cell phones, voice mail, pagers, incredible amounts of email, postal and interoffice mail, faxes, and meetings upon endless meetings — and all of it passing on "critical information?"

Are you worried that you will miss something if you don't see absolutely everything before making a decision? By getting organized and being selective about what which messages you return, you can stay informed.

To manage information overload effectively, you can use an information triage strategy. Doctors in hospital emergency rooms decide which patient needs immediate attention. They don't fix a broken finger before attending to a heart attack just because the broken finger came in first.

Triage applies to your work – even when lives are not at stake. It involves prioritizing, delegating and just letting things slide. Remember: all information is not created equal. What you want is the most current and critical information – only that information without which nothing else makes sense.

You are not alone if you feel overwhelmed or frustrated at not being able to find what you are looking for. Roper Starch Worldwide, a marketing firm, calls not finding what you want "web rage." A survey by Roper Starch Worldwide found that seventy-one percent of Internet users regularly encountered frustration during searches about twelve minutes after trying to make sense out of inaccurate or irrelevant search site results.

But there are lots of ways to organize your information and reduce information overload.

Managing Incoming Information

Managing Email

Email is great – until you're suffocating under the weight of too much of it! Here are some ways to take control.

Be Selective	Read the subject heading first and make your decision whether to open it or kill it based on that. Deleting unopened email is the only way to stay atop the mounting heap. It's ruthless but effective.
Note the Sender	Learn the difference between the person who sends you laughs and the person who controls your paycheck. Guess whose email belongs on top of your priority list?
Delegate	Delegate or forward email messages that shouldn't be yours in the first place – especially if you share email duties with others.
Filter	Some people can ignore their emails. If you can't, then eliminate the volume by filtering them as they come in. Either route them to folders of your choosing – eliminating unnecessary ones in the process – or use an email program that automatically routes your mail into folders. Pegasus Mail (a shareware program), Eudora Pro and Outlook all do this. Nearly all email programs allow you to sort mail by dates, by sender and, in some cases, by subject. Filtering will help eliminate spam (unsolicited email). Filtering tools vary, but most allow you to select words and throw out messages that contain them. Or, you can choose words and prioritize messages that contain them. For example, filter emails containing the phrases "make money" and "$$$" and the program will send them to your delete file without you having to read them. Filtering software, such as Forté's Free Agent is effective. (For more filtering programs, see the Filtering section of the Web Site Profiles index.)

➜*hot tip:*   **On your browser, locate the "Find" command when you are viewing your email messages. All email programs include a "Find" command that will locate messages containing specified words. Use it to save time.**

Managing Web Sites Using Bookmark Folders

Netscape calls them Bookmarks; Internet Explorer calls them Favorites. They're the web addresses that you want to save. Most people gather too many shortcuts and then can't find them when they're needed. Use the "Find" command in either of the major browsers to sort through your saved links. Better yet, both versions let you organize your bookmarks into folders and then let you create new names for the links – names that are easier to remember.

Managing Downloads

Some freeware/shareware programs help your browser schedule large file downloads while you're away. Programs such as Download Manager and Download Butler for PCs and the Midnight Download for Macs – can all be found at CNET's Download.com. They'll also automatically send you updates for the software.

Managing Your "Twinkie Time"

It is said that most Usenet content is as informative as Twinkies are nutritious. If you are going to subscribe to newsgroups, mailing lists and discussion groups, route them into folders where you can read them at your convenience. Learn to filter messages before you download them. When you do read them, apply the browsing tips described in the email section above. Usenet filtering software, like Forté's Free Agent can also help you manage the avalanche.

Managing Your Offline Life

What's the point of having an organized online life if you're just going to dump it into the dumpster of your real life? Here are some options for helping you manage your offline time.

Handheld or palm computers, also known as personal information managers (PIMs) or personal digital assistants (PDAs), help you get organized. They function as calendars/schedulers, address books, phone books, to-do lists, project or task managers and note takers. Most of them transfer data seamlessly to and from your laptop and/or desktop computer.

Many companies use the Internet to post employee schedules. Meetings can be coordinated electronically, insuring that everyone who needs to know is notified.

Software programs like Microsoft Outlook and Eudora Pro can be programmed to send you email reminders. Most palmtops have a reminder alarm function.

There are also hundreds of companies, news sites, and other web sites that will remind you or alert you to things you need to know by email. See the Alert Services section later in this chapter.

Helpful Hard-Drive Organizers

Can't keep up with the voice mail, email, pager and fax machines? Overwhelmed? What if they all came into a single mailbox? Several companies have new products coming out that will give you all of those in one unified manner.

Enfish Professional for the Desktop

This hard-drive organizing program coordinates everything on your hard drive by consolidating, collating and, most important, relating information from your email, web searches, your PIM or PDA. It works like a desktop interface. This US$229.95 program is like an automated assistant that can organize and file everything on your computer so you can find it when you need to.

Unified Messenger

Unified Messenger comes from Octel, a division of Lucent Technologies. It sells for about $200.00 per person, provides a single window into your email and voice messages on your PC screen. This can be a real asset while you are on the road, since you don't need a laptop to check it. You can call the messaging system from a phone and a computer-generated voice reads messages to you. Faxes are also being linked to this process. It has a downside: this technology is based on Microsoft's Exchange software, so you will need to run that program in order to use the Unified Messenger. Centigram and other companies are developing similar technologies.

CatchTheWeb
www.catchtheweb.com

CatchTheWeb.com offers a unique organizing tool. It offers a corporate organizing tool for passing information throughout an organization and for individuals to clip and maintain files through a computerized push-pin system. They offer a free trial and its worth a look.

Sageware
www.sageware.com

Sageware offers a product called Content Tagger, which uses predefined categories with the product, and allows customers to quickly tagging items without having to train the system to learn specific subjects. It is then able to compare web sites, news stories, and other resources — and help you follow specific subjects.

Time Matters
www.timematters.com

Time Matters is a hard-drive organizing tool geared to lawyers allowing them to track cases and all the paperwork tied to lawsuits. But the software can be moderated to work in all kinds of office environments as a tool to track deadlines and paperwork. It is expensive but very versatile.

Filtering: Controlling the Deluge

Filtering is the process of culling, sorting and routing information into useful categories. Structuring your filtering correctly will save time and keep you on top of things. Filtering is a personalizing tool.

Currently, most general filtering tools and services claim to give you news you can use when you need it. To a large extent, these products promise more than they deliver. Often, you'll receive mail you thought your filter would catch. Many times the filtering function is just too general to make the connection between what you need and what they deliver. At least not yet.

~~~~~~

➔ *hot tip:* Test filtering programs thoroughly. Most offer free trial periods. Remember, no one service is likely to meet every user's needs.

~~~~~~

Filtering for Kids

Companies have developed filtering software to enable parents to set content and access preferences for children. Most filters today act simply as content filters. Through coding and dozens of other ways, these filters prohibit access to web pages containing specified words or pictures.

As software companies begin to add privacy preferences to their content filters, upcoming software should enable consumers to access only Internet sites that match their privacy preferences.

Content-screening software uses either a filtering or rating method. The filtering method allows access to the Internet, but blocks the sites (or materials) that the software maker defines as objectionable. Typically, the software recognizes a database of banned sites and search words. This design is not foolproof. It does not prevent a user from clicking on a link to a site that is not in the database, and it cannot stop a clever search that avoids the search words listed in the database.

The rating method uses programs that identify a site's HTML code and permit access only to web sites with allowable ratings. Parents can, for example, restrict their children's access to sites that are rated as having no sexual material, foul language, or violence. The two currently operational rating systems are Recreational Software Advisory Council on the Internet (RSAC - now part of ICRA) at www.icra.org/about and SafeSurf at www.safesurf.com

Phrases with dual meanings or contexts can also cause unintentional blocking. For example, filtering out the word "breast" removes not only pornographic sites, but also breast cancer sites.

The following are among the best filtering tools for children, but remember they do not catch everything:

Cyber Patrol	www.cyberpatrol.com
Cyber Sentinel	www.securitysoft.com
Cyber Snoop	www.pearlsw.com
CYBERsitter	www.cybersitter.com
Arlington Browser	www.arlington.com.au
N2H2	www.n2h2.com
Net Nanny	www.netnanny.com

| SurfWatch | www.surfwatch.com |
| XStop | www.xstop.com |

Best Filtering Tools

Copernic

www.copernic.com

This is an interesting online search tool. You need to download free software from the web site to use it. It searches as many as eighty search tools and saves the results so that when you open the program, you have a list of previous searches. But you must view the banner ads. Copernic does your search, compiles the results, removes duplicates and then ranks them by relevancy. You can share the search results by sending them through email. Copernic offers two fee-based versions, which searches using a much larger search base. Some searchers swear by this tool as offering them an indispensable edge. It is very fast and results appear almost instantly, but it can be confusing in the information it returns.

Infominder

www.infominder.com/webminder/index.jsp

A newer service that enables users to track web sites and get notification when content changes.

Intellisync

www.pumatech.com

Intellisync from Pumatech offers several alert service that inform you every time there is a change to a web page. It is great if you routinely monitor web sites – such as your competitors' sites. You can also use it to monitor web coverage by submitting the proper names of people, companies, and so forth.

The company also offers other higher-end resources that monitors designated web pages, intranets or extra-nets, and emails, and synchronizes your electronic devices. The alerts monitor based on keywords, images and/or numbers.

Tracerlock

www.tracerlock.com

Tracerlock offers free monitoring of search engines, stock market information, newsgroups, 'for sale' ads, auction and employment sites and personal ads, emailing you when it has found new matches for your search terms. You need to download software and register. It also offers a fee-based version that will monitors hundreds of news sites - and emails you an alert that matches your search terms. It costs US$19.50 per month for any five search terms.

Newsalert.com
www.newsalert.com

An excellent alerting tool, geared toward business, Newsalert follows changes in the stock market, featuring quotes, research and market analysis for publicly-traded companies you select, all delivered as free email.

Webspector
www.illumix.com

This internet research and navigation tool automatically tracks an unlimited number of web pages for content changes. Everyone from business executives needing up-to-the-minute monitoring of their competitors' web sites to avid Internet users who want to be alerted when their favorite pages are updated. Costs US$79.00.

See Chapter 8, News Resources for additional news monitoring resources.

Bots as Personal Search Tools

Chapter 4 discussed search tools and the concept of robots or spiders worming their way through the Internet to permit keyword searching of indexed documents. There are personal spiders — also called "bots" (short for "robots") — that hunt through search tools and all kinds of web sites to retrieve information.

Bots are theoretically capable of three functions:

- Searching
- Monitoring
- Evaluating

Overnight while you sleep you can have a bot research certain criteria and keywords you have outlined, say, for acapella music, then wake up to a collection of sites and sounds that the bot has stored on your hard drive. Bots are particularly good at locating sound and picture files — a weakness of most search tools. Until recently, bots have been better at retrieving specific material than presenting overviews. Their ability to evaluate has been rudimentary.

But, that is changing rapidly. Now there are specialized bots that can be programmed to shop online for you, answer questions and retrieve music you may like based on your previous selections. Chat bots are adding dramatically to web site interactivity. Some bots host web site tours. Within the next few years, bots will become your servants on the Internet — carrying out orders that you've programmed from your computer, even when you're not actually online.

For considerably more information, go to **BotSpot** at www.botspot.com

Best Bots

Alexa
www.alexa.com

Alexa's free software lets you track web traffic patterns by telling you the next destination of people who have visited the site you're currently visiting. Alexa has partnered with Google on a search engine and is involved in an internet archive known as the Wayback Machine.

BotSpot
http://botspot.com

BotSpot is a clearinghouse for all kinds of bot research. Stop in and try one.

Agent Land
www.agentland.com/

Like Botspot, the Agent Land site monitors and highlights the best in intelligent agent technology – the tools that help you monitor changing technologies and other bots. A great resource.

Databots with Imagination
www.imagination-engines.com

These bots use their own independent judgments in finding and understanding complex databases. Using artificial intelligence capabilities, Databots are being used by a Swiss banking company to do stock market analysis and make prediction models from market data.

Infogist
www.infogist.com

A timesaving researching tool that uses intelligent agent software technology, this fee-based tool offers a free trial.

Intelliseek's Bullseye
www.intelliseek.com

Intelliseek's Bullseye combines many customized intelligent agents to tap 300+ search engines and 600+ plus databases on the Internet, simultaneously, to find, analyze, filter, report, manage and track information. Definitely one to watch when you are trying to weed through oceans of information. Intelliseek offers a thirty-day free trial.

Also:

For a terrific collection of resources for Intelligent Agents, see the Virtual FreeSites Search Agents collection at www.virtualfreesites.com/search.agents.html

Push Technology

In the past, search tools have been user-motivated, enabling a one-way communication to the Internet. Now, in addition to user-motivated information retrieval, sender-motivated material is sent to us via "push technology."

Push technology is a method of Internet data distribution in which information is "pushed" onto your computer screen, much like pre-selected television programs are broadcast onto your television set.

Email and instant messages are early forms of push technology. You can elect to block certain email addresses, or allow instant messages only from pre-selected names and/or addresses.

Information is being gathered *about* you at the same time other information is being *delivered to you*.

Push technology is only now coming of age, and the level and volume of interaction is increasing exponentially.

- Amazon.com and Barnes & Noble both use push technology quite successfully. They realized that ordinary book sales techniques wouldn't sustain their businesses. They needed to provide additional services. So, the Barnes & Noble web site at www.barnesandnoble.com lets you rank books you like. The site then identifies other users with similar tastes, then suggests their choices to you. You can also chat and exchange messages with readers with similar interests. Over time, the technology starts to recommend books based on your past preferences. It also takes into account your stated preferences. Amazon.com's site is similar.

- The Cinemax site at www.cinemax.com uses push technology to identify people with tastes similar to your own and shows their recommendations.

- Another company, iVillage at www.ivillage.com recommends chat groups for consumers based on their personal profiles and online footprints.

- Other companies can screen internet content and push it to various groups of employees, sending industry news to one segment and company announcements to another.

- Fidelity Management, a Boston-based mutual funds company, uses push technology to send volatile information, such as fund performance sales activities, to senior executives.

- Conference Plus of Illinois, which schedules and manages conference calls, pushes real-time customer statistics so managers know how long customers are waiting on the phone, and deploy backup operators so customers don't hang up.

Future intelligent marketing tools will ferret out new customers by tracking what groups of people are interested in and by aggregating the specific web sites people need quickly.

Push: The Downside

The downside of the new intelligent push agents is that they still rely on some form of interrupt to get the user's attention.

Interrupts in current push technologies include email messages, system beeps, alerts, animated icons, scrolling tickers, and screen savers. Interrupts can be turned off, but then push becomes much like email.

Though interrupts can take a user's focus away from the task at hand, the real problem is that they're too frequent and generally unscheduled. Scheduled interrupts a couple of times a day, plus emergency information, makes sense, but this level of control isn't always available.

Alert Services

Alert services (or alerting tools) are offered by hundreds of companies and they've already become significant features of companies selling books, airline tickets and other forms of e-commerce. If you want you can get email alerts on all kinds of subjects, from news to stocks to wakeup emails that make sounds.

While these notifications can be very helpful, they can also overwhelm your email box. So the most important tip is to keep the instructions on how to stop the alerts from coming once you have subscribed.

Remind Me, for example, notifies you a week or day before an event, or sends an alert for a specific time of a specific day, at your request. Need a nudge to make you remember it's time to take the cats to the vet for shots?

Ready for an off-beat but sure-to-save-frustration reminder service? Try Tow Zone from Phil Greenspun who also offers Remind Me. Tow Zone warns drivers when a city is cleaning its streets. Both sites are found at `http://photo.net/philg/services.html`. Here are a few more examples of interest:

- If you want to be alerted of bargain airfares, then visit `www.biztravel.com` or `www.travelocity.com` or `www.onetravel.com` or `www.etn.nl/hotfares.htm` or check the major airlines which offer discounted fares by email.

- Be the first to find and buy the latest new book from your favorite author using Amazon's alert service (`www.amazon.com`), or when your favorite music group is coming to town (`www.pollstar.com`).

- Business people use alert services to be notified when new documents on companies of interest are filed with the Securities and Exchange Commission (`www.freeedgar.com`). Alerts are also available from `www.edgar-online.com`, `www.10kwizard.com` and `www.hoovers.com`.

Here are more examples, by topic matter:

Computer Virus Alerts

Carnegie Mellon University's Cert Coordination Center
www.cert.org/nav/alerts.html

Need to know if there is a computer virus alert? The authority on that subject are the folks at Carnegie Mellon University's Cert Coordination Center and they will notify you by email

Competitive Intelligence Alerts
www.spyonit.com/Home

If you pay attention to competitors or monitor specific sites for changes, this site will really help you, by notifying you when something changes. It will send you an email, an instant message or a text message to your mobile phone or PDA.

Newsalert
www.newsalert.com

Lets you monitor when a company or industry is mentioned on the Web by news sites, or when a particular stock goes over or below a certain price.

Company Sleuth
www.companysleuth.com

This is an excellent site for monitoring public companies and will send you email alerts when those companies change their web sites.

Earthquake Alerts

National Earthquake Information Center
http://gldss7.cr.usgs.gov/neis/data_services/data_services.html

Want to know when a big earthquake hits anywhere in the United States? Chances are you won't need an email alert if it hits your neighborhood, but the Center's service will notify you if a quake measures 5.5. or larger anywhere in the U.S.

Government Alerts

More than twenty U.S. federal government agencies will notify you when policy changes or news happens. There are way too many to list, so go to the agency you care about and search for "alert."

Table of Contents Alerts

Infotrieve TOC Service

You must set up an account before you can start to use the TOC alert service. It alerts you to what is in the Table of Contents from hundreds of scholarly publishers. Registration is required.

```
www4.infotrieve.com
www4.infotrieve.com/users/createaccount.asp
```

News Alerts

Many of the major journalism organizations, including ABCNews.com, CNN.com, Washingtonpost.com, NYTimes.com, YahooNews.com and MSNBC.com, CBSMarket-watch.com all offer alerts several times a day with breaking news headlines. Some of them, like *The New York Times*, can be localized to subjects you care about. The British news resource Ananova at `www.orange-today.co.uk/promo/?id=Orange personal news` will let you choose topics and it will send you alerts on a variety of different news-related subjects. In addition to Yahoo!'s news alert, there is…

Yahoo!'s Business Headlines Page
`http://dailynews.yahoo.com/headlines/bs/`

This site takes you to the latest business news, and you can link to headlines from the past two weeks at the bottom of the page. Yahoo! Finance at `http://quote.yahoo.com/?u` links to stock market results.

World News Connection Alert
`http://wnc.fedworld.gov`

This subscriber-based alert comes from the U.S. government's world news connection and can be tailored by country or region of the world.

Other Alert Tools

Many of the news tools discussed in the News Chapter also offer email alerts. These include Moreover, NewsNow, Infobeat, Northern Light, and Daypop.

Need the latest news from Congress? *Congressional Quarterly* offers the latest news alerts from Capitol Hill at `www.cq.com/home/home.jsp`.

You can also find news alerts outside the U.S., including Channel News Asia, which provides news for Singapore, Malaysia and other Asian countries, `http://cna.mediacorpnews.com/enews/v3/index.htm`. For Pakistan, check out `http://paknews.com/alert.php`. A collection of dozens of Australian alert e-newsletters `https://f2members.f2.com.au/f2Reg/f2members/newsletter.jsp?topcat=4&newsid=44&urlto=www.SMH.com.au`

You can also get news alerts from the fee-based databases tailored to your own customized list of subjects.

Dialog News Alerts
`www.dialog.com`

Full-text articles delivered by email after you subscribe and establish keyword searches.

Factiva
www.factiva.com

Personalized email alerts with full-text or summaries of stories; they get saved into customized folders, with a maximum of 500 articles.

Lexis-Nexis
www.nexis.com

www.lexis.com

This is an incredibly deep resource with customized pages. Subscription required.

1stHeadlines
www.1stheadlines.com/business1.htm

This site posts links to free business news sources.

Yahoo! News
http://headlines.yahoo.com/Full_Coverage/Business

Another site that posts links to free current business news sources, including several major news wires, organized by subject, with a search feature at the top or bottom of the page.

Northern Light News Search
www.northernlight.com/news.html

Alternatively, you can limit a Northern Light News search to retrieve only business sources.

Also:

Quickbrowse.com and E-Library, two other fee-based news tools, offer news alerts.

Keeping-Up Tools

So how do you keep up with the latest resources on the Internet and find those incredibly useful hot new sites?

There are a series of truly outstanding keeping-up tools that will help. These are some of my favorites sites that I look at virtually every day and absolutely wouldn't want to live without.

The Virtual Acquisition Shelf and News Desk
http://resourceshelf.freepint.com

Gary Price's incredibly useful weblog, which lists a daily collection of resources he finds. Think of yourself as on the receiving end of an information hurricane. The gems he finds are often worth their weight in gold. Also remember to look at where Price finds these useful sites and studies for more places to find great resources.

The Virtual Chase
www.virtualchase.com

The Virtual Chase is an incredibly useful site from law librarian Genie Tyburski and is hosted by the law firm of Ballard, Spahr, Andrews and Ingersoll. Like Gary Price, anything Genie touches is must-read material for researchers. Absolutely worth reading, even if you never have any concern about legal issues.

Research Buzz
www.researchbuzz.com

Tara Calishain publishes a weekly research news weblog that is loaded with great resources about searching on the Web. She is an incredible researcher who has written several books including co-authoring *The Official Netscape Guide to Internet Research*, 2nd Edition. Like Price and Tyburski, this is a must read for anyone who wants to stay on top of the latest research tools for searching the web.

LLRX.com - Law Library Research Xchange
www.llrx.com

LLRX and its weekly alert, LLRX Buzz, are two incredibly useful research tools online. LLRX is a law librarian's gold mine. It is a collection of legal-related internet resources, but also looks at all kinds of other research and reference tools and has an outstanding archive of research material.

LLRX Buzz is Tara Calishain's regular column of legal research tips and sites to watch. It can be found at www.llrx.com/buzz/buzz101.htm

Neat New Stuff I Found on the Net This Week
http://marylaine.com/neatnew.html

Marylaine Block's wonderful collection of the latest new sites for research on the Web. She always seems to come up with something you need that you never knew about. Another must read from the former librarian at St. Ambrose University, who developed "Best Information on the Net," a great ready reference library.

InfoToday's News Breaks
www.infotoday.com/newsbreaks/breaks.htm

Info Today, which publishes many of the leading magazines and books about searching and research, brings you a weekly news research newsletter. Very useful.

Additional Keeping-Up Resources

All of these are free.

Search Day - Search Engine Watch
www.searchenginewatch.com/searchday/
www.searchenginewatch.com

Danny Sullivan and Chris Sherman pull together an incredible web site loaded with the latest information on searching and the technology behind search tools. Sherman's daily column is referred to above. Sullivan's site is a fee-based one, but if you are serious about understanding the nuances of search engines, it is required reading.

Free Pint
www.freepint.com

William Hann's collection of resources. It is particularly valuable for finding out what is happening with European resources.

Internet Resources Newsletter
www.hw.ac.uk/libwww/irn/irn.html

This monthly newsletter from the librarians at the British Heriot-Watt University is useful for always coming up with some excellent new worldwide resources.

Library News Daily
www.lights.com/scott/

This site from Canada's Northern Lights Internet Solutions, is also always on the cutting edge of new and useful web sites.

LII New This Week
www.lii.org/search/ntw

The wonderful Librarian's Index to the Internet puts together a great collection of the latest finds online, and sends out a weekly update of the latest sites. A great resource.

Scout Report & Scout Report Archive
www.scout.cs.wisc.edu

The Scout Report is one of the Internet's longest-running weekly publications, offering a selection of new and newly discovered online resources of interest to researchers and educators. It is available on a web site as a weekly alert. The archive is keyword searchable back seven years. It is available at www.scout.cs.wisc.edu/archives

USAToday's Hot Sites
www.usatoday.com/life/cyber/ch.htm

Sam Meddis' daily collection of hot sites is interesting, often useful, always entertaining and sometimes hysterically funny. Not an essential, but always entertaining.

About.com Web Search
www.websearch.about.com

About.com's collection of Web search resources is a good one, often with innovative and useful search techniques and research sites worth looking at. It is one of About.com's hundreds of guides, but they do a particularly good job at staying up on the latest of search tools.

Here are journalism sites worth looking at occasionally to find useful news-related and research-related sites:

Power Reporting
www.powerreporting.com

Bill Dedman, an editor at the *Chicago Sun Times* offers an excellent power reporting site.

A Journalist's Guide to the Internet
www.reporter.umd.edu

University of Maryland's Chris Callahan's web site for his book *A Journalists Guide to the Internet*[1] is also very useful.

JournalismNet
www.journalismnet.com

Canadian Journalist Julian Sher's superb JournalismNet site is an outstanding collection.

Mike Reilley's Journalismtoolbox.com
www.journalismtoolbox.com

This site, previously discussed in the news chapter, is always worth a look to see what new news tools Mike Reilley has uncovered.

Jenny's Cybrary
www.jennyscybrary.com/current.html

This is a terrific collection of useful links to places where you will find additional keeping-up tools.

---

[1] *A Journalists Guide to the Internet,* published by Allyn & Bacon, 1998. New edition scheduled for Spring, 2003.

Chapter 12

Evaluating Accuracy, Credibility, and Authority

Making Sure What You See Is What You Want

Credibility — Authority — How to Use ICANN to Trace Web Authority — Researching Domains — Finding Experts Online — Timeliness — Coverage and Objectivity — Evaluating Web Site Information — The Quick Link Credibility Test — Useful Evaluative Tools — Web Site Checklist — Still Not Sure? Take the Virtual Chase Test — Additional Sites for Evaluating Accuracy, Credibility and Authority

The reality of the Internet is that anyone can be a publisher. Web page content can — and often does — move straight from one person's fingertips into cyberspace. As more people discover that there is some bogus information on the Internet, they begin to question all online content. This poses a problem for professionals who object to their life's work being lumped together with what's been called "gossip roadkill on the information superhighway." Is it credible? Is it authoritative or second-hand or third-rate? How can you tell? There are some fundamental questions you can ask that will lead you to credible information.

- Who wrote the material? Is the author identified — or anonymous?

- What authority and credentials do they have?

- What are their biases?

- Has anyone checked the work?

- Has anyone else reviewed the page you are seeing?

- Is the data from a traditionally reliable source?

It's helpful to think of the Internet as the messenger, not the message. As Barbara Quint, editor of *Searcher Magazine* says, "...don't put in your head what you wouldn't put in your mouth. Ask: Where does this come from and why is this here?" She suggests, "Saying 'I got it from the

Internet,' is like saying 'I got it from the phone.' The quality of the information depends on who is on the line."

After something has been put online, *see if there has there been a reaction to it.* Can you find that reaction? In traditional newspapers, they print corrections if there were factual errors, but few newspapers even have correction policies when it comes to putting material on a web site.

When evaluating how accurate and reliable a web page is, there are several aspects to consider — credibility, authority and timeliness as well as coverage and objectivity.

➜ *hot tip:* **Consider the source. Professionals make mistakes, but behind them stands a professional organization, with editors, fact-checkers, and others who find and correct errors. At universities, original research is peer-reviewed before it's published, and often there is an internal review process as well. At many companies, many people's eyes see a statement before it is posted.**

Credibility

Good data can be verified. Suspect data can't.

There are no sure-fire indicators of reliability, but the nature of the information sources can provide a good initial hint. If the data comes from a traditionally reliable outlet, such as a well-known publisher or research center, chances are better that the report is credible than if that same data is cited in a web site of unknown origin. Here are some questions to consider:

- What can you tell from the web site about its accuracy and credibility? Are there footnotes, cited references or just bold unattributed or unverifiable statements?

- Are there spelling errors and grammatical mistakes? An absence of proofreading can be a tip-off. At the very least, it indicates inattention to detail that might carry over to the information itself.

- Why is this information being provided? Is the reason clear? Is the reason likely to be correct? If not, the web site author's motivation bears further checking.

➜ *hot tip:* **Verify web site authorship before using information from that site. A web site's main page — also called its home page — should identify its author/compiler. You can find a main page quickly by deleting parts of the URL, starting from the right and working your way toward the left. A tilde sign (~) embedded in an address usually signifies a personal home page. Try to verify the information elsewhere before assuming it's authoritative.**

To determine the credibility of something published, try *Ulrich's International Periodical Directory* available by subscription on the Web at `www.ulrichsweb.com/ulrichsweb`. *Gale's Directories*, similar to Ulrich's, are also online (`www.gale.com`) or through Dialog. Both are gated web sites that charge for service. You can always call a nearby library and check the print versions of these books.

Authority

Know where a web site's content originates. It can be difficult to identify the author of a web page and the author's qualifications. If there is no contact person, no credit taken for the web site, don't trust it. If someone won't stand behind their work or at least provide their name, be wary.

Is the information itself *authoritative*? Trust is critical.

For example, if you found these on the Internet, which would you trust more: a statement from John Smith, an employee of Cedar Hospital, *or* a statement from Cedar Hospital itself? Most people would agree that Cedar Hospital is far more trustworthy than John Smith, provided, of course, that the statement was in fact issued by the hospital.

If a company or organization is willing to put its reputation on the line, online, it should give the site's statements more credibility.

Another trick is to *go with a known brand*. If you regularly read *The New York Times* and count on its high standards of accuracy and credibility, its web site will likely hold to the same standard.

Use trustworthy organizations as guides to credible web sites. For example, government agencies, trade groups and professional associations and major universities all have web sites with credible links and references. So do reference tools like the Encyclopedia of Associations available on services such as Silver Platter (`www.silverplatter.com`) and the American Society of Association Executives (`www.asaenet.org`). Once you've identified the name of an authoritative source, use search tools to find their actual web sites.

Double-checking domain names via web and internet sources is also a valuable verification tool. If a document is supposed to be from a university but the domain name doesn't end in .edu, it might be legitimate.

Commercial online sources routinely compile source data and publications. Some fee-based companies compile several pieces of information – like phone numbers from phone companies, change of address forms and voter registration databases — into a single report. They may not identify the source of each item, but they will always tell you their sources, for instance, "state DMV records" as their source of driving records. But there are some databases that don't tell you directly where they get their information.

How much of an "authority" do you need? First figure out what you are going to use the information for. If you are taking something to court, you need a higher level of credibility than if you are just settling a bet. If it reads `www.whitehouse.net` and claims to be the official White House government site, be wary, because the official site's address should end in .gov.

> **→hot tip:** Check the URL! Usually, companies serious about establishing their presence on the Internet will buy a domain name that includes their company name in the address or a URL that includes a word that relates to their products or services. For example, `www.XYZ.com` if the company's name is XYZ, or `www.translation.com` if XYZ specializes in foreign language translations.

Genie Tyburski, a law librarian and the organizer of the superb Virtual Chase web site, `www.virtualchase.com`, suggests that before you rely on information, you need to run through a checklist of items to help you determine credibility.

She suggests you need to determine the web site's *origin*. Discover the author AND the publisher, ascertain the author's and publisher's credentials, discover the date of the writing. This gives the information historical context. You should also verify the document using another reputable source that provides similar information.

How to Use ICANN to Trace Web Authorship

Every time someone gets a web page, to secure their domain name or the first part of an Internet address, they must pay a fee to one of several federal government contractors who register all sites. Verisign (the contracted company who registers .com addresses), hosts a Whois page — a searchable list of anyone that has registered a domain name. While not foolproof, it often provides the real address, phone number, email information and contact person for each web site. Submit a domain name in the search blank then see what information comes up. Answers come directly from registrants so it may be outdated or incorrect.

Another place you can check the domain registration to figure out web site ownership is with Whonami, at `www.whonami.com`, an easy-to-use search interface, which also uses the Whois domain's registrar. Whonami also translates the registration pages into non-English languages.

Normally, there are two ways to find out who is responsible for such a web page:

1. Contact the Source

Often there is an email address, and you can write the person and ask for their credentials and information sources. Good content providers give you enough information to judge their authority.

2. Contact the Domain Registry

Check the domain registry to see who is paying for a site to be on the Internet. To do that, you go to Verisign at `www.netsol.com/cgi-bin/whois/whois` who regulates the registration of domain names. In 2000, a non-profit corporation known as ICANN took over responsibility for managing domain names. Its address is `www.icann.net`. Also, another way to get at the same information is through Inet's whois page at `www.allwhois.com` and Whonami.com, as discussed earlier.

For a comprehensive list of domain registries worldwide, check out these two sites:

`www.norid.no/domreg.html`

`www.iana.org/cctld/cctld-whois.htm`

An older but excellent example of when to use this domain lookup tool was the Heaven's Gate mass suicide in 1997. Margot Williams, a researcher at *The Washington Post*, and author of the excellent *Great Scouts* book, quickly went to the domain registration company then called InterNIC (now ICANN) to find out who had registered the cult's Higher Source web site. Further checking revealed that the names probably were faked and the telephone numbers rang to pay phones. If you looked now, you may find an entry created after the event that lists David Koresh, Jim Jones, and Jack Kevorkian as contacts. Google's caching capability now saves that page if you wanted to find it even though its no longer on the Web. Another search site for locating the Heaven's Gate web site would be the Wayback Machine, `www.archive.org/index.html`, which indexes pages no longer on the Web. The web archive is a project from Brewster Kahle, an early web pioneer and the man behind Alexa.com.

Also on the Network Solutions web site is the ability to search across multiple web sites to locate web pages associated with organizations from a database of almost two million entries. Enter the word "university" and the clue "California" and you will get a list of university sites in that state, along with clickable links.

You can also find a DNS Lookup on its site. This is how you translate a URL into its actual Internet protocol address which is a series of numbers. For example, the IP address of Ns.yourhost.com, a part of the Internet Planners web hosting site, is "216.147.43.224."

If your provider's DNS server isn't working, or if the URL isn't in there yet, you'll see an error message like "failed DNS lookup." If you type in the IP address instead, you will get into the site – unless some other problem caused the error.

You can use the DNS lookup to find a URL's valid IP address and do the reverse to find the web address from a mysterious series of numbers.

Researching Domains

Not long ago, a wonderfully off-beat creative site showed up on the Internet. `www.fractalcow.com/Bert`. The site is now down but it has been mirrored, and you can connect to the mirrored versions from the original address.

Called Bert Is Evil, it was a wickedly funny parody of Bert, the puppet character from *Sesame Street*. Its considerations of why Bert went bad included:

- Email relationship with mass murderer Jeffrey Dahmer.

- Participation in a lost Pamela Anderson video excerpt.

- Involvement in the JFK assassination.

- An appearance on *The Jerry Springer Show*.

- Secret connections to O. J. Simpson and terrorist Osama Bin Laden.

The site included photos of Bert in many compromising situations. The page contained no mention whatsoever of who put it up or why.

To find its creator, we looked up the URL: `fractalcow.com`. It belonged to a Dino Ignacio who has an address, phone number and email address in the Philippines. A graphic designer, he had built the web page for fun — and to promote his struggling graphics-design firm.

This kind of domain research can prove to be incredibly valuable as a backgrounding tool. Most people tend to provide real and accurate contact information because they want to make sure to get the bill in order to retain control of the domain name. However, there is no legal requirement to be accurate, so don't assume it is accurate. Also be aware that changing the registration information on the Network Solutions form is so complicated that many people will simply give up rather than go through the ordeal of retaining a domain name unless their company's business is at stake. Many other companies now also provide domain name registration.

Finding Experts Online

By Kitty Bennett

In my work as a news researcher for a daily newspaper, I'm requested to help unearth reputable, quotable experts for reporters in a very short amount of time. But journalists aren't the only ones with a need for experts — attorneys, writers, conference planners, medical researchers, engineers, and business people are also constantly on the prowl.

None of us has time to waste on "authorities" with questionable credentials, so what follows are some suggestions for finding experts and verifying their qualifications. While the ideal scenario would be to have Internet capability in addition to access to commercial online sources of information such as Lexis-Nexis and print resources such as *Who's Who*, in reality, the Internet may be the only tool available. Fortunately, much can be accomplished with a browser and a willingness to approach information sources with a fresh and innovative eye.

Here are some suggestions for getting started:

Check Directories of Experts Published Online by Universities, Think Tanks, and Government Agencies

These are typically found in a section of an organization's web site that is produced by the public affairs office. Authorities are usually searchable by their subject expertise, and listings may include photos, email addresses and home phone numbers. One of the best examples of this kind of directory is produced by the Wharton School of the University of Pennsylvania Faculty Director — `www.wharton.upenn.edu/actions/search.html`. For other such sites, see my "Sources and Experts" page at: `www.ibiblio.org/slanews/internet/experts.html`.

Think Creatively: Repositories of Experts Come in Many Different Forms

When you're looking for experts, Amazon.com isn't just a place to buy books. It's a database of more than a million experts, otherwise known as authors. Using Amazon's very sophisticated "Power Search" option, accessed by clicking "Book Search" on the opening screen, I recently found a forensic psychologist and author of a book called *Kids Who Kill* for a reporter who needed an expert to interview about a rash of school shootings. *The New York Times Book Review* (`www.nytimes.com/books`) is not only a great place to check an author's credibility, but also a good place to search for experts. A periodicals directory such as Mediafinder (`www.mediafinder.com`), can also serve as a database of nearly 100,000 magazine editors, who are often authorities in their fields.

Search in Newsgroup and Mailing List Postings — But Be Cautious

Newsgroups and mailing lists are usually unmoderated, and searching through them can swallow huge chunks of your valuable time. It's tedious to wade through irrelevant and trivial postings, and gauging credentials can be a dicey process.

Google (`www.groups.google.com`) is by far the best place to search for newsgroup postings. Learn how to search its database by printing out its "Group Google Help" page at `www.google.com/googlegroups/help.html` and placing it at your side so you can construct more advanced queries.

A good strategy is to search in particular hierarchies, or types, of newsgroups (see "A Newsgroup Primer" in Specialized Tools, Chapter 5). For example, if looking for experts on turtles, you might try searching like this: "`expert ^10 turtles and ~g sci*`" which means you're looking for the word "expert" within ten words of "turtle," and you only want to search in the "sci" hierarchy. The "~g" is Google News shorthand for "newsgroup."

The caret (^) means "near." In this case, I used the number "10" because I wanted the two search words to be within ten words of each other. If I hadn't specified the number "10," the query would have defaulted to "5" – meaning that Google would search and deliver newsgroup postings in which the two keywords were within five words of each other.

There are far fewer options for searching mailing lists. Topica (`www.topica.com`) is currently the best alternative, but even it has only a fraction of the estimated total number of mailing list postings. Unless it's vital that you keep your search project a secret, you can also poll newsgroup and mailing list members for their recommendations on experts.

Use Search Engines that Help You Focus on Particular Topics

Always use more than one search engine because each contains a unique database of records. AltaVista (`www.altavista.com`) supports proximity searching, truncation and all sorts of sophisticated options that make it ideal for finding experts. You can do seemingly complicated but effective searches, like this: "`(expert or author* or research* or professor) near astron* and (url:mit or url:princeton or url:stanford)`."

This search statement means you're looking for any one of several words that are synonyms for expert, like "author" or "authority" or "researcher," "near" (within ten words of) variations of the word "astron," like "astronomy" or "astronomical." The term "`url:mit`" means you're looking for a URL address containing the acronym "MIT." I typed "`mit`" in lower case, following AltaVista's directions to use lower case when submitting search terms.

If you did this search, you would find, among others, the faculty members of the Department of Astrophysical Sciences at Princeton University and of the Stanford Solar Center. From there you would be able to read descriptions their research.

While it's an excellent search engine, Google can't handle complete truncation in its basic search, which means you'd have to type in all the possible variations of words you're looking for. Still, you can't ignore Google because its database is huge. Some search engines that might help you focus on particular topics include Beaucoup! (`www.beaucoup.com`), Search.com (`www.search.com`) and About.com (`www.about.com`). This site, formerly the Mining Company, offers 500 interest areas about everything from the aviation industry to 'zines, all moderated by guides who are themselves experts. Check also Google Answers and Yahoo! Experts for experts.

Check Your Expert's Credentials and Credibility

If you found him or her at a reputable institution, you're on pretty firm ground. Somebody else checked them out before the organization hired them. See if your expert has been quoted in respectable publications, but don't use that as the sole criterion. Many publications have free searchable online archives that can be accessed via their web sites or through a compilation web site (see the Meta-Tools section of Chapter 4 and News Resources Chapter 8). For example, the News Division of the Special Libraries Association maintains a good publications guide at `www.ibiblio.org/slanews`. You can also run your expert's name through a couple of search engines. Northern Light (`www.nlresearch.com`), for example, offers a "special collection" of thousands of journals, books, and magazines. All abstracts in this collection are free and may give you a good sense of your expert's renown or lack thereof. Don't forget to check your expert in Google or use Teoma's expert links page when you run a search.

Be Aware that Some Directories of "Experts" Are Run by Businesses Who Charge a Fee for a Listing

These companies may do little or nothing to verify credentials. For example, recently I checked out the qualifications of an "expert" on aging issues listed on a site that specializes in providing guests for talk shows. The price for a listing here starts at US$199. This alleged expert claimed many qualifications, few of which could be verified. Among other things, he claimed to be a "senior associate" of a particular think tank.

It was a simple matter to go to the organization's web site and determine that the sole criterion for becoming a senior associate there was an annual donation of between US$250 and US$5,000. According to the person's biographical information, he held a Ph.D. in Psychology, so I looked for his dissertation in Dissertation Abstracts Online, which is available through Dialog and many other services. I found none. However, when I checked with the university listed on his resume, the school did confirm that he had indeed been awarded a Ph.D.

CompuServe's Knowledge Index (which no longer exists per se, but the databases are available through Dialog) used to be a great place to background someone who claims academic credentials. In this particular case, I checked for mentions of his name in Knowledge Index's Life Sciences Collection, Current Biotechnology Abstracts, ERIC, Academic Index, Medline (from 1966-present), PsycINFO, Mental Health Abstracts, Sociological Abstracts and Ageline. These are indices to mostly scholarly journals, dating back to the late 1960s. Using Knowledge Index, which cost US$21. an hour, I was able to search these databases in about five minutes, so the total search amounted to less than US$2. Although this expert had claimed to have "authored a number of scientific papers" in his web site biography, I found nothing that he had written and no references to him in anyone else's work.

By then, I had serious questions about this man's lack of substantial credentials. Still, since he made mention of a book he had written, I wanted to verify that it appeared in Books in Print (BIP), which is accessible through many online venues as well as through your local library. He was indeed the author of the book, but I discovered that he also owned the publishing company that had published it.

-- Kitty Bennett is a news researcher for *The St. Petersburg Times*.
Her email address is `Bennett@sptimes.com`

Timeliness

How can you tell when a web page was last updated? The date can be anywhere on the page.

If there is none, Netscape's browser's "View" menu will let you look at the document's page info. Look for a date in the "Last Modified" field. About half of the time, it will read "unknown," and in some cases, the "Last Modified" date will be more current than the date listed on the web page, because the author failed to update the date reference on the page itself. But when it works, it is a good way to check timeliness. Nothing similar is offered on Microsoft's Internet Explorer browser.

AltaVista's Range of Dates feature can check dates without your having to visit the actual site. The Range of Dates features is available on AltaVista's Advanced Search page. Google also allows you to date search from its advanced menu, but it is somewhat limited by how recently they located the page, not when it was written.

Network Solutions' Whois will tell you when the page was posted and/or last updated.

The web archives of most reputable periodicals will carefully note the coverage dates of the articles within the archives. This goes for both free and commercial database holdings.

Coverage and Objectivity

Veteran journalist David Brinkley once said that objectivity is not the determining criteria for journalism, fairness is. Being as fair as you can should hold for web pages as well.

If you see an article titled "Should you buy or lease your car?" find out who is writing the piece, and think about what they have to gain by convincing you. If it is written by an auto-leasing firm, you should be skeptical, but if it is written by the non-profit consumer organization Consumer Reports, which doesn't accept corporate advertising, it would have a little more legitimacy. It's always a judgment call.

In the wild, wild west of the Internet, the masking of biased information as objective data is a more common phenomenon than you might think.

Eyeball the entire web site to assess the breadth and depth of its coverage. Look for what it's not telling you, especially when it takes a position or editorializes. For example, some political advocacy pages neglect to mention their organizational sponsor(s).

Ask Yourself Why the Information is Being Published

Watch for these telltale clues, which should raise doubts as to a site's objectivity:

- sweeping statements like "most important, unquestionably the best."
- over-claims like "millions are being killed every minute."
- harsh language like "the shrill cries of my extremist opponents."

Over time you'll develop an instinct for statements that make you question the credibility of the entire site. Investigator Don Ray calls them JDLRs — *just doesn't look right*.

Because web sites change without warning, if you think you'll need proof that information existed on a certain date, download, print or save a copy of the source so that a record is preserved of your visit and your findings.

A few years ago, Stephen Miller of *The New York Times* developed a ranking scale for journalists to use when assessing the credibility of a web site. He suggests that, in general, government sources should be trusted more than other sources, with federal government resources being rated a little higher than state and local governments.

Next on his trust meter are university studies, because nearly all of them are peer-reviewed and many have footnotes attached detailing bibliographic information. Special interest groups appear next on Miller's list. He notes that they publish lots of data, and even if they have a political agenda, it doesn't mean that their data is flawed.

Finally, Miller suggests that all others, including personal home pages, are a toss-up in terms of validity. The saving grace of personal home pages is that there is usually some information about the owner and a way of contacting them, which allows for further research.

Regardless, you can always report something you've found on the Web, and accompany it with a citation as to where you found the information.

Evaluating Web Site Information

Here are several good sites for helping you better evaluate web site information:

Evaluating Quality on the Net
www.hopetillman.com/findqual.html

Babson College Library Director Hope Tillman has posted her thoughts on information assessment. This site offers a good overview of what critical evaluation skills should be.

Virtual Chase Accuracy Page
www.virtualchase.com/howto/assess_quality.html

Law Librarian Genie Tyburski's excellent site has a terrific page on how to assess the quality of information you find. It also has a superb checklist that will help you determine accuracy at:

www.virtualchase.com/quality/checklist.html

If you don't think credibility is a problem, see the incredible list of dozens of example links on page seven of the checklist at:

www.virtualchase.com/quality/checklist7.html

Evaluating Web Resources
www2.widener.edu/Wolfgram-Memorial-Library/webevaluation/webeval.htm

This is a practical tutorial from reference librarians at Widener University that indexes lists of questions and criteria to apply when evaluating sites.

Evaluating Information Found on the 'Net
`www.library.jhu.edu/elp/useit/evaluate/`

A good resource from the Johns Hopkins University Eisenhower Library.

Bibliography on Evaluating Internet Resources
`www.lib.vt.edu/research/libinst/evalbiblio.html`

A list of Internet and print resources, with links to example sites and newsgroups.

10 C's For Evaluating Internet Sources
`www.uwec.edu/library/Guides/tencs.html`

Criteria to consider when evaluating Internet resources.

Google Web Directory of Web Site Evaluation tools
`http://directory.google.com/Top/Reference/Education/Instructional_Technology/Evaluation/Web_Site_Evaluation/`

A great collection of tutorials on how to evaluate web sites credibility.

Getting It Right: Verifying Sources on the Net
`www.llrx.com/features/verifying.htm`

A terrific article by LLRX founder and editor Sabrina Pacifici, providing all kinds of tips on verifying information.

The Quick Link Credibility Test

You can judge a site by the company it keeps. Several search engines, including AltaVista and AllTheWeb offer a "Link" feature that allows you to do a quick and fairly reliable credibility test. In Business Tools, Chapter 9, Jennifer Kaplan describes a way to use the "Link" feature for free competitive intelligence research. The same principle applies to credibility research as well. Here are several examples:

> **Example 1:** Visit CataLaw (`www.catalaw.com`), self-described as the "Internet's Grand Central Legal Station" and "the catalog of catalogs of worldwide law on the 'Net." Go to AltaVista at `www.altavista.com` and type the following: `link:catalaw.com`. A list will appear of more than two-hundred sites that link to CataLaw. That means that 200+ other sites think CataLaw is credible enough to link to their web sites. Browse the sites. Notice that most are law schools, universities, libraries and other institutions — a good indication of credibility.

Let's try it again:

> **Example 2:** Say you're researching extra-terrestrial visits to earth, and you find the site `www.saucers.com`. On AltaVista, type the following: `link:saucers.com`.

A list of links appears, including a web site called the "Fringe Page." Jump to that web site and you'll notice references to a Dr. Saucer, who is "not, technically speaking, a real medical doctor, psychologist or even a dentist. In fact, he lacks a college degree of any kind but he does have enormous insight into the study of saucers. " The site says that "Dr. Saucer is an experienced potter and designer of fine porcelain vases, pots, plates and, yes, saucers." The lesson? Be aware that the credibility of the site is questionable. Satire pages and parodies abound on the Web.

Useful Evaluative Tools

Here are a few tools, listed alphabetically, that will help you *assess credibility*.

About.com
www.about.com

This site has more than 500 different subject areas, each maintained by a human. Essays are posted on key subjects. This site also features bulletin boards, chat groups on many subjects, and you can even subscribe to newsletters. While the quality level of the subjects varies, when it is good, it is very good. About.com is a solid starting point.

Argus Clearinghouse
www.clearinghouse.net

This site, affiliated with the University of Michigan, rates sites on a scale of 1 to 5. An email address is furnished for the evaluator. If contacted, the page's reviewer will usually respond.

HotBot
www.hotbot.com

Direct Hit is a software company that ranks sites based on how often they are visited. HotBot has a "Ten Most Requested List" (generated by Direct Hit), which is helpful when trying to find similar sites.

Yahoo!
www.yahoo.com

Yahoo! has a whole series of evaluation tools on its web site. Yahoo! is able to find large numbers of sites, but its recommendations are weak. Yahooligans! for Children (www.yahooligans.com), which is a subject directory that has been screened for children, does a good job.

→ *hot tip:* **Be wary of fake web sites, or sites that appear to be legitimate. They may be a parody, or worse, a deliberate attempt to mislead you away from the information and message of the true site.**

Web Site Checklist

In assessing credibility and evaluating accuracy, Virtual Chase's Tyburski uses a checklist of items to make sure things check out. Her recommendations are the best suggestions you will find and points to keep in mind in assessing any web site.

✓ Determine Objectivity

Lack of objectivity does not necessarily mean a source provides substandard information. To the contrary, a web page may use unimpeachable data to influence readers. Review all quality evaluation criteria — objectivity, timeliness, accuracy, and authority — when judging information. Beware of partiality; identify intent.

✓ Read Site Documentation

This advice especially applies to web sites offering primary documents, copyrighted works, works in the public domain, databases, or commentary.

✓ Ascertain Author or Publisher Credentials

Know the identity and expertise of the individuals or businesses behind a site. Discover whether the sources is a credible publisher and examine the author's credentials.

✓ Identify Citation Data

Locate the author, title, and publisher of the document or information. Ascertain creation and revision dates, record the date on which you visited a web page. Use the web citation machine, which will help determine if a web site provides enough data about itself for citation purposes.

Web Citation Machine
http://landmarks4schools.org/citation_machine/cm_web.php3

✓ Verify All Information

This suggestion pertains to all sources, whether well-known and reputable, or not. Confirm the documents or information's completeness and accuracy. Find two or more credible sources that say the same thing.

Learn from news stories about fraudulent, rogue, or questionable web sites. Tyburski's Virtual Chase web site lists more than fifty examples of examples where people were bamboozled by fake web sites.

Still Not Sure? Take the Virtual Chase Test

www.virtualchase.com/govdoc/verify.html

Other Sites for Evaluating Accuracy, Credibility, and Authority

Amnesi - The IDomain Name Search Engine

`www.amnesi.com`

Lets you search for internet server names (DNS names). You can type your best guess. The engine will try to match names to its extensive database and will give you a list of similar names.

CMP Media, Inc

`www.cmp.com`

Extensive computer resources and articles including evaluation sites, advice and how-to's.

Finding Information on the Internet: A Tutorial

`www.lib.berkeley.edu/TeachingLib/Guides /Internet/FindInfo.html`

Superb introduction to and tutorial on searching on the Web.

ICYouSee

`www.ithaca.edu/library/Training/ICYouSe e.html`

Another excellent accuracy tutorial on using the Web.

IDG.net

`www.idg.net`

Computer resources, valuable information, and articles including evaluation sites, advice, and how-to's.

Verisign

`www.netsol.com`

Regulates the registration of domain names. Includes WHOIS database.

Sam Spade.org

`www.samspade.org`

This site is terrific for helping you trace back the route of a web site or determine where something came from or its credibility.

Scout Report

`www.scout.cs.wisc.edu/report/sr/current /index.html`

Weekly roundup of new findings on the Web, geared to researchers and education. A must.

Top 100 Computer Magazines

`www.internetvalley.com/top100mag.html`

Links to online magazines about the Web and computers.

U.S. News Archives on the Web

`www.ibiblio.org/slanews/internet/expert s.html`

Univ. of NC's listings of newspapers offering access to archives.

Wharton Faculty Research Index

`www.wharton.upenn.edu/actions/search.ht ml`

Example of a searchable academic site.

White House.net

`www.whitehouse.net`

White House satire page.

Wired News

`www.wired.com`

Extensive computer resources and articles including evaluation sites, advice and how-to's.

ZDNet

`www.zdnet.com`

Extensive computer resources and articles including evaluation sites, advice and how-to's.

Chapter 13

Search Strategies

And Sample Searches

Sample Search 1: People Finder — Before Going Online: Q & A — People Finder Search Plan — Sample Search 2: Business Profile — Business Finder Search Plan — Sample 3: Problem Solving — Did You Find Enough "Right Information?" — More Search Strategies from Search Gurus — Super Searching Tips — "...Our Lives, Our Fortunes, and Our Sacred Honor" Protecting Yourself Online — Quick, Effective and Free Research Using AltaVista

It's time to see if you are ready for some creative searching. Here's where you can see how you would solve a few search dilemmas.

A lot of times, when you look for information, you don't know for certain whether it exists. In many cases you have only a minimal knowledge of the subject you need to research, so the terminology you use when searching may not match the jargon of experts on the subject.

If you've read the book most of the way through, you are now armed with knowledge about all the tools you can use to search with, a framework for how to research, and thousands of valuable research sites. Now it's time to put all the components together. But, realize you can conduct these searches many different ways. The key is getting the quality answer you are looking for.

These three sample searches are all types of searches you may need or want to do on your own. They are:

- Backgrounding a person

- Finding information about a business

- Learning about a medical condition.

While you may never have to conduct these particular searches, the tools and techniques used along the way will help you if you want to research people, a business, or health-related issues, and it will help you become more familiar with tools themselves and the techniques that work best for you.

Put yourself into "researcher mode," plan a strategy and then discover what you would do in each of these cases. Remember, there are no right or wrong answers, and most importantly, you should enjoy the process.

Sample Search 1: People Finder

The Assignment

For your people-finder search, you are a researcher who gets a call from some baseball fans who intend on hosting a reunion for the 1959 Los Angeles Dodgers team. Your clients have already located team members and the coaching staff, but they are missing the batboy from that year. You are asked to help find him.

So What Do You Do?

The solution involves two tasks. First, you must figure out his name, then you must locate him.

Given this situation, going online immediately would not be the best way to begin. If you do, it would be a swing, miss and strike one.

It would be a long shot to find anything online from that distant year. You could check for some kind of Los Angeles Dodgers history page, which might give you some leads to follow, but finding any "good" leads is a "long ball play" at best.

Rather, start by calling the Dodgers organization. Ask its employees if they would be willing to tell you his name by viewing the 1959 team photo. Remember, you don't always find everything online, and sometimes it's still easier to call someone or pick up a book.

After a little while, they tell you his name is Arnold Tesh, and that his nickname was "Red." Red could be his hair color, which might help if you find a driver's license or a picture provided that his hair hasn't turned gray. Later you may find out about a rumor that says he was called "Red" because he was a Communist. "Red" would certainly be consistent with sentiments of that era.

Can I Go Online Now?

Your instinct might be to go to a search engine and input "Dodgers." However, the result would be a wide range of links to pages that probably aren't specific enough to satisfy your search needs.

Getting hits on a search engine for "Arnold Tesh" would be relatively easy. However, finding connections between the names found and the 1959 Dodgers – which would be a grand slam – may be a daunting task.

A search on AltaVista for "batboy, Dodgers" returns 144 hits, including a link to a fascinating web page about an article in *The Brooklyn Eagle* newspaper. The Dodgers moved from Brooklyn, New York in 1958. The article, located at www.bayou.com/~brooklyn/batboy.html, relates the illustrious batboy career of Charlie Digiovanna, who was affectionately known as "the Brow" and was the batboy for the 1955 Dodgers season. At the very least, you've found someone worth trying to locate who might have information about other batboys. Put that on your "follow up later" list.

Next, on the Teoma search engine, you search for "batboy, Dodgers" and get 1,070 results. The first few are about the Dodgers. But, sometimes you don't always get close to what you want: several references are found about a Japanese man who calls himself the "batboy." Another is "Batboy sightings" at `http://bennyhills.fortunecity.com/elfman/660/ander son_batboy.htm`. Another site says "Batboy News Articles. BATBOY CAPTURED!/BAT BOY THREAT IS REAL – IF HE RUNS OUT OF BUGS, HUMANS WILL BE NEXT!" You'll find *The Weekly World News* headline with photo of the "Batboy wanted by the FBI" at `http://kulpatron.com/bboy.htm` or *The Weekly World News* tabloid site that chronicles the life of "The Batboy" at `www.weeklyworldnews.com/batboy/index.cfm`. These are not quite the baseball references you're looking for, but they're highly entertaining.

Another idea might be to check online phone books for all the Arnold Teshes in America. Such a search might result in a great deal of people across the country and you wouldn't know which one is the right one.

Essentially, although the above mentioned results might be helpful, they are the result of unfocused research. Before you search online, get "focused" by assessing what you know and what you need to know. This is the key to your ultimate success.

That leads to the next search question: What other clues do you have to eliminate people, like middle name, or age, or something unique?

Before Going Online – Q & A

The first thing you need is a clear question to help you figure out precisely what you are looking for. Then you need to determine if what you are looking for can be found online.

Before you spend hours searching for any tenuous connection between the Dodgers and batboys, you should ask yourself the questions suggested in Chapter 3, Framing Your Search Strategy.

What follows some of these questions and possible answers as they relate to this sample search:

Who?

Who is the research about?

Our subject is Arnold Tesh, a Dodger batboy in 1959.

Who is key to the topic you are researching? Are there any recognized experts or spokespersons you should know about?

Experts and other people who might know of Tesh include baseball aficionados, memorabilia collectors and former sports reporters. It is also worth determining if there is a batboy association of some sort.

Books about "the end" of the Dodgers in Brooklyn or the Dodgers' move to Los Angeles might also be worthwhile sources.

Who has the data I need? Does the database I'm considering include information from the time period I want?

There probably isn't a database of batboy statistics. Imagine it – statistics like "best handshake at home plate" or "fastest bat retrieval."

However, news databases may contain a mention. Likewise public records databases are likely sources of information about Arnold, the man, rather than Arnold, the batboy.

What?

What are you trying to do?

You are trying to find someone specific – Arnold Tesh.

What type of information will be useful: full-text articles or reports, specific facts, referrals to a person, public records?

Any of the above will suffice, provided that the materials can lead to Arnold Tesh. Essentially, you need as many good background leads as you can find.

What would be the best source of the information?

- Tesh's home page noting that he was once a batboy for the Dodgers.
- An article on "Where They Are Now," with leads.
- A batboy association.
- An article with a bio.
- California driver's license records 1959 to 1965 or so.
- Players from the 1959 Dodgers, or Dodgers' employment records for that year.
- A definitive history of the Dodgers with current contact names and addresses.

What information do you already have? What do you already know about the topic or person?

You know his name. Also, you can assume that Tesh was a teenager in 1959, and that if he's alive, he would be between fifty-five and sixty years-old.

Age is especially important because it is one of the few unique identifying features you have to distinguish him from anyone else named Arnold Tesh, aside from "Red," and you still aren't sure what that means.

Later, you should check the Social Security Death Index at www.ancestry.com to make sure Tesh is still alive.

What would the ideal answer look like?

Ideally, you would find "The Arnold Tesh Home Page," complete with a bio, photo, current address and phone number as well as a photo of him with the Dodgers.

When?

When did the event being researched take place?

1959 is the last date associated with Tesh by your clients. Nothing was online in 1959 and, as such, very little may be online for that year now. With that in mind, the use of information-rich archives from fee-based services may be necessary.

When will you know you should stop searching?

When you find him, and you can be sure you have the right guy.

Where?

Where is the biggest collection of the type of information you're looking for likely to be?

It's not exactly clear. A baseball historical group would be good. Someone at the Baseball Hall of Fame might have a Dodgers program from that year. However, a paper program would probably only reveal his name – a piece of information you already have courtesy of the phone call to the Dodgers.

Where did the person you're backgrounding come from?

Your clients informed you that Tesh lived in California back in 1959. Although it's unlikely, he could have moved to California along with the Brooklyn Dodgers when they relocated in the late 1950s. For all you know, he could be from New York originally.

Later, when you've narrowed down the list of Arnold Teshes, you could check past addresses using a fee-based tool. Using that information, you could try talking with neighbors. But remember, this is forty-year-old information; this could be a time-consuming task.

If time is not a critical factor, you could search Usenet newsgroups for baseball card collectors, Dodger fan discussion groups, etc. By doing so, you might find someone who knows something. From there, you could send out some emails and see what happens.

Where might there have been previous coverage: newspapers, broadcasts, trade publications, court proceedings, discussions?

A good library might have old *Los Angeles Times* newspapers on microfilm, but you have to consider the effort involved when going in-person and viewing reel after reel of microfilm. Maybe the Dodgers organization has more information; they got you his name pretty easily — maybe they have a photo?

➔*hot tip:*   Look where the light is best. If you lose your car keys in the parking lot, and there is a light source nearby, you first check under the light source before you start groping around on the ground in the dark. Same with searching – look first at sources that may have the most illuminating information.

How?

How much information do you need?

You just need the answer or information that will lead you to the target.

Information enough that lets you talk to Arnold Tesh.

How far back do you need to research?

Anything from 1959 to the present may be useful.

People Finder Search Plan

Okay, you get the idea about the importance of properly "framing" your query.

You have thought through what you want and how you might get it. You have considered many options, including whether to contact all the Arnold Teshes in America, go to the Dodgers' home page, contact baseball memorabilia collectors. You realize that the best way to go - after a quick few checks just to see what's there for free on the Internet - is to find all the Arnold Teshes and see if you can find someone who might fit the right age range. Lucky for us, his name isn't as common as John Smith.

Realize that you are not limited to searching online. Contacting baseball experts and lifelong Dodger fans might be the most productive option. However, among your online resources are Public Record Providers.

In this case, there are several public record providers that would be useful. Merlin, a west-coast-based search company, is regionally focused and terrific for California. KnowX is a national public records vendor, and Lexis-Nexis has some public records, but more importantly, they have extensive news clippings files. You will definitely want to spend some time rummaging through news clips to distinguish one Arnold Tesh from another.

The other key factor is time versus money. First, let's see what you can do for free or inexpensively.

You need to consider the Andy Warhol principle as it applies to searching. Warhol once said that everyone will be world-famous for fifteen minutes. In other words, you need to figure out if the person you are looking for is a celebrity of some sort.

As a batboy, Tesh was on "the edge of celebrity" in the sense that he was surrounded by those who had achieved fame. In fact, his glory might not have been as a batboy. He could been famous for his other accomplishments. Essentially, it's worth checking him out on the Web using a few search engines.

One option is to submit his name in double quotes (" ") to a search engine and see if you obtain any hits. Another initial search to do is to see if there is a picture of the 1959 Dodgers team online.

> **hot tip:** When searching, keep a notepad next to your computer. Make a running list of the URLs you've visited, and what links you should check out later. Check your browser History folder for recently visited URLs. Sometimes, at the end of a search, researchers realize that they were only a few keystrokes away from the information they needed. Keeping track of things to follow up on can prevent that crucial lead from getting lost.

So, you can begin by using a great search engine, Google

A search for "Arnold Tesh" with his name in quotes gets seventeen hits.

One of the first hits is www.cre.org/states/t_last.htm which lists an Arnold Tesh as the new head of the Counselors of Real Estate. It also mentions that he is a partner in Tesh & Daly Advisors, LLC, based in Washington, D.C. and lists his phone number. It says that the company specializes in counseling for litigation, investments in commercial-industrial portfolios, health care facilities, railroad and public utility acquisitions. It says he also does litigation consulting/strategy and works as an expert witness.

Darn! Nothing about squeeze plays.

MEMBER SEARCH

SEARCH BY AREA

SEARCH BY NAME

SEARCH NEW
MEMBERS

RETURN TO INDEX

MEMBER SEARCH

Alphabetical Index of CRE Members T

Send email to change your information: cre@interaccess.com

TESH, ARNOLD, Tesh & Daly Advisors, LLC, Washington, DC

Telephone: (202) 785-0635

Specializes in counseling for litigation, investments in commercial-industrial portfolios, health care facilities, railroad and public utility acquisitions, studies for resort and mixed-use projects. Assignments are both international and domestic.

Litigation Consulting/Strategy, Eminent Domain, Expert Witness

Resorts, Railroads

TESSLER, MARTIN, Chase Manhattan Bank, New York, NY

If this is our Arnold Tesh, three possible leads are gained from this information.

- His company is a limited liability corporation, which means there are papers filed that might provide more detail on the company.

- As a counselor for litigation, chances are he is a lawyer.

- As an expert witness, his conference presentations may be posted online.

Another of the top hits is at www.flrrt.com/results/law9810.txt which contains the results of the Lawyers Have Heart running race. It says that Arnold Tesh of Washington, D.C. finished 122nd overall. The site also says that he was second in the 55-59 age group, and he is 56.

```
121    2  MARY CATH MALIN    39 F ARLINGTON     VA   43:26   7:00
122    2  ARNOLD TESH        56 M WASHINGTON     DC   43:30   7:01
123    4  LY PHAM            33 F ALEXANDRIA     VA   43:32   7:01
124    3  JEFFREY ZAHLER     14 M BETHESDA       MD   43:33   7:01
125   17  BENJAMIN LIEBER    29 M WASHINGTON     DC   43:33   7:01
126    5  AMY JONES          31 F HEATHSVILLE    VA   43:35   7:02
127   40  TOM GILES          33 M CHEVY CHASE    MD   43:45   7:03
128   41  NICK PURINTON      34 M WASHINGTON     DC   43:45   7:03
129   16  WILLIAM KISSINGER  37 M WASHINGTON     DC   43:50   7:04
130   42  ROGER SHERMAN      32 M WASHINGTON     DC   43:50   7:04
131   17  FRED WHITE         38 M WALDORF        MD   43:52   7:05
```

This is an important finding because this Arnold Tesh fits the predicted age range. This could be your guy.

Also, having once been a batboy, the Arnold Tesh for which you are searching was, at least for a part of his life, interested in sports. The fact that this site mentions an athletic achievement could be a good sign. Maybe it is wishful thinking, but this Arnold Tesh's involvement in sports is certainly more encouraging than if the site mentioned that he was a chess champion.

Another hit, located on the same site as the previous one, is yet another road race. The site places him 759th at 1:11:53 for ten miles, which is really very good for someone his age. It also says he is from Vienna, Virginia, a bedroom community of Washington. The fact that these two hits mention that this Tesh is from Washington, D.C. suggests that the Arnold Tesh in all three of these hits is indeed the same person. We also find a few more running race results with an Arnold Tesh. Whether this Arnold Tesh is the one for which you are searching still remains to be seen.

Another hit you might find is `www.indigomagick.com` a web site for a company owned by Suzanne Snell Tesh, a writer who lives in Bethesda, Maryland, and Bradley Tesh. On the web site is a genealogy page that includes the following entry:

Bryon Arnold TESH	**Rebecca MATLOCK**
b. 17 Oct 1951 d. bur. occ. edu. rel. res. .	b. 2 Feb 1952 d. bur. occ. edu. rel. res. .

All of the remaining hits pertain to running. The Arnold Tesh of Washington, D.C. is definitely a serious runner.

Going for the "long ball," you decide to try another search engine. You choose AltaVista.

At this point you have two options. We can look for an image, using AltaVista's excellent "Image" search capability (`http://image.altavista.com/cgi-bin/avncgi`). If you go that way, make sure to check photos, color and black and white images, and realize that if you search for Dodgers, you will get hundreds of photos. If you search for batboy, you may get nothing you can use. Try "1959 LA Dodgers" but don't expect it to be fruitful. Try the same thing on HotBot, which is also great for finding photos. Make sure to check the "Image" box on the search engine.

The second option is to look for stories and references to the LA Dodgers from that year. Just on an instinct — and to avoid getting many references to the current LA Dodgers team — try looking for the LA Dodgers home page and/or sites that focus on the Brooklyn Dodgers, where you might find loyal followers and, possibly, references to batboys.

You discover an excellent memorabilia site at `www.brooklyn-dodgers.com.`. On that site there are some wonderful items, including a video of the 1959 season when the Dodgers won the World Series (`www.dodgers.com/1950.html`). However, you are unable to find a team photo. After looking at the Dodgers.com site, and knowing that you really need to link Tesh to the Dodgers, one option would be to write to the Dodger's webmaster and see if somewhere in the files there is a photo of the team. Dodgers webmaster Ben Platt sends you the following photo, but of course you won't get it until tomorrow – too late for your search.

Since, at the moment, you are unable to easily find the photo online, the next thing to try would be news clips. While at the Dodgers' site, you may have noticed a place to look up old newspaper clips, plus there's an option to subscribe to a regular newsletter. A subscription might result in the names of people who might have the information you need.

AltaVista's remaining hits for "Dodgers" are fruitless. Therefore, you decide to search for "Arnold Tesh."

You discover three more hits pertaining to the Arnold Tesh of Washington, D.C. Most noticeably, there is a reference to an Arnold Tesh in *The Pacific Business News* online service at `www.amcity.com/pacific/stories/081897/calendar.html` that says that Tesh was the keynote speaker at a conference of the National Association of Industrial and Office Properties, Hawaii Chapter's breakfast meeting. According to the site, Tesh was speaking about real estate investment trusts. This seems to be another link to Arnold Tesh of Washington, D.C.

At this point, you could use fee-based services to determine how many Arnold Teshes exist, but you decide to try additional search engines since they are free.

This time you choose HotBot. You submit Arnold Tesh without using quotation marks because HotBot does that automatically.

The first HotBot hit is for a JM Zell Partners site at `www.jmzell.com/apprais.htm`. A news subpage announces that they have built an alliance with the D.C.-based Arnold S. Tesh Advisors.

Once again the site seems to refer to the Arnold Tesh of Washington, D.C. However, this particular site gives you a very valuable tidbit – his middle initial. It also may have a bio on him or include links to several of Tesh's potential clients.

The links page for this site — `www.jmzell.com/links.htm` — also has several industry sources for the real estate world, including:

`www.inman.com`

`www.amrex.com`

and, *International Real Estate Digest :*
`www.ired.com`

These links are sources of information on people who work in real estate. They might be worth checking to find more information about the Arnold S. Tesh of Washington, D.C. It may be worth checking the Securities and Exchange Commission to do a search on owners' and officers' names, after you check to see if he is an attorney.

In addition, the Zell site has an extensive client list and names four key players in the company. These people may have information about Tesh, but if Arnold S. Tesh never mentioned or never had a past in baseball, contacting these people might be a waste of time even if you have the right person. The client list consists of hundreds of big-name companies, and it is still unclear what this particular Arnold Tesh does for them. Investigating this information could take hours, so, for now, it must be put on a back burner.

A hit from HotBot is `www.mrhat.simplenet.com/celeb101.htm` and it is certainly one of the most intriguing. It lists the "101 People we'd like to see on South Park by everyone who submitted to our survey." South Park is a racy, no-holds-barred, satirical television show on cable's Comedy Central. The names on the list include: Wayne Gretsky, Dilbert, Bill Murray, Sean Connery, William Shatner, Dan Akroyd, Tim Allen, and Gumby.

So why is Arnold Tesh on this list? It is not likely that the authors of this web site are roasting everyone and have worked their way to the batboys of forty years ago.

The site probably has the names John Tesh and Arnold Schwarzenegger together or "in proximity," leading the search engine to find Tesh and Arnold next to or near each other, which results in this HotBot hit.

After a brush with South Park, you decide to try a meta-search tool. You choose Profusion at `www.profusion.com` and get lots of hits concerning John Tesh, Arnold Schwarzenegger, and Saint Arnold Brewing but nothing new on the Arnold Tesh.

Now you decide to check him out using two lawyer look-up tools on the Web. Both of these tools offer biographies of every lawyer who practices. You go to the Martindale-Hubbell Lawyer Locator site at `www.martindale.com/xp/Martindale/home.xml` which may let you search, or you try the other lawyer site, Find Law's Legal Directory from Westlaw, located at `http://directory.findlaw.com`. To your surprise, you don't find anything. You thought that if the D.C. Arnold Tesh is advising lawyers on litigation strategy then he too might be a lawyer. Guess not.

He is either not a lawyer, or does not practice law.

Just to be thorough, you check `www.ancestry.com` to make sure Arnold S. Tesh is still alive. No matches. That means he is most likely still living.

Now you try the phone books. You do a quick search on InfoSpace.com and find three Arnold Teshes. One is in North Carolina. The other two are Arnold S. Tesh. One is in Santa Monica, California and the other in Vienna, Virginia. The latter is clearly the real estate/runner guy.

InfoSpace.com gives you phone numbers, addresses, maps, directions and can even send your "hits" a gift, if you want to. You're really curious who the California guy is because you haven't stumbled across him before, and the North Carolina person intrigues you.

So you check a couple of more phone books. You use Who Where (www.whowhere.lycos.com) and AnyWho (www.anywho.com), but come up with much of the same information.

Finally, you try yet one more phone book, just to see what you can find. You find seven people listed under Arnold Tesh, plus more detail:

- The Virginia Tesh's companion's name is Adriana.
- The Arnold in North Carolina is also listed under the name Solomon Tesh.
- There is an email address for the North Carolina Tesh.
- Four more A. Teshes from around the country are included in the findings.

At this point, re-evaluate the search and the plan. Assuming your man has a listed phone number, you've narrowed it down to three people pretty quickly and have not spent a dime to get there. What's your gut instinct?

Try the telephone — and for a few dollars you can contact all three and ask if they were ever a Dodger batboy.

Or, taking another approach, you proceed to some of the fee-based online services. Since you're curious about the Arnold Tesh in Santa Monica, you try Merlin, a regional company. You also try KnowX, a national web-based public records company. Both have a web presence.

Among the things you find are:

- Arnold S. Tesh Advisors, from D.C., has a Los Angeles office and that means the Santa Monica guy and the D.C. guy are probably one in the same, or father and son. Since the D.C. guy was 56, he looks like your best shot. It also looks like he has done well for himself and moved up in the world since his batboy days.
- He owns a house in Vienna, Virginia, had one in Hawaii as well as one in Arizona.

Then you go on to Lexis-Nexis. You find eight stories. Among them are:

- A 1994 *Baltimore Sun* piece saying Tesh had become the president of the Counselors of Real Estate, the professional consulting affiliate of the National Association of Realtors.
- Another piece from the same time period in which he was listed as that group's new vice president.
- A 1994 *Greensboro North Carolina News and Record* clipping showing that a Solomon Arnold Tesh sold a house. Now you know there is a second Arnold to seriously consider, and you need to check further. Is this is the right one? You can't rule him out.

- Another clipping shows the Washington, D.C. Tesh is the "financier" behind an ambitious $1 billion 1997 Costa Rican building project.

However, you still haven't found anything that links any of these Teshes to baseball.

Sometimes it is easier to use a dial-up service than the Web. In researching on Lexis-Nexis, experienced hands are much more comfortable using the dial-up version than the web version. You can also do considerably more advanced searching on the non-web version, including detailed Boolean searching, truncation, using wildcard and other precision searching techniques. So, you move to the dial-up version of Lexis-Nexis and start in the "All News" category of the News Library. Again, you are spending money, so be efficient with your time.

You input: **los angeles OR la OR l.a. OR l a OR dodgers W/15 1959 OR tesh OR arnold W/25 batboy OR bat boy**

Okay, it takes a while to get a sophisticated, narrow search like the one above. However, with the techniques in this book, you'll figure it out pretty quick.

In English, that means "Los Angeles" or "la" or "la or Dodgers" within fifteen words of "1959" or "Tesh" or "Arnold" and also within twenty-five words of "batboy" or "bat boy."

Unfortunately, there are no sources that identify Arnold Tesh as the batboy for the 1959 Los Angeles Dodgers. However, several documents identify Rene Lachmann as a batboy for the Los Angeles Dodgers in 1959. You theorize that there were several batboys that year and, maybe if you find Rene, he will know where Arnold is.

So to try something bold and different, we look at Dialog, another fee-based database and find something not found anywhere else, a caption from a photograph that ran in *The Los Angeles Times* in 1959 tied to a March 15, 2001 story pointing to the "honorary batboy" for the Dodgers in 1959, James Hahn, who was the son of well-known LA County Supervisor Kenneth Hahn at the time. Now, forty-plus years later, James Hahn is the Mayor of Los Angeles.

```
1/6,K/3 (Item 1 from file: 630)
DIALOG®File 630:© 2002 Los Angeles Times. All rts. reserv.

01650534 22791 (USE FORMAT 7 FOR FULLTEXT)
PROFILE: JAMES K. HAHN
Touting His Past, Vowing to Mold City's Future
Some see city attorney's record as a plus, others as a minus. The
son of a beloved county supervisor lacks his father's gregarious bent but
the
legacy resonates for many.
CAMPAIGN 2001
Thursday March 15, 2001
WORD COUNT: 2543
...CAPTIONS: the Church of Christ.; PHOTOGRAPHER: ROBERT GAUTHIER
/ Los
Angeles Times; PHOTO: James Hahn, L.A. Dodgers ' first honorary
batboy ,
in 1959 at the Dodger Stadium ground-breaking with, from left,
Gov. Pat
Brown, Kenneth Hahn, team...
```

So we could try and ask Lachemann or Hahn if they have any idea where Tesh is. Highly unlikely, but at least it's another lead.

In the process of researching using other fee-based tools, you also find out that

- The D.C. Arnold Tesh has two daughters.

- His Social Security Number was issued in California between 1955 and 1956.

- He has a Pennsylvania appraiser's license.

- He has no liens, judgments or bankruptcies outstanding.

- He and his wife have or had another house in Beaufort County, South Carolina.

- He has a Virginia driver's license.

- No links to baseball. Now, it's definitely time to make phone calls.

Other things you might do under normal circumstances include thoroughly checking back in *The Los Angeles Times* to see if you could make a link to his baseball career. That might include sending email to people you find on the newsgroup `alt.sports.baseball.la-dodgers`.

You could also check online biographies to see if he shows up in places like Marquis Who's Who (on Dialog or Lexis-Nexis), as well as looking for collectors' associations and baseball groups to contact.

Postscript to the Tesh Search

I called Arnold Tesh at his Washington, D.C. office and can now fill in some of the holes in the research. After getting permission to use his name for the book, he says that he went to Loyola Law School in Los Angeles, but didn't graduate, leaving instead for a job in the assessor's office. That led him to a real estate career. He does still have red hair, now mixed with gray. He was never a Communist. He has fond memories of the 1959 World Series Champion Dodgers team.

Rene Lachmann, by the way, was the batboy for the 1960 team, and ended up becoming a major league baseball manager.

Tesh said when he was a batboy, his photo was regularly in *The Los Angeles Times* and the now-defunct *Herald-Examiner* because it was a custom back then for the batboy to be the first person to congratulate players when they hit home runs. His grand Costa Rican project took two years out of his life, but never materialized.

Sample Search 2: Business Profile

The Assignment

A foreign-owned distributor of pet products is interested in buying half a million dollars worth of pet products from a company called Veterinarian's Best. They call you to "find out what you can" the company's track record, its stability and some background on the owners. The products, they tell you, are supposed to be all-natural and designed by an actual veterinarian. You have only hours to provide a response.

Again, as with any search, start by "framing" your research — figuring out what exactly you're trying to find. Less time is no reason to try shortcuts.

One of the first critical questions is whether or not this company is publicly held. As discussed in Chapter 9, if it is a public company, then you have a whole group of online resources to pull from, including government resources like the Securities and Exchange Commission, and then business-oriented web sites such as Hoover's, and others.

If Veterinarian's Best is a private company, the best places to start are the Secretary of State's office for the state where the company is located, and other public records vendors who would have some details on the company's track record. You'll check clippings to find out what's been written about the company. As you work through your framing the research checklist, there are several important things to consider.

- It is definitely worth checking to see if the company has a web site.

- Animal supply industry people, pet stores, magazines that cover those industries and analysts who follow the trends in those industries will be important contact points. So will veterinarians, groomers, pet activists, and of course, the company's competitors.

Always ask yourself the most important of the Nora Paul "framing" questions: if you could envision the perfect answer, what would it look like?

In this case it would be a research paper or an article detailing everything you ever wanted to know about Veterinarian's Best — a company history, details about product lines, its place in the marketplace. It is most important that this be from a credible independent business publication, research company or analyst.

Business Finder Search Plan

So, where to begin? All you have to start with is a name, a kind of product and that's about it. Here's are some thoughts:

Start on the Web just to see what can be found quickly. Later, move to fee-based tools, which are probably inevitable in this case.

If you're a subscriber, you would start out on the fee-based Dialog because you can search by company name. Dialog has great indices. You could do the same kind of research on Lexis-Nexis or Factiva. Go with Dialog on this because it is easier to maneuver around in.

I do the Dialog search before moving back to a free search engine because I know exactly what I need from Dialog, and I can find it quickly before I start ringing up big charges. If I wasn't familiar with Dialog or other of the fee-based services, then I would stick to the free services of the Web instead. But knowing how to maneuver Dialog can save time and won't cost a fortune.

Once you're comfortable with your findings about the basics about the company, then you can look for lawsuits and any kind of negative input just to make certain that you're giving your client everything they may ask for when you make your report to them later.

Turning your attention to the free search tools on the Internet, try company finders to locate Veterinarian's Best and, of course, look for their web site.

→ *hot tip:*   **The best researchers online always search using the rule of concentric circles. They start out by:**
1)   **Looking at the company.**
2)   **Then finding the key people in the company.**
3)   **Profiling the key people.**
4)   **Doing a layered search until they start coming back to the start. That will ensure they don't miss too much.**

Next, you will check for press releases involving Veterinarian's Best. You'll definitely need to look at public records, too. If you can find them, industry marketing reports on the pet food and pet supplies industry will be a great help. Also check the wire services to see how often and in what capacity news was written involving the company.

→ *hot tip:*   **There are two kinds of data on any company:**
1)   **Information a company wants you to find about them.**
2)   **Information they don't.**

Not being honest with stockholders can get you arrested, so public companies are pretty thorough in their reporting to the regulating agencies. That's one of the reasons the U.S. government's SEC site is so valuable. Few companies want to face off with their regulator over inaccurate information.

Private companies are held to a much lower standard of openness. That makes the finding of information about them a much harder research effort. In this sample, I chose a private company intentionally. The reasoning is, if you can find information on a private company, researching a public one will be much easier.

On a hunch, start with `www.veterinariansbest.com`

No luck. If they have a web site, this is not its URL.

Next, search the Internet to see if the company has a web presence. Several search engines bring up hits, but nothing that points to a specific web site for Veterinarian's Best company.

Once you find the names of some of their products, string together a search like: Veterinarian's Best, Vita-Derm Shampoo and HotSpot Spray. Just starting, try Dogpile, a good meta-search tool. Another option would be to go to a Yahoo! kind of index or subject directory site. There you may find lists of pet product vendors. That will give a list of potential competitors.

By searching on Excite first, just to see what comes up, you'll find thousands and thousands of pet-related sites. Among these sites are several places that carry the Veterinarian's Best line, and several more that post photos of the entire line. But, none of these sites link directly to a web site for the company. Even though you may not be zeroing in on the company's web site, the mere fact that you're finding so many of its products out there is, in itself, valuable information to your client.

Faced with so many pet sites out there, you can turn to Teoma at `www.teoma.com` because it puts sites into categories and links you to expert sites based on your search. When you search Teoma for "veterinarian's best," you quickly come up with several hits for a `www.vetsbest.com`.

The following image is the main screen for `www.vetsbest.com`

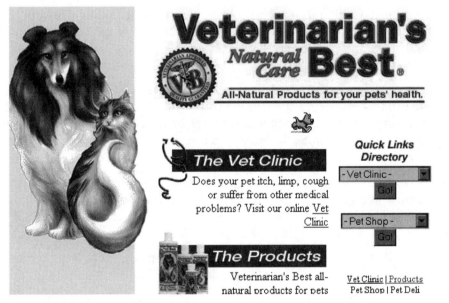

This company's web site is nicely designed and loaded with material about the company. Let's check some of the other sites first and come back to this in a moment.

At another site, you find that Veterinarian's Best has a hypo-allergenic shampoo that comes in several sizes, also three sizes of conditioner, three sizes of HotSpot Shampoo at US$47.50 a gallon, and Top Coat, a combination shampoo and conditioner.

Along the way, you're learning a lot about their products.

- These are all-natural products designed to avoid drugs, alcohol, steroids, pesticides and chemicals. They are gentle for dogs with sensitive skin, and help provide relief from itching and scratching.

- The HotSpot Shampoo is a natural, medicated shampoo with tea tree oil, whatever that is.

- The medicated stuff is supposed to provide relief from itching and relieves "hot spots" and red, raw, inflamed skin.

This all comes from sites that sell their products — sites that are found by simply doing a "veterinarian's best" search on the Google meta-search site. You may also find a People for the Ethical Treatment of Animals-related site that notes "The Santa Barbara-based Veterinarian's Best doesn't test its products on animals and their products are all vegan." At www.allforanimals.com/cruelfree1.htm you find *Veterinarian's Best, P.O. Box 4459, Santa Barbara, CA 93103 800-866-PETS.

Another directory of veterinarian products site at www.petgroomer.com lists the company address as Veterinarian's Best, Inc., 712 E. Mason Street, Santa Barbara, California 93193, Telephone: 805-963-5609, Fax: 805-963-2921. The "notes" include that they make kennel supplies and equipment, dog and cat products, veterinary products.

Look at their web site. The first thing to catch your attention is the little gray terrier frolicking around the web site in Java script. Nice touch.

In fact, this site is loaded with information about the company, including a history and profile. Of course, it's what they want us to know about them, but it says the company was founded by veterinarian Dr. Dawn Curie Thomas. It is a family-owned company with a full line of pet products including foods, dog cookies, flea and tick products, leashes, etc.

Their web site says the company owners are veterinarian Dawn Curie Thomas, DVM, (make a note to check the state agency for confirmation of her vets license) and her husband, William S. Thomas. He is a former newspaper editor and professor of journalism. If time permits, you can check the online archives for stories he once wrote, although with a name like Thomas, finding him quickly may be a long shot.

"Veterinarian's Best, Inc., was," the site tells you, "founded in 1989 when Dr. Thomas developed several very popular and effective all-natural skin care products for her dermatology patients at the Southern California Veterinary Hospital & Animal Skin Clinic in Los Angeles." So, there is another company to check out.

"There was such a demand for the products," the site continues, "that Veterinarian's Best, Inc., was formed to manufacture and distribute the products worldwide."

Now you have lots of leads to check out.

With this information, move to the company finders. A list of these is found in the Company Directories section of the Business Tools, Chapter 9. Assuming that Veterinarian's Best is a private company may be incorrect, so it's worth always doing a quick check of public companies on the U.S. government's SEC sites. And, much of this same information can be accessed via some free web-based public business finders that do capsule profiles of every company they list.

The SEC www.sec.gov/edgarhp.htm

Hoover's Online www.hoovers.com

CompaniesOnline
http://business.lycos.com/companyresearch/crtop.asp

Checking these, you find nothing about Veterinarian's Best, so you can begin to assume that it is a private company. Finding news clippings about the company is becoming even more important.

The Veterinarian's Best web site told you they're a California company, so, with a location, it's time to check fee-based tools, which are categorized by state locations. Start with Dialog Select at www.dialogselect.com, the lite version of the powerful Dialog database. Dialog Select is geared for web users who are not skilled in Dialog command language.

By starting with a search of Business News — Company News — you find three stories that talk about new Veterinarian's Best products:

- February, 1997 piece about "Nature's Creation," new dog cookies

- June, 1992 story about HotSpot, the anti-itch shampoo

- A similar story in the same issue about Vita-Derm food supplement.

These three stories all come from an industry newsletter called Marketing Intelligence Service. Put that on the list of people to contact later. The newsletter may have a reporter who covers the pet products industry who is worth getting some analysis from.

Next, run what is called a Duns profile. What you want is a profile of the Veterinarian's Best company put together from company information in the Dun & Bradstreet database. A Duns report on a company, which you could have run through Dun & Bradstreet on the Web — or through Lexis-Nexis, Dialog, Factiva or others — finds the company's address, phone number, employees, sales growth percentage, net worth, type of business, sales (current and historical), date of incorporation and state, president, size of property, and whether the property is owned or rented.

A more detailed Duns report on Veterinarian's Best includes information on sales, worth, payment history, type of business, president name (Dawn Curie Thomas), payment rating, payments by industry, assets, liabilities, ratio, working capital, other financial data, lien information, UCC filing information, when the business was started, whether there was a change of address, education and biographical information on Dr. Thomas, and information on a related company called Curie, Inc. Among the more interesting details, are:

- The company was incorporated in 1989.

- Annual sales were US$1.9 million in 1997, similar in 1996, US$675,000 in 1994, More current years are there as well.

- The company has five employees.

- The company has grown 18 percent over the past five years and also has a net worth statement.

- They have a 2,000 square-foot rented workspace, based in a single location.

- They have over one-hundred accounts.

- They export products overseas.

So far, you're getting general information and the business newsletter rewrites of Veterinarian's Best press releases. Now you need some objective information. Staying in Dialog, look for news clippings to see what's been written about the company. Let the search go as far back to 1988. This search finds a handful of articles. These include:

- A June, 1990 *San Francisco Examiner* story about how Dr. Dawn Curie Thomas of Veterinarian's Best has set up a fund to help animals caught in wildfires.

- A *Los Angeles Daily News* piece from 1990 that shows Dawn as the owner and director of the Southern California Veterinary Hospital in Los Angeles.

- Three other news clips.

News about her involvement in a veterinary hospital is worth going into other business files and checking. You'll also want to check property records.

Another news clip says she is the author of a book called *Ask The Vet* from BookWord Press. If there's time, the book company would be worth finding and talking to see if they have her bio, book sales figures, etc.

You may also find an August 13, 1995 *Arizona Republic* newspaper story that talks about Dr. Dawn as "Dawn Curie Thomas, a former Valley resident, in town for the grand opening of a PetSmart store at Pima and Shea. Thomas, a veterinarian who went to school at Camelback High and Arizona State University, will talk about a line of natural skin-care products for pets and will push her book, *The 100 Most Common Questions That Pet Owners Ask the Vet*."

Yet another story is a column she wrote where she claims to be the owner of the Southern California Veterinary Hospital and Animal Skin Clinic in Woodland, a Los Angeles suburb.

Now you have two more businesses to check out. Your best bet is to return to the fee-based service, which, by now, you're becoming very familiar with: Dialog. Go back and check out her other businesses to confirm them, and, if you still have time, you can turn to public records and the California Secretary of State's office. Among the public records of the California veterinary agency, you may want to find her veterinary license. You may be able to do this with a phone call, or you can move to Merlin at www.merlindata.com since it is a California search firm. Merlin can help you find all kinds of public records on the company. These include a Uniform Commercial Code filing showing that Dawn and her husband secured a loan with Wells Fargo Bank in San Jose, plus another from the Bank of Montecito. You may find considerably more detail on the company, including that Bill is the chief executive officer and Dawn is the president. You may find her veterinary medicine license dating back to 1981, and still current.

The Merlin filings, some of which come from the California Secretary of State's office, also include articles of incorporation for the Veterinarian's Best company as well as addresses for the company, its warehouse, and also information on another company they run called Curie, Inc.

Looking deeper, you also find family trust documents for the Thomases as well as a court record index showing two lawsuits in civil court. If you had more time, you could check details on these.

Now, focus on learning more about Bill and Dawn, the people. For this, quickly, you can move to another fee-based search tool, DBT Autotrack, a ChoicePoint product which provides limited access to public records, depending on if you are law enforcement, a lawyer, or an insurance person. But if you can get access, you would find:

- Dawn was born in Arizona in 1948.

- Her Social Security Number.

- Her last four addresses.

- Property records, including the value of their residency as well as the value of the warehouse they rent. This suggests that they are the owners and they rent the facility to themselves, a smart tax move.

A search reveals the same kinds of information on Bill, also the names, ages, and addresses of their children.

A couple of other pieces of information are quite interesting. While two lawsuits are found, you also find that she has no liens or judgments against her. Through public records you may also find that she has a Drug Enforcement Administration license to dispense certain kinds of drugs. This would make sense for a vet.

Next, run market analyst reports on their products and on the company, on tools like Investext and Dun & Bradstreet, then add those findings into your market reports about the pet supplies industry.

Among the other tools to use, given more time or instead of using the Web to find much of this, you could have looked at the Marketing and Advertising Reference Service on Dialog or the Publisher's, Distributors and Wholesalers Database. This would certainly have found some information about them and Veterinarian's Best. Additionally you could do some research on trademarks for their products, and might use the Web to look up some of their competitors to find some people to talk to who have opinions and perhaps some information not found on databases.

Now you are ready to produce a detailed report on the corporation, Veterinarian's Best. Some conclusions are:

- The people behind the company are upstanding community citizens.

- Veterinarian's Best is a solid company.

- Since everything checks out, you can recommend that your client go ahead with the purchases.

- You may wish to check into some of their products for your own cat and dog.

Postscript to the Veterinarian's Best Business Profile

When I talked to Bill Thomas and got his final okay to use Veterinarian's Best as a sample search, I asked him if anything was missed. As it turns out, had we gone further we might have found his erstwhile career as a political adviser to the UN Ambassador of Papau, New Guinea. It seems that Bill and a friend were asking directions to a hotel after a week out in the New Guinea jungle, when the person they asked the directions from volunteered to let them stay at his house.

Dinner was served, politics discussed, and in particular the conversation turned into a discussion of limited democracy and its potential. The next thing he knew, Bill was on a national radio program debating the merits of limited democracy.

You would have needed a few more minutes online to find that story.

Sample 3: Problem Solving

For our third scenario, I'll walk you through what I would do as I search on one topic, and leave it to you to pick a second topic, and you can do the actual searching on it. This lets you pick a medical or health topic of interest to you, rather than mine. The concepts involved in both my searches are the same, so your search should produce results, and, those results should be of some help to you.

My Assignment

Let's say my father is diagnosed with a prostate problem and is deathly scared of having surgery. He asks us to research alternative forms of treatment to the knife. He's going to see his doctor tomorrow morning. Time is the most critical factor.

Your Assignment

Your father, too, is diagnosed with a serious medical problem. He is concerned about the treatment he may receive, and would like to know more about all the alternatives.

So What Do You Do?

In the previous two searches I talked about using online tools to find specific information. But many times, you have something vague and general. Keep in mind, the Internet is about communication and using many of the human resources online like discussion groups, email, mailing lists and newsgroups. Among these we should find people who have had genuine experience with the same kind of medical conditions we are looking into.

These many online sources can help you find support groups, better doctors, and subject directory lists of inter-related web-sites — in addition to medical information and treatment prospects.

Online sources are also incredibly valuable in helping us figure out how to ask the right questions.

In this sample search, there is a pitfall. With every medical condition, there are frustrated consumers — loved ones who are often unsatisfied with the information they have. Often, the prognosis is not good. Many are willing to devote long hours to remedying the unfortunate situation, perhaps grasping for any shred of hope. Frustrated, "hurt" people are vulnerable to quackery. You must always be careful to ask ourselves who is behind a web site and why is it up there, with medical conditions especially, or anytime the stakes are high. Don't be led into doing the wrong things by the wrong advisors who might prey on our vulnerability.

Now, before we go further, this tip. If, at any time, you don't know much about a subject and are just foraging, it's suggested that you look at Barbara Quint's superb sidebar later in this chapter where she talks about protecting yourself by checking and double-checking online information. She speaks of how to deal with swimming in data, and the critical nature of it.

Can I Go Online Now?

Before we go online, let's plan your search.

Remember, while I'm researching alternatives to prostate surgery, you could be doing a similar search on your topic, perhaps diabetes, heart surgery or any other health or medical condition.

Let's think through the situation first. In a medical situation, the first key is to find out where good information can be found and to determine if you want or need to spend money for information.

There should be plenty of information for free, but if you want absolute credibility in our sources – and if it is your parent's life in the balance, you certainly do — a combination of fee-based and free resources is recommended.

In addition to finding the right focus for the search, you also need to figure out what keywords will help locate trustworthy, reliable documents. In this case, since you know little or nothing about the subject to start with, you'll need to do some preliminary searches to get familiar with the terminology in use.

Always ask yourself where the most reliable data would be found. In this case, the federal government should have some good information, but medical experts would be the first place to turn.

To get the right phrases and starting points, I turn to my medical expert of choice, Susan Detwiler and her wonderful compilation at `www.detwiler.com`.

Though this is getting ahead of ourselves and our search, a trip to her web site would be a good shortcut. She wrote the medical sidebar in Chapter 5, Specialized Tools, which includes many of her excellent web site links to the good medical sites online.

➜ *hot tip:*　**If you don't know much about a subject, find someone who does. When you find an authority – someone you trust or someone you think really knows what they are talking about – check to see if they have a list of favorite sites (and their links) before you turn to more general search tools.**

For this sample search, rather than compiling a long list of good sites, let's try finding one good medical site with the proper name for the medical condition you're researching. We'll use that web site to locate "alternatives to surgery."

You need a site that "speaks the right language" and contains what you're looking for — to find health information, preferably from the government. Put that all together in one URL: `healthfinder.gov`.

You're in luck: Healthfinder at `www.healthfinder.gov/default.htm` is a U.S. government list of previewed consumer health information sites. Here I can search for the scientific words for enlarged prostate, and you can search for whatever disease you are researching.

After finding some of the keywords, including

- Prostatitis
- BPH/ Benign Prostatic Hyperplasia
- PSA/ Prostate Specific Antigen
- TURP, TUNA and TUMT

The next thing is to think of all the terms we would expect to find in an ultimate results page. Make a list of them.

My list might include all the medical terms above as well as prostate, radiation, risk factors, symptoms, enlarged prostate, urinary, and also words like "alternate choice" or "alternative" or choice, blockage, diagnosis, and treatment.

→ *hot tip:* **Put several words in a search string, separated by commas and without quote marks, in a search field of a search engine. What comes back? Now, enter a somewhat different variation (add or subtract words) to your search string. What comes back? The results are different, but not all *that* different. Create another search string and see what sites the engine brings up again. Expert searchers use the list concept because if several of the search strings result in the same hits over and over, the search engines will rank those sites higher. This helps identify the top few sites.**

→ *hot tip:* **Switching search engines lets you see what else there is to find on a particular topic.**

One of the reasons to do this is to get the medical name or names for the condition you are trying to find out about. One warning about your medical list is necessary: you might want to specify "human being conditions" because an animal might have the same condition, which might lead you to a ton of veterinary sites.

When searching, you have to get into the right language to find what you're specifically looking for. For example, the dictionary of searchable sports terms is different from the terms in medicine. Further, the dictionary of terms for the sport of bowling are different from that of football. If you are trying to find out the best bowling score and you keyed in the phrase "highest points," you'd probably end up with the Bowling Green football score. Bowlers count pins, not points, so, for bowling scores, include the term "pins."

Knowing the differences between domain names, like .com, .org, .gov. and .edu, can make all the difference in the world when judging a site's credibility. Sites ending with .com are commercial vendors whose only goal may be to sell us products. Sites with .org may also be dependent on you for financial support, or they may be advocating something. Sites with .gov sites may be accurate, but they may not offer information about "alternatives."

Knowing the terminology also makes all the difference in successful searching.

Look for bias. Ask yourself, is this site one-sided or is there balance? As you consider the value of a site, ask questions, such as, are there contradictions and complications that someone with a differing viewpoint might point out?

Another way to pin down the disease and the technical lingo is to plow through medical journals. Here, you will find people who are familiar with your topics. Their work may be available for you to build on.

Since, at this point, you are searching by topic, using subject directories or indices like Yahoo! or About.com. Judging by the large number of hits your searches produce, it is clear you're not alone in looking for alternatives in medicine.

While searching the news features isn't likely to find many media stories unless someone famous has the same medical problem, celebrity news searches are a trick Carole Lane, the author of *Naked in Cyberspace* uses. Think of a few famous people who may have had the illness in question. In the case of prostate problems, there are quite a few cases, including former Sen. Bob Dole, baseball player Darryl Strawberry, two-time Nobel Prize winner Dr. Linus Pauling, civil rights advocate Stokely Carmichael, actors Don Ameche and Bill Bixby, Jordan's King Hussein and Time-Warner Chairman Steven Ross. Each made news for having or fighting prostate problems, yet they would not have if they weren't well-known first. An article listing them could also include the rest of what we're looking for.

As you visit sites in search of "our medical condition," you may find many "alternative treatments." This gives a "field" of possibilities to consider. Included in the list of prostate treatments is one that involves heat, another that involves microwaving, and several others. As you move forward, it would be wise to use our search engine tools to find more sites that contain these terms.

Not surprisingly, you'll find web sites that claim their procedure is best. But in looking at the domain name, quickly realize that many are from doctors advocating their own procedures. Only when you turn to the government and media sites do we find reliable information and both the upside *and* downside of each procedure.

Since some of the information you are finding for free on the Web has is a bit worrisome or troubling, the next move is to fee-based databases like Factiva, Dialog, or Lexis-Nexis, each with its own sections of reliable science, medical, and health information. The free sites on the Web have given us a lot of good terminology and background information, so, when you turn to the fee-based services, you won't be wasting time.

Lexis-Nexis has several medical resources that will help us find specific doctors, including:

- ABMS (The Official American Board of Medical Specialties Directory of Board Certified Medical Specialists)

- AMDIR (The American Medical Information's Physician & Surgeons Database

Dialog offers MANTIS, an incredibly good medical database for alternative and natural therapies. Dialog also has:

- The Dictionary of Substances and their Effects

- Drugs of the Future, which talks about side effects among other things.

- Many powerful medical-related databases.

- Information Access Corporation's Health and Wellness database, which is a terrific layman's guide to medical information.

Did You Find Enough "Right Information?"

Since the final sample search was about something you care about, by now you are more informed about something that, probably, affects your life and your future. How long did it take to collect that information? That's one of the true beauties of the Internet: it gives you same day access to information that, just a decade ago, would have taken you weeks to collect. And, the next time you're confronted with a medical emergency, you'll be able to take on tough search like this one and get results quickly.

Here's another beauty of the Internet: once you know what to look for, you have access to the "top experts." You can get to their published articles and news stories, ask them questions via email, find and compare their businesses, learn about their backgrounds, who they "link with." No longer do you have to rely on just one family doctor, or one phone call to one expert, or whoever puts out the most advertisements.

A crucial part of Sample Search 3 is evaluating the information once you get it. Since it was a health question, you have realized the absolute importance of being sure of the source. And, when you find a good source, you learn a lot. For medical questions, especially, if you really want to feel safe, a fee-based service can be the most helpful.

More Search Strategies from Search Gurus

Perhaps the most insightful conclusions I've seen on the "dos and don'ts" of searching come from two of the best search gurus in the business – Susan Feldman and *Searcher Magazine* Editor, Barbara Quint.

Susan Feldman has studied the uses of fee-based and free web searching and has some excellent tips on when to use which and what to look for from each. A few years ago she conducted The Internet Search-off for *Searcher Magazine,* comparing fee-based tools to free web-based resources. For the Search-off, Susan used experienced librarians, professional searchers, and real life examples and case studies.

While many of her findings may have changed over the past few years, Feldman found that one of the more interesting observations was that in using the Web or the fee-based tools, these highly-skilled searchers had different expectations from the different types of tools. In using the fee-based tools they *assume* that information exists on the subject, it is high quality, the information is current and expensive, and that it will take some training and know-how to find what you are looking for. Often, they were surprised when they could not find something as long as they searched.

On the Web, the expectations of the skilled professional searchers were much lower. On the Web there might be information on a topic, but its quality and timeliness is unpredictable. The information is free, but there's no telling how effectively search engines work. Many searchers thought it would be a surprise if they found something.

Feldman also notes that one major consideration is that time is money. "Free information that takes too long to find and format is expensive information," she says. But, there is no longer a clear dividing line between the fee-based services and the Web. Time is the most relevant factor. But she stresses that for most research jobs, you need to use a combination of the two toolsets.

If you want to look through thousands of newspaper articles to find what you want, you can do it on the Web and you will also find the graphics, charts and tables missing from the fee-based services. But, it will likely take you longer *and* you probably will not be as thorough as if you used the fee-based tools.

One thing that is not going to change is your need to understand how to use these tools to keep some sense of your own privacy while online, which is the topic of the next chapter.

➔*hot tip:* **When you do specific research on a subject you don't ever expect to come back to (for instance, you need to go out on Usenet to track down leads), set up your own separate email address just for this. Go to Hotmail or any service offering free email. Get a free password. When your project is over – and you no longer care – just ignore replies to that email service. That way, your regular email won't be cluttered with unwanted email replies.**

Super Searching Tips

By Susan Feldman

Web search engines all attach weights to different words and rankings in order to put the most valuable finding at the top of your results query. To do this, nearly every search engine uses a different formula. (See Chapter 4, Search Tools.)

Here are some rules that can be gleaned from some of the expert searchers who participated in the Internet Search-off:

- Since search engines generally have little overlap in coverage, use more than one search engine for your extensive searches.

- Rare or unusual words are easier to find than common ones.
  Try searching for the rare term first.

- Know the default parameters of the site: AND or OR, etc.

- Find and use synonyms for your most important concept. If you use only one term for your most important concept, and then use many synonyms for less vital aspects, you can skew the weighting of the query away from the most important term.

- Use AltaVista for finding foreign sites and information in foreign languages. While their translation feature may not be robust enough to try on Shakespeare, it does return a nice approximation of the original, unless you have idioms involved.

- Use HotBot if you need a specific format, date or field
  within a document such as the title or the URL.

- Use a meta-search engine to give you a quick overview of what might become a very broad search with many returns. Meta-search engines have one major drawback: they do not return enough information to make a considered decision of whether to view a page. Titles alone do not suffice usually.

- If too many pages come back, then add other concepts to the query.

- Ignore false drops. Don't waste time wondering why the German/English Running Dictionary showed up in a search on "the effect of jet lag on shining a light behind the knee." I never could figure that one out.

- Shorten a URL if you get a broken link,
  then use the features of the site to find the page you seek.

- Stick to a few search engines that work best for you. Knowing how to use them well will save searching time.

Don't let the numbers of results fool you. Each search service has its own idiosyncratic way of figuring out how many pages relate to a query. Some add all pages that have at least one of the query words. Others seem to limit that number or list only those which include all the concepts.

Product reviews, particularly for computer-related equipment are easy to find on the Web. Ask Jeeves often lists the best sites for reviews of various products.

-- Susan Feldman is Director of the Document and Content Technologies Program at IDC. Before coming to IDC in 2000, she was President of Datasearch, an independent information consulting firm. She is a former president and charter member of the Association of Independent Information Professionals. Her email is Sfeldman@IDC.com

"...Our Lives, Our Fortunes, & Our Sacred Honor" Protecting Yourself Online

By Barbara Quint

The signers of the *Declaration of Independence* defined the stakes they had riding on their actions very carefully. As Ben Franklin said, "If we don't all hang together, it's certain we'll all hang separately."

The warning applies as well to web work. If you have any of the above – life, fortune, or sacred honor – riding on the outcome of your web search, check and double check its quality. If you only plan to squander a pleasant hour or two in surfing the Web for amusement or entertainment, no problem, but if you plan to gather medical information or research your stock portfolio or hand someone your credit card data, *protect yourself.*

Rule One: Don't Put Anything Into Your Mind You Wouldn't Put Into Your Mouth.

- Where did this information come from?

- Who stands behind it?

- What axes are they grinding?

Approval of a source can vary from situation to situation. For example, an ardent environmentalist and a timber industry lobbyist might have widely different opinions as to the value of information from a Sierra Club web site, but both should appreciate verification that the material came from the actual Sierra Club.

Tips:

Check the entire URL. Clicking through to a document with a foot-long URL (usually ending in ".htm" or ".html") may expedite your trip to your target source, but it also skips the verification process. To check who or what brought you this far, just strip off the layers between the back slashes. Re-enter the URL up to the first back slash and see where you start.

Watch out for the domain name. If you're looking for a company site, it shouldn't end in ".org". If you're tracking government statistics, it shouldn't end in ".com". Sometimes there's a reasonable explanation. For example, one company selling laser printers might have a lovely collection of reference material, including poetry, quotations, statistics, etc., as a giveaway to lure users to its site. The data is probably reliable, but any smart searcher would have clicked around the site to see if anything "just doesn't seem right."

Look for contact information. The old-fashioned snail mail kind. Ignore this tip at your peril. In a desperate search for a cheap toner cartridge, I found a company that claimed to sell new ones $30.00 cheaper than my usual office supply house. But when I called the 800 number on a Saturday, the guy answered the phone, "Hello," and I could hear kids hollering in the background. When I rechecked the full web site, the contact section had no mailing address. I don't know about you, but I'm not handing over credit card data to businesses that don't tell me what state they're in. I need to deal with people who will stand behind the information they carry and the goods they sell.

Rule Two: Kick the Tires!

- Stay cynical.

- Ask embarrassing questions.

- Play devil's advocate.

Assume next Monday you'll face a board of inquiry or an angry boss with a set of questions designed to debunk the data. What questions would be on that list? Can you answer them?

Tips:

The old adage, **"You get what you pay for" doesn't hold true in web research.** Commercial services that charge high fees for data may offer wonderful, reliable data and solid information, but they can also carry lightweight or biased information. The free Web certainly has a sky load of cloudy data, but it can also carry rock-solid, reliable information – sometimes from the same sources as the commercial services. Look at each question and each answer.

Verify bias. Judge web output with at least the same rigorous standards you would apply to any other source of data. A professional searcher colleague of mine tells the story of a client who wanted a list of the top ten mutual funds. When she had cleared enough earlier projects to work on his question, the client told her he had already found the list he needed on the Web. Actually, he had gotten the data from a promotional piece on a single mutual fund's company web site. Do you believe phone company representatives when they tell you about studies that show their company has cheaper long distance rates than any other? Just because it comes off the computer doesn't make it more reliable. On the other hand, if the data came from an established financial journal or a trade association or a government study, then you might place more faith in it. But check them out too.

Identify critical factors. Timeliness and currency often affect the value of information. The perfect study from the most authoritative source filled with relevant detail may have little or no value if written three years ago. Sometimes web versions of reports may contain more current information than print ones, but you must verify the date of the most recent revision. If not apparent on the document, email the webmaster. Even if the study hasn't been updated recently, the webmaster may be able to suggest alternative sources. Remember built-in delay factors. Scholarly journals can have a two or three year delay between the submission of a research study and its publication. Again, contacting authors, their research organizations or their web sites may provide more current information, and perhaps more detailed reports.

Make sure you can find the information again. Too much material on the Web is ephemeral: here today, gone tomorrow. Newspaper web sites, for example, usually only carry one day's worth of data. Some offer archives, but rarely is the archived material complete or in an identical format. If you think you might face future questions about the information a transaction, then archive it or document it yourself. Print it out straight from the browser and stick it in a file. Download it into your computer. Find out whether and where archives appear. Many newspapers, trade press journals, company financial reports, etc. exist in commercial database archives. Libraries hold backruns of journals and magazines, government reports, etc.

Rule Three: When in Doubt, Hire It Out.

If you lack confidence in your ability to do quality research on the Web, get a professional searcher to do the job for you. This rule applies to non-web research as well. Your company may have a corporate library with expert searchers on staff. Your community may have a public library with a cost-plus-fee search service. Information brokers do research for hire.

Tips:

Use the searchers with the best match of skills and price. Don't let geography determine the hire. The Internet has eliminated distance as a barrier. If you have an institutional library available to you, its staff will probably know your subject area well and have a vested interest in serving you. If you need a personal search done, they may still offer help – at least, help to find you the right searcher. Check trade and professional associations. The American Library Association at `www.ala.org` has a section called FISCAL that lists all the intermediated searching operations at public and academic libraries around the country. The Association of Independent Information Professionals at `www.aiip.org` lists ethical information brokers from around the world.

Explain the full question to your searcher. Tell them how you plan to use the information. Online searching can offer a considerable range of choices.

Turn your search into a tutorial. Get double value from hiring a searcher by having them explain the logic and techniques they used to gather information. Next time, you can try doing it yourself. In fact, most searchers are happy to teach clients how to improve their research skills.

Rule Four: Just Do It!

A little knowledge is a dangerous thing, as the poet says, but the real enemy is ignorance. The most expensive and risky step you can take is just "going dumb." How many incurable diseases have cures that the patient or doctor just don't know exist? How many business losses result from not checking basic business data sources? How many mistakes can a person make in their life from sheer ignorance? The answers aren't pretty.

Tips:

Travel with the experts. Meta-sites are home pages that offer massive collections of links to related sites. Some come from libraries and academic institutions. Some come from individuals who have just said "No" when they were advised to "Get a life!" Some come from publishers working to retain their dominance in a print universe in the new digital world.

Check for update frequency. Whatever the source, webmasters behind major meta-sites have made a commitment to tracking the quality of their listings. Many of these sites will document when they last checked each and every listing.

Ask for help. The only bad question is an unasked question. If you find an expert, but don't find your answer or don't understand the answer you've found, contact them. Before the Internet had a web to hold all its research, it still held out open arms to connect all its people. Marvelous communities exist in the Internet. Use them. But watch out! Never let warm and fuzzy feelings about a friendly source deter you from cool-headed, critical examination of the information they give you.

Caveat searcher!

-- Barbara Quint is editor of *Searcher Magazine*. Her email address is `bquint@netcom.com`

The Five-Minute Challenge: Quick, Effective & Free Research Using AltaVista

By Jennifer Kaplan

For many people, conducting research sounds like a daunting and time consuming task, but it doesn't have to be either. And you don't need to become a search professional to quickly and effectively find the information you need to do your job. Using the knowledge you already have, applying basic search techniques, and focusing a critical eye on what you see can help you quickly uncover an amazing number of clues. Here's an example:

Blue Sage Home and Body, a company that provides one-of-a-kind home furnishing and decorative items, is launching a test email campaign to 1,200 selected friends. Since many of its items are unique pieces from all corners of the globe or selections from local artists, Blue Sage thinks a strong visual message is absolutely essential. That means an elegant "HTML email" with a few well-chosen high-quality photos to evoke the character of its stores and catalog. Blue Sage wants to execute an HTML email campaign but doesn't know how. But first it needs to quickly learn enough about HTML email to outline their options, set expectations, then build a plan for the next phase. This campaign will highlight unique pieces of Americana reflecting the western influence of the Blue Sage lifestyle, now so very popular in Germany, Russia, Asia and Australia. Let's help Blue Sage with The Five-Minute Challenge...

We've got to learn a lot in a little time. Let's take a moment to think about what we know and what we need to - and then jump right in. We won't launch an email campaign in five minutes, but we can learn quite a bit and really focus the next phase.

We know we need to design an HTML email and send it to a pre-existing list of people in the U.S., Germany, Australia, and Asia. Almost all of us have been bombarded with HTML email campaigns. So think about HTML emails you've received. Do any standout in your mind? Any specific characteristics that you might apply here? Better still, go to your inbox and pull up the promotional emails you received today. Notice what's similar, what's not. Does anything surprise you? Now that a minute is up, fire up your primary search engine - let's use AltaVista.

You will want to rely on your primary search engine when you embark upon a competitive intelligence assignment – particularly a Five-Minute Challenge - but don't do it to the exclusion of others. Be sure to use others to inform and narrow your search as necessary and don't forget about specialty search engines and directories for specific needs including in-language searches, country- and region-specific search engines and directories.

Go to www.altavista.com and type the phrase "html email." Don't spend too much time thinking about your search terms, first, just try the obvious. "I want to learn how to _____."

Looking at our search results page (see next page), we see five distinct and important areas to inform our search. Here's what we can learn without even scrolling on the page. Two areas catch our eye immediately. Not surprisingly, it's the advertisements. Don't ignore them, you can learn a lot. Area 1 on the top of the page, in prime banner ad location is a colorful banner for Verizon's SuperPages.com. Area 2 on the right side of the page is a vertical bar titled "html email sites" and it lists "Quicksoft E-mail Experts - The EasyMail Objects will enable your applications to send, retrieve, view, edit..." "We've gathered every major site that specializes in HTML email. We're ..." and "Turn Visitors into Prospects. Convert Prospects into Clients. Increase Back End ..." And, the middle site looks good, we'll definitely want to check that out.

What Have Learned Already?

The most expensive ad on this page – the banner on top – is not directly related to our search terms: "html email." That might mean we need more specific, even different terms. Let's keep that in mind as we go forward. Companies have a variety of ways to buy advertising. One of the ways they can do it is to buy phrases or keywords. So if you buy the keyword or phrase "home furnishing," your ads appear every time someone searches for home furnishing on the search engine you have purchased the words from. Because this is expensive, some advertisers don't buy 100 percent of the key words.

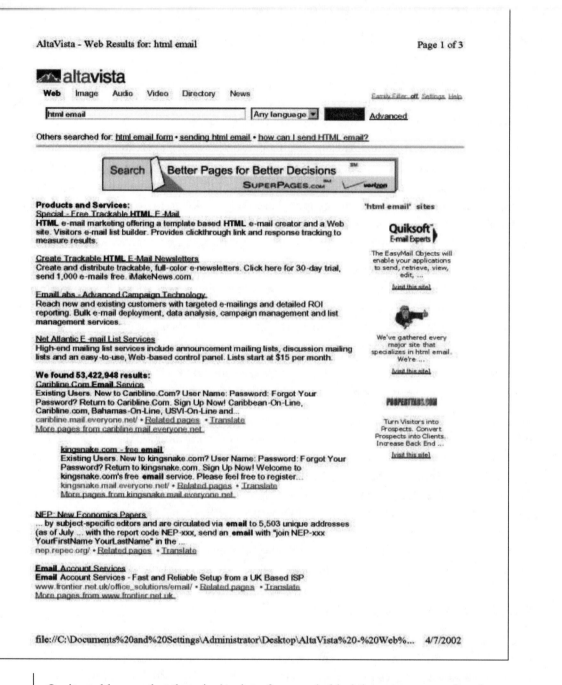

AltaVista - Web Results for: html email   Page 1 of 3

Or, it could mean that there isn't a lot of money behind these terms, so advertisers are not spending money on them. It could mean there are not many directly-related businesses, or that the margins are not strong enough to support keyword advertising.

We could refresh the page to see if other ads show up – it's possible that our key words were purchased for less than 100% of the instances.

By refreshing several times, we could see who else has purchased these words – a great way to find your competitors and see how much they may be spending on keyword advertising.

When you are doing this kind of quick research look at Area 1 to see who the sponsor is and how they frame their message. Although not for Blue Sage, you may find prime competitors, vendors, or customers for other similar challenges here. If the ad is related to your search terms, that sponsor is paying good money to be there. Key word advertising is among the most expensive banner advertising.

From the other ads, we can assume that there are folks offering both software and services, and that HTML email is used for customer acquisition - that's good because Blue Sage's ultimate goal is to acquire customers HTML email is one of the most important customer acquisition and retention tools because email is very effective and is targeted to specific people. Area 3 lists products and services.

Look at the headlines: by carefully reading the nuances of what is written, you can pick up some important clues about this field. The words, free and create are two good indicators.

We like "free," so let's keep the offer for free HTML email in mind. "Create" lets us know there are tools out there to help us do it yourself. Since we've already seen a few businesses advertising such tools, we know there have got to be a lot of people out there doing it themselves. If you read the ads clearly, it's obvious that there is a high-end, very complex, large-scale segment of HTML email marketing, and we might think that having a vendor do it for us would be expensive. Already we're thinking we'll probably have to look into creating and sending the HTML email ourselves, so let's keep our eyes out for other tools, resources, and free trials. And since we're seeing so many services, products, and vendors already, let's note where we see big solid brands. The solid brands connote trust and authority.

Quickly Scan The Descriptive Text

"Template" sounds like an important word and makes us wonder how the HTML email is created. Should a vendor do it? Should we do it? If we do it, a template sounds like an important tool. "30-day trial, send 1,000 e-mails free" is another free trial to keep in mind. And here's our first number: "1,000 emails free." Since 1,000 are free, we might assume that 1,000 is a low number. "Trackable, technology, bulk, data analysis, list management" all sound big. Where does Blue Sage fit in? Would we use these? Could this stuff apply or is our email campaign a small-scale endeavor that shares little with these scary sounding terms?

In our case, Blue Sage already has its own list and its only 300 people. There may be more to learn here at these four sites, but given the limited time we have (remember, your five minutes are almost up) and assuming this site is about purchasing lists and/or large-scale list management, our time is better spent elsewhere. We've already identified sites that look like they might have key info for us. But let's bookmark or save the URLs with free offers in case we want to investigate that route further. Again, we don't want to visit this site, but let's bookmark it for future use. If Blue Sage's pilot HTML email campaign is successful and it is rolled out on a large scale, these sites may be useful to us.

We're still on that AltaVista page. We haven't scrolled and we haven't clicked. Area 4 is a single line that says: *Others searched for: html email form • sending html email • how can I send html email?* Here we can see that we're not the only ones trying to figure out how to send HTML email. Since so many people are asking how to send HTML email, we might wonder how easy or difficult it is to do. We'll definitely want to click on the last two links in the next phase of our research since they are right on target and will certainly narrow our search.

Finally, we're at Area 5, the search results! Can you believe how much we've learned in so little time before we even see the search results? And it's a good thing because AltaVista found 53,422,948 results. Not to worry; we won't review them all in our remaining thirty seconds.

Quick Scanning in Thirty Seconds...

A quick scan shows there are a lot of vendors. There is enough in the description to learn more, to better focus our search and to bookmark for the next phase. You also may want to look for a few keywords that keep popping up in the brief site descriptions. These keywords may help you focus additional searches later. Also, don't forget to look at the URLs themselves; they're often ripe with clues.

What's in a URL? More than you might think. Size matters as does spelling, popularity, descriptiveness, prefix, suffix, domain. Generally, short domains are better than long ones, right? That's because shorter ones are easier to remember, spell, and type correctly. Each letter added to a domain increases the chances of misspelling and the possibility that people won't get there. Long or difficult to spell domains are too daunting, and searchers opt for a shorter alternative. It's true that people get to sites through linking more often than they do by typing in a URL. But what about URLs you see in print or hear on the radio or over the phone? Think about how you conduct research. If you're like me, then you jot down URLs all the time – perhaps you have an army of those little yellow sticky notes marching around the sides of your monitor? A URL list in your Palm Pilot? I'm always typing URLs in email or other documents. It's a lot easier and more inviting when they are short!

Shorter URLs and ones that are more descriptive or are popular words indicate that the site may have been around for a while. We've all heard the lament "all the good domain names were taken ages ago." If we're looking for HTML email guidance, are we more comfortable with an old faithful or a newcomer? When I see short URLs (for example, `x.com`) or ones that are really descriptive (`drugstore.com`), or really popular terms (`internet.com`), I assume the site publisher is an early pioneer, a good thinker or that they spent a lot of money to buy the domain. When I look for vendors, I keep this in mind. I may not like the big price tag, but surveying the big guys can help you see what is out there, what features and benefits are important. Big brands and market leaders often include a lot of data that's helpful for your research even if you don't intend to use them.

Prefixes and suffixes generally indicate the page does not belong to the site owner or is not the primary focus of the site. Our first result (`http://caribline.mail.everyone.net`) scares me a little; I'll quickly move on to the next. When looking for something very specific, however, a long URL with a lot of suffixes may be a clue that the web site may be worth further attention.

Our next search result (`http://nep.repec.org`) is a not-for-profit, indicated by the `.org` extension on the domain name. We can see quickly that this will not be useful to us or for Blue Sage and move on. Keep in mind that trade, professional, and non-profit organizations can be a great source of information. They're in the business of gathering and disseminating information, supporting members, contributors and constituents. They can be a great source of data and an effective way to find people or companies. *Gale's Encyclopedia of Associations* is available through Dialog and the American Society of Association Executives directory is available at `www.asaenet.org`.

URLs can indicate geography as well. Our third search result (`www.frontier. net.uk/office_solutions/email/`) is a U.K.-based site. It's not one of our target countries for this search, so we will ignore it.

Identifying High-Potential Resources, Vendors, and Free Stuff

Did our Five-Minute Challenge pay off? We know sending HTML email is popular: there are tens of million of pages about it, a lot of people are asking how to do it, there are a lot of resources available, a lot of vendors are offering free trials. We've identified high-potential resources, vendors, and free stuff. We may want to use a free or trial product or service to send the email. We'll probably want to create it ourselves, but we'll need help. That's okay; we know where to look. We were able to outline Blue Sage's options and set expectations. After five minutes, Blue Sage is ready to build a plan for the next phase.

Given Blue Sage's international reach, we'll have to make sure our efforts reflect the needs of customers and demands of business in Germany, Russia, Asia and Australia. Our search will include international sites, as we can see from the domains. But to better focus on a particular geographic area, we can add it to our search terms, "HTML email in Germany." Since I don't speak German, we will have to use a translator site to find appropriate material. (See Chapter 10, International Research for translation tools). AltaVista also allows us to search country-specific sites in Australia, Germany, India, Korea, New Zealand, and elsewhere, and we can search in twenty-five languages.

Remember the Web is a tool to leverage what you know and learn what you need to know. Go back to those HTML emails in your own inbox. Remember the ones you like? Take a look, scroll down to the bottom and look for information about how and by whom it was sent. These could be clues about prospective vendors, software tools, etc. Send off an email to your friend who works at that furniture company who does their weekly newsletter. Call your classmate from school who was profiled as a web marketing genius in the alumni magazine last month. The Web is a tool, a great one — but not the only one. And sometimes, not even "the best" or fastest.

-- Jennifer Kaplan is CEO of JKreative Solutions, Inc., a global consultancy that offers strategy, marketing and development services for business, education, government and non-profits. Her email address is `Jennifer@JKreative.com`. She has no personal stake in AltaVista.

A five-minute challenge at the beginning of a research assignment is one of the smartest time investments you can make. It is a chance to quickly get a lot of information and thoughtfully construct a plan for moving forward to better use your time and resources. It can help you immediately identify any risks, opportunities, ideas you need to consider, and also help you learn about potential competitors and customers in the field.

Rather than wonder aimlessly, this can give you the structure you need to save time as you move forward in your research.

Chapter 14

Privacy & Protection

Privacy discussions tend to be emotional ones. Who wants others to know what you paid for your house? But, we all want to know what our neighbors paid for theirs. You want to be able to check a potential caregiver's criminal history, yet you wouldn't want others checking on yours. It's an information age, and information *is* a double-edged sword.

Do you have any rights to privacy online? A few, and even those are narrowly defined. You should assume you have no privacy online whatsoever. It's wise to presume that any of your communications can be copied and posted throughout cyberspace without your knowledge or consent.

Most of this chapter is U.S.-focused. But, about fifty countries have enacted or are in the process of establishing privacy laws and specific data protection laws. About forty countries have enacted a legal right of access to government records through a Freedom of Information Act or Codes of Access.

More on that later in this chapter.

Online Interactions: A Reality Check

Web Browsing

As mentioned in Chapter 1, when you journey on the Web, you leave imprints all over cyberspace that identify you, your ISP, the sites you've visited and your movements within each web site. Some web browsers are programmed to transmit your email address to every web site you visit. Also, your browser's cache file is an ongoing record of everything you've viewed and read. Therefore, you should assume that everything you've sent or viewed can be accessed by someone somewhere out there.

The other half of the process occurs at the web site itself, which notes who you are and what you did at the site. Some sites make their logs available to anyone who wants access.

Internet Service Providers (ISPs)

Assume that all information you provide your ISP, other than your password, can and probably will be sold. That information includes online member profiles, directories, and preferences.

There have been some troubling incidents regarding ISPs and their self-perceived roles as information carriers. For example, an America Online subscriber posted her opinion about a Caribbean resort – which happened to be an unfavorable opinion – to an AOL bulletin board. The resort's lawyers demanded that AOL identify the woman to them. AOL complied. Needless to say, the resort is merely a private entity and posting an opinion isn't a crime – at least not yet.

So, if online providers will release names to anyone who asks, then how safe is your information that passes through an ISP?

A few years ago AOL announced it would sell its subscribers' information, including telephone numbers, to marketers – only to hastily retract the announcement under a firestorm of public outrage.

AOL is not alone. These kinds of problems happen with ISPs all over the world. All have different rules and policies on privacy.

Gated Communities

Safeguards such as passwords and registration processes are no guarantee of privacy in any forum. Additionally, content from your postings may be copied, stolen, mangled, reposted or sold – without your knowledge or consent. As a result, unless a web site has an explicit privacy policy (read the fine print!), consider your name and email address to be public property.

Discussion Groups and Bulletin Boards

When you post to a discussion forum, millions can see that message. Chat groups in particular are notoriously permeable forums – for example, jokes are transmitted like lightning through the Internet. Posting too much personal/identifying information is a hidden danger. For example, a male accountant harassed a woman through vindictive postings and foul language on a bulletin board for escorts/prostitutes and customers. Her ISP and the board's ISP warned him to cease. He didn't. So she posted his name, address, job title, and company on the bulletin board and in accounting forums. Legal? You bet. Though the man assumed his communications were private (perhaps because of the nature of the bulletin board), not only was he wrong, but thousands of his professional colleagues now know how wrong he was. So do the zillions of other people who can access his postings – and hers – through Google Groups and other archives. Now you know one way law enforcement officials track predators and other Internet criminals.

Mailing Lists

As a subscriber, you may feel camaraderie with your fellow enthusiasts. Fellowship doesn't prevent contents from being lifted, changed and/or reposted. Some lists prohibit their contents from being quoted or attributed to the list or its members – but that doesn't prevent information from re-appearing elsewhere.

Usenet Newsgroups

Your Usenet postings are readable by anyone. All Usenet postings are indexed automatically by Google Groups and other sites. Internet lore is rich with stories of people who posted casually only to find their words returning to haunt them. For example, an innocent posting to an AIDS newsgroup (perhaps you had a question or were doing research) posts your email address where any one can read it – including life insurance companies, potential employers, and others.

Instant Messaging

Instant Messaging is supposed to be safe from privacy violations because the messages don't get recorded on a server somewhere. But that is already changing. So you need to start thinking that someone is watching over your shoulder, because chances are they will be soon enough. Unlike email, the brief IM remarks that pop up on computer screens are not kept on central servers. But that hasn't stopped companies from developing software that snags every message — including those unflattering to the boss. Instant Messaging is especially valuable to business because companies are very worried about controlling information leaks and discourage cyber-slacking.

Like email or web traffic, Instant Messages can be monitored by corporate network administrators – whether the messages are sent on your companies proprietary software or to friends using programs from America Online, Yahoo! or Microsoft.

So far, at least, privacy advocates say they know of no major incidents involving disciplinary action for IM abuse. But last year a Radicati Group survey found that just twenty percent of all instant messenger accounts belonged to business users. That number is expected to grow to fifty percent by the end of 2004. And a Jupiter Media Metrix study finds Instant Messaging in U.S. businesses more than doubled from 2.3 billion minutes in September, 2000 to 4.9 billion in September, 2001.

Where this has really taken off is in the financial services industry, where monitoring IM traffic is essential because federal regulators require that all communications with clients be kept for auditing. While the Securities and Exchange Commission has not mandated requiring saving Instant Messages, some companies, like Thomas Weisel Partners are doing it voluntarily.

They are using FaceTime's monitoring software, which runs on their company's internal network and records all IM traffic. FaceTime also works with electronic archiving systems from companies like SRA International and Zantaz. It must be installed within a corporate network in order to capture all traffic that originates or is received by users of that network.

Another company, Communicator Inc., has signed up eight large financial institutions for its HUB IM, which controls communications among customers and competitors with encryption and authentication by using a trusted third party. None of these messages are done using public systems like AOL. For more details, see FaceTime at `www.facetime.com/main.shtm` or `www.zantaz.com`.

Privacy and Email

Normally, email is considered private just as regular mail is considered private. But every country regulates privacy differently. In the United States, the Federal Electronic Privacy Act makes it illegal for anyone to read or disclose the contents of an electronic communication unless one of the two people involved in the email has complained to law enforcement authorities about harassment. There are three exceptions to email privacy – and they are big exceptions.

- In cases of suspected crime, law enforcement officials can obtain warrants that enable them to access your email. Similarly, an online service can access your email if it suspects attempted damage or harm, even if no crime has been committed (as in the case of stalkers and predators).

- Your ISP can disclose private emails if it has the sender's consent. Most providers obtain that consent during the mandatory sign-up process. It's all in the fine print.

- If your employer owns your computer and/or the email system through which the emails are sent, then the emails belong to the employer, *not* to you. Repeat: in this case, your mail is not your mail. Several lawsuits are contesting the notion of full employer access to its employees' email, but they're treading shaky ground because most companies don't have a "bill of privacy rights" for employees and there is no legal presumption of employee privacy. Even if there were, you probably signed away your rights when you signed your employment contract. Generally speaking, whatever you do at work belongs to your employer, not you – and that goes for web site activity too, because your time at work is assumed to belong to your employer. Feeling nervous? You may have a good reason.

Commercial providers like America Online and the Microsoft Network routinely record email messages that pass through their networks. AOL and Microsoft say that when requested, they cooperate with law enforcement entities in criminal investigations involving stalkers, pedophiles, kidnappers and others. They say that when they are served with a warrant, they turn over information to law enforcement entities. The same applies to many of the large ISP companies.

The Ultimate Gold Mine: You

By now it should be clear that you are the answer to data miners' dreams and fortunes. Data miners, when in suits and ties, refer to the records of your online travels as "transaction-generated information." When they loosen their ties, they call them the "clickstream," and when they think you're not listening, they call them "mouse droppings." Whatever the name, the goal is to make an easy buck off your online navigational habits – actually, multiple bucks, since they can sell the information over and over again.

The Golden Trail of Cookie Crumbs

Here is how your data trail is generated:

When you visit a web site that is programmed to collect information about you, it creates a file about your browser called a "cookie." Cookies allow web sites to greet you personally ("Welcome back, Alan. It's been ten days since your last visit. If you're still interested in baseball, we have a special promotion just for you.") and furnish local weather, sports, and TV listings. Cookies enable companies to record your online activities every movement because they are placed on your computer's hard drive without your prior consent.

In reality, cookies are simply text files that are up to 255 characters long. They aren't software programs. They cannot scan your hard drive. Cookies from early versions of Netscape Navigator and JavaScript collected email addresses. Current versions don't. Future versions may.

In short, cookies are a convenience. They allow a site to remember your previously registered information, preferences and passwords. And they can facilitate interactivity. See a file on your hard drive called "`cookies.txt`" to look at what cookies have already been placed on your computer. Learn to delete this file regularly.

If you set your browser to warn you each time a web site tries to slip you a cookie, you'll be quite surprised at how often it happens in the course of a single online session.

➜ *hot tip:* Go to `www.geocities.com/SoHo/4535/cookie.html` for the **Great Cookie Taste Test. It will introduce you to many sites and the multitude of ways they use cookies.**

Get to Know Your Cache

When a browser retrieves a page you want to see, it stores the page on your disk. Go to the same page again ten minutes later, the program doesn't have to retrieve the page again because it can re-use the copy it already has stored. It actually retrieves the page from your cache (pronounced "cash"), which is the space your browser uses to store pages. The more space you tell your browser to use for its cache, the faster pages appear the next time you look at them. Google has turned this into an asset – recording a copy of every site it finds and then indexes them and offers you a chance to see the cached version if you can't get to the more current one. Where this is extremely helpful is finding notorious or important pages that are no longer live on the Web. But for individuals, there is a downside – places you don't want people to know you have visited – like porn sites – can remain in your cache until you clear them out. If you want to see what your child was looking at online while you were out, your cache is the place to find it.

> **➔ *hot tip:*** **Be aware that for your privacy, you want to clear your cache, or others who look at your computer can see where you have been.**

You can find details about the cache in Netscape Navigator under "Edit," "Preferences, Privacy & Security," or clicking on "Tasks, Privacy & Security" or "Edit," then "Options," then "Preferences," depending which version you use. For Microsoft Internet Explorer, you can find it under "View, Internet Options" and look at what's in the temporary files. More about disabling cookies and cache below.

In Netscape, you can also use the "Window/History" option from the pull down menu to track which sites you've already visited. You also want to delete sites from your history file that may prove embarrassing. Double click on any you want to visit again. Also, the "home" button on the top of the browser will take you back to the opening page, the home page.

Under most Windows operating systems, you can manually locate your cache, cookies and history files in the Temporary Internet Files subdirectory of your Windows directory (C:\Windows\Temporary Internet Files). The files contained in Temporary Internet Files include cookies and downloaded items necessary to view the pages visited on your computer. Anything in this subdirectory may be deleted in order to protect your privacy. Also, there can be multiple cache files, so you may want to go to "Find" in the Start Menu, then search on "cache." You definitely want to learn how to delete these and also to check out what information gets saved there after you have been online. By the way, Mac users will find the same menu options in IE and Netscape.

Major Privacy Threats

Essentially, federal privacy laws protect only certain types of records with personal information. Here are some examples:

- Your credit report can be released only to people you've authorized (as well as to banks, law enforcement people and some others).

- The American Disabilities Act (ADA) protects the release of personal information found in workers' compensation records.

- The Driver's Privacy Protection Act (DPPA) forbids access to personal information in motor vehicle records unless the need for request falls under one of the fourteen listed permissible uses.

- Your video rental records are protected – as a result of background checks of certain Washington politicians and a Supreme Court nominee as to whether they had ever rented adult movies.

- Also, the law protects your cable TV viewing habits.

In general, your other personal records are unprotected and undefended. Think about that. It means that you have no legal recourse even if you are able to prove abuse or misuse of your private information.

Identity Fraud: A Devastating Epidemic

Identity fraud artists use their victims' personal information to assume the victims' personas and rack up bills in their names. While no firm statistics are available, police, regulators, and privacy specialists say such crimes have become epidemic in recent years, with more than 500,000-700,000 incidents in the U.S. every year. And those numbers are growing.

How does this happen? Lots of ways, some that you can protect yourself from and others you can't. In the course of a typical day, you may write a check at the supermarket, charge tickets to a concert, rent a car, mail bills, and call home on your cell phone. You may not think much about it, but someone else may (see Don Ray's sidebar in Chapter 1).

The identity thief lives for your everyday transaction. The key is your personal information — your bank and credit card account numbers; your income; your Social Security Number, and your name, address and phone numbers.

These people procure some piece of your personal information and get it without your knowing it. Then they open a credit card with your name on it, change the mailing address on your credit card account, and run up the charges. Because your bills are now being sent to the new address, you may not immediately realize there's a problem. They could establish cellular phone service in your name, open a bank account in your name and write bad checks on that account. Again, for a while, you won't see this credit card and when you don't pay the bill, the delinquent account is reported on *your* credit report.

Other ways they get information is to fish credit card slips and loan or credit applications from your trash or that of a local bank or restaurant – or it could be hacked from sales information on commercial computers or, conceivably, intercepted somewhere over the Internet.

Online, the problem is also continuing to mushroom as identity thieves have managed to purchase or procure Social Security Numbers from companies despite the 1997 adoption of a voluntary privacy policy by the major information companies (see the Individual Reference Services Group at www.irsg.org for more details). So far, however, it has been ineffective in dramatically restricting the sale of sensitive personal information to the general public. It has, however, made it more difficult to get the information.

For much more information on identity theft, see the FTC's special consumer web site at www.consumer.gov/idtheft.

➜ *hot tip:* **Documented identity fraud cases are collected and archived by the San Diego-based Privacy Rights Clearinghouse at `www.privacyrights.org`**

Medical Records: A Privacy Meltdown Waiting to Happen

Nowhere are the stakes as high as when it comes to that most intimate of data: your medical records.

Nearly all U.S. (and Canadian) medical records are compiled by the Medical Information Bureau (MIB) into a single database. An estimated 15 million Americans and Canadians are on file in a database compiled by more than 750 insurance companies. The MIB – `www.mib.com` – is a consortium of insurance companies that maintains millions of records taken from insurance applications, doctors and hospitals. When you apply for a health insurance policy, insurers dive into MIB's computers for information about pre-existing health conditions that might affect their decision to issue a policy to you.

Imagine that you have a non-communicable disease but find that, all of a sudden, your co-workers won't work with you any more. And they won't tell you why. Or that a rumor causes your health insurer to cancel your policy. Or that you're fired – or not hired – for a job you deserve because someone took an unauthorized peek at your medical history and blabbed. You'll probably never know the real reason you were blacklisted.

In an effort to protect your medical records in 2001, the Clinton Administration established the first-ever legal protections for certain kinds of health-related information. In 2002, the Bush Administration made changes to the regulations, easing mandatory consent requirements for doctors to disclose patients' medical information. Since their implementation, it is already clear that the rules will not guard the privacy of Internet users when they are doing the most common health actions on the Internet. The rules only apply to web sites that are run by health care providers such as a hospitals or doctor's offices; or a health insurance plans such as Aetna U.S. Healthcare or Kaiser Permanente; or a healthcare clearinghouses like WebMD that process health insurance claims information.

But a study by the Pew Internet & American Life Project found that the vast majority of health web sites are not operated by such firms. That means that there still are no federal protections for those who use them.

So if you choose to use web sites providing information about general fitness, nutrition, medical conditions, and treatment options, or those selling drugs without a prescription, then these rules do not apply. Also online mental health counseling sites that accept only credit card payments and pharmaceutical company web sites are not covered by the regulations. And, because many of the health sites are hybrid sites combining different aspects of health, one site may be covered, while another may not and the consumer is left to figure out which sites have to comply with the regulations and which don't.

If you think this isn't an important area with gaping holes, the Pew study also notes that 65 million Americans have gone online for health information. Outside the U.S., there are few if any privacy regulations about health sites. Around the world, many people probably assume that the personal information they provide to health web sites is covered by the new regulation – and they are wrong.

As Janlori Goldman, director of the Health Privacy Project (which carefully monitors health and privacy issues) at Georgetown University suggests, American consumers may be misled to think their privacy is being protected when they are online.

"People often believe they are invisible and anonymous online, but in reality they are exposing their most sensitive health information to web sites that are not required by law to protect the information or keep it confidential," Ms. Goldman says. "The potential for abuse is enormous."

There are *some* state laws that do protect individuals' medical records.

Many people who develop illnesses use the discussion groups, chat rooms, and web forums to find others who have the same illness as a support group or to find out useful information about how to treat or deal with the illness. But remember these are public bulletin boards. So there's no guarantee that information you disclose in any of these forums is confidential. The best way to protect yourself is to always use a pseudonym and a non name-specific email address and to avoid registering your real name on web sites.

Another important way to protect yourself is to only agree to release your medical records to known parties. The Privacy Rights Clearinghouse, for example, suggests that when you are asked to sign a waiver for the release of your medical records, try to limit the amount of information released. So instead of signing a "blanket waiver" authorizing doctors, hospitals, and other medical providers to release your medical history, treatment, and exam information, change their form and authorize it to be released from a specific hospital or clinic for a specific treatment related to a specific date.

For more information, see the Health Privacy Project's web site at:

    www.healthprivacy.org

For a list of state laws related to medical privacy, see:

    www.healthprivacy.org/info-url nocat2304/info-url nocat.htm

Children: Prime Targets for Data Miners

Kids under eighteen spend more than $80 billion a year and influence another $160 billion in parental purchases, according to Federal Trade Commission (FTC) statistics.

Children are exposed to all kinds of powerful advertising images when they watch TV and also on the Internet. Clever animated characters, toys that come to life, bright colors and loud voices all carefully packaged to lure kids to consumer products and to convince their parents to buy them these goods. On the Internet, advertisers are routinely asking children to register in order to visit their favorite cartoon character or enter a contest. For a few years, web sites have taken the information provided by the kids and had their favorite characters send them email pitches, further blurring the differences between fiction and reality.

In addition, some of these web sites have invisibly gathered information about where the child looks online, and tailored marketing messages based on that information. In the worst cases, children have been asked to provide detailed personal information about their parents, like what kind of car does your parent drive, to derive income possibilities for the merchandizing or marketing companies. In effect, they have used children as data gathering possibilities – often without their parents' knowledge or consent.

It's not surprising, then, that eighty-nine percent of children's web sites in an FTC study in 1998 admitted to collecting personal information from child visitors.[1] The same survey found that forty-six percent of the sites didn't disclose their information collection practices; and fewer than ten percent let parents control the data mining. That last finding is echoed by the Center for Media Education (CME), a non-profit children's advocacy group, which discovered that more than ninety percent of child-oriented web sites didn't consult parents about the data taken from their children. A subsequent FTC study had similar findings. Children are favorite targets for marketing information about their families. One of the favorite tricks has been to lure kids with "rewards" in order to have them fill out questionnaires for marketable personal data. After all, how many children can recognize and reject the temptation of a "prize" or "free membership?"

Collecting online information from a child is very different from the cereal box forms you may have filled out as a child because computerized data can easily be sold or transferred elsewhere.

Soliciting online information from a child is unconscionable, according to *Privacy Journal* editor Robert Ellis Smith, because we don't allow strangers to ask children in a school playground for their names, addresses, phone numbers and family demographics. Many such sites solicit detailed information from children, such as home address, household size, birth date, and favorite TV programs. The FTC found the questions too invasive and restricted data mining of children without parents' consent. However, the Children's Online Privacy Protection Rule, approved by the U.S. Congress in 1998, has not really had much affect so far. The rules governing that law were not approved until April, 2000. The regulations require children's oriented web sites – those that are directed to children under age thirteen – to post their privacy policy and obtain parental consent before collecting, using, or disclosing personal information about a child. So far, the FTC, with authority to crack down on abusers, has enacted just five enforcement actions against companies for violating the law which prohibits the collection of personal information from children on web sites without parental consent. And repeated studies show few people read the fine print portions of the privacy policies.

Realizing that there's little the U.S. government can do to protect children outside the U.S., the 2002 Congress approved the creation of a new Internet domain aimed at protecting children online, "`kids.us`." Unlike previous efforts, the bill focuses on creating the new space within "`.us`," the U.S. country-specific Internet domain. It requires restricting content within this domain to that which is suitable for kids under the age of thirteen.

Workplace Privacy

Employers love to keep tabs on their workers. Technology now makes it easy for companies to monitor employees every minute of the workday. Employers can read your email, view your personal computer files, eavesdrop on your phone calls and watch you on video camera. There

---

[1] "Children And Privacy," Federal Trade Commission, June 1998.

are no laws regulating electronic surveillance in the private sector workplace. There simply is nowhere to hide. Employers are deemed to have a legitimate interest in monitoring work to ensure efficiency and productivity – even though the surveillance often goes well beyond legitimate management concerns.

Digital technology lets supervisors monitor employees' web use, keystrokes, phone call lengths, and time spent away from the desk. Olivetti and Xerox have developed an "active badge" that tracks employee movements on company property. Software programs like Sequel's Net Access Manager by Sequel (www.sequeltech.com) and Secure Computing's Smart Filter new URL (www.securecomputing.com/index.cfm?skey=85) enable employers to unobtrusively monitor employees' online activities in detail – and block certain online activities.

It's no accident that electronic surveillance is on the rise. It's not illegal, and it's facilitated by technology advances. Court rulings have deemed workplace time and output to be an employer's property. Since there's no strong legislation that specifically addresses electronic privacy concerns, it's not surprising that the courts have overwhelmingly supported employers in cases of workplace monitoring.

In one notable case, an Epson America Inc. employee named Alana Shoars discovered her supervisor reading and printing out other employees' emails. She questioned the practice and said she was told to mind her own business. A day later, she was fired for insubordination.

Shoars filed a class-action suit claiming invasion of privacy under California's constitution and a wiretapping statute – and lost. The state court ruled that state law didn't cover email and that the state constitution didn't apply to business information. She also lost her wrongful termination lawsuit. Yet, California's privacy laws are considered the most progressive in the country.

You are probably being monitored without your even thinking about it. Employers can use computer software that enables them to see what is on your screen or what is stored in your computer terminal and hard drives. They can monitor Internet usage and email. People who work in data entry jobs can be subject to keystroke monitoring, which tells their supervisor how many keystrokes per hour each employee is performing or employers may keep track of how much time an employee spends away from the computer or how much time the computer is idle.

Do you have any rights as an employee? Some, but it is very limited. Since the employer owns the computer network and the terminals, he or she is free to use them to monitor employees. Workers are given some protection from computer and other forms of electronic monitoring under certain circumstances. Union contracts, for example, may limit the employer's right to monitor. Some government workers have rights guarding against unreasonable search and seizure and some states have added additional rights, like California.

Your Data vs. Industry Concerns

Who owns your personal data trail? Is that information public and usable for any purposes by anybody who can pick it up and read it – or does it belong to you? Sadly, nobody seems to be talking about this subject. Rather, the industry discussion starts from the premise that the information should be standardized, so that all industry participants have an equal chance to obtain it.

That standard would function as an identification card attached to your online presence as you journey through cyberspace. It would eliminate the need for you to sign in or register at various sites (also eliminating any inconsistencies in your identity). It would allow you to control site access to your profile, which would include your name, address, phone number, email address, interests, hobbies and sites visited and activities at those sites. The entire profile would be stored and encrypted on your computer's hard drive, where you could view and modify it. Each time a web site requests your personal data, you can evaluate the request and offer some, all, or none of your information. The standard was proposed and endorsed in mid-1997 by sixty-plus online companies, with the notable exception of Microsoft, which subsequently added its endorsement.

The next step will likely be a proposed implementation plan and then a formal request for approval. But that could take several more years.

So, how can you really protect yourself? What concrete steps and actions can you take to prevent privacy invasion? Carole Lane, who has testified on privacy issues before the Federal Trade Commission and the California State Legislature, offers some terrific tips.

Ten Tips for Protecting Your Privacy Online

By Carole A. Lane

First of all, don't let online paranoia keep you up nights or stop you from enjoying the rich and remarkable resources of the Internet. Contrary to all of the horror stories circulated since the popular emergence of the Internet, most crime isn't perpetrated online, and your chances of becoming a crime victim are still greater offline. Although there's very little privacy left in life, these simple precautions will help to limit the risk factors that could put your in harm's way, as well as to defend what privacy you do have:

1. Protect Your Computer

Anyone with access to your computer can obtain information about you, read your documents, find out what you do online. They can read your cookies or cache), and otherwise compromise your security. Don't store your best-kept secrets on your PC. Delete and erase sensitive documents, cookies and cache files. (Sending them to your PC's trash file is not enough; delete them from there as well.) Change the passwords in the BIOS setup program of your PC and in Windows for added security, or consider purchasing one of the many security software packages available on the market.

2. Keep Your Private Life Away from the Workplace

Your employer has the right to monitor all of your online transactions, to intercept your email, read your files, and even to remove your PC altogether. If you don't want your boss to know that you're looking for a new job online, or checking out the latest porn sites during your coffee break, don't do it from work.

3. Carefully Select and Protect Your Passwords

Anyone having access to your passwords could pretend to be you online (a practice called "spoofing"), order products or services in your name, or invite the unwanted attention of others. Change your passwords often, and don't leave them on or near your computer. Don't select passwords that could be guessed by someone who knows you, and don't use the same password on more than one site. Combinations of eight or more alphabetic and numeric characters are your best bet when selecting a password.

4. Don't Tell Secrets

Much personal information gathered by companies is collected from warranty cards, "free" product offers, surveys, and other data that you may readily volunteer. Online, information about you is gathered when you sign up for services, select your preferences, sign guest books, register as a user of a site, or reveal your interests. If you don't want your personal information to be shared with the world, stop filling out surveys, stop giving your unlisted number to strangers, and stop filling in all of the blanks for marketers. Whether online or off, when sensitive information is requested (such as your Social Security Number, mother's maiden name, medical history, etc.) find out why it's needed and how it will be protected before you give it away. Assume that all of your personal information will be sold and resold by anyone who requests it, unless they tell you otherwise. Even then, there's no guarantee that it won't be sold later, so be cautious with whatever you consider private.

5. Find Your Own Records

Some information about you is probably already available online, even if you've never searched the Internet. Search all the online phone books for your listing. Check the web sites of each organization that you belong to in order to find out if they list your name, address, telephone number, or anything else about you in their directories. Remember to include alumni, professional, and even hobbyist associations, company sites of your current and previous employers, and the directory of your Internet service provider in your search. Use several search engines to find out if you are mentioned elsewhere on the Internet. If having information about you displayed at these sites makes you uncomfortable, ask that it be removed. In most cases, web site owners will comply with your wishes. (This is not true of public records, DMV records, and some other types of records, however.)

6. Stop Chatting or Become Anonymous

When you express opinions or reveal anything about yourself online, there's no telling who's listening or sending your thoughts on to others. When you participate in online (Usenet) newsgroups, the information is routinely archived and searchable for years to come. If you're determined to participate in newsgroups, an anonymous remailer can be used to strip the identifying information from your messages and send them on to the newsgroup, or even to an individual. A list of reliable anonymous remailers can be found at `www.epic.org/privacy/tools.html`. Another good anonymizer can be found at `www.gilc.org/speech/anonymous/remailer.html`

7. Stop the Archiving

You can request that one of the biggest archives, Google's Groups at `http://.groups.google.com` not archive your messages by following the steps at `http://services.google.com:8882/urlconsole/controller?cmd=reload&lastcmd=login`.

If you've already sent messages that you'd like to remove from Google Group's archive, follow the directions at `http://groups.google.com/googlegroups/help.html#9`.

8. Search Under Another Identity

If your Internet service provider allows you to set up more than one account, use one for correspondence with friends, family, business associates, and anyone else that you know and trust. NEVER search the Internet with that account or register it at web sites. Use another account for all Internet searching. NEVER give that email address to anyone, or connect it with your information in any way. Also, change your searching email address often, if possible. These steps will help to distance you from the data being gathered about you as you search, as well as keep your "real" email account mailbox free from spam email.

9. Hide Behind A Firewall

Even if you only have one email address, you can still search anonymously. A proxy server can be used to retrieve web pages and then pass them to you, serving as a firewall between you and the web site. If you access the Internet through a direct dial-up connection (rather than through a proxy server), Anonymizer at `www.anonymizer.com` can serve as your proxy server. Instructions for use are available at this site. (See J.J. Newby's firewall sidebar later in this chapter for more information on firewalls.)

10. For Added Email Privacy, Use Encryption Software

There are many types of encryption software available for use when sending private email, and some of these, such as PGP (Pretty Good Privacy) for Personal Privacy at `www.pgp.com` are available for a fee on the Internet, or may even be included with your current email software. If the information that you're sending is sensitive in nature, encrypt it before sending it.

-- Carole A. Lane is the author of *Naked In Cyberspace: How To Find Personal Information Online* (new edition July 2002, *Cyberage/Info Today*. Email Carole at `calane@technosearch.com`

More Ways to Protect Your Privacy

Visit Informational Resources

Visit the privacy demonstration project web site run by The Center for Democracy and Technology (www.cdt.org) a privacy advocacy group that monitors federal government activities. This excellent resource shows you what information your computer is giving away when you travel the Internet.

Visit the extensive resources of Junkbusters at www.junkbusters.com. Here you can have your browser checked, find form letters to end the flood of junk mail, read reports about the privacy wars, and so forth.

Visit the Privacy Rights Clearinghouse at www.privacyrights.org, another privacy advocacy group mentioned earlier, which offers excellent fact sheets on how to protect yourself. Other good privacy advocacy sites are the Electronic Frontier Foundation (www.eff.org) and the Electronic Privacy Information Center (www.epic.org).

Deep Clean Your Computer

Delete your email messages after you've read them from your computer and from the central server. This isn't a foolproof method, but it makes it harder for others to read your mail, for the time being.

Clean out your computer's hard drive. Password-protected files and deleted material can be recovered.

Clean your computer's cache through your browser's preferences. Purging your cache will delete the record of your online travels. It will also slim down and speed up your browser. While many computers work differently, for the most part, the way to clear your cache is to click on your browser's "Preferences" button – sometimes found under options and properties – then delete all files listed as "Temporary Internet Files." You also want to delete the "History" button on the browser.

Disable Your Cookies

You can search your hard drive for a file with the word "cookie" in it (cookies.txt) to view the cookies that have been attached to your computer. You will almost certainly be surprised to see how many show up on your hard drive. Most newer browsers allow you to recognize sites that send you cookies and reject them outright by accessing the "Advanced" screen of the "Preferences" menu.

Here are some instructions on how to delete cookies in several browsers. Most of them work the same way — for the most part, however, you need to go to the "Tools," "Internet Options" and delete cookies by clicking on the "delete files" button in the Tools area.

- If you're using a Netscape Navigator 3.x Browser, look in the "Options" menu for "Network Preferences," then "Protocols." Then click "Show an Alert before Accepting a Cookie." Then save your option settings.

- In Netscape Navigator 4.0 or higher, go to "Edit," then "Preferences," then "Advanced;" click on "Never Accept Cookies" or "Warn Me Before Accepting a Cookie." Some versions offer the option of accepting only cookies that are stored in the original server.

- If you're using a Microsoft Internet Explorer (IE) 3.0, look under "View," then "Options," then "Advanced," then check the box "Warn Before Accepting Cookies."

- In IE 4.0, go to "Edit/Preferences/Cookies/Never Accept" or "View Internet Options/Advanced/Security/Cookies/Disable all cookie use." You can also right-click IE Shortcut/Properties/Advanced/Cookies and then Options."

- In IE 5.0, go to your control panel, double click on "Internet Options," click on the "security" tab, click on "custom level." In the "cookies" section, select "Disable" or "Enable" then click OK. Then click yes and click OK to close the Internet properties window.

- To enable/disable cookies for Internet Explorer version 6 and up, click on "Settings," then "Control Panel," then double click on "Internet Options." Click the "privacy" tab and then click "Advanced." Next, click "Override Default Settings" and then specify how you want Internet Explorer to handle cookies for the different kinds of web sites.

- America Online does things a little differently, even though they own Netscape. You want to make sure you clear your cache or temporary files and delete your history.

- For AOL Versions 4.0 and 5.0, from the "My AOL Menu," click "Preferences." In that window, click "Toolbar" and then clear the history trail immediately by clicking "clear history now."

- For AOL Version 6.0 and 7.0, start at the "Settings" menu and click "Preferences," then go to the "Organization" column, and click "Toolbar and Sound." To clear the history trail immediately, click "Clear History Now."

- For AOL, you also want to delete your cookies, by going to "Settings," then click "Control Panel." Next, double click on "Internet Options." In the temporary Internet files area, click on "delete cookies" in the latest versions. In some versions, you need to go to the "Temporary Internet Files" bar, click "edit" and then click "select all." On the file menu, click "delete." Then click "yes" to delete the cookies.

- With Web TV, there is no way to block cookies.

If you use an early version of any of the above-mentioned browsers, upgrade. They are not secure.

Use Anonymizers and Encryption

There are dozens of encryption programs that can help you control who reads your messages when you send email or files. A great place to start is at `www.cnet.com` or at `www.shareware.com` and use the keywords encryption or anonymizer.

You can rid unwanted files so they can't be recovered by using Mutilate File Wiper, another shareware program downloadable from `www.cnet.com`. The program offers three defined security levels and a customizable level and includes an uninstall utility.

Buy one of the many memory protection programs designed to prevent unauthorized access to your home computer. They encrypt each directory with a different password that requires log-in from the user. Some include "audit trails" that record all activity on your computer's drives.

Become anonymous. Lists of more anonymous remailer sites, in addition to the one mentioned by Carole Lane on the previous page, can also be found at `http://dir.yahoo.com/Computers and Internet/Security and Encryption/Anonymous Mailers/`.

Padlock Your ISP

Request your ISPs policies about subscriber information. Inform it that you don't want your data sold, exchanged or given away. Request removal from your ISPs online directory, and check the fine print on its registration contract.

See Yourself as Others See You

Stalk yourself. Find out everything you can about yourself on the assumption that whatever you can discover, others can, too. Try every online tool you can. Then visit the courthouse and see what public records may eventually end up online. Again, you could be surprised at what public records are on file about you and members of your family.

Are you being fingered? Fingering is an old way of looking up someone's email address on the Internet. Fingering a user on the internet displays the last time the person logged in, and whether or not he or she has any mail to be read. There also may be special information displayed if the user has set up a Plan file. You need Finger Client (software) to use this feature of the Internet. This is not well-supported today.

To learn more, visit `www.emailman.com/finger`.

Check online web sites of conferences, trade shows, exhibitions and other events in which you participate. Sometimes event organizers will post information about you derived from registration forms without your knowledge – including home addresses and phone numbers. If you are a speaker or presenter, the posted content of your presentation may include personal information, as well.

End Marketing/Telemarketing

Request removal from marketing and telemarketing lists. The Direct Marketing Association lets consumers remove themselves from junk mail and telemarketers' lists. Contact DMA at www.the-dma.org.

Notify the three credit bureaus that you want no more pre-approved offers of credit. You can also request a copy of your credit report for $8.00 from any of the three. Their numbers:

- Equifax, 1-800-685-1111

- Experian, 1-800-682-7654

- Trans Union, 1-800-888-4213

Order a free copy of your Personal Earnings and Benefits Estimate Statement (PEBES) from the Social Security Administration once every three years or so. Make sure your earnings are accurately recorded and that no one else is using your Social Security Number. The SSA's toll-free number is 1-800-772-1213.

How to Stop Giving Out Your Personal Information

Give out your Social Security Number only when it's required (for banking/stock/real estate transactions). Don't carry the card itself in your wallet, don't list the number on business cards or checks, and don't give the number to merchandisers.

Government agencies that require your SSN must state in writing if the number is required or optional and how it will be used. Make private businesses do the same.

Don't participate in informal health screenings offered at pharmacies and shopping malls. They collect information that is sold to businesses that will solicit you to buy medications and related products.

Don't email or post confidential and/or personal information.

Read and Watch for Privacy Policies

An increasing number of web sites – especially commercial ones trying to sell things to you — have started to providing privacy policies that detail the sites' information practices. Be wary of sites that do not have them and are trying to conduct a transaction with you. They will give you some guidelines and can also serve as one indication of responsibility.

Make Sure Online Forms Are Secure

Online forms may be sent online in ways that can leave them and your information vulnerable. Most businesses use encrypted forms so that only the intended recipients can readily translate the information. Most browsers use graphic signs to determine if the page is insecure or locked. The graphic usually appears in the corner of the browser screen, and clicking on the lock or the key will inform you of additional security information about the page. Do not put sensitive personal information like your bank account numbers, credit card information, medical or personal financial information on pages that are not secure.

The State of the Law

Definitions of privacy vary widely around the globe. In many countries, the concept has been fused with data protection, which interprets privacy in terms of management of personal information. In some countries, however, privacy means human rights and how far the government can intrude into someone's personal life.

Two aspects of privacy – the rules governing the collection and handling of personal data like credit information, medical, and government records and the privacy of communication, including voice, email and use of the Internet are where there has been a great proliferation of activity around the world in the past few years.

In the European Union and Canada, there are comprehensive laws restricting how information is collected used and disseminated both by the government and the private sector. Australia was also considering adding a similar law. In Japan, Singapore and a few other countries, the emphasis has been on self-regulation by the agencies, while in the United States, there is a piece-by-piece approach, with laws covering children, some financial privacy, and some medical privacy, but no comprehensive statutes.

In 1995 and 1997, the European Union enacted two directives to ensure equal protection of all European citizens and to allow the free flow of personal information throughout those countries. These laws included the right to know where the data originated, the right to have inaccurate data rectified, a right of recourse in the event of unlawful processing, and the right to withhold permission to use data in some circumstances, like to opt-out of receiving direct marketing material. The European data law is especially aggressive in protecting the use of data about individuals.

In addition, the E.U. has been very aggressive in dealing with countries that refuse to adopt meaningful privacy laws themselves. The Europeans have also developed laws that restrict the transfer of data to countries that don't have similar privacy initiatives.

This requirement has put pressure on countries outside Europe to approve strong data privacy laws, or face not being able to conduct certain types of transactions with European businesses.

It has also caused anxiety for the United States, which has approved some industry-specific and self-regulatory privacy laws, but ones the Europeans questioned if they were strong enough.

The E.U.'s Directive on Data Protection bars the transfer of personal information from E.U. countries to the U.S. and other countries whose privacy regulation is deemed insufficient. To be able to deal with the lack of privacy laws in the United States, the E.U. commissioned a study, which pointed out many gaps in U.S. privacy protection. The U.S. then lobbied the Europeans and eventually an agreement to keep trade open was worked out in 2000. But it is subject to review and the E.U. promised to make sure that remedies are available to European citizens if any problems arise.

In the United States, there are still few federal laws that protect the online release of your medical records, phone logs, phone numbers, or your bank account numbers, The U.S. government's first broad effort to protect privacy on the Internet was approved late in 1998 with President Clinton signing the Children's Online Protection Act. That law prohibits web sites from collecting personal information from children without their parents' permission. But, aside from protecting children, there have been few successful efforts to protect the online consumer. While lawmakers have threatened to enact legislation to protect the consumer, in some cases they've simply passed on the power to legislate to the states.

Nonetheless, "E-tailing" or collecting information about consumers without their knowledge is rampant. Recent studies show that about eighty percent of all web sites use some form of information-gathering technique to track customers' purchases, likes and dislikes. Already this is a $3 billion industry, and it's growing dramatically. Companies that gather this kind of information have responded by offering to explain to consumers exactly what is being collected, and how they can opt-out of having their information shared. Lawmakers stress this does not go far enough. Since the early 1990s, lawmakers have continued to introduce bills designed to protect consumers and never seem to get the votes to pass them. So the best protection, of course, is to know what's being done to you and what you can do to protect yourself.

The only major legislation approved by the U.S. Congress in the past few years were amendments to the 1999 financial services bill, giving states the power to block banks, insurance companies, and securities industries right to share customer information with few restrictions. Since that time, there have been many legal challenges and state battles over the issues, but no clear trends yet.

Overall, the financial services bill makes it easier for companies to merge and share information about their accounts, transactions, stockholdings and so forth, without getting permission from individuals. In some cases, banks also would be able to give information to telemarketers as long as the marketers agree not to pass it along. Companies claim they would use such data, along with sophisticated computer systems, to create and market new consumer products and services.

Attorney Generals in twenty states, led by Minnesota, California, Washington and New York, have tried to trump the federal law and restrict the use of private information by financial firms. Privacy rights fights at the state and federal level are like an explosive brush fire, as an unusual coalition of civil liberties activists, social conservatives and Internet libertarians are making the issue a cause celebré by pressing for restrictions on personal data that is routinely swept up by computers. Fallout from the financial services fight could prompt much stronger action at the federal and state levels. During the congressional debate over the financial services bill, advocates seemed to persuade Democrats and a handful of Republicans to weigh-in for consumers' rights to stop the sharing of names, Social Security Numbers, account transactions and other details, but a fierce lobbying effort by banking, insurance and other industry officials temporarily fended off the strongest efforts for federal restrictions.

How long the freedom to use and abuse consumer information holds is anyone's guess. Already Europe is far ahead. The European Union (E.U.) views U.S. privacy laws as woefully inadequate.

One United States law approved in 1998 bars the transfer and/or use of someone's personal information if it is used to commit a crime. Penalties have been ratcheted up to twenty years in prison, and payment of restitution to the victim. Also, there are legal limits on the collection and transfer of personal data by U.S. government agencies. Citizens can sue agencies that violate those laws. For example, federal employees and agencies cannot perform a background check using someone's Social Security Number, credit history or other information without a legitimate work-related reason. While existing federal law also limits access to credit information to only those with legitimate need, such as banks and insurance companies, the law has been extended to include online use of personal information.

On the medical privacy front, the best privacy advocates have been able to do is get the White House to issue regulations that say patients must be notified if their electronic records are shared for reasons other than medical treatment or payment – the primary other reason being marketing. And patients must be allowed to see their medical records and correct errors.

Congress has also approved legislation on driver privacy, tightening rules limiting the disclosure by states of drivers' license information. Under the new law, states accepting federal transportation funds must obtain the expressed consent of a driver ("opt-in") before disclosing the person's photograph, Social Security Number, and medical or disability information for any purpose (with a few narrow exceptions); as well as the names of those requesting the information.

This battle will continue to rage in the near future.

For additional resources on international privacy laws, see: `www.privacyinternational.org/survey/`.

Some Perspectives on the Larger Debate

Do you have any rights related to how any released information will be used and disseminated? The absence of documented privacy policies by web sites and online entities represents a noticeable void on the Internet. Despite efforts by a non-profit, privacy rights organization called eTRUST, documented privacy policies continue to remain overwhelmingly absent on the Internet. Users beware. Your privacy concerns aren't a priority. There is no rule of thumb, no international information treaty, no United Nations commission on privacy. The technology and its capability to gather information has seriously outstripped any policies to protect you. Lawmakers around the world are only now starting to mull privacy policies to control the sale or barter of personal information online.

Meanwhile, the potential for abuse looms increasingly large. Nobody knows exactly who has access, or exactly what information can be accessed. Occasionally, bits of information do fall into public view, leaving everyone to wonder at the ramifications. For example, in the fall of 1996, Great Universal Stores, a U.K. company that owns Burberry Raincoats, bought the credit reporting agency Experian and with it, the credit reports of a 190 million Americans. Great Universal Stores now owns the financial profiles of 708 million people in forty countries and is, presumably, selling and reselling the data. But also, it is now a company that owns stores, does marketing and owns personal consumer data, including credit histories and other personal financial information. Surely the company must be tempted to use the confidential personal data to support its other operations. And even if not, surely the possibility exists for abuse of the confidential personal information.

Like the Great Universal Stores situation, the recent merger of advertiser Double Click and offline catalog tracking company Abacus Direct Corp. has privacy advocates extremely worried about potential information sharing abuses. The two companies combined would bring together online profiles obtained from an estimated 850 million Internet advertisements per day, and 88 million personally identifiable five-year catalog purchase histories. This, privacy advocates warn, would give advertisers unfair advantages in the marketing of products, impacting consumer decision making.

The centralization of information continues as data-holding companies buy smaller companies and the industry consolidates. The trend can only mean that personal information will become easier than ever to search and obtain. Your privacy – and expectations of privacy – will continue to shrink. Being aware of what is happening to you and how to use the technology remains your best weapon.

I Have Anti-Virus Software, Do I Need a Firewall Too?

By J.J. Newby

Imagine reading a news story about a family who was the victim of a burglary with this scenario: The thieves came into the house, read all the family's mail, rifled through their financial records, stole their identification, burned some of the family's files and even family photos in the fireplace, and then re-arranged the furniture. As a final act of deviance, they used the family's phone to place orders for merchandise, paid for by credit cards stolen from yet another house.

"How awful for them," you might think. But then your sympathy wanes a little when you find out the family regularly left the doors unlocked, and even open, despite warnings that this could result in such a crime.

Sounds unlikely? Well, yes, it is – but you may be doing practically the same thing every day by logging onto the Internet without a personal firewall. It's almost as if you are flinging your house doors wide open, just tempting someone to come in and wreak havoc – including reading your email and other files on your hard drive, stealing important bits of information to "lift" your identity and make it their own, destroying valuable files and rearranging hard drives. Most of us protect ourselves against viruses, but anti-virus software does not protect against hackers – people who connect directly to our computers and rummage around looking for information or just looking for trouble.

As our connections to the Internet have gotten faster and more sophisticated, we're leaving our computers connected for longer periods of time, which makes them even more susceptible to people looking either to copy information off our hard drives, or to use our computers as a starting point to launch attacks against other computers, disguising their identity by making it look like *you* are the person trying to break into another machine or commit other illegal acts.

If you think no one is interested in your computer, think again. A group of security experts launched a server with no business function, no links, no address, no advertisement, basically no reason to attract attention. It was compromised by hackers within fifteen minutes. That's just like having a house spring up in the middle of nowhere overnight and be burglarized within fifteen minutes.

The attacked server was part of Project Honeynet (`http://project.honeynet.org`), which launches "honeypots" — or different anonymous web servers — and studies the activities of "blackhat" or nefarious hackers (as opposed to "whitehat" hackers — security experts replicating hacking techniques to proactively find holes in a system). On an average day, Project Honeynet's systems have twenty or more unique scans a day, which means twenty or more attempts by a person or a piece of code to find a way to get past a computer's security system (`http://project.honeynet.org/speaking/know-your-enemy-1.3.zip`). What this means is that your computer doesn't have to be considered a particularly attractive target — *just by merely existing*, your computer can be found, broken into, and defaced or used for other bad acts any day, any hour.

Just as you would install and use deadbolts on your doors and even security alarms on your house, you should install a firewall on your system. A firewall can be a physical hardware device or a software program that monitors the information going in and out of your computer – carefully checking to see if the activity looks normal or suspicious. If it looks like activity or network traffic is suspicious, it can block that activity. This helps keep hackers from breaking into a computer and stealing or destroying information on it, or using it as a jumping off point to attack other computers.

A firewall is configured with certain rules and filters that it applies to every packet (see the Basics chapter for more information about packets) that it sees go by coming in from or going out to the Internet. For example, the act of opening a file on your computer is called an "access request." A firewall rule may restrict the number of access requests your computer can accept or the sections of the hard drive that may be accessed. If a packet meets certain rules, then it passes through unchanged. However, if it violates a rule then it is rejected outright and you may receive an alert via a pop-up window notifying you that something that shouldn't be allowed in is trying to get to computers on your network. Both the hardware and software types of firewalls come pre-configured with certain rules and filters that you can customize depending on your network needs and how much risk you're willing to take.

A hardware firewall is a device about the size of a small softcover book and is connected between the modem and the computer. It has two network connections and a small power cord. The advantage of the hardware firewall is that it allows you to configure a single firewall device once, yet protect all the computers connected to the same network equally. The disadvantages are that you are adding additional pieces of hardware onto your network that need to be maintained, you may need to run extra network cable, the device offers many more configurable options than are necessary for a small home network, it's more expensive than a software solution, and if you forget the administrative password you may have to send the device back to the manufacturer to get it reset. Manufacturers of hardware firewalls include: Linksys (www.linksys.com), Netgear (www.netgear.com), SMC (www.smc.com) and Cisco (www.cisco.com). Hardware firewalls cost between US$150- 500.

A software firewall functions just like a hardware firewall but only requires you to install a program on your computer. This is a good solution for smaller home networks, or networks that require different rules and filters for different individual computers. The cost is another advantage, since many software firewall programs are free or under US$75, low cost can be a deciding factor when deciding between hardware or software solutions. Other advantages include being able to easily uninstall and re-install the program as needed, and not having to add more cables and hardware to your existing system. The disadvantages are that as your network grows, you will need to configure each system individually, unlike a hardware firewall, which only requires configuration once. You can download software firewalls from the Internet or buy them from your local computer store. Free/shareware versions include BlackIce Defender (www.networkice.com), ZoneAlarm (www.zonelabs.com), Sygate (www.sybergen.com), and Tiny (www.tinysoftware.com). These versions may periodically post updates on the Internet that you can download and upgrade. You can also purchase Norton Personal Firewall (www.symantec.com/sabu/nis/npf) or ZoneAlarm Professional (www.zonelabs.com). Purchased versions will generally have a yearly subscription service that allows you to upgrade and patch as needed. Software firewalls cost between US$0 - $75 for home users.

Keep in mind that firewalls are just one part of your entire home security system. You will still need anti-virus software, the latest patches and upgrades for your operating system, and a regimen of protecting and changing your regularly-used passwords. In other words, just because you lock the front door, don't think the back door is secured too.

Firewalls are technical devices — and therefore to really understand them, you will need to delve a little deeper than I have here. A terrific collection of information regarding the different types of firewalls available, in addition to links to software download and vendor pages, is at Home PC Firewall Guide (www.firewallguide.com). If you are really interested in how hackers work, you may be interested in the book about Project Honeynet, *Know Your Enemy* by Project Honeynet. An interesting real life account of how hackers used university computers to hack into government computers is *The Cuckoo's Egg* by Clifford Stoll.

And remember, the hackers are out there, casing the Internet day and night, just looking for an unprotected computer with an "unlocked door" — make sure it's not yours!

-- J.J. Newby is a former television journalist and has spent the past seven years as a ghostwriter and consultant to Silicon Valley executives as well as a self-professed web addict. Email: jjnewby@aol.com.

Terrorism and Its Effects on Privacy

As far as privacy protections are concerned, the U.S. and perhaps the world changed on September 11, 2001.

In Europe and the Middle East, the fear of terrorism is something people have lived with for centuries. But in the United States, it is a new phenomenon with severe consequences to the rights of privacy.

Suddenly the issue was not whether the U.S. government should require U.S. companies to protect consumer privacy on the Internet, but instead whether the government would weaken privacy protections already in place in an effort to protect Americans from terrorism.

Before the Twin Towers came crashing down, political polls consistently showed Americans were worried about their privacy, and people were especially concerned about technology's ability to monitor your every move. Since the 9-11 attacks, sophisticated high-tech tools that were once considered too intrusive have become tolerable as part of the way of living. There's been a wholesale change of attitude about what level of personal privacy is acceptable. In the six months after 9-11, people who once fretted about their privacy suddenly were more willing to brush aside those qualms in exchange for a sense of safety.

The new reality in the United States is a shift from wired or wireless convenience to physical security – all in an effort to make Americans safer.

At major concerts, political or sporting events, video cameras capable of recognizing faces are being used to screen for terrorists. At the 2002 Super Bowl, the entire crowd was put through metal detectors, limits were imposed on what you things you could carry with you to your seat, and video cameras recorded and sent a photo identification of all individuals through a criminal database to identify known criminals and suspected terrorists. In many cities across the U.S., video surveillance cameras are being put up by local governments to monitor public streets.

At some U.S. airports, sophisticated X-ray devices that can "see" through a person's clothing to check for hidden weapons – are already being used. Video cameras have also been included on certain airplanes and outside airplane cockpit doors, And renewed efforts are being made in the U.S. Congress to establish a national identification card.

And money is also flowing to emerging technologies – everything from disposable surveillance cameras to systems that read brain waves for disturbing or unusual thought patterns.

Within a few months of 9-11, members of Congress approved some counter-terrorism measures which broaden the definition of terrorism and increases the penalties for it. Some of the more sweeping changes involve electronic surveillance. The act permits federal investigators to use more powerful tools to monitor phone calls, email messages, and even web searching and web usage. The new law, along with new surveillance tools, lets law enforcement create a dragnet wide enough that anyone's email note, text chat, or search inquiry might be recorded and used in a prosecution.

The Federal Bureau of Investigation has also stepped up their use of "Carnivore" and other internet surveillance technology, allowing them to record internet use, from emails to web searching to online chats.

The legislation approved by Congress also makes it easier for law enforcement to monitor an individuals phone calls, including cellular phone calls. In testimony on Capitol Hill, a Justice Department official told lawmakers that the law has also enabled police to obtain logs from Internet Service Providers.

So far, it is difficult to pin down the real implications of this new type of surveillance for your Internet privacy. That's because many of the laws key points have not been tested or challenged in court. For example, the law is also vague on many key points and understandably, law enforcement officials aren't eager to reveal details about tools like the controversial Internet surveillance system "DCS1000," more commonly recognized by its previous name, Carnivore. Unfortunately, no one really knows the details of how Carnivore works.

Under the new law, when an investigator wants to monitor email, no probable cause is needed and all kinds of information can be found about the person being investigated. In addition to the identify of the individual and the recipient's identity, they could also get details about the subject line and maybe even get the entire body of the message because the law does not clearly define what electronic content can be captured. The FBI's interpretation is to let the federal agent make the decision and take responsibility for getting rid of inadmissible information. So you can see where privacy rights could end up being trampled.

Surveillance, law enforcement officials say, will naturally focus on people about whom authorities have a solid basis for suspicion. So doing web searches on anthrax and terrorism and biological warfare will not be illegal. But, those searches, coupled with the purchase of the chemicals needed to develop such weapons, may cause law enforcement officials to show up unexpectedly at your door. There's no question that there is a reduction in a U.S. citizen's zone of privacy.

Political, legal, and technological changes in surveillance is outpacing discussion of its consequences.

And the effects – intended or unintended of this new technology are pushing some of the forward-thinking leaders of technology companies to call for a national identification card. Larry Ellison of Oracle Corp., the second-largest software company in the world and Scott McNealy of Sun Microsystems Inc., a maker of powerful computers that operate networks, argue that is necessary to protect individuals. "Absolute anonymity breeds absolute irresponsibility," McNealy said in October, 2001. "If you get on a plane, I want to know who you are. If you rent a cropduster, I want to know who you are."

While Ellison and McNealy believe a national ID card is a necessary protection, they also realize and acknowledge that it could generate considerable profits for their companies. Oracle and Sun could profit from the development of such an ID, which would be electronically linked to government databases. The irony is that their push comes from an industry that has steadfastly looked at governmental involvement with condescension.

Their view may reflect this post 9-11 changing view of the world. That shift is certainly reflected in some political polls. Some of the findings of a few polls are astonishing. A Zogby poll in December, 2001 found that fifty-four percent of Americans favored allowing telephone calls to be monitored in an attempt of protecting the country against terrorism, while eighty percent favor allowing video surveillance of public places.

These privacy changes are also being reflected in new and different attitudes toward using the Internet. A Harris-Teeter poll in February, 2002 found that fifty-seven percent of Americans believe Internet users should be willing to give up some privacy if it strengthens homeland security.

"We as a people are willing to trade a little less privacy for a little more security," Stewart Baker, former general counsel to the National Security Agency, the largest U.S. spy agency told the *Los Angeles Times* on February 19, 2002. "If using more intrusive technology is the only way to prevent horrible crimes, chances are that we'll decide to use the technology, then adjust our sense of what is private and what is not."

An example of the new reality of privacy is playing out in the subway system of San Francisco. In an effort to increase security, the Bay Area Rapid Transit (BART) commuter-rail system has upgraded its security, installing high tech cameras and monitors that can be rotated at a dispatcher's request. These images are then transmitted instantly via high speed fiber optic cable to BART police headquarters. With this new system, dispatchers can spot a criminal in the act, direct officers to the scene with precision and offer photos and detailed descriptions of the suspect –something they've never before been able to do.

But the potential of monitoring people without their express permission may also be cause for concern. George Orwell, author of the book *1984*, underestimated our enthusiasm for surveillance," said Baker, the former NSA counsel. "He correctly predicted that we'd have cameras everywhere. What he failed to imagine is that we'd want them so bad we'd pay for them."

The big question is whether all of this technology will really make us safer? Are you giving up personal privacy rights in exchange for a safer place to live or are you really getting that much more security. These questions will take some time to be determined. One thing is clear, however, the government, as a result of these new laws, could end up knowing a lot more about who you are, where you go, and what you do in the course of a day.

Additional Web Sites for Privacy and Protection

CDT - Internet Family Empowerment White Paper
www.cdt.org/speech/empower.html
A white paper on Internet Parental Empowerment Tools by the Center for Democracy and Technology.

CyberAngels.org Home Page
www.cyberangels.org
Safety and educational programming.

HNC Software Inc.
www.hncs.com
Fee-based site. Check fraud detection system software and other products.

KidsCom: Play Smart, Stay Safe & Have Fun!
www.kidscom.com
Children's resources and entertainment.

Lucent's Proxymate
www.proxymate.com
An anonymizer-style tool, for free, from Lucent Technologies.

MagusNet Public Proxy Server
http://proxy.magusnet.com/proxy.html
An anonymizer-style searching tool.

Privacy Times

www.privacytimes.com
Fee-based site. Privacy newsletter.

QSpace Inc

www.qspace.com
Fee-based site. An Oakland, CA company, allows you to fill out a form and within minutes you get your credit file on screen.

Rewebber

www.rewebber.de/
A Danish anonymizer - free.

Robert Brooks' Cookie Taste Test

www.geocities.com/SoHo/4535/cookie.html
Explanation of "cookies.".

Secure Computing's Smart Filter

www.securecomputing.com/index.cfm?skey=85
Smart Filter technology -- filtering tool.

Sequel's Net Access Manager by Sequel

www.sequeltech.com
Products that let you monitor internet usage, usually by employees.

Signature Finger FAQ launcher

www.best.com/~ii/internet/faqs/launchers/signature_finger_faq
Frequently Answered Questions about Signatures and Fingers.

Yahoo Finger Gateway

www.yahoo.com/computers_and_Internet/internet/World_Wide_Web/Gateways/Finger_Gateways
Yahoo links to Fingers gateways.

Indices

Private Online Sources of Public Records

Application Indices

Vender Profiles

Web Site Profiles

Contributors

Glossary

Page Index

Private Online Sources of U. S. Public Records

If you go to a search engine and search for "public records," you will find a myriad of sites offering access to public records. Many tout access to 10,000 databases and offer "national" searches. Most of these sites are legitimate, reputable vendors. However, the majority of sites you will find are usually intermediaries – companies that access records upon demand from either government agencies or from private enterprise, and then resell the data to the end user.

So, who are these private enterprise companies that have developed their own databases and how have they done this? Actually, there aren't that many – if you don't count all the direct marketing companies. BRB Publications classifies these firms into two categories:

- **Distributors** are automated public record firms who combine public sources of bulk data and/or online access to develop their own database product(s). Primary Distributors include companies that collect or buy public record information from its original source and reformat the information in some useful way. They tend to focus on one or a limited number of types of information, although a few firms have branched into multiple information categories.

- **Gateways** are companies that either compile data from or provide an automated gateway to Primary Distributors. Gateways thus provide "one-stop shopping" for multiple geographic areas and/or categories of information."

Companies can be both Primary Distributors and Gateways. For example, a number of online database companies are both primary distributors of corporate information and also gateways to real estate information from other Primary Distributors.

Distributors create their databases in one of two ways: they buy records in bulk from government agencies; or they send people to the government agencies and compile information using laptop computers or copy machines. This information can be sliced, diced and merged to create a powerful proprietary database for internal use or for resale purposes.

The pages that follow are profiles of nearly 200 of these distributor and gateway vendors. The profiles include product descriptions of their products, methods of distribution, and general statements regarding their capabilities. The profile will indicate if when a product is a *Database* or a *Gateway*. This list is not limited to only companies providing online access. You will find many media outlets, including CD-ROM, disk, tapes and microfiche.

Keep in mind many of these companies are sources and do not necessarily sell their products to casual or infrequent users. Typical clients include financial institutions, the legal industry, the insurance industry, and pre-employment screening firms among others. Regardless, people who use public records extensively will find these pages invaluable.

Application Indices

The first part of this section is a series of indices based on the "applications" or practical uses of the each company's services. Following these eighteen indices, there are full profiles of each company. The indices are:

Asset/Lien Searching/Verification

Background Info – Business

Background Info – Individuals

Collections

Competitive Intelligence

Direct Marketing

Employment Screening

Filing/Recording Documents

Fraud Prevention/Detection

Genealogical Research

General Business Information

Government Document Retrieval

Insurance Underwriting

Legal Compliance

Lending/Leasing

Locating People/Businesses

Litigation

Real Estate Transactions

If you find a company that may possibly fit you public record searching needs, call them or visit their web site.

For a more inclusive and updated list of online searchable gateways and distributors of public records, visit www.publicrecordsources.com.

Application Indices

Asset/Lien Searching/Verification

Access Louisiana Inc
ACS Inc
ARCountyData.com - Apprentice Information Systems
Attorneys Title Insurance Fund
Cal Info
Capitol Lien Records & Research Inc
ChoicePoint Inc
ChoicePoint, formerly CDB Infotek
Colorado Central Information System (CIS)
Commercial Information Systems Inc
CompactData Solutions
Confi-Chek
Conrad Grundlehner Inc
ConsumerInfo.com
Court PC of Connecticut
CourtExpress.com (RIS Legal Svcs)
CourtH.com
Courthouse Retrieval System Inc.
CourthouseDirect.com
Data Downlink xls.com
Datalink Services Inc
DataQuick
DCS Information Systems
Diligenz Inc
Dun & Bradstreet
eCCLIX - Software Management Inc.
Electronic Property Information Corp (EPIC)
First American Corporation, The
First American Real Estate Solutions East
First American Real Estate Solutions West
FlatRateInfo.com
GoverNet
Idealogic
IDM Corporation
Intercounty Clearance Corporation
Intranet Inc
KnowX
Law Bulletin Information Network
LEXIS-NEXIS
Logan Registration Service Inc
Merchants Security Exchange
Merlin Information Services
Motznik Computer Services Inc
National Service Information
Nebrask@ Online
NETR Real Estate Research and Information
Northwest Location Services
OPEN (Online Professional Electronic Network)

Pallorium Inc
Paragon Document Research, Inc.
Property Data Center Inc
Public Data Corporation
Publook Information Service
QuickInfo.net Information Services
Records Research Inc
Research Archives.com Legal Documents Library
Search Company of North Dakota LLC
Search Network Ltd
SKLD Information Services LLC
Southeastern Public Records Inc.
Superior Information Services LLC
Tenstar Business Services Group
The Search Company Inc
Thomson Financial
UCC Direct Services - AccuSearch Inc
Unisearch Inc
US Corporate Services
US Document Services Inc
US SEARCH.com
Westlaw Public Records

Background Info - Business

ADREM Profiles Inc
American Business Information
ARISTOTLE
Avantex Inc
Background Information Services Inc
BNA, Inc (Bureau of National Affairs)
Burrelles Information Services
Cal Info
CaseStream.com
CCH Washington Service Bureau
ChoicePoint, formerly CDB Infotek
CoCourts.com
Colorado Central Information System (CIS)
Companies Online - Lycos
Contemporary Information Corp.
Court PC of Connecticut
CourtExpress.com (RIS Legal Svcs)
CourthouseDirect.com
CourtLink
Criminal Information Services Inc
Daily Report, The
Data Downlink xls.com
Derwent Information
Dialog
Diligenz Inc
Discovering Montana
Dun & Bradstreet

eCCLIX - Software Management Inc.
EdVerify Inc
Electronic Property Information Corp (EPIC)
Experian Online
Fidelifacts
First American Real Estate Solutions West
Gale Group Inc, The
GoverNet
GuideStar
Hollingsworth Court Reporting Inc
Hoover's Inc
Idealogic
Information Network of Arkansas
Investigative & Background Solutions Inc
KnowX
KY Direct
Law Bulletin Information Network
LEXIS-NEXIS
LLC Reporter
Logan Registration Service Inc
Martindale-Hubbell
Merchants Security Exchange
Merlin Information Services
MidSouth Information Services
Motznik Computer Services Inc
National Credit Information Network NCI
National Service Information
Offshore Business News & Research
OPEN (Online Professional Electronic Network)
OSHA DATA
OSO Grande Technologies
Owens OnLine Inc
Paragon Document Research, Inc.
Public Data Corporation
Publook Information Service
Realty Data Corp
Records Research Inc
Research Archives.com Legal Documents Library
San Diego Daily Transcript/San Diego Source
SEAFAX Inc
Search Company of North Dakota LLC
Tax Analysts
Telebase
Tennessee Anytime
The Search Company Inc
Thomson & Thomson
Trademark Register, The
US Document Services Inc
US SEARCH.com
USADATA.com
Westlaw Public Records

Background Info - Individuals

Accurint
Accu-Source Inc.
ADP Screening and Selection Services
ADREM Profiles Inc
Agency Records
Alacourt.com
Ameridex Information Systems
ARCountyData.com - Apprentice Information Systems
AutoDataDirect, Inc
BiblioData
Cal Info
CaseStream.com
CCH Washington Service Bureau
ChoicePoint Inc
Circuit Express
CoCourts.com
Confi-Chek
Contemporary Information Corp.
Court PC of Connecticut
CourtExpress.com (RIS Legal Svcs)
CourtLink
Credentials Inc
Criminal Information Services Inc
Daily Report, The
Datalink Services Inc
Data-Trac Network Inc
Discovering Montana
eCCLIX - Software Management Inc.
Electronic Property Information Corp (EPIC)
E-Merges.com
Equifax Credit Services
Fidelifacts
First American Corporation, The
First American Real Estate Solutions West
Hogan Information Services
iDocket.com
Infocon Corporation
Information Inc
Informus Corporation
Innovative Enterprises Inc
Intellicorp Ltd
Interstate Data Corporation
Investigative & Background Solutions Inc
J B Data Research Co.
LEXIS-NEXIS
Logan Registration Service Inc
MDR/Minnesota Driving Records
Merchants Security Exchange
MidSouth Information Services
Military Information Enterprises Inc
National Background Data
National Credit Information Network NCI
National Student Clearinghouse
NC Recordsonline.com

NIB Ltd
Offshore Business News & Research
OneCreditSource.com
OPEN (Online Professional Electronic Network)
Owens OnLine Inc
Public Data Corporation
Rapsheets.com
Records Research Inc
Softech International Inc
Software Computer Group Inc
Tennessee Anytime
Texas Driving Record Express Service
The Official Providers Source
The Search Company Inc
Thomson & Thomson
tnrealestate.com KAL Software
US SEARCH.com
VitalChek Network

Collections

Accurint
Banko
Case Record Info Services
Commercial Information Systems Inc
CompactData Solutions
E-Merges.com
Equifax Credit Services
FlatRateInfo.com
Haines & Company Inc
Household Drivers Reports Inc (HDR Inc)
Informus Corporation
J B Data Research Co.
Merlin Information Services
National Background Data
National Credit Information Network NCI
Northwest Location Services
Owens OnLine Inc
Record Information Services Inc
Telebase
Trans Union

Competitive Intelligence

Accutrend Corporation
American Business Information
Aurigin Systems Inc.
BiblioData
BNA, Inc (Bureau of National Affairs)
Burrelles Information Services
CaseStream.com
CCH Washington Service Bureau
Confi-Chek
CountryWatch Inc.
Daily Report, The
Data Downlink xls.com
Derwent Information

Dialog
Experian Online
FOIA Group Inc
Gale Group Inc, The
Global Securities Information, Inc
GoverNet
Hoover's Inc
Intellicorp Ltd
KnowX
MicroPatent USA
Owens OnLine Inc
Plat System Services Inc
Public Record Research Library
Realty Data Corp
Research Archives.com Legal Documents Library
Telebase
Thomson & Thomson
US Corporate Services
USADATA.com
West Group

Direct Marketing

Accutrend Corporation
American Business Information
ARISTOTLE
Avantex Inc
Case Record Info Services
CompactData Solutions
Daily Report, The
DataQuick
E-Merges.com
First American Real Estate Solutions East
Haines & Company Inc
IDM Corporation
Intranet Inc
Kompass USA Inc
MDR/Minnesota Driving Records
Metro Market Trends Inc
Metronet
OSHA DATA
Property Data Center Inc
Record Information Services Inc
San Diego Daily Transcript/San Diego Source
SKLD Information Services LLC
Southeastern Public Records Inc.
Telebase
Thomson & Thomson
USADATA.com
Utah.gov

Employment Screening

Access Indiana Information Network
Accu-Source Inc.
ADP Screening and Selection Services
ADREM Profiles Inc
Agency Records
American Driving Records
AutoDataDirect, Inc
Avantex Inc
Background Information Services Inc
Campus Direct
CaseStream.com
ChoicePoint Inc
ChoicePoint, formerly DBT Online Inc
Circuit Express
Commercial Information Systems Inc
Conrad Grundlehner Inc
Contemporary Information Corp.
CourtExpress.com (RIS Legal Svcs)
CourtLink
Credentials Inc
Criminal Information Services Inc
Datalink Services Inc
Data-Trac Network Inc
DCS Information Systems
EdVerify Inc
E-Merges.com
Equifax Credit Services
Experian Information Solutions
Fidelifacts
Hogan Information Services
Hollingsworth Court Reporting Inc
iDocket.com
Industrial Foundation of America
Information Inc
Information Network of Arkansas
Information Network of Kansas
Informus Corporation
Innovative Enterprises Inc
Intellicorp Ltd
Investigative & Background Solutions Inc
IQ Data Systems
J B Data Research Co.
Landlord Protection Agency
Merchants Security Exchange
MidSouth Information Services
National Background Data
National Credit Information Network NCI
National Student Clearinghouse
NC Recordsonline.com
OneCreditSource.com
OPEN (Online Professional Electronic Network)
Owens OnLine Inc
Pallorium Inc
Rapsheets.com

Search Company of North Dakota LLC
Softech International Inc
Software Computer Group Inc
The Official Providers Source
TML Information Services Inc
US SEARCH.com
Verifacts Inc
Virginia Information Providers Network

Filing/Recording Documents

Access Indiana Information Network
Capitol Lien Records & Research Inc
CCH Washington Service Bureau
Colorado Central Information System (CIS)
CourtH.com
Daily Report, The
Diligenz Inc
Ernst Publishing Co, LLC
Fairchild Record Search Ltd
First American Real Estate Solutions East
Global Securities Information, Inc
Hollingsworth Court Reporting Inc
Idealogic
Intercounty Clearance Corporation
Law Bulletin Information Network
Metro Market Trends Inc
National Service Information
Nebrask@ Online
Paragon Document Research, Inc.
Plat System Services Inc
San Diego Daily Transcript/San Diego Source
Search Company of North Dakota LLC
Search Network Ltd
SKLD Information Services LLC
Tenstar Business Services Group
Trademark Register, The
UCC Direct Services - AccuSearch Inc
Unisearch Inc
US Corporate Services
US Document Services Inc
Utah.gov

Fraud Prevention/Detection

Cambridge Statistical Research Associates
Carfax
ChoicePoint, formerly CDB Infotek
ChoicePoint, formerly DBT Online Inc
Commercial Information Systems Inc
Conrad Grundlehner Inc
DCS Information Systems
FlatRateInfo.com
Household Drivers Reports Inc (HDR Inc)
IDM Corporation
Innovative Enterprises Inc
Investigators Anywhere Resource Line

IQ Data Systems
KY Direct
LEXIS-NEXIS
Merlin Information Services
Metronet
National Fraud Center
Offshore Business News & Research
QuickInfo.net Information Services
The Official Providers Source

Genealogical Research

Ameridex Information Systems
Ancestry
Cambridge Statistical Research Associates
Everton Publishers
Gale Group Inc, The
Infocon Corporation
Military Information Enterprises Inc
VitalChek Network

General Business Information

Accutrend Corporation
ACS Inc
American Business Information
Background Information Services Inc
Banko
ChoicePoint, formerly DBT Online Inc
CoCourts.com
Companies Online - Lycos
CountryWatch Inc.
Data Downlink xls.com
DCS Information Systems
Dialog
Discovering Montana
Dun & Bradstreet
Ernst Publishing Co, LLC
Experian Online
Fairchild Record Search Ltd
Gale Group Inc, The
GoverNet
Hollingsworth Court Reporting Inc
Hoover's Inc
Idealogic
Information Network of Arkansas
Information Network of Kansas
Interstate Data Corporation
Intranet Inc
Kompass USA Inc
KY Direct
LLC Reporter
MicroPatent USA
Nebrask@ Online
NIB Ltd
Offshore Business News & Research
OneCreditSource.com

Public Data Corporation
Public Record Research Library
Publook Information Service
Research Archives.com Legal Documents Library
San Diego Daily Transcript/San Diego Source
SEAFAX Inc
Tax Analysts
Telebase
Tennessee Anytime
Thomson Financial
Trans Union
Utah.gov
West Group

Government Document Retrieval

Access Indiana Information Network
ARISTOTLE
CaseClerk.com
CCH Washington Service Bureau
ChoicePoint, formerly DBT Online Inc
CoCourts.com
CourthouseDirect.com
Dialog
Diligenz Inc
Discovering Montana
eCCLIX - Software Management Inc.
Fairchild Record Search Ltd
FOIA Group Inc
Hollingsworth Court Reporting Inc
iDocket.com
Intercounty Clearance Corporation
KnowX
Loren Data Corp
Nebrask@ Online
OSHA DATA
Paragon Document Research, Inc.
Public Record Research Library
Publook Information Service
Software Computer Group Inc
Tennessee Anytime
The Search Company Inc
Thomas Legislative Information
Thomson Financial
UCC Direct Services - AccuSearch Inc
US Document Services Inc
Virginia Information Providers Network
West Group

Insurance Underwriting

A.M. Best Company
Access Indiana Information Network
Agency Records
American Driving Records

AutoDataDirect, Inc
ChoicePoint Inc
CompactData Solutions
Discovering Montana
Electronic Property Information Corp (EPIC)
Explore Information Services
Haines & Company Inc
Household Drivers Reports Inc (HDR Inc)
iiX (Insurance Information Exchange)
Information Inc
Information Network of Arkansas
Information Network of Kansas
MDR/Minnesota Driving Records
NC Recordsonline.com
Property Data Center Inc
Records Research Inc
Research Archives.com Legal Documents Library
Silver Plume
Softech International Inc
Tennessee Anytime
The Official Providers Source
TML Information Services Inc
Trans Union
Virginia Information Providers Network

Legal Compliance

Access Indiana Information Network
Access Louisiana Inc
Alacourt.com
ARISTOTLE
Aurigin Systems Inc.
Avantex Inc
Banko
Canadian Law Book Inc
CaseClerk.com
Colorado Central Information System (CIS)
CountryWatch Inc.
Derwent Information
Dialog
Ernst Publishing Co, LLC
First American Corporation, The
Global Securities Information, Inc
GoverNet
Information Network of Kansas
Innovative Enterprises Inc
Intercounty Clearance Corporation
Interstate Data Corporation
Investigators Anywhere Resource Line
KY Direct
LLC Reporter
MicroPatent USA
National Service Information
Nebrask@ Online
OSHA DATA
Public Data Corporation

Realty Data Corp
State Net
Superior Information Services LLC
Tax Analysts
Thomson & Thomson
Thomson Financial
UCC Direct Services - AccuSearch Inc
Unisearch Inc
US Document Services Inc
Utah.gov
West Group

Lending/Leasing

Agency Records
Banko
Capitol Lien Records & Research Inc
ChoicePoint, formerly CDB Infotek
Conrad Grundlehner Inc
ConsumerInfo.com
Contemporary Information Corp.
CourtH.com
DataQuick
Derwent Information
Equifax Credit Services
Ernst Publishing Co, LLC
Experian Information Solutions
Fairchild Record Search Ltd
First American Real Estate Solutions East
First American Real Estate Solutions West
Haines & Company Inc
Hogan Information Services
IDM Corporation
Information Network of Kansas
Intercounty Clearance Corporation
IQ Data Systems
Landlord Protection Agency
Law Bulletin Information Network
Metro Market Trends Inc
National Service Information
NETR Real Estate Research and Information
NIB Ltd
Property Data Center Inc
Publook Information Service
Rapsheets.com
Realty Data Corp
SEAFAX Inc
Search Network Ltd
Superior Information Services LLC
Tenstar Business Services Group
tnrealestate.com KAL Software
Trans Union
UCC Direct Services - AccuSearch Inc
Unisearch Inc
US Corporate Services
Westlaw Public Records

Litigation

Access Louisiana Inc
Accurint
ADREM Profiles Inc
Alacourt.com
BNA, Inc (Bureau of National Affairs)
Canadian Law Book Inc
Capitol Lien Records & Research Inc
CaseClerk.com
CaseStream.com
ChoicePoint Inc
ChoicePoint, formerly DBT Online Inc
CoCourts.com
Confi-Chek
Court PC of Connecticut
CourtExpress.com (RIS Legal Svcs)
CourthouseDirect.com
CourtLink
Diligenz Inc
Fidelifacts
FlatRateInfo.com
FOIA Group Inc
Global Securities Information, Inc
Household Drivers Reports Inc (HDR Inc)
Idealogic
iDocket.com
Infocon Corporation
Innovative Enterprises Inc
Interstate Data Corporation
Intranet Inc
Investigators Anywhere Resource Line
Juritas.com
Law Bulletin Information Network
MicroPatent USA
Motznik Computer Services Inc
Northwest Location Services
Offshore Business News & Research
OPEN (Online Professional Electronic Network)
OSHA DATA
Pallorium Inc
QuickInfo.net Information Services
Softech International Inc
Southeastern Public Records Inc.
Superior Information Services LLC
Tax Analysts
The Search Company Inc
Thomson Financial
Virginia Information Providers Network
Westlaw Public Records

Locating People/Businesses

Accurint
Accu-Source Inc.
American Business Information
Ameridex Information Systems
ARISTOTLE
Background Information Services Inc
Banko
Cambridge Statistical Research Associates
ChoicePoint, formerly CDB Infotek
Commercial Information Systems Inc
Confi-Chek
Court PC of Connecticut
CourtH.com
Data Downlink xls.com
DataQuick
DCS Information Systems
First American Corporation, The
FlatRateInfo.com
Haines & Company Inc
Hoover's Inc
Household Drivers Reports Inc (HDR Inc)
Information Inc
Informus Corporation
Intellicorp Ltd
Interstate Data Corporation
IQ Data Systems
KnowX
LEXIS-NEXIS
Merlin Information Services
Metronet
Military Information Enterprises Inc
Motznik Computer Services Inc
Northwest Location Services
OSO Grande Technologies
Pallorium Inc
Plat System Services Inc
Public Data Corporation
Public Record Research Library
QuickInfo.net Information Services
Rapsheets.com
Texas Driving Record Express Service
tnrealestate.com KAL Software
Trademark Register, The
US SEARCH.com
Utah.gov
Virginia Information Providers Network
Westlaw Public Records

Real Estate Transactions

Accu-Source Inc.
ACS Inc
ARCountyData.com - Apprentice Information Systems
Attorneys Title Insurance Fund
Capitol Lien Records & Research Inc
CompactData Solutions
ConsumerInfo.com
CourtH.com
Courthouse Retrieval System Inc.
CourthouseDirect.com
DataQuick
eCCLIX - Software Management Inc.
Electronic Property Information Corp (EPIC)
Environmental Data Resources, Inc. (EDR)
Ernst Publishing Co, LLC
Fairchild Record Search Ltd
First American Corporation, The
First American Real Estate Solutions East
First American Real Estate Solutions West
IDM Corporation
Infocon Corporation
Metro Market Trends Inc
Motznik Computer Services Inc
NETR Real Estate Research and Information
Paragon Document Research, Inc.
Plat System Services Inc
Property Data Center Inc
Realty Data Corp
Record Information Services Inc
San Diego Daily Transcript/San Diego Source
SKLD Information Services LLC
Southeastern Public Records Inc.
Tenstar Business Services Group
tnrealestate.com KAL Software
Trans Union
Unisearch Inc
US Corporate Services

Risk Management

Accurint
ADREM Profiles Inc
BiblioData
Carfax
CourtLink
Dun & Bradstreet
E-Merges.com
Environmental Data Resources, Inc. (EDR)
Hogan Information Services
Industrial Foundation of America
Infocon Corporation
Investigators Anywhere Resource Line
MDR/Minnesota Driving Records
National Background Data
National Fraud Center
Pallorium Inc
Public Record Research Library
Silver Plume
Software Computer Group Inc
The Official Providers Source

Vendor Profiles

555-1212.com

One Sarisome St, 39th Fl
San Francisco, Ca 94104
Fax: 415-288-2465
www.555-1212.com **Email:** support@555-1212.com
Clientele Restrictions: None reported
Products, Information Categories, Coverage Area
Proprietary Databases or Gateways:
Gateway Name: 555-1212.com
Addresses/Telephone Numbers (US)
Special Distribution Methods to Client: Internet

A powerful, free access, web site. Search the white pages,
yellow pages, phone reverse look-up, email reverse look-
up, and the web site finder. This site ranks among the top
1000 sites on the web, visit-wise.

A.M. Best Company

Ambest Rd
Oldwick, NJ 08858-9988
Fax: 908-439-3296
www.ambest.com **Email:** sales@ambest.com
Founded: 1899
Clientele Restrictions: Casual requesters permitted
Products, Information Categories, Coverage Area
Proprietary Databases or Gateways:
Database Name: Best Database Services
SEC/Other Financial (US)
Database Name: Best's Insight Global
Foreign Country Information (GB, Itl, Canada)
Special Distribution Methods to Client: CD-ROM,
Disk, Magnetic Tape, Software

A.M. Best Company, known worldwide as The Insurance
Information Source, was the first company to report on the
financial condition of insurance companies. A.M. Best
strives to perform a constructive and objective role in the
insurance industry toward the prevention and detection of
insurer solvency. The company's exclusive Best's Ratings
are the original and most recognized insurer financial
strength ratings. A.M. Best provides quantitative and
qualitative evaluations, and offers information through
more than 50 reference publications and services. Since its
inception a century ago, A.M. Best has provided financial
services to professionals with timely, accurate and
comprehensive insurance information. A.M. Best's London
office can be reached at 011-44-171-264-2260. A.M. Best
International, also based in London, can be reached at 011-
44-181-579-1091.

Access Indiana Information Network

10 W Market St #600
Indianapolis, IN 46204-2497
800-236-5446 Fax: 317-233-2011
www.ai.org **Email:** dnsadmin@ai.org
Founded: 1995 **Memberships:** NASIRE
Clientele Restrictions: Subscription required
Products, Information Categories, Coverage Area
General:
Environmental (IN)
Proprietary Databases or Gateways:
Gateway Name: Premium Services
Driver and/or Vehicle, Corporate/Trade Name Data,
Licenses/Registrations/Permits, Uniform Commercial
Code, Litigation/Judgments/Tax Liens (IN)
Gateway Name: Free Services
Legislation/Regulation (IN)
Special Distribution Methods to Client: Email, Internet

AIIN (or AccessIndiana) is a comprehensive, one-stop
source for electronic access to State of Indiana government
information. This network is owned by the state of Indiana.
Access to the public records listed here requires a
subscription fee and per-use fee. Specialties include drivers
records, vehicle title and lien information, vehicle
registration records, physician and nurse license
verification, Secretary of State records (including UCC,
lobbyist, and corporation information) and information on
the Indiana General Assembly. See the Internet site for
more information.

Access Louisiana Inc

400 Travis St #504
Shreveport, LA 71101
800-489-5620 **Email:** debois41@aol.com
Founded: 1981 **Memberships:** NPRRA, NFPA, PRRN,
Clientele Restrictions: None reported
Products, Information Category, Coverage Areas
General:
Bankruptcy (LA)
Proprietary Databases or Gateways:
Gateway Name: LA UCC
Uniform Commercial Code (LA)
Gateway Name: LA Corporate Data
Corporate/Trade Name Data, Trademarks/Patents and
Addresses/Telephone Numbers (LA)

Access Louisiana is a statewide legal research company with a physical presence in every Louisiana parish. Services include: public records (UCC, accounts, receivable, state/federal tax liens, suits, chattel mortgages, bankruptcy records), corporate filing/retrieval, court records and registered agent services. They have extensive knowledge of where information is recorded and how to effectively retrieve Louisiana public records.

Accurint

6601 Park of Commerce Blvd
Boca Raton, FL 33487
888-332-8244 Fax: 561-893-8090
www.accurint.com/ **Email:** sales@accurint.com
Parent Company: Seisint, Inc.
Clientele Restrictions: Subscription required.

Products, Information Categories, Coverage Area
Proprietary Databases or Gateways:
Database Name: Florida DL Search
Driver and/or Vehicle (FL)
Gateway Name: FAA
Aviation (US)
Database Name: UCC
Uniform Commercial Code (US)
Database Name: Property
Real Estate/Assessor (US)
Special Distribution Methods to Client: Internet

Accurint is a leading information management and technology company providing its customers with the accurate and complete information. Accurint's data stores contain billions of records that are searched, analyzed, and compiled in seconds. Because of our cutting-edge technology, we can conduct searches in an extremely cost-effective manner - batch and API services are also available. Accurint has access to over 20 billion records compiled from over 400 sources. Accurint can locate almost anyone, find deep background and historical information, and shorten research time and costs. Accurint provides aliases, historical addresses, relatives, associates, neighbors, assets, and more. Accurint is focused on helping collection agencies, companies with internal collections departments, lawyers, insurance professionals, law enforcement agencies, and corporations locate debtors, witnesses, suspects, and other persons critical to their work.

Accu-Source Inc.

8585 Stemmons #M26
Dallas, TX 75247
Fax: 214-637-1443
www.accu-source.com **Email:** as-sales@accu-source.com
Founded: 1990
Clientele Restrictions: Agreement required.

Products, Information Categories, Coverage Area
General:
Driver and/or Vehicle (TX, FL, OK, IL, LA, KS, NY, MI, NJ, PA)
Proprietary Databases or Gateways:
Gateway Name: Federal Bankruptcy Courts
Bankruptcy (AK, AR, AZ, CA, CO, FL, GA, HI, IA, ID, IL, IN, KS, KY, LA, MN, MO, NC, ND, NE, NM, NV, OK, OH, OR, SC, SD, TN, TX, UT, WA, WI, WY)
Gateway Name: National Pilot Registration
Aviation (US)
Gateway Name: Texas Voter Regisitration
Voter Registration (TX)
Special Distribution Methods to Client: Dial-Up (Other than Internet)

Accu-search provides a wide variety of searches, both locally and nationally, including fast return of criminal records in key Texas, California, and Kansas counties. They provide online access to a variety of DMV, aviation, bankruptcy records, some real time. It's suggested to visit their web site for a listing of records and services.

Accutrend Corporation

6021 S Syracuse Wy #111
Denver, CO 80111
800-488-0011 Fax: 303-488-0133
www.accutrend.com **Email:** info@accutrend.com
Founded: 1987 **Memberships:** DMA
Clientele Restrictions: None reported

Products, Information Categories, Coverage Area
Proprietary Databases or Gateways:
Database Name: New Business Database
Licenses/Registrations/Permits and Corporate/Trade Name Data (US)
Special Distribution Methods to Client: CD-ROM, Database, Disk, Email, FTP, Internet, Magnetic Tape

Accutrend Corporation compiles a new business database which each month adds 165,000 new business registrations, licenses and incorporations. Data is collected from all levels of government and is enhanced with demographic overlays.

ACS Inc

PO Box 4889
Syracuse, NY 13221
Fax: 315-437-3223
www.landaccess.com
Clientele Restrictions: Signed agreement required, must be ongoing account

Products, Information Categories, Coverage Area
Proprietary Databases or Gateways:
Gateway Name: BRC

Real Estate/Assessor, Uniform Commercial Code (MI, NJ, NY, OH)

Special Distribution Methods to Client: Dial-Up (Other than Internet)

ACS specializes in online access to Recorders, County Clerks and Registers across the country. Fees are involved except of Ohio.

ADP Screening and Selection Services

301 Remington St
Fort Collins, CO 80524
800-367-5933
www.avert.com **Email:** avert-info@avert.com
Founded: 1986
Clientele Restrictions: Casual requesters permitted
Products, Information Categories, Coverage Area
General:
Bankruptcy (US)
Proprietary Databases or Gateways:
Database Name: Workers Compensation History
Workers Compensation (IA, MD, MI, MS)
Gateway Name: Credit & Name Link
Credit Information (US)
Special Distribution Methods to Client: Dial-Up (Other than Internet), Email

Formerly Avert.Inc, ADP Screening and Selection Services provides pre-employment screening, job fit assessments and human resource solutions to clients nationwide. Combining innovative Internet technology and more than a decade of experience, ADP offers fast turnaround, current data and competitive pricing on background checking products including criminal court records, driving records, reference checks and more.

ADREM Profiles Inc

5461 W Waters Ave #900
Tampa, FL 33634
800-281-1250
www.adpro.com **Email:** adrem-sales@adpro.com
Founded: 1992 **Memberships:** SHRM, AIIP, PRRN, NPRRA, ASIS,
Clientele Restrictions: Signed agreement required, must be ongoing account
Products, Information Categories, Coverage Area
General:
Bankruptcy (US)
Proprietary Databases or Gateways:
Gateway Name: ADREM
Driver and/or Vehicle (US)
Special Distribution Methods to Client: Automated Telephone Look-Up, Dial-Up (Other than Internet), Email, FTP, Gateway via Another Online Service

ADREM Profiles is an international, full service public records research and retrieval company. Their comprehensive retrieval network allows access to information repositories within the 3,347 counties and independent cities throughout the United States. A staff of over 1,500 field researchers provides access to all counties within the US as well as to the Bahamas, Bermuda, Canada, the Caribbean and Europe. Utilizing ADREM's information ordering system, ADREM Advantage, research requests may be sent and retrieved securely and swiftly via the Internet 24 hours a day, 7 days a week.

Agency Records

PO Box 310175
Newington, CT 06131
800-777-6655 Fax: 860-666-4247
www.agencyrecords.com
Founded: 1972 **Memberships:** ARCO
Clientele Restrictions: Signed Agreement Required; Infrequent requesters permitted.
Products, Information Categories, Coverage Area
General:
Credit Information (US)
Proprietary Databases or Gateways:
Database Name: CT Criminal Records, MN Court Convictions
Criminal Information (CT, MN)
Gateway Name: ARI
Driver and/or Vehicle (US)
Database Name: FL Workers Compensation Claims (20 years)
Workers Compensation (FL)
Special Distribution Methods to Client: Dial-Up (Other than Internet), Disk, Email, FTP, Gateway via Another Online Service, Internet, Magnetic Tape

Agency Records or ARI is a business to business provider of public record information. They offer nationwide retrieval of driving records with instant access to MVRs for FL, AL, SC, NC, WV, NJ, NY, CT, VA, MS, NH, and ME. They also provide instant access to court convictions for Connecticut and Minnesota. They offer computer, fax and phone ordering as well as volume discounts. Public companies may be invoiced.

Alacourt.com

PO Box 8173
Mobile, AL 36689
877-799-9898
www.alacourt.com **Email:** info@alacourt.com
Parent Company: On-Line Information Services, Inc
Founded: 1990
Clientele Restrictions: Subscription required
Products, Information Categories, Coverage Area
Proprietary Databases or Gateways:

Gateway Name: Alacourt.com
Litigation/Judgments/Tax Liens, Criminal Information
(AL)
Special Distribution Methods to Client: Email, Internet

Alacourt.com is an Internet-browser driven way to access
the Alabama Trial Court records. All currently active cases
are maintained in the system as are disposed cases, some
going back as far as the late 1970's. The courts included are
civil circuit and district courts, criminal cases in circuit and
district courts, domestic relations & child support, traffic,
and small claims. The system includes outstanding alias
warrants, trial court dockets, attorney case information, and
other features. Search results include case summaries, party
& attorney names, dockets, judgments, claims, creditors &
charges.

American Business Information

PO Box 27347
Omaha, NE 68127
800-555-5335 Fax: 402-331-0176
www.infousa.com
Parent Company: InfoUSA Inc **Memberships:** ALA,
DMA, SIIA, NACM, SLA,
Clientele Restrictions: Casual requesters permitted
Products, Information Categories, Coverage Area
General:
Trademarks (US)
Proprietary Databases or Gateways:
Database Name: Business Sales Leads
Addresses/Telephone Numbers, Credit Information,
Foreign Country Information, News/Current Events and
SEC/Other Financial (US)
Database Name: Consumer Sales Leads
Addresses/Telephone Numbers, Credit Information,
Driver and/or Vehicle, Genealogical Information and
Real Estate/Assessor (US)
Special Distribution Methods to Client: CD-ROM,
Database, Dial-Up (Other than Internet), Disk, Gateway
via Another Online Service, Internet, Lists/Labels,
Magnetic Tape, Publication/Directory, Software

American Business Information, a division of InfoUSA,
compiles business information from telephone directories
and other public sources. Over the past 20+ years, they
have provided services to over 2 million customers. They
telephone verify every name in their database before they
offer it for sale. They phone-verify address changes from
the USPS NCOA. In addition, the provide business credit
reports. Their info is available in a variety of ways
including online (SalesLeadsUSA.com), CD-ROM, and by
telephone (Directory Assistance Plus). A division produces
the Pro-CD Disk and another operates Digital Directory
Assistance. For business leads call 800-555-5335. For
SalesLeads USA call 402-592-9000.

American Driving Records

PO Box 1970
Rancho Cordova, CA 95741-1970
800-766-6877
www.mvrs.com **Email:** sales@mvrs.com
Founded: 1986
Clientele Restrictions: Signed agreement required, must
be ongoing account
Products, Information Categories, Coverage Area
Proprietary Databases or Gateways:
Gateway Name: ADR
Driver and/or Vehicle (US)
Special Distribution Methods to Client: Dial-Up (Other
than Internet), Internet

American Driving Record (ADR) services include
accessing driving records and registration information.
Also, they provide special processing for the insurance
industry with such products as automatic checking (ACH),
calculating underwriting points, and ZapApp(tm) - an
automated insurance application from the agency to the
carrier. Driving records can be instant, same day or
overnight, depending on the state.

Ameridex Information Systems

PO Box 51314
Irvine, CA 92619-1314
Fax: 714-731-2116
www.ameridex.com **Email:** info@ameridex.com
Founded: 1988
Clientele Restrictions: Registration required, must be
ongoing account
Products, Information Categories, Coverage Area
Proprietary Databases or Gateways:
Database Name: Live Index
Addresses/Telephone Numbers (US)
Database Name: Military
Military Service (US)
Database Name: Death Index
Vital Records, DOB/DEATH/SSN (US)
Special Distribution Methods to Client: Dial-Up (Other
than Internet)

Ameridex presents several unique databases for people
tracing on the Internet. Over 260 million names and 230
million with a date of birth are compiled from multiple
public record sources. Speciality databases include a
nationwide death index with supplements, an active
military personnel database, and vital records (birth,
marriage, divorce) for several states.

Ancestry
266 W Center St
Orem, UT 84057
http://ancestry.com
Parent Company: MyFamily.com
Clientele Restrictions: Premium services require
subscription
Products, Information Categories, Coverage Area
Proprietary Databases or Gateways:
Database Name: Ancestry.com
Vital Records, Foreign Country Information (US, Intl)
Database Name: SSN Death Index
Vital Records (US)
Special Distribution Methods to Client: Internet

Ancestry.com is one of the leading Family History
genealogy web sites. Over 600 million records can be
searched from literally thousands of databases. One may
search by record type, or locality. Many free searches are
available, to access the entrie system, a subscription is
required. An editor's choice site.

ARCountyData.com - Apprentice Information Systems
900 N Dixieland, #102
Rogers, AR 72756
Fax: 501-631-9291
www.arcountydata.com **Email:** jason@apprenticeis.com
Founded: 1999
Clientele Restrictions: Signed Agreement Required.
Products, Information Categories, Coverage Area
Proprietary Databases or Gateways:
Gateway Name: Arkansas County Assessor Records
Arkansas County Assessor Records
Real Estate/Assessor (AR)
Special Distribution Methods to Client: Internet

ARCountyData.com provides access to county assessor
records in these Arkansas counties: Baxter, Benton,
Pulaski, and White. Future counties will include Craighead,
Faulkner, Lonoke, Saline, and Sebastian. Access is charged
by the minute; online registration and credit cards accepted.

ARISTOTLE
205 Pennsylvania Ave SE
(Administrative: 50 E St. SE)
Washington, DC 20003
800-296-2747 Fax: 202-543-6407
www.aristotle.org **Email:** sales@aristotle.org
Branch Offices:
San Francisco, CA, 415-440-1012; Fax: 415-440-2162
Atlanta, GA, 404-350-1675; Fax: 404-352-5757
Founded: 1983

Clientele Restrictions: Access to government
records.com databases is restricted to law enforcement
and news agencies
Products, Information Categories, Coverage Area
General:
Legislation/Regulation - Political (US)
Proprietary Databases or Gateways:
Database Name: ARISTOTLE
Addresses/Telephone Numbers (US)
Database Name: GovernmentRecords.com
Voter Registration (US)
Special Distribution Methods to Client: CD-ROM,
Magnetic Tape, Internet

GovernmentRecords.com is a comprehensive file of
registered voters, licenses drivers or government
identification card holders residing in 38 nations, including
the United States. Information is obtained directly from
government agencies at the federal, state or municipal level
at 3,400 locations. The US information is standardized and
enhanced with listed phone number, postal correction and
national change of address, census geography, and age and
is subject to laws governing access and use of driver license
information (DPPA) or registered voter information.
Access to the GovernmentRecords.com databases is
restricted to government, law enforcement and accredited
news organizations only.

Attorneys Title Insurance Fund
PO Box 628600
Orlando, FL 32862
800-336-3863 Fax: 407-888-2592
www.thefund.com
Founded: 1948 **Memberships:** ALTA, REIPA,
Clientele Restrictions: Signed agreement required, must
be ongoing account; however, certain products are
released to one-time clients
Products, Information Categories, Coverage Area
Proprietary Databases or Gateways:
Database Name: Online Data Service
Real Estate/Assessor, Litigation/Judgments/Tax Liens
(FL-40 counties)
Special Distribution Methods to Client: Dial-Up (Other
than Internet), Disk, Email, FTP, Magnetic Tape

Although the primary business of The Fund (as they are
called) is to issue title insurance, they offer access to over
100 million real estate records from 40 major counties in
FL. The Fund has 15 branch offices as wellas operations in
SC and IL. Online users can access public records
including mortgages, deeds, liens, assessments, right-of-
way data, and even judgment and divorce proceedings.

Aurigin Systems Inc.

10710 N Tantau Ave
Cupertino, CA 95014
Fax: 408-257-9133
www.aurigin.com **Email:** jross@aurigin.com
Branch Offices:
Princeton, NJ, 609-734-4300; Fax: 609-734-4352
Founded: 1992 **Memberships:** AIPLA, ABA, LES,
Clientele Restrictions: None reported
Products, Information Categories, Coverage Area
Proprietary Databases or Gateways:
Database Name: Aurigin
Patents (US, Intl)
Special Distribution Methods to Client: Dial-Up (Other
than Internet), Software

Aurigin, formally known as SmartPatents Inc, offers the
Aurigin Aureka® System to manage a company's
intellectual and innovation assets. Other important products
are Aurigin Electronic Patents, indexed patents from the
US Patent and Trademark Office, and the Aurigin
Workbench, a desktop software application.

AutoDataDirect, Inc

2940 E. Park Ave #B
Tallahassee, FL 32301-3427
www.add123.com **Email:** jtaylor@add123.com
Founded: 1999
Clientele Restrictions: Signed agreement required
Products, Information Categories, Coverage Area
Proprietary Databases or Gateways:
Gateway Name: ADD123
Driver and/or Vehicle, Vessels (FL)
Special Distribution Methods to Client: Internet

AutoDataDirect provides real time access to Florida motor
vehicle, vessel and driver's license records. ADD's services
are not available to individuals, but companies with a
permissible use of personal information as described in the
Federal Driver's Privacy Protection Act of 1994 are eligible
for ADD's service. To determine if you are eligible to
receive the vehicle records, please read the Federal Driver's
Privacy Protection Act of 1994 which can be found at our
Web site.

Avantex Inc

340 Morgantown Road
Reading, PA 19611
800-998-8857
www.avantext.com **Email:** dara@avantex.com
Founded: 1992
Clientele Restrictions: None reported
Products, Information Categories, Coverage Area
Proprietary Databases or Gateways:
Database Name: FAA Data

Aviation, Addresses/Telephone Numbers,
Legislation/Regulations (US)
Special Distribution Methods to Client: CD-ROM,
Internet

Avantext product line includes a line of powerful CDs for
the aviation industry. The Aircraft and Airman CD includes
a full listing of pilots and aircraft owners, schools,
technicians, dealers and much more.

Background Information Services Inc

1800 30th St #213
Boulder, CO 80301
800-433-6010 Fax: 303-442-1004
www.bisi.com **Email:** dawn@bisi.com
Founded: 1988 **Memberships:** ASIS, NHRA,
Clientele Restrictions: Agreement required
Products, Information Categories, Coverage Area
Proprietary Databases or Gateways:
Database Name: Criminal
Criminal Information, Credit Information (CO, OK, US)
Gateway Name: Filings
Corporation/Trade Name Data (CO)
Gateway Name: UCC
Uniform Commercial Code (CO)
Special Distribution Methods to Client: Dial-Up (Other
than Internet), Email, Internet

Background Information Services (BIS) is a nationwide
public records provider specializing in pre-employment and
tenant screening. BIS owns and maintains databases
containing criminal and civil records, especially for
Colorado and Oklahoma. Also serves as a gateway for
Colorado Secretary of State, Department of Revenue and
UCC Filings. Created in cooperation with state agencies,
database information is received electronically from the
courts. BIS allows online access to this information with
instantaneous results. Nationwide services that BIS offers
include civil, criminal, motor vehicle driving reports,
Workers compensation claims, credit histories, federal
records and UCC filings. BIS is a technologically advanced
company offering dial-up or telnet access to database
information and ordering screens. Orders can be placed on
a secured Internet site that can be tailored to the company's
needs.

Banko

100 S. 5th St #300
Minneapolis, MN 55402
800-533-8897 Fax: 612-215-7498
www.banko.com **Email:** sales@dolaninformaion.com
Branch Offices:
San Diego, CA
Parent Company: Dolan Information

Founded: 1987 **Memberships:** ACA, ICA, MBA, DBA,
Clientele Restrictions: Casual requesters not permitted; subscription for online searches is available

Products, Information Categories, Coverage Area
Proprietary Databases or Gateways:
Database Name: BANKO
Bankruptcy, Litigation/Judgments/Tax Liens (US)
Database Name: ACOLLAID
Addresses/Telephone Numbers (US)
Special Distribution Methods to Client: CD-ROM, Dial-Up (Other than Internet), Disk, Internet, Lists/Labels, Magnetic Tape

Dolan Information is a leading provider of public record information and record retrieval services for bankruptcies, civil judgments, tax liens, and deceased information. Receive electronic notification for bankruptcy and deceased through BANKO's batch process or login to www.banko.com for individual searches and nationwide access to bankruptcy dockets and documents. For more information, call 800-533-8897 or contact us at sales@dolaninformation.com

Better Business Bureau

4200 Wilson Blvd # 800
Arlington, VA 22203-1838
Fax: 703-525-8277
www.bbb.org **Email:** webwork@MAIL.BBB.ORG
Clientele Restrictions: Agreement Required to Join

Products, Information Categories, Coverage Area
Proprietary Databases or Gateways:
Gateway Name: Business Report
Corporate/Trade Name Data (US)
Special Distribution Methods to Client: Dial-Up (Other than Internet), Email, Internet

Business Reports are created and maintained by the BBB office where the business is located. Information reported includes time in business, complaint history, and information obtained through special Bureau investigations. Bureaus also have the option of reporting whether companies are Bureau members, or participate in any special Bureau programs, such as Alternative Dispute Resolution or BBBOnLine®. For additional information about the BBB reporting process, visit the BBB Help Desk online. If you desire a report from a BBB office that does not appear online, contact the office directly and request a verbal or printed copy of the report.

BiblioData

PO Box 61
Needham Heights, MA 02494
Fax: 781-449-4584
www.bibliodata.com **Email:** ina@bibliodata.com
Founded: 1989

Clientele Restrictions: Casual requesters permitted

Products, Information Categories, Coverage Area
Proprietary Databases or Gateways:
Database Name: BiblioData
News/Current Events, Addresses/Telephone Numbers (US)
Special Distribution Methods to Client: Internet, Publication/Directory

BiblioData publishes informative newsletters directly related to the online industry and publish the Cyberskeptic's Guide to Internet Research. Their products are targeted for researchers and librarians.

BNA, Inc (Bureau of National Affairs)

1231 25th Street, NW
Washington, MD 20037
800-372-1033
http://web.bna.com **Email:** icustrel@bna.com
Branch Offices:
Rockville, MD, 800-372-1033; Fax: 800-253-0332
Founded: 1929
Clientele Restrictions: Must be ongoing account

Products, Information Categories, Coverage Area
Proprietary Databases or Gateways:
Gateway Name: Intl Trade Daily, WTO Reporter
Legislation/Regulation, Foreign Country Information (Intl)
Gateway Name: Environment & Safety Library on the Web
Environmental (US)
Gateway Name: Class Action Litigation Report
Litigation/Judgments/Tax Liens (US)
Gateway Name: Corporate Law Daily
Corporate/Trade Name Data (US)
Special Distribution Methods to Client: Email, Internet, Publication/Directory

BNA is a leading publisher of print and electronic news and information, reporting on developments in health care, business, labor relations, law, economics, taxation, environmental protection, safety, and other public policy and regulatory issues. Its Class Action Litigation Report covers the most important developments in class action and multiparty litigation, in all subject areas. It monitors hard-to-find, significant litigation news acress all subject areas, including antitrust, consumer, employment, health care, mass torts, products and securities. The Report's timely notification is supplemented by analysis and practice pointers by outside experts and attorneys. Visit www.bna.com/new/ for additional products.

Burrelles Information Services

75 East Northfield Rd
Livingston, NJ 07039
800-631-1160
www.burrelles.com **Email:** info@burrelles.com
Clientele Restrictions: None reported
Products, Information Categories, Coverage Area
Proprietary Databases or Gateways:
Database Name: BIO
News/Current Events (US, Intl)
Special Distribution Methods to Client: CD-ROM,
Dial-Up (Other than Internet), Publication/Directory

For over 100 years Burrelle's has been monitoring,
organizing, and delivering media data to clients. Products
include Press Clipping, NewsExpress, NewsAlert, Media
Direcories, Broadcast Transcripts, and Web Clips. The BIO
- Burrelle's Information Office, is software to receive and
use information from Burrelle's.

Cal Info

316 W 2nd St #102
Los Angeles, CA 90012
Fax: 213-687-8778
www.calinfo.net **Email:** admin@calinfo.net
Branch Offices:
Washington, DC, 202-667-9679; Fax: 202-967-9605
Founded: 1986 **Memberships:** AIIP, AALL,
Clientele Restrictions: None reported
Products, Information Categories, Coverage Area
General:
Litigation/Judgments/Tax Liens (US, CA)
Proprietary Databases or Gateways:
Database Name: Guide to State Statutes
Legislation/Regulation (State Statutes) (US)
Database Name: Administrative Guide to State
Regulations
Legislation/Regulation (US)
Special Distribution Methods to Client: Email,
Publication/Directory

Cal Info offers an information research and retrieval service
that finds answers to questions that affect law firms and
businesses every day. Their personnel are trained to search
computerized databases as well as the more traditional
information sources, including libraries, publishers,
government agencies, courts, trade unions and associations.
They provide company reports, financial data, product
information, people information, journals and news stories,
real estate information, legal research, public records
research, government information and document retrieval.

Cambridge Statistical Research Associates

53 Wellesley
Irvine, CA 92612
800-327-2772
Founded: 1988
Clientele Restrictions: Must be ongoing account
Products, Information Categories, Coverage Area
General:
Addresses/Telephone Numbers (US)
Proprietary Databases or Gateways:
Database Name: Death Master File
Vital Records (US)
Special Distribution Methods to Client: CD-ROM,
Dial-Up (Other than Internet)

CSRA traces its origin to an actuarial and programming
service established in 1979. In recent years, its efforts
moved toward bringing large mainframe databases to the
desktop computing platform, including CD-ROM. CSRA
specializes in nationwide death index by name and Social
Security Number, death auditing service, database
consulting, genealogical and probate research, and address
trace service.

Campus Direct

One Plymouth Meeting, #610
Plymought Meeting, PA 19462
800-889-4249
www.campusdirect.com/ **Email:**
sales@campusdirect.com
Parent Company: Student Advantage Inc
Founded: 1990
Clientele Restrictions: Registration required.
Products, Information Categories, Coverage Area
Proprietary Databases or Gateways:
Database Name: Campus Direct
Education/Employment (US)
Special Distribution Methods to Client: Internet

Student Advantage's Campus Direct® division is one of the
nation's premier outsource provider of student information
services to colleges and universities. Search the client
schools list at the web site. Client schools utilize Campus
Direct® as a means by which to provide particular services
or as a coexisting backup system where services such as
transcript fulfillment are already provided in-house.
Campus Direct's knowledgeable staff and state-of-the-art
Internet and telephone technologies enable colleges and
universities to provide superior service for students and
information requesters.

Canadian Law Book Inc

240 Edward St
Aurora, Ontario, CD L4G 3S9
800-263-3269 Fax: 905-841-5085
www.canadalawbook.ca/ **Email:**
bloney@canadalawbook.ca
Branch Offices:
Vancouver, BC, 604-844-7855; Fax: 604-844-7813
Founded: 1855
Products, Information Categories, Coverage Area
General:
Foreign Country Information (Canada)
Proprietary Databases or Gateways:
Gateway Name: Canada Statute Service
Legislation/Regulation (Canada)
Gateway Name: Canadian Patent Reporter
Patents (Canada)
Gateway Name: Caselaw on Call
Litigation/Judgments/Tax Liens (Canada)
Special Distribution Methods to Client: Automated
Telephone Look-Up, CD-ROM, Internet,
Publication/Directory, Software

In Canada, dial 800-263-2037. Canada Law Book resources
have expanded to encompass a broad collection of material
from leading experts in the legal profession. They're
empowered with the latest technological tools to enhance
the delivery of the content. Get exactly the information you
need, in the manner that suits you best.

Capitol Lien Records & Research Inc

1010 N Dale
St Paul, MN 55117
800-845-4077
www.capitollien.com/clrridefault.asp **Email:**
tony@capitollien.com
Founded: 1990 **Memberships:** PRRN, NPRRA,
Clientele Restrictions: Casual requesters permitted
Products, Information Categories, Coverage Area
General:
Litigation/Judgments/Tax Liens, Criminal Information,
Driver and/or Vehicle, Real Estate/Assessor,
Corporate/Trade Name Data, (MN, WI, US)
Proprietary Databases or Gateways:
Gateway Name: UCC
Uniform Commercial Code (MN)
Special Distribution Methods to Client: CD-ROM,
Disk, Email, Magnetic Tape, Software, Internet

Capitol Lien Records & Research provides UCC, federal
and state tax lien searches, real estate searches, document
retrievals, bankruptcy searches, judgment searches,
corporate documents, a weekly tax lien report,
environmental lien searches, Phase 1, 2 and 3
environmental searches, watercraft, and aircraft and vessel
searches. An online ordering system accepting credit cards
is provided to clients.

Carfax

10304 Eaton Place, #500
Fairfax, VA 22030
Fax: 703-218-2465
www.carfaxonline.com **Email:** subscribe@carfax.com
Parent Company: R.L. Polk
Founded: 1986 **Memberships:** AAMVA, DMA,
Clientele Restrictions: Casual requesters permitted
Products, Information Categories, Coverage Area
Proprietary Databases or Gateways:
Database Name: Vehicle History Service, Motor Vehicle
Title Information
Driver and/or Vehicle (US)
Database Name: VINde (VIN Validity Check Program)
Software/Training (US)
Special Distribution Methods to Client: Dial-Up (Other
than Internet), Disk, Internet

With the largest online vehicle history database (over one
billion records), Carfax can generate a Vehicle History
Report based on a VIN in less than one second. They
collect data from a variety of sources including state DMVs
and salvage pools. Reports include details from previous
titles, city and state, odometer rollbacks, junk and flood
damage, etc, reducing the risk of handling used vehicles
with hidden problems that affect their value. Reports do not
contain personal information on current or previous
owners.

Case Record Info Services

33895 Cape Cove
Dana Point, CA 92629
Email: jeancris@aol.com
Founded: 1994
Clientele Restrictions: Casual requesters permitted
Products, Information Categories, Coverage Area
Proprietary Databases or Gateways:
Database Name: Judgment Lists
Litigation/Judgments/Tax Liens (CA)
Special Distribution Methods to Client: Dial-Up (Other
than Internet), Disk, Internet, Lists/Labels

Case Record Info Services provides judgment lists in
California. Their data is used by bulk data providers,
collection and mediation companies. They are also
members of the American Arbitration Association. Note:
The telephone number is to the residence of the principal.

CaseClerk.com

PO Box 1519
Dandridge, TN 37725
Fax: 865-397-5900
www.caseclerk.com **Email:** sales@caseclerk.com
Clientele Restrictions: None reported

Products, Information Categories, Coverage Area
Proprietary Databases or Gateways:
Gateway Name: Courtclerk.com
Bankruptcy, Criminal Information,
Litigation/Judgments/Tax Liens (TN)
Gateway Name: Caseclerk.com
Legislation/Regulation (US)
Special Distribution Methods to Client: Internet

CourtClerk.com serves as a gateway for case law and legal research. Cases back to 1900, cases, codes, statutes, local and federal rules, local and federal forms, court calendars, and contact information to available. Access is by subscription on a dail, monthly or yearly basis.

CaseStream.com

489 Devon Park Dr, #206
Wayne, PA 19087
800-500-0888 Fax: 610-254-9672
www.CaseStream.com **Email:** Info@MarketSpan.com
Parent Company: MarketSpan Inc
Founded: 1997 **Memberships:** ABA
Clientele Restrictions: Casual requesters permitted

Products, Information Categories, Coverage Area
Proprietary Databases or Gateways:
Database Name: CaseAlert for Federal Courts
Litigation/judgments/Tax Liens, Criminal (US)
Gateway Name: Delaware Chancery
Litigation/Judgments/Tax Liens (DE)
Database Name: CaseAlert for Federal Courts
Criminal Information, Bankruptcy (US)
Special Distribution Methods to Client: Dial-Up (Other than Internet), Email

CaseStream products include; Alert! which notifies you each day of activity in federal civil cases of interest to you; Historical which gives legal research on similar cases before the same federal judge; Docket Direct provides a fast and efficient means to retrieve federal civil or criminal docket on demand; and Delaware Chancery which provides a fully searchable database of the dockets in the Delaware Court of Chancery.

CCH Washington Service Bureau

1015 15th St NW, #1000
Washington, DC 20005
800-955-5219 Fax: 202-962-0152
www.wsb.com **Email:** custserv@wsb.com

Parent Company: Wolters Klower US
Founded: 1967
Clientele Restrictions: Casual requesters permitted.

Products, Information Categories, Coverage Area
General:
Legislation/Regulation (US)
Proprietary Databases or Gateways:
Database Name: SECnet
SEC/Other Financial, Bankrupcy (US)
Special Distribution Methods to Client: Internet, Microfilm/Microfiche, Publication/Directory

CCH Washington Service Bureau, has been serving the information needs of lawyers, corporate executives, brokers, accountants, and government officials since its inception in 1967. The company offers a number of products and services in a variety of practice areas to the legal and business professional. CCH Washington Service Bureau provides expedited information retrieval on filings made with the Securities and Exchange Commission. A pioneer in the area of "sample" securities research, our experienced research staff uses in-house proprietary databases and a library of SEC filings dating back to 1979 to fulfill the most difficult research request. CCH Washington Service Bureau offers watch services which are tailored by the individual needs of each client. We also offer "filex" services, enabling clients to file documents with federal regulatory agencies.

ChoicePoint Inc

1000 Alderman Dr
Alpharetta, GA 30005
Fax: 770-752-6005
www.choicepointinc.com
Founded: 1997 **Memberships:** AALL, ABI, ASIS,
Clientele Restrictions: Signed agreement required, must be ongoing account

Products, Information Categories, Coverage Area
General:
Workers Compensation (US)
Proprietary Databases or Gateways:
Database Name: Legal Information
Bankruptcy, Corporation/Trade Name Data, Criminal Information, Litigation/Judgments/Tax Liens, Uniform Commercial Code (US)
Database Name: Real Property
Real Estate/Assessor (US)
Database Name: Consumer Services
Addresses/Telephone Numbers ()
Database Name: Insurance Services
Driver and/or Vehicle (US)
Database Name: Information Services
Licenses/Registrations/Permits (Physicians) (US)
Special Distribution Methods to Client: Dial-Up (Other than Internet)

ChoicePoint is a leading provider of intelligence information to help businesses, governments, and individuals to better understand with whom they do business. ChoicePoint services the risk management information needs of the property and casualty insurance market, the life and health insurance market, and business and government, including asset-based lenders and professional service providers. The company, with many branch offices nationwide, was spun off from Equifax in 1997. They offer a variety of useful online products.

ChoicePoint, formerly CDB Infotek

6 Hutton Centre Dr #600
Santa Ana, CA 92707
800-427-3747 Fax: 714-708-1000
www.choicepointonline.com/cdb/ **Email:**
tony.mears@choicepointinc.com
Founded: 1997 **Memberships:** SIIA, NALV, NPRRA,
ASIS, ACA, IRSG
Clientele Restrictions: Signed agreement required, must be ongoing account

Products, Information Categories, Coverage Area
General:
Credit Information (US)
Proprietary Databases or Gateways:
Database Name: Real Property Ownership & Transfers
Real Estate/Assessor (US)
Database Name: Corporate & Limited Partnerships
Corporate/Trade Name Data (US)
Database Name: Uniform Commercial Code
Uniform Commerical Code (US)
Database Name: Legal Information
Bankruptcy and Litigation/Judgments/Tax Liens (US)
Database Name: Address Inspector
Addresses/Telephone Numbers (US)
Special Distribution Methods to Client: Dial-Up (Other than Internet), Internet

ChoicePoint (CDB Infotek) offers nationwide public records information, including instant access to more than 4 billion records and 1,600 targeted databases to efficiently locate people or businesses, conduct background research, identify assets, control fraud, conduct due diligence, etc. Subscribers learn search strategies at free, year-round seminars and have toll-free access to customer service representatives for help. ChoicePoint also offers direct marketing lists, monitoring services, hard copy document retrieval and high-volume processing services.

ChoicePoint, formerly DBT Online Inc

4530 Blue Lake Dr
Boca Raton, FL 33431
800-279-7710 Fax: 561-982-5872

www.dbtonline.com
Parent Company: DBT Online Inc
Founded: 1992
Clientele Restrictions: License required, must be ongoing account
Products, Information Categories, Coverage Area
Proprietary Databases or Gateways:
Database Name: AutoTrackXP
Addresses/Telephone Numbers, Real Estate/Assessor, Corporate/Trade Name Data (US)
Gateway Name: AutoTrackXP
Driver and/or Vehicle (US)
Special Distribution Methods to Client: Dial-Up (Other than Internet), Internet

ChoicePoint (DBT Online) offers nationwide public records information, including instant access to more than 4 billion records and 1,600 targeted databases to efficiently locate people or businesses, conduct background research, identify assets, control fraud, conduct due diligence, etc. Subscribers learn search strategies at free, year-round seminars and have toll-free access to customer service representatives for help. ChoicePoint also offers direct marketing lists, monitoring services, hard copy document retrieval and high-volume processing services.

Circuit Express

1200 Bigley Ave.
Charleston, WV 25302
800-795-8543 Fax: 304-343-6489
www.swcg-inc.com **Email:** info@swcg-inc.com
Parent Company: Software Computer Group Inc.
Founded: 1975
Clientele Restrictions: Registration required.
Products, Information Categories, Coverage Area
Proprietary Databases or Gateways:
Database Name: Circuit Express
Criminal Information, Litigation/Judgments/Tax Liens (WV)
Special Distribution Methods to Client: Internet

Circuit Express is the contract computer access provider of civil and criminal courts records for the West Virginia counties of Kanawha, Putnam, Hancock and Mineral, also Nicholas County, Ohio.

CoCourts.com

1033 Walnut St #300
Boulder, CO 80302
866-262-6878 Fax: 303-381-2279
www.cocourts.com **Email:** info@cocourts.com
Founded: 2000
Clientele Restrictions: Casual requesters permitted
Products, Information Categories, Coverage Area
General:
Criminal Information (CO)

Proprietary Databases or Gateways:
Database Name: Colorado Courts Information
Criminal Information, Litigation/Judgments/Tax Lien
(CO)
Special Distribution Methods to Client: Internet

CoCourts.com is a real-time statewide court records site
built specifically for the web. It is the official public-access
site for records maintained by the Colorado Judicial
Department. In addition to those listed above, other
applications include collections, employment screening,
and tenant screening.

Colorado Central Information System (CIS)

303 E 17th Ave, #900
Denver, CO 80203
Fax: 303-832-1119
www.cocis.com/main.htm
Clientele Restrictions: Casual requesters permitted.
Products, Information Categories, Coverage Area
General:
Uniform Commercial Code (CO)
Proprietary Databases or Gateways:
Gateway Name: State of Colorado
Uniform Commercial Code, Litigation/Judgments/Tax
Liens (CO)
Special Distribution Methods to Client: Internet

Colorado Central Information System (CCIS) maintains the
State of Colorado's databases of UCC information,
including lien records for all 64 Colorado filing offices.
Offers electronic filing of UCC statements to Secretary of
State. Images cost $1.00 per page viewed.

Commercial Information Systems Inc

PO Box 69174
(4747 SW Kelly #110)
Portland, OR 97201-0174
800-454-6575 Fax: 503-222-7405
www.cis-usa.com **Email:** cis@cis-usa.com
Parent Company: Openonline LLC
Founded: 1991 **Memberships:** SIIA, NACM, NALI,
Clientele Restrictions: Casual requesters permitted
Products, Information Categories, Coverage Area
General:
Addresses/Telephone Numbers (US)
Proprietary Databases or Gateways:
Database Name: Aircraft Registrations
Aviation (US)
Database Name: UCCs
Uniform Commercial Code (CA, ID, OR, WA)
Database Name: Corporations & Limited Partnerships
Corporate/Trade Name Data (CA, ID, OR, WA)

Database Name: Professional Licenses
Licenses/Registrations/Permits (ID, OR, WA)
Database Name: Real Estate Records
Real Estate/Assessor (ID, NV, OR, WA)
Gateway Name: Criminal & Civil Records
Criminal Information,Litigation/Judgments/Tax Liens
(ID, OR, WA, CA)
Database Name: Fish & Wildlife Records
Licenses/Registrations/Permits (ID, OR, NV)
Gateway Name: Driver's License & Registration
Driver and/or Vehicle (ID, OR)
Database Name: Hazardous Materials
Environmental (OR, WA)
Special Distribution Methods to Client: Dial-Up (Other
than Internet), Internet

Commercial Information Systems (CIS) is an online/on-site
database of public records serving business and
government entities. They provide direct access to selected
public and private database records on a national level
through special gateway relationships - for example,
gateway access to OJIN (Oregon) and JIS (Washington)
court records. The CIS integrated regional database
aggregates, commingles and cross-matches records at the
state level by name, address, city, state, ZIP Code, birth
date, driver's license, vehicle plates and other identifiers
with a search engine that allows a subscriber to return all
related records on a common identifier. CIS also provides
information on a manual retrieval basis, including credit
bureau products and services as well as special data mining
capabilities tailored to a clients' specific research or volume
searching needs.

CompactData Solutions

2800 W Mockingbird
Dallas, TX 75235
800-935-9093 Fax: 214-956-6350
www.emarqit.com **Email:** sales@nationsdata.com
Founded: 1993
Clientele Restrictions: Agreement is required.
Products, Information Categories, Coverage Area
Proprietary Databases or Gateways:
Database Name: EMarQit
Addresses/Telephone Numbers, Real Estate/Assessor
(TX)
Database Name: QuikList
Driver and/or Vehicle (TX, FL, OH)
Gateway Name: NationsData.com
Uniform Commercial Code (TX)
Special Distribution Methods to Client: CD-ROM,
Database, Gateway via Another Online Service, Internet

First created in 1993 as a CD-rom product, CompactData
Solutions now offers Internet access to its data, which is
based on appraisal district, and enhanced with address

standardization, telephone numbers, historical values of property, owner birthdates, geocoding, US Census Data. Available on a subscription or Charge-per-record basis as downloadable file in popular formats, display or Word format mailing labels. CASS Certification and other value-added features also available.

Companies Online - Lycos

400-2 Totten Pond Road
Waltham, MA 02451
Fax: 781-370-3412
www.companiesonline.com
Parent Company: Lycos, Inc.
Founded: 1995
Products, Information Categories, Coverage Area
Proprietary Databases or Gateways:
Gateway Name: companiesonline.com
Corporate/Trade Name Data (US)
Special Distribution Methods to Client: Internet

Excellent Internet site with free searching on over 900,000 public and private companies. This is a partnership of Lycos and Dun & Bradstreet, using information from the latter.

Confi-Chek

1816 19th St
Sacramento, CA 95814
800-821-7404
www.confi-chek.com **Email:** support@confi-chek.com
Founded: 1988
Clientele Restrictions: Must be ongoing account
Products, Information Categories, Coverage Area
General:
Litigation/Judgments/Tax Liens (US)
Proprietary Databases or Gateways:
Database Name: Confi-Chek Online
Criminal History (CA)
Special Distribution Methods to Client: Dial-Up (Other than Internet), Internet

Confi-Check provides instant access to national and local records throughout the US. They also offer asset services. Their web site has almost all state records. Dial-up, and, fax call-in services are also available.

Conrad Grundlehner Inc

8605 Brook Rd
McLean, VA 22102-1504
Fax: 703-506-9580
www.superiorinfo.com
Founded: 1984 **Memberships:** SIIA, NPRRA,
Clientele Restrictions: License required
Products, Information Categories, Coverage Area
Proprietary Databases or Gateways:

Database Name: Conrad Grundlehner
Bankruptcy, Litigation/Judgments/Tax Liens (DC, MD, NC, VA, WV)
Special Distribution Methods to Client: Database, Dial-Up (Other than Internet), FTP, Magnetic Tape

Conrad Grundlehner Inc (CGI) was among the first companies to use portable computers to collect legal data at courts and recording offices. The use of notebook computers combined with electronic transmission of data to the customer reduces the time between data collection and its availability to the customer. CGI's information processing expertise also allows it to provide a high degree of customized service to its customers. Data is available online from www.superiorinfo.com.

ConsumerInfo.com

1 City Blvd West #401
Orange, CA 92868
Fax: 215-785-3200
www.iplace.com **Email:** producer@creditmatters.com
Branch Offices:
San Francisco, CA
Founded: 2000
Clientele Restrictions: Registration required.
Products, Information Categories, Coverage Area
General:
Credit Information (US)
Proprietary Databases or Gateways:
Database Name: Qspace, Consumer info
Credit Information (US)
Database Name: e-neighborhoods, iplace
Real Estate/Assessor (US)
Special Distribution Methods to Client: Internet

Formerly iplace.com, they are a provider of personally relevant information about credit, home, neighborhood and other personal assets. The company's services, data, and technologies provide compelling information solutions, relationship building tools and transaction facilitation for more than 100,000 online and offline businesses. With its newly launched iPlace.com, the company introduced its proprietary infoStructure Technology™, enabling businesses to capture and deliver vital customer information while strengthening customer relationships via individually targeted communications.

Contemporary Information Corp.

25044 Peachland Ave #209
Newhall, CA 91321
800-754-0009
www.continfo.com **Email:** wbower@continfo.com
Founded: 1986 **Memberships:** NCRA,
Clientele Restrictions: none reported.

Products, Information Categories, Coverage Area
General:
Education/Employment, Credit Information, Tenant
History (US, CA)
Proprietary Databases or Gateways:
Database Name: Lexidate
Litigation/Judgments/Tax Liens (AZ, CA, NV, OR, WA)
Gateway Name: Continfo/Experiean/Equifax
Credit Information (US, CA)
Database Name: Criminal Scan
Criminal Information (CA)
Database Name: Continfo
Tenant History (US, CA)
Special Distribution Methods to Client: Dial-Up (Other
than Internet), FTP, Gateway via Another Online Service

CIC offers tenant screening and employment background
checks including credit, evictions (public records), criminal
history, drug testing, bad check search, criving records, and
reference verifications. In addition to the applications
mentioned above, their services are also of use in fraud
prevention, collections, legal compliance, and risk
management. CIC is an authorized agent of Experian
Business Credit; CIC sells a complete line of business
credit reporting solutions. The CA Eviction database is
searchable by defendant. CIC offers wholesale prices to
other credit reporting agencies. Other public record
databases are available.

CorporateInformation.com
440 Wheelers Farms Road
Milford, CT 06460
800-232-0013
http://corporateinformation.com **Email:**
regnery@wisi.com
Parent Company: The Winthrop Corporation
Clientele Restrictions: None Reported
Products, Information Categories, Coverage Area
Proprietary Databases or Gateways:
Database Name: Corporate/Trade Name Data
Corporate/Trade Name Data, Foreign Country
Information (US, Intl)
Special Distribution Methods to Client: Internet

Features include: research a company; research a
company's industry; research by country; and research by
state among others. A very informative web site with much
information available at no charge.

CountryWatch Inc.
Three Riverway #710
Houston, TX 77056
800-879-3885 Fax: 713-355-2008
www.countrywatch.com **Email:**
subscribe@countrywatch.com

Founded: 1997
Clientele Restrictions: Casual requesters permitted, but
subscription required for ongoing customers
Products, Information Categories, Coverage Area
Proprietary Databases or Gateways:
Database Name: Countrywatch.com db
Foreign Country Information (INTL – 193 Countries)
Special Distribution Methods to Client: CD-ROM,
Database, Internet

Countrywatch.com is a growing online publisher providing
original content and aggregated news to customers needing
real-time, quality, formatted political, economic,
cultural/demographic and environmental information and
data on each country of the world. In addition,
Countrywatch Inc provides a global forecast product that
covers 193 countries. The product, which is updated
monthly, is based on a standardized economic model that
projects key economic variables in a consistent manner
across every country in the world. This product is
interactive, integrated and visually oriented. Users can
agree with the default output or make their own
assumptions by varying the chosen parameters in a user
friendly Excel environment.

Court PC of Connecticut
PO Box 11081
Greenwich, CT 06831-1081
Fax: 203-531-6899
http://courtpcofct.com **Email:** jel@courtpcofct.com
Founded: 1992 **Memberships:** NPRRA
Clientele Restrictions: Casual requesters occasionally
permitted
Products, Information Categories, Coverage Area
General:
Bankruptcy (US, CT)
Proprietary Databases or Gateways:
Database Name: Superior Index
Litigation/Judgments/Tax Liens, Criminal Information
(CT)

Court PC is Connecticut's comprehensive source of docket
search information from Superior Court and US District
Court cases. Their Connecticut Superior Court database
contains records of civil filings since 1985, family/divorce
filings since 1989, and discloseable criminal convictions
since 1991. Microfiche indexes supplement PACER data to
provide complete USDC/CT civil and criminal searches
from 1970 forward. Court PC also provides current
corporation (also LPs and LLCs) and tax lien data from the
Connecticut Secretary of State database.

CourtExpress.com (RIS Legal Svcs)

701 Pennsylvania Avenue NW
Washington, DC 20004-2608
800-542-3320 Fax: 202-737-3324
http://courtexpress.com **Email:** info@courtexpress.com
Parent Company: RIS Legal Services
Founded: 2000
Clientele Restrictions: Registration required
Products, Information Categories, Coverage Area
Proprietary Databases or Gateways:
Gateway Name: US Court Records
Bankruptcy (US)
Gateway Name: State Court Records
Litigation/Judgments/Tax Liens
(AZ,CA,CT,FL,IA,MO,VA)
Special Distribution Methods to Client: Email, Internet

CourtEXPRESS.com delivers powerful U.S. Court searching and document delivery features to your desktop. They cover most of the U.S. Federal District and Bankruptcy Courts, also providing searching from the U.S. Party Case Index from three files: civil, criminal and bankruptcy, which they call the National Locator Service or "NLS." Every step is easier and more productive than all other traditional searching methods. Rather than waiting online for results, CourtEXPRESS.com will alert you via Email when your search is done. Each member has access to their last 100 searches, including Due Diligence for Federal cases and Case Tracker for current cases. Other searches can be set up to repeat daily or weekly. Document ordering takes only seconds. Try either a Guest Quick Search or get a Private Guest Account.

CourtH.com

PO Box 70558
Houston, TX 77270-0558
800-925-4225 Fax: 713-683-0493
www.courth.com **Email:** orders@courth.com
Branch Offices:
Richmond, TX
281-342-1777
Parent Company: Right-of-Way Acquisition Services Inc
Founded: 1982 **Memberships:** NACM
Clientele Restrictions: Casual requesters permitted
Products, Information Categories, Coverage Area
General:
Bankruptcy (TX)
Proprietary Databases or Gateways:
Database Name: Courthouse Research
Corporate/Trade Name Data, Real Estate/Assessor,
Litigation/judgments/Tax Liens (TX)

Special Distribution Methods to Client: Dial-Up (Other than Internet), Email, Internet

Our Internet service provides access to 30 databases of public information from marriage records to property records to bankruptcies. Our proprietary database consists of public records from Harris, Montgomery, and Fort Bend counties. These records are easily searched on our web site.

Courthouse Retrieval System Inc.

6700 Baum Dr #12
Knoxville, TN 37919
800-374-7488 Fax: 865-584-8047
www.crsdata.net **Email:** efinger@crsdata.net
Founded: 1985
Clientele Restrictions: Most requesters must sign agreement, but some casual, one-time requesters accepted,
Products, Information Categories, Coverage Area
General:
Real Estate/Assessor (AL, NC, TN)
Proprietary Databases or Gateways:
Database Name: CRSdata.net; ids™
Real Estate/Assessor (AL, NC, TN)
Special Distribution Methods to Client: CD-ROM, Disk, Internet, Lists/Labels

CR System Inc. provides real estate information (including tax records and mortgage information, but not limited to) on a subscription basis via the Internet to realtors, real estate appraisers, mortgage companies, etc. Specializes in AL, NC & TN, and limited counties in SC & VA. Various Internet and CD products available.

CourthouseDirect.com

9800 Northwest Fwy #400
Houston, TX 77092
Fax: 713-683-0493
http://courthousedirect.com **Email:** info@courthousedirect.com
Branch Offices:
Dallas, TX, 214-443-9355; Fax: 214-443-9207
Richmond, TX, 281-342-1777; Fax: 281-342-4485
Bryan/College Station, TX, 979-695-6504; Fax: 979-492-9664
Founded: 1982 **Memberships:** NAR, NPRRA, IRWA
Clientele Restrictions: Subscription preferred; credit card requestors accepted for casual requesters
Products, Information Categories, Coverage Area
General:
Litigation/Judgments/Tax Liens (US)
Proprietary Databases or Gateways:
Gateway Name: Real Estate/Assessor
Real Estate/Assessor (AZ, CA, FL, HI, IL, NY, OK, PA, TX, UT, WA)

Gateway Name: Real Property Documents
Litigation/Judgments/Tax Liens (AZ, CA, FL, HI, IL, NY, OK, PA, TX, UT, WA)
Special Distribution Methods to Client: Internet

CourthouseDirect.com, a specialized Internet portal based in Houston, provides electronic document images of Deeds, Mortgages, Releases, IRS Liens, Assignments, and other county Real Property and Official Record filings via the Internet. CourthouseDirect.com currently provides images for major counties in California, Florida, Arizona, Illinois, Michigan, New York, Oklahoma, and Texas. The current database contains 12 counties in Texas and 138 counties nationwide. CourthouseDirect.com expects to have images for 85% of the U. S. population online by the end of the year 2003. In addition to those listed above, other applications includes collections, geneology research, and litigation.

CourtLink

13427 NE 16th St, #100
Bellevue, WA 98005-2307
800-774-7317 Fax: 425-974-1419
www.courtlink.com **Email:** support@courtlink.com
Parent Company: Lexis-Nexis
Founded: 1986 **Memberships:** AALL, ABI, NACM, NAFE, SLA,
Clientele Restrictions: Casual requesters permitted
Products, Information Categories, Coverage Area
Proprietary Databases or Gateways:
Gateway Name: CourtLink®eAccess
Bankruptcy, Litigation/Judgments/Tax Liens (US)
Special Distribution Methods to Client: Dial-Up (Other than Internet), Disk, Email, FTP, Internet, Lists/Labels

CourtLink® has been developing, providing and refining online solutions for accessing court records and filing and processing court documents and case information. With a single online platform for both electronic access and filing, LexisNexis CourtLink is delivering on its mission to improve the speed, quality and overall effectiveness of connecting the legal and business communities to our nation's courts. We offer online access to more than 200 million court records. Our client base represents over 50,000 individual users in all 50 states, including 230 of the 250 largest law firms in the U.S. Our customers also include the largest banks, insurance companies and title insurance companies in the country.

Credentials Inc

550 Frontage Road #3500
Northfield, IL 60093
Fax: 847-446-7424
www.degreechk.com **Email:** tmckechney@degreechk.com
Founded: 1997

Clientele Restrictions: Casual requesters permitted
Products, Information Categories, Coverage Area
Proprietary Databases or Gateways:
Database Name: Degreechk
Education/Employment (US)
Special Distribution Methods to Client: Email, Internet

Credentials Inc offers 24 hour, 365 day Internet access to degree verification from participating colleges and universities. All verification transactions are uniquely audit-trailed and confirmed to the user via fax or email, often within the hour. In addition to online databases provided by participating schools, the system includes an off-line, archival search capability for degrees that are not included in the online database. This feature is important since most school databases only date back to the early or mid-1980s. All interactions with degreechk.com are fully encrypted. Growth in the number of school listed is expected; will broadcast email notifications of new school additions to the Degreechk.com menu.

Criminal Information Services Inc

PO Box 7235
Aloha, OR 97007-7235
800-973-5500 Fax: 503-642-7730
www.criminalinfo.com **Email:** crim@earthlink.net
Founded: 1993
Clientele Restrictions: Casual requesters permitted
Products, Information Categories, Coverage Area
Proprietary Databases or Gateways:
Database Name: CRIS
Criminal Information
(AZ,AR,CT,FL,GA,HI,ID,IL,IN,KY,MI,MN,MS,MO, NC,ND,NJ,NY,OH,OK,OR,SC,TX,UT,WA)
Database Name: CRIS
Tenant History (AZ,CA,ID,NV,OR,WA)
Special Distribution Methods to Client: Email, Internet

Criminal Information Services Inc (CRIS) offers Internet access to state-wide Department of Corrections conviction history databases from a growing number of states. More states will be added in the near future. Owned and operated by former criminal-justice professionals, CRIS provides real-time access to these databases, by alpha search and birthdate comparisons, with "hits" providing conviction date, county of offense, offense description and sentencing information. Reports, including "No Record Found" reports are easy to print. Prices, based on a name check basis and monthly volume, are very inexpensive and affordable.

Daily Report, The

310 H Street
Bakersfield, CA 93304-2914
Fax: 661-322-9084
www.thedailyreport.com **Email:** staff@thedailyreport.com **Memberships:** PRRN

Clientele Restrictions: Casual requesters permitted
Products, Information Categories, Coverage Area
Proprietary Databases or Gateways:
Database Name: The Daily Report
Addresses/Telephone Numbers,
Licenses/Registrations/Permits,
Litigation/Judgments/Tax Liens (CA-Kern County)
Special Distribution Methods to Client: Internet,
Publication/Directory

The Daily Report is a legal newspaper, published
continuously since August 21, 1907. Since publication
began, the volume of information filed with the Courts and
Hall of Records in Kern County has increased significantly.
This web site was developed in response to a growing need
expressed by our subscribers to easily search for
information filed in the Courts and Hall of Records
pertinent to their specific needs. With The Daily Report,
online subscribers can now browse for information filed
with the Courts such as New Suits or Judgments and the
Hall of Records, featuring most all recorded documents,
including Notices of Default, Deeds, Maps, Liens and Oil
and Gas leases. Other information such as Building Permits
and business Licenses are also available through our
specially designed search engine.

Data Downlink xls.com
c/o Alacra (and/or Angle Software)
88 Pine St, 3rd Fl
New York, NY 10005
www.xls.com **Email:** info@xls.com
Branch Offices:
London, GB, 44.(0)20.7398.1300
New York, NY, 888-333-0820
Paris, FR, 33 (0)1 44 71 36 72
Parent Company: Alacra
Founded: 1996
Clientele Restrictions: Subscription required.
Products, Information Categories, Coverage Area
General:
Business Information (US, Itl, Canada)
Proprietary Databases or Gateways:
Database Name: xls.com
Addresses/Telephone Numbers; Corporate/Trade Name
Data; SEC/Other Financial (US, FR, GB, Intl)
Special Distribution Methods to Client: Internet,
Publication/Directory

Data Dowlink, xls.com offers a wide range of company
information, much for investing purposes. They deliver
precise, current and reliable business information to the
corporate desktop via the Internet or a firm's Intranet. Their
Internet technology and sophisticated relational databases
(60) are tailored to meet business research needs. Their
diverse portfolio of products and services (Portal B is a

business search engine) is designed specifically for the
business information market.

Datalink Services Inc
PO Box 188416
Sacramento, CA 95818
Fax: 916-916-451-2623
www.imvrs.com **Email:** tohare@imvrs.com
Founded: 1983
Clientele Restrictions: Casual requesters not permitted
Products, Information Categories, Coverage Area
General:
Corporate/Trade Name Data (CA)
Proprietary Databases or Gateways:
Gateway Name: Driving, Vehicle & Dealer Records
Driver and/or Vehicle (CA)
Special Distribution Methods to Client: Email, Internet

Datalink specializes in processing and providinginstant
California DMV records with speed and accuracy, offering
one of the industry's most innovative web site for
California DMV data. Also, the web site processes driving
records from all states nationwide. For over nineteen years,
Datalink has been at the forefront of technological
advances, letting them ensure the quality and reliability of
their service. The mission of the highly-trained staff is
always to assist with the best and most efficient service
possible through loyalty and honesty, principles on which
their business is built.

DataQuick
9620 Towne Centre Dr
San Diego, CA 92121
888-604-3282 Fax: 858-455-7406
www.dataquick.com **Email:** smorga@dataquick.com
Parent Company: MacDonald Detwiler
Founded: 1978 **Memberships:** REIPA
Clientele Restrictions: Casual requesters permitted
Products, Information Categories, Coverage Area
Proprietary Databases or Gateways:
Database Name: DataQuick
Real Estate/Assessor (US)
Special Distribution Methods to Client: Dial-Up (Other
than Internet), Disk, Lists/Labels, Magnetic Tape

A leading name in real property information products,
DataQuick services the title, mortgage, real estate and
insurance industries. They provide property details such as:
ownership and address information; sale and loan details;
characteristics such as sq footage etc.; and historical sales
and data such as previous transactions for marketing and
research purposes. They cover household development
demographics and market trend data.

Data-Trac Network Inc

PO Box 488
Elmont, NY 11003
www.data-trac.com **Email:** support@data-trac.com
Founded: 1988
Clientele Restrictions: Access permitted only to the
Investigative and Security And Human Resources
Communities
an application and signed release with all confirmed
documentation
as to professional status is required before access can be
obtained.

Products, Information Categories, Coverage Area
General:
Criminal Information (US)
Proprietary Databases or Gateways:
Database Name: Profile Reports
Addresses/Telephone Numbers (US)

Database Name: NYC Criminal Records
Criminal Information (NY City)

Special Distribution Methods to Client: Dial-Up (Other
than Internet), Internet

Data-Trac is an online investigative network providing
instant access to public records. They also offer customized
pre-employment services and records searches. They
maintain a database and are a public record manufacturer.

DCS Information Systems

500 N Central Expressway #280
Plano, TX 75074
800-394-3274 Fax: 972-422-3621
www.dcs-amerifind.com **Email:** carroll@dcs-
amerifind.com
Founded: 1967
Clientele Restrictions: signed agreement required;
business or government agencies only

Products, Information Categories, Coverage Area
Proprietary Databases or Gateways:
Database Name: AmeriFind
Addresses/Telephone Numbers, Real Estate/Assessor,
Colorado Court Records (US)

Database Name: Texas Systems
Driver and/or Vehicle, Real Estate/Assessor, Vital
Records (marriage & divorce) (TX)

Special Distribution Methods to Client: Dial-Up (Other
than Internet), Internet

DCS' national product, AmeriFind, is a very effective and
comprehensive skip tracing, locating, fraud prevention and
investigation tools. Access to credit headers is provided for
GLB exception purposes. County courthouse criminal
history searches and online telephone directory assistance
is also available via DCS' products. The Texas product
provides comprehensive, up-to-date information on Texas

drivers and vehicle owners, with up to 13 years of history.
These systems provide the users with search capabilities
not available from other suppliers. DCS offers customized
information solutions for large volume users.

Derwent Information

1725 Duke Street #250
Alexandria, VA 22314
800-337-9368 Fax: 703-838-5240
www.derwent.com **Email:** custserv@derwentus.com
Parent Company: The Thompson Corporation
Founded: 1952
Clientele Restrictions: None reported

Products, Information Categories, Coverage Area
Proprietary Databases or Gateways:
Database Name: Derwent World Patents Index,
Trademarks/Patents, Corporate/Trade Name Data (US,
INTL)

Special Distribution Methods to Client: Dial-Up (Other
than Internet), Email, Internet, Publication/Directory

With offices in London, Japan, and Alexandria, Derwent
provides access to the over 200,000 patents filed each year
in the US alone while the European Patent office files
around 80,000 patents a year. Derwent makes this
information easily accessible by combining the world's
patents on one searchable database. During our editorial
process, a team of more than 350 specialist editors assess,
classify and index patent documents to provide concise
English language abstracts which are readily searched and
easily understood. With a wide range of delivery options,
Derwent ensures that companies are kept fully aware of the
latest developments in today's fast moving markets.

Dialog

11000 Regency Parkway
Cary, NC 27511
800-334-2564 Fax: 919-461-7252
www.dialog.com
Branch Offices:
London, 44-20-7940-6900; Fax: 44-20-7940-6800
Hong Kong, 852-2530-5778; Fax: 852-2530-5885
Founded: 1972
Clientele Restrictions: Casual Requesters Permitted

Products, Information Categories, Coverage Area
Proprietary Databases or Gateways:
Gateway Name: DIALOG Web; DataStar; Profound;
Intelliscope; Insite; IntraScope
Foreign Country Information, Corporate/Trade Name
Data, Trademarks, Legislation/Regulation, SEC/Other
Financial (US,Intl)

Gateway Name: NewsEdge
News/Current Events (US)

Special Distribution Methods to Client: CD-ROM,
Dial-Up (Other than Internet), Internet, Software

Dialog, a Thompson company, is a worldwide pioneer and leader in providing online information services to organizations seeking competitive advantages in business, finance and law, among others. With over 15 terabytes of data, Dialog's collection of 900 databases handles more than 700,000 searches and delivers over 17 million document page views per month. Dialog offers 35 products and services, including the Dialog, DataStar and Profound product lines and recent additions NewsEdge and Intelligence Data's Intelliscope. Content areas include intellectual property, government regulations, social sciences, food and agriculture, news and media, business and finance, reference, energy and environment, chemicals, pharmaceuticals, science and technology, and medicine. With operations in 32 countries, Dialog's global knowledge centers provide the highest levels of customer service to an international audience of 100,00+ professional researchers in over 103 countries.

Diligenz Inc

4629 168th St SE, #E
Lynnwood, WA 98037
800-858-5294
www.diligenz.com **Email:** sales@diligenz.com
Memberships: NPPRA, PRRN, UAEL, CFA,
Clientele Restrictions: Sign-up required.
Products, Information Categories, Coverage Area
General:
Bankruptcy (US)
Proprietary Databases or Gateways:
Database Name: Diligenz.com
Uniform Commercial Code, Corporate/Trade Name Data (US)
Gateway Name: Diligenz
Bankruptcy, Litigation/Judgments/Tax Liens (US)
Special Distribution Methods to Client: Email, FTP, Internet

Diligenz is a one-stop source for due dilligence needs from UCC and corporate searches to the management and tracking of filings, plus complete support services. They provide databases of public records, especially to the search and retrieval of Uniform Commercial Code and Corporate information. Financial statements, continuations, amendments are also here, also records pertaining to corporate status, ownership interests, business credit and business licensing information. Their web site offers rapid response and total reliability. The online search interface allows you to order and retrieve searches, and view and print documents online.

Discovering Montana

111 North Last Chance Gulch #3J
Helena, MT 59601
www.discoveringmontana.com/ **Email:**
rich@discoveringmontana.com
Founded: 2000
Clientele Restrictions: None, except for premium services which requires membership
Products, Information Categories, Coverage Area
Proprietary Databases or Gateways:
Gateway Name: Discoveringmontana
Driver and/or Vehicle, Corporate/Trade Name Data, Legislation/Regulation (MT)
Special Distribution Methods to Client: Internet

DiscoveringMontana.com, the official web site of the State of Montana, is a gateway to a myriad of state information and services. Many free services are available, as well as "premium services' which require fees and registration. Online certificates allows you to search all businesses registered in the state of Montana then print Certificates of Existence, Authorization, and fact. Registered Principal Search permits look up of officers and directors by name and by organization (app.discoveringmontana.com/rps). This site also gives pre-approved clients access to access driving records in both interatcive and batch modes. In the summer of 2002, Discovering Montana plans to introduce an online UCC filing and searching services.

Dun & Bradstreet

1 Diamond Hill Rd
Murray Hill, NJ 07974
800-234-3867
www.dnb.com
Branch Offices:
Murry Hill, NJ, 800-234-3867
Memberships: NPRRA
Clientele Restrictions: Casual requesters permitted
Products, Information Categories, Coverage Area
Proprietary Databases or Gateways:
Database Name: D & B Public Record Search
Addresses/Telephone Numbers, Bankruptcy, Corporate/Trade Name Data, Credit Information, Litigation/Judgments/Tax Liens and Uniform Commercial Code (US, PR, VI)
Database Name: Business Credit Information
Credit Information (US,PR,VI)
Special Distribution Methods to Client: Dial-Up (Other than Internet), Disk, Internet, Software

D&B is a leading provider of business information for credit, marketing, purchasing, and receivables management decisions worldwide. More than 100,000 companies rely on D&B to provide the insight they need to help build profitable, quality business relationships with their customers, suppliers and business partners. Dun & Bradstreet's Public Records Search database is one of the most extensive commercial public record information sites available. It is probably the only online database of corporate, UCC, litigation and tax lien information about businesses that covers all 50 states, the Virgin Islands, Puerto Rico and the District of Columbia. The 800 number listed above is for business credit information.

eCCLIX - Software Management Inc.

2011 Cobalt Ave.
Louisville, KY 40299
800-466-9445; Fax: 502-266-9445
www.ecclix.com **Email:**
sales@softwaremanagementinc.com
Parent Company: Software Management Inc.
Founded: 1998
Clientele Restrictions: Signed agreement required.
Products, Information Categories, Coverage Area
Proprietary Databases or Gateways:
Database Name: CCLIX-OptiMA and CCLIX System
Real Estate/Assessor, Litigation/Judgments/Tax Liens (KY)
Special Distribution Methods to Client: Internet

eCCLIX is the searchable internet version of CCLIX, a database produced for, and used by, about half the KY County Clerks for their electronic imaging and filing. Three Counties - Boone, Oldham, Warren - are available to non-government subscribers on eCCLIX. Availabe data includes real estate, liens, UCCs, marriage, and tax assessor records - UCC and liens back to 1987, real estate to 1989 (images to 1998).

EdVerify Inc

2240 W Woodbright Rd #412
Boynton Beach, FL 33426
877-338-3743 ; Fax: 516-746-9023
www.edverify.com
Founded: 1998
Clientele Restrictions: Signed agreement required, must be ongoing account
Products, Information Categories, Coverage Area
Proprietary Databases or Gateways:
Database Name: EdVerify.com
Education/Employment (US)
Special Distribution Methods to Client: Email, Internet

EdVerify has automated education and enrollment verifications for every accredited post secondary school in the nation, and quickly responds to verification requests via the Internet. The company offers the exchange of data to high volume clients through an FTP "batch" transfer protocol or by an HTTPS real time, server-to-server

protocol; and offers attractive pricing discounts to large accounts. EdVerify acts as the agent for educational institutions by consolidating Directory Information as defined by FERPA.

Electronic Property Information Corp (EPIC)

227 Alexander St #206
Rochester, NY 14607
Fax: 716-486-0098
Founded: 1987
Clientele Restrictions: None reported
Products, Information Categories, Coverage Area
Proprietary Databases or Gateways:
Database Name: OPRA
Real Estate/Assessor, Uniform Commerical Code, Litigation/Judgments/Tax Liens and Wills/Probate (NY-Erie, Monroe Counties)
Database Name: OPRA
Bankruptcy (NY)
Special Distribution Methods to Client: Dial-Up (Other than Internet), Internet

EPIC provides online access to their proprietary database of all public records affecting real property in Erie and Monroe Counties, NY and bankruptcy records for New York's Western and Northern Districts. In addition to helping create abstracts and write title insurance, the database has been used for collections, asset search, and individual and business screening applications.

E-Merges.com

1756 Ebling Tl #2000
Annapolis, MD 21401-6614
Fax: 801-437-3555
www.e-merges.com/ **Email:** info@e-merges.com
Clientele Restrictions: None reported
Products, Information Categories, Coverage Area
Proprietary Databases or Gateways:
Database Name: US Registered Voter File
Voter Registration
(AK,AR,CO,CT,DE,DC,FL,GA,IL,IN,IA,KS,LA,MA,MI MN,MO,NV,NJ,NY,NC,OH,OK,RI,SC,TX,UT,VA,WI)
Database Name: Hunting/Fishing Licenses
Licenses/Registrations/Permits
(AK,AR,CT,DE,FL,GA,KS,MS,MO,NV,NJ,NC,ND,OH, SC,UT,VA,WA)
Special Distribution Methods to Client: CD-ROM, Database, Disk, Magnetic Tape

E-Merges provides voter registration records with date of birth for unrestricted use from AK, AR CO, CT, DE, DC, LA, MA, MI, NV, NY, NC, OH, OK, RI, SC, UT, and WI (and other states with restrictions). They will sell by county, state, or entire file, which is updated annually and is internally compiled from 3600 towns and counties across the USA. They also track Hunting/Fishing data in 17 states; and organ donors for most states.

Environmental Data Resources, Inc. (EDR)

3530 Post Rd
Southport, CT 06490
800-352-0050
www.edrnet.com
Founded: 1991
Clientele Restrictions: Casual requesters permitted

Products, Information Categories, Coverage Area
Proprietary Databases or Gateways:
Database Name: NEDIS, Sanborn Maps
Environmental, Licenses/Registratoins/Permits, and Real Estate/Assessor (US)

Environmental Data Resources, Inc. (EDR) is an information company specializing in providing data on environmental liabilities associated with companies and properties. EDR provides this data to environmental consulting firms, banks, insurance companies, law firms, corporations and accounting firms. EDR has compiled and organized more than 600 separate government databases, obtained at the federal, state and local levels, into an environmental database referred to as NEDIS, the National Environmental Data Information System. On March 25, 2002, Environmental Data Resources, Inc. acquired certain assets of Fidelity National Information Solutions' (FNIS) environmental information operations including assets previously owned by VISTAinfo and EcoSearch. FNIS' environmental information businesses were also transitioned to EDR as of this date.

Equifax Credit Services

1600 Peachtree St NW
Atlanta, GA 30309
888-202-4025
www.equifax.com **Email:** customer.care@equifax.com
Parent Company: Equifax Inc
Founded: 1899 **Memberships:** AAMVA
Clientele Restrictions: Signed agreemnet required for Hoover's Online subscription

Products, Information Categories, Coverage Area
Proprietary Databases or Gateways:
Database Name: Credit Profile
Credit Information (US)
Database Name: Investigation System Persona
Addresses/Telephone Numbers, Education/Employment, Bankruptcy, Litigation/Judgments/Tax Liens (US)
Special Distribution Methods to Client: Dial-Up (Other than Internet), Internet

Equifax is a leading provider of consumer and commercial financial information worldwide. The database includes information on almost 400 million consumers and businesses around the world.

Ernst Publishing Co, LLC

2280 Grass Valley Hwy #215
Auburn, CA 9603
800-345-3822
www.ernst.cc **Email:** lrcanier@ernst.cc
Parent Company: Ernst Publishing Company, LLC
Founded: 1992 **Memberships:** AIIP, SIIA, NPRRA,
Clientele Restrictions: None reported

Products, Information Categories, Coverage Area
Proprietary Databases or Gateways:
Database Name: Uniform Commercial Code Filing Guide
Uniform Commercial Code Filing Guide (US)
Database Name: Real Estate Recording Guide
Real Estate/Assessor (US)
Special Distribution Methods to Client: Database, Internet, Publication/Directory

The Uniform Comemrcial Code Filing Guide™ is a practical "How To" reference for the preparation, filing and searching of Article 9 Financing Statements nationwide. This Guide provides information re: fees, forms, facts for all 4,316 filing jurisidictions and is designed for the high-volume multi-juridiction filer. Included are sections hosting the Model Act, Filing Fundamentals, Purchase Money Secured Interest snd Definitions. Subscription is annual with quarterly updates; a newsletter is provided in non-updating months. The new Revised Article 9 Alert assists filers and searchers to function in the new Revision environment. They also publish the Real Estate Recording Guide and National Release Guide and offer a database and web-based product – National Online Mortgage Assistance Database Program.

Everton Publishers

PO Box 368
Logan, UT 84323
800-443-6325
www.everton.com **Email:** leverton@everton.com
Founded: 1947
Clientele Restrictions: None reported

Products, Information Categories, Coverage Area
Proprietary Databases or Gateways:
Database Name: Everton's Online Search
Addresses/Telephone Numbers (US)
Special Distribution Methods to Client: Dial-Up (Other than Internet), Internet

Everton has offered online access since 1990. The company publishes the Everton's Genealogical Helper magazine and The Handbook For Genealogists.

Experian Information Solutions

500 City Parkway West #205
Orange, CA 92868
888-397-3742
www.experian.com
Parent Company: GUS, plc
Clientele Restrictions: Casual requesters permitted
Products, Information Categories, Coverage Area
Proprietary Databases or Gateways:
Database Name: File 1
Consumer File
Credit Information, Addresses/Telephone Numbers (US)
Special Distribution Methods to Client: Dial-Up (Other than Internet), Internet

As the consumer credit arm of Experian, data from Experian Information Solutions (formerly Experian Consumer Credit) may be used for a variety of purposes related to individuals, subject to permissible purposes. Individuals who need assistance with reports should call 888-397-3742.

Experian Online

505 City Parkway
Orange, CA 92868
800-831-5614
www.experian.com
Parent Company: GUS, plc
Clientele Restrictions: None reported
Products, Information Categories, Coverage Area
Proprietary Databases or Gateways:
Database Name: Experian Online
Addresses/Telephone Numbers, Driver and/or Vehicle, Real Estate/Assessor (US)
Database Name: Experian Online Business Records Reports
Uniform Commercial Code, Corporate/Trade Name Data, Bankruptcy (US)
Special Distribution Methods to Client: Dial-Up (Other than Internet), Disk, Internet, Magnetic Tape

Experian is an information solutions company. We help organizations to use information to reach new customers and to develop successful and long lasting customer relationships. We have built our business on the simple premise that commercial success is about getting close to customers. The more an organisation understands them, the more able it is to respond to their very individual needs and circumstances. This is the approach that we adopt in our own client relationships. It is also the underlying motivation behind everything we do as a company.

Explore Information Services

2945 Lone Oak Dr, #150
Eagan, MN 55121
800-531-9125 Fax: 651-385-2281
www.exploredata.com **Email:**
explore.info@exploredata.com
Clientele Restrictions: Signed agreement required, must be ongoing account
Products, Information Categories, Coverage Area
Proprietary Databases or Gateways:
Database Name: EARS and RiskAlert
Driver and/or Vehicle (AL, AZ, CA, CO, CT, DE, FL, ID, IA, KS, KY, MA, MD, ME, MI, MN, MO, MT, NE, NH, NV, NY, OH, OR, SC, TN, TX, UT, WI, WV, WY)
Special Distribution Methods to Client: Dial-Up (Other than Internet), Disk, FTP, Internet, Magnetic Tape

E.A.R.S. (Electronically Accessed Reunderwriting Service) monitors insured drivers for "moving violations" activity and notifies insurers prior to policy renewal. RiskAlert provides monthly notification of newly licensed youthful drivers.

Fairchild Record Search Ltd

PO Box 1368
Olympia, WA 98507
800-547-7007
www.recordsearch.com
Founded: 1980 **Memberships:** NPRRA, NFIB, PRRN,
Clientele Restrictions: Casual requesters permitted
Products, Information Categories, Coverage Area
General:
Uniform Commercial Code (US, AK, ID, OR, WA)
Proprietary Databases or Gateways:
Gateway Name: UCC
Uniform Commercial Code (US)
Gateway Name: Washington
Corporate/Trade Name Data (WA)
Gateway Name: Courtlink; Motznicks
Litigation/Judgments/Tax Liens (AK, WA)
Special Distribution Methods to Client: Email

Fairchild has specialized in public record retrieval service - emphasize "service" - in the US Northwest and in Alaska for more than 15 years. Primary capabilities include UCC/corporate document filing, retrieval and wildcard searching. Due to their long presence in the area they have established experience in filing and retrieval of virtually any public record documents in those states.

Fidelifacts

42 Broadway
New York, NY 10004
800-678-0007 Fax: 212-248-5619
www.fidelifacts.com **Email:** norton@fidelifacts.com
Founded: 1956 **Memberships:** EMA, SHRM, NCISS,
ASIS, PRRN,
Clientele Restrictions: Casual requesters permitted
Products, Information Categories, Coverage Area
General:
Bankruptcy (US, NY)
Proprietary Databases or Gateways:
Gateway Name: Fidelifacts
Credit Information (US, NY)

Among the oldest companies engaged in the business of
providing background reports on individuals for
employment purposes and on companies, Fidelifacts has a
network of investigators in offices around the country, and
local personnel who examine public records in less
populated areas. Fidelifacts specialty is conducting
background investigations, reference checks, screening
checks of job applicants and due diligence investigations.
They also provide asset location services, skip tracing and
other services on legal matters. Their in-house database
lists 1,500,000 names of persons arrested, indicted,
convicted, and otherwise had problems with the law. Data
is primarily for metro New York area, but also includes
SEC/NASD filings where unlawful activity may be a
question. They are located near the NY Office of Court
Admin. and pickup criminal record checks at the OCA
daily. They offer 24-hour service to these NY Counties:
New York, Queens, Kings, Bronx, Richmond, Nassau,
Suffolk, Rockland, Westchester, Dutchess, Orange,
Putnam, Erie.

First American Corporation, The

1 First American Way
Santa Ana, CA 92707
800-854-3643
http://firstam.com **Email:** jbandy@firstam.com
Branch Offices:
900+ offices in USA & abroad.
Products, Information Categories, Coverage Area
Proprietary Databases or Gateways:
Database Name: Real Estate Information
Real Estate/Assessor (US)
Special Distribution Methods to Client: Automated
Telephone Look-Up, CD-ROM, Gateway via Another
Online Service, Internet

First American Corp. is a leading provider of business
information and related products and services. Their 3
primary business segments include: title insurance &
services; real estate information & services, which includes

mortgage and database information and services; and
consumer information & services which provides
automotive, subprime and direct-to-consumer credit
reporting; residence and pre-employment screening, auto
insurance tracking, property & casualty insurance, home
warranties, investment advisory, and trust & banking
services. Visit www.firstam.com for further information.

First American Real Estate Solutions East

8160 Corporate Park Dr #200
Cincinnati, OH 45242
800-582-7300 Fax: 513-489-4409
www.firstamres.com **Email:** sales.res.ca@firstam.com
Branch Offices:
Columbus, OH, 614-277-9688; Fax: 614-277-9689
Detroit, MI, 248-348-8112; Fax: 248-348-8101
Cleveland, OH, 440-974-7863; Fax: 440-974-7935
Founded: 1980 **Memberships:** MBAA, NAR, REIPA,
Clientele Restrictions: Casual requesters permitted
Products, Information Categories, Coverage Area
Proprietary Databases or Gateways:
Database Name: PaceNet, MetroScan, Win2Data
Mortgage Data and Addresses/Telephone Numbers (KY,
MI, OH, MO, PA, IL, TN)
Database Name: PaceNet, Prospect Services
Real Estate/Assessor (KY, MI, OH)
Special Distribution Methods to Client: CD-ROM,
Dial-Up (Other than Internet), Disk, Lists/Labels,
Magnetic Tape

First Am. Real Estate Solutions maintains databases of
existing real estate ownership and gathers and verifies data
from courthouse public records and other sources on all
real estate sales. They collect most information manually,
assuring accuracy, completeness and timely information.
Property addresses are standardized and updated quarterly
to current CASS standards required by the USPS.

First American Real Estate Solutions West

5601 E. La Palma Ave
Anaheim, CA 92807
800-345-7334
www.firstamres.com **Email:** sales.res.ca@firstam.com
Parent Company: First American Financial Corporation
Clientele Restrictions: Casual requesters permitted
Products, Information Categories, Coverage Area
Proprietary Databases or Gateways:
Database Name: Real Property Database
Real Estate/Assessor (AL, AZ, CA, CO, DC, DE, FL,
GA, HI, IL, IN, LA, MA, MD, MI, MN, MS, NC, NJ,
NM, NY, NV, OH, OK, OR, PA, SC, TN, TX, UT, VA,
VI, WA, WI)

Special Distribution Methods to Client: CD-ROM, Microfilm/Microfiche

First American Real Estate Solutions is now part of the First American Financial Corporation. They are a leading provider of real estate information from major counties in most US states. Call for specific coverage and access via online database, CD-ROM and microfiche information.

First American Registry

11140 Rockville Pike #1200
Rockville, MD 20852
800-999-0350 Fax: 301-984-7312
www.registrycheck.com **Email:** sales@registrynet.com
Parent Company: First American Financial Inc
www.firstam.com
Founded: 1984 **Memberships:** NASA, NAA, NAHRO, NAREIT,
Clientele Restrictions: Casual requesters permitted

Products, Information Categories, Coverage Area
Proprietary Databases or Gateways:
Database Name: Trans Registry, Tenant Account Records,
Litigation/Judgments/Tax Liens (US)
Special Distribution Methods to Client: Dial-Up (Other than Internet)

The Registry provides tenant screening services to locate applicants with negative elements in their backgrounds. With fully-automated access to over 21 million landlord-tenant public records and online databases offering credit reports, The Registry database provides a method of predicting risk with applicants. This proprietary database includes major US metro areas. Affiliated with Trans Registry, a database of tenant history, evictions and related public record data.

FlatRateInfo.com

1033 Walnut #200
Boulder, CO 80302
888-259-6173 ; Fax: 303-381-2279
www.flatrateinfo.com
Parent Company: e-InfoData.com Inc.
Founded: 1996
Clientele Restrictions: Signed Agreement Required

Products, Information Categories, Coverage Area
Proprietary Databases or Gateways:
Database Name: QI National People Locator
Addresses/Telephone Numbers (US)

Database Name: QI
Bankruptcy, Litigation/Judgments/Tax Liens, Real Estate/Assessor, Fictious Business Names (US)

Database Name: US Merchant Vessels
Vessels (US)

Database Name: US Aircraft
Aviation (US)

Special Distribution Methods to Client: Internet

FlatRateInfo.com provides on-line access to nationwide databases to licensed professionals and qualified businesses with legitimate need for the information. FlatRateInfo.com is the source for accurate, up-to-date and highly searchable information for the investigative and collection industries. As the name implies, most of our databases are available at a flat rate, meaning no per-search fees. Available databases on FlatRateInfo.com include two national people locators; national bankruptcies, judgments and liens; national property; national fictitious business names; the Social Security death index, and others. At the heart of the FlatRateInfo.com system is the QI National People Locator, a powerful searching tool containing over 600 million records from most U.S residents, including SSN, current and previous addresses, date of birth and aliases. Unlimited searching subscriptions. Retrieve valuable and up-to-date information from all states. Call for a free demo.

FOIA Group Inc

1090 Vermont Ave NW # 800
Washington, DC 20005
Fax: 202-347-8419
www.foia.com **Email:** foia@foia.com
Founded: 1988 **Memberships:** ABA, SCIP,
Clientele Restrictions: Casual requesters permitted

Products, Information Categories, Coverage Area
General:
Associations/Trade Groups (US)
Proprietary Databases or Gateways:
Database Name: FOIA-Ware
Software/Training (US)
Special Distribution Methods to Client: Dial-Up (Other than Internet), Disk, Email, Internet, Software

FOIA specializes in the Freedom of Information Act and State Open Records Act protocols. They help prepare and file FOIA requests, monitor and review documents, and service the legal profession and others seeking information through the Act. They also offer agency and customer competitive research and surveys. FOIA Group attorneys provide whistleblower assistance.

Gale Group Inc, The

27500 Drake Rd
Framington Hills, MI 48331-3535
800-877-4253
www.gale.com **Email:** galeord@gale.com
Branch Offices:
Cambridge, MA,
Woodbridge, CT,
Foster City, CA,
Parent Company: Thomson Corporation
Founded: 1998
Clientele Restrictions: Casual requesters permitted

Products, Information Categories, Coverage Area
Proprietary Databases or Gateways:
Database Name: GaleNet
Associations/Trade Groups, Addresses/Telephone Numbers, Foreign Country Information, Corporate/Trade Name Data (US, Intl)
Special Distribution Methods to Client: CD-ROM, Dial-Up (Other than Internet), Microfilm/Microfiche

As a major publisher of academic, educational, and business research companies serving libraries, educational institutions, and businesses in all major international markets, The Gale Group provides much of its material online through products such as Associations Unlimited, Biography and Genealogy Master Index, Brands and Their Companies, Gale Business Resources, and Peterson's Publications. It was formed Sept. '98 with the merger of Gale Research, Information Access Co., and Primary Source Material.

Global Securities Information, Inc
419 7th St NW, #300
Washignton, DC 20004
800-669-1154 Fax: 202-628-1133
Founded: 1988
Clientele Restrictions: Casual requesters permitted.

Products, Information Categories, Coverage Area
Proprietary Databases or Gateways:
Gateway Name: Live Edgar
SEC/Other Financial (DC)
Database Name: International Prospectuses
Foreign Country Information (Intl)
Special Distribution Methods to Client: Email

Global Securities will scan and email documents to eliminate delay of overnight delivery. The SEC database contains searchable filings for both electronically filed documents and scanned paper images.

GoverNet
101 Technology Dr
Idaho Falls, ID 83401
208-522-2896
www.governet.net **Email:** pgy@governet.net
Founded: 2000
Clientele Restrictions: Approved registration required.

Products, Information Categories, Coverage Area
Proprietary Databases or Gateways:
Gateway Name: surfNV
Corporate/Trade Name Data,Litigation/Judgments/Tax Liens, Uniform Commercial Code, Real Estate/Assessor (NV)
Gateway Name: eregistry
Licenses/Registrations/Permits, (NV)
Special Distribution Methods to Client: Internet

GoverNet has packaged together Nevada state online resources including Secretary of State and county assessor/treasurer/recorders for Carson City, Churchill, Clark (licenses), Elko, Esmeralda, Eureka, Humboldt, Lander, Lyon, Mineral, Nye, Pershing, Storey, Washoe, and White Pine. Also availabe is building permits, contractors, licensees, and unsecured property. Register online with credit card. Also includes agency links for AZ and ID.

GuideStar
427 Scotland Street
Williamsburg, VA 23185
www.guidestar.org **Email:** administrator@guidestar.org
Parent Company: Philanthropic Research Inc
Clientele Restrictions: None

Products, Information Categories, Coverage Area
Proprietary Databases or Gateways:
Database Name: Charity Search
Corporate/Trade Name Data (US)
Special Distribution Methods to Client: Internet

GuideStar is a searchable database of more than 640,000 non-profit organizations in the United States. Type a name in the Charity Search box to find your favorite charity, or use the Advanced Search to find a charity by subject, state, zip code, or other criteria.

Haines & Company Inc
8050 Freedom Ave
North Canton, OH 44720
800-843-8452 Fax: 330-494-3862
www.haines.com **Email:** criscros@haines.com
Branch Offices:
Atlanta, GA, 770-936-9308; Fax: 770-455-1799
San Francisco, CA, 510-471-6181; Fax: 510-471-4910
Chicago, IL, 847-352-8696; Fax: 847-352-8698
Founded: 1932 **Memberships:** NAR, REIPA, DMA,
Clientele Restrictions: Casual requesters permitted

Products, Information Categories, Coverage Area
General:
Voter Registration (OH)
Proprietary Databases or Gateways:
Database Name: Criss+Cross Plus, Directory
Address/Telephone Numbers (US)
Database Name: Criss+Cross Plus
Real Estate/Assessor (US)
Special Distribution Methods to Client: CD-ROM, Dial-Up (Other than Internet), Disk, Lists/Labels, Magnetic Tape, Publication/Directory, Software

Varied products and full-service capabilities allow Haines & Company to satisfy the marketing and research needs of most industries. County Real Estate on CD-ROM has been noted for its ease of use, speed and marketing power. They also offer cross-reference directories in book form or on

CD-ROM in 71 major markets, also business and residential lists on labels, manuscripts, CD-ROM, off the Internet or bulletin boards (24-hour turnaround time available). Using their target list or a customer-provided list, they can provide complete direct marketing services, graphic design, printing and database maintenance -- all in-house. In addition to the branches listed above, they have offices in St. Louis, MO (800-922-3846, fax 314-429-2121), Cincinnati, OH (800-582-1734, fax 513-831-4286), Los Angeles, CA (800-562-8262, fax 714-870-4651) and in Washington, DC (877-889-1027, fax 301-780-3673).

Hogan Information Services

14000 Quail Springs Parkway #4000
Oklahoma, OK 73134
Fax: 405-302-6902
www.hoganinfo.com
Parent Company: Dolan Media
Founded: 1990
Clientele Restrictions: Signed agreement required, must be ongoing account
Products, Information Categories, Coverage Area
General:
Litigation/Judgments/Tax Liens (US)
Proprietary Databases or Gateways:
Database Name: Hogan Online
Bankruptcy, Litigation/Judgments/Tax Liens (US)
Special Distribution Methods to Client: Database, Dial-Up (Other than Internet), Disk, Lists/Labels, Magnetic Tape

Hogan Information Services offers one of the most complete, comprehensive, and current public record reporting in the country with a database of more than 100 million bankruptcies, tax liens, civil judgments, evictions, real estate deeds, and more. Hogan collects data in over 8,000 courthouses nationwide. Our collection processes combine court expertise with the latest technology to provide the most timely and accurate public record information in the US. Our extensive public record data is used by credit bureaus, tenant-screening agencies, mail houses, and other businesses to make smarter decisions and manage risk.

Hollingsworth Court Reporting Inc

10761 Perkins Rd #A
Baton Rouge, LA 70810
Fax: 225-769-1814
www.public-records.com **Email:** Nora@hcrinc.com
Founded: 1983 **Memberships:** NPRRA
Clientele Restrictions: None reported
Products, Information Categories, Coverage Area
General:
Tenant History (AL, AR, FL, GA, IL, LA, MS, TN)
Proprietary Databases or Gateways:

Database Name: Tenant Eviction/Public Record Report
Litigation/Judgments/Tax Liens, Tenant History (AL, AR, FL, GA, IL, LA, MS, TN)
Special Distribution Methods to Client: Dial-Up (Other than Internet), Email, FTP, Internet

HCR offers regional public record information including access to 25 million records. They have judgment, lien & eviction information. They also process criminal record searches with a 48 hour turnaround time.

Hoover's Inc

5800 Airport Blvd
Austin, TX 78752
800-486-8666 Fax: 512-374-4505
www.hoovers.com **Email:** info@hoovers.com
Branch Offices:
New York, NY, 212-632-1700; Fax: 212-246-6967/73
San Francisco, CA, 415-227-2512; Fax: 415-227-2501
Clientele Restrictions: Casual requesters permitted
Products, Information Categories, Coverage Area
Proprietary Databases or Gateways:
Database Name: Hoover's Company Profiles
Addresses/Telephone Numbers, Corporate/Trade Name Data, News/Current Events (US)
Database Name: Real-Time SEC Documents
SEC/Other Financial (US)
Database Name: Foreign Country Information
Foreign Country Information (Intl)
Special Distribution Methods to Client: CD-ROM, Dial-Up (Other than Internet), FTP, Gateway via Another Online Service, Internet, Publication/Directory, Software

Hoover's, is a leading provider of business information. Hoover's publishes authoritative information on public and private companies worldwide, and provides industry and market intelligence. This information, along with advanced searching tools, is available through Hoover's Online (www.hoovers.com), the company's premier online service that helps sales, marketing, recruiting and business development professionals and senor-level executives get the global intelligence they need to grow their business. Hoover's business information is also available through corporate intranets and distribution agreements with licensees, as well as via print and CD-ROM products form Hoover's Business Press.

Household Drivers Reports Inc (HDR Inc)

902 S Friendswood Dr Suite F
Friendswood, TX 77546
800-899-4437 Fax: 281-996-1947
www.hdr.com **Email:** sthomas@hdr.com
Founded: 1989

Clientele Restrictions: Signed agreement required, must be ongoing account

Products, Information Categories, Coverage Area
General:
Addresses/Telephone Numbers (TX)
Proprietary Databases or Gateways:
Database Name: Corp Data
Corporation/Trade Name Data (TX)
Database Name: Criminal Record Data
Criminal Information (TX)
Database Name: Driver & Vehicle
Driver and/or Vehicle (TX)
Database Name: Vital Records
Vital Records (TX)
Special Distribution Methods to Client: Dial-Up (Other than Internet)

Household Drivers Report Inc has been in the information business since 1989, at which time it pioneered its first online database. Subscribers can access the information available through HDR's online system with the slightest amount of information. The HDR system offers the unique capability of wildcard searches. With only a partial last name, plate, VIN or address, HDR can locate that person or business and identify a wealth of information. Information is updated weekly. HDR is an online, real time database system, providing results within minutes. They offer a "no-hit, no-charge" feature on their online searches as well as a competitive pricing structure. The system is available to qualified professionals in law enforcement, private investigation, insurance fraud investigation, business professionals and security investigations. HDR offers customize information solutions for large volume users. They operate strictly in compliance with state and federal laws. The HDR system allows access to the following: Texas: driver license records, vehicle registration records, business records, vehicle by manufacturer, automatic driver update report, criminal conviction records, sex offender records, marriage, death, divorce records; also,moving violation reports from various states. New databases are added periodically.

Idealogic
505 University Ave #1603
Toronto, Ontario, CD M5G 1X3
866-506-9900
www.idealogic.com **Email:** ideal@idealogic.com
Founded: 1980 **Memberships:** NPRRA, OAPSOR, PRRN,
Clientele Restrictions: Casual requesters permitted

Products, Information Categories, Coverage Area
General:
Foreign Country Information, Trademarks, Corporate/Trade Name Data (Canada)
Proprietary Databases or Gateways:

Database Name: Dynis-Cor:
Corporate/Trade Name Data (Canada)
Database Name: Dynis-Trademarks
Trademarks (Canada)

Idealogic is a full-service provider of public information from all jurisdictions in Canada. Corporate, personal property, UCC, real estate, motor vehicle and other registry information is available, including bankruptcy, civil and probate courts. Idealogic has knowledge about how to translate public information available in the US to its Canadian counterpart. One day turnarounds are common; credit cards accepted. Can perform service of process.

IDM Corporation
3550 W Temple St
Los Angeles, CA 90004
877-436-3282 Fax: 213-389-9569
www.idmcorp.com
Parent Company: Fidelity National Information Solutions
Founded: 1989 **Memberships:** REIPA
Clientele Restrictions: License required, must be ongoing account

Products, Information Categories, Coverage Area
Proprietary Databases or Gateways:
Database Name: Tax, Assessor and Recorders
Real Estate/Assessor (US)
Special Distribution Methods to Client: CD-ROM, Dial-Up (Other than Internet), Disk, Magnetic Tape

IDM Corporation is one of the largest source providers of real estate public records. They convert 900 tax/assessor counties and 500 recorder's counties to a uniform format. Their assessment files are updated once per year, and recorder's are updated weekly. Their business-to-business site is www.sitexdata.com, and their consumer site is www.smarthomebuy.com.

iDocket.com
P.O. Box 30514
Amarillo, TX 79120
800-566-7164 Fax: 806-351-2329
www.idocket.com **Email:** armandob@SIMAS.COM
Parent Company: Solutions, Inc
Founded: 1999
Clientele Restrictions: None reported.

Products, Information Categories, Coverage Area
Proprietary Databases or Gateways:
Distributor Name: iDockets
Criminal Information, Litigation/Judgments/Tax Liens (TX)
Special Distribution Methods to Client: Internet

iDockets gathers civil and criminal court case information from participating TX and OK counties each evening and posts it online for the Courts/Circuits. Basic information - name searching - is free; deeper case history information requires registration and fees. TX counties include: Bailey, Bandera, Brooks, Cameron, Eastland, El Paso, Guadalupe, Hays, Harris, Hidalgo, Hill, McCollough, Parmer, Potter, Brooks, Navarro, Randall.

iiX (Insurance Information Exchange)

PO Box 30001
College Station, TX 77842-3001
800-683-8553 ; Fax: 979-696-5584
www.iix.com
Parent Company: ISO
Founded: 1966
Clientele Restrictions: Must be ongoing account
Products, Information Categories, Coverage Area
Proprietary Databases or Gateways:
Database Name: UDI-Undisclosed Drivers, VIN
Driver and/or Vehicle (US)
Gateway Name: Motor Vehicle Reports
Driver and/or Vehicle (US)
Special Distribution Methods to Client: Dial-Up (Other than Internet), Internet, Software

iiX is an established provider of information systems to the insurance industry. Their services and products include MVR, claims, undisclosed driver, and other underwriting services. The Undisclosed Driver Information (UDI) and VIN are only available on Expressnet, the Internet ordering system. A new program offered by iiX is ExpressFill. Start with a phone number, and ExpressFill prefills information for that address for drivers, VINs and gives the option to order an MVR.

Indepth Profiles Inc

4528 S Sheridan #224
Tulsa, OK 74145
800-364-8319
www.idprofiles.com **Email:** sales@indepthprofiles.com
Founded: 1985 **Memberships:** NAWBO, NFPA, SHRM, PRRN, ASA, DAPA
Clientele Restrictions: Casual requesters permitted; agent agreement required
Products, Information Categories, Coverage Area
Proprietary Databases or Gateways:
Database Name: Arkansas Search
Criminal Information (AR)
Special Distribution Methods to Client: Email

Indepth Profiles specializes in pre-employment background investigations, national criminal record retrieval, motor vehicle records, credit reports, references, professional licensing verification and various other services. They offer 24-hour service on Arkansas and Oklahoma records.

Industrial Foundation of America

16420 Park Ten Pl #520
Houston, TX 77084
800-592-1433
www.ifa-america.com **Email:** ifa@ifa-america.com
Founded: 1960 **Memberships:** NHRA, SHRM, BBB,
Clientele Restrictions: Restricted to employers only
Products, Information Categories, Coverage Area
General:
Credit Information (US)
Proprietary Databases or Gateways:
Database Name: Member Records & Court Records
Workers Compensation (TX, OK, LA, NM)

The Industrial Foundation specializes as a database and clearinghouse of industrial accident histories on individuals, whether or not Workers' Comp is involved. Data is acquired from member employers' records and from state and federal records where litigated. No medical information is included. The Industrial Foundation provides free legal services for members, also professional safety and human reserve information for members from its library and key staff members.

Infocon Corporation

PO Box 568
Ebensburg, PA 15931-0568
Fax: 814-472-5019
www.ic-access.com
Clientele Restrictions: Casual requesters permitted
Products, Information Categories, Coverage Area
Proprietary Databases or Gateways:
Gateway Name: INFOCON County Access System
Criminal Information, Vital Records, Voter Registration, Litigation/Judgments/Tax Liens, Real Estate/Assessor (PA-15 counties)
Special Distribution Methods to Client: Dial-Up (Other than Internet)

The Infocon County Access System offers online access to civil, criminal, real estate, and vital record information in Pennsylvania counties of Armstrong, Bedford, Blair, Butler, Clarion, Clinton, Erie, Huntingdon, Lawrence, Mifflin, Potter, and Pike. Fees are involved, access is through a remote 800 number (internet access may be available).

Information Inc

PO Box 382
Hermitage, TN 37076
877-484-4636 Fax: 615-889-6492
http://hometown.aol.com/publicrecordstn **Email:** infomantn@aol.com
Founded: 1991 **Memberships:** PRRN, FOP,
Clientele Restrictions: Casual requesters permitted

Products, Information Categories, Coverage Area

General:
Criminal Information (US)
Proprietary Databases or Gateways:
Database Name: Arrest Database (Nashville)
Criminal Information (TN-Nashville)
Special Distribution Methods to Client: Dial-Up (Other than Internet), Email

Information Inc provides a real time criminal arrest database for Davidson County, TN. This includes all agencies in the 20th Judicial District of Tennessee. The database, updated weekly allows you to obtain results 24/7. Instant results let you know if there is more research to be done at the courthouse level, and often lets allows for the compilation of additional information such as former residences and license information. Free demos and audits are welcomed.

Information Network of Arkansas

425 West Capitol Ave #3565
Little Rock, AR 72201
800-392-6069
www.state.ar.us/ina.html **Email:** info@ark.org
Founded: 1998
Clientele Restrictions: Signed agreement required, must be ongoing account

Products, Information Categories, Coverage Area

Proprietary Databases or Gateways:
Gateway Name: INA
Driver and/or Vehicle, Workers' Compensation (AR)
Gateway Name: Secretary of State
Corporate/Trade Name
Data,Licenses/Registrations/Permits (AR)
Special Distribution Methods to Client: Internet

The Information Network of Arkansas was created by the Arkansas Legislature with the responsibility of assisting the state in permitting citizens to access public records. There is a fee for driving records, Nursing Registry, Lobbyist, and Workers' Comp record access, but none for Secretary of State Trademarks, Corporations, Banking and notaries. There may be fees for new record categories.

Information Network of Kansas

534 S Kansas Ave #1210
Topeka, KS 66603
800-452-6727 Fax: 785-296-5563
www.ink.org
Founded: 1991
Clientele Restrictions: Signed agreement required, must be ongoing account

Products, Information Categories, Coverage Area

Proprietary Databases or Gateways:
Gateway Name: Premium Services

Driver and/or Vehicle, Uniform Commercial Code, Corporate/Trade Name Data, Legislation/Regulations, Real Estate/Assessor (KS)
Gateway Name: Premium Services
Litigation/Judgments/Tax Liens (KS-Johnson, Sedgwick, Shawnee, Wyandotte)
Gateway Name: Premium Services
Criminal Information (KS- Sedgwick, Shawnee, Wyandotte)
Special Distribution Methods to Client: Dial-Up (Other than Internet), Internet

INK is the official source for electronic access to the State of Kansas government information. Access to public record information is a premium service and requires a subscription. Now includes Johnson, Shawnee, and Wyandotte Counties.

InforME - Information Resource of Maine

One Market Square #101
Augusta, ME 04330
877-463-3468
www.informe.org **Email:** info@informe.org

Products, Information Categories, Coverage Area

Proprietary Databases or Gateways:
Gateway Name: Bureau of Motor Vehicles Driver's Records
Driver and/or Vehicle (ME)
Special Distribution Methods to Client: Internet

InforME provides access to Maine's Bureau of Motor Vehicles Driver's Records on a subscription basis.

Informus Corporation

2001 Airport Rd #201
Jackson, MS 39208
800-364-8380
www.informus.com **Email:** info@informus.com
Parent Company: ChoicePoint
Founded: 1990
Clientele Restrictions: Signed agreement required, must be ongoing account

Products, Information Categories, Coverage Area

General:
Criminal Information (US)
Proprietary Databases or Gateways:
Database Name: Informus
Workers Compensation (MS, US)
Gateway Name: IntroScan
Addresses/Telephone Numbers (US)
Special Distribution Methods to Client: Dial-Up (Other than Internet), Internet

Informus provides an online pre-employment screening and public record retrieval service. Online access is available through the Internet. Some searches provide instant information, depending on state and category.

Innovative Enterprises Inc

PO Box 22506
Newport News, VA 23609
888-777-9435
www.knowthefacts.com **Email:**
innovate@knowthefacts.com
Founded: 1996 **Memberships:** PRRN
Clientele Restrictions: Casual requesters permitted
Products, Information Categories, Coverage Area
General:
Criminal Information (US, VA, NC)
Proprietary Databases or Gateways:
Database Name: Virginia Criminal Records Database
Criminal Information (VA)
Special Distribution Methods to Client: Email, Internet

Innovative Enterprises' staff brings forward more than 55 years of combined Virginia judicial, law enforcement, and military experience, making them qualified to service client's background research needs. MVR's retrieved from thirty states. Their proprietary VA Criminal Records Database includes millions of disposed court cases from every VA county.

Intellicorp Ltd

3659 Green Road #116
Beachwood, OH 44122
888-946-8355 Fax: 216-591-9578
www.intellicorp.net **Email:** info@intellicorp.net
Founded: 1996 **Memberships:** ASIS, SHRM,
Clientele Restrictions: Signed agreement required, must be ongoing account
Products, Information Categories, Coverage Area
General:
Addresses/Telephone Numbers (US)
Proprietary Databases or Gateways:
Database Name: Court, Inmate, & Booking Records
Criminal Information (OH, IN, IL IA, MN)
Special Distribution Methods to Client: Dial-Up (Other than Internet), Email, Gateway via Another Online Service

Intellicorp is an Ohio-based company providing online access to public records and other information. Their online systems are being used by law enforcement agencies, businesses, and professional organizations throughout the country. Their customers and markets include human resources, health care, insurance companies, investigators, financial, attorneys, government and general business needs for the information. All approved subscribers have been carefully screened and qualified under the company's enrollment process. By utilizing the latest technologies, Intellicorp can provide access to an array of information in

a fast and cost efficient manner. Intellicorp is one of a select group of companies licensed to provide access to Arrest and Booking records from OH, MI, IN, MN and IL county sheriff's offices. Intellicorp's information products are made available through its secured online system, accessible via the Internet or by dial-up methods. With over 700 million records available immediately online and access to millions of other records from other sources, Intellicorp services provide access to the right information to make more informed decisions.

Intercounty Clearance Corporation

111 Washington Ave
Albany, NY 12210
800-342-3676 Fax: 518-434-1521
www.intercountyclearance.com **Email:**
information@intercountyclearance.com
Branch Offices:
New York City, NY, 800-229-4422; Fax: 212-594-1304
Hartford, CT, 860-525-9238; Fax: 860-525-9280
Founded: 1935 **Memberships:** NPRRA, PRRN,
Clientele Restrictions: Must be ongoing business account.
Products, Information Categories, Coverage Area
General:
Driver and/or Vehicle (US)
Proprietary Databases or Gateways:
Gateway Name: Intercounty Public Records Portal
Uniform Commercial Code, Corporate/Trade Name, Real Estate/Assessor Data, Aviation/Vessels, Licenses/Registrations/Permits, Litigation/Judgments/Tax Liens (US)
Special Distribution Methods to Client: Dial-Up (Other than Internet), Disk, Email, Internet

Intercounty Clearance Corporation provides nationwide UCC and corporate services. They have experienced employees in each of the major metropolitan counties of New York. Intercounty's services include traditional and online UCC and corporate document retrieval, preparation (PowerLegal.com), online UCC database searching, online tracking/management of units of statutory representation, and corporate forms library. They also provide Revised Article 9 information and free Intercounty Informer Newsletter.

Interstate Data Corporation

113 Latigo Lane
Canon City, CO 81212
800-332-7999
www.cdrominvestigations.com
Founded: 1987
Clientele Restrictions: Must be ongoing account
Products, Information Categories, Coverage Area
Proprietary Databases or Gateways:

Gateway Name: CA Criminal
Criminal Information (CA)

Database Name: CA Professional Licenses
Licenses/Registration/Permits (CA)

Database Name: CA Corporate Records
Corporate/Trade Name Data (CA)

Special Distribution Methods to Client: CD-ROM,
Dial-Up (Other than Internet)

Intertstate Data Corporation provides primary access to
over 50 databases for the California area. Databases include
professional licenses, Board of Equalization, fictitious
business names, criminal and civil courts, and others.
Features online and CD-ROM technology at competitive
prices.

Intranet Inc

1321 Valwood Prky #420
Carrollton, TX 75006
800-333-8818 Fax: 903-593-8183
Clientele Restrictions: None reported

Products, Information Categories, Coverage Area
General:
Litigation/Judgments/Tax Liens (TX)
Proprietary Databases or Gateways:
Database Name: Bankscan
Bankruptcy (TX)
Special Distribution Methods to Client: Disk

Intranet specializes in bankruptcy research and retrieval
services for the state of Texas.

Investigative & Background Solutions Inc

4155 E Jewell Ave #901
Denver, CO 80222
800-580-0474 Fax: 303-692-8511
www.ibs-denver.com **Email:** info@ibs-denver.com
Founded: 1993
Clientele Restrictions: Casual requesters permitted

Products, Information Categories, Coverage Area
Proprietary Databases or Gateways:
Database Name: Resource Line (local private
investigators)
Addresses/Telephone Numbers (US, Intl)
Gateway Name: Colorado Court Records
Criminal Information (CO)
Special Distribution Methods to Client: Dial-Up (Other
than Internet), Software

With almost a decade of experience, IBS can tailor a
solution to any circumstance which will effectively ease the
applicant screening process in Colorado or nationally.

Investigators Anywhere Resource Line

PO Box 40970
Mesa, AZ 85274-0970
800-338-3463 Fax: 480-730-8103
www.investigatorsanywhere.com/ **Email:**
IONPRRN@IONINC.com
Parent Company: ION Incorporated
Founded: 1987 **Memberships:** ASIS, CII, ION, NALI,
NAPPS, NCISS
Clientele Restrictions: Casual requesters permitted

Products, Information Categories, Coverage Area
Proprietary Databases or Gateways:
Database Name: Resource Line
Addresses/Telephone Numbers,
Licenses/Registrations/Permits, Foreign Country
Information (US, Intl)
Special Distribution Methods to Client: Automated
Telephone Look-Up, Dial-Up (Other than Internet),
Internet

Investigators Anywhere Resources' Resource Line service
provides access to over 30,000 investigators, prescreened
for excellence of service levels. Connect direct to the web
page for 24 hour service. Callers are matched to appropriate
investigators. No fee to the callers except for international
and non-commercial projects.

IQ Data Systems

1401 El Camino Ave, 5th Fl
Sacramento, CA 95815
800-264-6517
www.iqdata.com **Email:** ballas@iqdata.com
Founded: 1996 **Memberships:** NPRRA
Clientele Restrictions: Must be ongoing account

Products, Information Categories, Coverage Area
Proprietary Databases or Gateways:
Database Name: IQ Data
Uniform Commercial Code, Bankruptcy, Real
Estate/Assessor, Litigation/Judgments/Tax Liens,
Addresses/Telephone Numbers, Corporate/Trade Name
Data (US)
Gateway Name: IQ Data
Driver and/or Vehicle, Credit Information (US)
Special Distribution Methods to Client: Internet

IQ Data Systems is a leading nationwide online public
record information provider. Accurate, up-to-date cost
effective and instant easy-to-access national data to verify
information and identities, conduct background checks,
locate people/business/assets, detect fraud, find
criminal/civil/financial records, assist law enforcement and
more. Empowering corporations, government agencies and
individuals to maximize the use and value of public record
information. IQ Data's cutting edge technology and

proprietary databases direct its customers to make better, timely and more informed decisions.

J B Data Research Co.

333 Haggerty Ln #6
Bozeman, MT 59715
Fax: 406-585-3323
www.eellis.net **Email:** jbdata@eellis.net
Founded: 1999
Clientele Restrictions: Casual requesters permitted.

Products, Information Categories, Coverage Area
Proprietary Databases or Gateways:
Database Name: Bankruptcy
Bankruptcy (ID, MT, ND, NV, OR, SD, UT, WA, WY)
Special Distribution Methods to Client: Disk, Email, Lists/Labels

J B Data Research can provide a quick 12-hour turnaround from their database of bankruptcy records from nine western states. They are also an expert document retrieval company in Southwest Montana.

Juritas.com

120 S State St, 2nd Fl
Chicago, IL 60603
888-877-9695 Fax: 312-424-0700
www.juritas.com **Email:** jparkman@juritas.com
Founded: 2000
Clientele Restrictions: Registration required.

Products, Information Categories, Coverage Area
Proprietary Databases or Gateways:
Database Name: Juritas
Criminal Information (CA, DE, FL, IL, NJ, WA)

Database Name: Juritas
Litigation/Judgments/Tax Liens (CA, DE, FL, IL, NJ, WA)
Special Distribution Methods to Client: Internet

The documents found on Juritas.com come directly from state and federal trial courts across the United States, and cover the 14 most litigated practice areas, including Antitrust, Personal Injury, Securities, Medical Malpractice, Tax, Insurance, Labor & Employment, Products Liability, White Collar Criminal, Environmental, Civil Rights, Intellectual Property and more.

KnowX

730 Peachtree St. #700
Atlanta, GA 30308
888-975-6699 ; Fax: 404-541-0260
www.knowx.com **Email:** support@knowx.com
Parent Company: ChoicePoint
Clientele Restrictions: Casual requesters permitted
Products, Information Categories, Coverage Area
Proprietary Databases or Gateways:

Database Name: KnowX
Addresses/Telephone Numbers, Vital Records, Real Estate/Assessor, Bankruptcy, Licenses/Registrations/Permits, Corporate/Trade Name Data, Military Svc, Aviation, Vessels, Litigation/Judgments/Tax Liens, Uniform Commercial Code (US (with limited Canadian))
Special Distribution Methods to Client: Dial-Up (Other than Internet), Internet

KnowX is one of the most comprehensive sources of public records available on the Internet, and as a subsidiary of ChoicePoint, they have 40 offices nationwide. KnowX provides public records on aircraft ownership, bankruptcies, business directories, partnerships, DBAs, DEAs, death records, judgments, liens, lawsuits, licensing, residencies, real property foreclosures, tax records, property transfers, sales permits, stock ownership, UCC and watercraft records. Often, they run promotions that offer free services.

Kompass USA Inc

1255 Route 70, #25s
Parkway 70 Plaza
Lakewood, NJ 08701
Fax: 732-730-0342
www.kompass-intl.com
Clientele Restrictions: Casual Requesters Accepted
Products, Information Categories, Coverage Area
Proprietary Databases or Gateways:
Database Name: Kompass.com
Addresses/Telephone Numbers, Corporate/Trade Name Data (US)
Database Name: Kompass.com
Foreign Country Information (Intl)
Special Distribution Methods to Client: CD-ROM, Database, Email, Internet, Lists/Labels, Publication/Directory

The Kompass Worldwide Database contains access to 1.5 million companies, 23 million product and service references, 600,000 trade and brand names, and 2.9 million executives' names. Many searches are free over the Internet.

KY Direct

101 Cold Harbor Dr, Dept.of Info. Systems
Frankfort, KY 40601
Fax: 502-564-1598
www.kydirect.net/ **Email:** bpuckett@mail.state.ky.us
Parent Company: Commonwealth of Kentucky
Founded: 2000
Products, Information Categories, Coverage Area
General:
Litigation/Judgments/Tax Liens (KY)
Proprietary Databases or Gateways:

Gateway Name: KYDirect
Corporate/Trade Name Data; Uniform Commerical Code;
Motor Vehicle Records; (KY)
Gateway Name: Vital Statistics
Vital Records (KY)
Gateway Name: Legislature Searching Service
Legislation/Regulation (KY)
Special Distribution Methods to Client: Internet,
Lists/Labels, Publication/Directory

KY Direct is the Commonwealth of Kentucky's
clearinghouse web site or the dissemination of state agency,
Secretary of State information, Motor Vehicle Dept, and
vital statistics. The site is also an excellent resource for
online and print directories such as state agencies lists,
resource directory, sex offenders lists, nuring registry, state
agency telephone directory, agency forms, maps, and more.

Landings.com
6280 S Valley View Blvd, #314
Las Vegas, NV 89118
Fax: 702-920-8298
www.landings.com/ **Email:** landings@landings.com
Founded: 1966
Clientele Restrictions: None
Products, Information Categories, Coverage Area
Proprietary Databases or Gateways:
Database Name: Landings.com, Aviation databases
Aviation (US)
Special Distribution Methods to Client: Internet

Landings.com is the the Internet's most comprehensive
collection of uniquely searchable Aviation Database's
including: N-Numbers, Pilots, Mediacl Examiners,
Designated Examiners, World Tail Number Registration, A
& P, detailed World Airport information and free flight
planning service, FAA regulations, NOTAMs, ADs, STCs,
TSOs, and TCDs. Also, NTSB accident reports and SDRs,
aircraft performance, flight related calculators, and 16,000+
external aviation links are all available free of charge.

Landlord Protection Agency
1075 W County Rd #E
St. Paul, MN 55126
800-358-3381 Fax: 651-765-2607
www.mnlpa.com/ **Email:** darrell@mnlpa.com
Branch Offices:
Houston, TX, 713-726-0141; Fax: 713-726-8337
Reno, NV, 800-450-2606; Fax: 888-329-5778
Redmond, WA
Parent Company: Sundberg Corporation
Founded: 1981
Clientele Restrictions: Service Agreement Required
Products, Information Categories, Coverage Area
General:
Education/Employment (US)

Proprietary Databases or Gateways:
Database Name: Unlawful Detainer Data
Tenant History (MN, ND, WI, CA, NV, WA, TX)
Database Name: Problem Renters
Tenant History (MN, ND, WI)
Gateway Name: Criminal Conviction Info
Criminal Information (MN, CA, NV, WA, TX)
Special Distribution Methods to Client: Email, Internet

Landlord Protection Agency offers FirstCheck©, an
automated Unlawful Detainer search system. They
specialize in false information (cross-referencing) and offer
instant access to unlawful detainer info (thorough data).
Complete tenant screening service includes unlawful
detainer info from 87 MN counties), and 3 bordering
counties (Fargo-ND, Superior-WI, Hudson-WI) credit
reports, current & previous landlord checks, current &
previous employment verifications. Complete criminal
info. LPA also offers an online system called "First Check"
that is available for use on PCs and allows the user to
perform self-service Unlawful detainer Checks. Automated
billing each month. Discounts offered for volume users.

Law Bulletin Information Network
415 N State
Chicago, IL 60610-4674
Fax: 312-644-1215
www.lawbulletin.com
Founded: 1854 **Memberships:** NALFM, NPRRA,
NFPA,
Clientele Restrictions: Casual requesters permitted
Products, Information Categories, Coverage Area
General:
Uniform Commercial Code (IL)
Proprietary Databases or Gateways:
Database Name: Access Plus
Real Estate/Assessor, Court Dockets, Uniform
Commercial Code (IL-Cook County)
Database Name: Access Plus
Litigation/Judgments/Tax Liens, (IL-Central, North
Counties)
Database Name: Access Plus
Addresses/Telephone Numbers (IL)
Special Distribution Methods to Client: Dial-Up (Other
than Internet), Email, Internet, Publication/Directory

The Law Bulletin Publishing Company's Information
Network's primary product, AccessPlus, provides both
online and access to Illinois Courts, vital public record
information, UCCs, corporate documents, court dockets,
realty sales, etc. They offer other document retrieval
services including licensed investigative services through
an affiliated licensed, private investigation agency. These
services can be requested online through the DocuServices
product at www.lawbulletin.com.

LEXIS-NEXIS

PO Box 933
Dayton, OH 45401-0933
800-227-9597
www.lexis-nexis.com **Email:** Greg.Noble@lexis-nexis.com
Parent Company: Reed Elsevier Inc
Founded: 1973 **Memberships:** AALL, ATLA, NALA, ABI, NPRRA, SCIP
Clientele Restrictions: Signed Agreement Required
Products, Information Categories, Coverage Area
Proprietary Databases or Gateways:
Database Name: LEXIS Law Publishing, Shepard's
Litigation/Judgments/Tax Liens (US)

Database Name: USBoat
Vessels (AL, AZ, AR,
CO,CT,FL,GE,IA,ME,MD,MA,MS,MO,MN,MT,NE,NV
,NH,NC,ND,OH,OR,SC,UT,VA,WV,WI)

Database Name: Congressional Information Service
Legislation/Regulation (US)

Database Name: ALLBKT
Bankruptcy (US)

Database Name: ALLOWN
Real Estate/Assessor (US)

Database Name: ALLUCC
Uniform Commercial Code (US)

Database Name: ALLSOS
Corporate/Trade Name Data (US)

Database Name: B-Find, P-Find, P-Seek
Addresses/Telephone Numbers (US)

Database Name: Professional Licensing Boards
Licenses/Registrations/Permits (CA, CT, FL, GE, IL,
MA,MI,NE,NJ,NC,OG,PA,TX,VA,WI)

Special Distribution Methods to Client: Dial-Up (Other
than Internet), Gateway via Another Online Service,
Publication/Directory

The LEXIS-NEXIS services offer one of the most
comprehensive aggregations of public records available
anywhere. Additionally, they compile and categorize these
records so that you find the information you need faster and
easier. With minimal effort, you can search one of the
largest and faster growing public records collections in the
United States. They offer industry-leading access to critical
information such as real and personal property records;
business and person locators; civil and criminal filings;
Secretary of State records; liens, judgments, and UCC
filings; jury verdicts and settlements; professional license,
bankruptcy filings; and much more.

LLC Reporter

Frontier Law Center, 1107 W 6th Ave
Cheyenne, WY 82001
800-282-4552 ; Fax: 307-637-7445
www.llc-reporter.com **Email:** WDBagley@LLC-REPORTER.com
Founded: 1993
Clientele Restrictions: Casual Requesters Permitted
Products, Information Categories, Coverage Area
Proprietary Databases or Gateways:
Database Name: LLC Reporter
Corporate/Trade Name Data (US)

Special Distribution Methods to Client: Internet,
Publication/Directory

The Limited Liability Company Reporter is a national
newsletter committed to assisting Lawyers, CPA's and
Business Planners who need to stay current in a fast
changing field. The Reporter Archive contains all issues of
the Reporter from January 1, 1993 to present, accessible by
a topic index and author index. The most recent events are
found under Current LLC News. The authors are a coast-to-coast network of limited liability company entity
practitioners and administrators who contribute their
expertise.

Logan Registration Service Inc

PO Box 161644
Sacramento, CA 95816
www.loganreg.com **Email:** contact@loganreg.com
Founded: 1976 **Memberships:** NFIB
Clientele Restrictions: Signed agreement required, must
be ongoing account
Products, Information Categories, Coverage Area
General:
Addresses/Telephone Numbers (CA)
Proprietary Databases or Gateways:
Gateway Name: Logan
Driver and/or Vehicle (CA,US)

Special Distribution Methods to Client: Dial-Up (Other
than Internet), Email

Logan has more than 25 years experience working with
California driver and vehicle records. They are an online
vendor that allows their DMV authorized clients to retrieve
driver and vehicle registration records in seconds with a
computer software program that is available free of charge.
Clients are also able to access needed records via phone or
fax.

Loren Data Corp

4640 Admiralty Way #430
Marina Del Rey, CA 90292
800-745-6736
www.LD.com **Email:** info@LD.com

Founded: 1987
Clientele Restrictions: Casual requesters permitted
Products, Information Categories, Coverage Area
General:
Licenses/Registrations/Permits (US)
Proprietary Databases or Gateways:
Gateway Name: Commerce Business Daily
Environmental, Military Svc, News/Current Events,
Legislation/Regulation (US)
Special Distribution Methods to Client: Email

Loren Data Corp provides customers with access to
government business, helping make bids and gain
government contracts. They offer free access and email
based subscription services for their publication Commerce
Business Daily, CBD.

Martindale-Hubbell

121 Chanlon Road
Providence, NJ 07974
800-526-4902 Fax: 908-464-3553
www.martindale.com **Email:** ccooper@martindale.com
Branch Offices:
London, GB, 44 20 7868 4885; Fax: 44 20 7868 4886
Parent Company: Reed Elsevier PLC Group
Founded: 1868
Clientele Restrictions: Casual requesters permitted
Products, Information Categories, Coverage Area
Proprietary Databases or Gateways:
Database Name: Martindale-Hubbell Law Directory
(Attorneys and Law Firms)
Addresses/Telephone Numbers, Education/Employment
(US, Intl)
Special Distribution Methods to Client: CD-ROM,
Lists/Labels, Publication/Directory

Martindale-Hubbell's database is now regarded as the
primary source for attorney and law firm information
around the world. Their flagship product, Martindale-
Hubbell Law Directory consists of more the 900,000
listings, organized by city, state, county, and province with
extensive cross-references and indexes. Products are
available in four media: hardbound print, CR-ROM, via
LEXIS/NEXIS (a sister company) and Internet via the
Martindale-Hubbell Lawyer Locator. Their data includes
corporate law departments, legal-related services such as
P.I.s, title search companies, law digests.

MDR/Minnesota Driving Records

1710 Douglas Dr. N #103
Golden Valley, MN 55422-4313
800-644-6877 Fax: 612-595-8079
Clientele Restrictions: Signed agreement required, must
be ongoing account
Products, Information Categories, Coverage Area
Proprietary Databases or Gateways:

Database Name: MDR
Driver and/or Vehicle (MN)
Special Distribution Methods to Client: Lists/Labels

MDR provides an automated touch-tone call-in service for
driver information in Minnesota, letting clients retrieve a
record with a verbal response in less than one minute,
followed by a fax hard copy within minutes. Service
available 24 hours a day every day. The service is endorsed
by the Minnesota Insurance Agents Assoc.

Merchants Security Exchange

20401 NW 2nd Ave #810
Miami, FL 33169
800-226-4483
www.merchants-fla.com **Email:** adobles@merchants-
fla.com
Branch Offices:
Tampa, FL, 800-226-7757
Orlando, FL, 800-226-7757
Parent Company: Merchants Association of Florida
Founded: 1916 **Memberships:** ACA, ASIS, MBAA,
Clientele Restrictions: Permissable users; agreement
required.
Products, Information Categories, Coverage Area
General:
Credit Information (FL, US)
Proprietary Databases or Gateways:
Gateway Name: Credit Reports
Credit Information (FL, US)
Database Name: Crime Online Database
Criminal Information (FL)
Database Name: Eviction
Tenant History (FL)
Gateway Name: Public Record
Litigation/Judgments/Tax Liens (FL, US)
Special Distribution Methods to Client: Database,
Dial-Up (Other than Internet), FTP

Merchants Security Exchange conducts various pre/post
employment verifications, such as criminal, MVR, credit,
etc. Since they are a credit bureau, they can produce a
credit report and SSN verification instantaneously. They
have gathered criminal information - felony &
misdemeanor - for the entire state of Florida, providing that
data instantaneously. They recently began tenant screening
and now provide eviction, credit, and criminal searches to
any business, per compliance with DPPA and FCRA. The
company holds a private investigation firm license.

Merlin Information Services

215 S Complex Dr
Kalispell, MT 59901
800-367-6646 Fax: 406-755-8568
www.merlindata.com **Email:** Support@merlindata.com

Founded: 1991 **Memberships:** ACA, CAC, CAPPS, NARM, SCRIA, NCSEA
Clientele Restrictions: Casual requesters permitted
Products, Information Categories, Coverage Area
Proprietary Databases or Gateways:
Database Name: Merlin Cross Directory
Addresses/Telephone #s, Credit Data, Driver and/or Vehicle, Vital Records, Voter Registration (US)
Gateway Name: National FlatRate, Collector's FlatRate
Civil/Criminal Indexes, UCC, Aviation/Vessels, MVRs, Real Estate/Assessor, Litigation/Judgments/Tax Liens, Addresses/Telephone #s, Corp./Trade Name Data, SSN, Bankruptcy, Credit Information, Licenses/Registration/Permits, Vital Records, Voter Regis. (US)
Gateway Name: Merlin Super Header
Addresses/Telephone #s, SSNs, Credit Information, Vital Statistics (US)
Gateway Name: QuikInfo.net FlatRate
Civil/Criminal (CA), UCC, Aviation/Vessels, Real Estate/Assessor, Criminal Data, Driver and/orVehicle, Wrokers' Comp, Addresses/Telephone Numbers, Corporation/Trade Name Data, SSN, Bankruptcy, Licenses/Registration/Permits, Vital Records, Voter Regis. (US)
Database Name: Nat'l Fictitious Business Names
Corporation/Trade Names, Addresses/Telephone #s (CA, US)
Database Name: CA Criminal Indexes, CA Brides/Grooms, CA Birth/Death Indexes, many other CA databases
UCC (Filing Index), Civil/Criminal Indexes, Vital Records, Licenses/Reg./Permits, Real Estate/Assessor, Litigation/Judgments/Tax Liens, Wills/Probate (CA)
Gateway Name: Link to America, DOB File
Addresss/Phone #s, Credit Data, Criver and/or Vehicle, Real Estate/Assessor, Vital Statistics, Voter Registration (US)
Database Name: Nat'l People Finder/Credit Headers/Criminal/Property
Addresses/Phone #s, Real Estate/Assessor, Litigation/Judgments/Tax Liens, Criminal Data, Credit Data, Vital Statistics (US)
Special Distribution Methods to Client: CD-ROM, Dial-Up (Other than Internet), Internet, Magnetic Tape

Merlin Information Services provides access to public records on the Internet. Their search and retrieval site and their software assists in obtaining results not found through traditional access. Merlin's extensive California databases are the most current and complete available. Their wide selection of national databases such as The Merlin Cross-Directory, Link to America, and Nat'l FlatRate rounds out their extensive skiptracing and investigative tools, helping you locate people, assets, neighbors, and associates.

Metro Market Trends Inc
PO Box 30042
Pensacola, FL 32503-1042
800-239-1668 Fax: 850-478-6249
www.mmtinfo.com **Email:** mmt@mmtinfo.com
Founded: 1990 **Memberships:** REIPA
Clientele Restrictions: Casual requesters permitted
Products, Information Categories, Coverage Area
Proprietary Databases or Gateways:
Database Name: Real Estate Activity Reporting System
Real Estate/Assessor (FL, AL)
Special Distribution Methods to Client: CD-ROM, Database, Disk, Email, Lists/Labels, Magnetic Tape, Software

MMTinfo is a leading provider of real estate related information products and software for Florida and south Alabama. Real estate information products include tax roll databases, updated real estate sales information systems, market share reports, comparable sales reports, property owner mailing lists, and custom data runs for economic and financial analysis. Real estate software products include tax roll programs and real estate sales information programs that are licensed to other real estate information providers.

MetroNet
500 City Parkway West #205
(Attn.: Pat Young)
Orange, CA 92868
888-397-3742
www.experian.com/yourmarket/collections/metronet.html
Parent Company: Experian
Founded: 1941 **Memberships:** DMA, ACA, ALA,
Clientele Restrictions: Casual requesters permitted
Products, Information Categories, Coverage Area
Proprietary Databases or Gateways:
Database Name: MetroNet, Cole's Directory
Addresses/Telephone Numbers, Real Estate/Assessor (US)
Special Distribution Methods to Client: Automated Telephone Look-Up, CD-ROM, Dial-Up (Other than Internet), Gateway via Another Online Service, Publication/Directory

MetroNet includes direct access to the electronic directory assistance databases of the Regional Bells (RBOC's). Regional editions of the MetroSearch CD-ROM products and call-in services are featured. At the US Experian web site, select "Subscriber" and click MetroNet.

MicroPatent USA
250 Dodge Ave
East Haven, CT 06512
800-648-6787 Fax: 203-466-5054
www.micropat.com **Email:** info@micropat.com

Branch Offices:
London, UK
Parent Company: Information Holdings Inc
Founded: 1989 **Memberships:** AALL, ATLA, AIPLA,
INTA, NALA, NLG
Clientele Restrictions: Casual requesters permitted
Products, Information Categories, Coverage Area
Proprietary Databases or Gateways:
Database Name: WPS, TradeMark Checker, Mark
Search Plus
Patents, Trademarks (US, Intl)
Special Distribution Methods to Client: CD-ROM,
Dial-Up (Other than Internet), Disk, Email, Internet,
Software

MicroPatent is a global leader in the production and
distribution of patent and trademark information.
MicroPatent is committed to developing intellectual
property systems with its sophisticated and talented
programming staff. MicroPatent Europe is located in
London, England.

MidSouth Information Services

116 Lakeview Drive
Greenville, NC 27858
Fax: 252-757-3184
www.midsouthinfo.com **Email:** ron@midsouthinfo.com
Founded: 1998 **Memberships:** ASIS, SHRM,
Clientele Restrictions: Casual requesters permitted
Products, Information Categories, Coverage Area
General:
Credit Information (US)
Proprietary Databases or Gateways:
Gateway Name: Carolina Information Inc
Criminal Information, Litigation/Judgments/Tax Liens
(NC)
Special Distribution Methods to Client: Dial-Up (Other
than Internet), Email, Gateway via Another Online
Service

MidSouth provides county criminal record checks for all 50
states and statewide criminal searches. They also provide
consumer credit reports, DMV reports, education and prior
employment reports, 24-48 hours for credit reports and up
to a week for DMV reports. They also provide access to
North Carolina's criminal and civil indexes through their
sister company Carolina Information, Inc.

Military Information Enterprises Inc

PO Box 17118
Spartanburg, SC 29301
800-937-2133 Fax: 864-595-0813
www.militaryusa.com **Email:** thelocator@aol.com
Founded: 1988 **Memberships:** SCALI

Clientele Restrictions: Casual requesters permitted
Products, Information Categories, Coverage Area
Proprietary Databases or Gateways:
Database Name: Nationwide Locator Online
Military Svc (US)
Special Distribution Methods to Client: Email,
Internet, Publication/Directory

Military Information Enterprises specializes in current and
former military locates and background checks, also
military reunions and service verifications. They also
publish books on locating people. The owner is a South
Carolina licensed private investigator.

Motznik Computer Services Inc

8301 Briarwood St #100
Anchorage, AK 99518-3332
Fax: 907-344-1759
www.motznik.com **Email:** sales@motznik.com
Founded: 1974 **Memberships:** NFIB
Clientele Restrictions: Casual requesters permitted
Products, Information Categories, Coverage Area
Proprietary Databases or Gateways:
Database Name: AK Public Information Access System
Aviation, Vessels, Bankruptcy, Licenses-Registrations-
Permits, Litigation/Judgments/Tax Liens, Criminal
Information, Corporate/Trade Name Data, Uniform
Commercial Code, Real Estate/Assessor, Voter
Registration and Driver and/or Vehicle (AK)
Special Distribution Methods to Client: Dial-Up (Other
than Internet)

Motznik Computer Services' product is a comprehensive
online information research system that provides access to
a wide selection of Alaska public files. Information that can
be researched includes: tax liens, UCC, address, real
property, Anchorage civil suits, commercial fishing vessels,
judgments, motor vehicles, partnerships, bankruptcies,
aircraft, permanent fund filing, businesses, Anchorage
criminal cases and commercial fishing permits. MV data
does not include driver's personal information.

National Background Data

303 SW 8th St
Ocala, FL 34474
www.nationalbackgrounddata.com/
Clientele Restrictions: Casual requesters permitted
Products, Information Categories, Coverage Area
Proprietary Databases or Gateways:
Database Name: Let's Check America, Nat'l Background
Directory
Criminal Information (US, FL)
Database Name: AIM (Address Information Mgr)
Addresses/Telephone Numbers (US, FL)
Special Distribution Methods to Client: Internet

NBD compiles The National Background Directory(TM) on line to fill emerging needs for criminal background searches across the nation. Currently provides criminal record information from 27 states, with more than 60% of the US population and more than 30 million criminal records. In the coming year, NBD anticipates having more than 100 statewide databases online from as many as 45 states and the District of Columbia that cover about 95% of the US population. Their AIM product provides information on individuals' past addresses and movement patterns.

National Credit Information Network NCI

PO Box 53247
Cincinnati, OH 45253
800-374-1400 Fax: 513-522-1702
www.wdia.com
Parent Company: WDIA Corporation
Founded: 1983
Clientele Restrictions: Signed agreement required; some searches available to non-members
Products, Information Categories, Coverage Area
General:
Bankruptcy (IN, KY, OH)
Proprietary Databases or Gateways:
Database Name: NCI Network
Tenant History (IN, KY, OH)
Gateway Name: NCI Network
Credit Information, Addresses/Telephone Numbers, Voter Registration, Driver and/or Vehicle (US)
Special Distribution Methods to Client: Dial-Up (Other than Internet), Email, Internet

National Credit Information Network (NCI) specializes in interfacing with credit and public record databases for online searches with immediate response time. Online ordering is available for setup and for searches using a credit card. Access is available through their Internet site. A variety of packages include applicant identity, SSNs, DMVs, education, reference and credential verification, criminal history, bankruptcy and civil history, workers comp claims, and more.

National Fraud Center

Four Horsham Business Center
300 Welsh Rd #200
Horsham, PA 19044
800-999-5658 Fax: 215-657-7071
www.nationalfraud.com
Email: email@nationalfraud.com
Branch Offices:
Dallas, TX, Minneapolis, MN, San Francisco, CA,
Parent Company: Lexis-Nexis
Founded: 1981 **Memberships:** ASIS, IAAI, CII, IFS,

Clientele Restrictions: Casual requesters permitted
Products, Information Categories, Coverage Area
General:
Litigation/Judgments/Tax Liens (US)
Proprietary Databases or Gateways:
Database Name: NFC Online
Software/Training, Publication/Directory (US, Intl)
Database Name: Bank Fraud/Insurance Fraud/Organized Crime
Criminal Information (US, Intl)
Database Name: The Fraud Bulletin
Criminal History (US)
Gateway Name: Cellular Fraud Database
Criminal Information (US)
Special Distribution Methods to Client: CD-ROM, Dial-Up (Other than Internet), Disk

National Fraud Center combines its diverse databases into a system: NFConline. They utilize a fraud prevention, an interdiction program, and risk management tools to discover and prevent fraud and risk. They also specialize in pro-active measures such as security policies, training, and installation of security devices to protect corporations from future losses.

National Marine Fisheries Service

Statistics & Economic Division (F/ST1)
1315 East-West Highway
Silver Spring, MD 20910
www.st.nmfs.gov/st1/commercial/index.html
Products, Information Categories, Coverage Area
Proprietary Databases or Gateways:
Database Name: Vessel Documentation Data
Vessels (US)
Special Distribution Methods to Client: Internet

This organization provides free searches to the US Coast Guard vessel database. Data is updated every quarter. Search by vessel number or name.

National Service Information

145 Baker St
Marion, OH 43301
800-235-0337
www.nsii.net
Branch Offices:
Indianpolis, IN, 317-266-0040; Fax: 317-266-8453
Founded: 1989 **Memberships:** NPRRA, REIPA,
Clientele Restrictions: Casual requesters permitted
Products, Information Categories, Coverage Area
General:
Uniform Commercial Code (US)
Proprietary Databases or Gateways:
Database Name: NSI - Online

Corporate/Trade Name Data, Uniform Commercial Code (IN, OH, WI)

Special Distribution Methods to Client: Internet

National Service Information is engaged in the search, filing and document retrieval of public record information. Having offices in Marion, OH and Indianapolis, IN, they consider Ohio, Indiana and Kentucky their local market in addition to 4300 different jurisdictions they search nationwide. They recently unveiled a comprehensive database to allow clients to perform public record searches via the Web. Their web site allows you to perform state level UCC lien and corporate detail searches for Ohio, and state level UCCs for Indiana. NSI also provides the option of requesting copies of microfilmed UCC lien images.

National Student Clearinghouse

2191 Fox Mill Rd #300
Herndon, VA 20171-3019
Fax: 703-742-7792
www.studentclearinghouse.com **Email:** service@studentclearinghouse.org
Clientele Restrictions: Registration required.

Products, Information Categories, Coverage Area
Proprietary Databases or Gateways:
Database Name: EnrollmentVerify, DegreeVerify
Education/Employment (US)
Special Distribution Methods to Client: FTP, Internet

They conveniently provide attendance, degree, and financial information about students of a wide number (2400+ or up to 80% of all students) of colleges and universities in the USA. Does not include addresses, SSN verification, or records "on hold" or "blocked."

NC Recordsonline.com

18125 W Catawba Ave
Cornelius, NC 28031
877-442-9600
www.ncrecordsonline.com
Parent Company: RSM Group LLC
Clientele Restrictions: Signed Agreement Required

Products, Information Categories, Coverage Area
General:
Criminal Information (NC)
Proprietary Databases or Gateways:
Gateway Name: ncrecordsonline.com
Criminal Information (NC)
Special Distribution Methods to Client: Gateway via Another Online Service, Internet, Software

NCRecordsonline.com offers a reliable link to the North Carolina Administrative Office of the Courts criminal and civil mainframe. This allows high volume users, research firms, employment screeners, attorneys, PI's, bondsmen, paralegals, etc to log on from any computer and access the same criminal and civil index system that is used by the NC Clerk of Court, 24-hours a day, 7 days a week. NCRecordsonline.com lets its users bypass all state required set-up costs, long distance charges, and equipment fees associated with a direct connection.

Nebrask@ Online

301 South 13th #301
Lincoln, NE 68508
800-747-8177 Fax: 402-471-7817
www.nol.org **Email:** info@nol.org
Founded: 1992
Clientele Restrictions: Signed Agreement Required
Products, Information Categories, Coverage Area
Proprietary Databases or Gateways:
Gateway Name: Nebrask@ Online
Driver and/or Vehicle, Corporate/Trade Name Data and Uniform Commercial Code (NE)
Special Distribution Methods to Client: CD-ROM, Email, FTP

Nebrask@ Online is a State of Nebraska information system that provides electronic access to state, county, local, association and other public information. Some agency and association data is updated daily, weekly or monthly, Subscribers connect via 800 #, local #s, or the Internet 24-hours per day. There are sign-up and connect fees if not accessing via the Internet. Interactive access to premium services (those with a statutory fee) requires an annual subscription.

NETR Real Estate Research and Information

2055 East Rio Salado Parkway, Suite 201
Tempe, AZ 85281
Fax: 480-966-9422
www.netronline.com/ **Email:** brett@netronline.com
Founded: 1993
Products, Information Categories, Coverage Area
Proprietary Databases or Gateways:
Database Name: Property Data Store
Real Estate/Assessor
(AL,AZ,CA,DC,FL,HI,IL,IN,MD,MS,MI,MN,MO,NV,NY,OH,PA,TN,TX,UT,WA,WI)

NETR Real Estate Research and Information (NETR), LLC provides real estate research and information services nationwide. Headquartered in Tempe, Arizona, NETR provides title services beyond that of conventional title insurance companies, without the costly addition of a title insurance policy or guarantee. Most common services are historical chain-of title-reports, images of recorded documents, and condition of title reports. Database completeness of the list above varies by state and county/city. They maintain an excellent list of web links to recorder's offices and tax assessors.

NIB Ltd

100 Canal Pointe Vlvd #114
Princeton, NJ 08540-7063
800-537-5528 Fax: 609-936-2859
www.nib.com **Email:** Info@nib.com
Parent Company: Bristol Investments LTD
Founded: 1993 **Memberships:** SIIA
Clientele Restrictions: Signed agreement required, must
be ongoing account
Products, Information Categories, Coverage Area
Proprietary Databases or Gateways:
Database Name: BACAS, BcomM, Courier
Credit Information (US)
Special Distribution Methods to Client: Dial-Up (Other
than Internet), Software

NIB has been providing credit processing information to
businesses for over 10 years. Courier is a combination of
the 5 accessible credit reporting agencies. Other state-of-
the-art products include BACAS and BcomM.

Northwest Location Services

PO Box 1345
Puyallup, WA 98371
Fax: 253-848-4414
http://legallocate.com
Founded: 1990
Clientele Restrictions: Agreement required, no casual
requesters permitted
Products, Information Categories, Coverage Area
General:
Criminal Information (WA)
Proprietary Databases or Gateways:
Database Name: Superior Courts
Northwest Online
Statewide Court Filings (WA)
Database Name: Business Licenses
Licenses/Registration/Permits (WA)
Database Name: People Finder
Name/Address/SSN/DOB (WA)
Special Distribution Methods to Client: Dial-Up (Other
than Internet), Email, Internet

Serving investigative, legal and business professionals,
Northwest Location Services specializes in witness
location, skip tracing, asset research and other information
services, with an eye on protecting privacy and the public
safety. Licensed and bonded in Washington, they are allied
with Northwest Online and Digital Research Company who
produces CD-ROM database products for investigators,
attorneys and collection agencies.

Offshore Business News & Research

123 SE 3rd Ave #173
Miami, FL 33131
Fax: 305-372-8724
www.offshorebusiness.com
Parent Company: Offshore Business News & Research
Inc
Founded: 1996
Clientele Restrictions: Casual requesters permitted
Products, Information Categories, Coverage Area
Proprietary Databases or Gateways:
Database Name: Courts and Businesses
Addresses/Telephone Numbers. Litigations (Bermuda &
Cayman Islands)
Special Distribution Methods to Client: Internet

OBNR supplies information on businesses and individuals
involved in offshore finance and insurance. OBNR owns
litigation databases covering Bermuda and the Cayman
Islands. They offer 24 hour daily access, year around via
the Internet. They publish investigative newsletters
covering Bermuda and the Caribbean.

OneCreditSource.com

PO Box 2228
Lake Oswego, OR 97035
800-955-1356
www.onecreditsource.com **Email:** support@biinc.com
Parent Company: Background Investigations
Founded: 1992
Clientele Restrictions: Agreement required, must have
permissible purpose
Products, Information Categories, Coverage Area
General:
Criminal Information (WA, ID)
Proprietary Databases or Gateways:
Gateway Name: OJIN, JIS
Criminal Information (OR,WA)
Gateway Name: Consumer/Employment Credit
Credit Information (US)
Special Distribution Methods to Client: Gateway via
Another Online Service, Internet

Through Background Investigation's online service,
OneCreditSource.com, users enjoy access to the three
national credit bureaus (Trans Union, Equifax, Experian)
with reports returned online in seconds. Plus,
OneCreditSource.com online has OJIN and JIS online for
up to the minute criminal information in OR & WA.
Finally, the company provides industry leading customer
service that allows all users to benefit from the myriad of
quality products.

OPEN (Online Professional Electronic Network)

PO Box 549
Columbus, OH 43216-0549
888-381-5656 Fax: 614-481-6980
www.openonline.com
Founded: 1992 **Memberships:** ASIS, NCISS, NSA, SHRM,
Clientele Restrictions: Signed agreement required, must be ongoing account
Products, Information Categories, Coverage Area
General:
Criminal Information (US)
Proprietary Databases or Gateways:
Database Name: OPEN
Real Estate/Assessor, Bankruptcy, Uniform Commercial Code, Corporate/Trade Name Data, Addresses/Telephone Numbers, Credit Information, Driver and/or Vehicle, Criminal Information (US)
Gateway Name: Arrest Records
Criminal Information (OH,IN,MI)
Special Distribution Methods to Client: Dial-Up (Other than Internet), Gateway via Another Online Service, Internet

OPEN provides real-time, direct access to a large range of nationwide public records, such as driver records, arrest & conviction records, commercial & consumer credit reports, bankruptcies, liens and judgments. The service is subscription-based and is available to professionals and businesses for a variety of applications including background checks, skip-traces, verification of information such as addresses, phone numbers, SSNs, previous employment and educational background. OPEN provides free software, account start-up, and toll-free technical support with no monthly minimum.

OSHA DATA

12 Hoffman St
Maplewood, NJ 07040-1114
www.oshadata.com **Email:** mcarmel@oshadata.com
Founded: 1991 **Memberships:** ASSE, AIHA,
Clientele Restrictions: Casual requesters permitted
Products, Information Categories, Coverage Area
General:
Environmental (US)
Proprietary Databases or Gateways:
Gateway Name: OSHA Data Gateway
Legislation/Regulation (US)
Special Distribution Methods to Client: CD-ROM, Dial-Up (Other than Internet), Disk, Lists/Labels, Publication/Directory, Software

OSHA DATA's database contains corporate regulator violation records for every business inspected since July 1972. Information includes not only OSHA data, but also wage and hour, EEOC, insurance, NLRB asbestos and other regulatory types. The database is updated quarterly. Consultation and software for the utilization of the data are available.

OSO Grande Technologies

5921 Jefferson NE
Albuquerque, NM 87109
Fax: 505-345-6559
www.technet.nm.org **Email:** info@nm.net
Parent Company: New Mexico Technet
Founded: 1984
Clientele Restrictions: None reported
Products, Information Categories, Coverage Area
Proprietary Databases or Gateways:
Database Name: New Mexico Technet
Driver, Vehicle, Litigation/Judgments/Tax Liens, Corporate/Trade Name Data, UCC, Legislation/Regulation (NM)
Gateway Name: NM Fed Courts/LegalNet
Bankruptcy, Criminal Information (NM)
Special Distribution Methods to Client: Dial-Up (Other than Internet), Internet

Oso Grande Technologie is the for-profit portion of a self-supporting, non-profit corporation operating to provide management of a statewide computer network serving New Mexico, its state universities and statewide research, educational and economic-development interests. OGT serves as the primary connection point to the Internet for other Internet Service Providers, business, government and private users. OGT offers a full range of Internet services from dial-up to direct connections and web page services, to co-located services and New Mexico MVR requests. LegalNet provides legal resources; Oso Grande provides premium services.

Owens OnLine Inc

6501 N Himes Ave #104
Tampa, FL 33614
800-745-4656 Fax: 813-877-1826
www.owens.com **Email:** email@owens.com
Founded: 1992
Clientele Restrictions: Casual requesters permitted
Products, Information Categories, Coverage Area
General:
Addresses/Telephone Numbers (US)
Proprietary Databases or Gateways:
Gateway Name: Owens OnLine
Credit Information (US, Intl)
Gateway Name: Owens OnLine
Foreign Country Information (Intl)
Special Distribution Methods to Client: Email, Internet

Owens OnLine specializes in international background checks and credit reports on businesses and individuals, and in international criminal checks. They provide worldwide coverage and also offer FreeDirectories.com where over 1 billion people, companies, and public records can be found free of charge.

Pallorium Inc

PO Box 155-Midwood Station
Brooklyn, NY 11230
Fax: 212-858-5720
www.pallorium.com **Email:** pallorium@pallorium.com
Founded: 1979 **Memberships:** ION, WAD, NAIS, BOMP, ASIS, NCISS
Clientele Restrictions: Casual requesters permitted
Products, Information Categories, Coverage Area
General:
SEC/Other Financial (US)
Proprietary Databases or Gateways:
Database Name: Skiptrace America
Addresses/Telephone Numbers, Driver and/or Vehicle, Vital Records and Voter Registration (US)
Database Name: People Finder
Aviation, Vessels, Driver and/or Vehicle, Vital Records and Voter Registration (US)
Database Name: Business Finder America
Corporate/Trade Name Data (US)
Special Distribution Methods to Client: Dial-Up (Other than Internet), Internet

Pallorium (PallTech Online) services are divided into three areas: the electronic mail system, which links all users (800 investigative/security professionals); the bulletin board system, which provides a forum for the free exchange of information among all approved subscribers (public or private law enforcement only); and the investigative support system, which provides investigative support to approved users. PallTech's searches include aircraft record locator, national financial asset tracker, bankruptcy filings locator, business credit reports, consumer credit reports, NCOA trace, criminal records, national vehicle records, current employment locator, NYC registered voters by address, court and governmental jurisdiction identifier, ZIP Code locator and more searches in the US, Canada, Israel and Hong Kong. New products of addresses and personal information for all states total more than five billion records.

Paragon Document Research, Inc.

PO Box 65216
St Paul, MN 55165
800-892-4235
www.banc.com/pdrstore **Email:** pdrinc@quest.net
Parent Company: PDR Inc

Founded: 1990 **Memberships:** NAFE, NALA, NPRRA, MSBA,
Clientele Restrictions: Signed agreement required for subscriber rates; casual requests permitted
Products, Information Categories, Coverage Area
General:
Addresses/Telephone Numbers (MN, ND, SD, MT, WI, US)
Proprietary Databases or Gateways:
Database Name: Pdrlog; Termination Database
Uniform Commercial Code (US)
Special Distribution Methods to Client: Database, Disk, Lists/Labels, Microfilm/Microfiche

Paragon Document Research's services include searches throughout state and county levels nationwide covering UCC and federal and state tax Liens, corporate documents, Bankruptcy filings,judgment searches, past and present litigation, searches for ownership of, and liens on DMV reports, aircraft/watercraft and vessel searches, assumed name searches, and name reservations. Registered Agent Services and weekly tax lien bulletin orders can be requested online through www.banc.com/pdrastore. Turnaround time is 48-72 hrs; some exception on MN UCC searches, terminations included from 1996 forward.

Plat System Services Inc

12450 Wayzata Blvd #108
Minnetonka, MN 55305-1926
Fax: 612-544-0617
www.platsystems.com
Founded: 1961
Clientele Restrictions: Casual requesters permitted for free trial, but license will be required.
Products, Information Categories, Coverage Area
Proprietary Databases or Gateways:
Database Name: PropertyInfoNet™
Addresses/Real Estate/Assessor (MN-Minneapolis/St Paul and nearby counties)
Special Distribution Methods to Client: Database, Disk, Internet, Lists/Labels, Publication/Directory

Plat System Services has a variety of services available including online services updated weekly, PID directories published annually, commercial sold reports monthly, residential sold reports monthly, custom reports updated weekly, and other monthly reports such as contract for deeds, and commercial buyers and sellers reports. They also offer mailing lists and labels, diskettes updated weekly, printed PLAT maps and PLAT books updated semi-annually. They provide computerized county plat maps.

Property Data Center Inc

7100 E Bellevue #110
Greenwood Village, CO 80111
Fax: 303-850-9637
www.pdclane.net
Founded: 1984 **Memberships:** NPRRA, REIPA, DMA, NAR,
Clientele Restrictions: Casual requesters permitted

Products, Information Categories, Coverage Area
Proprietary Databases or Gateways:
Database Name: Real Property Assessments, Taxes
Real Estate/Assessor (CO)

Database Name: Owner Phone Numbers
Addresses/Telephone Numbers (CO)
Special Distribution Methods to Client: Disk, Internet, Lists/Labels

Property Data Center's PDC database includes more than two million real property ownership and deed transfer records for the metro Denver area, plus counties of Adams, Arapahoe, Boulder,Clear Creek, Denver, Douglas, El Paso, Eagle, Elbert, Jefferson, Larimer, Mesa, Pitkin, Pueblo, Summit, Weld. Customized databases are accessible by owner, location, and indicators such as property value. They specialize in lender marketing data, new owners, sold comparables, mapping data and direct mail lists.

Public Data Corporation

38 East 29th St
New York, NY 10016
Fax: 212-519-3067
www.pdcny.com
Founded: 1988
Clientele Restrictions: Casual requesters permitted

Products, Information Categories, Coverage Area
General:
Bankruptcy (NY)
Proprietary Databases or Gateways:
Database Name: Public Data
Real Estate/Assessor, Environmental, Litigation/Judgments/Tax Liens and Uniform Commercial Code (NY)
Special Distribution Methods to Client: Disk, Email, Magnetic Tape

PDC maintains an online database of 60 million NYC real estate and lien records which are updated daily. Record include deed and mortgage recordings, bankruptcy judgments, federal tax liens and UCC filings. Searches can be ordered and received by email thru the company's web site at www.pdcny.com.

Public Record Research Library

PO Box 27869
(206 W Julie Dr #2)
Tempe, AZ 85285
800-929-3811
www.brbpub.com **Email:** brb@brbpub.com
Parent Company: BRB Publications Inc
Founded: 1989 **Memberships:** PRRN, AIIP, AALL, SIIA,
Clientele Restrictions: Casual requesters permitted

Products, Information Categories, Coverage Area
Proprietary Databases or Gateways:
Database Name: PRRS
Addresses/Telephone Numbers, Legislation/Regulations (US)
Special Distribution Methods to Client: CD-ROM, Database, Disk, Internet, Lists/Labels, Publication/Directory

The Public Record Research Library is a series of in-depth databases formatted into books, CDs and online. BRB is recognized as the nation's leading research and reference publisher of public record related information. The principals of the parent company are directors of the Public Record Retriever Network, the nation's largest organization of public record professionals. Over 26,000 government and private enterprises are analyzed in-depth regarding regulations and access of public records and public information. The Public Record Research System (PRRS) is available on CD, the Internet and as a customized database.

Publook Information Service

PO Box 670
Hebron, OH 43025
866-782-5665 Fax: 740-928-2036
http://publook.com **Email:** mail@publook.com
Founded: 1998
Clientele Restrictions: Signed Agreement Required

Products, Information Categories, Coverage Area
Proprietary Databases or Gateways:
Database Name: Publook
Uniform Commercial Code, Corporate/Trade Name Data, Addresses/Telephone Numbers, Trademarks/Patents, Licenses/Registrations/Permits (OH)
Special Distribution Methods to Client: Dial-Up (Other than Internet), Email

Publook.com features immediate Internet web access to its proprietary databases of Ohio Secretary of State corporations, trade names, trademarks and UCC filings information. Search corporation, debtor names by keywords, search by debtor address, secured party name, secured party address, filing number. Search corporations by agent/business address, agent/business associate name, charter number. Information is updated weekly. No subscription fees, no charge if no hits, pay a flat fee per search that hits results.

Questel-Orbit

8000 Westpark Dr
McLean, VA 22102
800-326-1710 Fax: 703-893-5632
www.qpat.com **Email:** help@questel.orbit.com
Branch Offices:
Paris, FR, 33 (0)1 55 04 52 00
Parent Company: Questal Orbit-France Telecom Group
Clientele Restrictions: License Agreement Required
Products, Information Categories, Coverage Area
Proprietary Databases or Gateways:
Database Name: QPAT-WW
Patents (US, Intl)
Special Distribution Methods to Client: Dial-Up (Other than Internet), Internet

Qpat-WW has the full text of all US patents since 01/01/74, along with most European patents since 1987. Access is available through a subscription service.

QuickInfo.net Information Services

1033 Walnut #200
Boulder, CO 80302
888-259-6173 Fax: 303-381-2279
www.quickinfo.net **Email:** info@quickinfo.net
Founded: 1996
Clientele Restrictions: Signed Agreement Required
Products, Information Categories, Coverage Area
Proprietary Databases or Gateways:
Database Name: QuickInfo.net
Voter Registration (AK, AR, CO, DE, GA, KS, MI, NV, OH, OK, TX, UT)
Database Name: QuickInfo.net
Corporate/Trade Name Data (AZ, AR, GA, ID, NV, NM, OR, TX, UT, WY)
Database Name: QuickInfo.net
Driver and/or Vehicle (FL, ID, IA, LA, ME, MN, MS, MO, NC, OR, SD, TX, UT, WV, WI, WY)
Database Name: QuickInfo.net
Real Estate/Assessor (FL, ID, IA, LA, MN, MS, MO, NV, NC, OR, TX, UT, WI, WY)
Database Name: QuickInfo.net
Licenses/Registrations/Permits (FL, ID, IA, LA, MN, MS, MO, NV, NC, OR, TX, UT, WI, WY)
Database Name: QuickInfo.net
Vital Records (CO, NV, TX)
Special Distribution Methods to Client: CD-ROM, Internet

QuickInfo.Net is a governmental and business network for licensed professionals with a need for "highly searchable"

access to critical public and proprietary information. The password-protected network takes you to county courthouses, state agencies, federal archives. Your agency or company will have easy, affordable and expert access to hundreds of millions of public records. Also, QuickInfo.Net is a leader in expanding the number of databases available to the public. Their databases are "word-indexed" to assure you're getting the best information. CD-Rom products available for some Colorado, Georgia, and limited Southwestern states records.

Rapsheets.com

PO Box 3663 (193 Jefferson Ave)
Memphis, TN 38173
Fax: 901-526-5813
www.rapsheets.com/index.html
Email: webmaster@rapsheets.com
Parent Company: The Daily News
Founded: 1999
Clientele Restrictions: Casual requesters permitted.
Products, Information Categories, Coverage Area
Proprietary Databases or Gateways:
Database Name: rapsheets.com
Criminal Information (AL, AZ, AR, CO, CT, FL, GA, IL, IN, ID. KS, KY, MI, MN, MS, MO, NC, NV, NJ, NY, OH, OK, OR, SC, TN, TX, UT, VA, WA)
Special Distribution Methods to Client: Dial-Up (Other than Internet), Email, Internet

The Daily News offers a variety of searches, many of them free or a small fee; rapsheets.com is a fee service. The Daily News specializes in information searches in the Memphis, TN area, and Nashville, including statewide MVRs for a fee. Rapsheets.com allows subscribers to access criminal records in most states.

Realty Data Corp

170 Old Country Rd #505
Mineola, NY 11501
Fax: 516-877-8724
www.realtydata.com
Email: customerservice@realtydata.com
Founded: 2000 **Memberships:** REIPA, ALTA, TAVMA, NHEMA,
Clientele Restrictions: Agreement required.
Products, Information Categories, Coverage Area
General:
Real Estate/Assessor (NY)
Proprietary Databases or Gateways:
Database Name: Realty Data Database
Real Estate/Assessor, UCC, Litigation/Judgments/Tax Liens, Bankruptcy, Environmental (NY)
Special Distribution Methods to Client: Internet

Specializing in NYC, Realty Data Corp. (RDC) is a B2B e-commerce aggregator of data that delivers online automated real estate data to the real estate and financial services industries. RDC has developed a proprietary system that has the ability to conduct "intelligent" searches, currently combing through more than 150,000,000 New York City records. RDC clients can order and receive complete on-line customized property reports and images 24/7 without the hassle of record examiners or the inaccuracy of the manual process. Data can be retrieved for any person, property or owner in New York County, Kings County, Queens County and Bronx County, NY. Images are available from counties in fifteen other states.

Record Information Services Inc

PO Box 894
Elburn, IL 60119
Fax: 630-365-6524
www.public-record.com **Email:** jmetcalf@public-record.com
Founded: 1993
Clientele Restrictions: Casual requesters permitted
Products, Information Categories, Coverage Area
General:
Uniform Commercial Code (IL)
Proprietary Databases or Gateways:
Database Name: IL Records, New Homeowners, Mortgages/Foreclosures
Litigation/Judgments/Tax Liens, Real Estate/Assessor, Mortgages, Foreclosures (IL)
Database Name: Bankruptcies
Bankruptcy (IL)
Database Name: Business Licenses, News Incorporations
Licenses/Registrations/Permits (IL)
Special Distribution Methods to Client: Database, Disk, Email, Internet, Lists/Labels, Software

Record Information Services provides complete and timely public record data that is delivered through state-of-the-art technology. Custom reports are available upon request. They also provide local document retrieval in Northeast Illinois counties.

Records Research Inc

PO Box 19300
Sacramento, CA 95819
800-952-5766
www.recordsresearch.com/
Email: recre@recordresearch.com
Founded: 1981
Clientele Restrictions: Signed Agreement Required
Products, Information Categories, Coverage Area
General:
Corporate/Trade Name Data (US)
Proprietary Databases or Gateways:
Gateway Name: RRI MVRs
Driver and/or Vehicle (CA, US)

Records Research (RRI) specializes in providing California motor vehicle reports (MVRs) to insurance and related industries. Driving histories and vehicle reports are available online, allowing instant response to client requests. Overnight service available. They offer a variety of searches including plate, VIN, automated name index, soundex searches, and financial responsibility reports. RRI offers MVRs from all other states with a 24-48 hour turnaround. RPI offers a wide range of other public record services including corporate and property searches. Clients must establish a commercial account with the state, which RRI will be happy to help expedite.

Research Archives.com Legal Documents Library

c/o Beard Group
PO Box 4250
Frederick, MD 21705
Fax: 240-629-3360
www.researcharchives.com **Email:** info@researcharchives.com
Parent Company: Beard Group
Clientele Restrictions: Subscription required.
Products, Information Categories, Coverage Area
General:
Bankruptcy (US, MD)
Proprietary Databases or Gateways:
DB Name: Legal Documents Library
Bankruptcy; Addresses/Telephone Numbers; Vessels; Corporate/Trade Name Data (US)
Special Distribution Methods to Client: Internet

ResearchArchives.Com is a powerful research tool for legal and business professionals. A convenient, fast and inexpensive online resource for copies of material contracts and agreements involving virtually all public companies in the United States. They have over 20244 bankruptcy documents and are adding 2,000 more every month.

San Diego Daily Transcript/San Diego Source

2131 Third Ave
San Diego, CA 92101
800-697-6397 Fax: 619-239-5716
www.sddt.com **Email:** tran@sddt.com
Clientele Restrictions: Casual requesters permitted
Products, Information Categories, Coverage Area
Proprietary Databases or Gateways:
Database Name: San Diego Source
Litigation/Judgments/Tax Liens and Uniform Commercial Code (CA)
Gateway Name: US Bankruptcy Court Filings
Bankruptcy (CA)

Database Name: Home Sales, Com. Real Estate, Leases
Real Estate/Assessor and Addresses/Telephone Numbers
(CA)
Special Distribution Methods to Client: CD-ROM,
Database, Email, Lists/Labels, Publication/Directory

The San Diego Source is a leading California web site for
public record information and business data. Site visitors
can perform customized searches on one or more than
fifteen databases. Links with Transcripts Online are
provided.

SEAFAX Inc

PO Box 15340
Portland, ME 04112-5340
800-777-3533 Fax: 207-773-9564
www.seafax.com
Founded: 1985
Clientele Restrictions: Casual requesters permitted
Products, Information Categories, Coverage Area
  General:
  Legislation/Regulation (US)
  Proprietary Databases or Gateways:
  Database Name: Business Reports
  Credit Information (US)
  Special Distribution Methods to Client: Internet

Seafax is the leading source of food industry-specific
information, thus a valuable credit reporting resource to
manage your exposure. Using Seafax, decision-makers
access timely and accurate information 24/7. More than
1200 food producers, processors and distributors use
Seafax services to minimize rick, save time and maximize
profits using products like Supersearch to perform
company, date or geography searches, or business report
services like Seafax Credit Appraisal & Risk Index, bank &
trade references, and unique financial data. Their
Bankruptcy Creditor Index allow the identification of
unsecured creditors of bankruptcies, receiverships and
assignments. Other products include Agriwire and Agriscan
Bulletin.

Search Company of North Dakota LLC

1008 E Capitol Ave
Bismarck, ND 58501-1930
Fax: 701-223-1850 **Email:** mkautzma@btinet.com
Founded: 1984 **Memberships:** PRRN
Clientele Restrictions: Casual requesters permitted
Products, Information Categories, Coverage Area
  Proprietary Databases or Gateways:
  Database Name: North Dakota Records
  Addresses/Telephone Numbers,
  Litigation/Judgments/Tax Liens,

Licenses/Registrations/Permits, Criminal Information and
Bankruptcy (ND)
Database Name: ND UCC
Uniform Commercial Code (ND)
  Special Distribution Methods to Client: Email,
  Lists/Labels

They will provide any and all city, county, state, or federal
record searching or filing in North Dakota. Over 15 years
of experience in all aspects of public record searching,
retrieval, or filing.

Search Network Ltd

Two Corporate Place #210
1501 42nd St
West Des Moines, IA 50266-1005
800-383-5050
http://searchnetworkltd.com **Email:**
lharken@searchnetworkltd.com
Branch Offices:
Topeka, KS, 800-338-3618; Fax: 785-235-5788
Founded: 1965 **Memberships:** NPRRA, PRRN,
Clientele Restrictions: Casual requesters permitted
Products, Information Categories, Coverage Area
  General:
  Litigation/Judgments/Tax Liens (US, IA, KS)
  Proprietary Databases or Gateways:
  Database Name: Search Network
  Uniform Commercial Code (IA, KS)
  Special Distribution Methods to Client: Dial-Up (Other
  than Internet), Lists/Labels, Microfilm/Microfiche,
  Publication/Directory

In business since 1965, Search Network provides full
service public record search information. The company
maintains an on-site UCC database for Iowa and Kansas.
Same day searches and copies are available as well as
personal filing service for UCC and corporate documents.
Since 1980, they have offered direct online access to their
databases of UCC filing/records information in Iowa and
Kansas

Silver Plume

4775 Walnut St #2B
Boulder, CO 80301
800-677-4442 Fax: 303-449-1199
www.silverplume.com **Email:** sales@silverplume.com
Founded: 1989
Clientele Restrictions: Signed Agreement Required
Products, Information Categories, Coverage Area
  General:
  SEC/Other Financial (US)
  Proprietary Databases or Gateways:
  Database Name: Insurance Industry Rates, Forms and
  Manuals
  Legislation/Regulations (US)

Special Distribution Methods to Client: CD-ROM, Internet, Magnetic Tape

Silver Plume is the leading provider of insurance-related reference and research material. Receive material in one subscription on CD-Rom or online.

SKLD Information Services LLC

720 S Colorado Blvd #1000N
Denver, CO 80246
800-727-6358 Fax: 303-260-6391
www.skld.com **Email:** sales@skld.com
Founded: 1961 **Memberships:** ATLA, DMA, National Association of Mortgage Brokers,
Clientele Restrictions: Casual requesters permitted but Agreement Required

Products, Information Categories, Coverage Area
General:
Bankruptcy (CO)
Proprietary Databases or Gateways:
Database Name: New Homeowners List, Deeds, Loan Activity, Notice of Demand
Real Estate/Assessor (CO-14 counties)
Special Distribution Methods to Client: Database, Disk, Magnetic Tape

SKLD Information Services maintains a complete database of public record information from documents recorded in fourteen County Recorder offices in Colorado since 1990. Information is available to enhance existing databases, create new homeowner mailing lists, report on real estate loan transaction information, and mortgage marketing data. With archived county recorded documents and plat maps in their in-house microfilm library, SKLD can provide quick turnaround time for document and plat map retrieval. Reports available include: real estate loan activity reports, warranty deed/trust deed match, trust deed report, owner carry reports, notice of election and demand, and new homeowners lists.

Softech International Inc

13200 SW 128th St #F3
Miami, FL 33186
888-318-7979 Fax: 305-253-1440
www.softechinternational.com **Email:**
reid@softechinternational.com
Branch Offices:
Chicago, IL, 312-654-8045; Fax: 312-654-1285
Founded: 1996
Clientele Restrictions: Casual requesters permitted; agreement required.

Products, Information Categories, Coverage Area
General:
Driver and/or Vehicle (AL, FL, NJ, NY, TN, GA, IN, IL)
Proprietary Databases or Gateways:
Gateway Name: MVRs and Registrations

Driver and/or Vehicle (FL, NY, NJ, AL, IN)
Special Distribution Methods to Client: Email, FTP, Gateway via Another Online Service, Internet

The provide MVR and registration information via the internet, real time.

Software Computer Group Inc

PO Box 3042
Charleston, WV 25331-3042
800-795-8543
www.swcg-inc.com/courts.htm **Email:** info@swcg-inc.com
Founded: 1975
Clientele Restrictions: Casual requesters permitted

Products, Information Categories, Coverage Area
Proprietary Databases or Gateways:
Gateway Name: Circuit Express
Criminal Information, Litigation/judgments/Tax Liens (WV)
Special Distribution Methods to Client: Dial-Up (Other than Internet), Internet

The Circuit Express product brings civil and criminal public information records from the Circuit Courts in West Virginia to you online. You can locate cases by name or case filing type. Not all counties are available. Fees include a sign-up fee, and monthly fee with connect charges. There is an additional system for magistrate courts; however, this service is only available to government agencies.

Southeastern Public Records Inc.

208 W Chicago Rd #4
Sturgis, MI 49091
Fax: 616-659-1169
www.publicrex.com **Email:** jimbarfield@msn.com
Founded: 1993
Clientele Restrictions: Casual requesters permitted

Products, Information Categories, Coverage Area
General:
Credit Information (MI, GA)
Proprietary Databases or Gateways:
Database Name: Michigan/Georgia Public Records
Addresses/Telephone Numbers, Bankruptcy, Litigation/Judgments/Tax Liens (GA, MI)
Special Distribution Methods to Client: CD-ROM, Database, Dial-Up (Other than Internet), Disk, Email, Internet, Magnetic Tape, Software

Southeastern Public Records can deliver bulk data up to 3,000,000 records within 48 hours of verifying customer specifications. Smaller batches of data available in 1 to 48 hours if needed. Verification of any judgment, tax lien, or bankruptcy at its original place of filing in all covered areas. All data is recorded from its original source by one of our certified collectors on software developed by us for that particular purpose. Our databases contain 15 years of historical data in Michigan and 10 years in Georgia. Our key personnel include: a full time onsite Internet/web specialist; full time onsite database development specialists; several full time personnel with extensive knowledge of legal recording, mortgages, major credit bureaus, and all civil public records at all levels.

State Net
2101 K Street
Sacramento, CA 95816
Fax: 916-446-5369
www.statenet.com
Branch Offices:
Washington, DC, 202-638-7999; Fax: 202-638-7291
Tallahassee, FL, 850-205-7710; Fax: 850-205-7714
Springfield, IL, 217-522-1188; Fax: 217-522-1195
Founded: 1978
Clientele Restrictions: Casual requesters permitted
Products, Information Categories, Coverage Area
Proprietary Databases or Gateways:
Database Name: State Net
Legislation/Regulations (US)
Special Distribution Methods to Client: Dial-Up (Other than Internet), Internet, Publication/Directory

State Net delivers vital data, legislative intelligence and in-depth reporting for people who care about the actions of government. Based in Sacramento, CA, they were created by legislative experts who invented a computerized tracking system that has evolved into what they feel is the nation's leading source of legislative and regulatory information. State net monitors 100% of all pending bills and regulations in the 50 states and Congress. Successful government affairs managers from small state associations to giant Fortune 500 companies rely on them to report activity on their issues in the 50 states. Backed by a three-decade commitment to providing fast, accurate legislative information. State Net publishes a variety of online and print publications.

Superior Information Services LLC
300 Phillips Blvd #500
Trenton, NJ 08618-1427
800-848-0489
www.superiorinfo.com **Email:**
lmartin@superiorinfo.com
Founded: 1987 **Memberships:** NPRRA, ICA, AALL, SLA, PRRN,
Clientele Restrictions: None reported
Products, Information Categories, Coverage Area
Proprietary Databases or Gateways:
Database Name: Superior Online
Litigation/Judgments/Tax Liens and Bankruptcy (DC, DE, MD, NC, NJ, NY, PA, VA)

Database Name: Corporate Files
Corporate/Trade Name Data (NY, PA, NJ)
Database Name: UCC Files
Uniform Commercial Code (PA, NJ)
Database Name: Real Property
Real Estate/Assessor (US)
Gateway Name: People Finder
Addresses/Telephone Numbers (US)
Special Distribution Methods to Client: Dial-Up (Other than Internet)

Superior Information Services is an online public record provider. In addition, we provide Nationwide Corporate Services, and Core Data Services, as well. Currently, we provide online public records through our new product, Superior Online PLUS, as well as our existing product, Superior Online. With Superior's new National property file you can access forty-eight states of data with just one search. You can now access Criminal Data when using Superior Online PLUS. Registered users can search criminal records in 27 U.S. states - including NJ and NY. A number of data sources are used to ensure as complete a dossier as possible. In addition, this search tool gives you the ability to download the information - allowing you to customize reports for your investigative needs.

Tax Analysts
6830 N Fairfax Dr
Arlington, VA 22213
800-955-3444 Fax: 703-533-4444
www.tax.org **Email:** cserve@tax.org
Founded: 1970
Clientele Restrictions: Casual requesters permitted
Products, Information Categories, Coverage Area
General:
Associations/Trade Groups (US)
Proprietary Databases or Gateways:
Database Name: Exempt Organization Master List
Corporate/Trade Name Data (US)
Database Name: The Tax Directory
Addresses/Telephone Numbers (US)
Database Name: The OneDisc,TAXBASE
Legislation/Regulations (US)
Database Name: TAXBASE, The Ratx Directory
Foreign Country Information (Intl)
Special Distribution Methods to Client: CD-ROM, Disk, Internet, Publication/Directory

Tax Analysts is a nonprofit organization dedicated to providing timely, comprehensive information to tax professionals at a reasonable cost. They are the leading electronic publisher of tax information. The Exempt Organization Master List contains information about more than 1.1 million not-for-profit organizations registered with the federal government. The Tax Directory contains information about 14,000 federal tax officials, 9000 private tax professionals and 8000 corporate tax professionals. Online databases include daily federal, state and international tax information as well as complete research libraries. Some products are available on DIALOG & LEXIS.

Telebase

1150 First Ave #820
King of Prussia, PA 19406
800-220-4664 Fax: 610-945-2460
www.telebase.com
Parent Company: Dun & Bradstreet
Founded: 1984 **Memberships:** SPA/IIA
Clientele Restrictions: Casual requesters permitted
Products, Information Categories, Coverage Area
Proprietary Databases or Gateways:
Gateway Name: Brainwave, I-Quest
Corporate/Trade Name Data, Addresses/Telephone Numbers, News/Current Events, Credit Information, Trademarks, SEC/Other Financial,Foreign Country Information (US)
Gateway Name: LEXIS-NEXIS CaseLaw @AOL
Litigation/Judgments/Tax Liens (US)
Gateway Name: Dun & Bradstreet @ AOL
Credit Information, Addresses/Telephone Numbers (US)
Special Distribution Methods to Client: Dial-Up (Other than Internet), Gateway via Another Online Service, Internet

Telebase, part of Dun & Bradstreet, offers company information from Dun & Bradstreet, corporate hierarchy information from LexisNexis and premium company and industry profiles from Datamonitor. Information Services are designed for people with little or no online searching experience and provide easy access to business information for sales prospecting, market analysis, competitive intelligence, product development, and other research. Several thousand sources, from over 450 databases, are available including credit reports, financial reports, company directories, magazines, newspapers, newswires, industry newsletters, etc. For a list of distribution partners visit www.telebase.com.

Tennessee Anytime

866-886-3468
www.tennesseeanytime.org/main/online/index.html
Founded: 2000
Clientele Restrictions: Premium services require registration
Products, Information Categories, Coverage Area
Proprietary Databases or Gateways:
Gateway Name: Free Services
Corporate/Trade Name Data,Trademarks, Uniform Commercial Code, Real Estate/Assessor (TN)

Gateway Name: Premium Services
Driver and/or Vehicle (TN)
Special Distribution Methods to Client: Internet

Tennessee Anytime, the official web site of the State of Tennessee, is a gateway to a myriad of state information and services. Many free services are available, as well as "premium services" which require fees and registration. A TennesseeAnytime subscription allows you to easily access Tennessee's eGovernment Online Services.

Tenstar Business Services Group

315 S College #245
Lafayette, LA 70503
800-960-2214 Fax: 337-235-5318
www.tenstarcorporation.com **Email:** tenstarco@aol.com
Branch Offices:
Baton Rouge, LA, 800-864-5154; Fax: 225-273-8987
Jackson, MS, 800-864-5154; Fax: 225-273-8987
New Orleans, LA, 800-856-8515
Parent Company: Tenstar Corporation
Founded: 1989 **Memberships:** ACE, RPA, NAPPS, NPRRA, ACA, PRRN
Clientele Restrictions: Casual requesters permitted.
Products, Information Categories, Coverage Area
General:
Bankruptcy (LA, MS)
Proprietary Databases or Gateways:
Database Name: ACB-1
Addresses/Telephone Numbers, Bankruptcy, Corporate/Trade Name Data, Criminal Information, Education/Employment, Litigation/Judgments/Tax Liens, UCCs, Real Estate/Assessor, Social Security Numbers, Tenant History, Wills/Probate, Workers Comp (LA, MS)
Datebase Name: ACB-1
Criminal Information (permissible users only) (MS)
Gateway Name: ACB-2
Credit Information, Driver and/or Vehicle (LA, US)
Special Distribution Methods to Client: CD-ROM, Dial-Up (Other than Internet), Disk, Email, FTP, Magnetic Tape

Tenstar specializes in research, retrieval, recording, corporate services, notary services, abstracting, process service, litigation support, paralegal services, court reporting, investigations, risk management and claims adjusting, and business office services. Add'l services not listed above are Tenant histories, and Wills/Probate records. Services statewide in LA, MS. All 64 Louisiana parishes researched in about 48 hours; 72 hours for Mississippi.

Texas Driving Record Express Service

7809 Easton / 7399 Gulf Freeway Plaza
Houston, TX 77017
800-671-2287 **Email:** www.txdrivingrecordexpress.com/
Parent Company: Ernest L Calderon dba CATS
Founded: 1992
Clientele Restrictions: License Agreement Required
Products, Information Categories, Coverage Area
General:
Driver and/or Vehicle (TX)
Proprietary Databases or Gateways:
Gateway Name: Certified MVRs
Driver and/or Vehicle (TX)

Texas Driving Records Express provides driving records statewide in 1-7 days, also original/state-certified documents for ticket elimination, restoration of Texas driving privileges from TX Dept of Public Safety, employment requirements, current addresses.

The Official Providers Source

4500 S 129th E Ave
Tulsa, OK 74134
800-331-9175 Fax: 918-664-4366
www.providerssource.com **Email:**
jeriw@dacservices.com
Parent Company: Total Information Services, Inc.
Founded: 1981 **Memberships:** SIIA, SHRM, AAMVA, ATA, PRRN,
Clientele Restrictions: Signed agreement required, must be ongoing account
Products, Information Categories, Coverage Area
General:
Credit Information (US)
Proprietary Databases or Gateways:
Database Name: Transportation Employment History; Drug/Alcohol Test Results, Security Guard Employment History; Drug/Alcohol Test Results, Security Guard Employment History
Education/Employment (US)
Gateway Name: Driving Records
Driver and/or Vehicle (US)
Gateway Name: 20/20 Insight
Criminal Information (US, CD, Itl, VI, PR)
Database Name: Claims and Injury Reports
Workers Compensation (AR, FL, IA, IL, KS, MA, MD, ME, MI, MS, ND, NE, OH, OK, OR, TX)
Special Distribution Methods to Client: Dial-Up (Other than Internet), Internet

They have serviced employers and insurance businesses for more than 16 years, providing employment screening and underwriting/risk assessment tools. CDLIS contains summary information on more than 6,000,000 drivers. Customers request information by PC and modem via toll-free lines. Computer access is available through networks and mainframe-to-mainframe connections. Customers may opt to call or fax requests to their service representative toll-free.

The Search Company Inc

25 Adelaide Street East #720
Toronto, Ontario, CD M5C 3A1
800-396-8241
www.thesearchcompany.com **Email:**
info@thesearchcompany.com
Founded: 1993
Clientele Restrictions: Must be ongoing account
Products, Information Categories, Coverage Area
General:
Foreign Country Information (Canada)
Proprietary Databases or Gateways:
Database Name: Property Ownership & Tenant Data
Real Estate/Assessor (Canada)
Special Distribution Methods to Client: Dial-Up (Other than Internet), Email, Software

The Search Company covers 2 distinct markets: 1) Canada wide public record retrieval; 2) Litigation related asset and corporate background reporting with or without a full narrative report, with analysis and opinion regarding the advisability of litigation.

Thomas Legislative Information

101 Independence S.E.
Washington, DC 20540
http://thomas.loc.gov **Email:** thomas@loc.gov
Parent Company: Library of Congress
Products, Information Categories, Coverage Area
Proprietary Databases or Gateways:
Database Name: Thomas
Legislation/Regulation (US)
Special Distribution Methods to Client: Internet

Although technically a government site, we have posted in this section due to the tremendous information available to the public. Free Internet access to legislative information (including bill summary, status, and text), congressional record, and committee information. A giant plus is the ability to search by bill number or by key word/phrase.

Thomson & Thomson

500 Victory Rd
North Quincy, MA 02171-3145
800-692-8833
www.thomson-thomson.com
Email: john.giaquinto@t-t.com

Branch Offices:
Antwerp, Belgium, 323-220-7211
Montreal, Quebec, CANADA, 800-561-6240; Fax: 514-393-3854
Parent Company: The Thomson Corporation
Founded: 1922 **Memberships:** INTA, SIIA, AALL,
Clientele Restrictions: Casual requesters permitted

Products, Information Categories, Coverage Area
General:
Litigation/Judgments/Tax Liens (US)
Proprietary Databases or Gateways:
Database Name: TRADEMARKSCAN
Trademarks and Foreign Country Information (US, Intl)
Database Name: Worldwide Domain
Foreign Country Information (US, Intl)
Gateway Name: Site Comber
Patents (US)
Database Name: US Full Trademark Search, Site Comber
Trademarks (US)
Database Name: US Full Copyright Search
Licenses/Registrations/Permits (US)
Database Name: US Title Availability Search, The deForest Report for Script Clearance
Corporate/Trade Name Data (US)
Special Distribution Methods to Client: CD-ROM,
Dial-Up (Other than Internet), Internet

Thomson & Thomson is a world leader in trademark, copyright and script clearance services, with over 75 years of experience and offices in the US, Canada, Europe and Japan. Accessing trademark records from more than 200 countries, T&T analysts provide reports to help clients determine if their proposed trademarks are available for use. Clients can perform their own trademark searches via Thomson & Thomson's TRADEMARKSCAN online databases. Thomson & Thomson also provides a complete offering of equally impressive copyright, title and script clearance services to help manage and protect your intellectual property assets.

Thomson Financial
1455 Research Blvd.
Rockville, MD 20850
800-847-4337
www.tfibcm.com **Email:** researchcenter@tfn.com
Founded: 1978
Clientele Restrictions: Casual requesters permitted

Products, Information Categories, Coverage Area
General:
Litigation/Judgments/Tax Liens (US)
Proprietary Databases or Gateways:
Database Name: Disclosure SEC Database
SEC/Other Financial (US)

Database Name: State & Federal Agency Filings
News/Current Events, Trademarks, Environmental, Legislation/Regulation, Litigation/Judgments/Tax Liens (US)
Database Name: Bankruptcy Filings & Reports
Bankruptcy (US)
Special Distribution Methods to Client: CD-ROM,
Email, Internet

Thomson Financial's Investment Banking and Capital Market Group is a nationwide research and retrieval company. Records and searches can be done on a state and federal basis at any court or agency around the country. Court services include monitoring companies for new cases and new pleadings in existing cases. SEC documents can also be ordered through our research centers. They have an extensive in-house collection of bankruptcy documents dating back to 1988 as well as other types of agency filings including FERC, DOT, & FCC.

TML Information Services Inc
116-55 Queens Blvd
Forest Hills, NY 11375
800-743-7891 Fax: 718-544-2853
www.tml.com **Email:** edarmody@tml.com
Founded: 1985 **Memberships:** AAMVA, IIAA, NAPIA, NETS,
Clientele Restrictions: Signed agreement required, must be ongoing account

Products, Information Categories, Coverage Area
Proprietary Databases or Gateways:
Gateway Name: Auto-Search
Driver and/or Vehicle (AL, AZ, CT, DC, FL, ID, IN, KS, KY, LA, MA, MI, MN, MS, NC, ND, NE, NH, NJ, NY, OH, SC, VA, WI, WV)
Gateway Name: Title File
Driver and/or Vehicle (AL, FL, SD)
Gateway Name: Driver Check
Driver and/or Vehicle (AL, AZ, CA, CT, FL, ID, KS, LA, MD, MI, MN, NE, NH, NY, NC, OH, PA, SC, VA, WV)
Gateway Name: Driving Records
Driver and/or Vehicle (US)
Special Distribution Methods to Client: Dial-Up (Other than Internet), Internet

TML Information Services specializes in providing access to motor vehicle information in an online, real-time environment. Their standardization format enables TML to offer several unique automated applications for instant access to multiple states' driver and vehicle information, including a touch-tone fax-on-demand service and a rule-based decision processing service for driver qualification for car rental. TML has online access to more than 200 million driver and vehicle records in more than 30 states and expects to add several more states soon. No third party use; professional license required.

tnrealestate.com KAL Software

PO Box 1375
Murfreesboro, TN 37133
www.tnrealestate.com **Email:** sales@tnrealestate.com
Parent Company: Kal Software LLC
Founded: 1996
Clientele Restrictions: Casual requesters permitted
Products, Information Categories, Coverage Area
  Proprietary Databases or Gateways:
  Database Name: Tennessee Real Estate Data
  Real Estate/Assessor (TN)
  Special Distribution Methods to Client: Dial-Up (Other than Internet), Internet

Tnrealestate.com provides free searches to Tennessee real estate for 91 of 94 counties for more than 3,000,000 parcels. Records reflect the tax assessor files and sales files.

Trademark Register, The

2100 National Press Building
Washington, DC 20045
Fax: 202-347-4408
www.trademarkregister.com/ **Email:**
trademarks@erols.com **Memberships:** ITA, SLA, NPC,
Products, Information Categories, Coverage Area
  Proprietary Databases or Gateways:
  Database Name: The Trademark Register
  Trademarks (US)
  Special Distribution Methods to Client: Internet, Publication/Directory

The Trademark Register is an annual volume consisting of over 1 million active trademarks in effect with the U.S. Patent and Trademark Office from 1884 to present. It was first published in 1958 when it contained approximately 200,000 registered trademarks. Each trademark entry gives the date of registration or filling date, international class, registration or serial number. A daily subscription is offered for Internet access.

Trans Union

PO Box 2000
Chester, PA 19022
800-888-4213
www.transunion.com
Founded: 1969 **Memberships:** SIIA
Clientele Restrictions: Signed agreement required, must be ongoing account
Products, Information Categories, Coverage Area
  Proprietary Databases or Gateways:
  Database Name: Trans Union Credit Data
  Credit Information (US)

  Special Distribution Methods to Client: Dial-Up (Other than Internet), Software

Trans Union is a primary source of credit information and offers risk and portfolio management services. They serve a broad range of industries that routinely evaluate credit risk or verify information about their customers. Their customers include financial and banking services, insurance agencies, retailers, collection agencies, communication and energy companies, and hospitals. They have strong relationships with every large and most medium and small credit grantors throughout the nation. Trans Union operates nationwide through a network of their own offices and independent credit bureaus. They also have many subsidiaries and divisions in the U.S. and abroad. The needs and desires of their customers and consumers directly shape Trans Union's products and services design. They have a competitive stance based on the highest levels of quality coupled with unmatched levels of service.

UCC Direct Services – (AccuSearch Inc)

PO Box 3248
2727 Allen Parkway, 10th Fl
Houston, TX 77253-3248
800-833-5778 Fax: 713-831-9891
www.uccdirect.com **Email:** info@uccdirect.com
Branch Offices:
Sacramento, CA, 888-863-9241; Fax: 916-492-6655
Austin, TX, 800-884-0185; Fax: 512-323-9102
Chicago, IL, 847-853-0892; Fax: 847-853-0893
Founded: 1985 **Memberships:** NPRRA
Clientele Restrictions: License required
Products, Information Categories, Coverage Area
  General:
  Litigation/Judgments/Tax Liens (CA, IL, TX)
  Proprietary Databases or Gateways:
  Database Name: AccuSearch
  Corporate/Trade Name, Uniform Commercial Code (TX,CA,PA,IL,WA,OH,OR,MO)
  Database Name: AccuSearch
  Bankruptcy (CA,IL,TX)
  Special Distribution Methods to Client: Dial-Up (Other than Internet), Internet

UCC Direct - formerly AccuSearch - provides immediate access to UCC, corporate, charter, real property and bankruptcy search services via the Internet. Instantaneous access is available for each online database listed. Each online or over-the-phone search is followed by same-day mailing or faxing of the search report. They also performs any of the above searches for any county or state nationwide. Their Direct Access system allows multi-page, formatted reports which eliminates print screens, and selective ordering of UCC copies. AccuFile UCC Filing and & Portfolio Managemnet allows UCC filing electronically.

Unisearch Inc

1780 Barnes Blvd SW
Tumwater, WA 98512-0410
800-722-0708
www.unisearch.com
Branch Offices:
Sacramento, CA, 800-769-1864; Fax: 800-769-1868
Salem, OR, 800-554-3113; Fax: 800-554-3114
St Paul, MN, 800-227-1256; Fax: 800-227-1263
Founded: 1991 **Memberships:** NPRRA, NRAI, PRRN,
Clientele Restrictions: Casual requesters permitted
Products, Information Categories, Coverage Area
General:
Bankruptcy, Litigation/Judgments/Tax Liens (US)
Proprietary Databases or Gateways:
Database Name: WALDO
Uniform Commercial Code, Litigation/Judgments/Tax
Liens (CA, WA)
Special Distribution Methods to Client: Dial-Up (Other
than Internet), Email, Internet, Microfilm/Microfiche

Unisearch is online with dozens of states' UCC and corporate databases, providing instant access to current information. Often, they provide document copies within 24 hrs. In areas where computer access is not yet available, Unisearch offers a complete range of UCC and corporate services, including national and international Registered Agent service. Additional branch offices are located in Hilliard OH (877-208-7193) and Reno NV (800-260-8118).

United State Mutual Association

4500 S 129th E. Ave., #200
Tulsa, OK 74134
888-338-8762 Fax: 912-828-9141
www.usmutual.com **Email:** corporate@usmutual.com
Parent Company: Total Information Services Inc.
Founded: 1996 **Memberships:** ASIS, SHRM, NRF,
NACS,
Clientele Restrictions: Agreement required
Products, Information Categories, Coverage Area
Proprietary Databases or Gateways:
Database Name: Retail Industry Theft Database
Criminal Information, Addresses/Telephone Numbers
(US)
Special Distribution Methods to Client: Automated
Telephone Look-Up, Dial-Up (Other than Internet), FTP,
Gateway via Another Online Service, Internet

USMA provides reports from a mutual and proprietary database containing documented incidents of theft. Applicant searches against this database provides member companies with a powerful tool that helps improve the quality and efficiency of the employment screening

process. USMA is a comprehensive source of employment screening products for human resource and loss prevention professionals. They provide unique access to background screening for retailers through automated phone, fax, web, dial-up and state-of-the-art call center services.

US Corporate Services

200 Minnesota Bldg, 46 E Fourth St
St Paul, MN 55101
800-327-1886
www.uscorpserv.com **Email:** info@uscorpserv.com
Branch Offices:
Portland, OR, 877-415-1822; Fax: 503-443-1056
Parent Company: Dolan Media Co
Founded: 1966 **Memberships:** NPRRA
Clientele Restrictions: Casual requesters permitted
Products, Information Categories, Coverage Area
General:
Bankruptcy (US)
Proprietary Databases or Gateways:
Database Name: MN Secretary of State Records
Corporation/Trade Name Data (MN)
Database Name: WI UCCs
Uniform Commerical Code (WI)
Special Distribution Methods to Client: Dial-Up (Other
than Internet), Disk, Lists/Labels, Publication/Directory,
Software

US Corporate Services is a full service UCC, tax lien, judgment, litigation and corporate search and filing firm. Their optical image library of Minnesota enables them to provide custom reports to their clients. They have nationwide correspondent relationships. Their turnaround time is 24-72 hours. They will invoice monthly; projects are generally billed by the number of names searched.

US Document Services Inc

PO Box 50486 (2817 Devine St #12)
Columbia, SC 29250
Fax: 803-771-9905
www.us-doc-services.com **Email:** info@us-doc-
services.com
Founded: 1990 **Memberships:** NPRRA
Clientele Restrictions: Casual requesters permitted
Products, Information Categories, Coverage Area
General:
Uniform Commercial Code (US, SC, NC)
Proprietary Databases or Gateways:
Database Name: Secretary of State
Corporation/Trade Name Data (NC, SC)

US Document Services is a nationwide public record search and document retrieval company specializing in North Carolina and South Carolina. They offer UCC, tax lien, suit and judgment, bankruptcy and asset searches, and provide legal, financial and commercial clients with a wide variety of services including formation, qualification and registrations of corporations, etc. With an in-house South Carolina and North Carolina microfilm and online database, they provide up-to-date results, with 48-hour turnarounds. They can also provide reports on DMVs, Workers Comp, watercraft and Real Estate transactions.

US SEARCH.com

5401 Beethoven St
Los Angeles, CA 90066
800-877-2410 Fax: 310-822-7898
www.ussearch.com/wlcs/index.jsp **Email:** corporate@ussearch.com
Founded: 1995 **Memberships:** PIHRA, SHRM,
Clientele Restrictions: Casual requesters permitted
Products, Information Categories, Coverage Area
General:
Addresses/Telephone Numbers (US)
Proprietary Databases or Gateways:
Gateway Name: US Search
Addresses/Telephone Numbers, Corp/Trade Names, Vessels, Bankruptcy, Criminal Information, Litigation/Judgments/Tax Liens, Real Estate/Assessor, Aviation (US)
Special Distribution Methods to Client: Dial-Up (Other than Internet), Email

US SEARCH.com is one of the leading public record providers on the Internet. In addition to comprehensive locate and background reports on people and businesses, US SEARCH.com also provides nationwide data on Corporate & Limited Partnerships; Uniform Commerical Code; Employer ID Numbers; Bankruptcies, Liens and Judgments; Death Records; Real Property; Watercraft; Aircraft and Pilots. US SEARCH.com also offers On-Site Civil and Criminal Records Checks.

USADATA.com

292 Madison Ave, 3rd Fl
New York, NY 10017
800-599-5030 Fax: 212-679-8507
www.usadata.com **Email:** info@usadata.com
Founded: 1995
Clientele Restrictions: Casual requesters permitted
Products, Information Categories, Coverage Area
Proprietary Databases or Gateways:
Gateway Name: Marketing Portal
Corporate/Trade Name Data, Addresses/Telephone Numbers, Real Estate/Assessor (US)
Special Distribution Methods to Client: Email, Lists/Labels, Software

USADATA.com's Marketing Information Portal (www.usadata.com) provides fast, easy access to the information you need to make critical business decisions. They provide mailing lists, research reports, consumer info,

and helpful information gathering solutions. They draw data from the top names in syndicated consumer data on both a local and national level, including Mediamark Research Inc (MRI), Scarborough Research, Arbitron, Acxiom, Competitive Media Reporting (CMR) and National Decision Systems (NDS). Marketers, planners and media buyers can order reports on a pay-per-view basis from the web site, or subscribe to unlimited Internet access.

Utah.gov

68 S Main St #200
Salt Lake City, UT 84101
877-588-3468 Fax: 801-983-0282
www.utah.gov/ **Email:** info@e-utah.org
Parent Company: Utah Electronic Commerce Council
Clientele Restrictions: Many free service, but must be ongoing account for premium services
Products, Information Categories, Coverage Area
Proprietary Databases or Gateways:
Gateway Name: TLRIS/MVR
Driver and/or Vehicle (UT)
Gateway Name: Business Entity List
Corporate/Trade Name Data, Addresses/Telephone Numbers (UT)
Gateway Name: UCC Filing Data
Uniform Commercial Code (UT)
Gateway Name: License Data
Licenses/Registrations/Permits (UT)
Special Distribution Methods to Client: CD-ROM, Database, Email, FTP, Internet

Utah.gov is the State of Utah's gateway providing a single access point, to all electronically available government information and services, to businesses and citizens via the Internet. Through Utah.gov, online users search the following databases: Business Entity, Principals, Business Name Availablity, Vehicle Titles, Leins and Tregistrations, Driving Records, Registered Notaries, and UCCs. In addition, online users can renew vehicle registrations, register a business name, buy hunting and fishing licenses, download offical forms, and access hundreds of government information sources and much much more. For more information, visit the web site at www.utah.gov.

Verifacts Inc

7326 27th St W, #C
University Place, WA 98466
800-568-5665
www.verifacts.com **Email:** jim@verifacts.com
Memberships: NACM, NASA, NARPM,
Clientele Restrictions: Casual requesters permitted for criminal or eviction searches w/ credit card
Products, Information Categories, Coverage Area
General:
Credit Information (US)

Proprietary Databases or Gateways:
Gateway Name: Statewide Criminal Records
Criminal Information (AK, AZ, AR, CA, CO, CT, FL, GA, HI, KS, ID, IL, IN, KY, MI, MN, MO, MS, NC, NJ, NY, OH, OK, OR, PA, SC, TN, TX, UT, VA, WA)
Gateway Name: Eviction/Unlawful Detainers
Litigation/Judgments/Tax Liens (AK, AZ, CA, CO, ID, KY, NV, OR, PA, TX, VA, WA)
Gateway Name: Registered Sex Offenders
Criminal Information (AK, AZ, CT, FL, GA, HI, ID, IL, IN, KS, KY, MI, MS, NC, NY, OH, OK, SC, TN, TX, UT, VA, WA)
Special Distribution Methods to Client: Email, Gateway via Another Online Service, Internet

A technologically advanced search company, Verifacts provide credit reports in three formats: standard, easy-to-read color-coded report, and totally-scored reports based on past credit behavior. Credit reports also include rick score information. Other services include SSN searches, nationwide criminal coverage, registered sex offender searches that include offender pictures, and eviction searches. Their pre-employment screening division is USAScreening.com.

Virginia Information Providers Network
1111 East Main Street #901
Richmond, VA 23219
877-482-3468 Fax: 804-786-6227
www.vipnet.org **Email:** webmaster@vipnet.org
Founded: 1996
Clientele Restrictions: Signed agreement required, must be ongoing account
Products, Information Categories, Coverage Area
General:
Associations/Trade Groups (VA)
Proprietary Databases or Gateways:
Gateway Name: VIPNet
Driver and/or Vehicle, Vessels, Legislation/Regulation (VA)
Gateway Name: Health Professionals (free)
Associations/Trade Groups (VA)
Gateway Name: State Employment Verification
Education/Employment (VA)
Special Distribution Methods to Client: Internet

The Virginia Information Providers Network was created by the state of Virginia to streamline and enhance the ways in which citizens and businesses access government information. VIPNet Premium Services includes access to state services including motor vehicle records, boat records, a value-added bill tracking service, state employment verification, and licenses health professionals data. VIPNet also provides an extensive range of free services for the public, including online election results, legisaltive tracking, and review of attorney disciplinary actions.

Vital Records Information
925 Cypress South
Greenwood, IN 46143
http://vitalrec.com **Email:** Corrections@vitalrec.com
Products, Information Categories, Coverage Area
Proprietary Databases or Gateways:
Gateway Name: vitalrec.com
Vital Records, Genealogical Information (US)
Gateway Name: vitalrec.com
Foreign Country Information (Intl)
Special Distribution Methods to Client: Internet

Although primarily a links list, vitalrec.com is a gateway to extensive information, especially oriented for geneology.

VitalChek Network
4512 Central Pike
Hermitage, TN 37076
800-255-2414
www.vitalchek.com **Email:**
vitals.comments@vitalchek.com
Clientele Restrictions: Casual requesters permitted
Products, Information Categories, Coverage Area
Proprietary Databases or Gateways:
Gateway Name: VitalChek
Vital Records (US)

VitalChek Network has a sophisticated voice and fax network setup to help people acquire certified copies of birth, death and marriage certificates and other vital records. VitalChek provides a direct access gateway to participating agencies at the state and local level.

West Group
620 Opperman Dr
Eagan, MN 55123
800-328-9352 Fax: 651-687-7302
www.westgroup.com
Parent Company: Thomson
Founded: 1872 **Memberships:** SIIA
Clientele Restrictions: Casual requesters permitted
Products, Information Categories, Coverage Area
Proprietary Databases or Gateways:
Database Name: West CD-ROM Libraries
Legislation/Regulations (US)
Database Name: Westlaw
Environmental, Legislation/Regulations, Corporate/Trade Name Data, Uniform Commercial Code (US)
Special Distribution Methods to Client: CD-ROM, Dial-Up (Other than Internet), Internet

West Group is one of the largest providers of information to US legal professionals. West Group includes renowned names such as Barclays, Bancroft Whitney, Clark Boardman Callaghan, Counterpoint, Lawyers Cooperative Publishing, West Publishing and Westlaw. Westlaw is a computer-assisted research service consisting of more than 9,500 legal, financial and news databases, including Dow Jones News/Retrieval. West Group produces a total of more than 3,800 products including 300 CD-ROMs.

Westlaw Public Records

P.O. Box 64833 (620 Opperman Dr)
St. Paul, MN 55164
800-328-4880
www.westlaw.com **Email:** admin@WESTPUB.COM
Memberships: NPRRA
Clientele Restrictions: Casual requesters permitted
Products, Information Categories, Coverage Area
General:
Driver and/or Vehicle (US)
Proprietary Databases or Gateways:
Database Name: Bankruptcy Records
Bankruptcy (US)

Database Name: Corporations and Partnerships
Corporate/Trade Name Data (US)

Database Name: Lawsuits, Judgments, Liens
Litigation/Judgments/Tax Liens (US)

Database Name: Professional Licenses
Licenses/Registrations/Permits (AZ, CA, CO, CT, FL, GA, IL, IN, LA, MA, MD, MI, NJ, OH, PA, SC, TN, TX, VA, WI)

Database Name: Real Estate, Liens & Judgments
Real Estate/Assessor, Litigation/Judgments/Tax Liens (US)

Database Name: UCCs
Uniform Commerical Code (US)

Database Name: Watercraft Locator/Aircraft Locator
Aviation/Vessels (US)

Database Name: Business Finder/People Finder
Addresses/Telephone Numbers (US)

Gateway Name: Motor Vehicle Records
Driver and/or Vehicle (AK, AL, CO, CT, DC, DE, FL, IA, ID, IL, KY, LA, MA, MD, ME, MI, MN, MO, MS, MT, ND, NE, NH, NM, NY, OH, SC, TN, UT, WI, WV, WY)

Special Distribution Methods to Client: Dial-Up (Other than Internet), Internet

Westlaw Public Records combines and links public records and courthouse documents with information from private sources to address the relationships between corporations, people and their assets. Banks, financial service companies, corporations, law firms and government agencies across the nation use their online and document retrieval services to obtain background data on businesses, locate assets and people, retrieve official public records and solve business problems. Westlaw Public Records was originally founded by a practicing attorney and a computer systems expert acquainted with the needs of government, legal and corporate customers.

Web Site Profiles

What follows are detailed profiles of EMPLOYMENT-RELATED and MISCELLANEOUS web sites. The information includes each site's title, its URL and a brief description. Unless otherwise noted, the content of the site profiled is available for free. The sites listed here were not mentioned within the main text of this book.

Employment

Miscellaneous

At the end of each chapter are profiles of additional web site. The topics of these additional web sites and the Chapter where they appear are listed below.:

Accuracy (Chapter 12)

Basics (Chapter 2)

Business (Chapter 9)

Creative Uses of the Internet (Chapter 1)

Government Records (Chapter 6)

Managing and Filtering (Chapter 11)

International (Chapter 10)

News (Chapter 8)

Privacy and Protection (Chapter 14)

Public Records (Chapter 7)

Search Engines (Chapter 4)

Specialized Tools (Chapter 5)

Employment Web Sites

Academic Employment Network
www.academploy.com
Online job classifieds for U.S. teachers from K-University, indexed by subject, geographic area and position level.

America's Employers
www.americasemployers.com
Comprehensive job search site for professionals, managers and executives.

America's Career Infonet
www.acinet.org/acinet/
State profiles, occupational and employment information from America's Job Bank. A good starting resource.

Best Jobs USA
www.bestjobsusa.com
Searchable employment ads database from USA Today.

Career Journal
www.careerjournal.com
thousands of searchable listing on all kinds of jobs.

Career Page from Princeton Review Online
www.review.com/career
A keyword searchable database with career profiles from the Princeton Review.

Career Resource Center
www.careers.org
Excellent starting point to begin your job search, including prepping tips.

CareerMosaic
www.careermosaic.com
Search by keyword - choose a company and check their available positions. Includes an index of Usenet jobs newsgroups.

careers.wsj.com
http://careers.wsj.com
Wall Street Journal and National Business Employment Weekly's deep career info and searchable database.

Craig's List
www.craigslist.org
Fee for postings. An outstanding job site, posting messages about jobs, leads, communities.

E-Span's Job Options
www.joboptions.com/esp/plsql/espan_enter.espan_home
Post a resume and look through their extensive directory of job listings.

Head Hunter
www.headhunter.net/jobseeker
Huge database of keyword searchable jobs.

Hotjobs.com
www.hotjobs.com
One of the larger job hunter sites, you post your resume and they do the rest.

Job Options
www.joboptions.com
Another outstanding collection of job leads.

Jobs In Government
http://jobsingovernment.com
Collection of government-related jobs, by geographic region.

JobSmart
www.jobsmart.org
Absolutely the best place to begin a job search. A library-sponsored guide to job-search resources on the Web. Geared to California, but has excellent national info as well.

Jobstar
http://jobstar.org
A truly outstanding job-finding site with all kinds of information about getting prepared to find jobs as well as job listings.

JobWeb
www.jobweb.com
Good site if you're a college student, recent graduate or alumnus and looking for work.

Monster.com
www.monster.com
Largest job database in the US and around the world - more than 400,000 openings in 1500 countries.

Online Career Center
www.occ.com
A database of job listings, searchable by geographic location, industry and keyword.

The Riley Guide: Employment Opportunities & Job Resources on the Internet
www.rileyguide.com
Directory of excellent employment sites compiled by librarian Margaret F. (Riley) Dikel.

Top 100 Electronic Recruiters
www.interbiznet.com/eeri
Thousands of sites were reviewed and these are the top 100.

What Color is Your Parachute
www.tenspeedpress.com/parachute/front.htm
Directory listings, resumes and career counseling by author Richard Bolles from his job-hunting book, *What Color is Your Parachute?*

Miscellaneous Web Sites

Expedia
www.expedia.com
A travel fare shopping and booking portal.

Federal Reserve Banks (FRB) Maps with Links
www.federalreserve.gov/pubs/frseries/frseri3.htm
Lists sites and information on banks in the FRB system.

FindLaw Supreme Court Decisions
www.findlaw.com/casecode/supreme.html
Search for a specific high court decisions.

History of the World Wide Web
www.w3history.org
An online history of the World Wide Web.

Illustrated Guide to Breaking Your Computer
http://members.aol.com/spoons1000/break/index.html
A humorous site demonstrating ways to break your computer, complete with photos.

Internet FAQ Consortium
www.faqs.org
All about frequently asked questions (FAQ).

Internet Gurus Central
http://net.gurus.com
Introduction to the internet. From authors of *The Internet for Dummies.*

Internet Public Library: Ready Reference Collection
http://ipl.si.umich.edu/ref/RR
Ready reference listing. Categories include almanacs, biographies, census data & demographics, dictionaries, encyclopedias, genealogy, geography, news, quotations and telephone numbers.

National Center for Supercomputing Applications
www.ncsa.uiuc.edu
An organization instrumental in the development of graphical browsers.

Northern Webs Tutorials
www.northernwebs.com/tutorials.html
An ongoing tutorial section, includes tutorials for people new to the Internet as well as for people wanting to learn

how to use scripting software. Check out the Articles section for other topics that may interest you.

Police Scanner

www.policescanner.com

Haven't had enough police drama on TV? If you want real life police drama, now you can listen to live police in several city departments using real audio streaming technology. Yahoo! Audio also offers rail, fire and airport control towers.

Ready Reference Using the Internet

http://k12.oit.umass.edu/rref.html

Ready reference listing. These files are alphabetical by subject -like a vertical file of pamphlets, and organized by reference librarians at the Winsor School in Boston.

SearchAbility

www.searchability.com

A list of specialized search engines with descriptions and some ranking.

Tech Corps

www.techcorps.org

A volunteer organization dedicated to expanding computer literacy by educating students and teachers about using computers and the Internet.

The Official Nerdity Test Homepage

http://home.rochester.rr.com/jbennett/nerd/index.html

A humorous online test to evaluate your "nerdity." The site also has other fun links for self-professed "geeks."

Travelocity

www.travelocity.com

A travel fare shopping and booking portal.

Virtual Reference Desk, The

www.lib.purdue.edu/vlibrary

Ready reference listing. Pulled together by Purdue University, well-organized, well researched.

WebCam Central

www.camcentral.com

Annotated guide to the live cameras on the Internet. More than a thousand webcams.

Contributors

Stephanie C. Ardito is President of Ardito Information & Research Inc. an information firm specializing in pharmaceutical, medical, and business information research as well as intellectual property and copyright matters. She is co-author of the "Legal Issues" column published in *Information Today*, and a past president of the Association of Independent Information Professionals. Address: sardito@ardito.com

Mary Ellen Bates is the owner of Bates Information Services, providing business research to business professionals and consulting services to the online industry. She is the author of five books, including *Super Searchers Cover the World*, *Researching Online For Dummies*, 2nd Edition, and *Mining For Gold on the Internet*. Prior to starting her business in 1991, she worked in specialized libraries for years and has been online since the late 1970s. Address: mbates@batesinfo.com and www.BatesInfo.com

Kitty Bennett is a news researcher for the *St. Petersburg Times*. Address: bennett@sptimes.com

Susan M. Detwiler is president of The Detwiler Group, an information consulting firm that has long specialized in the business side of medicine and health. She has testified before the White House Commission on Complementary and Alternative Medicine Policy, and is author of *Super Searchers on Health & Medicine: The Online Secrets of Top Health & Medical Researchers*. Address: sdetwiler@detwiler.com and www.detwiler.com

Susan Feldman is Director of the Document and Content Technologies Program at IDC. Before coming to IDC in 2000, she was President for twenty years of Datasearch, an independent information consulting firm. She is a former president and charter member of the Association of Independent Information Professionals. Address: Sfeldman@IDC.com

Jennifer Kaplan is CEO of JKreative Solutions, Inc., a global consultancy that offers strategy, marketing and development services for business, education, government and non-profits. Address: Jennifer@jkreative.com

Carole A. Lane is the author of *Naked In Cyberspace: How To Find Personal Information Online* (new edition July 2002, Cyberage. Address: calane@technosearch.com

Eva M. Lang is an authority on electronic research for business and litigation support services. Eva is also technology columnist for *CPA Expert Newsletter*. Address: lemay_lang@csi.com

John E. Levis is president of John E. Levis Associates, a long-time specialist in primary and secondary market research in healthcare and medicine, and a past president of the Association of Independent Information Professionals. Address: john@jelevisassoc.com and www.jelevisassoc.com

J.J. Newby is a former television journalist and has spent the past seven years as a ghostwriter and consultant to Silicon Valley executives as well as a self-professed web addict. Address: jjnewby@aol.com

Greg R. Notess is a reference librarian at Montana State University, a columnist for *Online* and *Database* magazines and the author of the Search Engine Showdown. He is also the author of the author of the first three editions of *Government Information on the Internet*. Address: notess@notess.com and www.searchengineshowdown and www.notess.com

Nora Paul is Director of the Institute for New Media Studies at the University of Minnesota, former Library Director of the Poynter Institute, a former *Miami Herald* librarian, a nationally recognized lecturer and co-author with Margot Williams of the *Great Scouts! Cyberguides For Subject Searching On The Web*, published by Cyberage Books, www.infotoday.com.

Lynn Peterson, President of PFC Information Services, Inc. in Oakland, California, is a well-known expert in public record research and retrieval. Address: `lpeterson@pfcinformation.com` and `www.pfcinformation.com`

Barbara Quint is editor of *Searcher Magazine*. Barbara's e-mail address is `bquint@netcom.com`

Don Ray is a multimedia investigative journalist and a sought-after speaker on the topics of information gathering, privacy and public records. He's written books on sources of information, interviewing, checking out lawyers and on document interpretation. Address: `donray@donray.com` and `www.donray.com/donray`

Chris Sherman is co-author of *The Invisible Web: Uncovering Information Sources Search Engines Can't See*, with Gary Price. He is President of Searchwise.Net and is the associate editor of *Search Engine Watch*. Address: `csherman@searchwise.net`

Danny Sullivan, an Internet consultant and journalist, edits *Search Engine Watch*, a highly-respected newsletter focused on search engines. Address: `Danny@calafia.com`

Drew Sullivan is the media advisor for IREX ProMedia in Sarajevo, Bosnia and Herzegovina. Address: `drew@drewsullivan.com`

Dave Wickham is creator of the Public Servant's Internet Abuse Page. Address: `davew@inlandnet.com` and `www.adsnet.net/states.htm`

Robbin Zeff, PhD is president of The Zeff Group, a research and training firm specializing Internet advertising and marketing. Robbin is author of the best-selling *Advertising on the Internet* and *The Nonprofit Guide to the Internet*. Address: `robbin@zeff.com` and `www.zeff.com`

Glossary

Terms and Definitions

Attachment Any file that is attached to an email message.

Back Slash Slash mark on your keyboard that goes from top left down to bottom right (\).

Boolean Method of searching a database or text in which Boolean operators (like AND, OR and NOT) are used to limit and specify the search criterion.

Browser Software that looks at various types of Internet resources. Browsers can search for documents and obtain them from other sources. A browser allows you to look at the World Wide Web. Common browsers include Netscape Navigator, Microsoft Internet Explorer; less common are Internet Chameleon and Internet-in-a-Box. Browsers are also called Web Browsers.

Chat Room Chat is the synchronous line-by-line communication (happening in real time, like a phone conversation but unlike an email exchange) over a network with another user or users. Chat rooms are the places wherein people conduct these online conversations.

Cyberspace A term coined by science fiction author William Gibson to describe the whole range of information resources available through computer networks.

Database A structured format for organizing and maintaining information that can be easily retrieved. A simple example of a database is a table or a spreadsheet.

DNS (Domain Name Service) An online distributed database responsible for mapping host names to their respective IP addresses. Also refers to Domain Name Server.

Domain The unique name that identifies an Internet site. The Internet is made up of hundreds of thousands of computers and networks, all with their own domain name or unique address. Domain names always have two or more parts separated by dots. For example, "whitehouse.gov" is the domain name belonging to the White House computer system. Domain names typically consist of some form of the organization's name and a suffix that describes the type of organization.

Download The method by which users access and save or "pull down" software or other files to their own computers from a remote computer, usually via a modem.

Email Short for electronic mail, email consists of messages, often just text, sent from one user to another via a network. Email can also be sent automatically to a number of addresses.

FAQ Acronym for Frequently Asked Questions. FAQs are online documents that list and answer the most common questions on a particular subject. FAQs were developed by people who got tired of answering the same questions over and over again.

Filter Is a program that allows certain messages or certain kinds of material to reach the user while eliminating other messages. Email filters separate email into categories. Other filters are used to pull out racy material so kids don't see it, and still other filters allow you to get just news on specific subjects you want, eliminating other irrelevant material

Firewall Security measure of the Internet that prevents users from doing any harm to underlying systems by protecting information and preventing access.

Forward Slash Slash mark on your keyboard that goes from bottom left to top right (/).

Frames Area of the screen of some graphical web browsers (such as Netscape Navigator and Microsoft Internet Explorer) that can be updated independently and may also scroll separately.

Freeware Software distributed for free with no fee required.

FTP A powerful tool that enables you to access computers anywhere in the world and copy files from them to your own computer – anything from information and pictures to full-fledged application programs. This process is known as "downloading."

Gateway A computer that interconnects and performs the protocol conversion between two different types of networks, bridging the gap between two otherwise incompatible applications or networks so that data can be transferred different computers. This is common with email that gets sent back and forth between Internet sites and commercial online services (like America Online) that has its own internal email systems. It can also be an online company that offers access to the internet as well as other online services.

Hits Refers to the number of files that are downloaded from a web server. It's a way of measuring traffic to a web site that can be misleading. The number of hits a site receives is usually much greater than the number of visitors it gets. That's because a web page can contain more than one file.

HTML Stands for Hyper-Text Markup Language. It is the basic language that web pages are created in. It is designed such that the basics are easy to learn. There are several good books about programming HTML, as well as a large selection of programs that generate it automatically for you.

Intranet Think of an intranet as an internal Internet, or "network," designed to be used within the confines of a company, university or organization. What distinguishes an intranet from the Internet, is that intranets are private.

IP Address Numeric code that uniquely identifies a particular computer on the Internet. Like your home address, every computer on the Internet has a unique address, too. Internet addresses are assigned to you by an organization called ICANN, formerly assigned by Internic. When you register an address, you get both a domain name like (whitehouse.gov), and a number (198.38.240.10), which is generally referred to as the IP address or IP number. Because the numeric addresses are difficult to understand or remember, most people use names instead.

ISP Acronym for Internet Service Provider; the company you get an account from in order to get access to the Internet.

Java An object-oriented programming language developed by Sun Microsystems, Inc. to create executable content (i.e self-running applications) that can be easily distributed through networks like the Web. Developers use Java to create special programs called applets that can be incorporated in a web page to make it interactive. When you see pages moving and jumping and dogs walking across pages on the Web, chances are good that it is a Java applet. Like a gateway (CGI) script, a special HTML tag on a web page activates Java.

Links A page link moves your browser from its current page to the page named in the link, whether on the same web site or not. A hyperlink goes a step further; if your browser is active, a hyperlink when activated from another document or program will launch your browser and take you to the hyperlinked page. Typically, links are underlined, often blue.

Mailing List A way of having a group discussion by electronic mail. Also used to distribute announcements to a large number of people. A mailing list is very much like a conference on a bulletin board system, except the conversation comes to you by email. Each time you or any member of the list posts a reply to the conversation, it is distributed to the email box of every member of the list. All of this traffic is automated and managed by programs called mailing list managers or mail servers. The two most frequently used programs are Listserv and Majordomo.

Meta-Tools Meta-tools are hybrids of search engines and subject directories that allow you to search several sites at once.

Portal Portal sites combine specialized content, free email, chat services and a variety of retail and consumer offers to draw users into making the site their starting point and principal destination on the Web. They make their money by getting huge amounts of web traffic and through ad revenue and commercial transactions.

Proxy Server Security measure that enables users behind a firewall to browse the web. Visited resources are actually downloaded by the proxy server and then viewed internally from there without exposing the contents of the material to public scrutiny

Push Technology A method of distributing information over the Web, by which updates are scheduled and then automatically sent to the user's screen or window, as if the content were being "broadcast" to a receiver.

Real Time The time used for synchronous communication, in which both participants must be available (as in a telephone conversation). It also means taking place at the present time, live, not delayed or recorded.

Search Tools These are the tools you use to search around on the Internet. They include search engines, which are a type of software that creates indexes of databases of Internet sites and allows you to type in what you are looking for and it then gives you a list of results of your search. Other tools include subject directories, which are catalogues of resources, pulled together and ranked by human being s and meta-tools, which allow you to search several search tools at once.

Searching The effort to find specific things online using a series of search tools to help you locate whatever it is you are interested in. Usually it is done by specifying key words to match

Server A network application or computer that supplies information or other resources to client applications that connect to it. In conventional networking, server usually refers to a computer; for Internet client/server applications, server usually refers to a program.

Shareware Computer programs that are available for a free trial with the understanding that, if you decide to keep the program, you will send the requested payment to the shareware provider specified in the program. You are on the honor system with the understanding that if you like the software and want to keep the inventor in business, you will pay for the software's continued development. Payment may also buy manuals, support, updates.

Signature Text automatically included at the bottom of an email message or newsgroup posting to personalize it. This can be anything from a snappy quote to some additional information about the sender, like their title, company name and additional email addresses they may have.

Snail Mail Internet slang for US Postal Service mail, so called for its relative slowness.

Truncation Shortening or cutting off of words, where search engines automatically use shortened versions of words in searching.

Upload Often confused with download, uploading a file means loading it from your computer onto a remote one. Most people do a lot more downloading than uploading.

URL Acronym for Uniform Resource Locator. URL is the address for a resource or web site. It is the convention that web browsers use for locating files and other remote services.

Usenet Usenet is the collection of newsgroups and a set of agreed-upon rules for distributing and maintaining them.

Web Browser A program used to navigate and access information on the World Wide Web. Web browsers turn HTML coding into a graphical display.

Web Page A web page is a document created with HTML (HyperText Markup Language) that is part of a group of hypertext documents or resources available on the World Wide Web. It usually contains hypertext links to other documents on the Web. Collectively, these documents and resources form what is known as a web site.

Web Site A collection of World Wide Web pages, usually consisting of a home page and several other linked pages

Webmaster Person in charge of maintaining a web site. This can include writing HTML files, setting up more complex programs, and responding to email.

Wildcard These are special characters used to represent either any single character or any number of characters. Usual wildcard characters are ? (for single characters) and * (for any number of characters). Using wildcards allows you to search when you do not have entire phrases or are missing a specific piece of your search criteria.

Index

Notes

Additional titles from
Facts on Demand Press

25 Essential Lessons
for Employee Management

25 Essential Lessons for Employee Management cuts through conventional practices and provides managers with easy-to-apply techniques that guide them through five essential processes: hiring, new employee integration, managing employee problems, termination, and compliance with regulations. Included in the book are recommended web sites and 22 essential employment forms.

Dennis DeMey • 1-889150-25-8 • 320 pgs • $22.95

Criminal Records Book

Criminal records provide essential information used for employment screening, locating people, fraud detection and other investigative purposes. This book is the complete guide to accessing and utilizing criminal records housed at the federal, state and county level. Learn how to:

- determine where criminal records are stored.
- obtain records at each jurisdiction level.
- select a record vendor.
- legally access criminal records.

Derek Hinton • 1-889150-27-4 • 320 pgs • $19.95

Public Records Online

The national guide to private and government online sources of public records! In this book you will find profiles on over 2,000 online government sources (county, state, and federal levels). Includes a sixty-page "Public Record Primer" to educate researchers on the complexities of public record research. Includes a directory of over one-hundred useful web sites to find information on businesses and people, and hundreds of private provider companies.

Edited by Michael L. Sankey and Peter J. Weber • 1-889150-21-5 • 576 pgs • $20.95

Available at Your Local Bookstore!

Also available from the publisher:
1-800-929-3811 • Facts on Demand Press • www.brbpub.com